EXCAVATIONS IN CHIOS 1938–1955

PREHISTORIC EMPORIO AND AYIO GALA

by

SINCLAIR HOOD

with contributions by
JULIET CLUTTON-BROCK and PERRY G. BIALOR

Volume I

SUPPLEMENTARY VOLUME NO. 15

Published by
THE BRITISH SCHOOL OF ARCHAEOLOGY AT ATHENS
THAMES AND HUDSON
1981

ISBN 0 500 96017 8

Printed in Great Britain at the Alden Press, Oxford

To the Memory of Philip Argenti, Citizen of Chios, and
Benefactor of the excavations at Ayio Gala and
Emporio,
and to that of George Choremis, friend and Benefactor of
the Emporio excavations,
and to the many other patriotic Chiots who joined with
them to help finance the excavations at Emporio,
and by their generosity made the work possible,
but who wished their names to remain unknown

Contents

Preface

These volumes are a sequel to *Greek Emporio* by John Boardman. They are concerned with the excavations at two prehistoric sites at opposite ends of Chios, at Ayio Gala in the north, where the late Miss Edith Eccles made soundings in a pair of caves in 1938, and at Emporio in the south where I directed work for the British School at Athens from 1952 to 1955.

The material from Ayio Gala is divisible into two chronological groups: an earlier, of which Dr. Audrey Furness (Mrs. Ozanne) has already published a careful study, and a later which appears to be assignable to the beginning of the Early Bronze Age. The earlier material is certainly Neolithic in Aegean terms, and has been assigned by Dr. Furness to a very early phase of the Aegean Neolithic. This assignation seems to me correct.

The great interest of Emporio is the stratified sequence for the early prehistoric periods obtained in the main Area A of the excavations. The oldest occupation levels of the site were not reached here, since they lay below the existing water table. The earliest pottery recovered has been classified by some of those who have seen it as Late Neolithic in Aegean terms, and that was my own view of it at first. But further study of this material has convinced me that it belongs to a much older horizon, and that it goes back in time before the earliest occupation at Ayio Gala. It is therefore I believe assignable to the beginning of the Early Neolithic in Aegean terms.

The bulk of the prehistoric material recovered at Emporio belongs to these early periods, that is (in Aegean terms) to the Neolithic and the beginning of the Early Bronze Age. This material has been divided among ten Periods, based upon major building developments in Area A. The ten Periods fall into five main groups which are marked by distinct changes in pottery fashions.

The first of these groups (Periods X–VIII) seems to cover a relatively early phase of the Aegean Neolithic, while the latest part of it (Period VIII) can be correlated with the earliest known phase of settled occupation in the Troad (Beşik Tepe and Kum Tepe I A). The pottery of the second group (Periods VII–VI) is closely related to that of Kum Tepe I B in the Troad. This second group (Periods VII–VI) appears to overlap with the end of the Middle Neolithic and part of the Late Neolithic on the Greek mainland. The third group consisting of Periods V and IV with pottery akin to that of the Trojan region seems to fall within the earlier part of Troy I. The fourth group (Periods III–II) follows a destruction of the Period IV settlement by fire. It should overlap with the later stages of Troy I and with the beginning of Troy II before the manufacture of wheelmade vases there. The fifth group (Period I) with the first appearance of wheelmade pottery at Emporio seems to correspond with a late stage of Troy II.

The pottery of Ayio Gala and that of the early periods at Emporio evidently reflect quite separate traditions. The pottery from the two sites is in fact so different that it is hard to establish a chronological relationship between the two sequences. The earliest pottery from Ayio Gala, however, appears to fall within Periods IX–VIII at Emporio; but occupation continued in the caves there into the time of Emporio Periods VII–VI and perhaps V–IV.

The marked divergences in the pottery from these two sites at opposite ends of Chios seems to be the effect of settlers reaching the island from different regions at different times. The first to arrive established themselves in the fertile south of Chios in the area of Emporio. They made dark-surfaced pottery distantly related to that of the earliest horizon known in Anatolia (e.g. Çatal Hüyük) and in Syria (from Amuq Phase A onwards). These immigrants probably came to Chios from the south or south-east. Early pottery from caves in the region of Antalya on the southern coast of Turkey has features reminiscent of pottery from the lowest levels reached by excavation at Emporio.

The earliest pottery of Ayio Gala on the other hand is red-surfaced and obviously related to that known from Hacilar in south-western Turkey. Similar pottery appears to have been noted at Morali in western Turkey opposite Chios. The immigrants who first occupied the north of the island and settled in the region of Ayio Gala may therefore have reached Chios from some neighbouring part of the Turkish mainland.

The later stages of the Early Bronze Age, the period of Troy III–V, were not certainly represented at Emporio by architectural remains or deposits in the areas excavated. But fragments of pottery suggest that there was continuity of occupation at the site throughout the Early and into the Middle Bronze Age overlapping with the opening phases of Troy VI. A little imported grey Minyan ware and some of the local matt-painted ware recovered at Emporio may be of Middle Bronze Age date; but the decoration of much of the matt-painted ware seems to reflect Cretan fashions of the earlier part of the Late Bronze Age (Late Minoan I).

There was some evidence for Mycenaean occupation at Emporio as early as Mycenaean III B. An important Mycenaean settlement undoubtedly existed there during the following Mycenaean III C period, and this was finally destroyed or abandoned in an advanced phase of Mycenaean III C. A number of complete or restorable Mycenaean III C vases was recovered from this horizon of destruction or abandonment.

These two volumes of Prehistoric Emporio and Ayio Gala were conceived as one, and the line of division between them is arbitrary. The pages, text figures and photo plates, as well as the pottery, have therefore been given consecutive numbers.

Volume I begins with a survey of prehistoric sites known in Chios, and describes the excavations at Ayio Gala with the pottery and other finds from the caves there. It continues with a discussion of the relationship between the sequence at Ayio Gala and that at Emporio, followed by an account of the excavations at Emporio, with a report on the pottery of the earlier periods from the main Area A there. This brings the story of Emporio down to the point where the settlement was destroyed by fire towards the beginning of the Early Bronze Age in the time of Troy I.

Volume II continues with the report on the pottery from Area A and from other parts of the site (Areas B–F) at Emporio. It includes a survey of what is known about occupation at Emporio in the latest phases of the Early Bronze Age and in the Middle and Late Bronze Ages together with an account of the Mycenaean pottery. Descriptions of other finds apart from pottery are followed by a report on the animal bones from Emporio by Juliet Clutton-Brock, and one on the chipped stone assemblages from Emporio and Ayio Gala by Perry Bialor. Volume II ends with a section on the chronological position of the Chian Neolithic and Early Bronze Age sequences as known from the excavations at Emporio and Ayio Gala.

Acknowledgments

The work of Miss Edith Eccles at Ayio Gala (1938) was financed by the late Dr. Philip Argenti and Mr. Eumorfopoulos. Excavations at Emporio (1952–55) were made possible in the first instance by the generosity of an anonymous donor. Other donors who wished to remain anonymous were inspired by his example to help finance the excavations. I and the other members of the excavation party would like to join the Committee of the British School of Archaeology at Athens in expressing our deepest gratitude to them all for what they did.

We are also most deeply grateful to that wise and good citizen of Chios, the late Mr. George I. Choremis, not only for his generous financial support of the Emporio excavations from year to year, but also for his active interest in the results, which extended to the problem of the eventual housing of the finds in a worthy manner. The fine new Museum which has since been built in Chios town represents a noble consummation of his dreams.

The soundings at Ayio Gala were made in 1938 by the late Miss Edith Eccles with the assistance of Miss Lilian H. Jeffery, and Mr. (now Sir) David Hunt. Illness prevented Miss Eccles from returning to Greece after the war to complete her work on the material, and she kindly invited me to undertake the publication of it in connection with the excavations at Emporio from 1952 to 1955. It is not possible to list by name all those who took part in the Emporio excavations; but among those who were in charge of trenches in the prehistoric sector were Miss Mary Williams (now Mrs. William Elliott), Miss Rachel Simmons (Mrs. Sinclair Hood), Miss Colina MacDougall, Dr. Michael Ballance, and Mr James Mellaart.

Our foreman at Emporio was Mr. Ioannis Theotokas, then mayor of the neighbouring village of Piryi, without previous experience of excavation work, but a man of great character, efficient in organisation, loyal and shrewd. Mr. George Laspis, his brother-in-law, was outstanding among the workmen. Mr. Michaeli Kokolis was in charge of the pot-washing. Our vase-mender and technician was Mr. Stelios Katsarakis. Some of the pottery from the Upper Cave at Ayio Gala was mended by Mr. Argyri Marinis.

All those who have worked on the archaeology of Chios since the Second World War owe much to the help and friendly interest of the local Epimelete of Antiquities, Mr. Antonios Stephanou, and it is a pleasure to record our indebtedness to him in connection with the excavations at Emporio where he was a frequent and welcome visitor. We also enjoyed the support of the Ephors of Antiquities for the region which included Chios, the late Professor Nicolas Kontoleon, and Mr. A. Vavritsas who succeeded him.

The earlier survey work at Emporio was done by the late Mr. David Smollett, but the final plans of the area were made in his own clear and uniquely strong and distinctive style by the late Dr. Michael Ventris, assisted by Mrs. Betty Ventris. The pottery was drawn by Miss Audrey Petty (now Mrs. Spencer Corbett), Miss Wendy Biggar (Mrs. Lardner-Dennys), Miss Rachel Simmons (Mrs. Sinclair Hood), and Miss Elizabeth Crowfoot. Drawings of the other finds were made by Miss Petty (Mrs. Corbett), Miss Christine Sapieha (Mrs. Freeman), and Miss Deborah Pawson (Mrs. Ruscombe-King). The final tracings of the pottery are mostly the work of Miss Elizabeth Crowfoot and Mrs. Patricia Clarke. Mrs. Clarke has also laboured with skill and patience to make the final ink drawings of most of the trench plans and sections. The arduous task of typing the text has been successfully completed by Mrs. E. T. Templeton.

Miss Olga Krzyszkowska has read through the accounts of bone objects and made some helpful suggestions in connection with them. Mrs. Helen Hughes-Brock has kindly answered questions and given advice and references about spindle whorls and beads, Dr. Oliver Dickinson about Minyan ware and ring pendants (METAL 17).

I am grateful to Dr. David French and to Dr. William Phelps for permission to cite their unpublished doctoral theses lodged respectively in the libraries of the British School of Archaeology in Athens and the Institute of Archaeology in London. The thesis of Dr. Phelps represents an important contribution to Aegean Neolithic studies. I am also obliged to Mr. J. A. MacGillivray for allowing me to refer to his unpublished account of pottery from the Mt. Kynthos settlement on Delos, available in the library of the London Institute of Classical Studies.

Abbreviations

The following abbreviations are used in addition to those current in *BSA*:

AAA	*Athens Annals of Archaeology*
AASyr	*Annales archéologiques arabes syriennes*
Åberg, *Chronologie* iv	N. Åberg, *Bronzezeitliche und Früheisenzeitliche Chronologie* iv: *Griechenland* (Stockholm, 1933)
Abydos i	W.M.F. Petrie, *Abydos* i (London, 1902)
Achilleion	M. Gimbutas, 'Achilleion: A Neolithic Mound in Thessaly; Preliminary Report on 1973 and 1974 Excavations', *Journal of Field Archaeology* i (1974) 277–302
Alaca 1935	R.O. Arik, *Les fouilles d'Alaca Höyük: rapport préliminaire sur les travaux en 1935* (Ankara, 1937)
Alaca 1936	H.Z. Koşay, *Ausgrabungen von Alaca Höyük: ein Vorbericht über die . . . im Sommer 1936 durchgeführten Forschungen und Entdeckungen* (Ankara, 1944)
Alaca 1937–39	H.Z. Koşay, *Les fouilles d'Alaca Höyük: rapport préliminaire sur les travaux en 1937–1939* (Ankara, 1951)
Alalakh	L. Woolley, *Alalakh* (Oxford, 1955)
Alishar 1927 i	E.F. Schmidt, *The Alishar Hüyük; season of 1927* i (O.I.P. vi) (Chicago U.P., 1930)
Alishar 1927 ii	H.H. von der Osten and E.F. Schmidt, *The Alishar Hüyük: season of 1927* ii (O.I.P. vii) (Chicago U.P., 1932)
Alishar 1928–29 i	E.F. Schmidt, *The Alishar Hüyük. Seasons of 1928 and 1929* part i (O.I.P. xix) (Chicago U.P., 1932)
Alishar 1930–32 i, ii, iii	H.H. von der Osten, *The Alishar Hüyük. Seasons of 1930–32* parts i–iii (O.I.P. xxviii–xxx) (Chicago U.P., 1937)
Amiran, *APHL*	Ruth Amiran, *Ancient Pottery of the Holy Land* (Jerusalem, 1969)
AntJ	*The Antiquaries Journal*
Anza	M. Gimbutas (ed.), *Neolithic Macedonia: As reflected by Excavation at Anza, Southeast Jugoslavia* (Los Angeles, 1976)
Arapi	H. Hauptmann and V. Milojčić, *Die Funde der Frühen Dimini-Zeit aus der Arapi-magula Thessalien* (Bonn, 1969)
AR . . .	*Archaeological Reports for . . .*, published by the Council for the Society of Hellenic Studies and the Managing Committee of the British School at Athens
Arene Candide i, ii	L.B. Brea, *Gli Scavi nella Caverna delle Arene Candide* (Istituto di Studi Liguri) (Bordighera, 1946, 1956)
Argissa iii	E. Hanschmann and V. Milojčić, *Argissa-magula* iii: *Die Frühe und Beginnende Mittlere Bronzezeit* (Bonn, 1976)
AS	*Anatolian Studies*

Asea E.J. Holmberg, *The Swedish Excavations at Asea in Arcadia* (Lund and Leipzig, 1944)

Asine O. Frödin and A.W. Persson, *Asine, Results of the Swedish Excavations 1922–1930* (Stockholm, 1938)

Aspripetra D. Levi, 'La Grotta di Aspripetra a Coo', *Annuario* viii–ix (1925–26 pub. 1929) 235–310

Athenian Agora xiii S.A. Immerwahr, *The Athenian Agora* xiii *The Neolithic and Bronze Ages* (Princeton, 1971)

Ayia Sofia Magula V. Milojčić and others, *Magulen um Larisa in Thessalien 1966* (Bonn, 1976)

Ayios Kosmas G. Mylonas, *Aghios Kosmas, an Early Bronze Age Settlement and Cemetery in Attica* (Princeton U.P., 1959)

Baden Symposium *Symposium über die Enstehung und Chronologie der Badener Kultur* (Bratislava: Slovak Academy of Sciences, 1973)

Berciu, *Contributii* D. Berciu, *Contributii la Problemele Neoliticului în Romînia în Lumina noilor Cercetári* (Bucharest, 1961)

Beycesultan i, ii S. Lloyd and J. Mellaart, *Beycesultan* i: *The Chalcolithic and Early Bronze Age Levels* (London, 1962); ii: *Middle Bronze Age Architecture and Pottery* (London, 1965)

BMA E.J. Forsdyke, *Catalogue of the Greek and Etruscan Vases in the British Museum* vol. i Part 1: *Prehistoric Aegean Pottery* (London, 1925)

Boll. d'Arte *Bollettino d'Arte*

Branigan, *Aegean Metalwork* K. Branigan, *Aegean Metalwork of the Early and Middle Bronze Age* (Oxford, 1974)

BRGK *Bericht der Römisch-Germanischen Kommission*

Buchholz and Karageorghis H.-G. Buchholz and V. Karageorghis, *Prehistoric Greece and Cyprus: an archaeological handbook (*London, 1973)

Burton-Brown 1970 *Third Millennium Diffusion* i: *Diffusion of Ideas* (Wootton, Oxford, 1970)

Byblos v M. Dunand, *Fouilles de Byblos* v (Paris, 1973)

*CAH*³ *Cambridge Ancient History* (3rd edition)

Cape Gelidonya G.F. Bass, *Cape Gelidonya: a Bronze Age Shipwreck* (Philadelphia, 1967)

Catling, *Cypriot Bronzework* H.W. Catling, *Cypriot Bronzework in the Mycenaean World* (Oxford, 1964)

Childe, *Danube* V.G. Childe, *The Danube in Prehistory* (Oxford, 1929)

Childe, *Dawn* V.G. Childe, *The Dawn of European Civilization* (6th edition) (London, 1957)

Childe, *New Light* V.G. Childe, *New Light on the Most Ancient East* (London, 1952)

CMS F. Matz and H. Biesantz (ed.), *Corpus der Minoischen und Mykenischen Siegel* i–   (Berlin, 1964–   )

Corinth xiii C.W. Blegen, H. Palmer, R.S. Young, *Corinth* xiii *The North Cemetery* (Princeton, 1964)

Cos L. Morricone, 'Coo—Scavi e Scoperte nel 'Serraglio' e in località minori (1935–1943)', *Annuario* l–li (N.S. xxxiv–xxxv) (1972–73 pub. 1975) 139–396

Davis and Cherry J.L. Davis and J.F. Cherry, *Papers in Cycladic Prehistory* (University of California, Institute of Archaeology, Monograph xiv) (Los Angeles, 1979)

Déchelette i — J. Déchelette, *Manuel d'archéologie préhistorique, celtique et gallo-romaine* (2nd edition) i (Paris, 1928)

Delos xi — A. Plassart, *Délos* xi: *Les sanctuaires et les cultes du Mont Cynthe* (Paris, 1928)

Dendra NT — A.W. Persson, *New Tombs at Dendra near Midea* (Lund, Leipzig, London, Oxford U.P., 1942)

Desborough, *LMS* — V.R. d'A. Desborough, *The Last Mycenaeans and their Successors* (Oxford, 1964)

Deshayes, *Les Outils* i, ii — J. Deshayes, *Les Outils de Bronze, de l'Indus au Danube* i, ii (Paris, 1960)

Dörpfeld, *Alt-Ithaka* — W. Dörpfeld, *Alt-Ithaka* i, ii (Munich, 1927)

Doumas, *Burial Habits* — Ch. Doumas, *Early Bronze Age Burial Habits in the Cyclades* (S.I.M.A. xlviii) (Göteborg, 1977)

DS — Ch. Tsountas, *Αἱ προϊστορικαὶ ἀκροπόλεις Διμηνίου καὶ Σέσκλου* (Athens, 1908)

Ehrich, *Chronologies* (1965) — R.W. Ehrich (ed.), *Chronologies in Old World Archaeology* (Chicago U.P., 1965)

Elateia — S.S. Weinberg, 'Excavations at Prehistoric Elateia, 1959', *Hesperia* xxxi (1962) 158–209

Emery, *Archaic Egypt* — W.B. Emery, *Archaic Egypt* (Harmondsworth, 1961)

Enkomi ii, iii a — P. Dikaios, *Enkomi, Excavations 1948–1958* (Mainz: Philipp von Zabern, 1971, 1969)

ESA — *Eurasia Septentrionalis Antiqua*

Eslick 1980 — Christine Eslick, 'Middle Chalcolithic Pottery from Southwestern Anatolia', *AJA* lxxxiv (1980) 5–14

Eutresis — H. Goldman, *Excavations at Eutresis in Boeotia* (Harvard U.P., Cambridge, Mass., 1931)

Festos i — L. Pernier, *Il Palazzo minoico di Festòs* i: *Gli Strati più antichi e il primo Palazzo* (Rome, 1935)

FMP — A. Furumark, *The Mycenaean Pottery, Analysis and Classification* (Stockholm, 1941)

French, *Pottery Groups* — D.H. French, *Notes on Prehistoric Pottery Groups from Central Greece* (Athens, 1972)

French, *Thesis* — D.H. French, *Anatolia and the Aegean in the Third Millennium B.C.* (Cambridge Ph.D. Thesis, 1968)

Gaul, *Neolithic Bulgaria* — J.H. Gaul, *The Neolithic Period in Bulgaria* (American School of Prehistoric Research Bulletin 16) (Cambridge, Mass., 1948)

Gawra i — E.A. Speiser, *Excavations at Tepe Gawra* (Philadelphia, 1935)

Gawra ii — A.J. Tobler, *Excavations at Tepe Gawra* (Philadelphia, 1950)

Gazetteer (1979) — R. Hope Simpson and O.T.P.K. Dickinson, *A Gazetteer of Aegean Civilisation in the Bronze Age* i: *The Mainland and Islands* (S.I.M.A. lii) (Göteborg, 1979)

Gimbutas, *Bronze Age Cultures* — M. Gimbutas, *Bronze Age Cultures in Central and Eastern Europe* (The Hague, 1965)

Gimbutas, *Prehistory* — M. Gimbutas, *The Prehistory of Eastern Europe* Part 1: *Mesolithic, Neolithic and Cooper Age Cultures in Russia and the Baltic Area* (Peabody Museum, Harvard University, Bulletin No. 20) (Cambridge, Mass., 1956)

Gonia	C.W. Blegen, 'Gonia', *Metropolitan Museum Studies* iii Part 1 (1930) 55–80
Gournia	H. Boyd Hawes and others, *Gournia, Vasiliki and other Prehistoric Sites on the Isthmus of Hierapetra* (Philadelphia, 1908)
Greek Emporio	J. Boardman, *Excavations in Chios 1952–1955, Greek Emporio* (British School of Archaeology at Athens, Supplementary Vol. 6) (London, 1967)
Hăbăşeşti	V. Dumitrescu, *Hăbăşeşti* (Bucharest, 1954)
Hacilar i, ii	J. Mellaart, *Excavations at Hacilar* i, ii (Edinburgh, 1970)
Hama ii. 1	E. Fugmann, *Hama: fouilles et recherches 1931–1938* ii 1 (Copenhagen, 1958)
Hammond, *Migrations*	N.G.L. Hammond, *Migrations and Invasions in Greece and Adjacent Areas* (Park Ridge, New Jersey: Noyes Press, 1976)
Hennessy, *Foreign Relations*	J.B. Hennessy, *The Foreign Relations of Palestine during the Early Bronze Age* (London, 1967)
Higgins, *Greek and Roman Jewellery*	R.A. Higgins, *Greek and Roman Jewellery* (London, 1961)
Hissar	E.F. Schmidt, *Excavations at Tepe Hissar Damghan* (Philadelphia, 1937)
Holmberg, *Neolithic Pottery*	E.J. Holmberg, *The Neolithic Pottery of Mainland Greece* (Göteborg, 1964)
Homolka	R.W. Ehrich and E. Pleslová-Štiková, *Homolka, an Eneolithic Site in Bohemia* (Prague, 1968)
Iasos i	D. Levi, 'Le due prime campagne di scavo a Iasos (1960–1961)', *Annuario* xxxix–xl (N.S. xxiii–xxiv) (1961–62) 505–571
Iasos ii	D. Levi, 'Le campagne 1962–1964 a Iasos', *Annuario* xliii–xliv (N.S. xxvii–xxviii) (1965–66) 401–546
Iasos iii	D. Levi, 'Gli scavi di Iasos', *Annuario* xlv–xlvi (N.S. xxix–xxx) (1967–68) 537–590
Iasos iv	D. Levi, 'Iasos. Le campagne di scavo 1969–70', *Annuario* xlvii–xlviii (N.S. xxxi–xxxii) (1969–70) 461–532
Ilios	H. Schliemann, *Ilios: the city and country of the Trojans* (London, 1880)
Ist. Mitt.	*Istanbuler Mitteilungen*
Izvoare	R. Vulpe, *Izvoare* (Bucharest, 1957)
Jacobsthal, *Greek Pins*	P. Jacobsthal, *Greek Pins and their Connexions with Europe and Asia* (Oxford, 1956)
Jarmo	R.J. Braidwood and B. Howe, *Prehistoric Investigations in Iraqui Kurdistan* (Studies in Ancient and Oriental Civilization no. 31) (Chicago O.I., 1960)
JFA	*Journal of Field Archaeology*
JNES	*Journal of Near Eastern Studies*
JRGZMainz	*Jahrbuch des Römisch-Germanischen Zentralmuseums Mainz*
Judeideh	R.J. Braidwood and Linda S. Braidwood, *Excavations in the Plain of Antioch* i: *The Earlier Assemblages, Phases A–J* (O.I.P. lxi) (Chicago, 1960)
Karo, *SG*	G. Karo, *Die Schachtgräber von Mykenai* (Munich, 1930)
Kephala	J.E. Coleman, *Keos* i *Kephala: a Late Neolithic Settlement and Cemetery* (Princeton, 1977)

Kerameikos i	W. Kraiker and K. Kübler, *Kerameikos* i: *Die Nekropolen des 12. bis 10. Jahrhunderts* (Berlin, 1939)
Khirokitia	P. Dikaios, *Khirokitia* (Oxford U.P., 1953)
KKh	Κρητικὰ Χρονικά
Kish i	S. Langdon, *Excavations at Kish* i: *1923–1924* (Paris, 1924)
Korakou	C.W. Blegen, *Korakou, a Prehistoric Settlement near Corinth* (Boston and New York, 1921)
Korucutepe ii	M.N. van Loon, *Korucutepe* ii (Amsterdam, 1978)
Kum Tepe	J.W. Sperling, 'Kum Tepe in the Troad: trial excavation, 1934', *Hesperia* xlv (1976) 305–364
Kutzían, *Körös-Kultúra*	I. Kutzían, *A Körös-Kultúra* (Budapest, 1944)
Kythera	J.N. Coldstream and G.L. Huxley, *Kythera* (London, 1972)
Lefkandi	M.R. Popham and L.H. Sackett, *Excavations at Lefkandi, Euboea, 1964–66* (British School of Archaeology at Athens) (London, 1968)
London BIA	*Bulletin of the Institute of Archaeology, London University*
MacGillivray 1979	J.A. MacGillivray, *Early Cycladic Pottery from Mt. Kynthos in Delos* (Edinburgh, 1979)
Marinatos and Hirmer	S. Marinatos and M. Hirmer, *Crete and Mycenae* (London, 1960)
Mat. și Cercetari	*Materiale și Cercetari arheologice*
Maxwell-Hyslop, *Western Asiatic Jewellery*	K.R. Maxwell-Hyslop, *Western Asiatic Jewellery c. 3000–612 B.C.* (London, 1971)
Megiddo i	R.S. Lamon and G.M. Shipton, *Megiddo* i: *Seasons of 1925–1934, Strata I–V* (O.I.P. xlii) (Chicago, 1939)
Megiddo ii	G. Loud, *Megiddo* ii: *Seasons of 1935–39* (O.I.P. lxii) (Chicago, 1948)
Mellaart, *Çatal Hüyük*	J. Mellaart, *Çatal Hüyük: a Neolithic town in Anatolia* (London, 1967)
Mellaart, *Neolithic Near East*	J. Mellaart, *The Neolithic of the Near East* (London, 1975)
Mersin	J. Garstang, *Prehistoric Mersin* (Oxford, 1953)
Milojcic, *Ergebnisse*	V. Milojčić, 'Ergebnisse der deutschen Ausgrabungen in Thessalien 1953–1958', *JRGZMainz* vi (1959) 1–56
Mochlos	R.B. Seager, *Explorations in the Island of Mochlos* (Boston and New York, 1912)
Mylonas, *Circle B*	G.E. Mylonas, Ὁ ταφικὸς κύκλος Β τῶν Μυκηνῶν i, ii (Athens, 1972, 1973)
Myrtos	P. Warren, *Myrtos, an Early Bronze Age Settlement in Crete* (British School of Archaeology at Athens, Supplementary Vol. 7) (Oxford, 1972)
Nea Makri	D.R. Theochares, 'Nea Makri: eine grosse neolithische Siedlung in der Nähe von Marathon', *AM* lxxi (1956) 1–29
Nea Nikomedeia	R.J. Rodden, 'Excavations at the Early Neolithic Site at Nea Nikomedeia, Greek Macedonia', *PPS* xxviii (1962) 267–288
Nemea	C.W. Blegen, 'Neolithic Remains at Nemea', *Hesperia* xliv (1975) 251–279
NMA	National Museum in Athens
Olynthus i	G.E. Mylonas, *Excavations at Olynthus* i: *the Neolithic Settlement* (Baltimore, London, Oxford, 1929)
Orchomenos ii	E. Kunze, *Orchomenos* ii: *Die neolithische Keramik* (Munich, 1931)

Orchomenos iii	E. Kunze, *Orchomenos* iii: *Die Keramik der frühen Bronzezeit* (Munich, 1934)
Otzaki-magula	J. Milojčić-v. Zumbusch and V. Milojčić, *Die deutschen Ausgrabungen auf der Otzaki-magula in Thessalien* i: *Das frühe Neolithikum* (Bonn, 1971)
Palaikastro	R.C. Bosanquet and R.M. Dawkins, *The Unpublished Objects from the Palaikastro Excavations 1902–1906* Part 1 (British School at Athens, Supplementary Paper 1) (London, 1923)
PBA	*Proceedings of the British Academy*
Pendlebury, *AC*	J.D.S. Pendlebury, *The Archaeology of Crete: An Introduction* (London, 1939)
Perachora ii	H.G.G. Payne, *Perachora* ii (Oxford, 1962)
Perate i, ii, iii	S.E. Iakovidis, Περατή: τὸ Νεκροταφεῖον i–iii (Athens, 1969, 1970)
Petrie, *Corpus*	W.M.F. Petrie, *Corpus of Prehistoric Pottery and Palettes* (London, 1921)
Petrie, *Tools and Weapons*	W.M.F. Petrie, *Tools and Weapons* (London, 1917)
Phelps, *Thesis*	W.W. Phelps, *The Neolithic Pottery Sequence in Southern Greece* (London Ph.D. Thesis, 1975)
Phylakopi	*Excavations at Phylakopi in Melos* (The Society for the Promotion of Hellenic Studies, Supplementary Paper No. 4) (London, 1904)
Piggott, *Neolithic Cultures*	S. Piggott, *The Neolithic Cultures of the British Isles* (Cambridge, 1954)
PM i–iv	A.J. Evans, *The Palace of Minos at Knossos* i–iv (London, 1921–35)
PMac	W.A. Heurtley, *Prehistoric Macedonia* (Cambridge U.P., 1939)
P.Nestor i	C.W. Blegen and Marion Rawson, *The Palace of Nestor at Pylos in Western Messenia* i: *The Buildings and their Contents* (Princeton U.P., 1966)
Poliochni i, ii	L. Bernabò-Brea, *Poliochni: città preistorica nell' isola di Lemnos* i, 1: i, 2: ii 1 and 2 (Rome, 1964, 1976)
PPS	*Proceedings of the Prehistoric Society*
Préhistoire française ii	*La Préhistoire française* ii: *Les Civilisations néolithiques et protohistoriques de la France* (ed. J. Guilaine) (Publis à l'occasion du IXe Congrès de l'U.I.S.P.P., Nice, 1976) (Paris, 1976)
Prosymna	C.W. Blegen, *Prosymna: the Helladic settlement preceding the Argive Heraeum* i, ii (Cambridge U.P., 1937)
Protesilaos	R. Demangel, *Fouilles du Corps d'Occupation Français de Constantinople exécutées de 1920 à 1923* i: *Le Tumulus dit de Protésilaos* (Paris, 1926)
PThess	A.J.B. Wace and M.S. Thompson, *Prehistoric Thessaly* (Cambridge U.P., 1912)
Renfrew, *Emergence*	C. Renfrew, *The Emergence of Civilization* (London, 1972)
Saliagos	J.D. Evans and C. Renfrew, *Excavations at Saliagos near Antiparos* (British School of Archaeology at Athens, Supplementary Vol. 5) (London, 1968)
Samos i	V. Milojčić, *Samos* i: *Die Prähistorische Siedlung unter dem Heraion: Grabung 1953 und 1955* (Bonn, 1961)
Samos xiv	Renate Tölle-Kastenbein, *Samos* xiv: *Das Kastro Tigani* (Bonn, 1974)
SCE	*The Swedish Cyprus Expedition* i–iv (Stockholm, 1934–72)
Schachermeyr, *Ältesten Kulturen*	F. Schachermeyr, *Die ältesten kulturen Griechenlands* (Stuttgart, 1955)

Schachermeyr, *Die myk.* F. Schachermeyr, *Die ägäische Frühzeit* ii: *Die mykenische Zeit* (Vienna,
Zeit 1976)
Schliemann, *Troja* H. Schliemann, *Troja* (London, 1884)
Schliemann, *Troy and its* H. Schliemann, *Troy and its Remains* (London, 1875)
Remains
Servia Cressida Ridley and K.A. Wardle, 'Rescue Excavations at Servia
1971–1973: A Preliminary Report', *BSA* lxxiv (1979) 185–230
Sotira P. Dikaios, *Sotira* (Philadelphia, 1961)
SS H. Schmidt, *H. Schliemann's Sammlung Trojanischer Altertümer* (Berlin,
1902)
Sukas iii P.J. Riis and H. Thrane, *Sūkās* iii: *The Neolithic Periods* (Copenhagen,
1974)
Sulimirski, *Prehistoric* T. Sulimirski, *Prehistoric Russia* (London, 1970)
Russia
TAD *Türk Arkeoloji Dergisi*
Tarsus ii H. Goldman, *Excavations at Gözlü Kule, Tarsus* (Princeton U.P., 1956)
Teleilat Ghassul i A. Mallon, R. Koeppel and R. Neuville, *Teleilat Ghassul. Compte rendu
des fouilles de l'Institut biblique pontifical* i *1929–1932* (Rome, 1934)
Theochares, *Auge* D.R. Theochares, *Ἡ αὐγὴ τῆς Θεσσαλικῆς Προϊστορίας* (Volos, 1967)
Theochares, *Neolithic* D.R. Theochares, *Neolithic Greece* (Athens: National Bank of Greece,
Greece 1973)
Thera i–vii S. Marinatos, *Excavations at Thera* i–vii (Athens, 1968–73)
Thermi W. Lamb, *Excavations at Thermi in Lesbos* (Cambridge U.P., 1936)
Thorikos iii H.F. Mussche, *Thorikos 1965: Rapport préliminaire sur la troisième Cam-
pagne de Fouilles* (Bruxelles, 1967)
Tigani 'Vorgeschichtliches in der Stadt Samos', *AM* lx/lxi (1935/36)
112–200: 'Fundtatsachen' by W. Wrede (112–24); 'Die Funde' by R.
Heidenreich (125–83); 'Nachträge' by W. Buttler (184–200)
Troy i–iv C.W. Blegen and others, *Troy* i–iv (Princeton U.P., 1950–58)
TuI W. Dörpfeld, *Troja und Ilion* i, ii (Athens, 1902)
Ucko, *Figurines* P.J. Ucko, *Anthropomorphic Figurines* (London, 1968)
Ugaritica iv C.F.A. Schaeffer, *Ugaritica* iv (Paris, 1962)
Ur ii C.L. Woolley, *Ur Excavations* ii: *The Royal Cemetery* (London, 1933)
Valmin, *SME* M.N. Valmin, *The Swedish Messenia Expedition* (Lund etc., 1938)
Vermeule, *GBA* E. Vermeule, *Greece in the Bronze Age* (Chicago, 1954)
Vinca i–iv M.M. Vasić, *Preistoriska Vinča* i–iv (Belgrade, 1932–36)
Vitelli 1977 Karen D. Vitelli, 'Neolithic Potter's Marks from Lerna and the
Franchthi Cave', *Journal of the Walters Art Gallery* xxxvi (1977) 17–30
Vrokastro E.H. Hall, *Excavations in Eastern Crete: Vrokastro* (University of Penn-
sylvania Museum Anthropological Publications III No. 3) (Phila-
delphia, 1914)
VTM S. Xanthoudides, *The Vaulted Tombs of Mesara: an account of some early
cemeteries of southern Crete* (London, 1924)
Wace, *Chamber Tombs* A.J.B. Wace, 'Chamber Tombs at Mycenae', *Archaeologia* lxxxii
(1932) 1–242
Wace, *Mycenae* A.J.B. Wace, *Mycenae: an archaeological history and guide* (Princeton
U.P., 1949)

Walker Kosmopoulos,   L. Walker Kosmopoulos, *The Prehistoric Inhabitation of Corinth*
   Corinth   (Munich, 1948)
Walker Kosmopoulos   L. Walker Kosmopoulos, 'Birch-bark technique: a possible prototype
   1953   for some Greek prehistoric wares?', in G.E. Mylonas (ed.), *Studies
                       Presented to D.M. Robinson* ii (St. Louis, 1953) 1–24
Warren, *MSV*   P. Warren, *Minoan Stone Vases* (Cambridge U.P., 1969)
Weinberg, *CAH*   S.S. Weinberg, 'the Stone Age in the Aegean', *Cambridge Ancient
                       History*[3] vol. i Part 1 (Cambridge, 1970) Ch. x
Zervos, *ACr*   C. Zervos, *L'Art de la Crète néolithique et minoenne* (Paris, 1956)
Zervos, *ACycl*   C. Zervos, *L'Art des Cyclades du début à la fin de l'âge du bronze, 2500–1100
                       avant notre ère* (Paris, 1957)
Zervos, *Nais* i, ii   C. Zervos, *Naissance de la Civilisation en Grèce* i, ii (Paris, 1962, 1963)
Zygouries   C.W. Blegen, *Zygouries, a Prehistoric Settlement in the Valley of Cleonae*
                       (Harvard U.P., Cambridge, Mass., 1928)

Notes

The material from other prehistoric sites in Chios apart from Ayio Gala and Emporio is numbered 1–15. That from Ayio Gala is numbered AG 1–390. The pottery from Emporio is numbered E 1–3000, and the other finds from Emporio apart from pottery have been given their own series of numbers (CLAY 1–41; WHORLS 1–56; STONE 1–54; METAL 1–19; BONE, SHELL, AMBER and FAIENCE 1–68). Chipped stone tools are only numbered if illustrated, with separate series of numbers for ones from Emporio and ones from Ayio Gala.

Where a sherd or other object which has no serial number is illustrated on a PLATE with a number referring to it in the text, the counting is in horizontal rows from left to right beginning at the top left.

All measurements of pottery and other finds are given in centimetres, unless otherwise stated.

For the Mycenaean pottery the term Mycenaean (Myc.) used by Furumark has been adopted in preference to Late Helladic (L.H.).

Part I

Prehistoric Chios

1. INTRODUCTION

The prehistoric antiquities of Chios were first brought to the notice of the public as early as 1888 when the island was still under Turkish rule. In that year Studniczka published an account of primitive handmade pottery which had been recovered by an entomologist, Eberhard von Oertzen, from the lower cave at Ayio Gala in the remote north-western corner of Chios (*AM* xiii (1888) 183–5). Von Oertzen visited the cave shortly after the time when Studniczka was in Chios in 1887. Excavations by Miss Edith Eccles in 1938 showed that this pottery belonged to the Neolithic and Early Bronze Ages as described in PART II.

The so-called 'Pelasgic Wall' (Fig. 1: A) by the main road from Chios town to Piryi, just south of Tholopotami, was first reported by Studniczka, but he did not have time to examine it (*AM* xiii (1888) 163. Cf. *BSA* xli (1940–45) 35 f.). From a distance it looks remarkably like a Mycenaean defence wall. A close inspection, however, reveals that it is in fact a natural formation of the rock, consisting of a stratum which has been forced by pressure into a vertical position, and which has then split into separate, roughly polygonal, fragments.

A tomb chamber built of squared stone was first noted by Dr Philip Argenti before the Second World War at the far end of the plain of Dotia above the little bay of Vroulidhia in southern Chios (Fig. 1: B). This was later seen by D.W.S. Hunt, who, from its striking resemblance to the Minoan built tombs at Isopata near Knossos, suggested that it might have been constructed in the Bronze Age as the last resting place of a Cretan sea-captain (*BSA* xli (1940–45) 38 f.). In 1951, however, I was able to clear away the earth from above the top of the tomb, which proved to date from Roman times. The tomb will be described in a future volume about Roman Emporio. A small rock-cut tomb of the Early Bronze Age was discovered inland from here by the shooting-box of the late Mr George Choremis, and was examined in 1936 by Miss Edith Eccles (site 5 (2) below).

In 1938 Hunt saw what he took to be ancient rock-cut tombs exposed by falls of the limestone rock on the summit of the Latomi (Quarry) hill north of Chios town (*BSA* xli (1940–45) 32). He compared these with the Bronze Age rock-cut tomb at Dotia; but they may have been of later, Greek or Roman, date, since the Bronze Age people of the Aegean area in general avoided excavating tombs in hard limestone, and Kourouniotis records a rock-cut grave of the Classical period found below a tumulus in this area (*ADelt* i (1915) 69).

An extensive search of the environs of Chios town has rather surprisingly failed to bring to light any other possible traces of prehistoric settlement, apart from the fragment of a stone axe from the Kofina ridge and a Mycenaean kylix foot from Frankomakhalas (site 11).

A Mycenaean sherd and a marble dagger pommel in Chios Museum appear to come from excavations at Kato Fana (site 7). There is a good deal of Mycenaean pottery together with some traces of earlier Bronze Age occupation at the important Archaic site (17) near Volissos discovered by Professor John Cook.

This site at Volissos and other prehistoric sites noted by us during the time of our work in

1

Chios from 1952–61 are listed below. Most of the pottery from these sites appeared to date from the earlier part of the Bronze Age, the horizon of Troy I–II. Traces of occupation assignable to the Middle Bronze Age were curiously rare. But there was evidence for Mycenaean occupation at a few other sites besides Volissos.

A small double-bladed axe, apparently of copper, is alleged to come from Chios (W. Ridgeway, *The Early Age of Greece* (Cambridge, 1931) 51 fig. 27).

2. SITES WITH BRONZE AGE OR EARLIER REMAINS
(FIGS. 1 and 2)

1. Emporio (see PART III).

2. Pindakas. One worn sherd that might be of Bronze Age date from the area of the Classical farmhouse excavated here in 1954 (J. Boardman, *BSA* liii–liv (1958–59) 295–309). The site, on a knoll in the middle of cultivable ground with a supply of good water to hand, is one calculated to attract occupation in early times.

3. Kalamoti (PLATE 1 (*a*)). Bearings: church at the northern end of Kalamoti village, 50°. Armolia church, 349°. Church on Profitis Ilias, 185°. Traces of an Early Bronze Age settlement noted in 1955 on a flat-topped hill in the middle of the valley south-west of the village, north of the church of the Panayia (the most northerly of three in this area) which has ancient blocks and mouldings built into its walls. The hill, the central one of three in a north–south ridge, overlooks the path from Kalamoti to Komi on the coast, and enjoys a fine view southwards to the sea. The Bronze Age settlement may have been an extensive one to judge from the scatter of stones from house walls; but the site is much eroded, and while a number of sherds are recognisably of Early Bronze Age date, there are traces of much later, Greco-Roman or mediaeval, occupation. Pottery assignable to the Bronze Age included the foot of a tripod cooking pot with thick oval section, and the rims (1, 2) below.

1. Rim of small carinated bowl (Emporio type 9) with low wart. Clay grey-black at the core, light brown at the edges; surface grey-brown burnished, worn. Cf. Emporio Period II.
2. Rim. Very irregular. Sandy orange clay with traces of a red wash.

4. Armolia. An isolated rim of a bowl of Troy IV–VI type (3) found in 1955 in flat ground due south of the village, in the area between the Kalamoti and Piryi roads, and about 100 m SE of the small church of Ayia Marina, which is hidden among mastica bushes and olive trees at the

FIG. 1. Chios, showing prehistoric sites

1. Emporio		S	C	M	10. Mesta	?		
2. Pindakas	?				11. Chios town	X		
3. Kalamoti		S			12. Nea Moni	X		
4. Armolia	X				13. Khalkios	X		
5. Dotia		S	C		14. Langadha: Ayios Isidhoros		S	
6. Piryi: Kastri tou Psellou		S		?M	15. Nagos		S	?M
7. Kato Fana	?			M	16. Ayio Gala		S	
8. Olimpoi: Petranos		S			17. Volissos: Levkathia		S	M
9. Olimpoi: Tripanos		S			18. Volissos: Anemomilos		S	
					19. Elinda	X		

KEY: S, Traces of Neolithic and/or Early Bronze Age settlement; C, Early Bronze Age tombs or cemeteries; M, Traces of Mycenaean occupation; X, Other prehistoric finds; ?, Doubtful prehistoric traces.

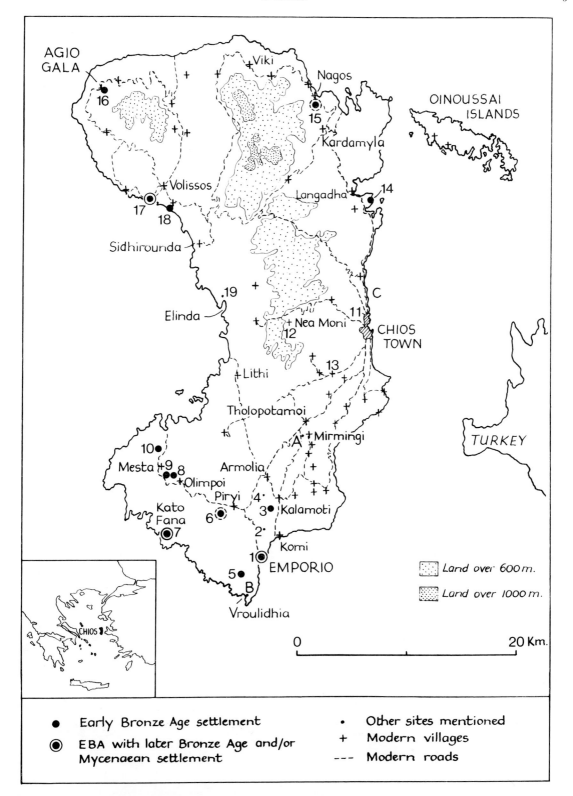

AGIO GALA

Viki

Nagos

OINOUSSAI ISLANDS

16

15

Kardamyla

Volissos

Langadha 14

17

18

Sidhirounda

.19

Elinda

C

11

Nea Moni

CHIOS TOWN

12

13

Lithi

Tholopotamoi

TURKEY

Mirmingi

10

A

Mesta +9 8

Armolia

Olimpoi

Piryi 4

Kato Fana

6

3 Kalamoti

7

2.

Komi

1 EMPORIO

5

B

Vroulidhia

CHIOS

Land over 600 m.

Land over 1000 m.

0   20 Km.

● Early Bronze Age settlement   • Other sites mentioned

◉ EBA with later Bronze Age and/or   + Modern villages
   Mycenaean settlement   --- Modern roads

eastern foot of a hill with a ruined windmill. A sherd of Classical black glaze and a piece of glazed tile were also noted here.

    3. Rim of bowl with side handle. Sandy orange clay somewhat dusky at the core. Surface originally it seems light-brown burnished, but now much worn. Cf. Troy IV–early VI (e.g. *Troy* ii fig. 183: 8–9 (Troy IV); ibid. fig. 254: 2 (Troy V); *Troy* iii fig. 424: 1 (early VI).

5. Dotia.

    (1) *Settlement.* Traces of an extensive Bronze Age settlement on the low hill where the shooting-box constructed by the late Mr. George Choremis stands and in the area of flat ground to the south of it. The inhabitants no doubt exploited the fertile valley of Dotia as the inhabitants of the deserted Mediaeval village at the eastern end of the valley did after them. The valley is now devoted to the cultivation of mastic bushes and belongs to the inland village of Piryi. The site was noted by Mr Choremis at the time the house was built, and he kept pottery found in digging foundations for its walls. This pottery, now stored in the Folk Museum above the Koraes Library in Chios town, is all handmade and Early Bronze Age (Emporio V–IV) in character. Two stone handles, one (4) found by me in 1952, the other (5) brought to me in 1954 as from the settlement here, are described below.

    4. Handle (PLATE 3 (*a*) right). Broken short at the lower end. L. 3. 2. fine-grained, yellowish translucent stone.
    5. Handle as 4 (PLATE 3 (*a*) left). Broken short at the lower end. L. 3. 5. Perforation 0.5 in diam. widening to 0.9 above.

    A similar object is illustrated from Palaia Kokkinia near Athens (*PAE* 1951, 113, 115 fig. 30: right, assigned to Late Neolithic or Early Helladic I). For a more elaborate stone handle, e.g. *AM* xi (1886) 20, 16 Beil. 1: D. 2, allegedly from Amorgos. See C. Renfrew, *AJA* lxxi (1967) 6 f., for this and other handles of anhydrite or calcite from the Cyclades.

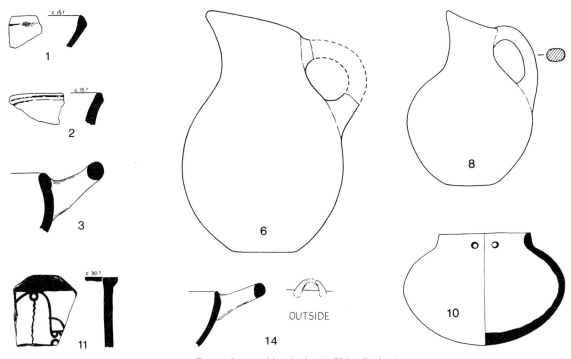

FIG. 2. Pottery from prehistoric sites in Chios. Scale 1/3.

(2) *Tombs.* In a gentle slope across a gully from the settlement and about 200 m west of the Choremis house. An Early Bronze Age rock-cut tomb was discovered here by chance and was visited by Miss Edith Eccles in 1936 (*BSA* xli (1940–45) 38). The chamber was intact, roughly oval in shape, some 2 m wide and 1.60 m long, but only about a metre high inside. The entrance, which was still visible in 1952, consisted of a hole about 0.70 m across. Its top was flush with the ceiling of the chamber, leaving a step down into it. The tomb was therefore probably very similar to that of comparable date excavated in Area E at Emporio (Tomb 1, FIG. 82). The entrance may have been at the bottom of a shallow pit, like the entraces of the Early Bronze Age tombs at Manika in Euboia (G.A. Papavasileiou, *Peri ton en Euboia Arkhaion Tafon* (Athens, 1910) pl. A); but all traces of this, if it ever existed, had been removed by erosion. The owner of the land, Mr. Georgios Ioannou Paplos, said that when he found the tomb the entrance was blocked by a flat slab of stone foreign to the Dotia region, and deriving perhaps from Thimiana about 5 km south of Chios town. He also told Miss Eccles about a 'kanali' leading into the tomb to the right of the slab, but he made no mention of this to me when I met him in 1952. Near the back wall of the chamber according to his description were five clay vases (6–10), together with some bones and a skull which broke when it was moved. The bones were apparently left in the chamber. The vases, all handmade, are comparable with ones of Periods V/IV–II at Emporio.

6–8. Jugs (PLATE 3 (*c*)). Hts. 19, 16.5, 14. Complete and unbroken, except for the handle missing from 6. The handle of 7 is more strap-like and rises above the rim. The clay, where exposed in the break in 8, is red-brown with large grit. Surfaces darkish brown, burnished but worn.

9. Pyxis with lid (PLATE 3 (*d*), (*e*)). Ht. of pyxis without lid 11. Diam. of rim 6.5, of body 14. Four vertically perforated lugs (two missing) on the belly were matched by four on the lid. The lid has a small depression in the top centre. Red-brown clay with grit. Surface shades of dark brown, well burnished. Fine rather shallow incised decoration with possible traces of an original white fill (reproduced with flour for the photos on PLATE 3 (*d*), (*e*)).

10. Pyxis (PLATE 3 (*b*)). Ht. 9 Diam. of rim 7.5, of body 13. Pairs of string-holes made before firing at opposite sides of the rim. Cracked down one side, but complete. Crudely made, with some large grit showing in the surface, which is shades of light and darker brown, burnished.

Miss Eccles recorded the position of another tomb to the north of this one and slightly higher on the slope. At the invitation of Mr. Choremis I made trials here for three days in the autumn of 1952 in a search for more tombs. An area of about 25 by 25 m was tested with trenches at intervals of 1.50–3.00 m in the spaces between the mastic bushes which clothed the slope. The only other traces of burials noted were higher on the slope some 17.50 m north of the tomb. Here I came upon a human jaw and part of a skull tucked away in crannies in the rock not far below the surface. There was nothing, however, to suggest the former existence of a rock-cut tomb in the area. Possibly natural cavities in the rock had been used for burials.

6. Piryi: Kastri tou Psellou (PLATE 1 (*b*)–(*d*)).

Settlement on a rocky hill west of Piryi village south of the junction of two paths, one leading to Karinda, the other to Kato Fana. The hill is in the range which divides the two plains lying to the south of the village. Below it on the north, in the angle between the paths to Karinda and Kato Fana, is the site of the deserted Mediaeval village of Managros. Several of its churches still survive. Ancient mouldings built into these were apparently brought from Kato Fana some 5 km away to the west (Boardman, *AntJ* xxxix (1959) 171 f.). But a fragment of fine Classical black glaze was noted here in 1961, and the Mediaeval village might have occupied the site of an earlier settlement.

Stones from house walls are much in evidence on the hill. The fortifications from which it gets its name of Kastri seem to date from Classical times. A stretch of defence wall some 2 m wide and built of rough stones is preserved to a height of about a metre on the west side of it (PLATE 1 (*d*)).

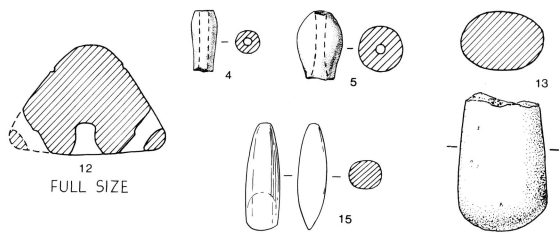

FIG. 3. Miscellaneous finds from prehistoric sites in Chios. Scale 1/2, except 12 (1/1).

While some of the pottery on the hill looks Classical, much of it is certainly prehistoric, although worn and undiagnostic. Most of the prehistoric sherds with any recognisable character seemed to be of Early Bronze Age types reminiscent of Emporio V–IV; but one plain base looked Mycenaean, and a fragment of pithos had a pair of hollow ribs like some late Bronze Age pithoi from Emporio (FIG. 276. PLATE 125).

7. Kato Fana. (1) Settlement (?). Scraps of what may have been Bronze Age pottery noted in 1954 on the slopes NE of the temple site. (2) Mycenaean sherd (11) and marble dagger pommel (12) from earlier excavations in Chios Museum. These excavations were made by K. Kourouniotis in 1913 and 1915, and by Miss Winifred Lamb in 1934 (*ADelt* i (1915) 72–85; ii (1916) 190–212. *BSA* xxxv (1934–35) 138–64. Cf. *Gazetteer* (1979) 370). The sherd and pommel do not appear to be illustrated in their reports; but the pommel may be Miss Lamb's 'marble boss with flat back, . . . pierced diagonally at the corners', which she tentatively suggested might have been the eye of an Ionic capital made as a separate piece (*BSA* xxxv (1934–35) 153). One of the fragments of pottery illustrated by Kourouniotis as Archaic Greek looks as if it could be Mycenaean (*ADelt* ii (1916) 205 fig. 24, third row from top on left. Cf. PLATE 119 (*a*) from Emporio).

11. Rim of Mycenaean krater (PLATE 3 (*f*)). Marked in ink φ Q 4.50–3.25. Orange clay; the surface orange-buff, smoothed but not burnished. Decorated in lustrous black. L.H. III C.
12. Conical dagger pommel (PLATE 3 (*g*)). Fine white translucent ?marble. Ht. 2.8. Diam. 4.3. Hole for the tang in the centre of the flat under side, and two diagonal holes (one broken) for rivets. The conical top decorated with a pair of irregular grooves.
   Pommels of Minoan and Mycenaean daggers normally seem to have been rounded on top. But the gold-plated pommel of the sword from a tomb of L.H. II date on Peparithos (Skopelos) is of this shape although flatter in profile (Marinatos and Hirmer pl. 173).

8. Olimpoi: Petranos (PLATE 1 (*f*)). Traces of Bronze Age occupation noted in 1961 on the south end of this small but dominating hill slightly north of west from Olimpoi village on the north side of the road to Mesta. Sherds, which were visible over a somewhat restricted area on the summit measuring about 50 m from north to south by about 25 m from east to west, tended to be large and well preserved, and included a good many pithos fragments. Traces of occupation did not seem to extend over the plateau to the north, but fragments of pottery and stones that might have come from ancient house walls were scattered down the steep eroded southern slope of the hill for a distance of 50 m or more from the summit. The pottery, as far as could be judged, seemed to correspond to that of Emporio V–II. The comparatively small area covered by traces of occupation, and the proximity of an extensive settlement which appears to date from the same period on the neighbouring hill of Tripanos (9), suggest that this might have been the site of an isolated farm or chieftain's house like that of the Troy I period at Karataṣ, Semayük in SW Anatolia (*AJA* lxix (1965) 245 ff.; lxx (1966) 245 ff.).

9. Olimpoi: Tripanos (PLATE 1 (*e*), (*f*)). Settlement noted in 1961 on the summit of a prominent hill *c.* 500 m due west of 8. The hill enjoys a view over a wide area: the villages of Mesta and Olimpoi are both visible from here, together with the sea on three sides. The site is much eroded, but the settlement appears to have been extensive, covering an area of about 100 m or more in all directions. Pottery included very worn sherds of distinctively Early Bronze Age (Emporio V–II) character, together with some of later periods. On the south side of the hill, about 50 m from the top, the line of a possible defence wall is indicated by a modern terrace wall with more stones than any of the others that traverse the slopes above and below it. Sherds and stones that might have come from ancient house walls are noticeably less in evidence on the slopes below this terrace wall than on those above it. Similar indications of a defence wall can be detected in places on the west and north sides of the hill.

10. Mesta. Possible traces of Bronze Age occupation on a hill to the left of the road leading from Mesta village to Pasha Limani. Scraps of pottery that might be of Bronze Age date were noted here in 1955. But shallow depressions cut in a flat rock on the summit are suggestive of an oil-press of the Greek or Roman periods.

11. Chios town. The only evidence for prehistoric occupation noted in this area was a broken stone axe (13) recovered in 1961 on the southern slope of the Kofina ridge below the site of the 1952 excavations, and a Mycenaean kylix foot from Frankomakhalas south-west of Kofina (*BSA* xlix (1954) 123–82. *Greek Emporio* 250 note 3. *Gazetteer* (1979) 370).

13. Axe blade (PLATE 3 (*h*) left). L. preserved 7.2.
   Hard, very dark grey-green crystalline stone mottled in places with red and containing fine shiny particles. The surface rough except for the blade which is highly polished.

12. Nea Moni. There is a stone axe, allegedly from this area, in Chios Museum.

13. Khalkios. A stone axe in Chios Museum is said to come from here.

14. Langadha: Ayios Isidhoros (PLATE 2 (*a*)). Traces of a Bronze Age settlement noted in 1961 on the promontory behind the church of Ayios Isidhoros south of Langadha. The promontory is now an island joined to the mainland by an artificial causeway. A few worn sherds of Bronze Age type are to be found in pockets in the rock over an area of about 50 × 25 m. To the north of the promontory there is a fine sandy beach suitable for drawing boats ashore.

15. Nagos (PLATE 2 (*b*)). Possible traces of a Bronze Age settlement noted in 1961 on a high, steep-sided hill, south of the road from Kardhamila shortly before it reaches Nagos. The hill occupies a dominating position, and catches the eye of anyone coming from Ano Kardhamila, which is visible from the summit. On the east and west sides it falls away into cliffs which descend into gorges running back into the mountains behind it to the south.

Traces of ancient walls could be detected on the slopes just below the northern edge of the summit area. All the way down the slopes on this northern or seaward side of the hill, as well as on the summit, was a scatter of small stones that might have come from ancient house walls. Occasional lumps of coarse pottery appeared to be of Bronze Age date. Some of the pottery looked as if it might be of the horizon of Troy II–VI or Mycenaean. But there was also evidence for occupation in later, Greek or Roman, times, and the remains of structures on the summit of the hill all seem to date from then rather than earlier.

Near the far southern end of the summit, and about 20 m south of the highest point, was a shallow circular sinking about 2 m in diameter and lined with stones. Another smaller circular sinking was visible next to it on the east. Some 30 m to the north traces of a curving stretch of wall were noted. Large fragments of a storage jar or small pithos, apparently Greco-Roman, were exposed in this area in 1961. About 20 m north of the curved wall, near the highest part of the northern end of the summit, was a kind of low stand, roughly square in shape and about 1.50 m across. The sides of this consisted of walling which was only preserved one or two courses high. It was somewhat reminiscent of the original open-air altar (A) of the Athena temple at Emporio (*Greek Emporio* 6–9).

Near the foot of the hill on the north there is a small church, and on the slopes below this fragments of Greek or Roman pottery and tile were thickly strewn for a distance of some 50 m.

16. Ayio Gala (see PART II).

17. Volissos: Levkathia (PLATE 2 (*d*)). Settlement on the promontory of Levkathia or Limnos which juts boldly into the sea west of the modern town. The important Archaic site here was first noted by Professor John Cook (*JHS* lxxi (1951) 247. R. Hope simpson, *A Gazetteer and Atlas of Mycenaean Sites* (London, 1965) 190. *Gazetteer* (1979) 371). While most of the pottery on the surface appears to be Archaic, Mycenaean sherds are also in evidence, especially at the far western end of the site. Mycenaean sherds recovered here in 1961 included a couple of kylix stems and a fragment of pithos with a pair of hollow ribs like some Late Bronze Age pithoi from Emporio (e.g. E. 2899–2901).

The promontory may have been occupied before Mycenaean times to judge from a fragment of bowl rim with a fine trumpet lug rising from it recovered here in 1961. The type of bowl is uncertain, but comparable trumpet lugs at Emporio were assignable to the horizon of Periods VII/VI–V/IV.

18. Volissos: Anemomilos (PLATE 2 (*e*), (*f*)). Settlement noted in 1961 on a low rocky hill by the sea at the end of the road from Khori. The hill projects into the wide sandy beach which stretches for several kilometres south of Volissos. The site was much eroded, but remains of Bronze Age occupation could be traced over an area of some 50 × 50 m. The road which leads to the beach cuts through the middle of the site, and three round-bottomed pits descending between 0.50 m and a metre into the rock were exposed on the south edge of it in 1961. The stone axe (15) was found just to the north of the road. While most of the prehistoric pottery appeared to be assignable to the earlier part of the Bronze Age (Emporio V–II), some might have been of Middle Bronze Age date. Greco-Roman sherds were also in evidence.

14. Rim of small carinated bowl (Emporio type 9) with side handle. Grey-brown clay; traces of a light-brown to red burnished surface. Cf. Emporio Period II.

15. Stone axe (PLATE 3 (*h*) right). Small, neatly made with sub-rectangular cross-section. L. 5. 7. Grey-green stone with fine crystals. The surface polished.

19. Elinda. The name is suggestive of a pre-Greek origin. In 1960 a scrap of obsidian was recovered from the hill on the north side of the valley. But pottery and traces of graves and buildings here all appeared to be Roman.

Part II

Ayio Gala (1938)

1. THE EXCAVATIONS

The excavations at Ayio Gala were made by Miss Edith Eccles in the spring and autumn of 1938. Two caves were explored, an upper and a lower one close by it, in the cliff above which the village lies (PLATE 2 (c)).

The lower of these caves was, curiously enough in view of the remoteness of the village, one of the earliest prehistoric sites to be recorded in Greece. A German entomologist, Eberhard von Oertzen, went to Ayio Gala and entered the lower cave shortly after Studniczka visited Chios in 1887. Von Oertzen collected some thirty fragments of primitive-looking pottery from the cave, together with the large clay head 309, which he sent to Berlin. The sherds were studied and described and the head illustrated by Studniczka in his article on the antiquities of Chios published in 1888 (*AM* xiii (1888) 183–5).

In the course of a search for prehistoric sites in Chios Miss Eccles and the Hon. Mercy Money-Coutts (now the Hon. Mrs Seiradaki) visited Ayio Gala in the summer of 1936. They explored the lower cave which von Oertzen had noted some fifty years earlier, and also found prehistoric pottery in the upper cave behind the chapel of Panayia Galactonosera. This title and the name of the village, Ayio Gala or Sacred Milk, were evidently inspired by the continuous drip of water from an impressive stalactite in the upper cave. Car roads now connect Ayio Gala with Volissos to the south and Kardhamila to the east; but at the time that Miss Eccles visited it, the village was still extremely remote. It lies over a kilometre inland from a rocky and inhospitable stretch of coast, without harbours or landing places, and is therefore difficult of access from the sea. The journey from Kardhamila on foot in those days took some eight hours.

Miss Eccles recognised the early character of the pottery lying on the surface in the caves, and through the generosity of the late Dr Philip Argenti and Mr Eumorfopoulos, she was able to return a couple of years later and undertake excavations there. The main excavations were made in the lower cave, which Miss Eccles explored with the assistance of Miss Lilian H. Jeffery and Mr (now Sir) David Hunt in the spring of 1938.

The entrance to the lower cave lies just to the north of the chapel of Panayia Galactonosera, above the path soon after the foot of the steps. A large chamber to the right on entering contained many sherds. To the left was a steep slope of earth and stones with fragments of pottery noted by von Oertzen. An area of about 25 sq. m was opened in this slope; and at the south end of it near the top, where the deposit appears to have been deepest, a sounding was carried down to the rock floor of the chamber which lay at a depth of some 7 m from the surface.

The deposit in the cave consisted throughout of earth and stones, without any sign of stratification in it. The pottery was kept separate by areas and depths; but it was observed that fragments of the same vase were recovered from very different levels. The bottom 2 m above the rock, however, in the deep sounding at the top of the slope were virtually sterile: the lowest metre here consisted of nothing but stones without sherds.

A hole in the roof of the cave at the top of the slope was blocked with compacted earth filled

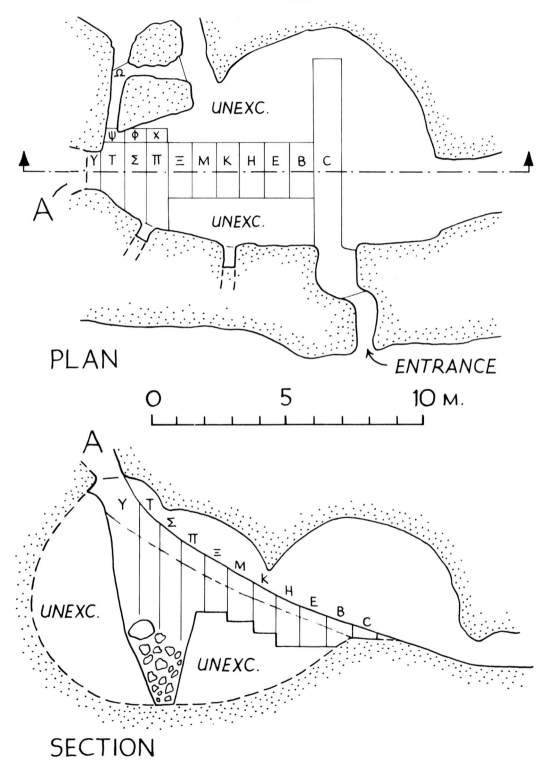

PLAN

SECTION

FIG. 4. Ayio Gala: Lower Cave.

with fragments of pottery. It therefore looks as if the earth with pottery which formed the slope below had fallen through this hole from somewhere above. The hole, it was thought, might connect with another cave at a higher level somewhere within the area of the modern village. No such cave has yet been discovered, but it may be concealed by one of the village houses.

The upper cave lies just above the lower cave and to the left of it. It is entered through the chapel of Panayia Galactonosera, and some of the annexes of the chapel are actually built inside the cave. On the right on entering the cave from the chapel is a large chamber with many sherds. A passage leading from this chamber also contains sherds. In October 1938, after the necessary permission had been obtained from the ecclesiastical authorities, a sounding was made by Miss Eccles in the large chamber, and was carried down through 4 m of deposit to the rock. Pottery was found throughout the deposit.

No traces of hearths, and no obvious floor levels, were detected during the excavations. But the character of the pottery and of other finds, including tools of stone and bone, suggests that the upper cave was used for habitation during prehistoric times. There is a marked difference between the pottery from the upper levels (2·90 m to the surface) and that from the bottom metre of deposit (4.00–2.90 m). The earlier pottery from the upper cave appears to correspond more or less to the bulk of the pottery from the lower cave.

A good many fragments of animal bone were kept with the pottery from the upper cave, and some of the bones had evidently been split to extract the marrow. Some bits of bone and skull from the upper group of levels had been burnt. At the time of the excavations Miss Eccles noted that some fragments of bone looked human, and among these were some which appeared to show traces of burning. If this was the case it might reflect the practice of a form of cannibalism, as attested in early times in many parts of Europe. The Kitsos Cave in Attica has produced some possible evidence for it during the Late Neolithic there (*BCH* xcv (1971) 725 f.).

There was nothing to suggest that the upper cave had been used for burials or for cult during prehistoric times. An isolated burial at a depth of 0.80–0.90 m below the surface is likely to date from the Christian period. A certain amount of wheelmade pottery, including Archaic Greek (367–76) and Roman with a little Mediaeval or later, occurred with the prehistoric material from the upper levels: most of it came from the top half-metre of deposit. Bits of lamps (377–81) ranging from Archaic to Roman, and some fragments of Classical and Hellenistic figurines (382–390), were also recovered. These suggest that the cave was already in use as a sanctuary by Greco-Roman times.

P. Demargne, *La Crète dédalique* (Paris, 1947) 60, refers to Mycenaean remains in Chios on the strength of the fact that Ayio Gala is included as a doubtful Mycenaean site by D. Fimmen, *Die kretisch-mykenischen Kultur* (Leipzig and Berlin, 1921) 15. Cf. Karo, *RE Suppl* vi col. 612. But there seems to be no evidence for Mycenaean occupation at Ayio Gala.

All the material from the lower cave, consisting of 84 sacks of sherds and 36 boxes of small finds, was taken by boat from Ayio Gala to Chios town, and thence to Athens in July 1938. The pottery was examined for joins during the winter of 1938–39 and several complete or largely complete vases were restored. These were photographed by Dr. F. H. Stubbings. Rim fragments, or most of them, and all decorated pieces, were kept aside, together with the small finds including tools of bone and stone. These and the restored vases survived the war in the National Museum at Athens. But the other fragments of pottery have not been identified since 1939 and may have been discarded during the war. It seems unlikely, however, that anything of real importance has been lost.

The material from the upper cave, excavated by Miss Eccles in October 1938, was left in the old mosque–museum in Chios. The pottery was stored there in open boxes marked with the excavation levels. But during the war years many of the boxes were removed: the sherds were dumped out of them, and evidence of their stratification was therefore lost. In 1952 I worked through this material from the upper cave at the request of Miss Eccles and with the help of the mender, Argyris Marinis, whose skilful exertions made it possible to restore some half-dozen profiles. Meanwhile in 1950 the surviving material from both caves had been seen and studied by Miss Audrey Furness (now Mrs. Ozanne) who published an account of it in her survey of early pottery from Samos, Kalimnos and Chios (*PPS* xxii (1956) 194–212).

2. THE POTTERY

(1) The Lower Cave (1–49)

The pottery from the lower cave which is considered here represents a selection of that found in the excavations. As it had evidently fallen from a third, as yet undiscovered, cave, it was in effect unstratified, and there is no reason why it should not cover a considerable span of time. Furness, *PPS* xxii (1956) 200, suggested that it might represent two or more phases rather than a single one. The series of complete or restored vases, however, appears to form a homogeneous group belonging to a relatively narrow horizon. In a general way this horizon seems to fall either within, or just before or after the period covered by the lower group of levels (4.00–2.90 m) in the upper cave. But isolated sherds from the lower cave may be earlier or later in date than the series of complete and restored vases. The fragments with punctuated decoration in particular (43 and PLATE 7 (*c*)) are comparable with fragments from the top levels of the upper cave (202, 285–9).

Fabric
(see *PPS* xxii (1956) 194 ff.)

The clay in general is tempered with abundant grit, dominantly greyish, or grey and red in colour, but white grit is noticeable in some fragments. Unlike most of the pottery of local manufacture from Emporio, that from the lower cave at Ayio Gala has mica, silvery or silvery and golden, in it. Straw temper does not seem to be as much in evidence in the pottery from the lower cave at Ayio Gala as it is in that from the early levels at Emporio.

The surfaces of the restored vases at any rate are basically red in colour, but are often mottled, shading to light or darker brown with splodges of black. The mottled surfaces of these vases are all burnished, and the marks of the burnishing implement are usually quite visible. While several of the vases are evenly made with a careful finish, some are rough with irregular surfaces and a comparatively poor burnish.

Bowls
(FIG. 5)

True bowls are not as much in evidence as jars in the material preserved from the lower cave. Bowls, however, seem to have been dominantly shallow, with rims either straight (cf. Emporio types 4 and 5) or slightly outward curving (as Emporio type 14). One shallow rim (6) had a pair of vertically perforated string-hole lugs below it. Deep bowls are represented by the profile 1, which might be classified better as a jar, and by the lug-handle 33 comparable with those on early bowls at Emporio.

1. Profile of small bowl cf. E type 5A. Clay grey at core, light brown at edges, with abundant grit, some large, grey and white, showing in surface which is slipped, red to dark brown with coarse burnish.

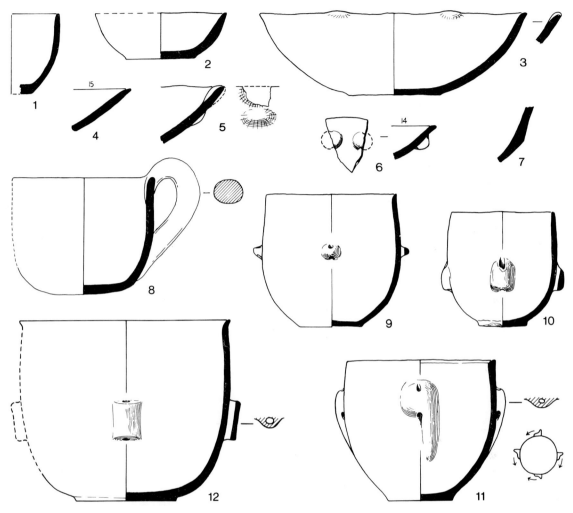

FIG. 5. Ayio Gala: Lower Cave. Bowls and small jars. Scale 1/3.

2. Profile of small shallow bowl cf. E types 5C and 14C. Irregular; the surface red to light brown with coarse burnish.

3. Shallow bowl as 2 (PLATE 4). About half of rim with an oblong wart on it and a non-joining scrap of base preserved. Ht. *c.* 6.5. Diam. 22. Coarse fabric with grit, some large, and mica showing in surface which is irregular and uneven, slipped and burnished, shades of light brown mottling to dusky and red.

   PPS xxii (1956) 210 fig. 12: 1.

4. Rim of shallow bowl cf. 3. Used as a rubber cf. 78. Abundant mica showing in surface, which is red to dark purple-brown with very fine burnish.

5. Rim of shallow bowl cf. 3 (PLATE 4). About half preserved. Diam. *c.* 20. A low irregular wart on the body with what appears to be the stump of another on the rim above it. Fabric as 3.

   PPS xxii (1956) 210 fig. 12: 2.

6. Rim of shallow bowl cf. E type 14C. Pair of small vertically perforated lugs. Surface light to dark brown with rather coarse burnish.

7. Fragment of open carinated bowl (PLATE 7) Grey clay with abundant grit including white and greyish. Some mica showing in surface which is grey-black inside, shades of dark brown to black outside, burnished. Above the carination on the outside, a hatched triangle in thin white paint, worn.

Carinated profiles resembling this are illustrated from Hacilar VI and I and from Can Hasan level 4 (*Hacilar* ii 252 f. fig. 51: 8; 362 f. fig. 111: 1–7. *AS* xvii (1967) 177 f. fig. 6: 1). Rather similar carinations are attested in the Early Neolithic on the Greek mainland (e.g. *Nemea* 265, 273 pl. 61: N 1). But the hatched triangle in thin white paint on 7 is suggestive of a later horizon.

Cups
(FIG. 5).

The handled cup 8 is unique at Ayio Gala, and provides the only example of a true handle to be found in the material kept from the lower cave. But there is nothing in the fabric to suggest that it is not contemporary with the other restored vases.

8. Handled cup (PLATE 4). Cf. 171 from upper cave. Base with part of rim and some of handle preserved. Ht. to rim 9.2. Diam. *c.* 11.7. Handle thick oval in section. Cup very irregular. Gritty clay; surface red mottling to shades of dark and light brown and dusky, well burnished outside, less well inside.
   PPS xxii (1956) 212 fig. 12: 17. Large cups of similar shape with bold thick-sectioned handles first appear in Crete in Early Minoan II (Pendlebury, *AC* 67. *PM* i 73 fig. 40: top right. *BSA* xxxvi (1935–36) 63 nos. 501–7, from Trapeza). But comparable handles are found on bowls at Mersin as early as the beginning of the Early Chalcolithic there (*Mersin* 56 f. fig. 34: 2).

Jugs

Some of the few fragments with white painted decoration, most of which evidently came from closed vases, might have belonged to jugs rather than jars. But evidence for the existence of jugs was lacking apart from these. No spouts or necks belonging to jugs were noted in the material from the lower cave.

Jars
(FIGS. 5–7)

Wide-mouthed bowl-like jars (bowl-jars) akin to Emporio type 30 were much in evidence as they were in the lower levels at Emporio. Those from the lower cave at Ayio Gala had vertically perforated lugs set well below the rim, on the shoulder or the swelling, and always where it was possible to judge four in number, either equally spaced round the body or in widely spaced pairs. This wide spacing of the lugs when they occur in pairs appears to be an early feature as Furness (*PPS* xxii (1956) 196) has noted. It is a characteristic of pottery assignable to the very beginning of the Bronze Age in the Cyclades (cf. *BSA* iii (1896–97) 45).

Rims of bowl-jars from Ayio Gala are mostly undifferentiated like those of Emporio class A. But 20 has a differentiated rim as class B III. Rims, mostly from large store jars, with a rib or a differentiated thickening round the outside (26–29), appear to be very characteristic of this early horizon at Ayio Gala. The exceptional thickened rim 48 from an unusually narrow-mouthed jar may be an import.

9. Small bowl-jar with four vertically perforated lugs (FIG. 5. PLATE 4). About one-third preserved, including profile, all four lugs, and most of base. Ht. *c.* 10.3. Diam. of rim *c.* 10.5. Well made, the lugs small and neat, equally spaced round the body. Fabric exceptionally fine, although clay has abundant grit, some large, which shows in surface, especially on underneath of base, together with some mica. Surface shades of light brown to red and dusky, stroke burnished outside, less well burnished inside.
   PPS xxii (1956) 211 fig. 12: 4.

10. Small bowl-jar with four vertically perforated lugs (FIG. 5. PLATE 4). Profile, base, parts of three lugs and about one-third of rim preserved. Ht. *c.* 9. Diam. of rim 8.5. The lugs appear to have been equally spaced as on 9. Roughly made and irregular. Coarse, rather reddish brown clay with grit, some evidently large. Some mica showing in surface, which is shades of light to darker reddish brown with dusky patches, apparently without any slip or wash, burnished outside, less well inside, the marks of the burnishing implement being clearly visible.
   PPS xxii (1956) 210 fig. 12: 3.

11. Small bowl-jar with thickened rim and four vertically perforated 'Ayio Gala' lugs (FIG. 5. PLATE 4). About half preserved including profile and parts of all four lugs and base. Ht. *c.* 11. Diam. of rim *c.* 12. The lugs are equally spaced as on 9, but in effect form two pairs, one with tails to left, the other with ones to right. Rather coarse fabric, with a good deal of grit and silvery mica showing in surface, which is shades of light and dark brown to black with somewhat poor burnish, the marks of the burnishing implement being visible in places.
   PPS xxii (1956) 211 fig. 12: 5.

12. Bowl-jar with rolled, everted rim (FIG. 5. PLATE 4). Profile with most of base preserved, but only small part of rim and one vertically perforated, slightly trumpet-shaped lug. Ht. *c.* 14.2. Diam. of rim *c.* 17.4. Perhaps with four equally spaced lugs like 9. Well and evenly made. Light grey to orange-brown clay with abundant grit, dominantly greyish, together with mica showing in surface, which is slipped and burnished, red to light brown with dark brown to dusky splodges.
   PPS xxii (1956) 211 fig. 12: 7.

13. Large bowl-jar with four long vertically perforated lugs in widely spaced pairs (FIG. 6. PLATE 5). About a third with most of three lugs preserved, but no complete profile. Ht. *c.* 24. 3. Diam. of rim *c.* 22. Well and evenly made; the lugs with neat triangular sections. Fabric as 12. Some greyish grit, and very abundant fine silvery mica showing in surface, which is red mottling to shades of light and darker brown, burnished inside and outside.
   PPS xxii (1956) 211 fig. 12: 8. Long vertical tubular lugs with relatively wide perforations as found on this and some other Ayio Gala bowl-jars (e.g. 14, 15) come on a Middle Neolithic vase from Lerna II (Vitelli 1977, 18 fig. 1).

14. Bowl-jar with four long vertically perforated lugs, in pairs as on 13 (FIG. 6. PLATE 5). Over half preserved, including profile and all four lugs. Ht. *c.* 20. Diam. of rim *c.* 16, of body *c.* 21.5. No traces of mica, but abundant grit, dominantly greyish, showing in surface, which is slipped and burnished, in places somewhat crackled, red to light and dark brown with several dusky blotches.
   PPS xxii (1956) 211 f. fig. 12: 11.

15. Rim of bowl-jar with long vertically perforated trumpet-lug (FIG. 6). Surface red to dark brown and black with fine burnish.
   PPS xxii (1956) 194 pl. xxi: 3.

16. Bowl-jar, apparently without lugs (FIG. 6. PLATE 5). About two-thirds preserved. Ht. *c.* 11.8. Diam. of rim *c.* 14, of body *c.* 15.8. Irregular in shape, but of good fabric with even surface, which is slipped and burnished, marks of the burnishing implement being clearly visible, reddish to light brown mottling to darker brown and dusky, with occasional grit and some mica showing in it.
   PPS xxii (1956) 211 fig. 12: 9.

17. Large bowl-jar with four vertically perforated 'Ayio Gala' lugs (FIG. 6. PLATE 5). About half preserved, including parts of three lugs and most of base. Ht. *c.* 24. Diam. of rim *c.* 20.3, of body *c.* 26. Lugs neat and evenly made, set in widely spaced pairs, the tails being on the outside of each pair unlike those on 11. Good fabric; occasional grit and some mica showing in surface, which is slipped and burnished, red to light and darker brown with many patches of black.
   PPS xxii (1956) 211 fig. 12: 10.

18. Bowl-jar with four vertically perforated 'Ayio Gala' lugs (FIG. 6. PLATE 5). About a third including profile and base preserved, but only one lug and part of another. The exact arrangement of the lugs is therefore uncertain, but they appear to have been evenly spaced. The perforation through the surviving lug runs at an angle. Ht. *c.* 19.5. Diam. of rim *c.* 13, of body, *c.* 20.5. Some grit and occasional mica showing in surface, which is well burnished, a deeper red than usual, mottling to light and dark brown and dusky. Four string-holes made after firing through the rim, apparently for mending the vase.
   PPS xxii (1956) 212 fig. 12: 12.

19. Large bowl-jar (PLATE 5). Less than one-third preserved, including profile and part of rim and base. Two thin sharp ridges at opposite sides of the vase may be the tails of unusually elegant 'Ayio Gala' lugs. Ht. *c.* 28. Diam. of rim *c.* 24, of body *c.* 32. Well and neatly made; some grit and mica showing in the even, regular surface, which is slipped and burnished, red mottling to light and dark brown and dusky outside, black inside.
   PPS xxii (1956) 212 fig. 12: 13.

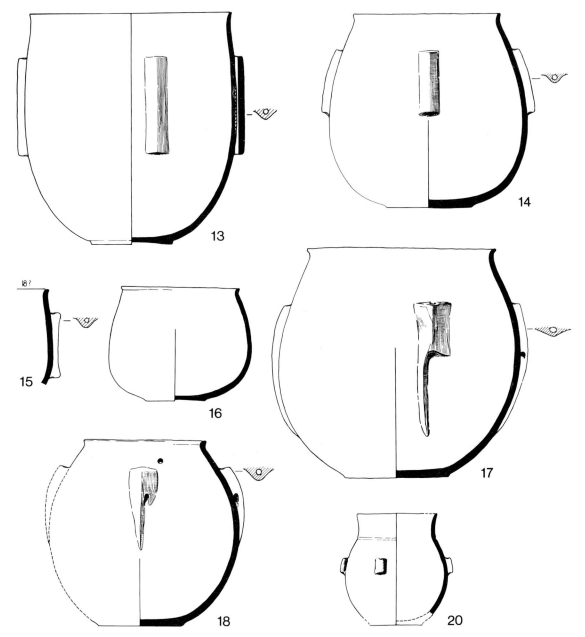

Fig. 6. Ayio Gala: Lower Cave. Jars. Scale 1/4.

19A. Another large bowl-jar (PLATE 5), very incomplete, appears to have been mislaid in NMA. It was not with the material seen by Miss Furness or myself.

20. Small jar with everted rim and four vertically perforated lugs (FIG. 6. PLATE 5). Three lugs and parts of rim and body preserved; base missing. Ht. as restored *c.* 11.5. Diam. of rim 8.5. The lugs in widely spaced pairs as on 13 etc. Thin-walled. Evenly made. Occasional mica showing in surface, which is regular and well burnished, vertical strokes of the burnishing implement being clearly visible, dark brown to red with dusky patches.

    PPS xxii (1956) 212 fig. 12: 16.

21. Tall jar (PLATE 5). Only parts preserved, but no complete profile; no sign of lugs or handles. Ht. restored *c*. 42. Diam. of rim *c*. 23. Surface with rather poor burnish, marks of the burnishing implement being visible, shades of light and dark brown to red with dusky patches.

Jar rims
(FIG. 7)

22. Rim, as E class A I (PLATE 7). Slightly thickened. Surface dark grey-brown with coarse superficial burnish. Incised decoration; a line below the rim and a diagonal line descending from it preserved.
23. Rim, as E class A II. Light greyish brown with fine burnish. Incised decoration; bold diagonal grooves.
24. Rim, as E class A III (PLATE 7). Shades of light and dark brown to dusky, well burnished inside and outside. Wide curving band in low relief with incised hatching, combined with other incised decoration.

    Comparable hatched relief bands appear on pottery from the Agora wells assigned to the Late Neolithic of the Greek mainland. In most cases, however, the hatching is much bolder, although in one or two examples it is not dissimilar (e.g. *Athenian Agora* xiii 41 f. pl. 11 nos. 159, 170).
25. Rim, cf. E class A III. Horizontal oblong wart on swelling. Red to light brown with coarse burnish.
26. Rim with rib on outside. Red to shades of brown with fine burnish. Another similar; red to light brown with fine burnish.
27. Rim, rolled outwards, with wide flat rib below it. Red to dark brown and dusky with fine burnish.
28. Rim, thickened and differentiated on outside. Clay with grit and mica in it. Inside surface dark greyish with little or no trace of burnish; outside light brown with a slight reddish tinge, coarsely burnished. Another similar; inside surface red with very poor burnish, outside light to dark brown, well burnished.

    Compare 80–82 from the lower levels of the upper cave. Cf. *Hacilar* i 106; ii 260 f. fig. 55: 18, from Hacilar VI, which is closely similar to those from Ayio Gala. Cf. ibid. ii fig. 64: 28, from Hacilar IV. Simpler versions of such rims occur in the Early Neolithic of Çatal Hüyük and Alan Hüyük (Beyşehir) (*AS* xi (1961) 165 fig. 3: 2; 169 fig. 5: 6). They are attested in Syria as early as Judeideh Phase B (*Judeideh* 79 fig. 54: 5). A somewhat comparable rim is illustrated from the upper Presesklo (E.N. III) level at Otzaki in Thessaly (*Otzaki-magula* pl. xxi: 2).
29. Rim with rib on outside. Shades of red and of light and dark brown with rather coarse burnish inside and outside.
30. Rim, as E class A III (PLATE 7). Light greyish clay with grit and some mica. Surface light to dark brown, burnished. Outside decorated with irregular bands in very thick, sandy paint, dirty white in colour, apparently applied after the surface was burnished.

    PPS xxii (1956) 197 pl. xxi: 10.

Lids
(FIG. 7)

One complete lid (31) with a pair of string-holes was recovered, together with the fragment 32 which may have belonged to another.

31. Lid with two perforated lugs set opposite each other (PLATE 8). Complete and unbroken except for chips round edges. Diam. *c*. 12. Roughly made and irregular. Clay reddish to grey-brown at core with abundant grit, dominantly grey and red, some showing in surface together with silvery mica. Surface red to light brown with dusky patches, coarsely burnished.

    PPS xxii (1956) 211 fig. 12: 6. It might pass for a remoter ancestor of the Trojan shape D 11, only recognised in the Early Subperiod of Troy I; but this has four high pointed lugs (*Troy* i 74).
32. Fragment of lid (?). Diam. *c*. 7. Clay with much grit, some showing in surface together with abundant mica. Surface light to dark brown and reddish, coarsely burnished.

Handles and lugs

Handles were evidently rare. The only example of a true handle was in fact on the cup 8, but this was a large one. The solitary lug-handle (33) with its diagonal perforation appears to have risen from a bowl rim like those characteristic of the early levels at Emporio. The clay head (310) with a perforation right through it may have been a lug of this type set on a vase.

Vertically perforated string-hole lugs were very much in evidence on the bodies of bowls and jars, and especially on the bowl-jars characteristic of this early horizon. They were of many different types, including simple round or oval lugs as on 6 and 9, and on the lid 31, and tubular lugs (e.g. 10, 14, 20) which might be very long (13) or trumpet-shaped (15). Some tubular lugs (e.g. 13) were sharply triangular rather than rounded in cross-section. The distinctive tailed lugs (11, 17, 18 and PLATE 7(*f*)), christened by Miss Furness 'Ayio Gala lugs', are not common. The actual lug to which the tail has been added may be a simple round knob (as on 11), or more or less tubular (18 and PLATE 7(*f*)), or even trumpet-shaped (17). The single tail may descend from the left or right side of the lug. There is one double 'Ayio Gala lug' (34) with a tail each side. These 'Ayio Gala lugs' may be local equivalents of the single lugs with a pair of tails found on some bowl-jars of Period VIII at Emporio (E 172, 228, 358–360).

In contrast to those with vertical perforations, horizontally perforated lugs appear to be rare, and only two or three possible examples of them (e.g. 37) were noted in the surviving material.

Lugs were evidently applied to the surface of the vase, and not bonded into it. This is clear in cases where the lug has come away from the vase as in 39.

String-holes

A number of fragments have V-shaped perforations made after firing (38, 39). These may have been rivet-holes for mending cracked or broken vases with string. Perforations of this kind were a marked feature of the earliest levels (X-VIII) at Emporio.

33. Lug-handle with diagonal perforation (FIG. 7). Apparently projecting from a bowl rim. Surface light and dark brown to dusky, well burnished.
     Cf. Emporio 113 (Period X).
34. Double 'Ayio Gala lug' (PLATE 7). Apparently from a large jar. Somewhat coarse fabric. Surface slipped, light brown to red, with rather poor burnish.
     PPS xxii (1956) 196 pl. xxi: 9. Cf. *Athenian Agora* xiii 5, 23 no. 7, 24 no. 12, and 8 note 42, referring to *Kephala* 16 pl. 78: 97. Lugs of this type, but more refined and sophisticated in appearance with long tails in very low relief, occurred on some intact red burnished jars from the Agora wells (nos. 1, 3, 7). No. 1 was one of those which Milojčić, *JdI* lxv-lxvi (1950–51) 32 f. fig. 12: 8, assigned to an advanced phase of Sesklo (Middle Neolithic). These Agora lugs and the comparable ones from Kephala in Kea look more evolved and later than 34. A similar lug from Thessaly assigned to the Bronze Age is not so closely comparable (*DS* 265 fig. 174).
35. Vertically perforated lug, associated with feature in relief (PLATE 7). Surface red to light and dark brown with coarse burnish.
36. Small lug, apparently with vertical perforation, but perhaps as 37 (PLATE 6). Fabric cf. 48. Clay orange to reddish throughout, with abundant grit, including reddish and white, and some mica, showing in surface. Remains of thick dark red wash inside and outside, with little or no trace of burnish.
     Possibly from an imported vase.
37. Lug, apparently with horizontal perforation (PLATE 6). From a large vase. Surface red to light brown with rather coarse burnish. Possible traces of encrusted decoration in white paint on the right.
38. Rim of bowl or jar with five V-shaped perforations (rivet-holes?) made after firing (PLATE 6). Red to light brown with fine burnish.
39. Rim of bowl-jar with stump of vertical cylindrical lug and two V-shaped perforations as 38 (PLATE 6). Red to light brown with fine burnish.
     PPS xxii (1956) 194 pl. xxi: 1.

Bases

These might be flat, as on 1, but were normally more or less sharply differentiated (10, 12, 13), and often, but not always, sunk. One fragment of a base (40) has the impression of a mat on the bottom.

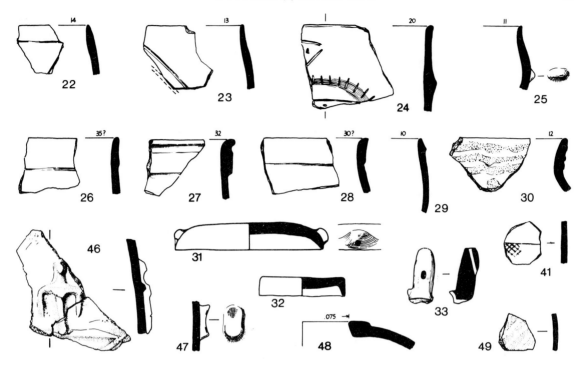

FIG. 7. Ayio Gala: Lower Cave. Jar rims, lids, handles and misc. Scale 1/3.

40. Fragment of base with mat-impression (PLATE 6). Evidently from a large jar. Coarse clay, grey to light brown, with abundant grit including white marble-like chips.

PPS xxii (1956) 197 pl. xxi: 7. For mat impressions on the bases of early Aegean pottery see Jill Carington Smith, *Kephala* 118 ff. Mat-impressed bases are found in the Early Neolithic at Servia and Nea Nikomedeia in Western Macedonia (*Servia* 193). They occur at Saliagos (*Saliagos* 71 f.), and are well represented in the later Neolithic and Early Bronze Ages of the islands and Greek mainland. Schliemann, *Ilios* 667, implies that there were many vases with mat or basket impressions from Beşik Tepe in the Troad (cf. *TuI* 547 fig. 468. W. Lamb, *PZ* xxiii (1932) 128); but they do not appear to be attested at Troy and Thermi. Only three examples were noted at Emporio: one from level 158 of Period IX in Area A; and two (1860, 1942) from levels of Periods V and II in Area B.

Decoration

Incision and relief, sometimes combined as on 24, were evidently the commonest forms of decoration, but white painted decoration also occurs. Pattern burnish, however, is conspicuous by its absence from the lower cave, and is hardly attested in the material from the upper cave.

Paint. Some eight or nine fragments have designs in white paint. They include the fragment of a carinated bowl (7) and the jar rim 30. The other fragments with white paint mostly appear to come from closed vases of some kind (41 and PLATE 7 (*b*): bottom row). The designs consist of groups of diagonal stripes, except in the case of 41 with a lattice band. The paint is apt to be rather thin, dirty white in colour: it was evidently applied after the surface of the vase had been burnished. The scrap 49 with decoration in red on a white slip clearly belongs to an imported vase.

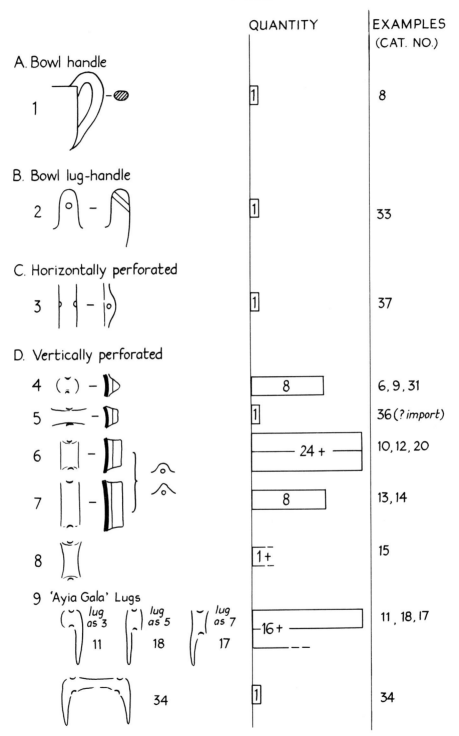

FIG. 8. Ayio Gala: Lower Cave. Handles and lugs.

FIG. 9. Ayio Gala: Lower Cave. Relief decoration: rib sections.

Incision. Some forty fragments had remains of incised decoration. In its general character this seems to correspond to that of the early levels (X-VIII) at Emporio. Most of the fragments are more or less well burnished on the inside, and must come from bowls or bowl-jars; but some with rough insides may have belonged to jugs or jars with narrow necks. The incisions are usually bold, sometimes very bold resembling grooves or channels. But fine incision also occurs.

Designs are almost entirely confined to groups of diagonal lines and multiple chevrons, as characteristic of the early levels at Emporio (examples on PLATES 6 and 7). In one instance (43) a curved line, which may have been part of a curvilinear design, appears to be combined with an area of punctuated decoration. Six other fragments, including the jar rim 24, have punctuated decoration with lines of dots or dot-filled zones or bands (PLATE 7). Traces of white fill were only noted in two instances, once on a fragment with punctuated decoration: the other fragment (42) is exceptional.

41. Fragment, apparently from a closed vase (FIG. 7. PLATE 7). Grey clay, reddish at the edges, with abundant grit, some large, and mica showing in surface, which is light reddish with rather poor burnish. Decorated with band of lattice in white.

42. Fragment, perhaps from bowl-jar (PLATE 7). Coarse gritty clay; surface red to light brown with somewhat rough burnish. A pair of bold diagonal grooves *c.* 3 mm. wide with remains of thick white paste in them.

43. Fragment, perhaps from bowl-jar (PLATE 7). Surface burnished, greyish inside, light pinkish brown outside. Incised decoration, including a curved line and punctuation.

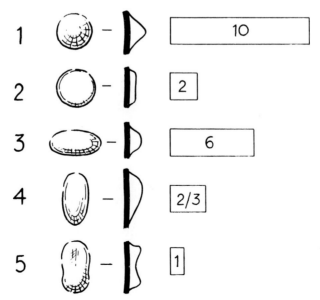

FIG. 10. Ayio Gala: Lower Cave. Warts: types and frequency of occurrence.

Relief. Decoration with ribs or warts in relief is much in evidence as in the early levels at Emporio. As in the case of lugs, ribs appear to have been applied to the surface of the vase, not bonded into it or moulded out of it. Ribs are characteristically triangular in section with a sharp ridge as FIG. 9: 1. But rounded and rectangular-sectioned ribs occur (FIG. 9: 2, 3). Relief decoration might be elaborate, with diagonal and curving as well as straight ribs in evidence (44, 45 and PLATES 7 and 8 for others). The jar rim 24 combines a curving rib in relief with incised decoration. One fragment (46) has a human figure, apparently female, in relief on it.

Warts (PLATE 6, bottom right) are for the most part circular (FIG. 10: 1), usually rather bold and sharply defined, somewhat conical in profile. But two flat-topped discs (FIG. 10: 2) were recovered. There are about half a dozen horizontal oblong warts (FIG. 10: 3) (e.g. 5, 25), and two or three vertical, somewhat nose-like ones (FIG. 10: 4). One wart (47), which seems to have been vertical, is horned (FIG. 10: 5).

44. Fragment of large jar with ribs in very bold relief (PLATE 7). Thick-walled. Coarse gritty clay, greyish to brown. Inside surface rough, outside with traces of coarse burnish.
    PPS xxii (1956) 196 pl. xxi: 6.

45. Fragment of bowl or bowl-jar with pair of curving ribs in relief (PLATE 6). Surface grey-brown with rather coarse burnish inside and outside.
    PPS xxii (1956) 196 pl. xxi: 5.

46. Fragment, apparently from large jar, with figure in relief (FIG. 7. PLATE 8). The figure is female to judge from the projecting breasts and might represent a goddess. Surface red, with rather coarse burnish outside; less well burnished inside.
    PPS xxii (1956) 196 pl. xxi: 11. The arms hanging downwards appear to be unusual. Figures in relief with upraised arms occur on fragments of large vases of red burnished ware from Paradimi in Eastern Macedonia, and also on vases in the Balkans: they seem to be related to the goddess in childbirth as found in relief on walls at Çatal Hüyük (Theochares, *Neolithic Greece* fig. 235. M. Gimbutas, *The Gods and Goddesses of Old Europe* (London, 1974) 174 ff. *AS* xiii (1963) 61 ff. fig. 8; 70 ff. fig. 14). An Early Neolithic (Körös Culture) vase fragment from Hungary has a figure in relief with the left arm raised and the right down (P. Raczky, *Szolnok Megyei Múzeumi Évkönyv* 1978, 10 fig. 1). Animals, birds and insects appear in relief on vases from Hacilar VI and V (*Hacilar* ii 286 fig. 57 pl. lxviii: 4). There is even a goddess in relief from Hacilar, but she is less schematic than 46 (ibid. 264 no. 9, 266 fig. 57: 5).

47. Fragment, apparently from bowl or bowl-jar, with small horned wart (FIG. 7. PLATE 6). The wart appears to have been vertical like 57 rather than horizontal. Surface slipped, red to light and dark brown, with fine burnish inside and outside.
    PPS xxii (1956) 196 fig. 13: 2. But the parallels cited there from Troy and Dhimini are much larger and basically different in shape. Similar warts, however, are attested in the Late Chalcolithic of Anatolia, and in the Late Neolithic on the Greek mainland (*AS* xiii (1963) 264 fig. 3: 13, Late Chalcolithic from the Konya plain. Phelps, *Thesis* 262 fig. 38: 24, 325 fig. 51: 25, from Gonia and Klenia, his Periods III and early IV). There is a boldly projecting wart of this kind on the belly of a jar from Karagyös-Magula in Thessaly assigned to the Rakhmani horizon (*Ayia Sofia Magula* 60 pl. 28: 21).

Imports

The unusual rim 48 may be from an imported vase, unless it is a stray of some later period. The small scrap 49 with painted decoration in red on white is unique at Ayio Gala and almost certainly comes from an import, either of Sesklo ware from the region of Thessaly, or of some corresponding ware from Anatolia akin to the painted wares of Hacilar.

48. Flat-topped and thickened rim of narrow-mouthed jar (FIG. 7. PLATE 7). Fabric cf. 36. Very coarse clay, fired orange to reddish all through, with much grit, some large, red, grey and white in colour, showing in surface, which is red inside. Outside light brown, but with traces of a thick dark red slip, which may have been burnished, but is now worn.

49. Scrap, evidently from a closed vase (FIG. 7. PLATE 7). Thin-walled, of fine fabric. Well fired. Dark brown to

reddish clay with abundant grit or sand, but no sign of mica. Outside with a white slip, decorated with diagonal stripes in red paint before being given a high polish-like burnish. Inside somewhat dark red in colour, with marks of rather superficial burnishing or wiping; these, which were evidently horizontal, indicate the angle of the sherd.

PPS xxii (1956) 197 fig. 13: 3. This appears to be of rather finer fabric than any of the sherds of Middle Neolithic Sesklo (A 3β) ware from Thessaly in the collection of the British School at Athens. The finish on the inside, however, is exactly the same as that on the inside surfaces of fragments of Thessalian Sesklo ware. Mellaart, *Hacilar* ii 437 fig. 156, classifies 49 as 'West Anatolian painted ware', and even as Hacilar I ware (*Studia Balcanica* v (1971) 126). This is doubted by French, *AS* xix (1969) 58 at bottom; but the decoration of thick close-set diagonal lines is more easily matched perhaps in the painted ware of Hacilar V-I than on Thessalian Sesklo ware or the Chaeronea ware of Central Greece.

A few later sherds, including some of the Geometric and Archaic periods (PLATE 14), were recovered from the lower cave as from the upper one.

(2) The Upper Cave

All the pottery recovered from the upper cave was stored after the excavation in open boxes in Chios Museum. During the war a number of these boxes were removed, and the sherds were dumped out of them in piles on the floor of the museum. As a consequence out of more than 6,000 sherds, about 3,600, or three-fifths, were virtually unstratified when I came to study them in the summer of 1952. Some 580, representing about a quarter, of the 2,470 sherds of which the stratigraphy was preserved, were from the lower group of levels which accounted for the lowest metre of deposit (depth 4.00–2.90 m) in the cave. The remaining three-quarters of the stratified material were from the upper group of levels, roughly the top three metres of deposit.

The pottery from the upper cave has been classified according to the types defined at Emporio, and the type numbers refer to these. Depths at which the pottery was found are given in brackets. Material of which the context has been lost, and which is therefore virtually unstratified (US), has been included with that from the upper group of levels above 2.90 m, since there is a 75% chance that in fact it came from there.

All of the prehistoric pottery from the cave was handmade, and even vases from the upper levels might be irregular in shape. But there was a noticeable difference in character between the pottery from the lower group of levels below 2.90 m and that from the levels above. The change in the character of the pottery seemed to be clearly marked, if not abrupt. The differences between the two groups of pottery both in shapes and fabric were quite sharp and clear. This might suggest a gap of time between them, indicating an appreciable interval during which the cave was not inhabited. But it could equally reflect the supplanting of one group of inhabitants by another with different pottery traditions; and other explanations for the change are possible.

The characteristics of the pottery and the stratigraphic evidence are presented on the charts, FIGS. 11–15.

(a) Lower levels (below 2.90 m) (50–89)
(FIGS. 16–18)

A significant feature of the pottery from the lower levels was the comparatively high proportion of fragments from small, thin-walled vases. This was especially noticeable in the case of the pottery from the lowest part of the deposit. At the same time the deposit below 2.90 m seems to have been more or less homogeneous in character, and in several instances fragments of the same vase were in boxes of material labelled as found at the bottom and near the top of it.

	(A) BOWLS — RIMS OF TYPES													(B) JUGS cf.		(C) JARS — RIMS OF CLASSES										(E) PITHOI	(F) LIDS		(G) MINIATURE VASES
	2	3	4	5 A	5 B,C MIN	6	7	8	10	12	13	14 A	14 B,C MIN	Type 20	Type 23	A I	A II	A III	B I–II	B III a high	B III a low	B III b low	B III c	B III d	B III f		Type 60	Type 62	
UPPER LEVELS																													
1 0.50 – 0	70	1			1	2	1											1										1	
2 0.90 – 0 N.W. Corner	1	1																											
3 0.60 – 0.50	28	1	1	1	1	8	2	2	2					1		1	1	3	4			3	1				1	1	
4 0.70 – 0.60 / 0.95 –			1		1	1	1	1					1			1	1		2	1		1	1	1					
5 0.90 – 0.80	1	4	4	4	3	2	1	1				1		1	1	1	3	3	3	1						1	1		
6 Burial at 0.90 – 0.80			1	1		4		5							1				8		1			1					
7 1.10 – 0.90 / 1.20 – 1.10		3		3		9	1									2		1	2	1			1				1	1	
8 1.20 – 1.10	1			1		1	2												1										
9 1.30 – 1.20	8	1		4			3	2			1					2	1		4		4				1				
10 1.50 – 1.30								2																					
11 1.60 – 1.45		1	1	1	2	1	2																1	1	1				1
12 1.90 – 1.80		1	1					1																			1		
13 2.05 – 1.90				1									2			1	1	2	1				1						
14 2.15 – 2.05		1	1	2			1									1	1	1		1							1		
15 2.70 – 2.60	1			1		1	1	1				1	1			1			2							2			
LOWER LEVELS																													
16 3.00 – 2.90				1 2	1			1			1	1	1			2	1	8	1		1		1 1	1					
17 3.20 – 3.10					1						1	2	5			1	1	9	1				1		1				
18 3.45 – 3.20 / 3.60 – 3.50					1							2	4					7	1				4						
19 3.80 – 3.70			2	2				1				2	4			2	4	1	4							2			
20 4.00 – 3.95		1	1	1		1	1					1	3				3	1					1						
WITHOUT CONTEXT		2	8	27	30	19	2	18	3	2	3	11	14	5	8	1	13	10	17	28	27	4	1	6	1	12	2	1	1
TOTAL	110	11	13	42	50	48	16	34	3	3	6	19	36	8	10	21	22	34	57	61	6	8	2	11	12	3	17	5	4	1

FIG. 11. Ayio Gala: Upper Cave. Pottery types (numbers of rims).

Column key — (1) BOWL HANDLES & LUG-HANDLES (see Fig.13): B1–B11. (2) PERFORATED LUGS (see Fig.14): (A) VERTICAL VA1–VA6, (B) HORIZONTAL HB6–HB9. (3) SOLID LUGS & WARTS: S1–S6. (4) VERTICAL HANDLES: Thick (oval to circular), Thin (oval), Horned, With wart, Rivet holes. (Small italic numbers are catalogue references.)

UPPER LEVELS	B1	B2	B3	B4	B5	B6	B7	B8	B9	B10	B11	VA1	VA2	VA3	VA4	VA5	VA6	HB6	HB7	HB8	HB9	S1	S2	S3	S4	S5	S6	Thick	Thin oval	Horned	With wart	Rivet holes
1 0.50 – 0	1 /135											3 /269						2 /295	1			1 /191								1		
2 0.90 – 0 NW Corner																																1
3 0.60 – 0.50									1			1						2 /151				2 /196								1	1	1
4 0.70 – 0.60 / 0.95						1 /251			1	1 /252	1 /250														1 /142					1	1 /260	
5 0.90 – 0.80									1													1 /300						12		1		3
6 Burial at 0.90 – 0.80					1										1			1				3	1	1				5	1	1		2
7 1.10 – 0.90 / 1.20 – 1.10				1					1													1 /95	2 /95	1				5	1			
8 1.20 – 1.10											3 /129											3						10	4			1
9 1.30 – 1.20												2										2	2 /141	2				3				
10 1.50 – 1.30																		1							1 /239							
11 1.60 – 1.45			1 /140									1 /268						1											1			
12 1.90 – 1.80																							1 /94					3	1	[1] /140		
13 2.05 – 1.90															1							1						1	1			
14 2.15 – 2.05							1					3						2										1			1	
15 2.70 – 2.60												1						1				1						5			1	
LOWER LEVELS																																
16 3.00 – 2.90												2			2			4				1										2
17 3.20 – 3.10												1			2			2		1 /84		1		1								
18 3.45 – 3.20 / 3.60 – 3.50															2			2				1										
19 3.80 – 3.70															2			2				1						1	1			
20 4.00 – 3.90															2			2									1 /57	5			
WITHOUT CONTEXT	1	2 /114, 147	1 /115	1 /253	1 /254	1 /256	1 /255	1	13 /148			c.6? /117	2 /267	1 /85	c.7 /265	1 /263		c.8? /297		1 /270	1 /116	17	3	10 /98		2 /187, 301	1 /57	44	8	12	12	13
TOTAL	1	1	2	2	1	1	1	1	1	21	1	c.20	2	1	c.19	1		c.28	2	2	1	33	3	17	2	2	1	85	16	20	20	24

FIG. 12. Ayio Gala: Upper Cave. Handles and lugs etc.

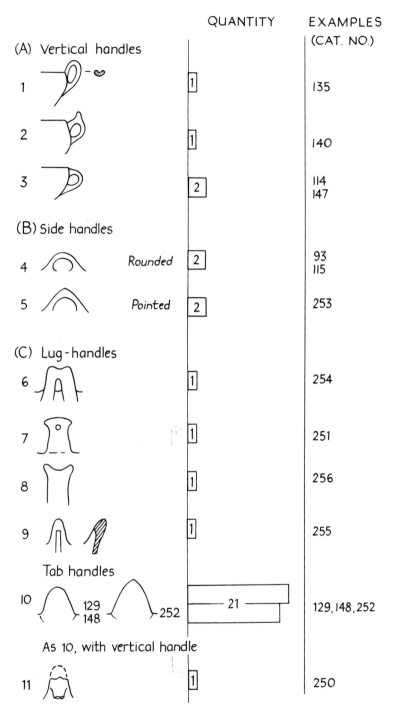

QUANTITY   EXAMPLES
                  (CAT. NO.)

(A) Vertical handles

1   1   135

2   1   140

3   2   114
                                         147

(B) Side handles

4   Rounded   2   93
                                         115

5   Pointed   2   253

(C) Lug-handles

6   1   254

7   1   251

8   1   256

9   1   255

Tab handles

10   129   252   ——— 21 ———   129,148,252
      148

As 10, with vertical handle

11   1   250

FIG. 13. Ayio Gala: Upper Cave. Bowl handles and lug-handles.

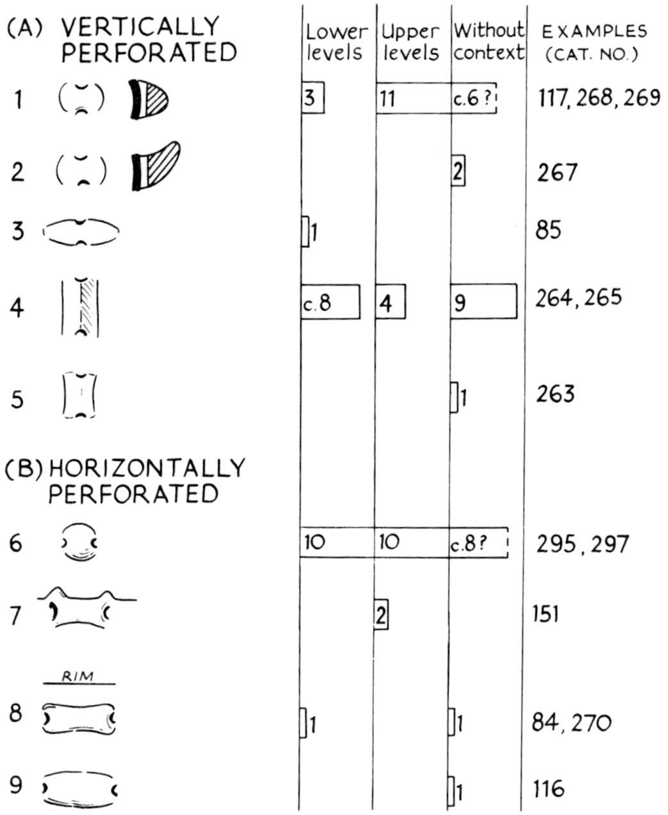

(A) VERTICALLY PERFORATED		Lower levels	Upper levels	Without context	EXAMPLES (CAT. NO.)
1	(͜)	3	11	c.6 ?	117, 268, 269
2	(͜)			2	267
3		1			85
4		c.8	4	9	264, 265
5				1	263
(B) HORIZONTALLY PERFORATED					
6		10	10	c.8?	295, 297
7			2		151
8	*RIM*	1		1	84, 270
9				1	116

FIG. 14. Ayio Gala: Upper Cave. Perforated lugs.

Fabric

This tended to be soft, and the firing of the vases was uneven and in general less thorough than in the upper levels. The clay was greyish to reddish brown, tempered with grit and finely chopped straw. Grit of various colours—white, grey, purplish and red—was noted even in the same vase. Large lumps of grit regularly appeared in fragments from thick-walled vases, and sometimes occurred in those from vases with thin walls and finely burnished surfaces. Shining particles of mica were often prominent in the surfaces of vases.

Outside surfaces were almost invariably burnished. Red was the dominant surface colour in the case of the finest burnished ware, the clay being characteristically grey at the centre of the break, light brown near the edges. Red may be the colour to which the burnished surfaces naturally fired, but some vases at any rate appear to have had a red wash. The burnish might be very fine, like a polish, with the marks of the burnishing implement scarcely visible. But normally the marks of the burnisher are quite obvious on the surface.

Owing to the haphazard nature of the firing, the surfaces even in the case of the finest burnished wares might be richly variegated, ranging from crimson red through orange and shades of brown to black and whitish. Brown burnished surfaces were also well represented, but grey and black were less in evidence.

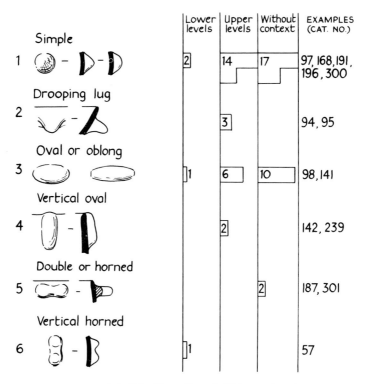

	Lower levels	Upper levels	Without context	EXAMPLES (CAT. NO.)
Simple 1	2	14	17	97, 168, 191, 196, 300
Drooping lug 2		3		94, 95
Oval or oblong 3	1	6	10	98, 141
Vertical oval 4		2		142, 239
Double or horned 5			2	187, 301
Vertical horned 6	1			57

FIG. 15. Ayio Gala: Upper Cave. Solid lugs and warts.

Bowls (FIG. 16)

The bowls from the lower levels of the upper cave at Ayio Gala are classifiable under Emporio types 5, 13 and 14.

5. Open bowls with curving sides

A. Deep

    50. (4.00–3.90) Rim with vertical rib (PLATE 8). Light grey clay, shading to reddish brown near outside edge. Surface pitted with little holes, and with mica showing in it; reddish brown inside, crimson red outside, burnished.

    51. (3.20–3.10, 3.00–2.90) Profile (PLATE 9). Fine clay, grey to brown. Surface dark crimson red, well burnished.
        Cf. two bowls from Phlius near Nemea assigned to the Early Neolithic (*Hesperia* xxxviii (1969) 449 f. pl. 114 nos. 24, 28).

B, C. Medium and shallow

    52. (3.00–2.90) Flat-topped rim. Light grey clay, red-brown near the edges. Fine mica shining in surface, which is light brown mottling to purplish inside, crimson red outside, burnished.

    53. (3.80–3.70) Rim. Light grey to brown clay. Some mica showing in surface, which is light brown inside, crimson red to light brown outside, finely burnished.

12. Bowls with straight rims thickened and differentiated on the inside. Three rims in all were recovered from the upper cave. The only example of which the context was recorded

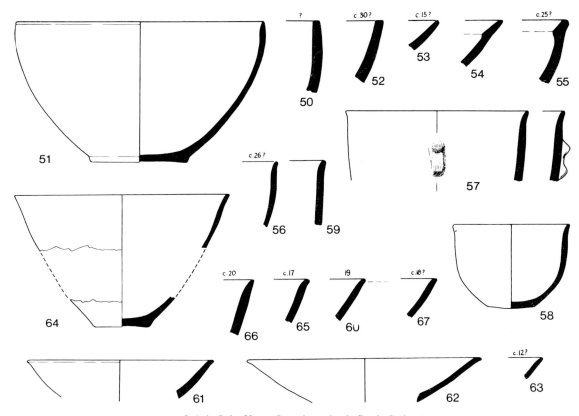

FIG. 16. Ayio Gala: Upper Cave: lower levels. Bowls. Scale 1/3.

(not illustrated) came from 3.45–3.20 m of the lower group of levels. The other two rims, including 153, were unstratified, but may belong to the early group of levels rather than to the later one.

13. Bowls with outward curving rims, internally differentiated and thickened. Two of the three rims of this distinctive type with recorded contexts were in boxes marked as from the lower levels. Such rims are well attested in the Early Neolithic of Thessaly from the beginning of the Preseklo phase (see under Emporio type 13).

54. (3.45–3.20) Rim. Angle not certain. Coarse greyish brown clay with large grit. Abundant mica showing in surface, which is red to light brown, well burnished but worn.

55. (3.20–3.10) Rim. Gritty grey to purplish brown clay. Surface light purplish brown inside, dark brown to black outside, burnished. Straw impressions showing in outside.

14. Bowls with outward curving rims. Rims of bowls of this type appeared to be very common in the lowest group of levels. The rim 57 has a solid vertical horned lug resembling 47 from the lower cave.

A. Deep

56. (3.80–3.70) Rim. Gritty red-brown clay. Inside surface reddish to light brown, outside reddish brown shading to dark brown, finely burnished.

57. (US, but a non-joining fragment apparently from the same vase in 3.80–3.70) Rim with solid vertical horned lug. Light grey clay, red-brown at the edges. Some mica showing in surface, which is light brown shading to red with darker brown and dusky patches, finely burnished.
    Cf. the lug 47 from the lower cave.
58. (3.30–3.20) Profile (PLATE 9). Fine clay, grey to light brown, with tiny particles of mica showing in surface, which is light brown mottling to black, burnished.
59. (3.20–3.10) Rim. Dark grey clay. Outside surface crimson red shading to orange, burnished; inside dusky with poor burnish.
60. (4.00–3.90) Rim. Light grey to red-brown clay. Mica showing in surface, which is crimson red shading to light brown round the rim inside, light brown mottling to red outside, finely burnished.
61. (4.00–3.90) Rim. Light grey clay, red-brown at the edges. Inside surface grey, outside light brown, finely burnished.
62. (4.00–3.90, 3.80–3.70) Rim. Fine grey-brown clay, well burnished.
63. (3.80–3.70) Rim. Fine light grey-brown clay, well burnished.

B, C. Medium and shallow

64. (3.45–3.20, and base from 3.20–3.10) Rim and base, apparently from same vase. Fine grey to light brown clay. Surface shades of light brown to dusky, wiped and afterwards given a superficial burnish.
65. (3.45–3.20) Rim. Gritty dark grey clay, red-brown at the edges. Occasional mica showing in surface, which is crimson red inside, light brown outside, finely burnished.
66. (3.30–3.20) Rim. Grey to red-brown clay. Mica showing in surface, which is crimson red to light brown, finely burnished.
67. (3.20–3.10) Rim. Orange clay with grit. Surface light brown to crimson red with very fine polish-like burnish

Jars (FIG. 17)

Bowl-like jars of Emporio type 30 with rims of class A I were especially characteristic of the lower group of levels. Their surfaces tended to be well burnished, dominantly red to light brown in colour, mottling or shading to dark brown, grey and dusky white or black.

(1) A. Undifferentiated rims

Class A I

68. (4.00–3.90). Brownish grey clay. Surface dark brown, shading to light brown with dusky patches inside and red outside, well burnished.

Class A II

69. (4.00–3.90). Gritty greyish brown clay. Inside surface black, outside dark purplish brown, burnished.

Class A III

(A) Upright rims

70. (3.80–3.70, 3.30–3.20) Profile (PLATE 9). Fine light grey clay shading to light brown at the edges. Surface red to light brown mottling to black, finely burnished.
71. (3.45–3.20) (PLATE 10 (*a*)). Dark grey clay, light brown at the edges. Surface crimson red shading to light brown with very fine burnish.
72. (3.45–3.20) Fine grey clay. Surface black inside, light brown shading to red outside, finely burnished.
73. (3.30–3.20) (PLATE 10 (*a*)). Red-brown clay shading to light grey with grit. Surface shades of light brown to red and black, finely burnished.
74. (3.20–3.10) Grey to light brown clay. Surface black inside, light brown shading to red outside, finely burnished.

(B) Inward leaning rims

75. (3.20–3.10, with one fragment from 4.00–3.90) Profile (PLATE 9). Fine dark grey clay. Surface shades of light brown mottling to black and red, burnished

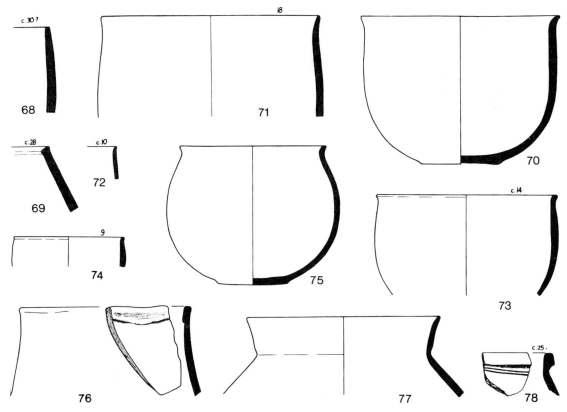

FIG. 17. Ayio Gala: Upper Cave: lower levels. Jars. Scale 1/3.

(2) B. Differentiated rims

76. (3.00–2.90) Two fragments of rim cf. Emporio class B III c. Rim made by folding back the clay so as to leave a ridge on the inside. Red-brown clay fired an even colour throughout. Mica showing in surface, which is light brown to crimson red, finely burnished.

77. (Mostly from 3.80–3.10, with one or two fragments from 4.00–3.90) Rim cf. Emporio class B III f, and fragments including parts of sunk base, apparently from same vase (PLATE 10 (a)). Grey clay, brown at the edges, with occasional mica showing in surface, which is pitted and unburnished inside. Outside finely burnished, crimson red mottling to light brown, deep purplish brown and black.

Cf. E 282 from Emporio X. Similar everted jar rims are attested from the beginning of the Neolithic in Crete and on the Greek mainland (e.g. Knossos: *BSA* lix (1964) 163 fig. 22: 18; 179 fig. 30: 46–8. *Elateia* 169 f. fig. 5: 17, 18. *Otzaki-magula* pl. i: 13). Offset jar necks resembling these occur in Hacilar VI but are said to be rare (*Hacilar* i 106; ii 258 f. fig. 54: 8). They are found, however, in very early contexts in Syria (e.g. *Judeideh* 75 fig. 47: 12, Phase B. *Byblos* v 57 fig. 26: 20100, Early Neolithic).

78. (3.80–3.70) Rim with two rough grooves or incisions below it. Hard light-grey clay. Inside surface red-brown, outside red to dark brown, well burnished. The top of the rim is worn as if the fragment had been used as a rubber cf. 4 from the lower cave.

Pithoi and large store jars (FIG. 18)

A number of fragments of pithoi were decorated with ribs in relief in the manner characteristic of pithoi from the earliest levels X–VI at Emporio. Rims with a rib below them like 79 are matched

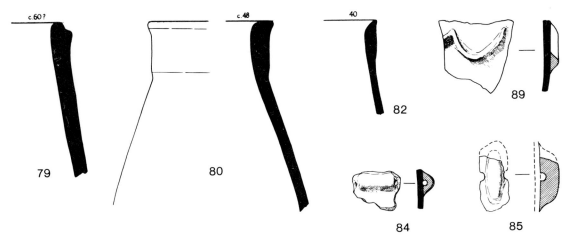

FIG. 18. Ayio Gala: Upper Cave: lower levels. Pithoi, lugs and decoration. Scale 1/3.

at Emporio by ones from the earlier levels, notably E 749–751 of Periods VII–VI, and have Early Neolithic parallels on the Greek mainland. The peculiar thickened rims 80–82 resemble the somewhat smaller jar rims 26–28 from the lower cave. No rims exactly corresponding to these were recognised at Emporio.

79. (3.80–3.70, US) Two rims with rib round outside and vertical ribs descending from it (PLATE 8). Hard gritty greyish red-brown clay. Surface red-brown to light brown, with rough burnish.
   Cf. *Athenian Agora* xiii 40 pl. 10 no. 152, assigned to the Late Neolithic. But there are close Early Neolithic parallels for 79 from Phlius near Nemea (*Hesperia* xxxviii (1969) 446 ff. fig. 2: 4, 6). Rims with ribs below them like this were at home in very early times in Syria (e.g. *Ugaritica* iv 169 fig. 6: 9, bottom, from Ras Shamra V A (Late Neolithic). *Judeideh* 48 fig. 21: 3–5; 50 fig. 22: 17; 74 fig. 44: 15–20; 75 fig. 46: 12, 13).
80. (3.80–3.70) Thickened rim. Hard, gritty light grey clay. Surface light brown mottling to red. Outside finely burnished.
81. (3.80–3.70) Thickened rim. Fine light grey clay, light brown at outside edge. Surface light grey to light brown and purplish, finely burnished.
82. (3.20–3.10) Thickened rim. Gritty dark brown to black clay. Surface shades of brown and purplish to red-brown, finely burnished.

Handles

These were not much in evidence in the material from the levels below 2.90 m in the upper cave. But two horned handles including 83 came from boxes labelled as from the lower levels. The other three stratified examples of such handles, however, were in boxes of the upper levels, two being probably from jars, the third (140) apparently from a bowl of type 8.

83. (3.80–3.70) Horned handle (PLATE 10 (b)). Light grey clay. Surface light greyish brown with very fine burnish.

Lugs

Simple perforated lugs, more or less round or oval in shape, were common in the lower levels of the upper cave as they were in the lower cave. In contrast to the lower cave, however, lugs with horizontal perforations here seemed to outnumber vertically perforated ones. Horizontally perforated lugs might resemble miniature handles like similar lugs of Period VIII at Emporio.

But the perforation through the unique elongated lug 85 may have been vertical rather than horizontal.

Tubular lugs were evidently a characteristic of the lower levels of the upper cave as of the lower cave. About half the twenty tubular lugs from the upper cave were of the red burnished ware characteristic of the earliest horizon of pottery at Ayio Gala, and these tubular lugs were often triangular in cross-section like several from the lower cave and from early levels at Emporio. Eight tubular lugs were noted in boxes with material from the lower levels below 2.90 m, as opposed to only four in those of the upper levels. Tubular lugs, it seems, might be set vertically or horizontally.

Tubular lugs merge into incipient trumpet-shaped lugs like 84. But no developed trumpet lug was recorded from the lower levels, although the fabric of the unstratified lug 263 suggests that it might belong with this early horizon of material from Ayio Gala.

Lugs were normally at any rate applied to the surface of the vase (e.g. 85), as noted in the lower cave and clearly seen in the case of 39 (PLATE 6).

84. (3.20–3.10) Trumpet lug (FIG. 18). Dark grey clay. Surface dark purplish brown, burnished.
85. (3.20–3.10) Lug (FIG. 18). Originally applied to surface of vase from which it has become detached. Perforation probably vertical rather than horizontal as drawn. Dark grey clay. Surface light reddish brown, well burnished.

String-holes

The upper cave produced some twenty-four rims and other fragments with holes made at some point after firing, evidently for string used to repair or strengthen the vases. But only eleven of these were stratified; and only two of the eleven came from the lower group of levels, and they were from the top of the deposit (3.00–2.90 m.). Some of the thirteen unstratified examples, however, are probably from the lower levels. Repair holes (rivet-holes) of this kind occurred in the lower cave (e.g. 38, 39), and were a feature of the earliest Periods X–VIII at Emporio.

Bases

Simple flat bases (Emporio class 6) occurred. Two or three bases which may have been meant to be flat were somewhat convex like 58. These convex bases evidently came from bowls, as they were burnished inside and out. More often, however, bases were sunk, as Emporio class 5. Four bases of the flat splayed Emporio class 7 A were recovered from the lower levels, and four others from the lowest deposits of the upper group of levels. Such bases were also at home in the earliest levels at Emporio, especially in those of Emporio IX. But the type of base most characteristic of the lower levels of the upper cave at Ayio Gala was differentiated like 51, so that it resembled bases of Emporio class 8. Similar bases were also much in evidence on the bowl-jars of fine burnished ware from the lower cave (e.g. 10, 12. 13). All the twenty-six stratified examples of such bases from the upper cave were from the levels between 4.00 and 2.90 m. As in the lower cave, these differentiated bases belonged to vases of more or less fine burnished ware, while the splayed bases akin to Emporio class 7 A mostly seemed to come from large thick-walled jars. One or two bases from the lower group of levels were markedly oval, like the unstratified 272. The small bowls 118–120 with rounded bases, one of them at least (118) oval, may also be from the lower levels.

Decoration

This was mostly, it seems, in relief as in the lower cave. Incised decoration is also attested.

Decoration in white paint may have occurred, as in the lower cave and in levels of Periods X and
IX at Emporio, but it seems to have been exceptional.

Paint. No example of white painted decoration was noted in the boxes with material from the
levels below 2.90 m. But the unique bowl rim 163 combining grooved decoration with white
paint appears to belong with the early material from the cave.

Incision. The rim 78 and the fragment 86 bear incised decoration. The interesting bowl rim 163
decorated with a combination of bold grooves and white paint also seems to belong with the
material from the lower levels. Two or three sherds from vases with thick walls like 163 had a pale
reddish burnished surface and decoration consisting of wide grooves with traces of a white paste
fill. The only one of these with a context was from the lowest level in the cave (4.00–3.90 m.).

   86. (3.80–3.70) Jar fragment (PLATE 10 (*d*)). Fine light grey clay shading to red-brown at outside edges. Surface
      purplish brown, burnished inside and out.

Relief. This was evidently the commonest type of decoration. Ribbed decoration was especially
favoured for large storage jars and pithoi. It was no doubt ultimately derived from the rope
cradles used to strengthen and protect such vessels. Several large jar rims (e.g. 79) had a rib
round the outside like similar rims from early levels at Emporio (E 306, 749–751, of Periods
VIII, VII and VI). Storage jars and pithoi decorated with ribs are also attested from the upper
levels of the cave above 2.90 m, but smaller vases of fine burnished ware with this type of
decoration seemed more at home in the lower group of levels. Many of the unstratified fragments
of small vases with ribbing were of the fine red burnished ware characteristic of the lower levels
and may have come from them. Ribs were normally it seems applied to the surface of the vase,
not bonded with it.
    There was much variety in the character of the ribbing, especially in the case of the fine
burnished wares which appeared to come from the lower group of levels. Thus the ribs varied
much in section, sometimes being in high relief (e.g. 88), sometimes low, flat and almost
imperceptible. Designs mostly appear to have consisted of simple combinations of horizontal,
vertical or diagonal ribs. But a number of fragments, including several of fine burnished ware,
had curved ribs (e.g. 87–89, and the unstratified fragments 305, 306, which may belong with the
early material).
    Ribs in relief were in evidence in levels of the earliest Period X at Emporio, and they included
curving motifs like E 297 which is reminiscent of 89. Relief ribs of this kind are also a feature of
the Early Neolithic on the Greek mainland (e.g. *Elateia* 171, 172 pl. 53: c, 7–10; d, 6, all from the
earliest Phase 1 of E. N. there. Nemea 267 pl. 64: 19. Corinth: Babbius Area: *Hesperia* xlvii (1978)
433 no. 2, red-slipped and burnished ware. *Otzaki-magula* i 21 pls. 6: 7; iii: 23, from the house in A
and B 17 which appears to be earlier than the Tiefe Schicht of Protosesklo. Cf. *Prosymna* i 374; ii
156 fig. 632: 3, of coarse unpainted ware from the 'Pyre' on the West Yerogalaro ridge,
associated with pattern burnish ware. The group was assigned by Blegen, although with every
reserve, to the earlier Neolithic horizon, but Coleman, *Kephala* 103, thinks it more likely to date
from a time near the end of the Neolithic). Such ribs also appear on Early Neolithic pottery from
Knossos in Crete (e.g. *BSA* lix (1964) 214 pl. 49 (2): 1, from Stratum IV (E. N.II), which closely
resembles the E. N. example from Otzaki). But they occur later, and are a feature of the evolved
Blue period at Poliochni (*Poliochni* i pls. lxii–lxiii. Cf. J. D. Evans, *BSA* lxiii (1968) 273).
    Warts and solid lugs included a small horned lug set vertically below the rim of a bowl (57) of

type 14, which appears to come from the early group of levels. A similar lug (47) was recovered from the lower cave.

87. (4.00–3.90) Jar (?) fragment with curving rib (PLATE 8). Coarse light grey clay. Surface light brownish grey with rough burnish.
    The curving rib might have formed part of an unperforated crescentic lug, like those found on type 5 bowls from Emporio IX and VIII (e.g. E 58, 78).
88. (3.00–2.90) Jar (?) fragment with curving rib (PLATE 8). The rib is unusually high in relation to its width. Light grey clay. Surface shades of brown, burnished.
89. (3.00–2.90) Jar (?) fragment with curving ribs (FIG. 18). Light grey to red-brown clay with grit and straw. Mica showing in surface, which is purplish, burnished but worn.

(b) Upper levels (above 2.90 m) (90–308)

Fabric

The firing has improved, and the fabric tends to be harder. The clay in the break is normally dark grey or black, often changing to red-brown at one or both edges. Burnished surfaces are now dominantly dark, brownish grey or grey-brown, often with a purplish tinge. But light grey, and light brown and red burnished surfaces are also in evidence. The burnishing is sometimes very fine and polish-like. Even at the bottom of this group of levels, however, cooking pot type ware is found with surfaces unburnished. In the highest levels the proportion of unburnished ware is considerable.

A certain amount of material of which the context has been lost has been included with that from the upper levels. In the case of this unstratified (US) material no depth is given in brackets.

Bowls
(FIGS. 19–27)

Most of the types common at Emporio are represented. But it is interesting and perhaps significant that there are no examples of the two standard Troadic types, Emporio type 11 with inward curving and internally differentiated rim, common in Kum Tepe I B and Emporio VII–VI, and the carinated type 9 dominant in Troy I and Emporio V–IV.

2. Dishes. Only one example was noted.

90. (0.90–0. NW) Profile (FIG. 19). Very coarse light grey clay red-brown at the edges with straw and large grit showing in surface. Inside deep red, burnished. Outside purplish, less well burnished. Underneath of base red-brown, burnished.

3. Baking pans (FIG. 19). Some nine rims of this distinctive type were recognised from the upper levels, but none from the material labelled as from the lower group of levels in the cave (cf. Furness, *PPS* xxii (1956) 200). The situation here is therefore the reverse of that at Emporio, where baking pans were abundantly represented in the earliest levels, but may have been no longer made by Periods V–IV. Baking pans are a feature of the Late Neolithic of the Greek mainland, however, with which this later horizon at Ayio Gala seems to have connections.

91. (1.30–1.20) Rim. Coarse greyish brown clay with large grit. Surface deep purplish brown, rough and unburnished.
    Cf. (US) Rim 91A, as 91 and perhaps from same vase (PLATE 10 (*b*)).
92. (0.90–0.80) Rim. Fabric as 93 below. Other similar rims.
93. (0.50–0.) Rim with stump of large horizontal side handle. Irregular. Coarse grey clay with large grit. Surface brown to red-brown, rough and unburnished, with grit and straw impressions showing in it.

4. Open bowls with straight or slightly curving sides. Rims assignable to this type merge with those of types 5 on the one hand and 14 on the other. Several of the rims grouped here have circular or drooping or oblong warts on the outside. One has a string-hole made after the vase was fired.

From stratified contexts (FIG. 19)

94. (2.05–1.90) Rim with large unperforated drooping lug of class 2 on outside. Dark grey clay, red-brown near the outside edge. Inside surface dark brownish grey, burnished. Outside brown, rough without any trace of burnish.
    Others similar, including one (2.15–2.05) with stump of large round vertically perforated lug. Coarse light grey clay. Inside surface light brown, burnished. Outside dark brown to black with little or no trace of burnish.
95. (1.20–0.90) Two rims, which may come from the same bowl, with large drooping lugs like that on 94 on outside. Grey clay with mica showing in surface, which is light grey inside, greyish brown outside, burnished.
    Drooping lugs of the kind found on 94 and 95 are said to be at home in the Middle Neolithic of the Greek mainland (e.g. Corinth: *Hesperia* xlvii (1978) 433 no. 5 pl. 105, from a Middle Neolithic context, but could be Early Neolithic according to Lavezzi).

Without context (FIG. 20)

96. Rim. Hard grey clay, red-brown at outside edge. Inside surface black, burnished. Outside dirty brown to black, rough as if wiped with a bunch of twigs and afterwards given a superficial burnish.
97. Rim with circular wart on outside. Dark grey clay with large grit. Inside surface greyish brown, outside dark purplish brown, burnished.
98. Rim with oblong wart on outside (PLATE 10 (*b*)). Dark grey clay. Surface dark brownish grey, burnished.
99. Rim with string-hole bored after firing. Light brownish grey clay. Surface light brown, burnished.

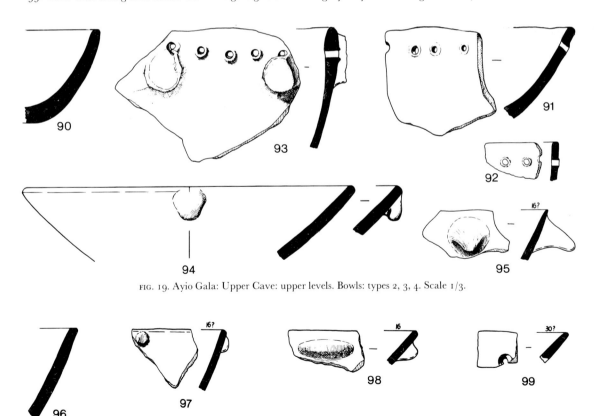

FIG. 19. Ayio Gala: Upper Cave: upper levels. Bowls: types 2, 3, 4. Scale 1/3.

FIG. 20. Ayio Gala: Upper Cave: without context. Bowls: type 4. Scale 1/3.

5. Open bowls with curving sides. These were well represented in the later group of levels, as they were in those below 2.90 m. Some bowls of this type from the later group of levels evidently had handles. The miniature bowls (118–120) were all more or less round-bottomed. The largest (118) at least was oval in shape. None had a context.

A. *Deep*

From stratified contexts (FIG. 21)
100. (1.60–1.45) Rim, and fragment which may be from same vase. Light grey clay, light brown at edges. Straw impressions prominent in break. Surface seems to have a slightly lustrous wash, reddish to light brown inside, dark purplish brown to black outside. Possibly an import.
101. (1.20–0.90, 0.90–0.80, 0.60–0.50) Large parts of rim, and stump of lug. Grey-brown clay. Surface shades of dark purplish brown with fine polish-like burnish. Several other similar rims.
102. (1.20–0.90) Rim. Hard clay, light grey throughout. Surface dark grey, finely burnished.
103. (0.90–0.80) Rim. Light grey clay, red-brown at edges. Surface shades of light brown, finely burnished.
104. (0.90–0. NW Corner) Rim. Grey-brown clay. Inside surface dark brown, outside light brown mottling to red and purplish and greyish brown, finely burnished.

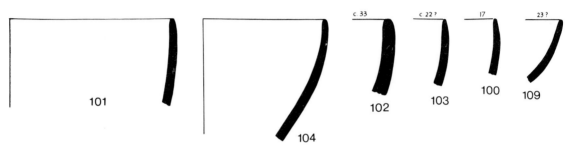

FIG. 21. Ayio Gala: Upper Cave: upper levels. Bowls: type 5. Scale 1/3.

Without context (FIG. 22)
105. Rim. Coarse gritty grey clay. Inside surface light brown, outside reddish to dark brown, burnished.
106. Rim. Black clay. Inside surface black, outside brown, burnished but worn.
107. Rim. Dark brownish grey clay. Surface dark greyish brown with rather poor burnish.
108. Rim. Brownish grey clay, burnished.

B, C. *Medium and shallow*

From stratified context (FIG. 21)
109. (1.30–1.20, 0.60–0.50) Rim. Grey clay. Surface black, burnished but worn. Other similar rims.

Without context (FIG. 22)
110. Rim. Dark grey clay. Surface dark brownish grey with fine burnish.
111. Rim. Coarse grey clay, reddish brown at edges. Surface reddish to dark brown with poor burnish. Many other similar rims from all levels.
112. Rim. Light grey clay. Surface grey without any trace of burnish. Other similar rims from all levels.
113. Rim. Greyish brown clay. Surface light brown shading to crimson red and mottling to dark brown and black, well burnished. Many other similar rims from the upper levels.

Handles and lugs (all without context) (FIG. 22)
114. Rim with stump of vertical strap handle. Angle uncertain. Dark grey clay. Surface greyish brown, burnished.
115. Rim with stump of horizontal side handle. Grey-brown clay. Inside surface dark grey, outside greyish brown, with fine polish-like burnish.

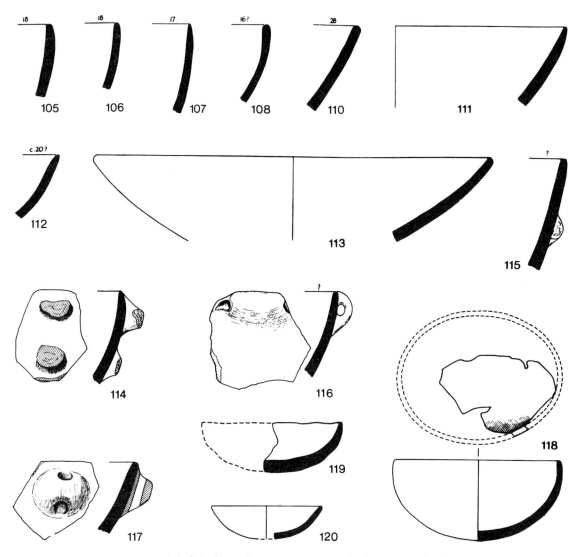

FIG. 22. Ayio Gala: Upper Cave: without context. Bowls: type 5. Scale 1/3.

116. Rim with horizontally perforated lug. Grey-brown clay. Surface shades of dark brown with fine burnish.
117. Rim with vertically perforated lug. Gritty red-brown clay. Surface dark purplish brown, burnished.

Miniature bowls (diam. less than 15) (all without context) (FIG. 22)

118. Profile of small oval bowl (PLATE 9). Grey-brown clay. Surface dark brownish grey, burnished.
  Oval vases were already being made in Syria in the Early Neolithic there (e.g. *Byblos* v 51 fig. 19). They come in the Early Neolithic of Anatolia at Çatal Hüyük (*AS* xii (1962) 54 f., 53 fig. 9: 16), and occur at Hacilar from Level IX onwards, reaching their fullest development there in Levels V–I (*Hacilar* i 103 f., 110).
119. Profile. Very irregular. Possibly oval like 118. Coarse brown to red-brown clay with large grit and straw. Surface brown, rough and uneven.
120. Profile. Fine grey to brown clay. Surface shades of darkish brown, burnished but worn.

6. Bowls with inward leaning rims (FIG. 23)

From stratified contexts

With somewhat upright rims (cf. type 5)

121. (Burial at 0.90–0.80) Rim (PLATE 10 (*a*)). Grey clay. Surface red-brown and purplish brown mottling to light brown and black, finely burnished.
122. (0.90–0.80) Rim. Grey clay. Surface dark purplish brown to black with very fine polish-like burnish.
123. (0.60–0.50) Rim. Grey clay, reddish brown at edges. Surface light brown shading to red, finely burnished.
124. (0.50–0.) Rim. Grey clay. Surface light brown mottling to black, finely burnished.

With distinctly inward leaning rims

125. (1.90–1.80) Rim. Dark grey clay. Surface grey-brown, burnished.
126. (1.20–0.90) Rim. Grey clay, reddish brown at edges. Surface shades of dark and light brown, finely burnished.
127. (0.90–0.80) Rim. Dark purplish grey-brown, burnished.

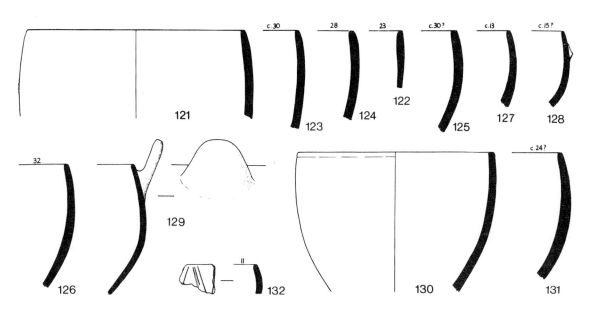

FIG. 23. Ayio Gala: Upper Cave: upper levels and without context. Bowls: type 6. Scale 1/3.

Handles and lugs

128. (1.20–0.90) Rim with stump of handle or lug. Grey clay. Inside surface black, outside brown, finely burnished but worn.
129. (1.20–1.10) Rim with tab handle. Light grey clay. Surface grey-brown, burnished.

Without context

130. Rim. Grey clay. Inside surface black, outside greyish brown mottling to red, brown and black, finely burnished.
131. Rim. Grey clay. Surface purplish brown, finely burnished but worn.
132. Rim with incised decoration. Soft greyish brown clay with grit, including some fairly large lumps of white. Surface dark purplish brown, finely burnished. The decoration appears to have been cut after the burnishing of the surface.

7. Bowls with inward leaning rims and high shoulders. Rims of this type merge with those of types 6 and 8. About a third of the rims assignable to this type were markedly thickened, as 134. The rim 135 from the top level is unburnished and has a kidney-sectioned vertical handle.

From stratified contexts (FIG. 24)

133. (1.30–1.20) Rim. Grey clay. Inside surface deep chestnut brown, outside shades of light brown mottling to black, finely burnished.
134. (1.20–0.90) Rim. Dark greyish brown, finely burnished.
135. (0.50–0.) Rim with vertical handle. Dark grey clay with grit including large lumps of white. Surface light greyish brown, unburnished.
    For the handle cf. E 93 from a level of Emporio IX.

Without context (FIG. 25)

136. Rim. Dark grey clay, brown at edges. Surface dark brown shading to light brown round outside of rim, finely burnished.

8. More or less carinated bowls with high rims and often ogival profiles.

The rims of these were very common, and included one example (139) of an exceptionally shallow variety that was not recognised at Emporio. The rim 149 assigned to this type was unique in having pattern burnish.

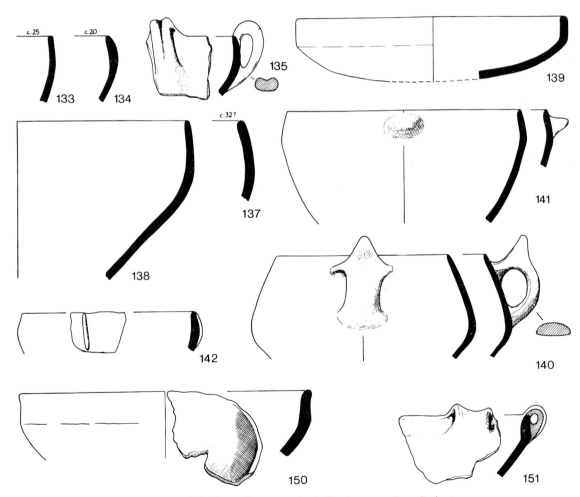

FIG. 24. Ayio Gala: Upper Cave: upper levels. Bowls: types 7, 8, 10. Scale 1/3.

From stratified contexts (FIG. 24)

137. (2.70–2.60) Rim. Gritty grey clay. Inside surface dark greyish brown, outside a lighter shade, well burnished.
138. (1.20–0.90) Rim (PLATE 10 (a)). Brownish grey clay. Inside surface light brownish grey, outside dark brown shading to black, burnished.
139. (1.20–0.90) Profile of shallow variety of type 8. Black clay with white grit and straw. Surface dark purplish brown, finely burnished.
140. (1.90–1.80) Rim with vertical horned handle (PLATE 10 (a)). Light grey clay. Surface light greyish brown, finely burnished.
141. (1.50–1.30) Rim with oval wart. Grey clay, brown at edges. Surface irregular with poor burnish, brownish black inside, greyish brown with patches of light brown outside.
142. (0.60–0.50) Rim with vertical rib. Dark greyish brown, burnished.

Without context (FIG. 25)

143. Rim. Grey clay, brown at edges. Surface dark brown to black, finely burnished.
144. Rim. Grey clay. Surface dark grey-brown, burnished.
145. Rim. Black clay with white grit and straw. Inside surface dark grey to black, outside light greyish brown, well burnished.

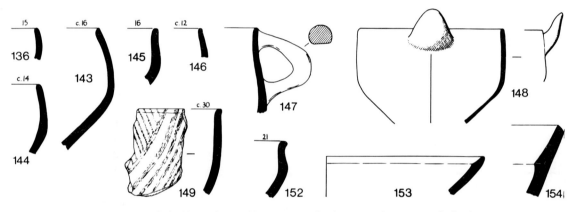

FIG. 25. Ayio Gala: Upper Cave: without context. Bowls: types 7, 8, 10, 12, 13. Scale 1/3.

146. Rim. Grey clay. Inside surface dark grey to black, outside light greyish brown, finely burnished.
147. Rim with vertical handle. Brownish grey clay, red-brown at edges. Inside surface deep purple, outside dark purplish brown, burnished.
148. Rim with tab handle. Rather soft grey to red-brown clay tempered with finely chopped straw and some grit. Surface dark grey to reddish brown, burnished but worn.
149. Rim with pattern burnish (PLATE 10 (c)). Dark grey clay with straw and some large grit. Inside surface black to dark brown, finely burnished. Outside dark brown with pattern burnish.

10. Bowls with short S-shaped, usually thickened club-like rims. This type, characteristic of Periods VII–VI at Emporio, is only represented at Ayio Gala by three rims from the upper cave. None of these is very typical, but 151 has a trumpet lug like bowls of type 10 from Emporio, and the rather soft fabric with abundant straw temper of the other rims is also reminiscent of this type at Emporio. It is noteworthy that two of the rims assignable to this type (150, 151) are from boxes labelled as from near the top of the deposit (0.60–0.50 m) in the upper cave, the third (152) being unstratified. But the surface of 151 at least is markedly worn, which might indicate that it was a stray of earlier date.

From stratified contexts (FIG. 24)

150. (0.60–0.50) Rim. Brownish grey clay with grit and straw. Surface with straw impressions showing in it, black inside, shades of light and dark brown outside, well stroke burnished.
151. (0.60–0.50) Rim with horizontal trumpet lug (PLATE 10 (*b*)). Dark grey clay. Surface light brown, burnished but worn.

Without context (FIG. 25)

152. Rim. Grey clay shading to red and light brown at edges. Grit and straw showing in surface, which is light brown, burnished but worn.

12. Bowls with straight rims thickened and differentiated on the inside. Like type 10 this type was only represented by three rims in the upper cave at Ayio Gala. Two of these including 153 had no context, but the third came from the lower group of levels (3.45–3.20 m). All three rims may therefore date from the earlier horizon in the cave.

153. Rim (FIG. 25). Gritty grey clay with straw impressions showing in surface, which is black shading to brown inside, dark brown outside, finely burnished

13. Bowls with outward curving rims, internally differentiated and thickened. Two of the three rims (54, 55) of this distinctive type with a context came from the lower group of levels. The third (not illustrated) was in a box labelled 1.30–1.20 m of the upper group. Three more including 154 were of unknown context.

154. Rim (FIG. 25). Greyish brown clay with mica showing in surface, which is shades of light brown, finely burnished.

14. Bowls with outward curving rims. These were very common in the lower group of levels, but distinctly rare in levels above 2.90 m. Most of the examples of which the context is unknown may therefore come from the lower group of levels. Traces of bold grooved decoration were noted on four rims of this type including 162, 163, both without context. The grooves on 163 had afterwards been emphasised with a thick creamy white paint. The inside of this rim had bold hatching in white.

From stratified contexts (FIG. 26)

155. (2.15–1.90) Rim. Dark grey clay, brown at edges. Surface dark greyish brown, finely burnished.
156. (0.95 NW Corner) Rim. Gritty grey clay, red-brown at edges. Surface dark brown to black, burnished.

Without context (FIG. 27)

A. Deep

157. Rim. Coarse grey clay, red-brown at edges. Occasional straw impressions and lumps of grit showing in surface, which is brown, burnished.

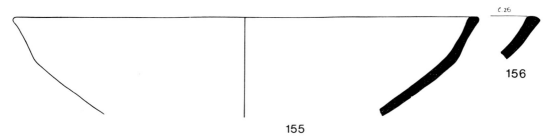

C.26

156

155

FIG. 26. Ayio Gala: Upper Cave: upper levels. Bowls: type 14. Scale 1/3.

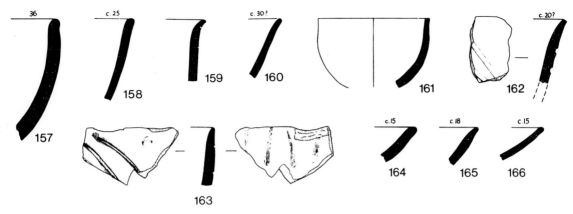

FIG. 27. Ayio Gala: Upper Cave: without context. Bowls: type 14. Scale 1/3.

158. Rim. Grey clay, red-brown at edges. Abundant large grey and purple grit showing in surface, which is orange mottling to red in patches, burnished but worn.
159. Rim. Gritty greyish brown clay. Surface dark purplish brown mottling to dark red, finely burnished.
160. Rim. Grey clay, red-brown at edges. Occasional mica showing in surface, which is shades of light brown mottling to red, burnished but worn.
161. Rim. Grey clay with white grit. Inside surface dark grey, outside greyish brown, burnished.
162. Rim with bold grooved decoration (PLATE 10 (d)). Dark grey clay. Mica showing in surface, which is black inside, dark purplish brown outside, burnished.
163. Rim with bold grooved decoration combined with white paint (PLATE 10 (d)). Very hard fabric. Fine light grey to purplish brown clay. Surface shades of light brown, burnished. On outside, three bold diagonal grooves overpainted in thick creamy white, with traces of a small circle or spot in white just below rim; bold vertical hatching in white on inside of rim. Two unstratified fragments of similar fabric may come from the same vase (below 163 on PLATE 10 (d)).

B, C. Medium and shallow
164. Rim. Soft light grey clay. Small grit and straw impressions showing in surface, which is light brown, finely burnished.
165. Rim. Light grey to brown clay. Inside surface dark purplish brown to black, outside brown shading to red, burnished.
166. Rim. Soft orange clay with fine grit including some white. Surface light brown shading to reddish, finely burnished

Jugs

One or two fragments like 172, 173, from the highest levels of deposit in the upper cave evidently belonged to jugs akin to type 23 characteristic of Periods VII–VI at Emporio although attested there earlier. In fabric as well as in shape these jugs appear to have resembled ones of Emporio VII–VI. But in general the handled jugs in use at Ayio Gala would seem to have had straight sloping necks and flat mouths like the earlier Emporio type 20. A number of fragments of rims with handles apparently belonged to jugs akin to this type. Most of these were unstratified, but two at least, including 167, came from the upper levels in the cave.

20. Jugs with straight necks and flat mouths

From stratified contexts (FIG. 28)
167. (1.20–1.10) Neck with handle. Hard grey clay. Surface light brownish grey, well burnished outside and round inside of rim.

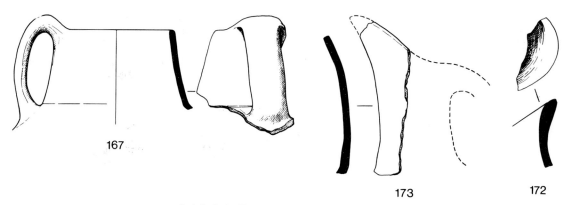

FIG. 28. Ayio Gala: Upper Cave: upper levels. Jugs Scale 1/3.

Without context (FIG. 29)

168. Fragment with neck and stump of handle. There is a large low circular wart on the shoulder opposite the handle. Irregular. Greyish brown clay. Outside surface dark grey-brown, well burnished.
169. Neck with stump of handle. Outside surface shades of brown, finely burnished.
170. Fragment with stump of handle. Soft greyish brown clay with white grit. Outside surface brown to black, burnished but rather worn.
171. Fragment with handle. Cf. 8 from lower cave. Grey to light-brown clay. Surface reddish brown to grey, well burnished inside as well as outside.

23. Jugs with sloping mouths (FIG. 28)

172. (Burial at 0.90–0.80) Spout. Dark grey clay tempered with straw. Brownish black surface with fine polish-like burnish.
173. (0.60–0.50) Neck. Red-brown clay with grit and straw. Black surface with fine polish-like burnish.

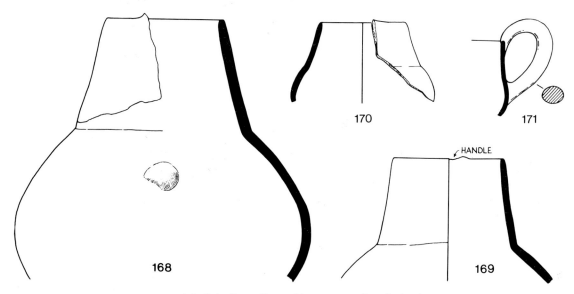

FIG. 29. Ayio Gala: Upper Cave: without context. Jugs. Scale 1/3.

Jars

Rims of class A I include some from large storage jars like 179. Some rims with vertically perforated lugs (e.g. 268, 269) may come from bowl-jars of the kind prevalent in the lower group of levels below 2.90 m and in the lower cave. But bowl-jars with rims of type A III akin to Emporio type 30 were hardly represented in the levels above 2.90 m. At least one rim of class A I had a single wart, and 187 boasts a double wart. The rim 191 of class A III from the top of the deposit in the cave has a bold conical wart, while a group of fragments (202), without a context but apparently from the same vase as 191, carry elaborate punctuated and incised decoration.

While bowl-jars akin to Emporio type 30 are characteristic of the lowest horizon at Ayio Gala, jars of types 41–42 seem more at home in the upper group of levels of the upper cave there. Many rims and some profiles of jars of these types were recovered from the levels above 2.90 m. The larger of these jars tended to have sloping as opposed to upright necks. One large jar (205) evidently had a pair of neat horned handles. A number of these jars including 205 had been decorated with simple linear designs in white paint.

Jars with collar rims (class B III) were in evidence. But rims of the kind standard at Emporio in Periods V–IV did not seem to occur.

(1) A. Undifferentiated jar rims

Class A I

From stratified contexts (FIG. 30)

174. (2.05–1.90) Hard dark grey clay. Surface shades of brown and red-brown, burnished.
175. (2.15–2.05) Gritty dark grey to red-brown clay. Inside surface unburnished, outside shades of brown and red-brown, burnished.
176. (1.60–1.50) Grey clay. Surface greyish brown, burnished.
177. (1.30–0.90) Dark grey-brown, burnished.
178. (0.90–0.80) Hard gritty dark grey clay. Surface unburnished, light purplish brown inside, dark purplish grey outside.

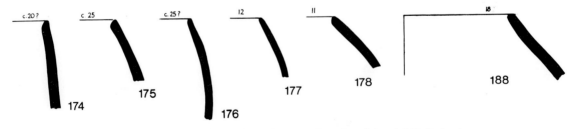

FIG. 30. Ayio Gala: Upper Cave: upper levels. Jars: rims of class A I–II. Scale 1/3.

Without context (FIG. 31)

179. Hard gritty grey to red-brown clay. Surface dark reddish brown with rough burnish.
180. Hard gritty grey clay. Surface light brown, burnished.
181. Coarse dark grey clay. Surface dark brown, burnished.
182. Hard red-brown clay. Outside surface red-brown to dark brown, burnished.
183. Light grey clay. Outside surface light brown with rough burnish.
184. Hard light grey clay, red-brown at edges. Some mica showing in surface, which is smoothed rather than burnished, purplish inside, light brown mottling to black outside.
185. Hard grey clay. Inside surface light grey, outside brownish grey, burnished.

186. Profile with vertically perforated lug, probably one of a pair (PLATE 9). Dark grey clay. Inside surface unburnished. Outside dark brown, burnished.
187. Large fragment with double wart (PLATE 9). Hard dark grey clay. Surface shades of light and dark brown with rough burnish.

Class A II

From stratified contexts (FIG. 30)
188. (0.95 NW Corner) Stump of handle on shoulder. Coarse clay with large grit and straw. Some mica and straw impressions showing in surface, which is shades of brown and red, burnished but worn.
Without context (FIG. 31)
189. Hard dark grey clay, red-brown at outside edge. Some mica showing in surface, which is dark brownish grey inside, reddish brown outside, burnished.
190. String-hole apparently made while clay soft before firing of vase. Fine brownish grey clay. Some mica showing in surface, which is shades of dark and reddish brown, finely burnished inside and outside.

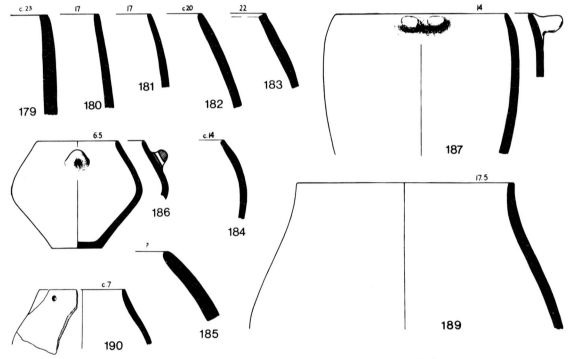

FIG. 31. Ayio Gala: Upper Cave: without context. Jars: rims of class A I–II. Scale 1/3.

Class A III

From stratified contexts (FIG. 32)
191. (0.50–0.). Bold wart on outside. Gritty dark grey clay. Straw impressions and some grit showing in surface, which is light brown, rough.
192. (1.30–1.20) Greyish brown clay. Straw impressions showing in surface, which is dark brown with poor burnish.
193. (0.60–0.50) Grey to red-brown clay. Surface dark purplish brown, burnished but worn.
194. (0.60–0.50) Grey clay. Surface dark brownish grey, burnished.
195. (0.95 NW Corner) (PLATE 9). Stump of lug or handle on swelling. Soft fabric. Clay shades of brown and grey

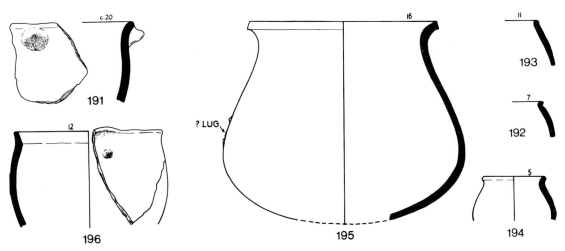

FIG. 32. Ayio Gala: Upper Cave: upper levels. Jars: rims of class A III. Scale 1/3.

with abundant large grit (white, orange, grey and purplish), some showing in surface, especially on inside, which is unburnished. Outside orange-brown to dusky, burnished.

196. (0.60–0.50) Rim internally thickened and differentiated, with slight projection rising from it and small wart below. Grey clay. Surface light brown mottling to dark brown and purplish black in patches, well burnished.

Without context (FIG. 33)

197. Hard brownish grey clay. Inside surface crimson red, outside light brown, finely burnished.

198. Brownish grey clay. Surface dark purplish brown to black, mottling to crimson red on outside, finely burnished.

199. Light grey clay. Inside surface red mottling to light brown and black, outside light brown to black, finely burnished.

200. (PLATE 10 (a)). Grey clay. Mica showing in surface, which is reddish brown, burnished.

201. Fine light greyish brown clay. Surface shades of light brown, finely burnished.

202. Fragments, seven in all, apparently from same vase (PLATE 10 (d)). Dark grey clay. Inside surface black, outside brown with fine polish-like burnish. Decorated with punctuations made with the end of a small bone and framed by incised lines. Traces of white fill in the decoration. The rim fragment has vertical ripples.

    PPS xxii (1956) 202 pl. xxiii: 1–3.

203. Greyish brown clay. Mica showing in surface, which is dusky shading to light brown and crimson red. Outside finely burnished.

204. Stump of horizontally perforated lug on swelling. Surface greyish brown, finely burnished.

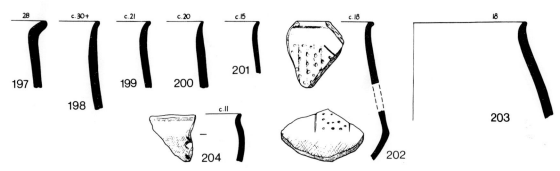

FIG. 33. Ayio Gala: Upper Cave: without context. Jars: rims of class A III. Scale 1/3.

(2) B. Differentiated jar rims

Classes B I–II

Some rims were markedly curved like 205, 210, 213–14. But the majority were more or less straight and fairly upright.

From stratified contexts (FIG. 34)

205. Profile (restored from many non-joining fragments, mostly US but including one from 1.20–0.90). Dark grey clay with small grit and straw. Outside surface black with fine polish-like burnish; decorated with groups of thin diagonal stripes in white.

   Jars of comparable type with necks of this kind and handles on the swelling or shoulder were very much at home in the Middle Chalcolithic Level XVI at Mersin (*Mersin* 146 ff. figs. 91, 92). Similar jars of red burnished ware from a well by the Beulé Gate of the Acropolis at Athens are assigned to the Late Neolithic or Subneolithic (*ADelt* xxi (1966) Chron. 42 f. pl. 63. *AR* 1967–68, 4 fig. 3. *Athenian Agora* xiii 3). Flattened shoulders as on 205 were common in the Late Neolithic of Southern Greece according to Phelps, *Thesis*. Cf. *Aspripetra* 303 fig. 91: top row, second from right. *Orchomenos* ii 12 f. figs. 9, 10: Class A, Black Polished Ware.

206. (1.30–1.20) Light grey clay, red-brown at edges. Surface with purplish tinge, well burnished.

207. (1.30–1.20) Grey to brown clay. Surface dark greyish brown, burnished.

208. (0.90–0.80) Dark grey clay, red-brown near edges. Surface dark purplish brown to black, finely burnished.

209. Profile (restored from fragments from between 0.90–0.60) (PLATE 9). Dark brownish grey clay. Outside surface black shading to brown in places with fine polish-like burnish. Traces of decoration in white; triple chevrons on rim and shoulder.

   Cf. *AS* vi (1956) 194 f. no. 3, of comparable shape with similar decoration in white, from Gökçe Boğaz east of Sinope, and *AS* xiii (1963) 206 fig. 4: 3, from the Konya plain, both assigned to the Late Chalcolithic. A fragment of white-painted ware from Level XXXIX (Late Chalcolithic 1) at Beycesultan could have belonged to a vase of this shape (*Beycesultan* i 72 f. fig. P. 1: 21). Compare also a Late Neolithic jar of red burnished ware from the Kitsos Cave in Attica (*BCH* xcvi (1972) 828 f. fig. 14).

210. (0.80–0.70) Grey clay red-brown at edges. Outside surface light brown, finely burnished. Traces of decoration in white.

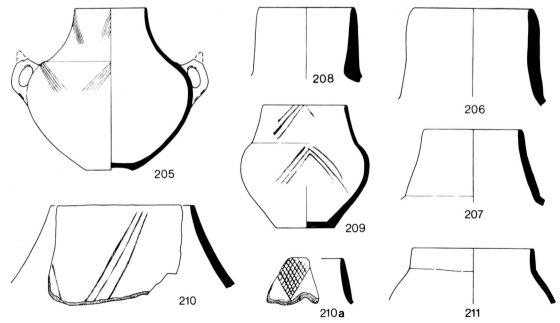

FIG. 34. Ayio Gala: Upper Cave: upper levels. Jars: rims of class B I–II. Scale 1/3, except 205 (1/6).

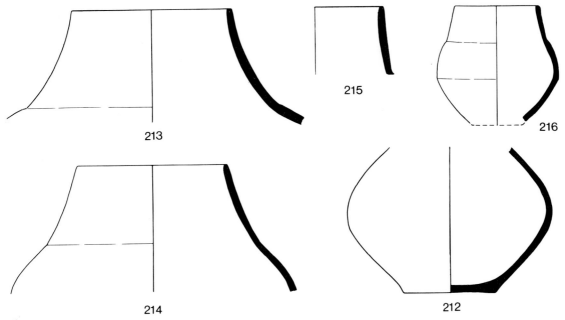

FIG. 35. Ayio Gala: Upper Cave: without context. Jars: rims of class B I–II. Scale 1/3.

210a. (0.60–0.50) Grey clay, red-brown at outside edge. Outside surface purplish black, burnished. Inverted cross-hatched triangle in white.
211. (2·05 1.90) Gritty grey clay. Outside surface light brown mottling to black and red, burnished.
212. Body which may have belonged to jar with rim of this type (restored from fragments coming from different levels between 2.70–2.60 and 0.60–0.50) (FIG. 35). Fine brownish grey clay. Outside surface black, finely burnished.

Without context (FIG. 35)
213. Three fragments of rim. Gritty grey clay, red-brown at edges. Inside surface red, outside shades of light brown, burnished.
214. Dark grey clay. Surface brown shading to black, burnished but worn.
      For the rim profile compare a type 41 jar from Poliochni evolved Blue (*Poliochni* i 571 pl. liv: d).
215. Black with fine polish-like burnish.
216. Fragment of small jar with carinated body. Soft grey clay, red-brown at edges. Outside surface dark purplish brown, finely burnished.

Class B III

A. Rims cf. E class B IIIa: high

From stratified context (FIG. 36)
217. (2.70–2.60) Dark greyish brown, well burnished.

Without context (FIG. 37)
218. Grey clay, red-brown near inside edge. Surface dark brown to black, finely burnished.
219. Grey clay. Surface shades of brown, burnished.
220. Two fragments, apparently from same vase. Line impressed by cord round outside of rim. Light grey to brown clay. Surface light greyish brown, burnished.
221. Dark grey to brown clay. Surface dark grey to light brown, finely burnished.

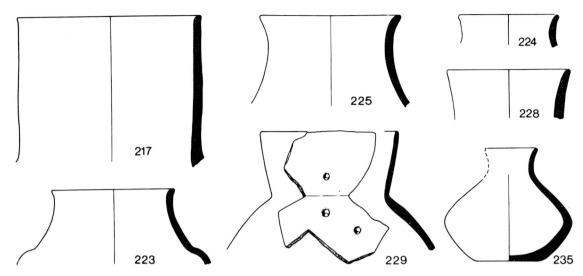

FIG. 36. Ayio Gala: Upper Cave: upper levels. Jars: rims of class B III. Scale. 1/3.

B. Rims cf. E class B III a: low

Without context (FIG. 37)

222. Gritty dark grey to red-brown clay with some large grit. Surface shades of brown and red-brown with rough burnish.

C. Rims cf. E class B III c

From stratified context (FIG. 36)

223. (0.95 NW) Very soft dark grey clay. Outside surface black with fine polish-like burnish, but worn.
224. (0.90–0.80) Black clay with fine grit and straw. Surface black with very fine polish-like burnish.
225. (0.60–0.50) Soft light grey clay, red-brown at edges. Straw impressions showing in surface, which is light brown to crimson red on outside, well burnished.

Without context (FIG. 37)

226. Coarse grey clay, red-brown at edges. Surface shades of brown and red-brown with dusky patches, burnished.
227. Hard fabric. Coarse grey clay with grit and abundant straw impressions showing in surface. Outside purplish grey-brown with poor burnish.

D. Rims cf. E class B III d

From stratified context (FIG. 36)

228. (1.60–1.45) Light grey clay with large white grit and straw. Surface shades of light brown, well burnished.
229. (Burial at 0.90–0.80) Three string-holes bored after firing. Hard gritty black to light brown clay with abundant white grit, some showing in surface, which is light brown with traces of burnish inside and outside.

Without context (FIG. 37)

230. Hard grey clay, red-brown at outside edge. Inside surface light grey mottling to light brown, burnished. Outside orange-brown, finely burnished but worn.
231. Grey to red-brown clay. Inside surface light brown, outside light brown to red, finely burnished but worn.
232. Grey clay. Inside surface brownish black, outside brown shading to red with black patches, well burnished.

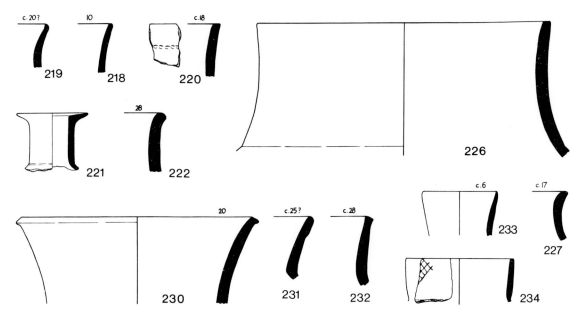

FIG. 37. Ayio Gala: Upper Cave: without context. Jars: rims of class B III. Scale 1/3, except 230 (1/6).

233. Light greyish brown clay with mica showing in surface, which is red to light brown, finely burnished inside and outside.

234. Grey clay, red-brown at outside edge. Surface dark brownish grey, finely burnished. Traces of cross-hatching (? inverted triangle) in white.

E. Rims cf. E class B III f

235. (1.30–1.20) Profile of small jar (FIG. 36. PLATE 9). Black clay with abundant fine grit. Occasional mica showing in surface, which is blackish and rough on inside except round rim. Outside white with some dusky and reddish patches, burnished.

Pithoi and large store jars
(FIG. 38)

There were no rims of the everted class characteristic of Periods V–IV at Emporio.

From stratified contexts

236. (0.90–0.80) Rim with flattened top. Coarse gritty grey clay, red-brown at edges. Abundant straw impressions in surface, which is uneven, light brown, with very poor burnish.

237 and 237a. (Burial at 0.90–0.80) Rim rising in projection with rib below it on outside. Coarse gritty grey clay. Surface red-brown with rough burnish.

Without context

238. Gritty black clay. Surface black, burnished outside.

239. Rim with large vertical wart. Hard gritty grey clay. Some mica showing in surface, which is reddish brown with rough burnish.

240. Rim with flattened top. Hard very coarse light grey clay containing grit and straw. Surface brownish grey with poor burnish.

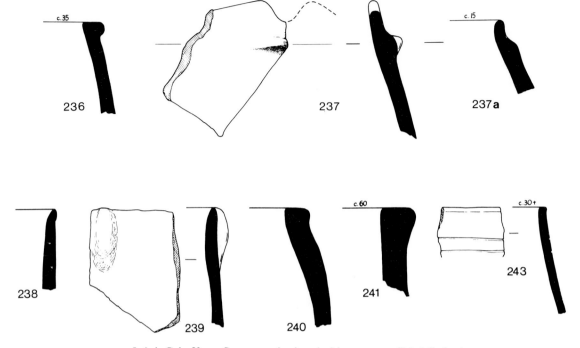

FIG. 38. Ayio Gala: Upper Cave: upper levels and without context. Pithoi. Scale 1/3.

241. Rim with flattened top. Hard light brown clay with fine grit. Some mica showing in surface, which is light brown, well burnished.
242. Fragment with ribs in relief (PLATE 8). Coarse gritty light brown clay. Inside surface light brown, outside black, burnished.
243. Rim of large jar with two bold horizontal grooves round outside. Mica showing in surface, which is reddish brown, well burnished.

Lids (FIG. 39)

No fragments of lids were recognised from the lower levels below 2.90 m., and they were not common in the upper levels of the cave. Most of the fragments recovered came from flat lids (type 60), but several belonged to flanged cover lids cf. type 62.

From stratified contexts

244. (1.20–1.10) Fragment cf. type 60. Coarse gritty grey clay. Straw impressions showing in surface, which is red-brown inside, dark brown outside, unburnished. Decorated with three deep punctuations with traces of white fill.

   Flat lids (types 60, 61) were hardly attested at Emporio before Period II, when they were common. But they were much in evidence at Troy (shape D 14) from the beginning of Troy I onwards.
245. (1.20–1.10) Fragment cf. type 62. Coarse grey to red-brown clay. Straw impressions showing in surface, which is red-brown shading to dark purplish brown with slight traces of burnish.
246. (0.50–0.) Fragment cf. type 62. One of a pair of string-holes through the flange preserved. Coarse gritty grey clay. Straw impressions in surface, which is greyish brown, burnished on outside but worn.

   This and 245 come from flat-topped covers like the earliest lid fragment (E 754) at Emporio and some rare examples from the Neolithic of the Greek mainland listed under Emporio type 62.

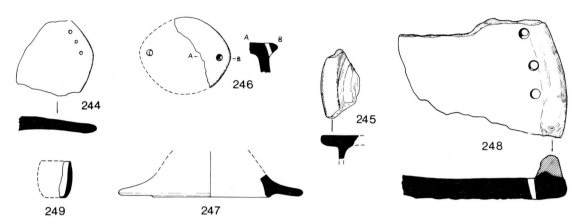

FIG. 39. Ayio Gala: Upper Cave: upper levels and without context. Lids and miniature vases. Scale 1/3.

Without context

247. Fragment cf. type 62. Coarse grey clay with straw and fine white grit. Mica showing in surface, which is shades of light brown, burnished inside and outside.

For the shape of this variation of type 62 compare a Late Neolithic lid of polychrome ware from Corinth noted by Phelps, *Thesis* 280 fig. 45: 12.

248. Fragment of large lid cf. type 60. Diam. *c.* 20. Round outside edge, low rib with oval wart. Inside this, row of three holes made while clay still soft before firing. Coarse grey clay, light brown at edges. Surface light brown, very uneven, rough and unburnished.

Possibly the lid of a baking pan of type 3 (*PPS* xxii (1956) 200).

Miniature vase

The only fragment of a true miniature vase recognised from the upper cave came from one of the levels above 2.90 m.

249. (1.60–1.45) Profile (FIG. 39). Rough and irregular. Red-brown clay. Outside surface reddish with poor burnish.

Bowl handles and lug-handles
(FIG. 40)

Vertical handles do not seem to have been common on bowls. The only example of a vertical handle rising above the level of the rim was 135 from a bowl of type 7 recovered from the very top of the deposit (0.50–0.). With its kidney-shaped section this resembles a bowl handle from Emporio IX (E 93). A few other vertical handles were set below the rims of bowls (e.g. 114 on a bowl of type 5, and 147 on one of type 8). The rim 140 from a bowl of type 8 had a vertical handle of the horned type. Horizontal side handles also seem to have been rare on bowls. Only three examples were recognised, two of them being of the pointed variety like 253.

Lug-handles or tab handles of various kinds seem to have been standard on bowls from the upper levels of the cave to judge from their fabric and the stratigraphic evidence such as it is. They resemble those from the earliest levels (Periods X–VIII) at Emporio, where parallels for them are discussed. But these Ayio Gala tab handles appear to be decidedly more elegant and more evolved in character. The most common variety rose from the top of the rim or from a point

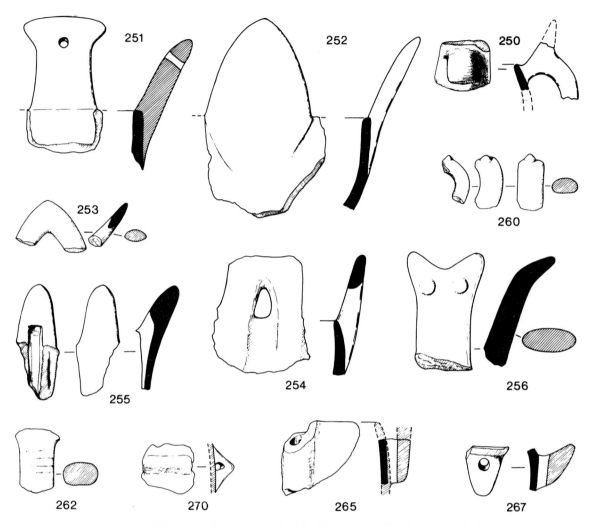

FIG. 40. Ayio Gala: Upper Cave: upper levels and without context. Handles and lugs. Scale 1/3.

just below it. All the stratified examples of these tab handles came from levels above 1.20 m. They varied in size, measuring from 3.5 (e.g. 148) to 10 across the base. Some like 252 were very large. One (250) seems to have had a vertical handle springing from its back.

From stratified contexts

250. (0.080–0.60) Tab handle with vertical handle of thick oval section springing from back. Set below rim of (?) bowl of type 6 or 7. Sandy light grey to light brown clay. Surface dark brownish grey to black with fine polish-like burnish, but worn.

       Saliagos fig 59: 10 looks as if it may be a similar projection with the stump of a strap handle at the back.

251. (0.80–0.70) Lug-handle rising from bowl rim (PLATE 10 (*b*)). Greyish brown clay. Surface dark purple-brown, finely burnished.

252. (0.70–0.60) Tab handle (PLATE 10 ((*b*)). Rising from rim of bowl, apparently of type 6. Dark grey clay. Surface dark grey-brown, finely burnished.

Without context

253. Pointed side handle (PLATE 10 (*b*)). Gritty black clay. Some mica showing in surface, which is black with slight traces of burnish.

    For somewhat comparable horizontal side handles see E 759 and *Kum Tepe* 324 nos. 215, 216 fig. 9 pl. 73, Phase I A 2.

254. Horned handle (PLATE 10 (*b*)). Rising from rim of bowl of type 5 or 6. Dark grey clay. Surface greyish brown, finely burnished.

255. Lug-handle (PLATE 10 (*b*)). The rectangular-sectioned groove may be the top of a vertical perforation. Grey clay. Surface dark brownish grey, finely burnished.

256. Fish-tailed lug-handle (PLATE 10 (*b*)). Two low warts on what is evidently the upper side. Dark grey clay. Surface shades of light and dark brown, burnished but worn.

    For the type cf. E 1823.

Jar handles

These were mostly thick oval in section. But some eight or nine handles of circular section appeared to come from jugs or jars rather than bowls. In addition there were about fifteen handles of thin oval or strap-like section. All of these handles, where the stratification was recorded, came from the upper levels above 2.90 m. But two of the five stratified examples of the characteristic horned handles were from the lower group of levels (e.g. 83), the other three being from the upper ones. Most of the horned handles evidently came from jars, but 140 seemed classifiable as a bowl of type 8. Handles surmounted by warts like 260 appeared to be at home in the upper levels: the three stratified examples of such handles were all from levels above 0.90. Some wart-surmounted handles, including one from 0.60–0.50, were very small like those of Period VIII at Emporio.

257. (Burial at 0.90–0.80) Horned handle (PLATE 10 (*b*)). Light grey to brown clay, Surface light brown, finely burnished.

258. Horned handle (PLATE 10 (*b*)). Circular section. Grey clay. Surface dark greyish brown with fine polish-like burnish.

259. Handle surmounted by large wart (PLATE 10 (*b*)). Light brownish grey clay. Surface light grey, burnished.

260. (0.95 NW Corner) Handle surmounted by wart (FIG. 40). Gritty grey clay. Straw impressions showing in surface, which is shades of brown with rough burnish.

261. Small handle surmounted by wart (PLATE 10 (*b*)).

262. Handle to rim (FIG. 40). Grey clay. Surface shades of brown, finely burnished. Traces of stripes across top in white paint.

Lugs

Simple perforated lugs, round or oval in shape, were common in the upper levels above 2.90 m as well as in the lower ones. But in the upper levels the proportion of lugs with horizontal perforations seemed to be about equal to that of lugs with vertical ones. Some vertically perforated lugs were set on rims of bowls, but others (266, 268–9) belonged to jars. Two without context including 267 were markedly upturned.

    Four tubular lugs occurred in boxes with material from the upper levels, but such lugs were more characteristic of the levels below 2.90 m. The unstratified tubular lug 270 with triangular cross-section may belong with material from the lower levels.

    Trumpet lugs were rare, and the only three developed examples were all from the highest levels of deposit above 0.60 m. All three seem to have been set horizontally and to come from bowls. Two, including 151 from a bowl of type 10, rose above the rim; the third was set below rim level.

263. Fragment with (?) vertically perforated trumpet lug (PLATE 10 (*b*)). Gritty red-brown clay. Mica showing in surface, which is crimson red, finely burnished inside and outside.
264. (0.60–0.50) Fragment with (?) vertically perforated rubular lug (PLATE 10 (*b*)). Light grey to brown clay. Surface purplish brown, burnished.
265. Rim with part of large tubular lug, which appears to have risen above it (FIG. 40). Hard grey clay, red-brown at edges. Surface light brown, burnished.
266. Crescentic lug with vertical perforation (PLATE 10 (*b*)). From a jar. Fine greyish brown clay. Inside surface red-brown, rough. Outside dark brownish grey, burnished.
    Vertically perforated crescentic lugs are found in Middle Neolithic Urfirnis ware at Corinth (*Hesperia* xlvii (1978) 407). They are very much at home at Saliagos (*Saliagos* 39 fig. 47 pl. xxxvi (*b*)), and occur in the Early Chalcolithic of Çatal Hüyük West in the Konya region of Anatolia (*AS* xv (1965) 152 shape 13). Unperforated lugs of this shape come on bowls of type 5 in Emporio IX–VIII (e.g. E 58, 78).
267. Lug with vertical perforation (FIG. 40. PLATE 10 (*b*)). Apparently upturned. Gritty grey clay. Surface dark brownish grey, burnished.
268. (1.60–1.45) Rim with vertically perforated lug, from a bowl of types 6–8 or a jar (class A I) (PLATE 10 (*b*)). Dark brownish grey, finely burnished inside and outside.
269. (0.50–0.) Rim as 268 (PLATE 10 (*b*)). Gritty orange-brown, burnished but worn.
270. Incipient trumpet lug with triangular section (FIG. 40). Possibly vertical rather than horizontal. Greyish brown clay. Surface dark reddish brown, well burnished.

String-holes

Rims of baking pans (type 3) (FIG. 19) had rows of holes made while the clay was still soft before firing, perhaps for string to strengthen the rims and provide handles. One fragment of a large store jar had a pair of small holes made while the clay was soft like those on baking pans, and these may also have been for string handles. But in every other case the holes had evidently been bored later with a view to mending or strengthening the vase with string. These repair holes (rivet-holes) were regularly hour-glass (e.g. 99) or V-shaped in section. About half the total of twenty four rims and fragments with them came from large store jars or pithoi. But such holes were also found on smaller jars (190, 229) and on bowls like 99.

Bases

These were in general flat (e.g. 209). But more or less sunk bases akin to those of Emporio class 5 also occurred. The small round-bottomed bowls 118–120 were unstratified and may belong with the material from the lower levels. Bases with a marked differentiation like that of the bowl 51 characteristic of the levels below 2.90 m were only represented by a single untypical example from a deposit of 1.60–1.50 m of the upper levels. The oval base (272) of this class is without a context, and its fabric suggests that it belongs with the earlier material. Oval vases were being made from very early times in Syria and Anatolia (see under 118); and oval ring bases occur in the Early Neolithic of Thessaly (e.g. *Otzaki-magula* i pls. xvi: 1–4; 15: 14–17). Two or possibly three (if 174 is included) long feet were recovered from the highest part of the deposit in the cave above 0.90 m. Their fabric suggests that they belonged to tripod cooking pots. Feet of this kind are not attested at Emporio until Period VIII, and they are rare before Period V there.

271. Ring foot cf. E class 4 B (FIG. 41). Coarse gritty brown clay. Inside surface black, outside dark brown, with rough burnish.
272. Oval differentiated base cf. E class 8 B (FIG. 41). Light grey to red-brown clay. Inside surface black, outside brown to reddish, burnished.
273. (0.50–0.) Tripod foot (PLATE 10 (*b*)). Coarse light brown to red-brown clay, well burnished.
274. (0.80–0.) (?) Tripod foot (FIG. 41). Gritty red-brown clay. Surface light brown with slight traces of burnish.

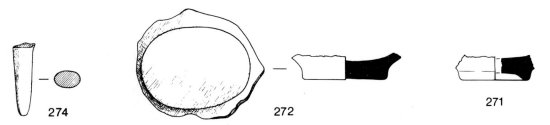

FIG. 41. Ayio Gala: Upper Cave: upper levels and without context. Bases. Scale 1/3.

275. Fragment from rounded side or base of small vase with thick walls (PLATE 10 (b)). Coarse light greyish brown clay with some large grit. Surface rough. Riddled with deep perforations made from outside, but not all continuing through to inside.

Decoration

This was in relief, white paint, or incision. Pattern burnish is curiously rare. Ribs in relief may have been the commonest form of decoration on large storage jars and pithoi as they were in the levels below 2.90 m. But smaller jars, it seems, were regularly decorated with white paint.

Pattern burnish. The only good example of this distinctive type of decoration from the upper cave was on the bowl rim 149 (FIG. 25. PLATE 10 (c)). This was lacking a context, but the shape of bowl (type 8) and the pattern burnished design would have been at home at Emporio in Period VIII. Another scrap, also apparently from a bowl, with grey-brown surface and wide bands of pattern burnish on the outside, came from a deposit of 3.00–2.90 m.

Paint (PLATE 10 (c)). Decoration in white paint seems to have been characteristic of the upper group of levels, and is only attested from the earlier horizon in the cave by the exceptional bowl rim 163. The use of white painted decoration was virtually confined to jars of types 41–42, but on these it appears to have been not uncommon. About sixty fragments assignable to such jars had traces of white painted decoration, and some thirty of these, about half, were from stratified contexts: all thirty came from the upper group of levels, most of them being from the top metre of deposit above 0.90 m; but one fragment was in a box of the lowest level (2.70–2.60 m) of the upper group, while another was from 2.10–2.00 m, and three from 1.60–1.45 m. Both the rims and the bodies of these jars might be decorated. Designs seem to have been virtually confined to groups of diagonal lines, normally between three and six in number, and cross-hatching or lattice pattern (e.g. 210a, 234). One unstratified rim (283) with a group of diagonal lines in white paint might have belonged to a bowl of type 8 rather than to a jar of types 41–42.

From stratified contexts

276. (2.10–2.00) Body of jar (PLATE 10 (c)). Grey to red-brown clay. Surface shades of light and dark brown, finely burnished on outside, which has groups of diagonal lines in chalky white.

277. Fragment with stump of handle, perhaps from same vase as 276 (PLATE 10 (c)). Outside surface greyish brown, finely burnished. Groups of diagonal lines crossing to make lattice pattern in white.

278. (0.80–0. NW Corner) Rim of jar of type 41–42 (PLATE 10 (c)). Dark grey clay. Inside surface dark brown, burnished. Outside shades of light brown, finely burnished. Three diagonal stripes in creamy white.

279. (0.90–0. NW Corner) Rim as 278, but with outside surface a darker shade of brown (PLATE 10 (c)). Four diagonal stripes in white.

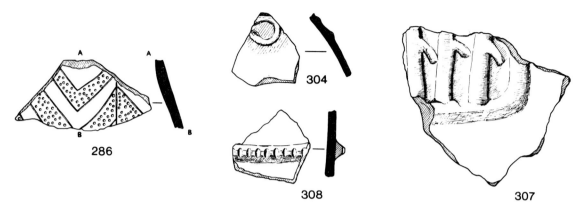

FIG. 42. Ayio Gala: Upper Cave: upper levels and without context. Decoration. Scale 1/3.

280. (0.60–0.50 and US) Fragments, apparently from neck and body of same jar (PLATE 10 (c)). Light greyish brown clay. Inside surface red-brown, unburnished. Outside light brown, burnished. Lattice and groups of diagonal stripes in chalky white.

Without context
281. Fragment, perhaps from neck of jar of type 41–42 (PLATE 10 (c)). Light grey clay shading to red-brown at inside edge. Surface light greyish brown, burnished. Lattice in chalky white.
282. Rim as 278, but with black surface, finely burnished but worn (PLATE 10 (c)). Six diagonal stripes in white.
283. Rim, perhaps from bowl of type 8 (PLATE 10 (c)). Diam. c. 18. Surface brownish black with very fine polish-like burnish inside and out. Outside with diagonal stripes in white.

Incision (PLATE 10 (d)). Incised decoration was noted on some seventy or more fragments. A few came from boxes of material of the lower group of levels (e.g. 78, 86). Three rims assignable to bowls of type 14 (e.g. 162, 163) had bold diagonal grooves on the outside: these were unstratified, but may also belong with the earlier horizon of material from the cave. Nearly all the remaining fragments with incision appeared to come from jars, mostly akin to Emporio types 30–31 (e.g. 295, 297) and 41–42.

On some forty-four fragments, about two-thirds of the total, the decoration consisted of broad shallow grooves or channels made before or at the time that the surface of the vase was burnished. Designs seemed to be confined to groups of horizontal or diagonal lines as on 296. This type of decoration occurred for the most part on fairly large vases with thick walls, mostly it would seem jars of types 41–42. These jars often appear to have had a shallow groove or channel round the base of the neck at the point of junction with the shoulder.

On the remaining third of the fragments the incised decoration took the form of deep cuts made while the clay was still soft, but after the surface of the vase had been burnished, as on 297–8: neither of these has a context, but the stratified pieces with this type of incision all come from the latest of the upper group of levels, which suggests that it may be characteristic of material belonging to the last phase of occupation in the cave. Patterns in this type of incision might be elaborate, and included hatched chevrons (e.g. 290–2), and perhaps hatched loops (294). In three or four cases the incision was exceptionally fine and narrow (e.g. 299).

Punctuation was not uncommon, occurring on about a dozen fragments; but more than half of these, unfortunately without context, may have belonged to the same vase 202. Several of the stratified fragments with punctuated decoration (e.g. 286–7) came from the top half-metre of deposit in the cave, although one at least (284) was recorded from a depth of 2.15–2.05 m. The punctuations were sometimes circular, sometimes long and jab-like as on 289: in some cases (e.g. 202) they seem to have been made with the end of a small bone.

284. (2.15–2.05) Fragment of bowl-jar (PLATE 10 (d)). Fine dark grey clay. Surface light grey, finely burnished. Small deep punctuations flanked by bold grooves.

285. (1.20–1.10) Fragment of bowl-jar (PLATE 10 (d)). Purplish brown clay. Surface deep purplish, burnished inside and out. Punctuations flanked by incised lines.

286. (0.50–0.) Fragment of large jar (FIG. 42). Hard dark grey clay. Inside surface black, rough and unburnished. Outside light brown, well burnished. Chevrons filled with punctuations.

Elaborate punctuated decoration of this kind is at home at the end of the Late Neolithic on the Greek mainland (e.g. Zervos, *Nais* figs. 839, 841–2, from the Cave of Pan at Marathon).

287. (0.50–0.) Fragment, apparently from same vase as 286 (PLATE 10 (d)).

288. Fragment, perhaps from same vase as 286–7 (PLATE 10 (d)). Possible remains of white paste fill in punctuations.

289. Fragment of bowl-jar (PLATE 10 (d)). Dark grey clay. Surface dark brownish grey, burnished inside and out. Jab-like punctuations flanking bold incised line.

290. (0.50–0.) Fragment of jar (PLATE 10 (d)). Light grey clay, orange-brown at edges. Surface unburnished. Bold hatched chevrons.

291. (0.95 NW Corner) Fragment of jar (PLATE 10 (d)). Light grey clay. Inside surface dark grey, outside light grey, burnished. Bold hatched chevrons.

292. (0.50–0.) Fragment of jar, probably from same vase as 291 (PLATE 10 (d)).

293. (0.50–0.) Fragment of jar (PLATE 10 (d)). Light grey clay. Surface purplish brown, burnished on outside. Very bold hatched chevrons, apparently made after burnishing of surface.

294. Fragments of jar (PLATE 10 (d)). Grey clay. Inside surface dark greyish black, outside light brownish grey, burnished. Bold hatching contained by curved lines.

295. (0.50–0.) Fragment of jar with horizontally perforated lug (PLATE 10 (d), where misplaced on side). Gritty brown clay. Surface black, unburnished.

296. Fragment of jar (PLATE 10 (d)). Gritty dark grey clay. Inside surface rough and unburnished. Outside black, finely burnished. Bold U-shaped grooves made while clay soft but apparently after burnishing of surface.

297. Fragment of jar with horizontally perforated lug. (PLATE 10 (d), where misplaced on side). Gritty light grey clay, red-brown at edges. Inside surface rough and unburnished. Outside light brown, burnished. Bold deep incisions apparently made after burnishing of surface.

298. Rim of jar cf. E type 30 (PLATE 10 (d)). Surface brown, finely burnished inside and out. Groups of diagonal lines, apparently incised after firing.

299. Fragment of jar (PLATE 10 (d)). Gritty dark grey clay. Inside surface dark greyish black, outside brown, unburnished. Very finely incised multiple chevrons.

Relief (PLATE 8). Ribs in relief were the commonest form of decoration from the cave, being represented by 105 examples as against about 60 of white paint and 70 of incision. But whereas most of the incised, and most if not all of the white painted decoration, seemed to come from the upper levels, a large proportion of the ribbed decoration evidently belonged to the earlier horizon of material.

Virtually all the stratified examples of ribbed decoration from the upper levels were on fragments of large storage jars or pithoi. Rims of these might have ribs set below them like 237a; but apart from this designs seem to have been almost entirely confined to combinations of horizontal, vertical or diagonal ribs, as in the lower levels. The unstratified fragment 307 has an elaborate design in relief, however, vaguely suggestive of three figures upright in a boat. One exceptional fragment of fine burnished ware with a shallow curving rib (304) came from a deposit of 1.30–1.20 m; but the unstratified fragments 305–6 with comparable ribs may belong with the earlier horizon of material. The notched rib on 308 was unique.

Warts on vases of various types were usually circular (e.g. 300), but sometimes oval or oblong as on the unstratified bowl rim 98. Solid unperforated lugs included several markedly projecting or drooping ones, two of them set below the rims of bowls (94, 95). Solid drooping lugs like FIG.

15: 2 as found on 94 and 95 were not attested in levels of Periods X–VIII at Emporio. According to Phelps, *Thesis* 157, such lugs were popular during the middle phase of his Period II (Middle Neolithic) especially at Koufovouno near Sparta (ibid. 133 fig. 11: 15). Cf. *Orchomenos* ii 28 fig. 26: class D, Red Monochrome and Red Burnished Ware. Double horned warts or lugs (FIG. 15:5, 6) might be horizontal (e.g. 187, 301, both unstratified), or vertical as on 57 which appears to belong with the material from the lower group of levels.

300. (Burial at 0.90–0.80) Fragment of jar with circular wart (PLATE 10 (*b*)). Outside surface brownish black with fine polish-like burnish.
301. Fragment of large bowl or jar with double horned wart (PLATE 10 (*b*)). Grey to light brown clay. Inside surface light brown, outside dark purplish brown, burnished.
302. Fragment of large jar with horizontal and diagonal ribs (PLATE 8). Fine light grey to red-brown clay. Inside surface crimson red, burnished. Outside reddish to purple with very fine burnish and abundant mica showing in it. Probably from lower group of levels.
303. As 302, and apparently from same vase (PLATE 8).
304. (1.30–1.20) Fragment from shoulder of jar with shallow curving rib (FIG. 42). Fine red-brown clay. Outside surface black with fine polish-like burnish.
      This motif appears in relief on vases of coarse ware from Saliagos (*Saliagos* 43: 3–8 pl. 28 (*b*)). A similar motif occurs on a sherd from the 'Pyres' on the East Yerogalaro ridge at Prosymna assigned to the Late Neolithic (*Prosymna* 372 fig. 626: 9).
305. Fragment of jar with curving rib (PLATE 8). Light grey to red-brown clay. Inside surface red-brown, unburnished. Outside light brown to purple with poor burnish. Probably from lower group of levels.
306. Fragment of (?)jar with curving rib (PLATE 8). Grey clay. Straw impressions and mica showing in surface, which is dark brown to light reddish brown, well burnished. Probably from lower group of levels.
307. Fragment of large jar or pithos with elaborate relief design (FIG. 42. PLATE 8). Coarse gritty brown to red-brown clay. Surface purplish brown, rough and unburnished.
      Elaborate relief decoration of a comparable type from the Agora wells is assigned to the Late Neolithic (*Athenian Agora* xiii 41 nos. 155, 156, pl. 10). Cf. *BCH* xcvi (1972) 824 fig. 9, from the Kitsos Cave.
308. Fragment of jar with notched rib (FIG. 42). Coarse clay, brown at inside, grey at outside edge. Mica showing in surface, which is dark brownish grey, burnished.
      Rows of notches and notched ribs akin to this are well represented on Agora pottery assigned to the Late Neolithic (e.g. *Athenian Agora* xiii pls. 10, 11 esp. no. 159).

Imports

The rim 100 classified as from a bowl of type 5 seemed to have a lustrous red wash reminiscent of that on some Early Helladic II vases.

3. OTHER PREHISTORIC FINDS (309–390)

(1) **The Lower Cave**

Some of the objects from the lower cave were seen and studied by me in the National Museum at Athens in 1961. These included the clay head (310) and fragments of stone vases (312–4) together with the flaked stone implements. But the bone industry, and the pendants of stone and shell, are only known to me from the photographs taken for Miss Eccles before the war (PLATES 12 and 11 (*b*)).

Clay

The remarkable clay head (309) was found by von Oertzen in 1887 and went to Berlin. A head of about the same size (310) was recovered during the excavations by Miss Eccles in 1938. This may have served as a vertically perforated lug on the rim of a vase, since it is indistinguishable in fabric from some of the pottery, and has a hole right through it from the crown to the back of the neck. A clay head from Kephala on Kea assignable to the Late Neolithic is similarly perforated (*Kephala* 8 no. 98 B pls. 26, 71). A perforated lug in the shape of a bull's head was recovered from a level of Period II at Emporio (CLAY 7).

309. Head (PLATE 9). Found by E. von Oertzen and sent to Berlin. Described by Studniczka (*AM* xiii (1888) 184) as being of coarse dark red-brown clay, well fired; the surface burnished. Eyes, eyebrows and crown on top of head incised. Mouth only indicated by a dot.

  PPS xxii (1956) 197 fig. 13: 1, traced from AM xiii (1888) 184.

310. Head (FIG. 43. PLATE 8). Ht. 4.7. Coarse grey-brown clay with grit, some large, showing in surface together with mica. Surface with a red shading to light brown wash, well burnished.

This head (310) in its modelling is reminiscent of three from Ayios Petros in the Sporades published by Theochares and assigned by him to the end of the Early Neolithic or beginning of Middle Neolithic in Thessalian terms (*ADelt* xxv (1970) Chron. 274 f. pl. 235). The Ayios Petros

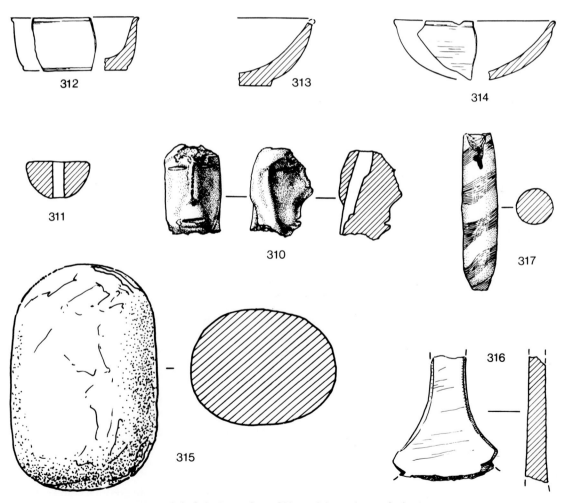

FIG. 43. Ayio Gala: Lower Cave. Objects of clay and stone. Scale 1/2.

heads all have similar large noses and horizontal slits for eyes and mouths. Theochares suggested that the horizontal eye slits might be a peculiarity distinctive of an island type. The figurines from Hacilar, for instance, have their eyes applied or outlined by incision. But an Early Neolithic figurine from Otzaki is not dissimilar (*Otzaki-magula* pl. S: 2 (16: 3)), and heads like *PThess* 200 fig. 141: a–c, from Chaeronea, although stylized in shape, exhibit the same principle of projecting noses and horizontal slit eyes and mouths.

The head 309 found by von Oertzen is also reminiscent of those from Ayios Petros in the way it is modelled, while the flat-topped crown is comparable with those worn by two of the Ayios Petros heads. But the mouth is only indicated by a dot, and the eyes, like those of the more stylized heads 320–1 from the upper cave, are incised in outline according to the convention which was standard at Hacilar (e.g. *Hacilar* ii pl. 238: 2, from Level V).

Spindle whorls

The only spindle whorl from the lower cave (311) was of clay, and hemispherical in shape like No. 6 of type 4 from a level of Period IX at Emporio. It is noteworthy that spindle whorls of clay or stone were excessively rare at Emporio before Period V, and hardly became common there until Period IV.

311. Hemispherical (FIG. 43. PLATE 11). Coarse grey-brown clay. Surface dark grey-brown, burnished.

Stone

The stone objects from the lower cave were of considerable interest. They included the bowl fragments (312–14), part of a schematized figurine (316), and the unique stalactite (317) painted like a barber's pole with spiral bands in black and red.

Bowls (FIG. 43). There were three fragments of small bowls made of steatite (soapstone). These all had neat bead rims, and parts of offset bases were preserved on two of them.

312. (PLATE 11). Profile. Ht. 2.8. Diam. *c.* 7. Dark brown steatite.
313. (PLATE 11). Profile. Ht. *c.* 3.6. Top of rim missing, but it was evidently beaded like 312. Black steatite.
314. (PLATE 11). Rim. Diam. *c.* 9. Translucent pale green steatite.

Bowls with similar rims but made of other kinds of stone were common in the lower levels of Neolithic (A I–II) at Nea Makri on the eastern coast of Attica, and especially in those of A II there (*Nea Makri* 24 fig. 45 pls. 16–7). Cf. Rims of one or two of the later marble bowls from Hacilar (*Hacilar* ii fig. 163: 1, 2, from Level II). Stone vessels with comparable rims and bases occur as early as Phase A in the Amuq (*Judeideh* 58 fig. 32).

Pounder
315. (FIG. 43). L. 11. Hard stone like granite with yellow to reddish veins. Surface much pitted. Ends chipped by use. Found by me inside the cave in 1959.

Figurine
316. (FIG. 43. PLATE 11). Broken at top and bottom. Ht. preserved 6.7. Max. W. 6. Light greyish schist-like stone. Violin or fiddle-shaped like 339. Cf. Renfrew, *AJA* lxxiii (1969) 5, class I, A–B.

Stalactite

317. (FIG. 43. PLATE 11). Broken short at one end. L. 8.5. Painted with a pair of spiralling bands in matt black and red.
    Stalactites were used in cult at Neolithic Çatal Hüyük (*AS* xiv (1964) 73). For stalactites in cult in Bronze Age Crete see N. Platon, *AE* 1930, 160–8. Stalactites standing points upwards on an altar may be represented on a sealing from Ayia Triadha (*Annuario* viii–ix (1925–26) 139 no. 136 fig. 152).

Pendant

318. Small triangular pendant (PLATE 11). Apparently made of schist-like stone.

Chipped stone and obsidian

The chipped stone assemblage from the lower cave, consisting of 164 pieces of which only 7 were obsidian, is discussed by Perry G. Bialor in Part IV.

Bone

Bone tools were numerous to judge from working photographs taken before the war (PLATE 12). I did not see any bone objects when I went through the material from the lower cave in the National Museum in 1952. These bone tools may reappear one day, however, and clearly deserve study. The needle in the centre of the bottom row on PLATE 12 (*e*) is like Emporio Bone type 16.

Shell

A number of simple pendants of bone or shell are illustrated on PLATE 11 (*b*) taken before the war. The irregular fragment of shell with a couple of perforations is reminiscent of the shell bead Emporio 60 (FIG. 298). There is a worn cardium shell perforated for use as a bead like Emporio 65 with the material from the lower cave in the National Museum.

(2) The Upper Cave

The objects from the upper cave are with the pottery from it in Chios. But there is a danger that some of the objects that were associated with the material from the upper cave when I came to study it in 1952 were really from elsewhere and had strayed into that association during the war. This seems especially probable in the case of the metal objects including the bronze knife 340 described below.

Clay

The only clay objects from the upper cave apart from the spindle whorl 323 are two heads of figurines (320–1). These are both of a much more stylised type than the moulded heads (309, 310) from the lower cave, and they are almost certainly a good deal later in date. While 320 was without a context, 321 came from the top metre of deposit.

The noses of these heads are the only features modelled. The eyes are indicated by incised ovals, reminiscent of the eyes of the head 309 from the lower cave. The eyes of some figurines from Hacilar are represented in a similar manner (e.g. *Hacilar* i 176; ii fig. 235 pl. clxi no. 455). But a clay head from Demircihüyük assigned to Phase I of the early Bronze Age or later, although of quite a different shape, is even more closely comparable with its blob nose and eyes and eyebrows rendered by incision in this way (*Ist. Mitt.* xxvii–xxviii (1977–78) pl. 9: 6). Other Early Bronze Age figurines from Demircihüyük have similar incised eyes and eyebrows (e.g. *Ist. Mitt.* xxix (1979) 31 fig. 5: 3). Heads of clay figurines resembling 321 in shape are found in the Neolithic of the Greek mainland; but these have the eyes represented by mere slits (e.g. Corinth: *Hesperia* vi (1937) 521 f. fig. 42. Cf. *DS* 299 fig. 224. *PThess* 201 fig. 141: a–c. Ucko, *Figurines* pls. lxviii–lxxii).

320. Head (FIG. 44. PLATE 11). Broken short at bottom. Ht. preserved 5.5. Dark grey shading to brown clay. Surface plain and unburnished. Nose applied in relief. Eyes and eyebrows marked by deep incisions. A bold dot in centre of each eye. On the back at the point of the break, a horizontal incision with upturned ends.
321. (0.90–0.80) Head (FIG. 44. PLATE 11). Broken at top and bottom. Ht. preserved 3.2. Brown clay, grey at core. Surface light brown shading to reddish brown with rough burnish. Nose made by applying a small lump of clay. Nostrils indicated by a couple of punctuations. Mouth incised. Eyes as on 320.

Spindle whorls

Only two spindle whorls were recovered from the upper cave, and their rarity supports the evidence of the pottery to suggest that prehistoric occupation ended there before the beginning of Period IV at Emporio. One of the whorls (322) is made of stone and flat like Emporio type 6. A stone whorl of this type was found in a level of Period IX at Emporio, and similar whorls are attested in early contexts at Mersin and elsewhere in the Near East. The second whorl (323) of clay has the biconical shape which did not occur at Emporio until Period VI or later, but was very common there from Period IV onwards. It is significant that 323 comes from the top half-metre of deposit in the upper cave.

322. (FIG. 44. PLATE 11). Flat (E type 6). Diam. 3.8. Dark grey schist. Edges chipped in places. Surface smooth except for scratch marks from tool used to work it. Hour-glass perforation.
323. (0.50–0.) (FIG. 44). Biconical (E type 9). Ht. 3.3. Diam. 4.5. Coarse grey-brown clay with large grit. Surface light greyish brown, burnished.

Stone

Stone objects apart from the spindle whorl 322 included a number of celts (324–8), mostly axes; but one of them (328) with a rectangular cross-section has an adze-like blade. The rectangular cross-section of 328 is suggestive of metal prototypes, and a broken whetstone (329), unfortunately without a context, hints at the existence of metal tools. At the same time the four fragments of stone bracelets (330–3) are in harmony with the early date suggested by the character of the pottery from the cave.

A broken plaque with four holes (338) from an early level of the upper cave might be part of a figurine. A small stylized female figurine resembles the large fragmentary one of this type from the lower cave (316). Other stone finds, without a context and not illustrated, were a lump of pumice (reminiscent of two from levels of Emporio V and IV) and a roughly spherical pounder of marble akin to Emporio type 1. One or two smooth worn stones may have been used as rubbers, unless they were regarded as figures (cf. C. Renfrew, *AJA* lxxiii (1969) 5 type I. D pl. 2: a, b).

The large well-shaped cylindrical bead of rock crystal (334) may come from some other site like Kato Fana. The cylindrical shape can indeed be paralleled from Neolithic contexts in the Aegean (e.g. *Saliagos* 65 fig. 78: 4, but this is smaller and made of green stone). A hard material like crystal, however, was probably not used for sophisticated beads like this until a mature phase of the Bronze Age in the Aegean area.

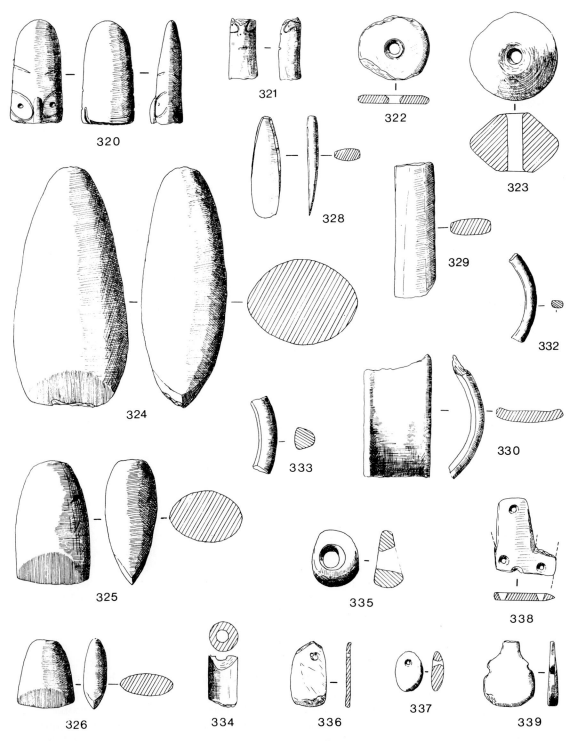

FIG. 44. Ayio Gala: Upper Cave. Objects of clay and stone. Scale 1/2.

Celts (FIG. 44)

324. L. 12.5. W. 6. Grey crystalline stone like granite. Most of blade missing. Pointed butt. Oval section. Axe-like blade. Surface rough, except for blade which is smoothed.

325. L. 6.5. W. 4.2. Dark green stone mottled with black, as 328. Axe-like blade slightly chipped. Oval section. Pointed butt. End of butt flat, with possible signs of hammering. Rest of surface more or less rough, except for blade of which both faces are well smoothed.

326. (PLATE 11). L. 3.5. W. 3. Green stone. Blade trapeze-shaped with flattened oval section; more or less central, axe-like rather than adze-like; rather blunt and very slightly chipped through use. Butt rough, but rest of surface well smoothed.

327. (PLATE 11). Only blade preserved. L. 2. W. 2.2. Light green stone. Oval section. Blade axe-like rather than adze-like. Surface well smoothed.

328. (PLATE 11). L. 5.3. W. 1.5. Stone same as 325. Long, chisel-like shape with rectangular cross-section and adze-like blade, chiped along edge by use. Surface smoothed.

Whetstone

329. (FIG. 44. PLATE 11). Broken short at each end. L. 7. Grey stone. Traces of wear through use.

Bracelets (FIG. 44). Fragments of four stone bracelets or circlets (330–3) were recovered from the upper cave. None was recognised from the lower cave, and only two were found at Emporio, both of them in relatively early levels (Periods VIII and VII) (Emporio STONE 33, 34). The only fragment of a stone bracelet from the upper cave at Ayio Gala of which the context was preserved (331) came from the top metre of deposit (0.70–0.60 m).

Whether these stone rings were really bracelets is uncertain. Some like 333 are large enough, and the wide strap-like section of 330 suggests that it was made as a bracelet; but others (e.g. Emporio STONE 33) are too small in diameter to have been worn even by children, as noted by J. D. Evans, *BSA* lix (1964) 237, apropos of those from early Neolithic levels at Knossos in Crete. Possibly these small stone rings, and some at any rate of the larger ones, were used as pendants, variants of the ring-pendants which have a separate hole for suspension (see Emporio METAL 17).

Stone bracelets or rings of this kind occur in Predynastic Egypt and elsewhere in the Near East (Childe, *New Light* 53, 192). They are found at a very early date in the Zagros region of Mesopotamia, being common at Jarmo where they were usually made of marble (Mellaart, *Neolithic Near East* 74, 77, 79 ff. *Jarmo* 46 pl. 21: 1–6). There is a stone ring from the Neolithic at Tell Ramad in Syria (*AASyr* xiv (1964) pl. i A: 11, opp. 122). But the only one reported from Judeideh came from a level of Phase H (*Judeideh* 388 f. fig. 298). Those from Tarsus in Cilicia are similarly from Early Bronze Age levels (*Tarsus* ii 279). There are several, however, from early contexts at Mersin (*Mersin* 43, 65 f. (Levels XXV, XXIV). Cf. *LAAA* xxvi (1939) pls. xxxiii: 17, 32; xxxiv: 23). They have also been found on Neolithic sites in Cyprus like Khirokitia and Sotira (*Khirokitia* 304 pls. ci, cxlii, three fragments. *Sotira* 201 pl. 102 no. 687, Phase IV). They occur at Çatal Hüyük (*AS* xiv (1964) 95, bracelet of white marble with burial of Level VI). One is illustrated from Hacilar VI (*Hacilar* ii 171 pl. cxii: c). A marble bracelet is reported from Can Hasan Layer 2 A assigned to the Middle Chalcolithic (*AS* xv (1965) 90).

Fragments of four stone circlets or bracelets were recovered from the earliest Neolithic levels (X–VIII) at Knossos in Crete (*BSA* lix (1964) 237 fig. 59: 1–4). The Neolithic settlers at Knossos might have brought exceptionally fine personal ornaments like these with them from their original homes beyond the seas. Sections of one stone and one Spondylus shell bracelet were found at Saliagos in the Cyclades (*Saliagos* 65 fig. 78: 6, 7, pl. xlvi: 1, 3). Bracelets of stone and shell are reported from the Neolithic of Thessaly and Macedonia (*PThess* 43, Rakhmani; 125, 129 fig. 78: a, e–g (shell), c, d (stone), Tsangli. *PMac* 65, 79, 164 fig. 34: m, Early and Late Neolithic. *Olynthus* i 77 fig. 81: d, e; 81 fig. 93 (shell)). There are marble and Spondylus shell bracelets from the Middle Neolithic destruction level at Servia in western Macedonia, and shell and clay ones from Late Neolithic deposits there (*Servia* 202, 212, 217 pl. 26 (*c*)). Large numbers of Spondylus shell bracelets were found at Ayia Sofia in Thessaly from the surface down into deposits of the Arapi (Dhimini 2) phase of the Late Neolithic (*Ayia Sofia magula* 12 f.): it was noted that ones with broad sections like 329, 330, seemed to be the earliest. A shell ring from Troy presumably dates from the Early Bronze Age there (*Ilios* 414 no. 491, assigned to the Third, Burnt City, probably end of Troy II).

Bracelets or rings of stone and Spondylus shell are also found in the Neolithic of the Balkans (Childe, *Danube* 31, 53, 55, 70; *Dawn* 61, 91. R. Tringham, *Hunters, Fishers and Farmers of Eastern Europe, 6000–3000 B.C.* (London, 1971) index sv Spondylus). They occur as far west as Liguria and the south of France (*Arene Candide* i 212 f. figs. 66, 67: none stratified, but common in Liguria and thought to belong to the horizon of vases *a bocca quadrata* (Arene Candide levels 24–14). *Préhistoire française* ii 258 fig. 2: 19).

330. (PLATE 11). L. preserved 6.7. W. 3.5. Diam. estimated *c.* 7.7. Elegant strap-like section. White marble with brown veins.
331. (0.70–0.60) (PLATE 11). L. preserved 5. Diam. estimated *c.* 7.2. Rectangular section. Light brown stone. Surface smoothed.
332. (PLATE 11). L. preserved 5. Diam. estimated *c.* 7. Dark grey stone shading to brown and reddish brown. Surface smoothed.
333. (PLATE 11). Two fragments, apparently from same bracelet. L. preserved 4.2. and 3.2. Diam. estimated *c.* 10. Triangular section. White marble.

Beads and pendants (FIG. 44. PLATE 11)

334. In a box marked 'X below Gray' along with the fragments of a faience object (363). Cylindrical bead, broken short at both ends. L. 2.8. Diam. 1.6. Rock crystal. Probably not from Ayio Gala.
335. Bead or pendant. L. 2.7. W. 2.5. Soft white to yellow stone. Hour-glass perforation. Surface much weathered and pitted.
336. Pendant. L. 3.5. W. 1.8. Grey schist. Thin roughly rectangular plaque. The surfaces on both faces may have flaked away, since they are rough and uneven. Hour-glass perforation.
337. Pendant. L. 2. W. 1.5. Small smooth pebble of white marble-like stone. Hour-glass perforation.

Figurines (FIG. 44. PLATE 11).

The remarkable fragment 338 from a deep level of the cave may have been part of a pendant representing a goddess with upraised arms.

338. (3.80–3.50) Flat plaque. Broken. L. 4. W. 3.3. Silvery grey stone. Surface smoothed. Four hour-glass perforations.
     Cf. *Saliagos* 64 fig. 78: 1, 2, perforated figurine pendants of bone and stone, but of a different shape with outstretched arms.
339. Plaque in shape of female figurine with notched waist. Top missing. Ht. preserved 3.5. W. 2.8. Soft flaky greenish stone.
     Cf. Renfrew, *AJA* lxxiii (1969) 5 types I. B and C. *Saliagos* 63 fig. 76: 1.

Chipped stone and obsidian

The material, consisting of 95 pieces of flint or chert and 9 of obsidian, is discussed along with the chipped stone assemblages from the lower cave and from Emporio in PART IV.

Metal

Metal objects found by me in 1952 in association with the material from the upper cave at Ayio Gala in the mosque-museum in Chios included the interesting bronze knife or sickle (340), a bronze buckle, evidently Roman, and scraps of bronze sheet. A large bell, made of bronze inside and iron outside, all much corroded, may be of Roman date or later. None of these objects was with stratified material. But a large iron nail with rectangular-sectioned shaft was in a box of 1.35–1.30 m, and a bronze ring, which may have formed part of a penannular brooch, in one marked 1.60–1.50 m. These and the other metal finds may all have strayed into the company of Ayio Gala material during the confusion of the war years. Miss Eccles had no record or memory of their discovery in the course of her excavations in 1938. She also noted that the soil in the cave was damp, and that the bronze knife would hardly have survived in such good condition if it had been lying there for three thousand years or more. All of these objects are therefore probably from other sites. Some may be chance finds, but some at any rate may come from the excavations at Kato Fana: this seems highly probable in the case of the crystal bead (334) and the scraps of faience (363) found in a box with it. Although it may not come from Ayio Gala the bronze knife (340) is certainly prehistoric and of some interest.

340. Bronze single-edged knife or sickle (FIG. 45). L. 12. Short flanged hilt plate with three rivet-holes. The rivets still in position in two of these may have replaced an original hafting system with a single rivet in the remaining hole.
    This knife approximates to Deshayes type J, which appeared in the Aegean during the Middle Bronze Age (Deshayes, *Les Outils* 312 f.). Some of the earlier examples resemble knives of type C, which flourished in the second half of the third millennium. A knife from Amorgos, classified by Deshayes, *Les Outils* no. 2363, as type C 2 c, somewhat resembles 340. But 340 seems closest to examples of his sub-type J 1 a as found in the Mycenae shaft graves (Karo, *SG* nos. 154, 227, pls. cxlix, lxxii). A comparable knife from a Middle Helladic grave at Sesklo has a blunted tip like 340 (*DS* 144, pl. 4: 14, Tomb 50). A knife from the Anthedon hoard is similar in shape and has only one rivet (*AJA* vi (1890) pl. xv: xviii. I am grateful to Dr. H.W. Catling for drawing this to my attention).

Bone
(FIG. 45. PLATE 13 (*b*))

1. Emporio type 2. Hollow leg bones of small animals, with a head as handle, and shaft cut diagonally to form a point.

341. (3.20–3.10) L. 5.5.
342. L. 7.1.

2. Emporio type 4. Hollow bones, split so as to leave a U-section, with a head as handle and the opposite end cut to a point.

343. L. 8.8
344. L. 7.7.
345. (3.20–3.10, 2.90–2.80, US) Broken tips of four others similar.

3. Emporio type 6. Pointed tools made from ribs carefully split lengthwise.

346. (1.60–1.50) L. 15.8.
347. Broken short. L. 6.5.

4. Cf. Emporio type 9. Ribs, split and with rounded tips at each end.

348. Broken, but complete except for small chip from side. L. 11. Inside rough, outside smooth.
349. (1.60–1.45) Broken, but complete. L. 9.8. Both sides smoothed.
350. (1.60–1.45) Broken short. L. 7.7. Inside rough, outside smooth.

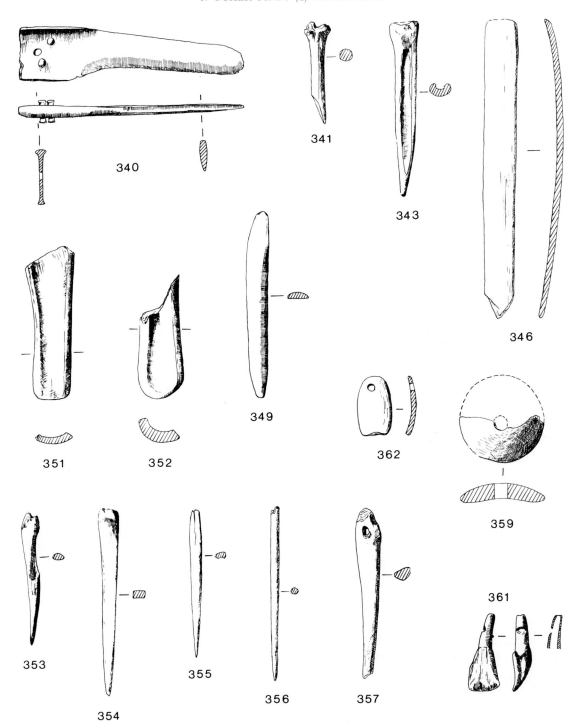

FIG. 45. Ayio Gala: Upper Cave. Objects of metal, bone and shell. Scale 1/2.

5. Cf. Emporio type 10. Slices of large bones used as rubbers or chisels.

351. L. 8. The narrow end cut square with rounded corners, as if for use as a rubber or chisel of some kind, but without many signs of wear. The outer convex side with striations down its length as if from use.
352. Broken short at top end. L. 6.7. The lower end splayed and worn smooth by use. The bone dark brown all through as if burnt.

6. Emporio type 13. Leg bones of small animals with the joints used as heads, rounded shafts and single points.

353. Broken, but complete. L. 7.

7. Cf. Emporio type 14. Pins with rectangular, sub-rectangular or circular shafts, and plain heads.

354. (1.60–1.50) Broken, but complete. L. 9.9. Rectangular section.
355. (1.60–1.50) Apparently complete. L. 7. 9. Subrectangular section.
356. Broken, head missing. L. preserved 9.3. Neat circular section.

8. Cf. Emporio type 16. Needle, with perforated head.

357. (2.90–2.80) Tip missing. L. preserved 9. Shaft with slightly triangular section.

9. Cf. Emporio type 18. Wide, flat instrument, made from a rib with a hole through one end.

358. (2.90–2.80) Broken. L. Preserved 7.5.

10. Cf. Emporio type 29. Spindle whorl, cut from joint of a thigh bone.

359. Only half preserved. Diam. 4.6. Flat somewhat concave section.

11. Cf. Emporio type 30. Perforated teeth.

360. L. 2.5.
361. L. 4.2. One side cut through to the centre, which is hollow, to make a hole for suspension.

Shell

The shell pendant 362 is one of the few objects apart from pottery known to come from the lower group of levels in the cave.

362. (3.80–3.50) (FIG. 45. PLATE 11). L. 3.1. W. 1.8. Probably made from a scrap of shell worn to this shape by the sea.

Faience

The scraps of faience (363) were in a box with the crystal bead 334. It seems unlikely that either the bead or the faience came from Ayio Gala.

363. In a box marked 'X below Gray' with 334. A few fragments of some small object of light bluish green faience. Possibly a scarab like those from Kato Fana (*BSA* xxxv (1934–35) 163 f. pl. 32).

Wood

364. (PLATE 13 (*b*)). Pointed tip. Broken short. L. 4.1. Rectangular section. Probably not from Ayio Gala.

4. POST-BRONZE AGE FINDS

(1) Lower Cave

There was a little Archaic pottery with the prehistoric material from the lower cave in the National Museum at Athens.

365, 366. (PLATE 14 (c)). Fragments of large vases, such as amphoras and hydrias. Cf. *Greek Emporio* 137 ff. pls. 44–45.

(2) Upper Cave

A certain amount of wheelmade pottery was recovered from the higher levels and mostly from the top half-metre of deposit. This ranged from Archaic (367–376) to Roman with a little Mediaeval or later. In addition there were fragments of lamps, Archaic (377–8), Hellenistic (379) and early Roman (380–1), and of Classical and Hellenistic terracotta figurines (382–390).

367, 368. (FIG. 46). Cups. Handles missing. Cf. *Greek Emporio* 127 f. fig. 78 Nos. 369–70. *AM* liv (1929) 33 fig. 25:2, from Samos Heraion.

369. (FIG. 46). Small jar with two handles. Rim and handles missing. Cf. *AM* liv (1929) 31 fig. 23:2, from Samos Heraion.

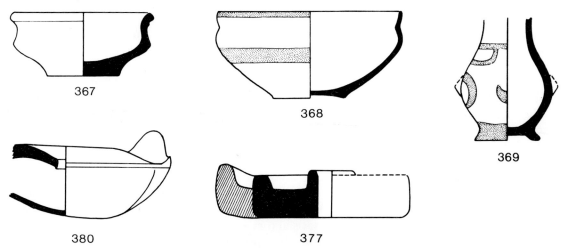

FIG. 46. Ayio Gala: Upper Cave. Post-Bronze Age pottery and lamps. Scale 1/2.

370–376. (PLATE 14 (d)). Fragments of large vases, as 365–6.

377–381. (FIG. 46. PLATE 14 (e)). Lamps: 377 Archaic. Cf. *AM* liv (1929) 52 f. fig. 44: 1, 2, earliest form of lamp from Samos Heraion; 378 Archaic. Cf. *Greek Emporio* 234 no. 505; 379 Hellenistic; 380–1 Early Roman.

382–390. (PLATE 14 (f)). Terracottas. Classical to Hellenistic. Dr. Reynold Higgins has kindly examined this photograph and notes: Nos. 382, 384 and 385 are probably mid-fourth century B.C., while the rest are standard 'Tanagra' types of 330–200 B.C. A closer dating is not possible for the Tanagras, but all *could* go into the last quarter of the fourth century, which would bring them close to the earlier group.

5. RELATIONSHIPS OF AYIO GALA WITH EMPORIO AND OTHER AREAS

It is not easy to assign Ayio Gala to its place in relation to other sites in Greece and Turkey, but it is even more difficult to correlate it with Emporio at the opposite end of Chios. Since the lowest occupation levels at Emporio lay below the present water table and were not reached in excavation, it might be argued that the equivalent of the Ayio Gala sequence was to be found at a still greater depth there, and that it antedated Emporio X. This was indeed my own view until I came to study the material in detail. It seems unlikely, however, for reasons which may become clear in considering the parallels for the Ayio Gala material.

The alternative is to accept that the sequences at Ayio Gala and Emporio reflect entirely different cultural traditions. Indeed it looks as if Ayio Gala at the northern end of Chios was settled by people from the neighbouring parts of Turkey at a time roughly corresponding to Emporio VIII or IX; while Emporio itself in the more fertile south of the island was occupied some time before this by immigrants from Samos, or from further afield along the southern coast of Turkey, if not directly from the shores of the Levant.

The pottery from Ayio Gala can be divided between two main horizons: an earlier consisting of material from (1) the lower cave together with that identified as from (2) the lower group of levels below 2.90 m in the upper cave; and a later with the material from (3) the upper levels in the upper cave, to which the bulk of the unstratified material from the upper cave considered with it may also be assigned. While the connections of the later horizon of material (3) are reasonably clear, there are many difficulties when it comes to deciding the relations of the material from the earlier horizon which includes (1) and (2). In dealing with the material from these three groups of deposits their character must be kept in mind:

(1) The material from the lower cave is only a selection of what was found during the excavations. It was essentially unstratified, and the pottery kept may therefore belong to more than one archaeological period. The series of complete vases, however, looks homogeneous and is probably assignable to a single and relatively early period. But some of the individual fragments appear to be of considerably later date, contemporary perhaps with material from (3) the upper levels of the upper cave.

(2) The material of which the context was preserved from the lower group of levels (4.00–2.90 m) in the upper cave was only about one-third in amount of what was recorded as being from (3) the upper levels above 2.90 m. Very few complete vase shapes could be restored from this material.

(3) The material from the levels above 2.90 m in the upper cave was clearly different in character from that assignable to (2) the lower levels. But more than one archaeological period may have been covered by the deposits which were nearly 3 m thick. The material was too scanty and fragmentary, however, to allow any satisfactory scheme of subdivision.

The pottery from (3) the upper levels in the upper cave offers many points of comparison with Emporio VII–VI and with the Late Chalcolithic of Anatolia, as well as with the Late Neolithic of the Greek mainland. This much seems reasonably clear, and since there is no certain evidence of Trojan influence there, occupation at Ayio Gala may have come to an end before the beginning of Troy I or Emporio V. But some of the latest elements in the very top levels of the upper cave have parallels in the latest phase of the Late Neolithic (Final Neolithic) on the Greek mainland, and this appears to overlap in time with the early part of Troy I. The possibility of a survival of earlier traditions in the pottery of this somewhat remote area must therefore be kept in mind. It might have continued to remain unaffected by the Troadic influences which prevailed as early as Period VIII at Emporio in the south of the island. The end of occupation in the upper cave at Ayio Gala could therefore date from the time of Troy I, contemporary with Emporio V–IV.

The evidence bearing upon the relationship between the sequence at Ayio Gala and that at Emporio will be considered first in isolation before an attempt is made to set Ayio Gala in a wider context.

(A) Relationship between Ayio Gala and Emporio

The distinctive features which Emporio shares with the sequence in the Troad from Period VIII onwards appear to be almost entirely lacking at Ayio Gala. Thus decoration by means of pattern burnish, characteristic of Emporio VIII and of the earliest phase yet identified (at Beşik Tepe) in the Troad, is rare at Ayio Gala, where it is only represented by a few scraps and the rim (149) of type 8 from the upper cave. Similarly bowls of type 11, with inward curving anti-splash rims, characteristic of Periods VII–VI, and especially of VII, at Emporio, and of the Kum Tepe I B phase which immediately precedes Troy I in the Troad, are lacking at Ayio Gala. So are bowls of type 9 with short carinated rims, and jars of type 43 with collar necks, both standard in Emporio V–IV which are closely related to Troy I and contemporary with it.

Jars of type 41, however, characteristic of Periods X–VI at Emporio, and bowl-jars akin to types 30–33, which were at home in the same horizon there, were also in evidence at Ayio Gala. This suggests that the sequence at Ayio Gala falls within the horizon of Emporio X–VI or earlier. The analysis which follows will conclude that it was probably contemporary with Emporio VIII–VI, but may have begun in Emporio IX and may have continued later into the time of Emporio V–IV contemporary with Troy I. Since, however, the Ayio Gala material belongs to a different pottery tradition from that found at Emporio, it is by no means inevitable that a given type or feature will have appeared or flourished in the same horizon of time at the two sites. The observations which follow must therefore be considered as tentative until they are viewed against the background of the wider relationships of Ayio Gala discussed under (B).

The evidence such as it is suggests that the latest horizon at Ayio Gala represented by the material from (3) the upper levels in the upper cave overlaps with Emporio VII–VI. Fragments of fine black burnished ware from the top metre of deposit in the upper cave (172, 173) appear to come from jugs corresponding in fabric and shape to ones which were at home in Periods VII–VI at Emporio, although already attested there earlier in levels of VIII if not of IX. The presence of one or two feet of tripod cooking pots (273, 274) in the top metre of deposit in the upper cave is in harmony with the evidence of these jugs of black burnished ware. Such feet do not occur at Emporio before Period VIII, and only begin to be reasonably common there in VI. The prominence of white painted decoration in (3) the upper group of levels above 2.90 m in the upper cave, and especially in the top metre of deposit, also points to a correlation between the later occupation at Ayio Gala and the horizon of Emporio VII–VI.

Three rims of bowls from the upper cave at Ayio Gala were classifiable as of type 10, which occurred at Emporio in Period VIII but was most characteristic of VII–VI and especially of VII. One of these rims was unstratified, but the other two (150, 151) came from the very top of the deposit (0.60–0.50 m) in the upper cave. This, taken in conjunction with the complete absence of type 10 bowls equally characteristic of Emporio VII–VI, and of the type 9 ones which begin to be at home in Emporio VI and are common in V–IV, might suggest that the sequence at Ayio Gala had come to an end by the time of Emporio VI or earlier.

Some of the incised decoration from the upper cave, however, is suggestive of a date contemporary with Emporio VI or even later for the end of occupation in it. The hatched bands of 290–4 from the top metre of deposit can hardly be paralleled at Emporio before Period VI. Similarly the panels filled with punctuation, as on 202, 285–9, are scarcely if at all represented in the great mass of incised ware assignable to Emporio VIII, and only become current it seems in Emporio VI. The fabric of the pottery from the upper levels also gives a relatively late impression. There is evidence of improved firing, and the burnished surfaces, dominantly brownish grey or grey-brown, often with a purplish tinge, have an Early Bronze Age look.

It therefore seems as if the end of occupation in the upper cave at Ayio Gala may have fallen as late as the horizon of Emporio VI or even within Emporio V–IV. But what of the earliest occupation in the upper cave, reflected in the pottery that survives with an ascription to levels between 4.00 and 2.90 m?

Some features in the pottery from (2) this lower group of levels in the upper cave point to the horizon of Emporio X–VIII rather than later. No fragments of jugs were attested from (2) the earlier levels in the upper cave, but there were some fragments of jugs of type 20 from (3) the upper group of levels above 2.90 m, and nearly all the jug fragments recovered from the upper cave were assignable to this type. This is the earliest type of jug found at Emporio, where it was already current by the beginning of Period X (e.g. E 161).

Elegant horned handles like 83 were most common at Emporio in Period X, although they were not rare in IX, and still occurred in VIII; but only two examples were recovered from levels of Emporio VI. The handle 83 comes from a depth of 3.80–3.70 m in the upper cave at Ayio Gala. There are two other horned handles (140, 257) from the upper group of levels there; 140 at any rate with its thin strap-like section looks relatively late.

Bowl rims of type 13 are not attested at Emporio before Period VII, and are very rare until Emporio V. No less than six rims of this distinctive type were recovered from the upper cave at Ayio Gala, and two out of three of the stratified examples (54, 55) came from the lower group of levels (3.45–3.10 m).

This is not the only evidence to suggest that the beginning of occupation in the upper cave may fall in a relatively late horizon of the sequence at Emporio. Bowls of type 14 with simple outward curving rims are very well represented in the levels below 2.90 m in the upper cave at Ayio Gala. At Emporio, however, bowls of this type hardly occur before the last phase of Period VIII, although they are not uncommon in Emporio VII–VI.

The material which has been preserved from (1) the lower cave remains to be considered. The series of complete and restored vases appears to belong to a single and relatively narrow horizon of time. The vases of this series are mostly bowl-jars of the kind at home in the earliest levels at Emporio, and especially in those of Periods VIII and VII. A distinctive feature of these bowl-jars from the lower cave are the tailed 'Ayio Gala' lugs which some of them boast. Ayio Gala lugs cannot be exactly paralleled at Emporio, but they seem to reflect the same general idea as the pair of tails found descending from the bottom edges of lugs (and handles!) in Period VIII there. Clay lids, however, represented by the complete example 31 and by a possible fragment (32) from (1) the lower cave are not attested at Emporio before Period VI, and then only by a single scrap (E 754).

While the complete and restored vases from (1) the lower cave appear to belong to a single relatively early horizon of time, the fragments of pottery preserved with them may not all be of the same early date, and some of them at any rate show distinctly late features. Thus some of the incised ware, notably the fragments with punctuated decoration (43 and PLATE 7 (c) Nos. 6–9), resembles that from the top levels in the upper cave (202, 285–9). Punctuated decoration of this kind is hardly attested at Emporio before Period VI there.

(B) General relationships of Ayio Gala

Before considering the relationships of the earlier groups of material (1) and (2) from Ayio Gala it is necessary to face the problem of how the series of complete vases from (1) the lower cave relates to the material from (2) the lower levels of the upper cave. Both groups of material clearly belong to a relatively early horizon in time. The dominance of red and light brown surfaces, the preponderance of bowl-like jars or bowl-jars akin to Emporio type 30, and the simple character of the open bowls largely confined to varieties of types 5 and 14, are features shared in common. But the parallelism is not exact, as Furness has noted (*PPS* xxii (1956) 199).

There are slight indications that the earliest material from (2) the lower group of levels in the upper cave may antedate the series of complete vases from (1) the lower cave. The shapes of the few restorable vases from (2) are rather closer than those of the complete vases from (1) the lower cave to ones of the Sesklo horizon of Thessalian Middle Neolithic. The (1) lower cave vases on the other hand appear to have some affinities with pottery from the Athenian Agora assigned to the Late Neolithic, although they are almost certainly a good deal earlier in date. At the same time elegant horned handles like 83 from (2) are reminiscent of ones from levels of Emporio X and IX.

The earliest material from (2) the lower group of levels in the upper cave may therefore overlap with Emporio IX in time, while the complete vases from (1) the lower cave seem to look rather towards Emporio VIII. But the parallels for both the complete vases of (1) and for the material assignable to (2) appear to point in a general way to Hacilar in Anatolia and to the later part of the Early Neolithic and the Middle Neolithic on the Greek mainland.

A horizon of red burnished pottery related, although only perhaps in a distant way, to that of Hacilar IX–VI, has been charted by D.H. French in western Anatolia ('Early Pottery Sites from Western Anatolia', *London BIA* v (1965) 15–24). This pottery, and especially that from Morali which lies inland from Smyrna, looks extremely close to that of the earlier horizon represented by (1) and (2) at Ayio Gala. J. Mellaart has indeed included Ayio Gala among sites with Hacilar VI type monochrome ware (*Hacilar* ii 437 fig. 156: a). But there are points of resemblance linking the pottery of this early horizon at Ayio Gala with that of the earlier group of levels IX–VI at Hacilar as a whole, as well as with that of the Kizilkaya culture of southern Anatolia which may overlap with Hacilar IX–VI if it is not earlier (*AS* xi (1961) 166 ff.).

(1) **Lower Cave**

The bowl-jars, of which several complete or restorable examples were recovered from the lower cave, may all belong to a single relatively early horizon in time. In shape they are reminiscent of vases from Hacilar, and more especially of ones from the earlier levels IX–VI there. But their bases are more like Early Neolithic bases from Çatal Hüyük, although this may not be significant (e.g. *AS* xi (1961) 165 fig. 3). The lugs on the Ayio Gala bowl-jars are normally arranged in widely spaced pairs, which may be an early feature; although in the case of 6 the paired lugs are set close together, a system which in the past has been regarded as a relatively late development: but pairs of lugs set close together in this manner appear on some vases of Hacilar IX.

Triangular-sectioned lugs like the ones on 13 are a feature suggestive of an early date for the series of complete vases from the lower cave. Vertical tubular lugs with a marked ridge giving a triangular section occurred in the Early Neolithic at Çatal Hüyük, but according to Mellaart were more common in the Kizilkaya culture, although still found in Late Neolithic Hacilar (Levels IX–VI) where they gradually developed rounded sections (*AS* xi (1961) 164 f. fig. 3: 11). Two jars with triangular-sectioned lugs from Hacilar VI were among possible imports (*Hacilar* i 106; ii 260 f. fig. 55: 9, 11).

A short lug (264) which may have been vertical from a high level in the upper cave is somewhat triangular in section, and is matched by one from Kum Tepe I B 2 (*Kum Tepe* 330 f. no. 416). A long horizontal lug from a level of Emporio VII (E 767) also has a triangular section. The vertical lugs with triangular sections from the lower cave at Ayio Gala might therefore represent a survival of an earlier fashion in this peripheral area into a period contemporary with the painted ware of Hacilar V–II. If the fragment of painted ware 49 is an Anatolian import rather than one of Middle Neolithic date from the Greek mainland it should be assignable to this horizon at Hacilar. But the isolated fragments of pottery from the lower cave are not all necessarily of the same date as the series of complete vases, and some of them certainly appear to be later. This might be the case with 49.

Looking westwards there are affinities for the pottery from the lower cave with that of the later part of the Early Neolithic and the Middle Neolithic on the Greek mainland. The red burnished surfaces of much of the pottery recall Thessalian A 1 ware. The mottling on some of the complete vases (e.g. 16–19 etc.) brings to mind the variegated (Rainbow or Buntpoliert) Ware of the Greek Early Neolithic. The shapes of the Ayio Gala bowl-jars are reminiscent of vases of the Thessalian Protosesklo (E.N. II) and Sesklo horizons. Some of the vases of red-slipped ware from Nea Nikomedeia in Western Macedonia contemporary with Thessalian Protosesklo recall ones from the Lower Cave at Ayio Gala. Compare 9 for instance with *ILN* 11 April 1964, 564 f. fig. 6, from Nea Nkomedeia. But in some respects the Ayio Gala vases seem more primitive than their Thessalian or Macedonian counterparts. Thus ring or pedestal bases are absent from Ayio Gala, although they have already made their appearance in the Proto-sesklo (E.N. II) if not in the Early Pottery (E.N. I) phase of the Early Neolithic in Thessaly.

Flat bowls resembling 3–6 were at home in the Early Neolithic of the Greek mainland (e.g. *Nemea* 264 f., 269 fig. 5: a–c). Bowl rims with warts on them like 3 were a feature of the earliest pottery of Period I at Elateia in Central Greece (*Elateia* 170 pl. 52: d). A lug with triangular section was recovered from the deep levels of the Neolithic hut on the Acropolis at Athens; it is described as horizontal, but illustrated as vertical (*Annuario* xiii–xiv (1930–31) 450 fig. 52: p).

Some of the complete vases from the lower cave, however, are suggestive of a later date, notably the cup with a large vertical handle (8) and the lids (31, 32). Clay lids are hardly attested at Emporio until Period V, apart from one possible fragment (E 754) from a level of VI. They do not seem to occur at Hacilar (see *Hacilar* i 103), and they are not in evidence in the Late Chalcolithic at Beycesultan. There are a few examples of lids, however, from the Neolithic of the Greek mainland, mostly assignable to the Late Neolithic, but one at any rate apparently being of earlier date (*Nea Makri* 15 f. fig. 26).

Other features with a late aspect from the lower cave at Ayio Gala include the vertical horned wart 47 with parallels in the Late Chalcolithic of Anatolia and the Late Neolithic on the Greek mainland. There are also a number of parallels for the lower cave pottery from the wells in the Athenian Agora assigned to the Late Neolithic. Thus the tailed Ayio Gala lugs, which appear on some of the series of complete vases from the lower cave, are matched by one from the Agora, although the Agora lug is horizontally instead of vertically perforated (*Athenian Agora* xiii 26 no. 30 pl. 3). Parallels are also available from the Agora as well as from the Late Neolithic site of Kephala on Kea for the unique double-tailed lug 34.

In a more general way the relief and incised decoration on fragments from the lower cave are reminiscent of the Agora wells. Compare for instance the fabric and pointillé decoration of 43 with the fragment of a high foot of white slipped ware, *Athenian Agora* xiii 34 no. 99 pl. 7; or the ribbed decoration on PLATE 8 (*b*) with ibid. 41 nos. 155, 156 pl. 10. But the Ayio Gala ribs are all plain, except in the case of 24 for which there are again possible parallels from the Agora wells. On the other hand the bowl-jars from the lower cave have Early and Middle Neolithic counterparts on the mainland, and are distinctly earlier in appearance than their Agora equivalents which are virtually pyxides with short collar rims.

The evidence of other finds agrees with that of the pottery in suggesting a horizon which overlaps with Emporio VIII and perhaps IX and with the Early to Middle Neolithic on the Greek mainland for much of the material from the lower cave. Thus the remarkable clay heads 309, 310, and especially 310, are reminiscent of ones from Ayios Petros in the Sporades assigned by Theochares to the end of the Early Neolithic or beginning of the Middle Neolithic in Thessalian terms. The only clay spindle whorl (311) from the lower cave was hemispherical like one from Emporio VIII. The stone bowl fragments (312–314) are comparable with ones from Nea Makri assigned to the Early Neolithic.

(2) Upper Cave: lower levels

The material from the lower levels in the upper cave shares several distinctive features with that from (1) the lower cave. These include thickened rims (80–82) like 27–28, and a vertical horned wart or lug (57) like 47, which has parallels in the Late Chalcolithic of Anatolia and the Late Neolithic of the Greek mainland. Rims of type 13 like 54 and 55 can most easily be paralleled in the horizon of Troy I and Emporio V–IV. Such rims are not attested at Emporio before Periods VII–VI and do not become common there until V. But similar rims occur on Halafian pottery in the Levant, and they are found as early as the beginning of the Presesklo phase (E.N. III) of the Early Neolithic in Thessaly.

In a general way the parallels for the material from these lower levels of the upper cave appear to be with the earlier levels at Hacilar and the Early Neolithic of the Greek mainland. The bowls 58 and 64 are reminiscent of *Hacilar* ii 272 f. fig. 60: 6, from level V there, while 70 is very much like ibid. 252 f. fig. 51: 4, from Hacilar VI. Bases like those of 51, 64 and 70 resemble ones of Hacilar IX–VI.

Looking westwards the bowl 51 is closely paralleled by two Early Neolithic bowls from Phlius near Nemea. Its neat bead rim is also very much like some rims on vases of the Protosesklo (E.N. II) phase of the Thessalian Early Neolithic (e.g. *Otzaki-magula* pl. vii esp. No. 23). Shallow bowls with slightly outward curving rims like 61–67 are at home in the Early Neolithic of Southern Greece and in Thessalian Protosesklo (e.g. *Elateia* 169 fig. 5: 6, 9. *Otzaki-magula* pl. viii: 4–11). But such relatively evolved-looking features of Protosesklo as ring feet and everted bowl rims are absent from the earlier horizon of material at Ayio Gala.

Jar rims like 77 occur in the Early Neolithic of the Greek mainland and in Emporio X (e.g. E 282). The rim 79 with a rib below it is similarly paralleled in the early Neolithic of the Greek mainland, although such rims are also attested from later contexts including the Agora wells and Emporio VII–VI (E 749–751). The ribbed decoration from (2) in general has many parallels in the Early Neolithic of the Greek mainland as well as in the earliest levels at Emporio. The fine horned handle 83 resembles ones from Emporio X–IX.

(3) Upper Cave: upper levels

The material from the later horizon in the upper cave appears to be relatively homogeneous in character, although certain features like tripod feet are only attested from the topmost levels. As in the case of the material from (2) the lower group of levels in the upper cave and that from (1) the lower cave, it is not easy to find many parallels at Emporio. On the other hand a number of features afford links with the Late Neolithic of the southern part of the Greek mainland, and, to a lesser extent, with the Late Chalcolithic of south-western Anatolia as represented at Beycesultan. The Troadic elements, however, so prominent at Emporio from Period VIII onwards, are lacking at Ayio Gala. Nevertheless this horizon at Ayio Gala would appear to correspond to

Periods VII–VI at Emporio, and the end of it may even overlap with Emporio V–IV contemporary with the early part of Troy I.

Baking pans (91–93) are only attested at Ayio Gala in these upper levels of the upper cave, but they are well represented there. This is in striking contrast to the situation at Emporio, where baking pans were at home in the lowest levels (Periods X–VIII) and less in evidence later. They were a characteristic feature of the Late Neolithic on the Greek mainland, however, and continued to flourish there in the Early Bronze Age.

The few rims (150–2) assignable to type 10, characteristic of Emporio VII–VI, may all come from the topmost levels. One (151) with a trumpet lug is comparable with examples from Emporio and from the Late Chalcolithic of Beycesultan. Bowls of type 14, which, although attested at Emporio in Period VIII, first become common there in VII–VI, are well represented in the upper levels of the upper cave and look evolved in character. Jars like 205 and 209 have good parallels in the Late Neolithic of the Greek mainland and in the Late Chalcolithic of Anatolia.

The presence of clay lids (244–6) in the upper levels of the upper cave is in harmony with the view that the material from them belongs to a relatively late horizon contemporary with Emporio VII–VI, the Late Chalcolithic in south-western Anatolia, and the Late Neolithic on the Greek mainland. On the other hand very few tripod feet were recovered, and they were only noted in the topmost levels (273–4).

The tab handles (129, 250–6) might be interpreted as an early feature. Handles of this kind were at home in the earliest levels (Periods X–VIII) at Emporio. But the ones from the upper levels of the upper cave at Ayio Gala look more elegant and evolved in character. In addition to the tab handles some horned handles were recovered from the upper levels in the cave. Such handles were characteristic of the two earliest periods (X–IX) at Emporio, and a horned handle (83) closely resembling the early Emporio ones came from (2) the lower levels in the upper cave. But horned handles also seem to be very much at home in the Late Chalcolithic of Anatolia and in the Late Neolithic of the Greek mainland, which may overlap with (3) the upper levels in the upper cave at Ayio Gala. The neat thin strap-like section of the handle with a horn on the bowl fragment 140 suggests that the horned handles from the upper levels may belong to a relatively advanced date. On the other hand solid drooping lugs like 94 and 95, which are not attested in the earlier horizon of (1) and (2) at Ayio Gala, are said to be a feature of the Middle Neolithic on the Greek mainland.

The white painted decoration from the upper levels in the upper cave is reminiscent of Emporio VII–VI and the Late Chalcolithic of south-western Anatolia, while the incised decoration in a general way resembles that on pottery from the Agora wells, assigned to the late Neolithic of the Greek mainland, except that pointillé is perhaps more in evidence at Ayio Gala. Elaborate pointillé decoration as found on 286 from the top level of the deposit in the upper cave is a feature of the latest phase of the Late Neolithic (Final Neolithic) on the Greek mainland which appears to overlap with the beginning of Troy I. The mainland Late Neolithic similarly offers parallels for the elaborate relief decoration of 307 and for the notched rib on 308.

The evidence of other finds from the upper cave apart from pottery confirms the lack of Troadic influence at Ayio Gala and weighs in favour of a relatively early date for the end of occupation there. The rarity of spindle whorls is noteworthy: only two were recovered; one (322), a flat disc of stone, without context, resembles a stone whorl from Emporio IX; the other (323), biconical, of clay, came from the very top level (0.50–0. m). Stone bracelets like 330–3 were found in levels of Periods VIII and VII at Emporio, but have a wide range in time and place in the Aegean and elsewhere in the Near East. The only one with a context from the upper cave (331) was from a high level (0.70–0.60 m).

Summary of conclusions

On balance therefore it looks as if the earliest occupation at Ayio Gala does not antedate that at Emporio; it may be contemporary with Emporio VIII or even IX. It seems to overlap with the Early Neolithic on the Greek mainland, but not perhaps with the earliest (Early Pottery) phase of it. Some of the material from (2) the earliest group of levels in the upper cave may be earlier than the complete vases from (1) the lower cave. But the latest occupation represented in the topmost of the upper levels in the upper cave (3) appears to overlap with Emporio VI and may even come to an end after the beginning of Emporio V. The end of occupation at Ayio Gala seems to fall within the horizon of the Late Neolithic on the Greek mainland and before or soon after the beginning of Troy I.

Part III

Emporio (1952–1955)

I. INTRODUCTION

(1) History and aims of the Emporio excavations

The decision of the British School at Athens to embark on a further programme of excavations in Chios after the Second World War was inspired by generous offers on the part of an anonymous donor. The work was placed under my direction, and the site chosen in the first instance was an open space on the Kofina ridge on the northern edge of the ancient city of Chios, which appears to have occupied much the same situation as the modern town. Excavations were made here in the summer of 1952, and the results of these were published by J.K. Anderson two years later (*BSA* xlix (1954) 128–82).

At the same time, at my suggestion the British School had applied for a permit to search for and make soundings in a prehistoric settlement which it was assumed must exist at the place where rock-cut tombs assignable to the Early Bronze Age had been disclosed in the south of the island at Dotia (FIG. 1: 5) some years before the war. In June 1952 I visited the site of the tombs, but (fortunately as it happened) was unable upon that occasion to locate the settlement to which they belonged, as the fields were then under corn.

On the walk to Dotia, however, I had noticed a likely hill (our so-called Acropolis) by the sea at Emporio, and on the way back to Piryi I stopped with my guide to visit it. The situation of the hill by an excellent harbour, and the sherds littering its lower slopes, suggested the existence of an important prehistoric settlement, and trials allowed by a generous interpretation of the Dotia permit confirmed this a few weeks later. Excavations were continued at Emporio during three successive summers from 1953 to 1955. The mending and study of the prehistoric material from the excavations occupied me during several months of every summer after that until the autumn of 1961.

The main objective of the Emporio excavations was the exploration of the prehistoric settlement with special reference to its stratigraphy, since it proved to have important Late Bronze Age (Mycenaean) deposits superimposed on earlier Bronze Age levels, with remains of still earlier, Chalcolithic or Neolithic, occupation below them. It became clear, however, that Emporio with its excellent harbour had attracted settlers during almost every period of later antiquity. In 1953 an early Greek town with a walled acropolis and a temple within it was discovered on the hill of Profitis Ilias above the harbour on the north, while the foundations of another and architecturally more splendid temple came to light below the apse of a large Early Christian basilica church whose baptistery showed above ground before the excavations began in a field on the western side of the harbour (FIG. 48. PLATE 15 (*c*)). The remains of the Greek period, including the town on Profitis Ilias, the temple there, and the one by the harbour, have been published by John Boardman in a separate volume (*Greek Emporio*). The account of the Early Christian basilica church and the Late Roman fortified settlement on the Acropolis hill overlooking it is to follow.

The following brief reports and notices have already appeared about the Emporio excavations: *ILN* 30 Jan. 1954, 159–61; 31 Dec. 1955, 1144–5. *JHS* lxxiii (1953) 124; lxxiv (1954) 162–4. *AR* 1954, 20–3; 1955, 35–8. *AJA* lviii (1954) 240; lix (1955) 228 f.; lx (1956) 273 f. *BCH* lxxviii (1954) 147–9; lxxix (1955) 286–8; lxxx (1956) 326–8. *ADelt* xvi (1960) Chron. 243 f. M.S.F. Hood and J. Boardman, 'Chios Excavations, 1954', *Antiquity* xxix (1955) 32 f. J. Boardman, 'The Island of Chios. Recent Discoveries', *Archaeology* viii (1955) 245–51. S. Hood, 'Excavations at Emporio, Chios, 1952–55', *Atti del VI Congresso Internazionale delle Scienze Preistoriche e Protostoriche* ii (Rome, 1965) 224–7. See also *Greek Emporio. Gazetteer* (1979) 369 f., 381.

(2) **The site of Emporio**

Emporio lies on the southern coast of Chios in the territory of the important village of Piryi from which it is about an hour's walk distant. A car road, constructed a few years before the period of our excavations, leads down from Piryi village to the hamlet which clusters round Emporio harbour. The area plan (FIG. 47) shows the hamlet as it was in the 1950s. Since our excavations ended in 1955 a number of new houses and villas have been constructed at this inviting spot.

The little harbour at Emporio offers the only good anchorage and landing place on the southern and eastern coasts of Chios between Chios town and Kato Fana (FIG. 1: 7) which is some 10–12 km by sea (but only 9 km as the crow flies) away from it to the west. The harbour is bag-shaped, with the opening toward the sea on the south-east. It is protected on the south by the rocky promontory (named by us the Acropolis hill) on which the prehistoric and Late Roman settlements were based, and on the north by the southern spur of Profitis Ilias with a mediaeval *vigla* or watch-tower on it. The enclosed bay which forms the harbour is some 250 m or more in length and nearly 200 m across at its widest extent from north-east to south-west (see Hunt, *BSA* xli (1940–45) 48 f.).

Emporio had not attracted much scholarly attention before the time of our excavations. About the middle of the eighteenth century it was visited by the Dutch traveller, J. Aegidius van Egmont, who noted the ruins of a temple in the 'plain' adjacent to the harbour and saw an inscription to Artemis (J. Aegidius van Egmont, *Travels* (English translation, London 1759) i 252 f. The inscription is *BSA* lviii (1963) 60 no. 12). He conjectured that his temple belonged to Apollo, but he was evidently confusing it with the temple of Apollo at Kato Fana to which Strabo refers. Moreover, what van Egmont saw and took for a temple was almost certainly the Early Christian basilica church, which was in fact largely constructed with materials from the Greek temple that had once stood on the same site. His conjecture that Apollo was worshipped here was indeed confirmed by our excavations, which also brought to light more dedications to Artemis (*Greek Emporio* 62 f.). In 1938 D.W.S. Hunt visited Emporio and saw what were evidently curved blocks from the temple re-used in building the apse of the basilica church (*BSA* xli (1940–45) 37).

The first human settlers in Chios must have come there by sea, and the Anatolian affinities of the earliest pottery from Emporio and Ayio Gala suggest that they arrived from various parts of the mainland of what is now Turkey. Emporio may well have been the site of one of their earliest stations. The harbour would have been ideal for the small boats of ancient times: when not in use they could have been hauled ashore on its well-protected shingle beaches. The little valley behind the harbour is comparatively fertile, and would have been easy to cultivate some thousands of years ago as it is now.

An attraction which may not have been without its weight with the earliest settlers in this part of Chios is the fact that the quail stop here on their annual migration southwards. This southern end of Chios is also the heart of the mastic country, and the settlers no doubt soon came to appreciate some of the varied uses of the gum which exudes through the bark of this attractive bush.

Drinkable water is easily reached by wells at Emporio, but today there are no springs there. It seems likely, however, that when the first human settlers arrived, they found a spring of fresh water at the base of the Acropolis hill by the harbour.

The earliest occupation deposits at the western foot of the Acropolis hill at Emporio were never reached by excavation, as they lay below the present water table. This is now considerably higher than it was in ancient times owing to the rise in sea level. There has been a general rise in sea level throughout the world as a result of continued melting of the polar ice caps; but in many parts of the Mediterranean area the tendency has either been accentuated, or in some cases reversed, by local volcanic or tectonic movements.

It is not possible to estimate by how much the sea level has risen at Emporio since any given period of antiquity without further work there. Traces of house walls were visible under the water on the southern side of the harbour at the time of the excavations in the 1950s. The houses submerged here were certainly ancient, and might have belonged to the Bronze Age or Neolithic settlements, but they could have been later, Greek or Roman, in date (R. Garnett, *BSA* lvi (1961) 103 f. fig. 2).

(3) The prehistoric excavations at Emporio
(Plan, FIG. 47)

In the first season of work at Emporio in the summer of 1952 a set of trenches was opened down the north-east side of the Acropolis hill (Area B), and trials were made in the field below this in trenches G and H of Area A. In the following seasons Area A with its deep early deposits was enlarged and excavation was carried down in places to the water level there. The trenches on the slope above in Area B were cleared to the rock, and smaller soundings were opened in Area C to the north (C. 1), west (C. 2) and south (C. 3) of Area A. At the same time shallow deposits with remains of Early Bronze Age and Mycenaean houses were explored on the west slope of the Acropolis in Area D, and the Mycenaean and earlier Bronze Age deposits preserved below the Roman occupation levels in Area F on the north side of the Acropolis were excavated to the rock. Trials for tombs were made in Area E across the valley from the Acropolis hill to the west.

(4) Prehistoric Emporio

The prehistoric occupation at Emporio appears to have lasted from an early phase of the Aegean Neolithic to the end of the Bronze Age in Mycenaean III C. But only the earlier and the later parts of this long period of time were well represented in the material from the excavations.

The best stratified sequence and the earliest was revealed in the main Area A. A series of deposits was uncovered there ranging from the Neolithic to the beginning of the Early Bronze Age when pottery comparable with that of Troy I–II was in use. Ten successive periods, labelled X–I, could be distinguished on a basis of differences in the pottery or major architectural changes in Area A.

These ten periods appear to reflect more or less continuous occupation without any significant break in time. The periods fall into five groups (FIG. 50). The earliest (Periods X–VIII) ranges from what may be called Neolithic in Aegean terms to a horizon (VIII) with material comparable with that of the Kum Tepe IA phase in north-western Anatolia classified there as

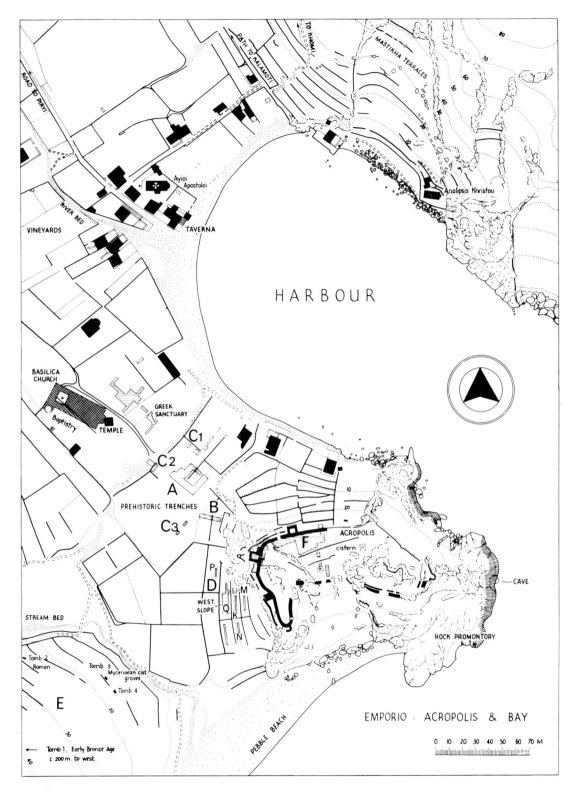

FIG. 47. The harbour at Emporio showing the prehistoric excavations, Areas A–F: A. Main trenches at the foot of the Acropolis hill on the north-west side; B. Subsidiary trenches on the slope of the Acropolis hill above Area A to the south; C. Little trenches in flat ground (1) north, (2) west and (3) south of Area A; D. Soundings on the western slope of the Acropolis hill; E. Trials for tombs on the slopes across the valley from Area D to the west of the Acropolis hill; F. Soundings below the Roman occupation levels on the northern edge of the Acropolis hill.

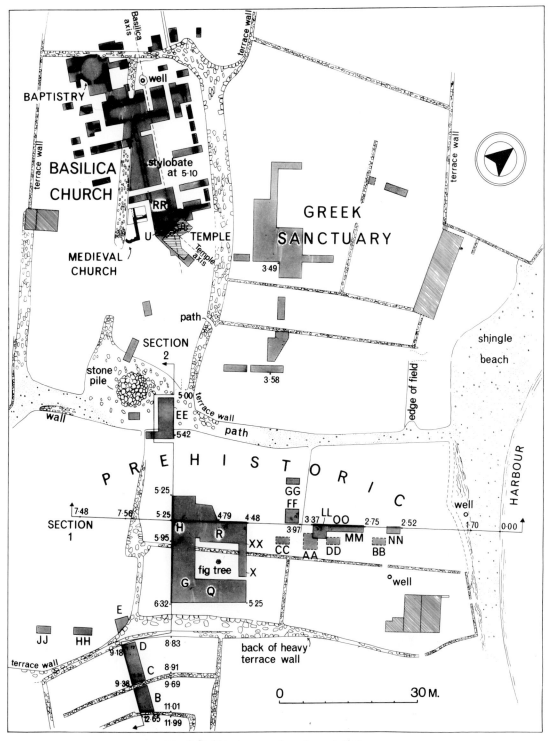

FIG. 48. Prehistoric excavations: Areas A, B, C. 1–3.

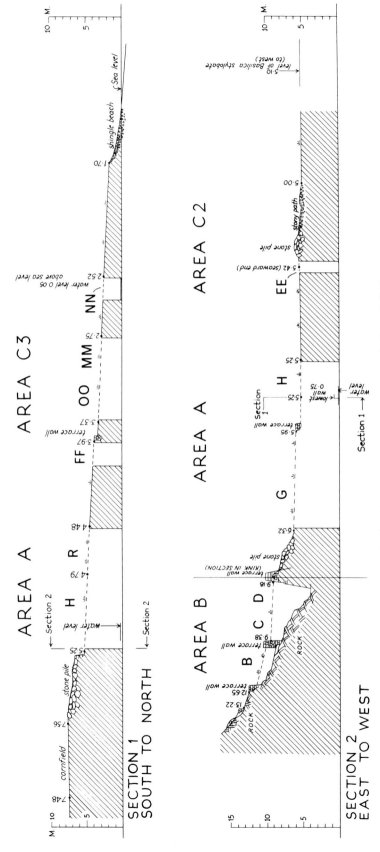

FIG. 49. Sections through the prehistoric excavations in Areas A, B, C. 2–3.

Late Chalcolithic. The second group of periods (VII–VI) has features which connect it with the Late Chalcolithic (or Early Bronze Age) Kum Tepe I B phase of north-western Anatolia, while the third (Periods V–IV) is closely comparable with the developed Early Bronze Age of that area as reflected in the First City of Troy (Troy I). The fourth group of periods (III–II) with pottery which is still entirely handmade may be roughly parallel with the end of Troy I and the beginning of Troy II.

The horizon of Period II at Emporio appears to have been a relatively long and important one to judge from the different phases of it detected in Areas A, B, C and F, and the noble character of some of the pottery assignable to it. This raises the possibility that it lasted for a considerable time after the fast potter's wheel had already come into use at Troy in Troy II b. On the other hand there are no features in the pottery of Period II to suggest an overlap with an advanced phase of Troy II, while the pottery of Period I, when the fast wheel is first attested at Emporio, has characteristics which indicate links with Troy II rather than with later Trojan phases.

Period I was only represented by a little pottery from the fill of the well in Area A. But house floors and pottery of Period I were identified in Area F on the northern edge of the Acropolis above earlier Bronze Age deposits contemporary with those of Periods V/IV–II in Area A. The pottery from these house floors of Period I seems to belong to a developed phase of Troy II.

Emporio appears to have been occupied during the latter part of the Early Bronze Age (the horizon of Troy III–V) and into the Middle Bronze Age contemporary with Troy VI. A small amount of pottery assignable to this horizon was recovered, notably in the soundings on the Acropolis hill (Area F), and also in some of the little trenches (Area C) to the north, west and south of Area A. But no architectural remains or deposits that could certainly be placed within this long period of time were identified in the course of the excavations.

Two or three successive building levels assignable to the Late Bronze Age topped the prehistoric deposits in Area F. The latest of these at any rate was finally abandoned in a mature phase of Mycenaean III C. In addition two levels of Mycenaean III C houses were revealed together with Early Bronze Age (Period IV) deposits in the soundings on the western slope of the Acropolis hill (Area D). The slopes across the valley to the south-west of the Acropolis (Area E) appear to have been used as a cemetery area from the Early Bronze Age onwards. One small rock-cut tomb of Early Bronze Age date (tomb 1), and a pair of Mycenaean cist graves (tombs 3, 4), were discovered here. The clay vases in tomb 3 dated from Mycenaean III B.

There is no evidence for Mycenaean settlement at Emporio before Mycenaean III B in the thirteenth century B.C. The Mycenaean settlement appears to have come to an end late in Mycenaean III C c. 1100 B.C. if not later. The site by the harbour was then deserted; and the next traces of settlement in the area are on the western slopes of Profitis Ilias and assignable at the earliest to the eighth century B.C. (*Greek Emporio* 40).

The earliest settlement at Emporio may have occupied a space of relatively flat ground by the harbour to the west of the Acropolis. It has already been suggested that there was probably a spring of fresh water on the site of the later well here. The original settlement may not have extended over the top of the Acropolis hill: no occupation deposits earlier than the beginning of the Early Bronze Age (Periods V–IV) were identified in the trenches carried down to the rock in Area F. But stray sherds from the Acropolis assignable to Periods VIII–VI could reflect some occupation there by then. How far the earliest settlement extended at the foot of the Acropolis beyond Area A was not ascertained.

In the Early Bronze Age, during Periods IV–I, the settlement appears to have covered a considerable area on top of the Acropolis as well as at its foot by the harbour, extending perhaps

DATE B.C.	PERIODS	AREA A (Group)	AREA A (Period)	B	C	D	F	AREA E (TOMBS)
1000						Tr. Q / II / I	8 / 7	
	MYC. III C							
	MYC. III B						6B	Tomb 3
						Pre I?	6A	
1500	TROY VI				6?		5?	
	TROY III-V	Group	Period					
2000	TROY II	5	i		5?		4	
				10 / 9 / 8 / 7	4 / 3 / 2	Tr. M 2	3 / 2	Tomb 1
		4	II / III					
	TROY I			6 / 5 / 4	1	1	1A? / 1?	
		3	IV* / V	3 / 2				
	KUM TEPE IB	2	VI / VII					
	KUM TEPE IA BEŞIK TEPE	1	VIII / IX / X	1				

* P-273   2025 ± 92 B.C. + 5568 half-life

over more than 150 m from north to south and 200 m from west to east. This would have made it rather larger than Troy at the time: the walls of Troy II for instance enclose an area of only about 100 × 100 m. The Late Bronze Age and Mycenaean settlements also appear to have been relatively large in size.

2. THE EXCAVATIONS

(1) **Area A: trenches G, H, Q, R, X, XX**
(FIGS. 51–73)

(a) Summary

A total area of about 220 sq. m was opened here at the foot of the Acropolis hill on the north-west side (PLATE 15 (*b*), (*c*)). After the preliminary trials in 1952 a couple of trenches (G, H) 3 m wide were run down the slope from south-east to north-west. These were eventually linked by the removal of a field wall which separated them. Two trenches (Q, R) each 4.50 m wide were then dug on the northern sides of G and H at right angles to them. The space between G and Q had already been used as a dump, and a very fine fig tree, taking advantage of the moisture from the concealed Bronze Age well, grew in the north-western corner of this area. The stratigraphy in these subsidiary trenches (Q, R) proved to be extremely complicated and difficult to relate to that in the main trenches, G and H, in spite of the connecting trench (X, XX) which was dug to link Q with R. The removal of the island of unexcavated ground with the fig tree might have made the stratigraphic situation clear, but it was beyond our resources in the final season of work, by which time it had been decided to bring the excavations to a close.

In the deepest part of the excavated area, the southern corner (D) of trench G, the deposits examined reached a depth of over 6 m (PLATE 16 (*c*)). The actual depth of the occupation deposits here may have been considerably more, but the bottom of them was never reached, since the water level was met at 5.90 m below the surface. In the sequence of deposits excavated in this southern corner of trench G it was possible to distinguish some fifteen or more occupation levels of all Periods from X–III (FIGS. 67, 70: Sections 1 and 4 at D). Deposits of Period II were not preserved here, and Period I was only represented in Area A by the material from the fill of the well.

The stratigraphy in the southern corner of trench G was the most complete and easily read in the whole of the area excavated. It was therefore taken as a key for the rest. Deposits of the six main Periods (IX, VIII, VI, V, IV, II) could be identified in most parts of the area where the

FIG. 50. Prehistoric Emporio.

Area A: Group 1. Periods X–VIII; Group 2. Periods VII–VI; Groups 2/3. Periods VI/V (trench R level ?83); Group 3. Periods V–IV; Group 4. Periods III–II; Group 5. Period I.

Area B: Stage 1 (Periods IX–VIII with some later admixture); Stage 2 (Period V with earlier elements); Stage 3 (Period V); Stage 4 (Period IV); Stage 5 (Period IV (?)); Stage 6 (Period IV (?)); Stage 7 (Period II: early phase); Stages 8 and 9 (Period II: classic); Stage 10 (Mixed, but dominantly Period II: late (?)).

Area C: (1) Area C. 1—Stage 1 (Periods V/IV and IV destruction); Stage 2 (Period II; early phase (?), with some admixture of IV); Stage 3 (Period II: classic); Stage 4 (Period II and later). (2) Area C. 3—Stage 5 (Period I (?)); Stage 6 (Middle Bronze Age (?), mixed with Late Bronze Age including Mycenaean).

Area D: Stage 1 (Period IV); Stage 2 (Period II with later intrusions).

Area F: Stage 1 (Period IV (?)); Stage 1A (Period IV (?)); Stage 2 (Period II: early phase (?)); Stage 3 (Period II: classic). Mixed levels in Area F: material assignable to (1) Periods VIII–VI; (2) Periods V–IV; (3) Period II rather than earlier. Stage 4 (Period I) (Troy II?)

Area E: Tomb 1 (Period II (?)); Tomb 3 (Mycenaean III B).

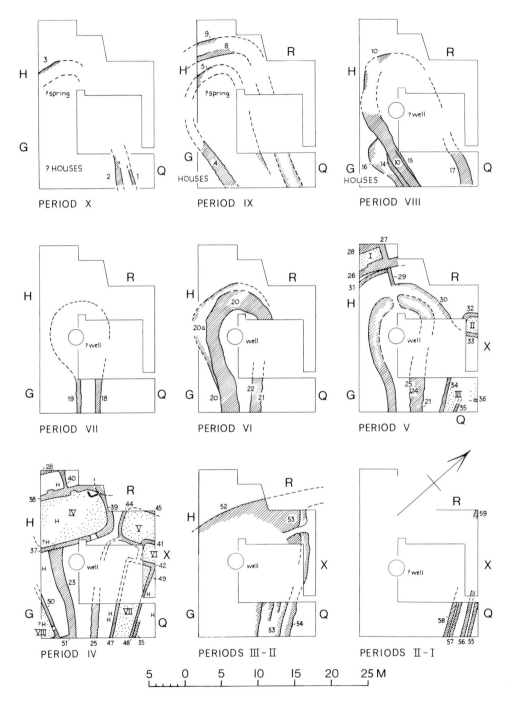

FIG. 51. Area A: main trenches. Key to Periods.

excavation was carried down in depth. But it was not always easy to correlate the stratigraphy in other parts of Area A with that in the 'key' in the southern corner of trench G. This was owing to the complex nature of the site, which was on a slope, with deposits of the same period on different levels. The stratigraphic difficulties were enhanced by the successive defence and terrace walls.

For this area of the main trenches (A) was evidently an exceptional one. It seems that it was only covered to any large extent with houses in two Periods, in X (the earliest) and again in IV. In every other period most of the area had been occupied by successive walls which had surrounded a well and flanked the approach leading down the slope to it from the east. The well may have replaced a spring which, it was assumed, must once have existed here at the foot of the Acropolis hill. Such a spring, and the protection from wind and weather afforded by the steep slope of the hill above it, may have attracted settlers to the spot in the first instance.

Substantial house walls were revealed in the earliest levels of Period X reached by excavation. Skulls (PLATE 16 (b)) found underneath the lowest floor that could be identified in trench Q may reflect a custom of burial within the settlement at this time as at Neolithic Çatal Hüyük in Anatolia and Khirokitia in Cyprus.

Two walls (8, 9) uncovered at water level in trench H might have formed the inner and outer skins of a defensive rampart of Period IX, but could have belonged to houses. But wall 4 assignable to Period IX was the first of a series of relatively massive walls which were built descending the slope from east to west to surround the site of the well. These walls were well defined on the south in trench G, and the nose that curved round the site of the well to the west in trenches H and R could be identified clearly enough for Period VI and with some degree of confidence for the earlier Periods from IX–VII. But it was more difficult to recognise any return of these walls on the north in trench Q.

At the time of the excavation these relatively massive walls were called 'defence walls'. But it seems doubtful whether defence was their main function. They were in effect terrace walls. The earlier series assignable to Periods IX and VIII seem to have been constructed with the aim of holding back the accumulating debris of the settlement from invading the area round the spring which is assumed to have existed here. During Period VIII houses were built in trench G outside the walls surrounding the site of the later well, and the floors of these houses were eventually at any rate at a higher level than that of the surface of the ground inside the wall to the north of them.

The arrangements at Emporio at this time seem to have resembled on a miniature scale those found at a number of early sites in the Near East, where, as the occupation debris of the settlement accumulated, an original spring or well was protected by retaining walls so that it eventually came to be at the bottom of a wide open walled pit with steps winding down into it, as seen at Byblos.

The lower part of the stone fill (level 153) against the northern face of wall 4 of Period IX continued below the water level, and the assumed spring was therefore probably some distance below the present water table and below any level reached by our excavations.

An interesting D-shaped house-room of Period VIII (FIG. 53. PLATE 18) produced evidence of obsidian working in this early period at Emporio. But metal was already in use by then, and indeed before the end of Period IX, to judge from the bronze ring-pendant (METAL No. 17) found below the level of wall 17. The burial of an adolescent, which was partly below the floor and partly covered by the curving wall 12 of the D-shaped room (PLATE 18 (b)), might suggest that the custom of burial inside the settlement that seems well attested for Period X was still practised as late as this at Emporio; but it is more likely perhaps to have been some kind of foundation sacrifice made when the house with the D-shaped room was built.

In Period VII, when pottery with features akin to that of the Kum Tepe I B phase of north-western Anatolia came into use at Emporio, a road or path seems to have been made leading down to the well from the east. The road in course of time became in effect a causeway raised above the level of the ground to the north and south of it. This system of a raised causeway descending the slope to the well from the east was to remain in use throughout the following Periods VI and V and until the end of Period IV. Throughout these Periods there was a very marked slope of the ground down to the north towards the harbour. The slope to the south was less marked.

Only two walls (18, 19) were certainly assignable to Period VII. These flanked the road leading down to the well, but wall 19 might have belonged to a house with an apse at the north-west end. In any case the settlement must surely have spread in this region at the foot of the Acropolis hill during Period VII as it did both earlier and later. Some house walls in trenches Q and X seem to be assignable to Period VI. The spaces north and west of the well were certainly occupied by houses during Periods V and IV. In IV the houses seem to have encroached upon the area round the well. At that time, if not already in Period V, there was access to the well from the west as well as by a road down the slope from the east. The pottery in use during Periods V and IV was closely akin to that of Troy I.

At the end of Period IV the settlement was destroyed by fire. Large numbers of clay vases were recovered from the floors of the fire-destroyed houses. Whether the destruction was due to war or to accident is not clear. Immediately after the destruction, however, the ruins of the houses in Area A were deliberately filled with stones to make a wide platform at a higher level (Period III). This platform occupied almost the whole of the excavated area, the well being left in one corner of it. The edges of the platform were identified on the west and north in the shape of the terrace walls 52, 53. The wall (53) on the north was eventually extended by about 1.50 m (wall 54). There was access to the platform from the north by means of a narrow sloping passage which could be closed with a wooden gate.

After what may have been a relatively short interval of time the platform was extended again for a considerable distance northwards (Period II). The retaining wall which must have existed to support this extension lay beyond the area excavated in trenches Q, X and R. The fill of the extension (levels 5–14) consisted of ashy earth with pebbles and masses of fragments of pottery incorporated in it. None of the pottery of Period II was wheelmade, and it appears to be contemporary with the end of Troy I or the beginning of Troy II.

At some point after the platform had been enlarged part of it was occupied by houses to judge from the scanty traces of walls (55–58) just below the surface at the northern end of trench Q. About this time, or not long afterwards, the well was filled with stones and earth. Perhaps the well had become too deep for convenient use through successive raising of the platform which surrounded it. It may have been replaced by a new well or wells in lower ground to the west or north.

(b) Periods X–VIII
(FIGS. 52, 53. PLATES 16–18)

Levels of the earliest Periods X–VIII were exposed in three separate places within the area of excavation: (A) at the eastern end of trench G, (B) in trench Q, and (C) in trench H.

Very little pottery was recovered from levels of Periods X and IX. But that assignable to Period VIII was abundant, with a characteristic type of incised decoration and pattern burnish much in evidence. The pattern burnish in particular suggests that Period VIII should be equated with the horizon of Kum Tepe I A in the Troad.

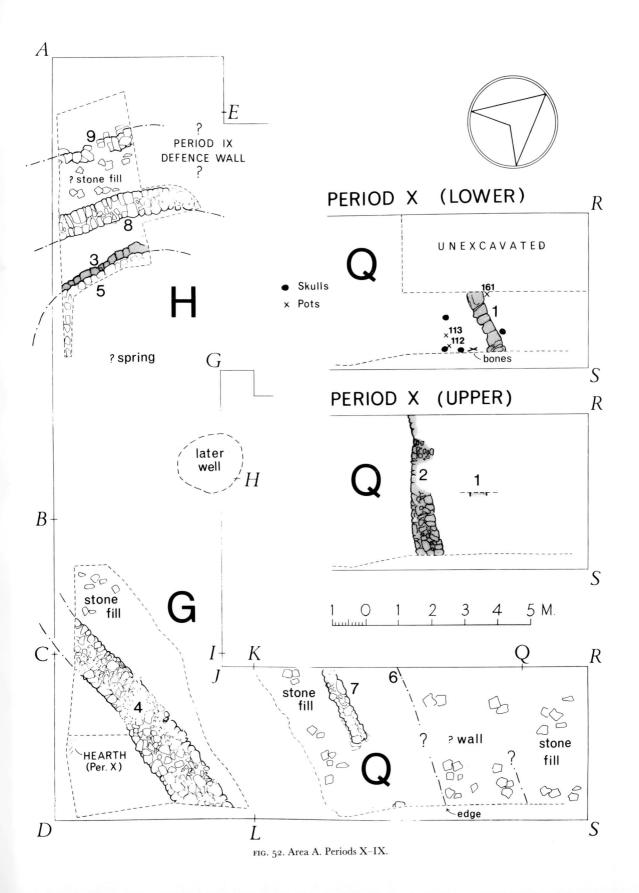

FIG. 52. Area A. Periods X–IX.

i. **Period X** (Plan, FIG. 52)

A small sounding over an area of about 5 sq. m was carried down into levels of Period X in (A) trench G (PLATE 16 (*c*), (*d*)). The top of level X here lay at a depth of about 5.40 m from the surface and 0.60 m above the modern water level. No walls assignable to Period X were encountered in this sounding. But a hearth consisting of a shallow pit filled with ash showed in the southern section 1 (FIG. 67), and this was associated with a floor or occupation surface about 0.20 m above the water level. Excavation was carried down to a depth of about 0.40 m below the level of the water table (level 164) without it being possible to detect an earlier floor or reach the bottom of the occupation debris here.

In (B) trench Q an area of about 20 sq. m was opened in deposits of Period X, and excavation continued some 0.30 m below the water table. Two walls (1, 2) were detected running across the trench from west to east. These were not on the same alignment, and may have belonged to different phases of Period X. At the time they were excavated, and before the water rose to find its level in the trench, the bottom of wall 1 was observed to be lower than that of wall 2. Wall 1 was only noted as a single row of large, roughly rectangular, flattish slabs. These were observed to make a corner at the eastern edge of the trench at the time of excavation. Other courses of walling were noted above this corner, and a wall several courses high remained clearly visible in Section 4 (FIG. 70). This (wall 1 in Section 4) may be a later wall contemporary with wall 2 and built on top of an earlier wall 1 at this point. No traces of such a wall, however, were detected during the excavation above wall 1 in the centre of trench Q to the west. Wall 2 was neatly built of small stones set in greyish earth (PLATE 16 (*b*)). The southern face of the wall was untidy, descending in three ill-defined steps.

In the space between walls 1 and 2 an occupation surface was noted about 0.20 m above the water level (FIG. 70: Section 4, at the bottom of 166). Underneath this occupation surface, and at the water level or below it, four human skulls were recovered together with the remains of several clay vases, including 112, 113 and 161 (PLATE 16 (*b*)). One vase (112) was found partly overlying a skull. But apart from this doubtful instance, there was nothing to suggest a connection between the skulls and the vases. The skulls seemed to be on their own, and might therefore reflect some version of the custom of burying the skulls of the dead inside the houses where they had lived, as noted in early times elsewhere in the Near East, at Jericho for instance and Çatal Hüyük. A number of human skulls in aceramic Hacilar appeared to have been set up inside the settlement for cult reasons (*Hacilar* i 6). But it looks as if the skulls at Emporio had been buried immediately below the floor of a house. At one spot on the eastern side of the area opened in trench Q some other human bones were detected among the skulls. It might be argued from this that skulls, bones, and vases, were all lying together upon an earlier floor which was not detected because of the water in the trench. In that case their presence could be taken to reflect some catastrophe, such as slaughter by enemies, overwhelming the settlement. But a similar scatter of skulls and bones has come to light in the Early Neolithic settlement of Prodromos I in Thessaly (*AAA* iv (1971) 167 and 165 fig. 1. Cf. *AR* 1971–72, 15). Two successive deposits of skulls in one of the houses there were thought to reflect a rite of secondary burial.

A face of wall (3) below wall 5 assignable to Period IX in (C) trench H may have belonged to Period X (PLATE 17 (*b*), (*c*)). The three courses visible of this were neatly built with flat slabs, and it continued below the water level. It might have been the outer face of a defence wall, or of a wall round the site of the assumed spring, like wall 5 of Period IX which was built on top of it. It was noticeable that this and the other walls assignable to Periods X and IX tended to be more neatly built than later walls at Emporio.

An interesting find from a low level of Period X was a fragment of bone of a brown bear

(*Ursus arctos*). Juliet Clutton-Brock notes in her report that the bone is slightly polished, and the fragment may therefore have been part of some imported artifact or talisman (PLATE 144 (*a*)).

ii. Period IX (Plan, FIG. 52)

Wall 4 of Period IX was the first of a series of large walls running down the slope from east to west and cutting diagonally across the south end of the excavated area in trench G. These walls seem to have been built to enclose the site eventually occupied by the well. Wall 4 was about 1.00–1.50 m wide, and at the eastern end of trench G it was preserved to a maximum height of 0.85 m. The southern face of it was constructed of large stones set in very irregular courses. An uneven occupation surface appeared to abut against the wall on the south (FIG. 70, Section 4, below level 155). Part of the northern face of wall 4 was exposed by excavation on the west at the point where it disappeared into Section 1 (FIG. 67). The face descended below the water level which was reached at a depth of 1.50 m from the top of the wall at this point. The space beyond wall 4 to the north was filled with a solid mass of stones (levels 152, 153) which may have been dumped to raise the level after the wall went out of use. Wall 10 of Period VIII was built over this stone fill.

A face of wall (5) exposed in (C) trench H rested on top of wall 3 assignable to Period X (PLATE 17 (*b*), (*c*)). This face was preserved to a maximum height of 0.50 m with five courses of flattish stones which had evidently been selected with some care. The style of the construction differed somewhat from that of wall 4 and looked rather better. Nevertheless it seems possible that this wall face 5 represents the western continuation of wall 4. If there was a northern return of wall 4 it was no doubt concealed by the hump of stones underneath wall 17 in trench Q. What seems to have been a scrap of wall (6) visible in Section 5 (FIG. 71) above the western end of wall 2 of Period X might indicate the southern edge of it. No such line of wall was noted during the excavation, but in Section 4 (FIG. 70) on the opposite side of trench Q the stone fill underneath wall 17 appeared to end on the south in an irregular vertical face.

A stretch of possible walling in (B) trench Q (Plan, FIG. 52, wall 7) which was not identified in the sections could have bounded the northern edge of a stone fill to the north of wall 4. This fill may have been continuous with the deep fill of stones (levels 152, 153) against the northern face of wall 4 in Section 1 (FIG. 67).

To the west of wall 3 in (C) trench H were two stretches of wall (8, 9) which ran roughly parallel from north to south. Wall 8 was about 0.75 m wide standing to a height of some 0.50 m with three courses. Wall 9 was badly preserved, but appeared to have been of rough construction, with boulders of medium to large size set in mud. These may have been two house walls; but the space between them was apparently filled with large stones and clay (level 162). Mr. Mellaart therefore suggested that walls 8 and 9 might conceivably represent the inner and outer skins of a defence wall some 2.50 m thick. A mass of stones beyond wall 9 on the west may have fallen from it. An occupation surface defined by a layer of charcoal (at the bottom of level 161) ran against the eastern face of wall 8 and was evidently associated with it. This occupation surface could be traced eastwards running over the top of wall 3 of Period X and abutting on wall 7.

iii. Period VIII (Plan, FIG. 53)

Wall 4 of Period IX appears to have been deliberately slighted and the level of the ground enclosed by it raised with a fill of stones (levels 152, 153). A new wall (10) was now built in (A) trench G on more or less the same alignment as wall 4 but at a higher level and slightly to the north of it. It might have been at this time rather than later that the assumed spring was replaced by a well.

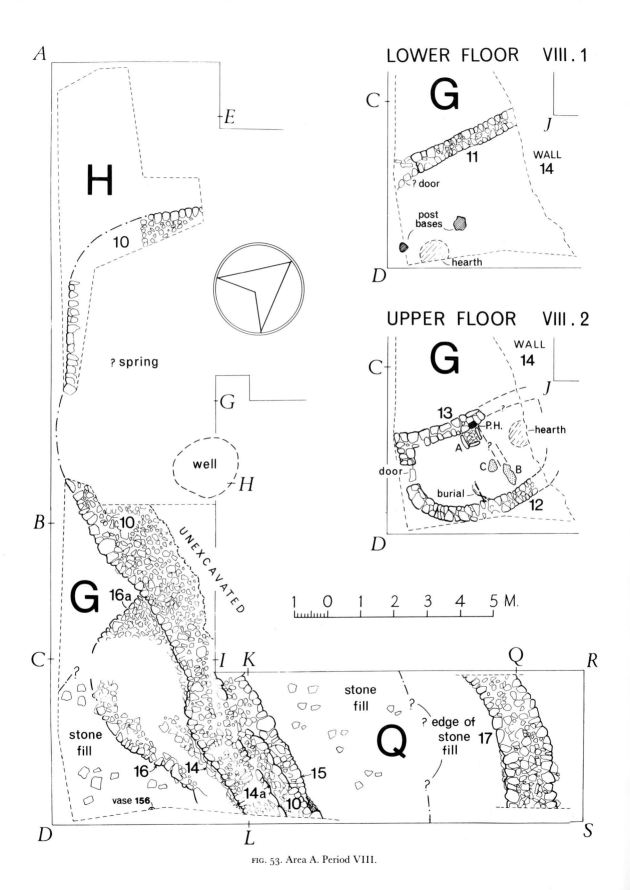

LOWER FLOOR VIII.1

UPPER FLOOR VIII.2

FIG. 53. Area A. Period VIII.

Wall 10 was obscured by subsequent additions to it. But in its original form it seems to have been about 1.00–1.50 m wide. Its northern (inner) face exposed by excavation at the eastern side of (B) trench Q (FIG. 70: Section 4) was standing to a height of 1.65 m with some twelve irregular courses of large stones. The interior of the wall was filled with smaller stones and earth.

The western (outer) face of what was evidently the continuation of wall 10 could be traced in (C) trench H running in a curve about 0.75 m west of the face of wall 5 of Period IX and at a slightly higher level. The southern part of this stretch of wall 10 in trench H was unfortunately removed in error before it could be planned during the clearance of stones fallen from it (level 149). The outer face of wall 10 here was only preserved to a maximum height of about 0.30 m with two courses built of large rough stones. Its rude style of construction formed a marked contrast to the neat and careful system of the earlier wall 5 in this area. The same fill of stones and earth was noted behind the face of wall 10 here as in the section of it exposed in (B) trench Q.

A wall (17) at the northern end of (B) trench Q may be a continuation of wall 10 returning eastwards up the slope of the Acropolis hill. Wall 17 was between 1.25–1.50 m wide. It had a fill of small stones between faces built with larger ones. Only the stump of it was preserved, standing to a maximum height of 0.55 m with one to four courses. Wall 17 had been erected on top of the mounded debris which may conceal the return of wall 4 of Period IX. As a consequence its base was at a considerably higher level than the bottom of the lowest course of wall 10 (about 0.90 m higher on the east in Section 4 and over 0.50 m higher on the west in Section 5). While this wall (17) may have been built at the same time as wall 10 it is always possible that the continuation of wall 10 lay somewhat further to the north nearer the harbour. If so the line of it must have cut across trench X, where its top may have been concealed in the stones uncovered at the bottom of our excavations there. In that case wall 17 might have been erected at the time of one of the subsequent additions to wall 10, contemporary with the construction of walls 14 and 15, or even later.

Two successive building levels were associated with the first stage of wall 10 in (A) trench G.

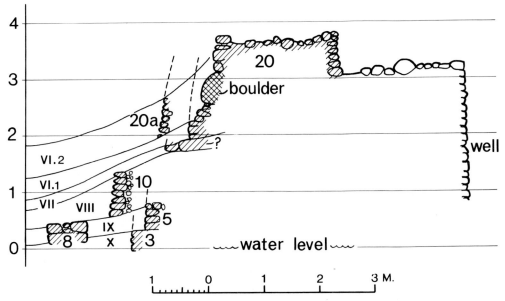

FIG. 54. Apparent relationship of walls to the west of the well in trench H.

These continued under wall 14, which was not removed in excavation, but it may be assumed that they abutted against the concealed southern face of wall 10 (FIG. 55). The earliest of these levels (VIII. 1) was associated with a stretch of house wall (11) running north-south and built immediately on top of wall 4 of Period IX (PLATE 16 (e)). Wall 11 was about 0.50 m wide, constructed of flat slab-like stones laid in more or less regular courses of which five or six were preserved to a maximum height of 0.60 m. At the southern end of the wall were traces of what may have been a doorway, where pebbles which had evidently been strewn on the floor of the house (on the eastern side of wall 11) could be traced running over a row of stones that could indicate the position of a threshold (FIG. 67: Section 1). A patch of pebbles might well have been laid just inside the doorway where the earth floor would get worn and become muddy in damp weather. But it is always possible that the wall at this point had been destroyed to its foundations, and that pebbles from the floor had later drifted over them.

With this house floor (VIII. 1) east of wall 11 were associated a hearth (FIG. 70: Section 4, below level 142) and two stones that may have supported wooden posts. The larger of these stones was roughly hexagonal in shape, about 0.40 × 0.45 × 0.12 m thick. The smaller on the southern side of the trench was four-sided, some 0.30 × 0.30 m across and 0.20 m thick.

Some 0.30–0.40 m above this floor was another (VIII. 2) belonging to a D-shaped room (PLATE 18). The curving wall (12) which formed the eastern side of this was between 0.45–0.52 m wide and was standing to a maximum height of about half a metre with five or six courses. A disused saddle quern (STONE No. 12) had been incorporated in it. Wall 12 had a distinct inward lean, with an overhang on the western side of as much as 0.10 m (1 in 5 of the height). This may have been due to subsequent pressure of the deposit on the slope behind it to the east: it cannot be taken as evidence that the D-shaped room was covered with some kind of half-dome, although the roof may very well have been of this kind, with a frame of wooden beams overlaid with branches.

The straight wall (13) which formed the western side of the D-shaped room was about 0.45 m wide and was only preserved one or two courses (0.15 m) high. There was no trace of a wall continuing westwards at right angles to wall 13 to make the D-shaped room the apse of a long house of the type known at Troy and elsewhere in Anatolia and the Near East as well as in the Balkans in early times. In view of the poor state of preservation of wall 13 it is always possible that

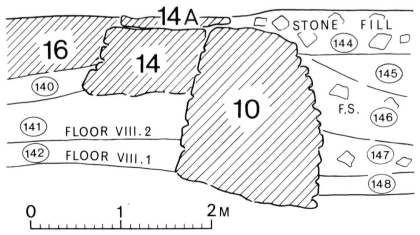

FIG. 55. Relationship of Period VIII walls 10, 14, 14A, 16.

traces of such a wall, if it existed, might have disappeared over the small part of its course exposed in trench G. But in that case the house would have been constructed with its long axis running down the slope from west to east. Moreover, there was no sign of a door leading through wall 13 into the D-shaped room, which was in fact entered through the southern end of the curving wall 12. The doorway here was just over 0.50 m wide, with a threshold block 0.42 × 0.20 × 0.06 m thick still in position in it (PLATE 18 (c)). The bottom of this threshold block was set 0.14 m above the bottom of the wall at this point. It is interesting that the apsidal long house (House 103) in the earliest level of Troy I appears to have had a doorway in the same position in the side of the apse (*Troy* i 83 fig. 425).

The D-shaped room was just over 2 m across at its widest point inside. Its length could not be ascertained as it continued northwards below wall 14, but it is unlikely to have been much over 4 m. Built against what may have been the middle section of wall 13 was a low rectangular stand on platform (Plan, FIG. 53: A) consisting of a fill of stones enclosed by three upright slabs and measuring 0.44 m from east to west by 0.50 m from north to south (PLATE 18 (d)). A rectangular hollow 0.28 × 0.20 m across and about 0.15–0.20 m deep in the edge of wall 13 by the northern face of the stand (A) appears to have contained a large wooden post which helped to support the roof of the house: it may indicate the middle point in the length of wall 13.

There may have been a partition wall abutting on this post and dividing the D-shaped room into two more or less equal compartments. The stand (A) would then have occupied a corner in the southern one of these. Possible traces of such a wall were noted in excavation, and the large slab (FIG. 53: B) might have served as the threshold of a door through it. Alternatively, if no partition wall existed, slab B could have been a seat by the fire-place at the northern end of the room, within reach of the saddle quern (FIG. 53: C) which was lying upside down on the floor beside it (PLATE 17 (d), (e)). The saddle quern may have been deliberately placed upside down on the floor to keep the grinding surface clean when it was not in use. Stone mortars appear to have been left upside down on the floors in this way in the Akrotiri settlement on Thera at the time of its abandonment before the eruption *c.* 1500 B.C. (e.g. *Thera* i 28 fig. 37; vi (1974) 21).

Apsidal houses are attested at various sites in the Cyclades in the Early Bronze Age. Some of these were certainly long houses like the apsidal house in Troy I a. But small one-room horse-shoe shaped houses were the rule in the Mt. Kynthos settlement on Delos (*Delos* xi 11 ff., 21 ff.). Comparable one-roomed D-shaped or apsidal houses are found at certain sites on the Greek mainland at the end of the Early Bronze Age in Early Helladic III and into Middle Helladic times (e.g. Orchomenos: H. Bülle, *Orchomenos* i (Munich, 1907) 34 ff. fig. 9, Typus C. Malthi: Valmin, *SME* 25 ff.; R.J. Howell, *Hesperia* xliv (1975) 111, for the date). The D-shaped building of Emporio VIII might be a remote ancestor of these.

It seems very possible in the absence of information to the contrary that apsidal houses of one kind or another were at home in western Anatolia from the earliest times. No complete house plans were recovered from levels of the Black period assignable to the Late Chalcolithic at Poliochni, but fragments of curving walls revealed by the soundings into deposits of it suggest that the houses of that horizon may have been apsidal rather than circular or oval (*Poliochni* i 53 ff. figs. 25–28; 86 ff. figs. 45–55. Cf. Jane Warner, *AJA* lxxxiii (1979) 138).

The apsidal house of Troy I a is in fact the earliest house of which the plan could be recovered at Troy. A number of early houses at Karataş were apsidal. It would be interesting to know if the houses at Beşik Tepe in the Troad contemporary perhaps with Emporio VIII were apsidal or D-shaped. The D-shaped structure of Period VIII is the only one from the early levels at Emporio of which any kind of plan could be restored. There is no reason why the fragments of house walls assigned to Periods X and IX might not have belonged to apsidal structures. Wall 19 of Period VII was at first taken to belong to an apsidal house with the apse at the north-west end, and this idea may after all have been the correct one.

It is therefore possible that this distinctive shape of house plan with an apse was introduced to Chios by the earliest settlers. Like many features of the early pottery of Emporio the apsidal house plan may have been ultimately derived from the Levant. Long houses with apses are well attested in Palestine and Syria at the end of the Chalcolithic and the beginning of the Early Bronze Age there. Such houses are found at Byblos in the Late Aeneolithic (e.g. *Byblos* v 224 fig. 139, 244 ff. fig. 146). But one well-preserved long house with an apsidal end is assigned to the Early Neolithic there (*Byblos* v 24 f. fig. 9 pls. ix: 2, xvi: 3). The apse of this is flattish, but unmistakable and evidently deliberate, It was thought that this apsidal building might have been a shrine, associated with burials in the area.

It is significant perhaps that when relatively complete house plans are again recoverable at Emporio in the horizon of Period IV contemporary with Troy I they appear to retain distinct vestiges of an apsidal tradition. The plan of House IV for instance might almost be called sub-apsidal. Similar vestiges of an apsidal tradition can be observed in buildings of the Blue period at Poliochni which seems to overlap with Troy I and Emporio IV (e.g. *Poliochni* i atlas pl. 4: areas 206, 211, 212).

Some 0.20 m below the earth floor of the D-shaped room was the complete skeleton of a child or adolescent lying on its back with the legs crossed to the west and with the head and shoulders underneath wall 12 (FIG. 56. PLATE 18 (*b*)). The bones were in a fairly good state of preservation except for the skull of which only a few fragments were found: it may have been damaged when wall 12 was built. The body was evidently placed here before the construction of wall 12, but it must have been buried from the level of the floor of the D-shaped room. It looks as if we are dealing with a foundation sacrifice of some kind rather than with a continuation of the practice of

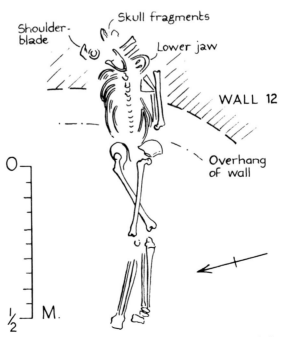

FIG. 56. Burial underneath wall 12 of Period VIII in trench G.

burial inside the settlement for which there was evidence in (B) trench Q in Period X. The ritual emplacement of the unique vase 156 almost immediately above this spot later in Period VIII strengthens this suspicion.

A large number of flakes and several cores of obsidian were recovered from above the floor of the D-shaped room. These indicate that obsidian working was among the activities practised here as well as cooking and making flour. Perry G. Bialor in PART IV remarks that the way in which the cores have been used to the limit suggests that obsidian must have been precious. The obsidian found at Emporio was presumably imported from Melos. Theochares noted evidence for working obsidian at two spots in the settlement assigned to the end of Early Neolithic or beginning of Middle Neolithic on Ayios Petros off Kira-Panayia in the Sporades (*ADelt* xxv (1970) Chron. 274). Other finds from the area of the D-shaped room included the fragment of a stone bracelet (STONE No. 33).

The ruins of the D-shaped room were buried when wall 10 was enlarged on the south by the addition of wall 14 (FIG. 55). It may have been at this time that a section of the northern face of wall 10 was strengthened by the addition of a skin (15) some 0.50 m thick. These additions (14, 15) on both sides of wall 10 increased its width to over 2 m. The enlarged wall may have been strictly defensive in character, since there were no traces of houses contemporary with it in the part (A) of trench G which was excavated to the south of it. The apparent stump of a wall (14A) about 1.00–1.20 m wide built on top of wall 14, with its southern face coinciding with that of wall 14, but its northern face overlapping the top of the original wall 10, might have been all that was left of a parapet erected at the time that wall 10 was enlarged and leaving a narrow rampart walk between 0.60–1.00 m wide on the northern side. In that case the wall was a very low one with the rampart walk only about 0.70 m above the level of the ground beyond it to the south. The significance of wall 14A remains doubtful.

The way down to the assumed spring or well in (B) trench Q, represented by the surface below level 148 between the enlarged version of wall 10 and wall 17, was still at this stage about a metre lower than the level of the ground beyond the enlarged wall to the south in (A) trench G. Eventually, however, it seems to have been decided that the approach to the source of water should be transformed from a sunk way into a raised platform. This decision may well have been taken in conjunction with a scheme for replacing the assumed spring by a well. The enlarged version of wall 10 was now levelled, and the space between it and wall 17 was partly filled with stones from it (levels 146, 147). Above the stones was a thick deposit of hard gritty earth (level 145) which might be the remains of mud walling or mud-brick. This could have come from the upper part of the enlarged version of wall 10, or from wall 17, or from both walls. Over this fill, represented by levels 148–145 and in places nearly 1.50 m deep, a layer of loose stones (level 144) was piled. On the west side of trench Q there were traces of what might have been a wall or kerb forming the edge of these loose stones (FIG. 71: Section 5, A). On the east side of the trench the fill ended below the Period V wall 34, which may have been built on top of a kerb here (FIG. 70: Section 4, A).

The deposits above the occupation surface (at the bottom of level 140) associated with wall 14 in (A) trench G corresponded to those in (B) trench Q to the north. The earth fill (level 140) here was similar in character and in the type of pottery of an advanced phase of Period VIII recovered from it to level 145 in (B) trench Q. Above level 140 was a curving face of wall (16) preserved to a height of between 0.35–0.60 m with two or three courses. This was roughly built and had a distinct inward batter. A number of large boulders had been set upright at close intervals in the wall face or just inside from it (FIG. 70: Section 4). A similar use of large upright boulders was noted in the construction of the Period VI wall 20. The face of wall 16 may never have been meant to be visible, since a compact fill of stones (level 139) continued beyond it to the south at the same level, and appeared to have been deliberately placed there before any debris had accumulated. The great terrace wall (53) of Period II in trench Q seems to have been built with several contemporary faces set one behind the other in this manner. A system of construction with internal wall faces had obvious advantages for retaining walls built of rubble and subject to pressure from a fill of loose stones behind them.

No traces of retaining walls bounding the stone fills (level 139 in trench G and level 144 in trench Q) were remarked during the excavations. But in trench G the stone fill tailed away more or less on the line of a face of rough walling (16A) running from north to south and perhaps continuous with the wall face 16. It is always possible that wall 17 in trench Q was built at this time rather than earlier as a northern retaining wall for the stone fill, level 144.

At the base of the stone fill (level 139) in trench G and resting on the surface below it was the curious bowl 156 with its unique multi-horned handles (FIG. 70: Section 4. PLATE 18 (e)). The bowl was found unbroken, and it looks as if it must have been placed on the ground here and immediately afterwards buried among the stones of the fill with some care. Perhaps it was some kind of foundation deposit. A vase buried in one of the bastions which may have marked the approach to Town II at Thermi appeared to have been placed there for some ritual purpose (*Thermi* 21). At the same time the position of 156 is suggestive, since it had been placed more or less over the spot occupied by the head of the body buried under the wall of the D-shaped room earlier in Period VIII.

(c) *Periods VII–VI*
(FIG. 57. PLATES 19, 20)

There seems to be a fairly abrupt change in the character of the pottery in use at Emporio with the advent of Period VII. It is always possible, although by no means certain, that this reflects some degree of dislocation and an influx of newcomers from the mainland of Anatolia. Incised decoration and pattern burnish are no longer so much in evidence as they had been during Period VIII, and they are largely replaced by decoration in white paint. At the same time new shapes of vase, notably large bowls with thickened or antisplash rims as type 11, now become fashionable and may be compared with ones characteristic of the Kum Tepe I B phase of the Troad definable as Late Chalcolithic in Anatolia. A type of fabric with a light brown slip and rough stroke burnish (Light Brown Burnished Ware) which occurred earlier, but is now much in evidence, is reminiscent of the 'Urfirnis' ware of the Middle and Late Neolithic on the Greek mainland.

The well was almost certainly in existence from the beginning of Period VII if not earlier. The system of a raised path or road leading down the slope to it from the east appears to be an innovation of the end of this period. The road was gravelled and flanked by walls that may have been in some way defensive in character in spite of their comparatively small size. Throughout the time covered by Periods VII–VI the space beyond the well and the road down to it on the south, west and north, appears to have been open ground: no traces of houses that could safely be assigned to this horizon were identified in the area excavated, unless wall 19 belonged in fact to an apsidal house which ran down the slope from south-east to north-west.

A curious feature that first became apparent in the debris assignable to the end of Period VII was the abundance of fragments of jugs. This continued to be a characteristic of the pottery of this part of Area A all through Period VI and into Period V and later. Handled jugs may have been brought to the well for water. But breakages on such a scale can hardly have been the result of accidents, even assuming that the inhabitants, or those of them whose business it was to draw water, were quite precociously clumsy. The breaking of the jugs must therefore have been deliberate and may reflect some kind of cult or ritual which took place from time to time by the source of water and in connection with it.

i. Period VII (Plan, FIG. 57)

At the end of Period VIII there appears to have been a relatively extensive area of raised platform in the eastern part of the excavated area (trench Q). This sloped down rather steeply from east to west to the site of the well. The well itself may have been in existence by this time. At some point—it may have been soon after the creation of the raised platform—a layer of fine gravel (level 135) was dumped to make a path or road leading down the slope to the well from the east. This layer of gravel was only some 0.10 m thick at the eastern end in Section 4, but reached a thickness of 0.40 m as it neared the well.

On the north side this road may have been retained from the first by wall 18 (FIG. 71: Section 5), which appears to have been built before the gravel was deposited. Wall 18, which ran below the later wall 21, was between 0.70–0.90 m wide in trench Q, where it was preserved to a maximum height of about 0.70–0.80 m.

There was no evidence for any wall forming a kerb for the gravel of level 135 on the south. But at some stage a wall (19) was built on top of the southern edge of it (PLATE 19 (a)). Wall 19 cannot have been built before the gravel (level 135) was laid; but it might have been erected

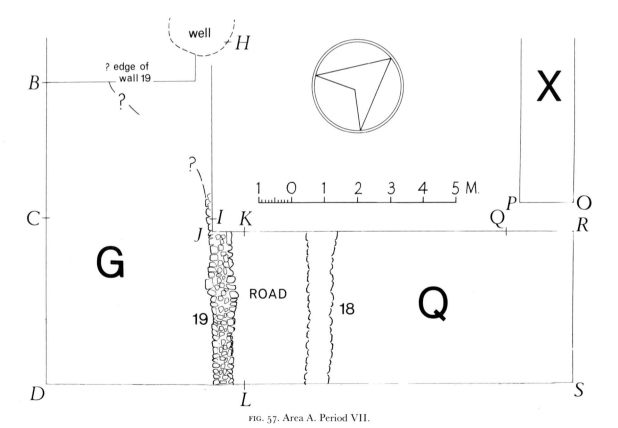

FIG. 57. Area A. Period VII.

immediately afterwards. This wall was between 0.60 and 0.90 m wide and stood to a maximum height of about 0.60 m; it may never have been much higher, since the top of it was more or less flat, and there were comparatively few stones that could have tumbled from it in the deposit round it. It was roughly built and irregular, most of the stones used in it being very small, unlike those employed for constructing house walls in earlier and later periods at Emporio. But as in the case of wall 18, some larger stones and one or two small boulders had been incorporated in the faces of the wall.

The gravelled roadway between walls 18 and 19 in trench Q was about 2.20–2.30 m wide. The surface of the ground on the southern side of wall 19 (below level 123) in trench G was uneven and irregular as if it had been an open space. Nothing in the nature of a house floor was noted here. This seems to weigh the balance against the idea that wall 19 belonged to an apsidal house. If it was not a house wall it might have been constructed to serve as a boundary for the road on the southern side as wall 18 appears to have done on the north.

Wall 19 curved southwards as it neared the well. This part of the wall was unfortunately removed during excavation before it could be planned. What seemed to be the continuation of the wall, however, was traced in Section 6 (FIG. 72) where its outer edge was about 2 m from the side of the well.

The line of wall 19 westwards beyond this point was masked by the later wall 20 of Period VI which was left standing here. But a stump of walling exposed at the base of the western face of wall 20 in trench H might have belonged to Period VII (FIG. 54). Possibly therefore wall 19 continued round the well like the Period VI wall 20, returning eastwards to appear as wall 18 in trench Q.

Eventually it seems it was decided to build a new and more massive wall (20) at a higher level. The whole area of the road leading down to the well was therefore raised to make a platform for this. The tops of walls 18 and 19 may have been levelled: stones in the fill by them evidently came from them. In places the fill ran over the top of wall 18.

The material used for the fill included beach pebbles like those employed for the roadways (FIG. 71: Section 5, level 121); but it mostly consisted of ashy earth (levels 122, 123), and in places of almost pure white ash, that may have been collected from the fire-places of the settlement. In this fill was a large amount of broken pottery with fragments of jugs much in evidence.

On the south the ashy fill (levels 122, 123) extended into Section 1 (FIG. 67). No trace of it was noted to the north of wall 18, but some fallen debris from wall 18 seems to have piled against its north outer face (FIG. 71: Section 5, level 128). Stones, apparently from the wall, were in a deposit (levels 127, 128) of earth with pebbles like those used for the make-up of the successive roads leading down to the well.

A deposit of similar character (level 99) seemed to be traceable continuing down the slope northwards above the stump of wall 17 into Section 3 (FIG. 69). This deposit looks like debris from the roadway and its retaining walls which may have fallen down the slope at the end of Period VII or later in Period VI.

A fragment of an obsidian arrow-head was recovered from Q130 of Period VII (FIG. 303: 14).

ii. **Period VI** (Plan, FIG. 59)

Period VI was inaugurated by the construction of the massive wall 20 on the southern side of the approach leading down to the well (PLATE 19 (d), (e)). This was much more substantial than wall 19 of Period VII, being on average c. 1.80 m wide at the base but attaining a width of over 2 m in places. The south (outer) face of it in trench G was found standing to a maximum height of 1.30 m with ten or more courses visible in it. Like most walls of all periods at Emporio, wall 20

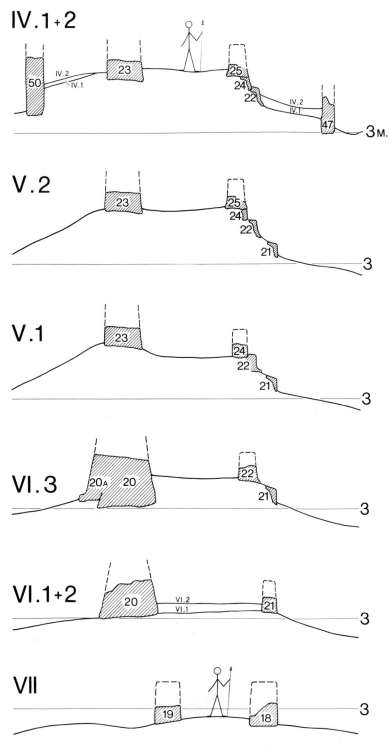

FIG. 58. Area A. Sections through the roadway to the well (Periods VII–IV).

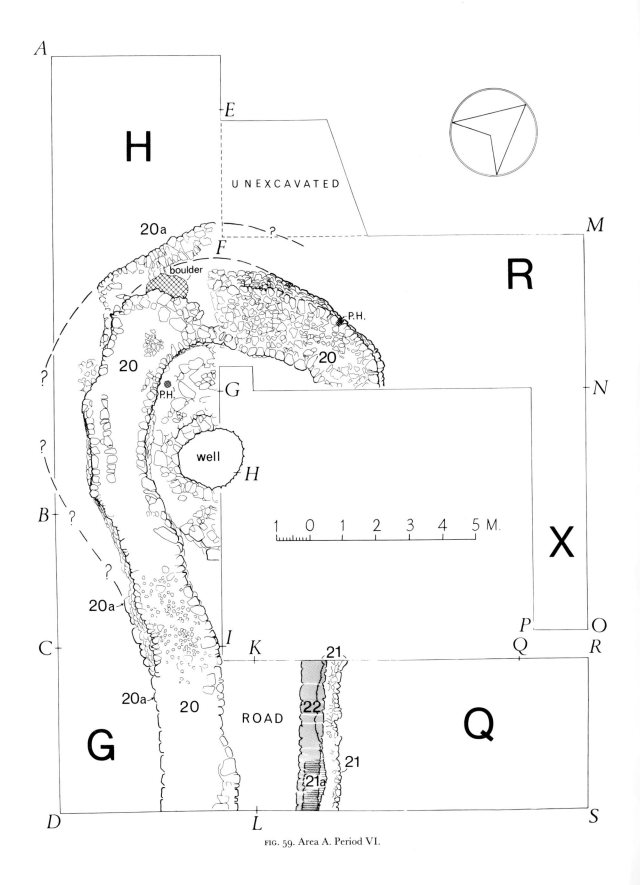

FIG. 59. Area A. Period VI.

was built without any foundations, the bottom course of stones resting immediately on top of the ashy fill (level 123) spread to level the site.

Wall 20 resembled the earlier terrace or defence walls (4 and 10) in the area in its somewhat rough and irregular construction. Like them it had an outer and inner face built of larger stones with a fill of smaller stones and earth or clay packed into the space between them. Both faces of the wall had been given a slight inward batter, but in some places the wall had bulged outwards in course of time. The faces were somewhat roughly built with medium-sized stones, although some larger ones up to 0.80–0.90 m in length had been incorporated in them. The lowest course on the southern, which was evidently the exposed, outer face of the wall, consisted of large flat blocks. Most of the stones in the faces were laid more or less flat, with a slight inward tilt to increase the strength of the wall; but some were set on their edges. Behind each face of the wall and concealed from view in the fill was a line of massive boulders, set upright or on edge at intervals along its length (FIG. 71: Section 5). The same system of construction with boulders at intervals behind the wall face was observed in the case of wall 16, added to the southern side of wall 10 in Period VIII. Such boulders would have served as a kind of framework helping to keep the fill of small stones and earth forming the interior of the wall in place.

It is not altogether clear what happened on the northern side of the roadway leading down to the well at the time that wall 20 was built. But it looks as if a new parapet (wall 21) was erected on top of wall 18 of Period VII. This parapet, however, was not in any way comparable in size or strength with wall 20, which certainly looks as if it had a defensive purpose. If wall 21 was really the northern return of wall 20 its comparatively slight character might be explained by the existence of a steeper slope on this northern side towards the harbour. Perhaps it was felt that the slope here made it unnecessary to build more than a breastwork on top of the old wall (18) on this side.

The roadway between walls 20 and 21 on the eastern side of trench Q (FIG. 70: Section 4) appears to have been about the same width (some 2.25 m) as that which had existed between walls 18 and 19 in Period VII. But owing to the line adopted for wall 20, diverging from that of the Period VII wall 19, the roadway of Period VI splayed to become some 3 m wide by the time it entered the section (FIG. 71: Section 5) on the western side of the trench.

Wall 20 continued round the western side of the well. In connection with the building of wall 20 the mouth of the well was surrounded with a rough pavement composed of large rounded beach stones. This may have replaced an earlier pavement which had already existed here at a lower level in Period VII. In some places the pavement of Period VI seemed to run below the bottom of wall 20, as if it had been laid before it was built, but elsewhere it clearly abutted against the face of the wall. The paved area surrounding the well was about 5.50 m across.

Eventually, but within the duration of Period VI, the level of the roadway to the well was raised with deposits of beach pebbles by some 0.70–0.80 m in all. This raising of the level of the road could have been a gradual process, thin layers of gravel being spread over it every few years or as it became necessary to effect repairs. But it seems more likely that the roadway was raised in two stages, in the first instance by some 0.30 m. (level 111 above VI. 1), and after an interval of time by some 0.50 m more (level 108 above VI. 2). An increase in the height of the roadway may have become desirable owing to an accumulation of debris raising the level of the paths in the settlement on the slopes of the hill above it. In conjunction with this raising of the roadway the stone pavement surrounding the well became buried in gravel (FIGS. 68, 72: Sections 2 and 6). But the deposit of gravel in the area round the well does not seem to have been as deep as it was on the roadway to the east of it.

As the level of the roadway was raised the parapet on the northern side of it had to be increased in height. Thus when the roadway was first raised by the deposition of level 111 above VI. 1, wall 21 was strengthened to carry the new parapet by thickening it on the inside (wall 21A). This thickening was clearly visible in Section 4 (FIG. 70) on the eastern side of trench Q, although it was not detected in the western Section 5. In conjunction with this first stage in raising the level of the roadway the inner northern face of wall 20 appears to have been patched or repaired (FIG. 70: Section 4).

When the level of the roadway was raised the second time (level 108) by as much as half a metre, the new parapet (wall 22) on the northern side of it was set back from the face of the old one (wall 21) by some 0.60 m. But the outer northern face of the new parapet continued to run parallel with that of wall 21 below it.

At some stage—perhaps when the level of the roadway was raised for the second time and the parapet wall 21 was built, but it may have been earlier—the western end of wall 20 was strengthened in places by the addition of an outer skin (20A). This was only added after a certain amount of debris, that looks as if it had fallen from wall 20, had accumulated against its southern outer face. Wall 20A seems to have diverged away from the original face of wall 20 as it descended the slope to the west, but it was not detected in excavation. It showed, however, as an irregular face of wall entering and leaving Section 1 (FIG. 67). The fill behind the wall face consisted of earth mixed with stones and pebbles.

What seems to have been the continuation of this face of wall (20A) was noted in the area immediately west of the well in trench H and appears to be recorded in Section 2 (FIG. 68). But it was not traced beyond this point to the north. Section 2 suggests that wall 30 was later than wall 20A and separated from it by a layer of debris (level 83a). Wall 30 exactly overlies wall 20A in Section 2, and the continuation of wall 20A into trench R may therefore lie concealed below it there. The stretch of wall 30 in trench R was not removed in excavation.

What seemed to be a vertical hole for a wooden post was noted in the outer edge of wall 20 in trench R just north-west of the well. The hole was rectangular, about 0.16 m across, and set about 0.16 m into the wall. It could be traced running down the full height of the wall which was about 0.75 m here. The top of the hole was found covered with stones from the wall, but this may be accidental, and the post probably projected above it, unless it was part of a system of wooden beams incorporated in the wall to strengthen it. No evidence for such a system, however, was noted in the long stretch of wall 20 that was removed in trench G.

A similar post-hole was found on the edge of the platform round the well and just to the west of it in trench H. This was also rectangular, measuring about 0.22 × 0.16 m across. It was visible in the latest gravel surface (below level 89) that seemed to be associated with wall 20 in the area round the well, and could be traced for a depth of 0.32 m with traces of carbonised wood in it. At the time of the excavation it was thought that a post here might have served as the upright for a balanced pole used like a crane to draw vessels of water from the well after the manner of an Egyptian *shaduf*. Post-holes suggestive of a *shaduf* were found by a stone-lined well in Hacilar II (*Hacilar* i 35). But our post-hole was only a metre from the edge of the well, which seems very close for such an arrangement; and in Egypt itself the use of the *shaduf* does not appear to be certainly attested before the New Kingdom (*CAH*[3] ii Pt. 1, 374. Cf. H.E. Winlock, *The Rise and Fall of the Middle Kingdom in Thebes* (New York, 1947) 164 ff., and despite F. Hartmann, *L'agriculture dans l'ancienne Égypte* (Paris, 1923) 117 f.).

Ultimately wall 20 in its enlarged form with the additional face 21 was destroyed. The destruction of the wall appears to have been deliberate and due to human agency rather than the result of an earthquake or some other natural cause. The debris from the wall was pushed over to make a sloping pile against its southern outer face. At the same time material appears to have been spread on the surface of the road leading down to the well to bring it level with the top of the slighted wall. The material is represented by a deposit of clay with some pebbles about 0.30–0.40 m thick (level 88) above the latest gravelled road surface (VI. 3) associated with wall 20. In contrast to the fairly clear situation on the southern side of wall 20 there was virtually no deposit that could be assigned with certainty to the time when the wall was slighted on the slope to the north of the roadway in trench Q.

The decision to level wall 20 may have been taken in conjunction with a plan to expand the settlement and build houses at the foot of the Acropolis hill in the area round the well. Houses certainly existed here in the following Period V. On the other hand there was no positive evidence for houses in this area during Periods VII and VI. This seems virtually certain as far as the space south of the roadway in trench G is concerned. But the situation is admittedly less clear when it comes to the space north of the roadway in trench Q. The houses in trenches R and X, however, must have been built after wall 30 was erected, and this wall seems to date from a period after the ruin of the enlarged wall 20 of Period VI. Some doubt remains in the case of the building (Plan, FIG. 60: III) with flimsy walls (34, 35) in trench Q. But on the whole it looks as if this house also dates from a time after the slighting of wall 20, when it would seem houses were once again built in the area at the foot of the Acropolis hill as they had been in Period VIII and earlier.

The deposits of Period VI like those of the previous Period VII were distinguished by the vast quantity of jug fragments in them. These jug fragments mostly came from the sand and gravel layers of the successive roadways assignable to Period VI. But fragments of jugs were also abundant in rubbish immediately above the debris from the ruin of wall 20 on the south and west.

(d) Periods V–IV
(FIGS. 47, 48. PLATES 20–25)

The pottery of these periods is closely akin to that of Troy I. From now onwards and for many centuries Emporio is in effect a province of the Trojan culture. The evanescent white painted decoration of Periods VII—VI is largely replaced by incisions filled with white paste. The Light Brown Burnished Ware reminiscent of the Urfirnis of the Middle and Late Neolithic periods on the Greek mainland is no longer in use, and bowls of Kum Tepe I B types become obsolete. The change in the character of the pottery may have been gradual rather than abrupt, but this was not altogether clear from a study of the stratified deposits.

In Period V houses were built in the areas beyond the roadway and the platform surrounding the well. This process of house building was consolidated during the following Period IV, when deep fills were dumped in order to level ground in the neighbourhood of the roadway and the well to make it more suitable for houses. No complete house plans were recovered, but it looks as if the houses of Period V may have been of a slightly different type from those of Period IV; smaller, narrower, and perhaps trapeze-shaped. The houses typical of Period IV on the other hand appear to have been wider in relation to their length than those of Period V.

The space of time covered by Periods V–IV may have been considerable. The roadway to the well was raised at least twice during this time, while in places as many as four or five successive floors or occupation surfaces could be distinguished in and around the houses.

Period IV ended with a great destruction by fire. Since traces of this fire were also found in Areas B, C and E, the whole settlement may have been involved in it. Large numbers of clay vases were recovered from above the floors of the fire-destroyed houses, which suggests that the destruction was rather sudden; but whether it was the work of enemies remains uncertain. The pottery in use during the following Periods III–II shows no real break in development. On the other hand immediately after the fire considerable changes were made in the arrangements round the well. It could also be significant that Juliet Clutton-Brock noted some evidence for the introduction of a new and larger type of goat to Emporio in Period II.

i. Period V (Plan, FIG. 60)

After the slighting of the massive wall 20 of Period VI a new wall (23) was built directly on top of it. This wall was constructed in the same way as wall 20 and the earlier walls of this kind which preceded it in the area. It was rather rough and irregular with an inner and outer face of comparatively large stones enclosing a fill of smaller ones (PLATE 22 (b)). Its rough appearance was in marked contrast to the neater style of construction of more or less contemporary house walls.

Wall 23 was about a metre wide and preserved to a height of four or five courses at the point where it entered the eastern side of trench G (FIG. 70: Section 4); but it became wider and stood considerably higher lower down on the slope to the west. It was not recognised west of where wall 37 of Period IV cut across the line of it. But at the point where it was cut by wall 37 it was about the same width as wall 20 on top of which it was built. It probably continued round the well following the same line as wall 20, or the part of wall 20 round the well may have been left standing into Period V.

When wall 23 was built a new layer of gravel (level 87) seems to have been deposited on the eastern end of the roadway in order to raise the level of it. A new parapet (wall 24) was then constructed on the northern side of the road with its inner face resting on top of the re-gravelled surface, and with its outer face set inwards slightly from that of the Period VI wall 22 below it. Wall 24 was a metre wide, about the same width, that is to say, as the contemporary wall 23 on the opposite side of the road to the south (FIG. 70: Section 4).

The situation round the well was not altogether clear. But it looks as if a path now led up to the platform round the well from the area below it to the west through a gap in the ruined wall 20. The level of the platform round the well may have been raised with gravel at this time. But there was some uncertainty as to how the deposits of gravel to the west of the well were to be related with those in the roadway to the east of it (FIG. 68: Section 2).

Eventually the level of the roadway and of the platform round the well were raised by a new deposit of gravel (level 85) some 0.30–0.40 m thick. When this was done, the height of the parapet wall on the northern side of the roadway was evidently increased. On the western side of trench Q (FIG. 71: Section 5) the southern inner edge of the new parapet (wall 25) was set back some 0.25 m from the face of the previous one (wall 24). This latest parapet wall (25) was built with large stones, and was about 0.70 m wide at the bottom. On the western side of trench Q in Section 5 it stood to a height of 0.40 m with two or three courses, but only a stone or two of it survived at the eastern side of the trench (FIG. 70: Section 4) where it was virtually on the surface at the time of excavation. The northern outer face of this parapet wall (25) appears to have had a distinct batter.

In the top of wall 25 was found the block of stone (STONE No. 52) with a group of fourteen roughly parallel lines cut in one face of it. Since the lines were cut in the eastern face they would have been hidden from sight in the wall. The lines must therefore have been incised before the block was incorporated in the wall, and it may have come from some earlier structure on the site.

Area to the west of the well (trench H) (PLATE 23)

It seems that a house represented by walls 26, 27 and 28, was constructed in this area

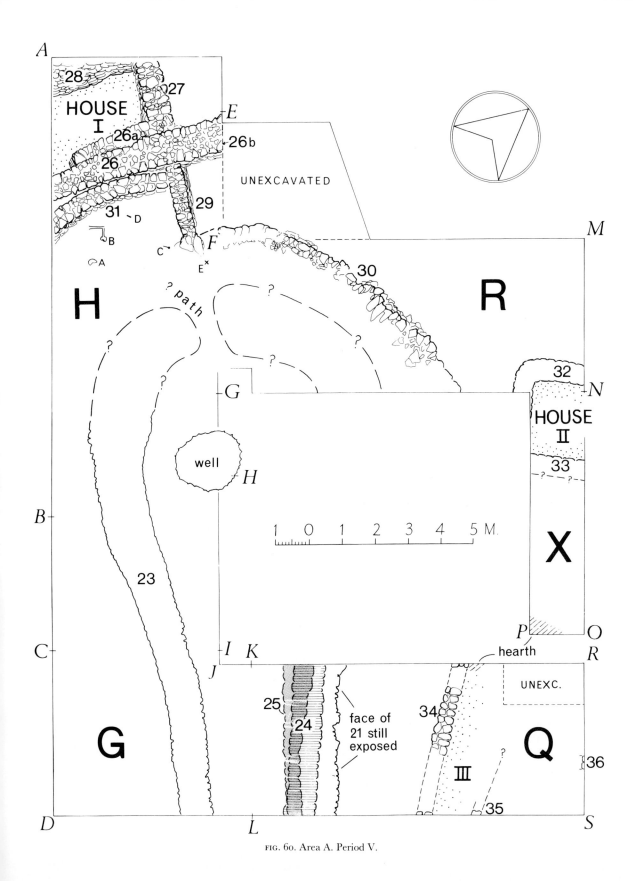

FIG. 60. Area A. Period V.

immediately after the overthrow of wall 20. Wall 26 was built on top of what appears to be debris from it. It had a foundation course of large stones which projected beyond the line of the wall on the western side facing down the slope. In addition the western side of the wall was strengthened for part of its length by a kind of buttress (wall 26A) about 2.50 m long and 0.50 m thick. This appeared to have been built at the same time as wall 26, and to have been bonded with it.

After wall 26 was built a loose fill of earth and stones (level 90) was dumped against its eastern face. This fill was clearly traceable in Section 2 (FIG. 68), but it did not seem to extend far northwards into trench R, and it was not apparent on the southern side of trench H (FIG. 67: Section 1). It may have been placed here in order to raise the level of the ground in the space between wall 26 and the well at the point where there may have been a path leading upwards to the platform round the well over the stump of the ruined wall 20. A large amount of fragmentary pottery was recovered from this fill (level 90). It was distinctly Period V in character and included many fragments of jugs. Others finds from the fill included what appears to be one end of a pounder of the waisted type (STONE No. 17), and a bronze pin (METAL No. 4) (Plan, FIG. 60: C). Just to the south of where the pin was found were several fragments of human skeletons, including the skull and teeth of an infant, and part of an adult skull (FIG. 60: A). About a metre away to the west of this skull (A) were two leg bones (B) which seemed to be in articulation, together with the traces of what may have been a pelvis. This group of bones (B) and the adult skull (A) might have been the relics of a burial in the flexed position; a mother, perhaps, buried with her child. But they gave the impression, not of orderly burial, but of the remains of bodies which had been tumbled into the fill of loose stones along with fragments of pottery and other rubbish. It is interesting that disjointed human remains, both adult and infant, were similarly found at various places in Town III at Thermi (*Thermi* 11, 28).

A skin of wall (26B) was added to the eastern face of wall 26 after the fill (level 90) had been deposited. But in places wall 26B looked as if it were bonded into wall 26; and wall 26, the fill (level 90), and walls 26A and 26B, may all have been part of a single building operation. Walls 27, 28 and 29, as well as the retaining wall 30, seem to belong to the same scheme and may all be contemporary with wall 26.

Walls 26, 27 and 28 appear to have enclosed one end of a long house (I) running in a roughly north–south direction across the slope. The width of this house as exposed in trench H was about 2.50 m. The earliest floor (below level 47) appears to have been level with the top of the projecting foundation course of wall 26.

Wall 29, which continued the line of wall 27 on the eastern side of wall 26, appeared to be of the same date. It abutted against wall 26B, but its foundations were set deeper in the fill of loose stones (level 90). These foundations consisted of a row of larger stones, many of which had been set on edge. The wall itself was built of relatively small stones, and was about 0.50 m wide with a maximum height of 0.90 m. At its eastern end it abutted onto and overlapped the top of the retaining wall 30 (PLATE 23 (a), (b)).

Wall 30 was of very rough construction (PLATE 20 (b)). The outer face, which had a slight inward batter, was extremely uneven, with rather large stones incorporated in it. This rough facing was backed by a fill of earth and pebbles, which appears to be debris from the Period VI wall 20. Wall 30 was evidently built with the object of keeping this debris in place so that it did not slip down against the walls of the houses that were now being erected in the area below the well on the northern side. As it is, many of the house walls here were found to lean in the direction of the downward slope, and the tendency to lean that way may have made itself felt while the houses were still in use.

No traces of this retaining wall 30 were noted in the area south of wall 29 and of the presumed path leading up to the platform round the well. Perhaps a retaining wall was not considered necessary here where the slope of the ground was less marked.

Wall 31 (PLATE 23 (*a*), (*b*)) was *c*. 0.55 m wide and preserved to a height of *c*. 0.90 m. It was built in front of the eastern face of wall 26 after some 0.20 m of ash (level 76) (FIG. 67: Section 1) had accumulated or been deposited at the foot of it. A mass of fragmentary pottery was recovered from the original ground surface at the bottom of this ashy layer. This included a jar (1190) and the miniature bowl 1303. The ash may have come from fires lit in the sheltered space of ground here, but no fire-places (hearths) were recognised in the area excavated. Alternatively it may have been dumped from fire-places in the neighbouring houses. In this ashy layer (level 76) was found a bronze awl (METAL No. 8) (Plan, FIG. 60: D).

Area to the north of the well (trenches R and X) (PLATES 24, 25)
The area directly north of the retaining wall 30 also appears to have been open ground during Period V. But walls 32 and 33 were evidently built in connection with wall 30, and enclosed what must be one end of a narrow rectangular house (II) with roughly the same alignment as House I. Wall 32 was about 0.60 m wide, and on the south ended in a corner which was rounded on the outside. Wall 33 may have been the same width as wall 32, but the eastern face of it was hidden below wall 42 of Period IV. The space enclosed by these walls was just over 2 m across from east to west. Two successive earth floors were noted in this space associated with the walls. The first of these (V. 1, below level 77) was only indicated by a few scraps of pottery and some pithos fragments scattered on it. The second (V. 2), about 0.25 m above V. 1 and below level 60, was marked by a thin layer of ash.

In the area of trench X to the east of wall 33 there were no walls until Period IV. The space here may have been open ground during the time that walls 32 and 33 were in use, but this remains uncertain. The earliest occupation surface assignable to Period V was associated with a shallow pit used as a fire-place in the south-eastern corner of the trench (FIG. 71: Section 5, *P–O* below level 60). Patches of clay formed a thin layer over this occupation surface. The clay was yellow, except for a very thin red patch at the eastern end of the trench. This red patch may have been discoloured by the heat of the neighbouring fires, if the clay was floor material. But the clay may be dissolved mud or mud-brick from walls like the deposit (level 75) in trench Q which appears to be assignable to the same horizon.

Area to the east of the well (trench Q)
The surface with the fire-place and patches of clay above it could be traced continuing into the north end of trench Q (FIG. 69: Section 3, below level 61). Here in trench Q the stratigraphy appears to have been much telescoped, and was not altogether clear. But the stretch of flimsy wall 34 running at an angle across the trench seems to be assignable to Period V rather than to Period VI. The surviving stretch of this wall consisted of a single course of stones about 0.35–0.50 m wide. The wall showed clearly in Section 5 (FIG. 71), and what may have been the continuation of it eastwards was identifiable in Section 4 (FIG. 70) on the eastern side of the trench.

This wall 34 appears to have been constructed at the foot of a bank of debris from the successive terrace walls (18, 21 and 22) which had supported the roadways of Periods VII–VI on the north. It was clearly the southern wall of a building, presumably a house (III), the floor on the northern side of it being marked by a thin streak of brown clay that was visible in Section 4 (FIG. 70, below level 75). In section 5 (FIG. 71) this same floor could be detected sloping down towards the north. Traces of burning above it here may be connected with the fire-place (hearth) in the south-eastern corner of trench X. Wall 34 was on the same alignment as the return at the southern end of wall 32 in trench R, and may have continued westwards to join it.

There were hardly any traces of fallen stones that might have come from walls above the floor of House III associated with wall 34. A fill of clean sandy yellow clay (level 75) some 0.40–0.50 m thick appears to be the remains of dissolved mud or mud-brick walling. It therefore looks as if wall 34 and any other walls associated with it must have been constructed of mud or mud-brick on low stone foundations or socles.

The floor of House III stopped on the north by the southern face of another stretch of flimsy walling (35). At the time of the excavation there seemed to be evidence that this walling, which was only c. 0.40 m wide, might have been contemporary with wall 34. It was noted that a thin layer of the same yellow clay (level 75) that covered the floor of House III could be distinguished in places running over the top of 35 and below the stones (level 24) fallen from the Period IV wall 48. But the space between walls 34 and 35 at the point where they enter Section 4 is only c. 1.20 m across, which seems very narrow for a house, and 35 could not be traced as far as the western side of trench Q or beyond it into trench X. It therefore seems possible that it was in fact a structure of Period IV adjacent to wall 48, or of one build with it, although with its bottom resting on a surface some 0.30 m lower.

In the area to the north of 35 in trench Q the occupation surface assignable to this horizon seemed to dip rather abruptly downwards under a thin layer of sandy yellow clay (level 74) which might be the remains of decayed mud or mud-brick walling like level 75 and the layer of yellow clay noted in trench X immediately to the west. This sandy yellow clay of level 74 stopped in Section 3 (FIG. 69) at a pair of stones (36) which could have been the stump of another flimsy wall running from north to south across trench Q, but no such wall was noted in excavation.

The floor of house III (below level 75) was some 2 m lower than the level of the earliest Period V roadway (V. 1, below level 85). The latest Period V roadway (V. 2, below level 70) was as much as 2.30–2.40 m higher than this floor. The face of wall 21 assigned to Period VI seems to have remained visible during Period V at the base of the later parapets (walls 22 and 24). There was a slope downwards from the foot of wall 21 to the back of wall 34.

Area to the south of the well (trench G)
The area exposed by excavation to the south of the roadway in trench G appears to have been open ground in Period V. An ashy fill (level 51) assignable to Period V underlay the deposits of Period IV here.

ii. Period IV
This period was inaugurated by a major planning development in the area round the well. The levels of the roadway and of the platform round the well were raised once again by some 0.30–0.50 m. At the western end of the well platform the new fill (level 71) backed against the outer face of wall 37 of House IV. This implies that wall 37 was built before the fill (level 71) was deposited, although it may have been built only a short time before in conjunction with the raising of the platform round the well and of the roadway leading down to it from the east. It seems that at some point during Period IV the upper part of the lining on the eastern side of the well collapsed. It was repaired (PLATE 19 (*b*)), and a fill of stones (level 30) was dumped into the gap behind the restored section of lining (FIG. 68: Section 2). A layer of white gravel (level 28) was then laid over the top of this fill of stones.

As a prelude to the building of the Period IV houses most of the area to the south, west and north of the well was levelled up with fills of ash or stones. The walls of the houses were sometimes

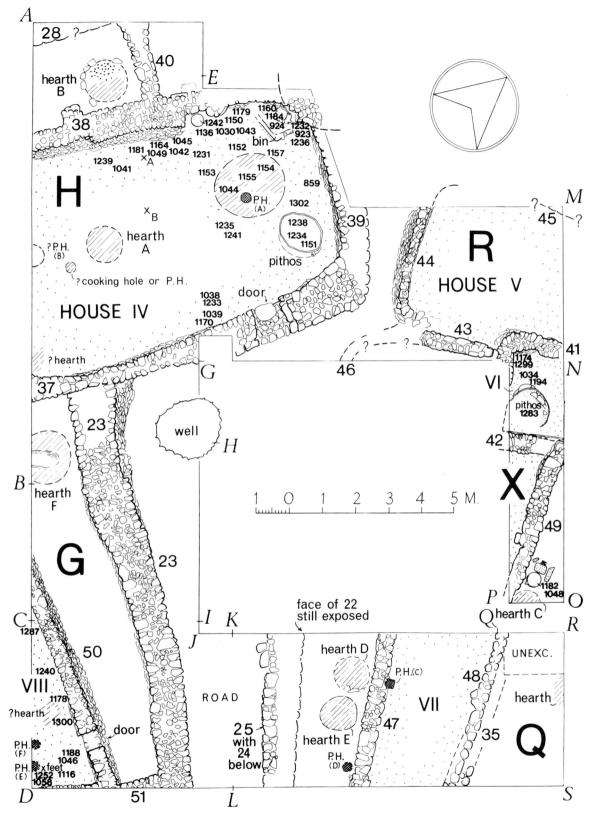

FIG. 61. Area A. Period IV.

built on top of house walls of Period V. But many of the new house walls were on different lines. In spite of what was done in the way of levelling the site the floors of the Period IV houses were still a good deal below the level of the platform round the well and of the roadway leading down to it. Thus the top of the threshold in the doorway through the north end of wall 37 of House IV was more or less flush with the latest stage of the platform round the well, but some 0.40 m above the latest floor of the house.

Houses

No complete house plans were recovered. But most of one house (IV) and a large part of another (House V) were cleared. These two houses appear to have been rectangular and about twice as long as they were wide. The corners were rounded inside and outside. Large single-roomed long houses akin to those of Emporio IV were also characteristic of the more or less contemporary Troadic settlement at Thermi on Lesbos, as of Troy itself and of other Anatolian settlements of the time like Karataş-Semayük in Lycia. Such houses would have been suitable dwelling places for extended families. The rounded corners of Houses IV and V may reflect a tradition of apsidal buildings like the D-shaped room of Period VIII in trench G (FIG. 53). Similar vestiges of an apsidal tradition have been noted at Poliochni in the Blue period which should overlap with Emporio IV and Troy I, and later in the Kastri settlement at Chalandriani on Syros contemporary with Troy II or III (*Poliochni* i atlas pl. 4: areas 206, 211, 212. Eva-Maria Bossert, *ADelt* xxii (1967) 59).

The floors of houses were of earth, or might be covered wholly or in part with a thin layer of clay, whitish, greenish or red in colour. On occasion at any rate (e.g. House IV) the clay floor was laid on top of an original earth floor after this had been in use for a time. Gravel was only noted in patches on the floors of houses: fine gravel may have been used as in earlier periods to fill hollows or cover spots which had become muddy owing to leaks in the roof or proximity to doorways or washing activities, or as stands for vases as suggested at Thermi (*Thermi* 9).

House walls were built of rubble and were normally about 0.50 m or more in thickness, narrowing somewhat towards the top where they were preserved to any height. One or two walls (44, 50) had survived in places to a height of 2 m or more, and this may have been virtually their full height. These walls at any rate may have been built entirely of stone. It seems that at Thermi mud-brick was never used in any quantity, and the evidence for its use at all in the earlier Towns I and II contemporary with Troy I is inconclusive (*Thermi* 7 f., 21 f.). But it was almost certainly in regular use at Troy from the earliest times (e.g. *Troy* i 83, 90, 91). The upper parts of some of the house walls of Emporio IV may therefore have been constructed of mud or mud-brick like wall 34 assigned to Period V.

None of the walls appears to have had sunk foundations, although the lower parts of some walls were concealed more or less immediately after they were built with fills of earth or stones dumped on one or both sides of them (e.g. wall 50 of House VIII). As in earlier periods at Emporio the lowest course of the wall was simply placed on top of the existing ground surface; but it was usually constructed with larger blocks of stone than the rest of the wall, and might project beyond the wall face, as noted in the case of some earlier walls (e.g. 26 of Period V). The lowest course of the unusually well-preserved wall 44 of House V consisted of single stones about 0.65 m long set lengthwise and extending the whole width of the wall. But there was a considerable range of variation in the size of stones used for building house walls. Sometimes at least (e.g. wall 47) upright timbers may have been combined with the wall to strengthen it or help support the roof. Holes for large posts which look as if they may have been roof supports were found sunk in the floors of some houses (IV and VIII) (PLATE 24 (*d*), (*e*)). It is curious, however, that at Thermi in Lesbos, where large numbers of comparable houses were cleared, roof supports of this kind seem to have been virtually absent, and only one post-hole was identified there (*Thermi* 9, 21). Post-holes seem to be similarly ill-attested at Troy.

The houses appear to have had flat roofs as suspected at Troy and Thermi (*Thermi* 9. *Troy* i 91 f.). The ruin debris immediately above the floors of the fire-destroyed houses of Period IV at Emporio normally consisted of a layer of red clay and charred wood about 0.30–0.40 m thick. This seems to represent the remains of the collapsed roof, built like the flat roofs of Bronze Age houses in Crete with a layer of waterproof clay above earth laid on branches and brushwood which had been placed across the rafters (*BSA* x (1903–04) 205. Cf. *Greek Emporio* 36). Thus in Section 2 (FIG. 68) the ruin debris of House IV showed as a layer of clean red clay (level 25) overlying one of clay and charred wood (level 26) from the rafters and brushwood.

There was no evidence to suggest the existence of upper floors in any of the houses, and the thin layer of ruin debris above the floors taken in conjunction with the relatively narrow walls suggests that they were single storeyed. No traces of staircases were noted inside or outside the houses; but if the roofs were flat there was no doubt access to them, whether by means of permanent wooden staircases or by movable ladders of some kind.

Fire-places (Hearths)

Many hearths or places where fires had been lit were noted in levels of Period IV. Some of these fire-places were indoors, others out of doors. Several were merely irregular areas with traces of burning on the surface of the ground or floor, while others were defined by shallow circular hollows. But a number of hearths had been more or less elaborately constructed with a foundation of sherds or pebbles surrounded by a ring of stones. The more elaborately constructed hearths tended to be in open spaces outside the houses and not indoors. These open-air hearths were no doubt used for cooking, and most of the serious cooking was probably done out of doors as it is today in many parts of Greece, where cooking places and bread-ovens are regularly found outside the houses. At Servia in western Macedonia it was noted that hearths of the Middle Neolithic period seemed to occur in open yard areas (*Servia* 195, 198). Many of the Neolithic cooking-holes at Knossos were similarly in the spaces between the houses (*BSA* lxiii (1968) 268).

No remains of ovens were detected in levels of the Early Bronze Age at Emporio. Similarly at Troy domed ovens are not certainly attested until the beginning of Troy IV (*Troy* ii 90, 103). But they appear to have been in use much earlier than this in other parts of Anatolia and the Aegean area (Renfrew, *Emergence* 309 f. *DS* 52 f., fig. 10, 91 f., 104, for Late Neolithic examples from Dhimini and Sesklo. *BSA* lix (1964) 148; lxiii (1968) 268, for possible Early Neolithic ones at Knossos in Crete). Some of the more elaborately constructed hearths at Emporio, however, may have been designed specifically for the baking of bread. This seems highly probable in the case of the open-air Hearth F in trench G with a neat oblong sinking in the middle.

Area to the west of the well (trench H)

The space east of wall 26 which appears to have been open ground in Period V was now filled with ashy earth (levels 48, 49, 50). This ashy fill merged into one of loose stones (level 54) on the east. The fill of stones (level 54) and the ashy fill (levels 48, 49, 50) appeared to be contemporary and part of the same scheme of rebuilding in the area.

This ashy fill was nearly a metre deep in places against the eastern face of wall 26. It covered the retaining wall 30, together with the site of the path which is assumed to have existed here leading to the platform round the well in Period V. Two bronze pins (METAL Nos. 2, 3) and a bone needle (BONE No. 41) were found close together in the fill (FIG. 60: E); other objects from it include a group of shell buttons (SHELL No. 60).

The floor of the new House IV of Period IV was above this fill. At first the top of the fill itself appears to have served as its floor. Patches of pebbles were spread in places above this floor, either where it was damp and muddy, or to level hollows in it, or for other reasons. Soon, however, and before any debris had been allowed to accumulate above this original floor, a thin layer of green clay, less than 0.05 m in thickness, was laid as a floor (IV. 1) over it. Patches of pebbles were also noted in places on top of this floor (see FIG. 68: Section 2).

At some point before the house was destroyed by fire at the end of the Period IV a new floor (IV. 2) was made by spreading a layer of red clay some 0.10–0.15 m thick over the earlier green clay floor (IV. 1). It seems likely that the clay in this case was also originally green, but was turned red by the heat of the fire which destroyed the Period IV settlement.

Wall 38 forming the western side of House IV was built directly on top of the Period V wall 26 (PLATE 23 (a), (b)). It was about 0.80 m wide, and was standing to a height of about 0.90 m at the time of excavation. The stones used in its construction were noticeably smaller than the ones employed for wall 26 of Period V below it. A small buttress projecting from the western outside face of wall 38 may have been meant to strengthen it against the tendency to lean with the slope, like the larger buttress associated with the earlier wall 26.

The southern end of House IV lay beyond the area excavated in trench H. But the house appears to have been rectangular in shape with the longest dimension from north to south. The part of the house that was cleared was about 6 m wide from west to east inside. The length from north to south may have been in the region of 12 m or more. The two corners of the house exposed by excavation were rounded. The north-west corner seemed to incorporate the rounded south-eastern corner of another house which lay beyond the area of excavation to the north.

House IV seems to have been larger than most of the houses at contemporary Thermi. Its width was certainly greater than that of House A 1 of town I at Thermi, one of the most impressive houses revealed there (*Thermi* 15). But even larger houses of comparable type have been uncovered at Karataş Semayük in south-western Anatolia.

In the eastern wall (37) of House IV, near its north-eastern corner, was a doorway about a metre wide leading to the area round the well. The threshold of this was level with the surround of the well, but the top of it was about 0.40 m above the latest floor level (IV. 2) in the house, and as much as 0.60 m above the earlier green clay floor (IV. 1). There may have been a wooden step or steps in front of the doorway inside the house to facilitate entering or leaving by it.

The roof was evidently supported with the help of wooden posts. The hole for a large post was identified at the northern end of the house (FIG. 61: P.H. (A). PLATE 24 (d), (e)). This was circular in shape, with a diameter of about 0.30 m, and sunk to a depth of 0.55 m below the level of the latest floor (IV. 2). One or two sherds on edge at the side of the hole had been put there in order to help wedge the post, if they had not slipped down into cracks which had later formed at its sides. The hole was filled with burnt red clay and soft black ash, suggesting that it still held a post at the time the house was destroyed by fire. But it was not entirely clear from the section (FIG. 73: Section 7) that the latest floor (IV. 2) did not run over the top of the hole and seal it. Moreover, a deposit of black ash together with reddish cinders some 0.10 m deep over an area about 2 m in diameter above the latest floor in the area round the hole was taken to be debris from a hearth at the time of excavation. The ash, however, might represent the carbonised remains of a post; a large lump of charred wood was in fact noted on the western edge of the presumed hearth area.

A pit about 0.60 m wide and some 0.20–0.25 m deep (? P.H. (B)) visible in the southern section (FIG. 67: Section 1) seems too shallow for a post hole, but might have contained the stone base for a wooden post at the time the earlier green clay floor (IV. 1) was in use. But if so, the stone was removed before the laying of the later floor (IV. 2), which appeared to run over the top of the pit.

A circular fire-place (hearth A) paved with small stones was in use in connection with the earlier floor (IV. 1). It was about 1 m in diameter, and was surrounded by a rim of ash formed by raking back the debris from the fires lit on it. When the new floor (IV. 2) was laid the fire-place remained in use, but it was not considered necessary to repave it at a higher level. A humped ridge of hardened ash about 0.25 m wide and 0.06 m high had formed on the eastern side of the fire-place above the red clay floor (IV. 2) by the time House IV was destroyed. Just to the south of hearth A was a small hole full of burnt debris. This may have been used for cooking; unless it held a post which replaced one in ? P.H. (B) during the last phase of occupation in the house. A shallow pit filled with ash (level 31) showing in Section 1 (FIG. 67) near the south-eastern corner of the house also appeared to mark a place where fires had been lit in connection with both floors IV. 1 and IV. 2.

Set into the curve of the opposite north-western corner of the house was a clay-lined bin or chest (FIG. 61. PLATE 23 (d)). This was roughly the shape of a triangle which had the curving house wall as a base. The other two sides of the triangle were formed by thin clay walls, about 1 m long on the east and some 1.35 m in length on the south. The bottom of the bin was c. 0.20 m below the level of the later floor (IV. 2), which was very uneven in this area, and 0.10 m or more below that of the earlier green clay floor (IV. 1). The tops of the clay walls projected in places some 0.25 m above the surface of the later floor (IV. 2). These walls and the lining of the bin were made of coarse clay tempered with abundant straw. The clay had been reddened and baked by the fire which destroyed the house. A bin made of unbaked clay at Hacilar was similarly hardened by the fire which destroyed the Level II settlement there (*AS* viii (1958) 133). A small circular hole c. 0.08 m in diameter, visible in the top of the eastern side wall of our bin, might have held an upright post or stick.

A large storage jar (1184) was found lying shattered on its side in the bin. It held traces of some whitish substance, apparently the remains of its original contents. Around the base were fragments of another smaller clay jar (1232). Other finds from the bin included a deer antler, and, at a higher level, five large clay loomweights like CLAY No. 27, together with the vases 923, 924, and 1160. Some of these objects might have been sitting on top of a wooden cover placed over the bin; or they might all have fallen from a shelf or sleeping platform that ran above it.

Clay bins have a long history in Anatolia, and large numbers of bins and boxes made of clay were found at Çatal Hüyük (*AS* xxvii (1977) 147 f.). Our bin is more immediately reminiscent, however, of the clay-lined 'house-pits' or 'bothroi', common at Thermi in houses of Periods III–IV, although not found there earlier (*Thermi* 61 ff.). It is true that none of these Thermi 'house-pits' is reported as having a rim which projected above floor level. But some of them were very shallow, with bottoms as little as 0·05 m below the level of the associated floor in a few instances. It looks as if these shallower pits at any rate might have had rims like our bin. Such rims, made of unfired clay, would be difficult to detect in excavation, unless they had been hardened and differentiated by fire, as happened in House IV at Emporio.

There was no certain indication as to how the 'house-pits' at Thermi were used. The use for which our bin was intended is similarly obscure. It seems too small for a granary; and if it was employed for storing food, some carbonised remains of this ought to have survived as a result of the fire which destroyed the house. Some comparable clay-lined pits in houses of Troy I it was

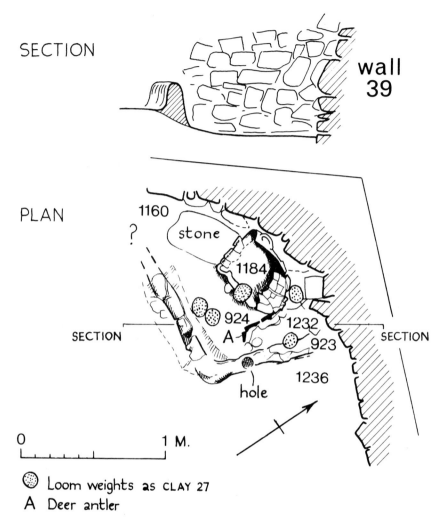

SECTION

wall
39

PLAN

1160

?

stone

1184

924
A

1232

923

SECTION   SECTION

hole

1236

0   1 M.

⊚ Loom weights as CLAY 27
A Deer antler

FIG. 62. Bin in north-west corner of House IV of Period IV in trench R.

suggested might have been used for setting bread dough to rise, similar pits being still used for
that purpose in the Troad; the quality of the clay was said to have much to do with the flavour of
the bread (*Troy* i 84, 94). The bin may have been simply a cupboard, however, for general
purposes, or for clothes: an early version of the under-floor storage chests which are a feature of
the Bronze Age palace at Knossos in Crete. It is just possible that it had some kind of sacred
function, like the house shrines of Minoan Crete or of later Greek times, or the corner with an
icon found in houses throughout the Balkans to this day. this was suggested in the case of the
'bothroi'—clay-lined pits, mostly circular—found at Orchomenos and assignable it seems to
Early Helladic III (*Orchomenos* i 25 ff. esp. 30 f.). There was a deer antler in our bin, and it is
curious that deer antlers appear to have been conspicuous in the 'house-pits' at Thermi (*Thermi*

63). But deer antlers were used as tools in early times, and the presence of an antler pick might seem more suggestive of the family tool chest than of a shrine. A whetstone (STONE No. 28) was also recovered from the area of the bin, but it appears to have come from the ashy deposit (level 48) below its floor.

The north-eastern corner of House IV was occupied by a large pithos (PLATE 23 (e), (f)). The rounded base of this was found sunk to a depth of c. 0.20 m below the level of the later floor (IV. 2). But both the clay-lined bin and the pithos may have already been in use in connection with the earlier floor levels in the house. The shattered remains of a number of smaller clay vases were recovered from above the latest floor (IV. 2) at the northern end of the house between the clay bin and the pithos. A large jar (1236), which had evidently been standing on the floor just to the east of the bin, contained remains of carbonised grain. But remains of two large jars, 1234 and 1238, were actually recovered from inside the pithos, indicating that they had fallen from above. This suggests that many of the vases of all sizes found in this area were resting on shelves, or on a raised sleeping platform of some kind, which may have run along the north wall; the bowls might have been hanging by their handles from pegs on the wall here.

Other vases were found along the western wall of the house to the south of the bin. Some of these (e.g. 1041) were upside down between 0.10 and 0.15 m above the floor, indicating that they had fallen from above. But the large jar 1242 was standing on the floor in a kind of niche in the wall. Near the wall just to the south of this niche a mortar like STONE Nos. 8–9 was found resting upside down on the floor (Plan, FIG. 61: A). It was the earliest example of a mortar of this type noted at Emporio, and like the saddle quern on the floor of the D-shaped house of Period VIII (FIG. 53: C) it may have been left upside down to prevent dust accumulating in it when it was not in use. A pounder (STONE No. 18) of the waisted type 3 from the same area may have belonged with it.

Another pounder (STONE No. 14) of type 1 came from the ashy deposit round P. H. (A). Several clay spindle whorls (including WHORLS Nos. 16 and 36 of types 9 and 10) were recovered from the debris above the floor in the northern part of the house where the vases were concentrated. Among other finds from the ruin debris above the floor was a bronze awl (METAL No. 10) (Plan, FIG. 61: B).

When House IV was built the space to the west of it was raised with a fill of small stones (level 47) between 0.80 m and 1.00 m deep. The surface above this was level with the bottom of wall 38 of House IV. A new wall (40) of rather rough construction was built on top of wall 27 of Period V. Wall 28 of Period V survived or was restored to define the space on the west. The space here may have been part of a house during Period V, but in Period IV it was evidently open ground, serving possibly as a yard in connection with House IV. Eventually, perhaps when the latest floor (IV. 2) was laid in House IV, the level in this space was raised again by means of a fill of yellowish clay (level 38) with a deposit of small stones (level 37) above it. The surface in the space was now about level with the latest floor (IV. 2) in House IV. This final Period IV surface was over 1.50 m higher than the surface in use during Period V here.

Associated with this final surface of Period IV was a built fire-place (FIG. 61: Hearth B), consisting of a circular patch of pebbles c. 1.30 m in diameter, with a ring of stones round it. The fire-place was in the sheltered corner made by the angle of walls 38 and 40, and had the buttress projecting from wall 38 to the south of it. A thin layer of white ash had accumulated on the south and west sides of this fire-place by the time of the destruction at the end of Period IV. The existence of a built fire-place close to the walls in this space is in harmony with the idea that it was open ground at the time. The fire-place may have been used for cooking out of doors. No clay vases were found in this area.

Area to the north of the well (trenches R and X)

An ashy fill 0.50–0.60 m deep (level 60) was dumped into the space enclosed by walls 32 and 33 of Period V, and new, rather narrower walls (41, 42) were built on top of them. The width of the space enclosed by the new walls (House VI) was thus about 2.40 m, rather wider than it had been in Period V. A gap at the northern end of wall 42 by its point of junction with wall 49 might have been occupied by a wooden beam: remains of charred wood were noted here.

The earliest floor (IV. 1) associated with the new walls (FIG. 69: Section 3, *N–O*, below level 40) was clearly defined by a sandy layer in places. A large pithos had been sunk into this floor, and fragments of it were found scattered above the floor throughout the space cleared between the walls (PLATE 25 (*c*)). In the pithos and above the floor associated with it were the shattered remains of several smaller vases. No signs of burnt destruction were noted above this floor, which appears to belong to the earlier part of Period IV.

A later floor (IV. 2) was identified *c.* 0.25–0.30 m above the earlier one (IV. 1). This later floor had been subsequently destroyed in places by erosion down the slope to the north. But where it had survived it was marked by a layer of small pebbles. Another pithos set above the earlier one was evidently associated with this floor (PLATE 25 (*b*)). While this floor had no obvious signs of burnt destruction on it, the charred wood, which may indicate the existence of a wooden beam in the gap at the northern end of wall 42, suggests that House VI was destroyed by fire like House IV.

When House VI was built, or almost immediately afterwards, a spacious house (V) appears to have been added on the west side of it. Wall 41 of House VI served as part of the east wall of House V, and a new wall 43 extended from it southwards. Wall 43, and wall 44 forming the southern end of House V, were sunk into the top of a deep fill of ash and large stones (levels 56–59) which appear to have been dumped to raise the level here. Wall 44 was eventually incorporated in the raised terrace of Period III and was found standing to a height of 1.75 m at the time of excavation. It had a projecting foundation course 0.65 m wide. The wall resting on this was 0.55 m in width at the bottom, but at the top it narrowed to 0.35–0.40 m.

A ragged gap at the southern end of wall 43 before the point where it began to form a rounded corner with wall 44 marks where it was destroyed by the passage (Plan, FIG. 65: Postern Gate) which led through the Period III terrace wall to the area round the well. What appeared to be a scrap of wall (45) in the north-western corner of trench R (FIG. 73: Section 7) might have belonged to House V, which would then have been *c.* 4.00–4.50 m wide across the inside. But this apparent wall did not seem to be associated with the earlier floor (IV. 1) in House V, and it may have been nothing more than fallen stone, or some construction of Period III which cut into the later floor (IV. 2).

House V was almost certainly smaller than House IV, and its walls were less massive in construction. But these two houses were evidently similar in type and appear to have been erected at the same time. A space was left between them for a narrow path mounting the slope to the platform round the well. This path would have replaced the one which is thought to have existed further south in trench H in Period V, but which was now covered by House IV. After this path had become worn into a trough by use, or by rain water tearing down the slope, it was filled with pebbles to a depth of *c.* 0.40 m (FIG. 73: Section 7, level 44) to make a flat surface (IV. 1). Eventually the path was raised again with another layer of pebbles (level 43) some 0.30 m thick. This path seems to have sloped upwards towards the east until it merged with the pebble-strewn surround of the well.

The stump of what appears to have been a wall (46) keeping back the pebbled surround of the well from a surface at a somewhat lower level between it and wall 43 of House V was distinguished in Section 6 (FIG. 72). The traces of burning above this surface (level 26) were assignable to the destruction marking the end of Period IV. This burnt debris above it suggests that the surface was the floor of a house rather than open ground at the time. It would be logical in that case to expect wall 46 to bend northwards and meet the south-eastern corner of House V. No trace of it was noted here in excavation, but the Postern Gate of Period III had cut deep into this area, as we have seen.

Area to the east of the well (trench Q)

A new house (VII) was eventually built above the ruins of House III assigned to Period V. On the eastern side of trench Q (FIG. 70: Section 4) the floor of this house seemed to lie immediately on top of the sandy yellow clay (level 75) which may be the debris of mud or mud-brick walling from House III. But on the western side of the trench (FIG. 71: Section 5) a possible occupation surface, with a layer of yellow clay mixed with ash (level 65) some 0.10–0.20 m thick above it, could be detected between the sandy yellow clay (level 75) and the floor of House VII (at the bottom of level 26).

A pit (level 66), which appears to have been sunk from this level, was recognised in Section 5 (FIG. 71). It was partly filled with ash, and a scatter of ash could be traced in the section to the south of it (level 64), and to the north above the ruin debris of House III (bottom of level 65). The pit may have been used for lighting fires, a precursor of the series of fire-places which came to occupy the space between the northern retaining wall of the road leading to the well and wall 47 of House VII. But the activities connected with it evidently date from a time before House VII was built. The ashy layer at the bottom of level 65 was traceable in Section 5 northwards as far as the southern face of wall 48 of House VII which may have been cut through it.

Occupation surfaces which appear to have been in use during Period IV to the north of House VII were a good half-metre lower than the level of its floor. As in earlier times the ground evidently sloped away down to the north and west here. At the northern end of trench Q (FIG. 69: Section 3) two successive occupation surfaces (IV. 1 and 2) could be distinguished with a fill of earth (level 41) some 0.20–0.30 m thick between them. Both these surfaces continued westwards into trench X to abut against wall 49, which appears to have been the westward extension of wall 48 (Plan, FIG. 61).

It is not clear whether the area north of walls 48 and 49 was open ground or incorporated in a house at the time of the Period IV destruction. It may have been open ground, however, since it was evidently used for cooking. At the eastern end of trench X there were successive fire-places in Period IV above the spot where fires had been lit during Period V (FIG. 71: Section 5, *P–O*). The latest of these fire-places (hearth C) consisted of a shallow circular hollow filled with ash. Beside it on the west a large tripod cooking pot (1182) had been sunk into the occupation surface (IV. 2); this had been packed round with small stones, and almost touched the northern face of wall 49 (PLATE 25 (*c*)). A couple of large flat blocks of stone had been set in the earth by it to serve as pot-stands or seats, their tops being level with its rim. A small bowl (1048) with a hole deliberately bored through the bottom after firing was found in the area, and may have been used in connection with the cooking pot.

Another fire-place consisting of a shallow hollow filled with ash was noted in the north-western corner of trench Q (FIG. 69: Section 3, *R–S*). This was associated with the latest occupation surface (IV. 2) of Period IV there. But the edge of a fire-place that was in use in connection with the earlier occupation surface (IV. 1) appeared in the north-eastern corner of trench X (FIG. 69: Section 3, *N–O*, at the bottom of level 41).

House VII seems to have been long and narrow, and somewhat trapeze-shaped. The width of the floor between the walls at the eastern side of trench Q was *c.* 2.30 m, widening to *c.* 2.80 m at the western side. The walls, like those of the other houses in use at the time of the Period IV destruction, appear to have been constructed to a considerable, if not to their full height, in stone. When House VII was destroyed by fire the north wall (48 in trench Q and 49 in trench X) evidently collapsed outwards, covering the cooking place (hearth C) in trench X. No clay vases (apart from the cooking pot 1182 set in the earth by hearth C) and no burnt debris were noted on the surfaces covered by the collapsed walls. The lack of vases and of signs of burning here in contrast to what was found inside House VII supports the idea that the space to the north of it was open ground at the time of the Period IV destruction.

Collapsed walling (level 24) occupied the northern end of trench Q. This must have come from walls 48 and 35, or from 48 alone, if 35 was of Period V date and not contemporary with 48 or part of it. The surface on top of which the walling (level 24) had collapsed ran against the bottom of 35. If therefore 35 was the remains of a wall of Period V date, it was still exposed at the time of the Period IV destruction.

A thin deposit of white plaster-like material was noted here and there above 35, either immediately on top of the stones, or in the yellow clay over them. At the time of excavation this white deposit was taken to be the remains of plaster. But the white deposit was actually incorporated in the layer of yellow clay in places, and there was nothing else to suggest the use of lime plaster at Emporio as early as this. Similar white deposits were eventually found in trench G (FIG. 64), where a careful study suggested that they had been formed by water seeping down from above and meeting comparatively hard surfaces.

The floor of House VII consisted of a thin layer of green clay which could be traced rising in a curve against the northern face of wall 47. Some twenty-five or more clay vases were recovered from the burnt debris resting on this floor in the area at the foot of the wall (FIG. 63. PLATE 21 (*a*), (*b*)). They included some of the finest and most interesting vases found during the excavations. All had been shattered, and a number of the fragments had been much discoloured by the fire which destroyed the house. Several of the vases were found lying upside down, notably the fine bowls 1073, 1081, 1082. Perhaps they had been placed that way to prevent dust from accumulating inside them when they were not in use, whether on the floor like the stone mortar in House IV (Plan, FIG. 61: A), or on a wooden bench or shelf of some kind set against the wall. A rectangular post standing in a hole about 0.20 m wide by 0.26 m deep against the face of wall 47 might have had some connection with such a bench or shelf (PLATE 21 (*c*)). The green clay floor could be traced running against the edge of the post-hole. The post would have projected about one half its width beyond the face of the mud plaster which appears to have coated the wall. Traces of smaller wooden beams or planks, about 0.10–0.12 m wide, could be detected above the floor of the house among the vases and beyond them to the north. These beam traces ran more or less from north to south at right angles to wall 47. They might have come from a bench or shelf, if they were not rafters which helped to support the roof.

When House VII was built some debris (levels 62, 63) seems to have been piled into the space between its south wall (47) and the north retaining wall of the road leading to the well. This narrow space, about 1.30 m across on the eastern side of trench Q (Section 4), but widening to 2.00 m where it disappeared into the western Section 5, was clearly open ground. An elaborate fire-place (hearth D) was constructed in the sloping surface here (PLATE 20 (*d*), (*e*)). This was *c.* 0.95 m in diameter. The base of it was formed by a layer of stones, with four alternate layers of pebbles and clay on top of them. Above the uppermost layer of clay was one of potsherds. The whole was surrounded by a ring of stones.

By the time of the Period IV destruction hearth D had been replaced by another fire-place

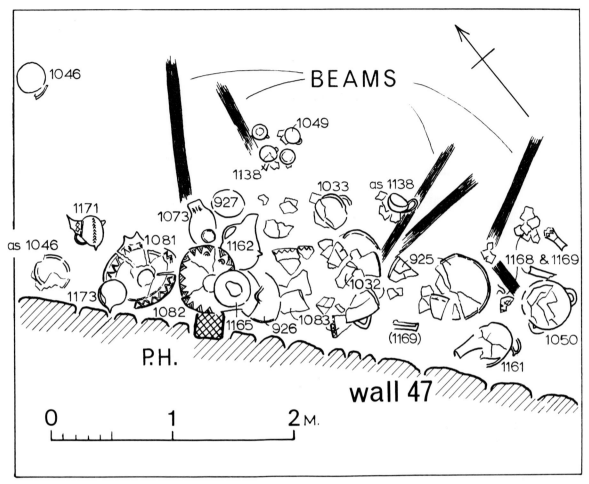

FIG. 63. Vases on floor of House VII of Period IV in trench Q.

(hearth E) of similar type at a slightly higher level just to the east of it (PLATE 20 (c)). This had no stone kerb round it, and was somewhat oval in shape, measuring 1.00 × 1.08 m across. It was sunk about 0.20 m from the latest Period IV occupation surface, cutting into the earlier surface associated with hearth D. Above a foundation of stones was a layer of potsherds serving as the base for three alternate layers of pebbles and clay. The sides of the shallow pit in which this hearth was built had a thin clay lining (c. 0.01 m thick).

These fire-places (hearths D and E) were evidently built for cooking in what appears to have been a narrow strip of open ground sheltered by high walls. Their elaborately constructed foundations were no doubt meant to help retain the heat from the fires lit on them. The embers would have been raked aside, and bread or other food baked on the hot surface. Such hearths would therefore have fulfilled some of the functions of enclosed ovens, of which there were no traces as early as this at Emporio.

About 1 m to the east of hearth E was a hole, more or less circular, about 0.30 m in diameter at the top but tapering downwards to a rounded end. It had evidently been sunk from the latest

Period IV occupation surface to a depth of *c.* 0.43 m. The upper part of it was packed round with stones, the lowest of them coinciding with the earlier surface associated with hearth D. The hole appears to have held a large post, although there were no traces of carbonized wood in it. It was filled with soft dark red earth.

Area to the south of the well (trench G)
No deposits assignable to Period V were recognised in trench G on the southern side of the roadway leading to the well. The walls (50, 51) of Period IV here were built directly on top of the ruin debris (levels 91, 93) of the massive Period VI wall 20. After these walls had been erected the space to the north of wall 50 was levelled with a fill of small stones and pebbles (level 54), while a thick deposit of ash with burnt debris and stones (levels 51–53) was dumped on the southern side of the wall as make-up for the floor of a house (VIII). This deposit below the floor of House VIII corresponds to the ashy deposit (levels 48–50) below the earliest floor of the contemporary House IV immediately to the west. The ashy deposit under the floor of House IV merged into the fill of stones (level 54) on the northern side of wall 50 of House VIII. From this stoney fill (level 54) a large amount of fragmentary pottery was recovered.

Wall 50 was exceptionally well preserved (PLATE 22 (*d*)). It was found standing to a height of nearly 2 m above the latest floor of House VIII. This may have been the full height of the wall in its original state, since the top of it was flat and regular, as if prepared to receive the rafters supporting the roof of the house. Like the equally well preserved wall 44 (PLATE 24 (*b*)) of the contemporary House V, wall 50 measured between 0.50–0.65 m at the bottom narrowing to *c.* 0.42 m at the top. A doorway about 0.50 m wide led through it from House VIII into the space to the north.

Only the north-eastern corner of House VIII lay within the area of excavation in trench G. It is therefore uncertain whether the house was rectangular like House IV, or narrow and trapeze-shaped as House VII in trenches Q and X appears to have been. But the position of the associated post-holes (P.H. (E) and (F)) seems more in harmony with the idea of a narrow house with the length running down the slope from east to west. The doorway in wall 50 would then have been at the eastern end of one of the long sides of the house.

Two successive floor levels could be distinguished in the part of House VIII excavated. The earlier of these (IV. 1) was marked by a thin layer of green clay, like the green clay floor (IV. 1) in the contemporary House IV just to the west. At the western end of the part of the house excavated the two floor levels merged, and the original green clay floor was still in use here at the time of the final destruction of the house by fire. Elsewhere the latest floor (IV. 2) was only separated from the green clay floor (IV. 1) by a few centimetres.

Even the latest floor (IV. 2) in House VIII was some 0.70 m lower than the contemporary occupation surface north of wall 50. This meant that the threshold in the doorway leading from the house into the space north of it was set comparatively high in wall 50, like the doorway in wall 37 of House IV. As in that case, there were probably wooden steps by which the threshold was reached from inside the house.

Two post-hoes were identified on the southern edge of trench G. One of these (P.H. (E)) may have been associated with the earlier green clay floor (IV. 1) in House VIII, the other (P.H. (F)) belonging with the latest floor (IV. 2). The earlier post-hole (E), which showed in Section 1 (FIG. 67), was between 0.25–0.35 m in diameter and *c.* 0.60 m deep. The hole for the post was packed round with stones and fragments of pottery. All traces of the post itself had disappeared. Perhaps it was removed when the floor was remade at a slightly higher level and a new post-hole (F) was dug some 0.60 m to the west. Post-hole (F) was also packed round with stones.

A patch of dark grey ash just to the west of the doorway in wall 50 may indicate a place where fires were lit in association with the earlier floor (IV. 1) of the house. Above the latest floor (IV. 2) in the area between post-hole (F) and the eastern wall of the house were fragments of a large pithos which had evidently been standing in the corner here. A curious find was made on the floor below some fragments of this. It consisted of the bones of three feet, in two cases at least very well articulated, from a young adult pig (PLATE 22 (*e*), (*f*)). These were presumably ready for cooking, although, as Juliet Clutton-Brock observes in her report, they could hardly have been a delicacy. A few other small animal bones were noted in this corner of the house. A number of fragmentary clay vases were recovered from the burnt debris above the latest floor here.

Another curiosity in this area was a succession of thin layers of white deposit which had formed at various levels at a depth of between about 1.60 m and 2.20 m below the surface (FIG. 67: Section 1, and FIG. 64). This white deposit was clearly akin to that already noted above the

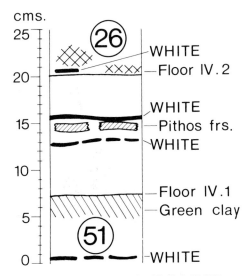

FIG. 64. Water-laid deposits in levels of Periods V–IV in trench G.

stump of wall 35 in trench Q. In trench G the deposit was in evidence over a wide area immediately on top of the debris of the Period IV fire-destruction, above level 25 that is to say, and below the stone fill (level 19) of Period III. But a thin layer of it covered much of the latest floor (IV. 2) of House VIII below the burnt debris (level 26) of the final destruction. Patches of the same white deposit were also observed below the latest floor (IV. 2) in House VIII, and just below the earlier green clay floor (IV. 1) there. In some places as many as three or four distinct layers of white deposit were observed in a depth of 0.15–0.20 m in this horizon. In the extreme southern corner of trench G for instance two layers of it some 2 or 3 cm apart were noted in the space of 0.15 m separating the latest floor (IV. 1) from the earlier green clay floor, while another layer was observed just below the green clay floor (IV. 1) in level 51 (FIG. 64).

These layers of white appear to be natural sediments of lime, deposited by water seeping through from above, and forming where comparatively hard surfaces were met. A white calcareous deposit like plaster was also noted at Thermi (*Thermi* 7, 32). What sounds like a comparable phenomenon appears to have been observed at a depth of about 1.50 m from the surface at Jarmo in Iraq, where it was noted that this was also the approximate maximum depth of the deeper-rooted plants (*Jarmo* 40).

At one spot on the south inner side of wall 50, just to the east of the doorway into House VIII, a vertical patch of white deposit was noted running parallel to the wall and only about 0.035 m away from it. This certainly looked very much like a coat of whitewash or thin lime plaster on the clay facing of the wall. But it may have been a natural deposit of the same kind as the horizontal ones in this area, forming in a crack between the wall and the fill beyond it.

The space to the north of wall 51 appears to have been surrounded by walls on all sides (PLATE 22 (*c*)). It may have been open ground serving as a yard for House VIII, since the only access to it seems to have been through the doorway in wall 50. Two occupation surfaces could be identified in this space separated by 0.20 m or less of ashy earth (level 36) which may have accumulated from the lighting of fires here. At the western end of the space and associated with the latest of these occupation surfaces (IV. 2) was a carefully prepared fire-place (hearth F). This consisted of a circular area of fire-hardened clay about 1.15 m across. As in the case of hearths D and E in trench Q, the clay had large flat fragments of pottery incorporated in it, and was laid on a basis of pebbles. A sinking about 0.40 m wide and 0.20 m deep ran across the centre of the fire-place and into Section 1. Our foreman, Mr. Ioannis Theotokas, suggested that the hollow may have been made for baking bread, the ashes being raked out of it, while the clay with its backing of potsherds retained the heat after the manner of an oven. Three circular clay discs (diam. 0.65–0.85 m) assignable to the Late Neolithic from the Alepotripa cave near Diros in the Mani were thought to have been used for baking bread, ashes from a nearby hearth being piled on top of them to heat them: one appears to have had a hollow in the top like our hearth (*AAA* iv (1971) 300 f.).

Like the contemporary hearths D and E this elaborately built fire-place, designed perhaps for baking, appears to have been in the open air. The virtual absence of any traces of burnt debris in the space also strongly suggests that it was open ground at the time of the Period IV destruction. On the other hand the remains of a number of smashed clay vases were recovered from above the latest occupation surface (IV. 2) of Period IV here (PLATE 22 (*c*)). Elsewhere in this horizon clay vases were only found in any numbers above floors that were clearly inside houses.

(e) Periods III and II
(FIG. 65. PLATES 21–25)

The pottery of these periods is still handmade, and seems to belong to a horizon contemporary with the end of Troy I and the early part of Troy II.

The relatively sophisticated character of much of the pottery from levels of Period II, notably of the large elaborately incised jars with lids of which only fragments were recovered, might suggest the possibility of a later date for this horizon. But the wheelmade pottery of the succeeding Period I seems to equate with that of Troy II rather than later.

i. Period III

The fire at the end of Period IV destroyed the houses, but in many cases at any rate left the walls standing and relatively undamaged, so that only some 0.30–0.40 m of burnt debris covered the floors. It would not have been difficult to restore the houses by repairing the walls and roofs and laying new floors on top of the burnt debris. Instead of this, however, the decision was taken to extend the raised area round the well into a wide terrace. The western face of this terrace (wall 52) seems to have formed part of a massive defence wall.

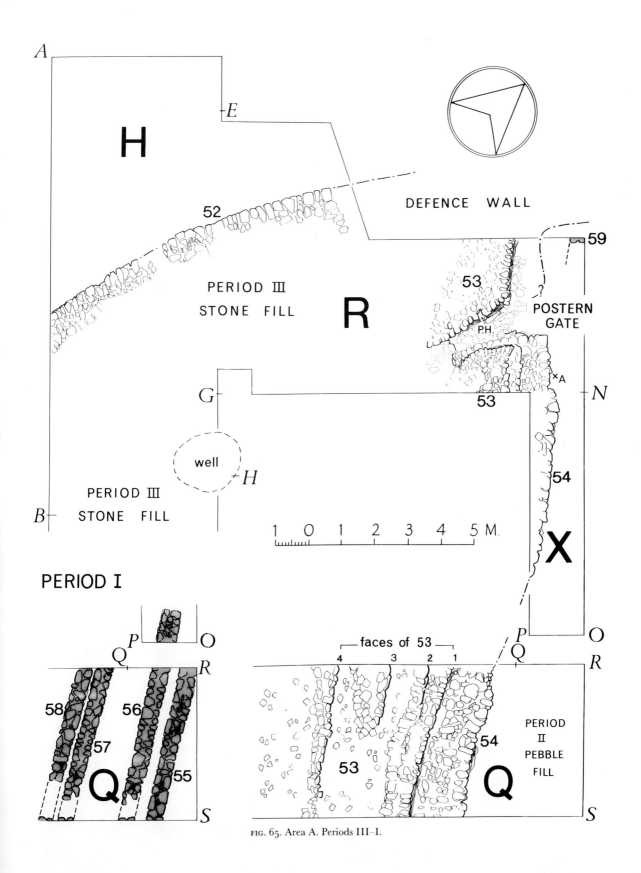

FIG. 65. Area A. Periods III–I.

The terrace was made by dumping a close-packed fill of stones (level 19) into the spaces between the walls of the fire-destroyed houses of Period IV (PLATE 22 (*a*)). The stones used for this fill did not appear to have come from destroyed houses elsewhere on the site: they tended to be a good deal larger than the stones used for building the walls of houses in Period IV. The fill of stones was dumped into the ruins of the houses before any rubbish had accumulated on top of the burnt debris there. This indicates that the terrace was constructed almost immediately after the fire-destruction at the end of Period IV.

There was hardly any pottery in the fill of large stones (level 19) which formed the terrace. What is published as being from deposits of Period III evidently includes a good deal that really came from the Period IV destruction level. Pottery, however, from deposits in other areas of the excavation, resembling that of Period II in character, but stratified below deposits of classic Period II, may in fact date from the time when the Period III terrace round the well was in use and before it was extended on the north by the great Period II fill. Such deposits are stage 7 in Area B, and perhaps stage 2 in C. 1 and stage 2 in F.

The line of the façade of the stone-filled terrace could be traced on the west (wall 52) and on the north (wall 53). The terrace retaining wall on the north (53) was found standing at the time of excavation to a height of *c.* 1.75 m, and it may never have been much higher than this. The western retaining wall (52) was less well preserved, being represented by a single line of stones in Section 2 on the northern side of trench H (FIG. 68), although it survived to a height of 1.20 m on the southern side of the trench (FIG. 67: Section 1).

Wall 53 at any rate seems to have been built with a system of multiple faces. Four such faces could be distinguished set one behind the other at intervals of about 1 m. These showed most clearly on the western side of trench Q in Section 5 (FIG. 71) (PLATE 21 (*e*), (*f*)). The four faces of wall here were evidently part of a single building scheme: they do not reflect successive extensions. Stones were piled behind each wall face during the course of its construction, so that the successive faces of wall had no back to them: an obvious way of building terrace walls, and one still found in use in Chios and other parts of Greece today. a similar system of multiple faces appears to have been adopted in building the town walls of Thermi V (*Thermi* 43 f. figs. 18, 19 and Plan 6). It is not in fact actually stated that these walls at Thermi were multiple faces; but this seems likely from the stone-by-stone plans. Since Thermi V may date from the period of Troy II before the use of wheelmade pottery, it could have been roughly contemporary with Period II at Emporio.

The faces of these walls were constructed with large and medium-sized blocks of stone placed in a somewhat irregular manner, which contrasted with the comparatively neat and professional-looking style of the walling of the Period IV houses. The difference in construction may reflect, not a change of population, but the fact that house walls were erected by experts, while the building of defence works and terrace walls of a public character was something in which the whole community shared.

Wall 52 seems to have continued northwards beyond the limits of trench R to merge into the western face of a massive defence wall about 2.50 m thick. This could be traced in the small soundings FF, LL, OO, running down the slope in the direction of the harbour. Like the terrace walls (52, 53) of the platform round the well, this defence wall was built without any foundations, its bottom courses resting on top of the debris of the fire-destroyed houses of Period IV. Its faces were constructed in the same rather crude and irregular manner as the faces of the terrace walls (52, 53). But the latter appear to have been more or less vertical, while both faces of the contemporary defence wall had a distinct batter like the Period VI wall 20.

In the lee of the defence wall at the northern end of trench R was the entrance to a sloping passage which led through the western part of the terrace wall 53 to the platform round the well (Plan, FIG. 65: Postern Gate). At its narrowest point this passage was only about 0.50 m wide. A vertical slot *c.* 0.15 m wide and 0.20 m deep in the wall flanking it on the western side had evidently housed a wooden beam (Elevation, FIG. 66) (PLATE 25 (*e*)). This may have formed part of a gate that could be closed to bar access to the well.

At some point, whether as part of the original scheme of the terrace round the well or later, an outer skin (54) about 0.50 m thick was added to the face of wall 53 (PLATE 21 (*e*)). This was only traced with certainty in the area to the east of the passage leading to the well. It seems likely, however, that it also existed on the western side of the passage, but was removed during the course of excavation under the impression that it was a mass of fallen stone.

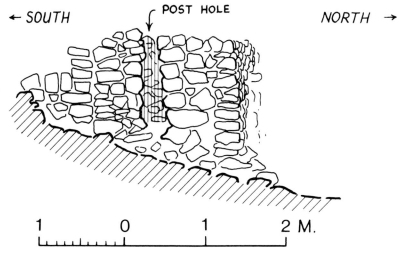

FIG. 66. Postern Gate of Period II in trench R: elevation of west side.

ii. Period II (Plan, FIG. 65)

Parts of the latest outer face (wall 54) of the northern terrace wall round the well eventually collapsed. The wall does not appear to have been repaired after this. Instead the platform round the well was extended it seems for some distance towards the north. A great fill of pebbles and rubbish was dumped at the northern ends of trenches Q and R and in trench X to make this extension. This fill was presumably held in place by a new terrace wall which lay further north beyond the excavated area.

Vast quantities of potsherds (but no complete vases) were recovered from the fill. The pottery from the different levels in the fill was kept apart, and that from the upper group of levels was studied separately from that from the lower levels; but no obvious differences could be distinguished. The pottery assignable to Period II was noticeably more evolved, less rugged in appearance than what had been in use at the time of the Period IV destruction. But it was still handmade, and seemed to date from a late phase of Troy I or the early part of Troy II. Other finds from the fill included numbers of spindle whorls and a shell button (SHELL No. 61) from trench R (Plan, FIG. 65: A).

Metal tools must have already been in general use by this time. The almost complete lack of obsidian from levels of Period II is in harmony with this. But it was surprising to find a large amount of flint, including a high proportion of cores and core fragments, as Perry G. Bialor has noted in PART IV. The flint must have been brought to the site for some purpose, and it is tempting to wonder if chips of it may not have been employed for arming wooden threshing sleds (*tribula*) of the type still in use in Greece into recent times.

(f) Period I

The only deposit of pottery assignable to Period I (the horizon of Troy II) in Area A came from the fill of large stones and earth (level 4) in the well in trench G (FIG. 68: Section 2). The well appears to have been closed during or at the end of Period I. Very little pottery was recovered from the fill; but it included one or two fragments of wheelmade vases with a red wash like those from Area F on the Acropolis assignable to Period I.

The well was an irregular oval in shape. It had been lined with stone from top to bottom. The south side of it had collapsed at some point down to the level of the stone platform dating from the beginning of Period VI. At this level the well measured *c.* 2.30 × 2.10 m across. The stone-lined sides were more or less vertical, but with bulges and irregularities owing to the rough character of the lining, which was built with medium-sized rubble. Below the level of the platform made at the beginning of Period VI the stone lining seemed to be homogeneous, all of one construction; which suggests that the well may have been lined with stone for the first time then, even if it was already in use earlier in Period VII. In contrast to this, the 2 m of walling preserved above the level of the Period VI platform on the northern side of the well showed clear traces of various phases of construction, which corresponded to the successive rises in the level of the pebbled area round the well and of the roadway leading down to it from the east. When the well finally went out of use and was closed in Period I it was presumably replaced by another well or wells, which may have been in lower ground to the north or west included in the area of the settlement at the time.

Remains of four walls (55–58) running parallel down the slope from east to west were noted in the top of the Period II fill at the northern end of trench Q. These walls being just below the surface were only preserved one course high at the eastern end (FIG. 70: Section 4) rising to two courses in the western Section 5 (FIG 71). They were narrow, only *c.* 0.40–0.50 m wide, built of quite large stones, some of which extended the full width of the wall. No floors or occupation surfaces which belonged with them could be detected. Possibly they were not the walls of houses, but had formed the successive outer skins of some later defence wall. The space between walls 56 and 57 was only *c.* 1.20–1.30 m at its widest, while the maximum distance from the northern face of wall 55 to the southern face of wall 58 was *c.* 3.60 m, not unduly wide for a wall of defence. Wall 56 could be traced into the eastern end of trench X. A scrap of walling (59) just below the surface in the north-western corner of trench R (FIG. 73: Section 7) might have been a continuation of wall 58.

Owing to the lack of floors or stratified deposits associated with these walls it was impossible to date them with accuracy. They were probably built at the end of Period II or in Period I, but may have been of even later construction. The evidence from trenches HH and JJ of Area C. 3 to the south of Area A suggests that occupation continued in this part of the site into the Middle and Late Bronze Ages. No Bronze Age deposits later than Period I were identified in Area A, although sherds of Middle Bronze Age matt-painted and of Mycenaean wares were recovered from surface levels along with Greek and Roman debris. Area A would have continued to form a

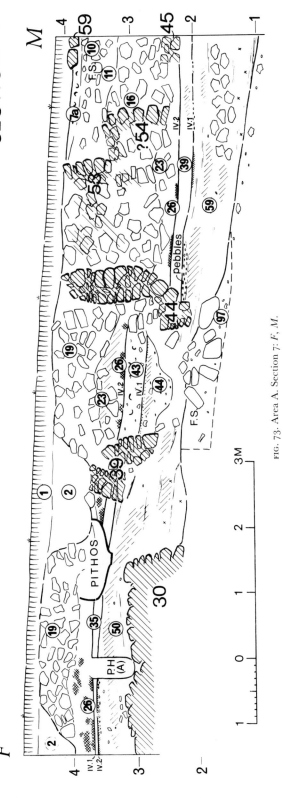

FIG. 73. Area A. Section 7: *F, M.*

FIGS. 67–73. Area A. Sections 1–7. Levels:

Post-Bronze Age: (1) Disturbed surface soil (all Sections); (1a) Disturbed surface soil with stones (Section 6); (2) Blackish with small stones. Recent hill wash (Sections 1, 2, 7); (3) Dark brown with stones, later Greek pottery, and tile fragments (Section 1).

Period I: (4) Earth with large stones. Fill of well (Sections 2, 6).

Period II: (5) Ashy white with some pebbles and sherds (Sections 3, 4, 5, 6); (5a) Band of grey ash in level 5 (Sections 3, 6); (6) Hard sandy (Sections 3, 5); (7) Light brown ashy with pebbles, small stones, and sherds (Sections 3, 4, 5, 6); (7a) Light brown ashy with masses of sherds (Sections 3, 7); (8) Hard reddish brown ashy (Section 3); (9) Soft reddish brown ashy with pebbles and small stones (Sections 3, 6); (9a) Grey ash in level 9 (Section 3); (10) Stones (Sections 3, 7); (11) Brown with stones (Section 7); (12) Reddish ashy (Section 3); (13) Yellow clay, loose pebbles and small stones, with pockets of white ash (Sections 3, 6); (14) Soft light brown ashy (Sections 3, 4); (15) Fallen stone, apparently from wall 54 (Sections 3, 4, 5); (16) Fallen stone, apparently from walls 53, 54 (Sections 3, 7); (17) Layer of sherds (Section 3); (18) Large stones and earth. Possibly fall from wall 52 (Section 1).

Period III: (19) Reddish with stones. Fill behind walls 52, 53 (Sections 1, 2, 4, 5, 6, 7).

Period IV: (a) *Period IV. 2*—(20) Thick reddish clay with stones. Possibly fall from wall 38 (Section 1); (21) Red-brown with charcoal (Section 4); (22) Stones, apparently fallen from wall 47 (Section 4); (23) Red with large stones (Section 7); (24) Light brown with large stones, apparently fallen from wall 48 (Sections 3, 4, 5); (25) Red clay (Sections 1, 2, 3, 4, 5, 6); (26) Red clay with charred wood (all Sections); (27) Hard sandy yellow (Section 5); (28) Hard white with pebbles, apparently a new surface after the collapse of the well lining (Section 2); (29) Whitish with pebbles. Possibly the same as level 28 (Section 6); (30) Fill of large stones and pebbles, apparently placed behind the well lining after it was renewed in Period IV (Section 2). (b) *Period IV. 1/2*—(31) Hearth, associated with floors IV.1 and 2 in House IV (Section 1); (32) Burnt red with ash. Debris from hearths D and E (Section 4); (33) Ash from hearths D and E, as level 32 (Section 5); (34) Light brown, with abundant flecks of charcoal and sherds, against wall 23 (Section 5). (c) *Period IV. 1*—(35) Red clay above IV.1 floor (Sections 1, 2, 7); (36) Brown earth with charcoal and ash, and occasional patches of red clay, above IV. 1 floor (Sections 1, 5, 6); (37) Fill of small stones below IV. 2 surface and above level 38 west of House IV (Section 1); (38) Yellow clay with ash above IV. 1 surface west of House IV (Section 1); (39) Reddish above IV. 1 floor in House V (Sections 3, 7); (40) Gritty reddish with some charcoal above IV. 1 floor in House VI (Sections 3, 6); (41) Dark brown streaked with red with flecks of charcoal, above IV. 1 surface east of House VI (Sections 3, 4, 5); (42) Reddish with ash above IV. 1 pebble floor on east side of trench R (Section 6); (43) Light brown with pebbles and sherds in path in trench R (Section 7). (d) *Below floors and surfaces of IV. 1*—(44) Reddish with pebbles with clean sand above, below level 43 (Section 7); (45) Reddish, pebbly, make-up for IV. 1 floor, below level 42 (Section 6); (46) Shallow pit with ash, apparently a hearth, below the green clay IV. 1 floor in House IV (Section 2).

Period V: (a) *Fill before building of Period IV houses*—(47) Loose fill of small stones with bands of ash below IV. 1 surface west of wall 26 (Section 1); (48) Ashy fill below IV. 1 floor of House IV. Grey and reddish ash (Section 1); (49) As level 48, but reddish brown with occasional stones and pebbles (Section 1); (50) As level 48, but reddish with stones and pebbles (Sections 1, 2); (51) Ashy fill below floor of House VIII. Grey ashy (Sections 1, 4, 5); (52) As level 51, but hard reddish (Section 1); (53) As level 51, but soft reddish with charcoal, stones and pebbles (Section 1); (54) Loose fill of stones below IV. 1 surface north of House VIII (Section 1); (55) White ash with flecks of charcoal (Section 2); (56) Ashy fill below IV. 1 floor of House V. White and black ash with burnt red earth, and pebbles forming make-up for floor (Section 3); (57) Reddish brown with stones below level 56 (Section 3); (58) Reddish with grey ash below level 57 (Section 3); (59) Ashy fill below IV. 1 floor of House V. Equivalent of levels 56–58. Reddish and whitish ash with abundant charcoal and some pebbles (Section 7); (60) Light brown ashy streaked with red, with some stones, above V. 2 floor in House II (House VI of Period IV) (Sections 3, 6); (61) Yellowish light brown below IV. 1 surface north of House VII (Section 3); (62) Loose fill of small stones and dark brown earth, behind wall 47 of House VII of Period IV (Section 4); (63) Brown earth with stones and stone chips, behind wall 47 as level 62 (Section 5); (64) Brown earth with black and red ash and some stones, below level 63 and running under wall 47 (Section 5); (65) Hard sandy yellow above a thin layer of ash, apparently continuous with level 64 (Section 5); (66) Pit, sunk from bottom of level 65. Yellow with ash (Section 5); (67) Brown clay with stones and pebbles, running under wall 43 (Section 6); (68) Yellow clay with small stones and pebbles, behind wall 32 and below level 67 (Section 6); (69) Light brown clay with stones and pebbles above a layer of ash, below level 68 (Section 6). (b) *Roadway above V. 2 surface*—(70) Reddish with pebbles and some ash (Sections 2, 4, 5, 6); (71) Brown with large stones and ash, apparently the equivalent of level 70, west of the well (Section 2); (72) Red clay with stones. Possibly the equivalent of level 71 (Section 6, *G–N*); (73) Reddish with some pebbles and sherds. Possibly the equivalent of level 70 (Section 6, *G–N*). (c) *Ruin debris above V. 2*—(74) Yellow clay, apparently dissolved walling of mud or mud-brick, above surface of Period V (Sections 3, 4); (75) Hard clean sandy yellow, apparently dissolved walling of mud or mud-brick, above floor of House III (Sections 4, 5). (d) *Above surfaces assignable to Period V. 1*—(76) Ash, with burnt reddish above, running below wall 31 (Section 1); (77) Light brown with occasional streaks of red and some charcoal, below V. 2 floor in House II (Sections 3, 6). (e) *Before the building of wall 30 and below V. 1 floors*—(78) Loose stones with sherds and pebbles behind wall 30 (Section 2); (79) Dark brown sand behind wall 30, below level 78 (Section 2); (80) Large stones, apparently fallen from wall 20, behind wall 30 (Section 6); (81) Brown with stones and sherds below V. 1 surface, north of wall 30 and west of House II (Sections 3, 6); (82) Dark brown, sandy, with charcoal, below V. 1 floor of House II. Possibly the equivalent of level 81, although different in character (Section 3); (83) Layer of sherds under level 81, running below wall 30 (Section 6); (83a) White ash with abundant sherds, running below wall 30 in trench H. Presumably the equivalent of level 83 (Section 2); (84) Hard light brown with pebbles, above a thin layer of charcoal, running below level 83 (Section 2). (f) *Road below V. 2 surface*—(85) White pebbles and stones (Sections 2, 4, 5, 6); (86) Reddish with pebbles and stones, apparently the equivalent of level 85 west of the well (Sections 2, 6).

Period VI: (a) Roadway above VI. 3—(87) White with pebbles (Sections 2, 4, 6); (88) Brown clay, probably the equivalent of level 92 (Sections 2, 4, 5, 6); (89) Brown to yellow clay, apparently continuation of level 88 west of the well (Sections 2, 6). *(b) Debris of wall 20A*—(90) Soft black with loose stones, north of wall 29, and apparently overlying level 91 (Section 2); (91) Hard bright yellow clay (Sections 1, 4, 5, 6); (92) Soft brown earth with large stones (Section 1); (93) Hard light brown clay with stones and pebbles, below level 92 (Sections 1, 4, 5); (94) Light shading to dark brown clay with large stones and pebbles, apparently the equivalent of levels 92 and 93 (Section 2); (95) Yellowish clay, north of wall 20. Probably the equivalent of level 91 (Sections 3, 6); (96) Dark brown with stones and pebbles below level 95 (Sections 3, 6); (97) Brown with stones and pebbles. Possibly the equivalent of level 96 (Section 7); (98) Brown with pebbles and some charcoal below level 74 (Sections 3, 5); (99) Dark brown with small stones and largish pebbles, apparently continuation of level 98 to east in trench Q (Sections 3, 4); (100) Light sandy brown with some small pebbles. Possibly continuation of level 98 to south (Section 5); (101) Brown with some small stones behind wall 34 (Section 5); (102) Fill inside wall 20A. Clean dark brown clay with stones and pebbles (Sections 1, 6). *(c) Debris of wall 20 below that of wall 20A*—(103) Gritty light brown with stones and pebbles (Sections 1, 4, 5, 6); (104) Hard reddish clay with some stones and pebbles, continuing level 103 to west in trench H (Section 1); (105) Dark brown clay with large stones, west of level 104 in trench H (Section 1); (106) Light brown to yellow with stones and pebbles. Probably equivalent of level 103 (Section 2); (107) Red clay with stones, cf. level 104 (Section 2). *(d) Roadway below VI. 3 surface*—(108) Hard light brown with some pebbles (Sections 2, 4, 5, 6); (109) Hard light brown with whitish and reddish streaks; sandy with small pebbles and occasional stones and sherds. Apparently continuation of level 108 west of well (Section 2); (110) Soft brown with pebbles, stones and sherds. Equivalent of level 108 (Section 6); (111) Soft whitish brown with some pebbles below VI. 2 (Sections 2, 4, 5, 6).

Period VII: (a) South of roadway and well—(112) Soft whitish below road surface assignable to VI. 1. Probably equivalent of level 121 (Section 2); (113) White with pebbles and many sherds. Possibly equivalent of level 112 west of well (Section 2); (114) Layer of pebbles. Possibly equivalent of level 113 (Section 6); (115) Loose earth with stones, pebbles and many sherds (Sections 1, 6); (116) Light brown with small stones and pebbles. Possibly continuation of level 115 to west in trench H (Section 1); (117) Dark reddish brown, with patches of large stones and pebbles, speckled with white. Probably continuation of level 116 to west (Section 1); (118) Yellowish speckled with white, cf. level 117 (Section 2); (119) Soft reddish with white ash and sherds (Section 1); (120) Soft whitish brown with charcoal and pebbles. Continuation of level 119 to east (Sections 1, 5); (121) Hard pebbly below level 120. Probably equivalent of level 112 (Section 5); (122) White ashy (Sections 1, 2, 4, 5); (123) Soft light brown to whitish ashy below level 122 (Sections 1, 4); (124) Dark brown with stones and many sherds, south of wall 19 (Section 5); (125) Hard light brown with pebbles. Probably equivalent of level 124 (Section 6); (126) Soft brown whitish with stones. Probably equivalent of levels 124, 125 (Section 2). *(b) North of roadway and well*—(127) Brown with pebbles and small stones, apparently fallen from wall 18 (Section 4); (128) Brown with stones fallen from wall 18. Equivalent of level 127 (Section 5); (129) Dark brown with pebbles and small stones, cf. level 127. Possibly continuation of levels 127, 128 (Section 5); (130) Dark brown with charcoal and some pebbles. Probably continuation of level 129 (Sections 3, 4, 5). *(c) Roadway and well area*—(131) Soft ashy, reddish and whitish, with stones and many sherds (Sections 2, 5); (132) Soft light brown with pebbles and many sherds, apparently continuation of level 131 (Section 2); (133) Very hard light brown, sandy with pebbles. Probably equivalent of upper part of level 131 (Section 4); (134) Soft brown whitish with pebbles and stones, apparently fallen from walls 18, 19. Probably equivalent of lower part of level 131 (Section 4). *(d) Below wall 19*—(135) Hard light brown pebbly (Sections 2, 4, 5, 6); (136) Pebbles, below level 135 (Section 6); (137) Brown with large stones and pebbles (Section 6).

Period VIII: (a) Area A (trench G)—(138) Dark brown with stones and small pebbles, apparently fallen from wall 10 complex (Sections 1, 5); (139) Loose fill of stones with dark brown earth, south of wall 16 (Sections 1, 4); (140) Fill of hard brown with some stones and pebbles, below level 139 (Sections 1, 4, 5); (141) Brown with stones above floor VIII. 2 (Sections 1, 4); (142) Yellowish brown above floor VIII. 1 (Sections 1, 4); (143) Very hard reddish brown clay with occasional pebbles, above wall 4 (Sections 1, 5). *(b) Area B (trench Q)*—(144) Loose fill of small stones with dark brown earth. Apparently equivalent of level 139 north of wall 14A (Sections 2, 4, 5); (145) Fill of hard light brown, gritty, with small stones and pebbles (Sections 2, 4, 5); (146) Fallen stones from wall 15 (Sections 4, 5); (147) Brown with stones and pebbles at bottom of level 146 (Sections 4, 5); (148) Yellowish sandy with small pebbles and stones. Possibly accumulation against face of wall 10 before building of wall 15 (Sections 4, 5). *(c) Area C (trench H)*—(149) Clay with large stones (Section 1); (150) Red clay with small stones. Probably equivalent of upper part of level 149 (Section 2); (151) Yellow clay with stones. Probably equivalent of lower part of level 149 (Section 2).

Period IX: (a) Area A (trench G)—(152) Fill of soft reddish brown earth with large stones, below wall 10 (Sections 1, 5); (153) Yellowish brown earth with large stones below level 152 (Sections 1, 5); (154) Dark yellow brown with pebbles. Fill below floor VIII. 1 (Sections 1, 4); (155) As level 154, with small stones (Sections 1, 4). *(b) Area B (trench Q)*—(156) Light brown, gritty, with some pebbles (Sections 4, 5); (157) Dark brown with some stones and pebbles. Possibly continuation of level 156 (Section 3); (158) Yellow clay with stones (Sections 4, 5); (159) Dark brown, gritty, with pebbles (Section 5); (160) Stone fill (Sections 3, 4, 5). *(c) Area C (trench H)*—(161) Earth with stones, above floor with charcoal associated with walls 5 and 8 (Section 1); (162) Yellow clay with stones between walls 8 and 9 (Section 1).

Period X: (a) Area A (trench G)—(163) Dark yellow brown with some fallen stones, above floor with hearth (Sections 1, 4); (164) Yellow clay (Sections 1, 4). *(b) Area B (trench Q)*—(165) Yellowish speckled with white, with pebbles and stones, south of wall 2 (Sections 4, 5); (166) As level 165, but without stones, north of wall 2 (Section 4); (167) Yellow clay with skulls and vases, below level 166 (Section 4); (168) Yellow clay, below level 165 (Sections 4, 5). *(c) Area C (trench H)*—(169) Yellow clay at water level, west of wall 3 (Section 1).

kind of raised platform projecting from the foot of the Acropolis hill and dominating the parts of the settlement to the north, west and south of it. Its exposed situation would have led to the disappearance through erosion of any later deposits which might once have existed there.

(2) Area B: trenches B–E on the slope of the Acropolis hill above Area A to the south
(Plan and Sections, FIGS. 74–76. PLATE 26)

During the first year of the excavations in 1952 a line of four trenches (B, C, D, E) 3 m wide was opened on the steep slope of the Acropolis hill to the south of Area A (Plan, FIG. 48).

Trench E at the lower western end of the line was not carried down below 1.40 m, since a deep layer of hard stoney earth was found to have accumulated on top of the Bronze Age deposits here. The highest building level, which began to appear at a depth of 1.25 m below the surface, seems to have been Mycenaean, as in trench HH which was opened in 1954 a few metres to the south.

Stage 1

Trench B at the upper end of this line of trenches hit the rock at a depth of between 0.50 m and 1 m. Pottery recovered from immediately above the rock here (FIG. 75: level 5) seemed to be early in character, mostly assignable to Periods IX–VIII, although with a mixture of some later elements. This suggests that the early settlement extended up the slope of the Acropolis hill at least as far as trench B. A stump of wall preserved in the north section (FIG. 75) may have belonged to the same horizon (stage 6) as the granary in trench C described below.

Stages 2–5

Trenches C and D were also excavated to the rock, which sloped sharply down at the western end in D. The lowest deposit above the rock here (level 28) consisted of a stoney fill with pottery assignable to Period V (stage 2). A thick band of yellow clay (27) above this fill appears to have been put as make-up for the floor of a house which was eventually destroyed by fire in Period IV. On this floor was a layer of black ash (20) with charred wood and burnt red debris (19) above it (stage 4). From the burnt debris came a number of clay vases comparable with ones from the Period IV destruction level in Area A.

The contemporary floor up the slope to the east appears to be level 21, although this lies some 2.00–2.50 m higher. Large fragments of characteristic Period IV vases were recovered from the debris (13) above it (stage 5). Below this floor, which consisted of a thin layer of gravel (level 21), were two similar floors (23 and 25) assignable it seems to Period V (stage 3). These floors had evidently abutted against a wall (1) running across the trench from north to south (Plan, FIG. 74: 1). The wall was very irregular, and only preserved to a height of two courses, built on the rock with medium-sized to large stones. At right angles to it on the eastern side were the remains of a contemporary wall (2) which was also based upon the rock. Wall 2 was of poor construction, built with small stones, and only c. 0.30 m wide. It was found standing to a maximum height of 0.55 m.

Stage 6

At some point after the buildings represented by walls 1 and 2 went out of use, what appears to have been a granary was erected on top of the ruin debris from them (Plan, FIG. 74:2. PLATE 26

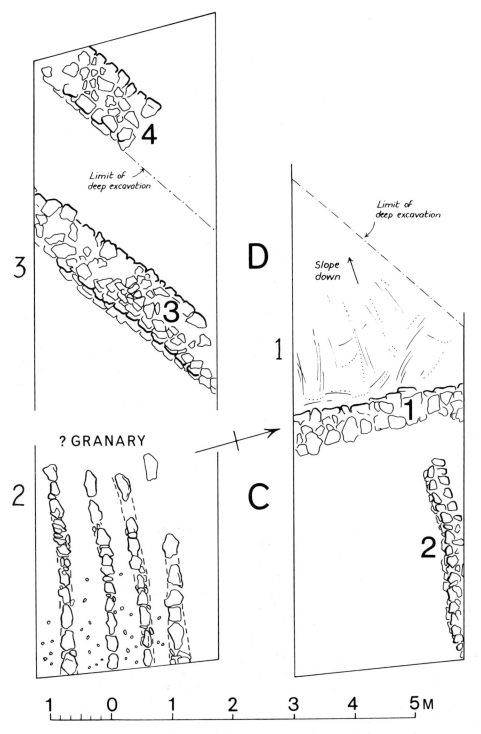

4

*Limit of
deep excavation*

3

3

D

*Limit of
deep excavation*

*Slope
down*

1

1

? GRANARY

2

C

2

| 1 | 0 | 1 | 2 | 3 | 4 | 5 M |

FIG. 74. Area B: trenches C, D. Plans 1–3.

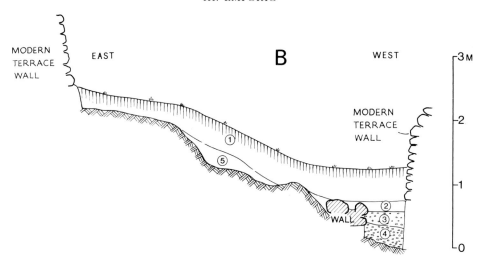

FIG. 75. Area B: trench B. Section (north side). Levels: (1) Surface; (2) Hard brown; (3) Soft blackish with pebbles. Possibly the equivalent of level 7 in trenches C, D; (4) Reddish with pebbles. Possibly the equivalent of level 11 in trench C; (5) Sticky yellow clay (Stage 1).

(*a*)–(*c*)). This consisted of a system of parallel channels running from east to west down the slope and filled with small pebbles, which merged in places into fine shingle, but not into sand. The pebble fill (11) (PLATE 26 (*a*), (*b*)) was between 0.10 m and 0.30 m deep, the deepest part of it being on the southern side of trench C where it showed in the section (FIG. 76). Red clay had been used to line the sides and even the bottoms of the channels. In places a layer of red clay mixed with pebbles (level 10) was noticed above the channels, and this may represent the remains of a floor; but only patches of it had survived. This floor must have been raised some 0.30 m or more above the level of the surrounding ground, because the channels filled with pebbles had not been dug from the surface but constructed on top of it. The walls separating the channels were c. 0.15–0.25 m wide, and preserved to a maximum height of 0.35 m. They had been constructed on the sloping surface with large stones set on edge, supplemented with small stones, all bonded together and coated with red clay. The original ground surface could be traced as a thin blackish layer running underneath the channels and continuing under the bottoms of the walls which divided them.

Little pottery was recovered from the channels and the dividing walls, and that little consisted only of scraps. The scraps from the pebble fill in the channels were mostly rolled and worn by water action. These rolled and water-worn sherds had no doubt been brought along with the pebbles from some beach or stream-bed near the settlement. The pottery from this complex seemed more akin to that of Period IV in character than to that of Period II. The complex may have been built in Period III soon after the Period IV destruction and about the same time as the great terrace round the well in Area A.

Similar constructions, with close-set parallel walls evidently supporting raised floors, were found in the more or less contemporary settlement at Thermi in Lesbos. These structures appear to have been peculiar to the earlier settlements, Thermi I and II (*Thermi* 10). The larger ones, which most closely resemble ours, were evidently free-standing (e.g. *Thermi* Plan 1 (Thermi I): one NE of Z (p. 14), two or three in E 7, and probably the large example in A 3 (p. 15); Plan 2 (Thermi II): one in Λ 1 (p. 22)). But some smaller platforms supported in this way were inside houses (e.g. *Thermi* 21 f. fig. 7 in Δ 1). Comparable raised floors inside houses of the Middle

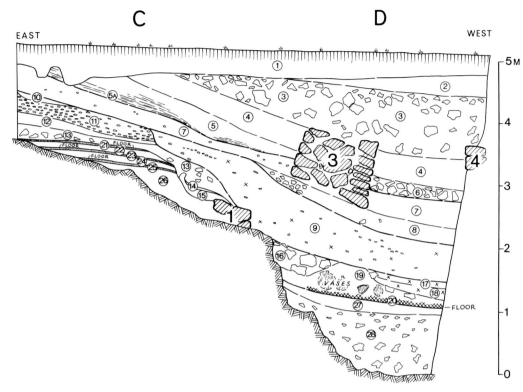

FIG. 76. Area B: trenches C, D. Section (south side). Levels:

Stage 10 (Period II, late ?): (1) Surface; (2) Hard brown with small stones; (3) Sticky dark brown clay with large stones.

Stage 9 (Period II, classic): (4) As (3), but without stones; (5) Grey ashy, shading into 5A on the east; (5A) Thick black ash; (6) Stones, apparently fallen from wall 3.

Stage 8 (Period II, classic): (7) Light greyish brown with small pebbles; (8) Loose earth with small stones.

Stage 7 (Period II, early): (9) Reddish with small pebbles and flecks of charcoal.

Stage 6 (Granary) (Period IV?): (10) Red Clay, above the pebbles of level 11; (11) Pebbles in channels.

Stage 5 (Period IV ?): (12) Blackish with small pebbles; (13) Hard gritty yellow clay with small stones; (14) Fallen fragment of floor; (15) Fallen fragment of debris below level 14.

Stage 4 (Period IV): (16) Fallen stones; (17) Greyish with specks of charcoal; (18) Reddish grey with specks of charcoal; (19) Burnt red, debris of fire-destroyed building, with vases; (20) Black ash above floor of fire-destroyed building.

Stage 3 (Period V): (21) Floor of fine gravel; (22) Hard yellow clay; (23) Floor, as level 21; (24) Gritty reddish clay; (25) Floor, as level 21; (26) Hard gritty reddish clay with small stones and pebbles.

Stage 2 (Period V, with earlier elements): (27) Yellow clay, make-up of floor of fire-destroyed building; (28) Dark brown earth with stones.

Bronze Age at Argissa (Gremnos) certainly belonged to structures for the storage of grain (*AA* 1955, 202 f. fig. 10; 1956, 144 fig. 1).

Our raised floor seems to have belonged to a free-standing granary, like the larger platforms of Thermi I and II. Granaries of this type may have already existed in the Aegean in the Neolithic. Parallel walls set close together in this way were noted at Saliagos where it was thought that they had supported floors (*Saliagos* 25 pl. xi (*a*), in L 3/4). But such granaries were probably not confined to the Aegean in early times. Similar groups of parallel walls were found at Hama in Syria in Phase K there (*Hama* ii. 1, 38 fig. 45: right). The great Hellenistic granaries at Pergamon had floors raised on comparable systems of parallel walls (e.g. G. Rickman, *Roman Granaries and Store Buildings* (Cambridge, 1971) 252 ff. fig. 61).

Stages 7 and 8

After the granary went out of use some degree of erosion evidently took place on the slope here. Following this a deep fill (levels 9–7) accumulated or was dumped in the area. The abundant pottery from this fill was assignable to Period II; but the pottery from level 9 seemed to reflect an earlier phase of II than that from levels 8 and 7 which was comparable with the classic Period II pottery from levels 5–14 in Area A. A fragment of baked mud (0.18 × 0.12 m) with the impression of a branch or reed 0.03 m wide in it was recovered from level 7 of Stage 8 (PLATE 28 (*e*)). This and some of the pottery from deposits of Stage 8 may come from a building higher on the slope destroyed in the fire which ended Period IV. The fire would have hardened and preserved the mud. The fragment is probably from a ceiling or roof rather than from a wall (cf. *Troy* i 374 f. fig. 351, end of Troy II. *DS* 80 f. figs. 15, 16).

Stage 9

A substantial wall (3) was eventually built with its foundations in the top of level 7 (Plan, FIG. 74: 3). This wall ran diagonally across the trench from north-east to south-west. It was *c.* 0.65–0.75 m wide, with four or five courses of large stones preserved to a maximum height of 0.90 m. Like many of the walls in Area A it was found to be leaning at a marked angle in the direction of the slope. Behind wall 3 on the east was a hard and clearly marked occupation surface (below level 5) with pebbles, sherds and bones, trampled into it. A layer of black ash (level 5A) had accumulated in places above this surface to a depth of *c.* 0.25 m or more. This area behind wall 3 may have been open ground used for lighting fires for cooking like the patches of open ground in Periods V–IV in Area A. But a number of large fragments of vases were recovered from levels 5 and 5A. The pottery from this horizon was still assignable to Period II, and hardly distinguishable in character from that of stage 8 (levels 8–7).

Stage 10

Another wall (4), running more or less parallel to wall 3 but at a higher level 1.50 m to the west, appears to have been constructed after wall 3 went out of use and may have replaced it. This wall only survived to a height of two or three courses in the north-western corner of trench D. No occupation surface was noted in connection with it. Pottery from a deep fill of stones (level 3) above walls 3 and 4 was still assignable to Period II, although to a distinctly late phase of it.

The successive levels and the depth of deposit ascribed to Period II here and elsewhere on the site suggest that this phase at Emporio before the introduction of the fast potter's wheel in Period I may have been a comparatively long and important one.

(3) Area C: little trenches in flat ground (a) north,
(b) west and (c) south of Area A
(Plans and Sections, FIGS. 77, 78)

In 1953 a row of four trial trenches (CC, AA, DD, BB) was opened in the field north of Area A (FIGS. 48 and 77). The evidence from these indicated that the Bronze Age settlement had extended for a considerable distance in that direction towards the harbour; but since no time was left to carry the trenches down below the surface levels, they were refilled again at the end of the season.

A new series of trenches (HH, JJ, EE, GG, FF, LL–OO) was opened in the following year, 1954, to the south, west and north of Area A. One aim of these trials was to ascertain the extent of the prehistoric settlement at different stages in its history. It was also hoped to come upon floors of houses of Period II with complete vases of the remarkable fine incised ware of which only fragments had been recovered in Areas A and B.

The trenches measured 3.00 × 1.50 m, unless otherwise stated.

(a) C.1. Trenches AA–NN north of Area A (FIG. 77)

The latest Bronze Age occupation for which there was any evidence in this area dated from Period II. In the southern part of the area (trenches CC, AA, DD) traces of house walls and floors assignable to Period II were encountered immediately below the surface. The walls (1–4) were on more or less the same alignment as walls 55–59 in Area A immediately below the surface at the northern end of trench Q there. These walls in Area A may have also belonged to a developed phase of Period II if they were not still later in date. The walls (5, 6) further north in trenches BB and NN assignable to Period II were probably contemporary with walls 1–4, although they were at a considerably greater depth; the ground appears to have sloped away here in the Bronze Age as it still did in later Greek times.

A pair of walls (8, 9) in trenches FF and LL might have formed the inner and outer faces of a defence work dating from the time of these houses or from an earlier phase of Period II. Between these walls was a deposit of pebbles (level 9). Such a defence wall could have been built in connection with the expansion of the terrace round the well by the addition of the Period II fill (levels 5–14) at the northern end of Area A. If these walls (8, 9) were part of a defensive rampart it would have been some 5 m or more thick. But the true character of walls 8 and 9 remains uncertain, since the upper levels here were much eroded.

Wall 10, however, immediately below wall 9 was certainly a defensive rampart some 2.50 m wide. It evidently continued the line of wall 52 in trench H of Area A, and may have been erected at the same time as the great Period III stone-filled terrace round the well there. The northern outer face of wall 10 could be traced into trench OO, but it was obscured in trench MM by later pits (levels 4–6). This outer face of wall 10 was very roughly built, and it had a distinct batter.

A wall (7) in trench AA at a lower level than walls 1 and 2 may have belonged to a house dating from the time when the defence wall 10 was built. The Period II house to which wall 6 in trench NN belonged must have been outside the line of the defence wall 10, unless (as may have been the case) this took an abrupt turn northwards somewhere in the space between trenches OO and NN.

Immediately below the bottom of wall 10 were buildings of the fire-destroyed Period IV settlement (Plan, FIG. 77). The lowest levels reached by excavation at a depth of three metres or more from the surface in FF and LL–MM were still Period V–IV in character.

In later Greek and Roman times this part of the site appears to have been open ground used for industry of one kind or other. Pits of the Hellenistic and Late Roman periods were encountered in trenches MM, NN and DD. That in MM seems to have housed a kiln engaged in firing bricks for the Early Christian basilica church or the settlement on the Acropolis hill. The pit in trench DD may have been occupied by a similar kiln. That (level 3) in trench NN, however, produced fragments of tile and pottery assigned to the Hellenistic period.

Trench GG (Plan, FIG. 48) was carried down to a depth of 1.50 m from the surface without reaching deposits earlier than Hellenistic. Traces of walls which may have belonged to buildings of the Hellenistic period were noted at a depth of 1.00–1.50 m.

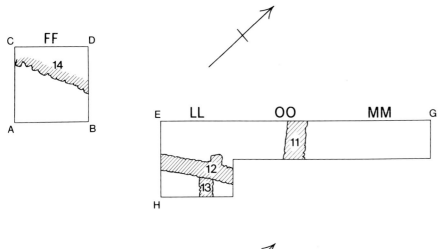

PERIODS V – IV

FF

C — D

14

A — B

E LL OO MM G

11

12

13

H

PERIODS III – II
and later

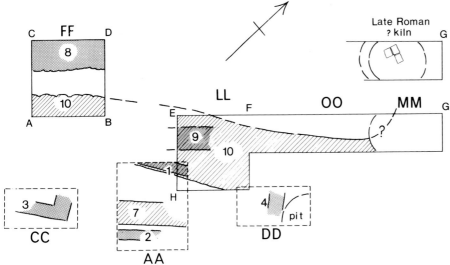

Late Roman ? kiln

G

FF

C — D

8

10

A — B

LL

E F OO MM G

9

10

?

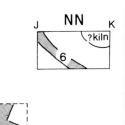

NN

J — K

? kiln

6

CC

3

AA

7

1

2

H

DD

4

pit

BB

5

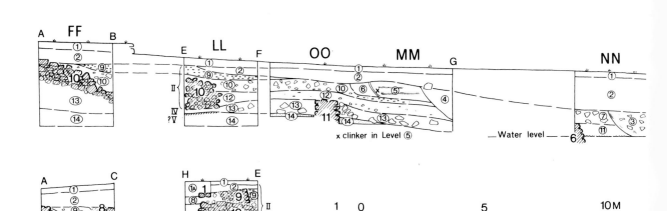

A FF B E LL F OO MM G NN

1

2

9

10 10

13

14

II

IV

?V

1

9 2

10

12

13

14

1

2

10 6 5

12

13

14 11

4

x clinker in Level 5

Water level

1

2

7 3

6 11

A FF C H E

1

2

9 8

10 10

13

14 14

Water level

1A 1

8 9 9

12 10 II

13 IV

13 ?V

14 12

Water level

1 0   5   10 M

Trench FF (3.00 × 3.00 m). At a low level here was a collapsed house wall (14) of the fire-destroyed Period IV settlement. Deposits beneath the Period IV destruction level seemed to be assignable to an earlier phase of Period IV or to Period V like those in trench LL. Wall 14 continued down through these earlier deposits.

The western outer face of the Period III defence wall (10), continuing the line of wall 52 in Area A, was identified on the eastern side of the trench. The face was irregular, roughly built with large stones, like the faces of the corresponding walls 52–54 in Area A.

The rather ill-defined face of another wall (8) was noted at a higher level on the western side of the trench running on a somewhat different line from wall 10. This later wall seemed to date from Period II, and had a deposit of pebbles (level 9) against it on the east. It may have been the outer face of a Period II defence wall of which wall 9 in trench LL formed the inner face, the space between them being filled with pebbles. Alternatively the pebbles could represent a roadway bounded by walls 8 and 9.

Trench LL. The original 3.00 × 1.50 m sounding here was enlarged to form a square 3.00 × 3.00 m in order to ascertain the width of the Period III defence wall 10. The corners of the extension overlapped the corners of trenches AA and DD opened in 1953. Wall 10 ran across LL from south-west to north-east, and was about 2.50 m wide. Its inner face on the east was standing to a height of nearly 1 m and had a distinct batter. Above wall 10, and running at a similar but not identical angle across the trench, was another, thinner wall (9), which also had battered faces. Only a short stretch of this wall (9) was preserved at the southern end of the trench. Against it on the west was a fill of pebbles (level 9) corresponding to that against the eastern face of wall 8 in trench FF. Wall 9 may therefore represent the inner face of a later defence wall of which wall 8 served as the outer face, as suggested above.

Wall 10 was built on top of the ruin debris of the fire-destroyed Period IV settlement (level 13) associated with the house walls 12 and 13. The floors which belonged with these walls were reached at a depth of *c*. 2.25 m from the surface. Wall 12 was about 0.75 m wide. A thin layer of yellow clay on its collapsed north-western face (FIG. 77: Section H–E, left of level 13) appears to be a relic of the mud plaster with which it was once coated.

Beneath the floors in use at the time of the Period IV destruction here was a black ashy deposit (level 14) as found in trench FF with pottery assignable to an early phase of Period IV or to Period V.

Trenches OO and MM (8.00 × 1.50 m). The western face of the Period III defence wall 10 continued through OO, but was not traced in MM. Wall 10 may have turned abruptly northwards in trench MM, although this remains uncertain. Below wall 10 was a house wall (11) of the fire-destroyed Period IV settlement which had collapsed down the slope to the north-east.

Most of trench MM was occupied by what appeared to be a Late Roman brick kiln. This was roughly circular in shape with an internal diameter of *c*. 2.00 m. A good many bricks were found in it, and it looked as if the floor at a depth of 1.25 m from the surface had been deliberately paved with bricks. The sides of the kiln curved upwards from the floor, which was covered with a deep layer of ash below a mass of burnt red clay with two successive layers of hard burnt green clay in

FIG. 77. Area C 1, North: trenches AA–OO. Plans and Sections. Levels: (1) Surface; (1A) Trench AA (1953); (2) Hard brown; (3) Pit (trench NN). Brown with tile and stones; (4) Pit (trench MM). As level 3; (5) Late Roman kiln? Burnt red clay, with layers of hard greenish clay, and some clinker (x); (6) Hard reddish; (7) Brown with some large stones (trench NN); (8) White with occasional pebbles (trench LL); (9) Pebbles; (10) Brown with large and small stones; (11) Dark brown (trench NN); (12) Reddish brown with pebbles and stones; (13) Burnt red with stones (Period IV destruction debris); (14) Soft black ashy.

it (Section, FIG. 77: level 5). The bricks from this burnt fill resembled those used in the Early Christian basilica church and in the Late Roman settlement on the Acropolis hill. They were roughly square, measuring an average *c.* 0.30 × 0.30 × 0.10 m in thickness. Nearly all had finger-made patterns of some kind on them.

Trench BB. A complex of house walls (5) here with their tops at a depth of 1.60 m were evidently of Period II date and may have been contemporary with the Period II wall 6 in trench NN.

Trench NN lay 5 m to the north of MM. The top of the Bronze Age deposit (level 11) assignable to Period II was some 2 m or more below the surface, and this deposit continued under the water level which was reached at a depth of just over 2.50 m. The pottery from it seemed to correspond to the classic phase of Period II as known from the fill (levels 5–14) at the northern end of Area A. Fragments of two or more very large vases with the elaborate incised decoration characteristic of Period II were recovered from the water level and immediately above it at the foot of wall 6.

A pit (level 3) at the northern end of the trench contained fragments of tiles and Hellenistic sherds. It had been dug through a level (7) of earth with large stones and some Classical Greek pottery in it. From deep in the fill of the pit came three pieces of slag with traces of green glaze, identical with lumps found in the area of the Greek Sanctuary to the west (Plan, FIG. 48).

(b) C.2. Trench EE west of Area A (FIG. 48)

Trench EE (3.00 × 9.00 m) was carried down through later Greek deposits to a depth of some 2 m or more from the surface. Scraps of Mycenaean and earlier Bronze Age pottery were recovered from the lower part of these deposits. The last half-metre excavated at a depth of *c.* 2.25–2.75 m appeared to be entirely Bronze Age with scraps of pottery assignable to the horizon of Troy II–V rather than earlier.

(c) C.3. Trenches JJ and HH south of Area A (FIG. 78)

Trench JJ was carried down to a depth of 3.25 m from the surface without encountering any occupation level or structure. The lowest metre of deposit (level 4) produced scraps of Bronze Age pottery which might have been of Period II date but was certainly not earlier. Above this was a horizon (level 3) with pottery assignable to Period I (Troy II) or later. These deposits appear to represent accumulations of rubbish, which may have been beyond the limits of the prehistoric settlement, unless the ground fell away in a very sharp slope in the space of 5 m which separated trench JJ from HH.

Trench HH (4.00 × 1.50 m) was evidently within the limits of the Bronze Age settlement during most periods of its history. What seemed to be two successive Late Bronze Age or Mycenaean building levels were identified here. The walls (8 and 9) which belonged with these ran at different angles, like the walls of the two Late Bronze Age or Mycenaean building levels on the Acropolis hill (Area F). A layer of pebbles (7) about 0.40 m thick associated with wall 8 may indicate the position of a street. Some fragments of matt-painted ware assignable to the Middle Bronze Age were recovered at a higher level from a deposit of material (2) which had evidently washed down from the slopes above over the tops of the latest walls. Below the Late Bronze Age horizon was an occupation level associated with walls (5, 6, 7) which appeared to date from Period II. Apart from some later strays, the pottery recovered in removing walls 6 and 7 looked

SECTIONS : East side

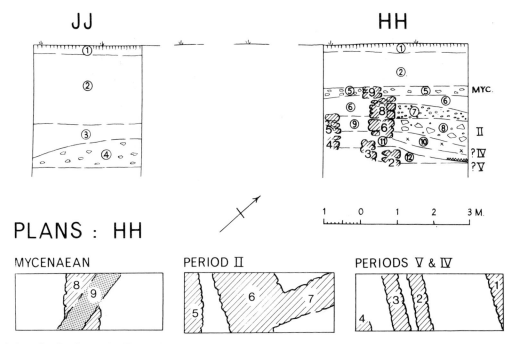

FIG. 78. Area C 3, South: trenches HH, JJ. Plans and Sections (east side). Levels: (1) Surface; (2) Brown earth; (3) Dark brown earth; (4) Brown earth with small stones; (5) Earth with small stones; (6) Brown earth; (7) Small pebbles (road ?); (8) Loose stones and pebbles; (9) Light brown clay; (10) Light brown flecked with charcoal; (11) Burnt red with charcoal; (12) Dark brown earth.

homogeneous in character and of early Period II date. Similarly the pottery associated with the two successive building levels identified below walls 5, 6 and 7, was not older than Periods V–IV. Level 11 with burnt debris seemed to belong to the same horizon of fire-destruction as that which ended Period IV in Area A. Level 12 associated with wall 2 below level 11 should then be assignable to an early phase of Period IV or to Period V.

(4) Area D: soundings on the western slope of the Acropolis hill
(Plan and Sections, FIGS. 79–81. PLATES 26, 27)

From sherds exposed on the surface it seemed likely that remains of the Bronze Age settlement existed immediately below it on the western slope of the Acropolis hill beyond the Roman defence walls. Trials were therefore made in 1954 on the terraces sparsely planted with mastic bushes there. A deposit of the fire-destroyed Period IV settlement was revealed at the northern end of the middle terrace, and a trench (M) 3 m square was opened to examine this. Two large pithoi together with a number of smaller Period IV vases were recovered from the debris of the burnt destruction (PLATE 27 (a)). A few later sherds, including some assignable to Period II and some Mycenaean, were clearly intrusive.

On the lower terrace immediately south-west of trench M important remains of the Mycenaean settlement were uncovered, but no earlier Bronze Age deposits had survived at this spot. A trench (L) was opened here in 1954, and in the following year this was enlarged and

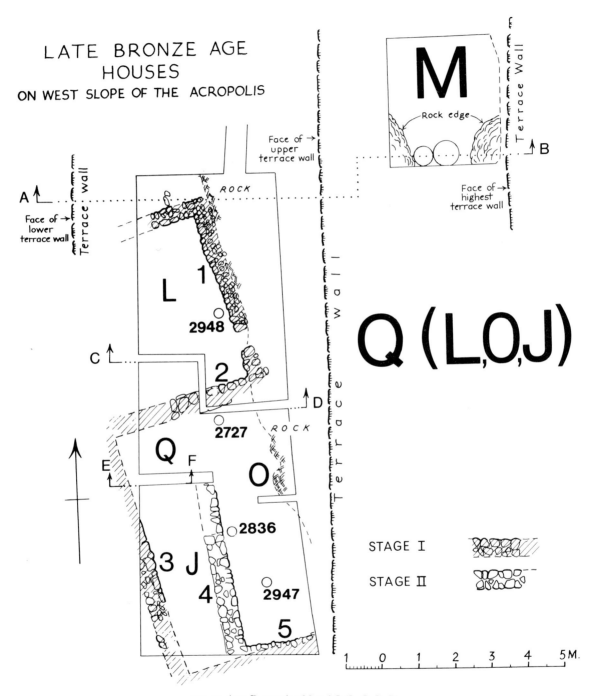

LATE BRONZE AGE
HOUSES
ON WEST SLOPE OF THE ACROPOLIS

Face of
upper
terrace wall

ROCK

M

Rock edge

Terrace Wall

Face of
highest
terrace wall

A

Face of
lower
terrace wall

Terrace wall

L 1

2948

C

2

D

2727

ROCK

Q (L,O,J)

Q   F

E

O

2836

3 J

4

2947

5

Terrace wall

STAGE I

STAGE II

1   0   1   2   3   4   5 M.

FIG. 79. Area D: trenches M and Q (L, O, J). Plan.

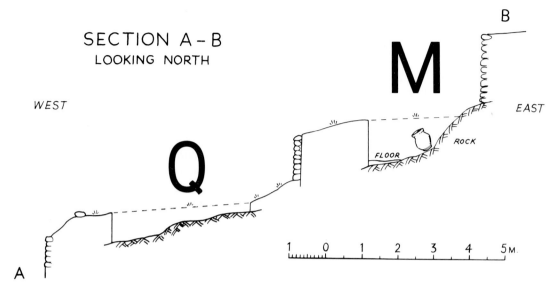

FIG. 80. Area D. Trench M. Section A–B.

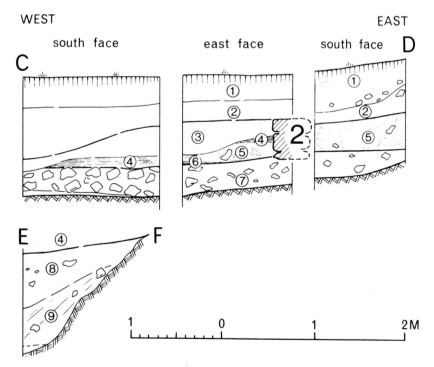

FIG. 81. Area D. Trench Q (L, O, J). Sections C–D, E–F. Levels: (1) Surface; (2) Dark brown hill wash; (3) Hard light brown; (4) Black, burnt debris (Mycenaean stage I destruction); (5) Burnt red (Mycenaean stage I destruction); (6) Grey ash above floor of Mycenaean stage I; (7) Brown with stones and some Mycenaean sherds, below floor of Mycenaean stage I; (8) Brown, possibly same as level 7, below floor of Mycenaean stage I (Section E–F); (9) Soft burnt red. Possibly debris of Period IV destruction as met in trench M (Section E—F).

extended southwards to embrace an area some 13 m long and 4–5 m wide (trench Q). Two Mycenaean building levels could be distinguished. The earlier of these (stage I) had ended with a destruction by fire. Parts of two large rooms of this horizon were uncovered. Below their floors was a fill of earth and stones (levels 7, 8) with Mycenaean sherds in it, except at the northern end of the excavated area (Section A–B) where the floor was on the rock.

Wall 1 of the northern room was built so as to back against a low shelf of rock on the eastern side (PLATE 26 (d)). It was about 0.37 m wide, standing to a maximum height of 0.82 m, and constructed of large irregularly shaped stones without any obvious courses. The lower part of the exposed western face of the wall had been marked by the fire which destroyed the building and brought stage I to an end. Only one or two courses of the dividing wall 2 (Section C–D) were preserved to a maximum height of 0.34 m, and the surviving section of wall 3 consisted of a single course of stones 0.22 m high.

From above the floors of stage I in trench Q (L) came a number of clay vases assignable to Mycenaean III C, including a small bowl of the Mycenaean type 2 (2727) and two plain cooking pots, one of them (2947) made on the fast wheel, the other (2948) from the northern room a rough version of the same shape made by hand.

The bottoms of walls 4 and 5 of the later Mycenaean building were set between 0.05 m and 0.10 m above the top of the burnt ruin debris of stage I and not sunk into it (PLATE 26 (e)). This suggests that the ruins of stage I were levelled to make a platform for the building of stage II. Only a corner of the stage II structure was preserved at the southern end of the trench; but while only one course of wall 4 had survived here, wall 5 was standing to a height of 0.47 m with a five courses of small irregular stones.

No clearly defined floor of stage II was distinguishable. But the unique bird-shaped askos 2852 came from a comparatively high level at the southern end of the trench and appears to have belonged to this horizon.

(5) Area E: trials for tombs on the slopes across the valley from Area D to the west of the Acropolis hill
(FIGS. 47, 82, 83. PLATE 29)

Burials were said to have been found in the past on the gentle terraced slopes planted with mastic bushes west of the Acropolis hill (FIG. 47). Slabs which seemed to belong to a tomb of some kind led to the making of trials here in 1954. The slabs evidently came from a destroyed cist grave (tomb 4), and another better preserved cist grave (tomb 3) with four clay vases assignable to Mycenaean III B came to light a few metres along the slope to the north (PLATE 29 (d), (e)).

A small rock-cut chamber tomb (1) of Early Bronze Age date was discovered higher on the slope to the west (PLATE 29 (a)–(c)). Finally an isolated Roman tomb (2) was revealed some 60 m to the north-west of the Mycenaean cist grave 3. Other tombs no doubt once existed on this hillside, but it looked as if they had been largely destroyed by cultivation and erosion of the soft rock here since ancient times. Cultivation and erosion may also explain our failure to locate any tombs of later Greek periods at Emporio in spite of a careful search throughout the area.

Tomb 1 (FIG. 82. PLATE 29 (a)–(c)). This lay quite high on the slope some 350 m from the western edge of the Bronze Age settlement. A small oval chamber about 1.70 m long and 1.30 m wide, large enough to hold one body, had been dug into the soft white and yellowish rock here. The chamber had long ago collapsed, but it could hardly have been over a metre, and may have been little as 0.80 m high inside. The entrance to the tomb was a mere hole c. 0.50 m across.

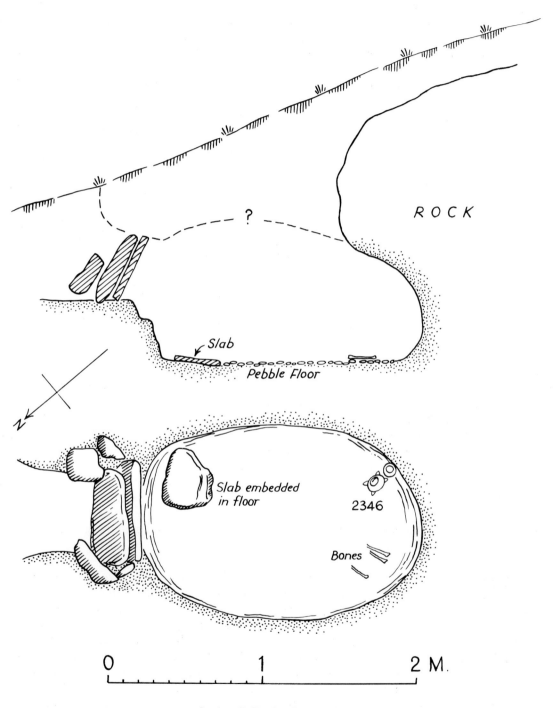

ROCK

?

Slab

Pebble Floor

N

Slab embedded
in floor

2346

Bones

0   1   2 M.

FIG. 82. Area E. Tomb 1. Plan and Section.

The bottom of this hole was *c.* 0.35 m above the floor of the chamber. The top of the entrance had disappeared, but a couple of blocking slabs were still in position in it. A large stone had been placed each side of the entrance concealing the edges of the outer slab.

The floor of the tomb was covered with a layer of small pebbles. A slab of stone embedded in the pebble floor just to the left of the entrance (PLATE 29 (*c*)) may have served as a pillow for the head of the body; but all traces of this had disappeared, except for a few much decayed bones in the far south-west corner of the chamber. At the side of the chamber near them were a couple of small clay jars of the pyxis type. The tomb had been cleaned for drawing and photography on the eve of a public holiday, and the vases being left in position over-night one of them was stolen. It had fine incised decoration, and three or four small feet, one of which was left behind in the tomb. The surviving jar (2346) is of a type assignable to the Early Bronze Age, Period II, or Period IV at the earliest.

Fragments of pottery from the collapsed fill of the tomb chamber appeared to be of Period II date. Among them were several pieces of a large pithos of good fabric, including the rim 2345. Other fragments of the same pithos were found just inside the entrance of the tomb beyond the blocking slabs. The pithos may have been used to contain a burial somewhere on the slope above tomb 1; and then, after it had become exposed through erosion, the fragments of it may have washed down into the hollow left by the collapse of the tomb chamber. A flat stone disc 0.38 m in diameter may have served as its lid. A complete jug (2343), and a bowl (2342) and jar (2344) of which large fragments were recovered from the fill in the chamber at a height of *c.* 0.30 m above the floor, may have come from this pithos burial or from some other grave on the slopes above the tomb.

Small rock-cut tombs of this kind assignable to the Early or Middle Bronze Age have been found at various sites in the Aegean, such as Phylakopi in Melos, Manika in Euboia, and perhaps Pavlopetri in the southern Peloponnese (*Phylakopi* 234 ff. esp. nos. 5, 6. Vermeule, *GBA* 43. *BSA* lxiv (1969) 127 ff., 139 f.). The custom of pithos burial, which is only found on the mainland of Greece from Early Helladic III times onwards, had a long tradition in Anatolia (Tamara S. Wheeler, *AJA* lxxviii (1974) 415 ff.). At the spot Asklupis on Cos two large pithoi came to light, one containing three, the other four burials, accompanied by vases of Anatolian Early Bronze Age type (*Boll. d'Arte* xxxv (1950) 323 ff. fig. 98). It is interesting to have evidence for the practice of pithos burial apparently alongside that of burial in rock-cut chambers in the Early Bronze Age at Emporio.

Tomb 2 of the Roman period will be described in the volume on Roman and later discoveries at Emporio.

Tomb 3 (FIG. 83. PLATE 29 (*d*), (*e*)). The survival of this Mycenaean cist grave was evidently due to the fact that it lay at the foot of one of the terrace walls which ring the slope, and it had therefore escaped with relatively little damage from cultivation in modern times. The grave had been set in a cutting in the soft yellow rock. Its sides, and also it seems its ends, had been lined with slabs backed with large stones. The slab forming the south side of the grave had survived intact and was 1.75 m long and 0.05 m thick. Part of the slab lining on the north side of the grave was missing, and the slabs which had formed the ends of the grave had entirely disappeared except for a few displaced fragments which may have come from them.

The floor of the grave was only *c.* 0.45–0.60 m below the surface of the terrace. It consisted of a layer of small beach pebbles about 0.05 m thick. The bottoms of the slabs lining the grave were set *c.* 0.10 m below the top of this pebble floor. No traces of a body had survived, but resting on

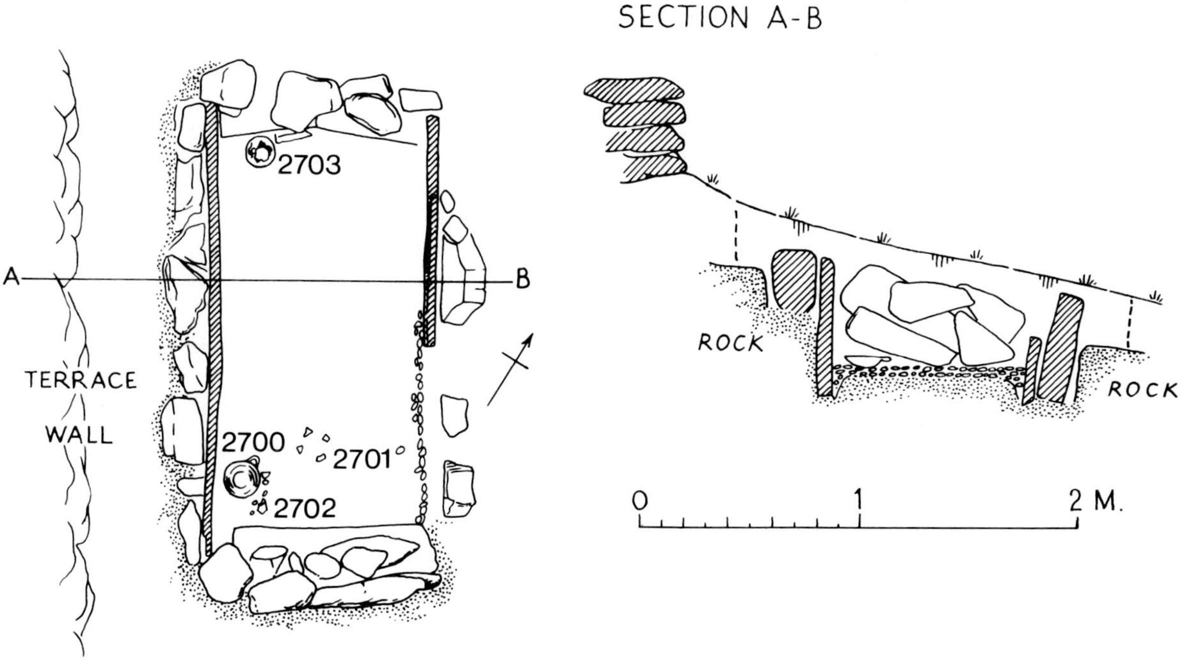

SECTION A-B

FIG. 83. Area E. Tomb 3. Plan and Section.

the floor were the remains of four clay vases (2700–3) assignable to Mycenaean III B. At the southern end of the grave were a shallow semi-globular cup with horizontal handle (2700), a small cylindrical cup (2701) and a plain handleless conical cup (2702); at the northern end a straight-sided alabastron (2703).

Tomb 4. The shattered remains of another Mycenaean cist grave were noted some 10 m south-east of tomb 3. Nothing was recovered here, but the owner of the land reported that he had once found a child's burial in the area.

Cist graves, apparently of the same Mycenaean (Late Helladic) III B date as tomb 3, have also been discovered at Arkhontiki on the island of Psara to the north of Chios (*ADelt* xvii (1961–62) Chron. 266 pl. 321). It seems unlikely that these cist graves on Chios and Psara had anything to do with the custom of single burial which appears to have been brought with them into the Aegean by intruders from the north in the period after *c.* 1200 B.C. They are more likely to reflect a survival of an earlier Bronze Age system of burial continuing into Mycenaean times in parts of the Greek mainland if not in some of the islands and introduced to Chios and Psara by Mycenaean settlers (cf. A.M. Snodgrass, *The Dark Age of Greece* (Edinburgh, 1971) 180 ff. esp. 182. V. Desborough, *The Greek Dark Ages* (London, 1972) 108. O.T.P.K. Dickinson, *The Origins of Mycenaean Civilisation* (SIMA xlix) (Göteborg, 1977) 65, for early Mycenaean examples). It is interesting to find cist graves here at Emporio instead of rock-cut chamber tombs, which were more usual in the Mycenaean world, since the soft rock of the hillside was suitable for the excavation of chamber tombs as the earlier Bronze Age inhabitants of the area had shown.

(6) Area F: soundings below the Roman occupation levels
on the northern edge of the Acropolis hill
(FIGS. 47, 84–95. PLATES 27, 28)

Most of the area opened inside the Late Roman defence wall on the northern edge of the Acropolis hill was carried down into the Bronze Age levels wherever these still existed. But the greatest depth of Bronze Age deposits encountered (in trench B) was only some 2 m, and the deposit assignable to each building period tended to be thin. The stratigraphy was further complicated by the slope, and by robbing of earlier walls for their stone.

In the trenches against the inside of the Late Roman defence wall (K, B, D, F, and S) traces of at least two successive building levels (stages 6 and 7) could be distinguished above that (stage 4) assignable to Period I. The latest of these (stage 7) was Mycenaean, ending with a horizon of destruction and final abandonment in Mycenaean III C. Parts of two long houses of this stage had survived in trenches F and B, J, K. That in trench F at any rate may have had an apse.

The walls of stage 6 were on a totally different alignment. The deposits of this stage were preserved to a maximum depth of 0.40 m with two successive floors in trench B. At the time of the excavation the pottery from this stage was taken to be Mycenaean, and assignable to the same general horizon as that from stage 7. But in fact this stage may have been earlier, and non-Mycenaean in character. The latest pottery from deposits of it appears to date from the early part of the Late Bronze Age contemporary with Late Minoan I in Crete. The two relatively complete matt-painted jugs (2658, 2659), and the fragmentary jug or jar of grey Minyan ware 2653, were from deposits of stage 6. The plain wheelmade cups (classified as Mycenaean types 10 and 11) and the pithoi with channelled ribs like 2900 also belong to this horizon.

It is not clear when the houses of stage 6 were built. Stage 4 (Period I) seemed to belong to the horizon of Troy II. Some fragments of pottery assignable to the horizon of Troy III–V/VI might suggest that occupation continued on the Acropolis without a break after the end of stage 4. But it seems difficult to believe that the buildings of stage 6 in Area F had survived for all that length of time. Stage 4 seems unlikely to have lasted very long after the end of Troy II, and even on a short chronology that can hardly be placed much after c. 1900 B.C.; while stage 6 is unlikely to have ended much before c. 1500 B.C., the conventional date for the end of Late Minoan I A in Crete.

There must have been a similar gap of time between the end of stage 6 and the building of the long houses of stage 7 which seems unlikely to have taken place before the twelfth century B.C. The cist grave with Mycenaean III B vases in Area D, however, indicates that there was occupation of some kind at Emporio then. Possibly there were buildings of intervening stages on the Acropolis, but all traces of them had disappeared in Area F. Alternatively the settlement, or the main part of it at any rate, may have moved in the intervals to the foot of the Acropolis by the harbour, where the evidence suggests that it must have been in later Greek and early Roman times. The gap of some 1,500 years separating the latest Mycenaean occupation on the Acropolis from that of the Late Roman period will then have been preceded by similar, although rather shorter gaps in the Bronze Age.

The houses of stage 4 (Period I) were better preserved than those of any later period of the Bronze Age on the Acropolis. They appear to have consisted of several rectangular rooms with doors between them (PLATE 27 (b)–(d)). The large number of complete or restorable vases recovered from the floors of stage 4 suggests that the settlement may have come to a violent and abrupt end then.

The earlier Bronze Age deposits, corresponding to the horizon of Periods II–IV in the main

Area A, were only examined in trenches K, B and S. In trench B, where the stratigraphy was most clearly distinguishable, three successive building levels were noted below that of stage 4. The latest of these (stage 3) was assignable to Period II. Stage 2 may have belonged to an early phase of Period II, and stage 1 to Period IV. In trench S as in trench B the lowest deposits above the rock seemed assignable to Period IV. But stray sherds found unstratified on the Acropolis suggest that there may have been occupation of some kind there during Periods VII–VI if not earlier.

All the buildings of which traces were revealed in the Bronze Age levels on the Acropolis appear to have been houses. Their walls were built of rubble, although the upper parts of the walls may have been constructed of mud (pisé) or mud-brick. There was no evidence for the use of timber in the construction of any of these walls, although some possible examples of timber incorporated in walls were noted in buildings of Period IV (Houses VI and VII) in Area A. The stone used for the Bronze Age houses on the Acropolis was never dressed and was evidently the grey limestone of the hill itself. The walls of the Late Roman houses by contrast were mostly built with a lighter coloured limestone which may have been quarried from elsewhere in the area.

The walls of one Bronze Age stage on the Acropolis had usually been ransacked for stone by the builders of the next stage. Whole stretches of wall had disappeared as a consequence of this, leaving isolated stumps of walling or bits of foundations here and there. The walls running along the line of the slope from east to west at the southern end of houses of all periods in trenches B, D and F, had usually been constructed with their backs (on the south) against a fill of earlier debris. These walls were often found to have collapsed northwards down the slope owing to the pressure of the fill behind them.

The floors were normally of stamped earth. But a floor of stage 1 (Period IV) in trench B was marked by a thin layer of yellow clay with pebbles (FIG. 91: Section 2, below level 14), and patches of green clay floor were noted in stage 2 and in the Late Bronze Age stage 6 there (FIG. 91: Section 2, below levels 12 and 6).

Stage 1 (? Period IV) (Plan, FIG. 84)

A wall (1) in trench S built upon the rock and running from north to south appeared to belong to Period IV. The earliest building level immediately above the rock in trench B may also have been of this period. Wall 2 of this level was built on rock. It was *c.* 0.50 m wide and preserved to a height of two or three courses. Two other walls (3, 4) appeared to branch from it at right angles

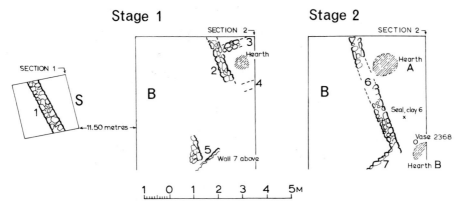

FIG. 84. Area F. Stages 1 (Period IV) and 2 (Period II ?early) (trenches B, S).

on the east. The rock seems to have been deliberately cut back to accommodate the southern wall 4 (FIG. 91: Section 2). The small room formed by these three walls had traces of a floor represented by a thin layer of pebbles just above the rock. A deposit of ash some 0.10 m thick over this floor (Section 2, level 14) indicated the position of a hearth or fire-place. An angle of wall (5) built on the rock higher on the slope to the south may have belonged to this earliest period. It turned and ran eastwards underneath the later wall 7.

Stage 2 (Period II: early phase (?)) (Plan, FIG. 84, right)

Wall 6, running on the same alignment as wall 2 of stage 1, belonged to this horizon. Only one or two courses of it had survived, and a stretch of it was missing. With it may have gone wall 7 preserved to a height of 0.40 m with three courses and running at a wide angle from it above the continuation of wall 5. There was a fire-place (hearth A) on the eastern side of wall 6. Another fire-place (hearth B) on the surface of the rock where it sloped upwards at the southern end of trench B appeared to be of this horizon rather than earlier. Beside it was found the complete cup 2368. The seal (CLAY No. 6) comes from this horizon or from stage 1 A.

Stage 3 (Period II: classic) (Plan, FIG. 85)

Walls 8, 9 and 9A of this horizon in trench B were on the same alignment as the walls of stages 1 and 2. They were only preserved one or two courses high, and in places all traces of them were missing. But they evidently enclosed three sides of a room about 2.75 m wide from east to west and as much as 5 m or more in length from north to south. At the southern end of the room by the back wall (9) was a fire-place (hearth C), and near it against the side wall (8) a rectangular structure (D) 0.70 m long and 0.50 m wide flanked by small slabs of stone set on edge. This may have been a box or bin of some kind, or the slabs may have served as the revetting for a seat or a stand for cooking utensils in connection with the fire-place (C).

A stretch of wall (11) on the southern side of wall 9 and roughly parallel to it might have belonged to a contemporary building higher on the slope. Another stretch of walling (10) behind wall 17 of stage 4 in trench D may have been of this horizon.

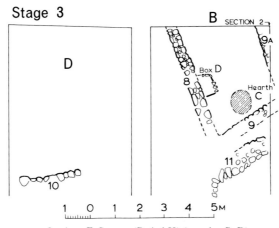

FIG. 85. Area F. Stage 3 (Period II) (trenches B, D).

Stage 4 (Period I) (Plan, FIG. 86. PLATE 27 (b)–(e))

An area of about 75 sq. m assignable to this horizon was exposed in trenches B, D and F, where parts of six rectangular rooms (I–VI) were identified. Numbers of clay vases were recovered from the floors of these.

About a dozen complete or largely complete vases were lying on or just above the floor in the eastern part of room I in trench B (FIG. 87). The large jars (2543, 2555, 2556) appear to have been standing on the floor, and were evidently thrown on their sides when disaster came. The three bowls (2483, 2484, 2494) which were found upside down may have been serving as covers for the jars. It is remarkable that these vases had survived at all, since the deposit left above the floor of room I was only some 0.10–0.20 m deep (e.g. PLATE 27 (e) showing the goblet 2531 with wall 22 of stage 6 above it). The walls (12, 13, 14) bounding room I were only preserved one or two courses high at the most. The back wall (13), which had evidently been constructed against an earlier fill (level 10A) on the south, survived as a single row of large stones c. 0.40 m wide. The tops of these stones were in most places barely 0.10 m above the level of the earth floor of the room. Much of wall 14 forming the western side of the room had disappeared.

It is not clear whether room I belonged to the same house as rooms II and III to the west of it. Walls 14A and 16 here were better preserved, standing to a height of over 0.60 m above the level of the floors. They were c. 0.50–0.60 m wide and reasonably well built of rubble. The sides of the doorway between rooms II and III leant inwards, the door being 0.82 m wide at the bottom narrowing to 0.68 m at the top c. 0.65 m above the floor level (PLATE 27 (b), (c)). This inward lean must have been deliberate. An inward lean of this kind may have been a standard feature of doorways in the Aegean area during the Bronze Age. It is a feature reproduced in the portals of some of the great Mycenaean tholos tombs like the Treasury of Atreus and in the rock-cut entrances of contemporary chamber tombs.

A large pithos had been standing in the middle of room III (FIG. 93: Section 4). The wall (15) bounding this room on the south had been built on the rock which sloped upwards here (FIG. 93: Section 4). Along most of its length in trench D this wall had eventually collapsed northwards into the room owing to pressure from the fill behind it. But what seemed to be a continuation of it in trench B had survived to a height of 0.68 m with five courses. This possible continuation of wall 15 in trench B was also built against an earlier fill on the south. On the north it was associated with a patch of pebble floor.

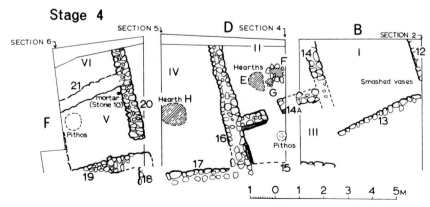

FIG. 86. Area F. Stage 4 (Period I) (trenches B, D, F).

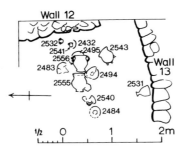

FIG. 87. Area F. Stage 4 (Period I). Vases in room I (trench B).

The large room IV west of rooms II and III seemed to belong to another house. It was c. 3.25 m wide and over 5 m long from south to north. A fire-place (hearth H) was indicated by a somewhat rectangular patch of burnt material about 0.10–0.15 m thick with reddish earth and stones. A door 0.73 m wide at floor level in the south-west corner of room IV led into a smaller room V which had a large pithos standing against the north wall (21) (PLATE 27 (d), at the back). The base of the pithos had been sunk into the earth floor of the room. Wall 21 was only preserved one course high, but walls 20 and 19 on the east and south sides of the room were in a better state (PLATE 27 (d)). A stone with a small hollow in the top (STONE No. 10) recovered from above the floor of room V against wall 20 near the corner with 21 appears to have been a mortar. Wall 18 running southwards from the eastern end of wall 19 was neatly bonded with it. Only a short section of this wall was cleared; it was c. 0.60 m wide and stood to a height of c. 0.69 m with six courses.

Stage 5 (Troy III–VI)

Some fragments of pottery suggested that the Acropolis, or at any rate parts of it, might have been occupied during the period between stage 4, assignable to the horizon of Troy II, and stage 6, which appears to begin in the earlier part of the Late Bronze Age. This period would have overlapped with the horizon of Troy III–V and the early phases of Troy VI. No deposits or structures certainly assignable to it were identified in the course of the excavations. But it is possible that the oven (M) and scraps of walling which appeared to be associated with it in trench D of Area F (FIG. 88), and the apse (wall 30) in trench F there (FIG. 89), belonged somewhere within this period rather than in stages 6 or 7.

Stage 6 (pre-Mycenaean) (Plan, FIG. 88)

Two successive floors in trench B were assignable to this stage (FIG. 91: Section 2, stages 6A and B). These floors were separated by a gap of between 0.10–0.15 m, and were both associated with the walls 22 and 23. Wall 22 was c. 0.60 m wide, and was still standing to a height of 1 m with some seven courses of rubble at the western end where it made a corner with 23; but on the east where it ran below wall 36 of the later (stage 7) Mycenaean building it was only preserved one course high (FIG. 91: Section 2). It was constructed of large undressed stones against an earlier fill (level 10A) on the south where no face of it could be distinguished. The west side of wall 23 was also apparently built against earlier ruin debris. Wall 23 stood to a maximum height of c. 0.75 m with four courses above the latest floor of level 6 in trench B.

A number of pithoi had been ranged against wall 22 at different times, their bases, as was usual, being sunk below the floor level. The sunk bases of three of these pithoi (J, K, L) had been

Stages 5 & 6

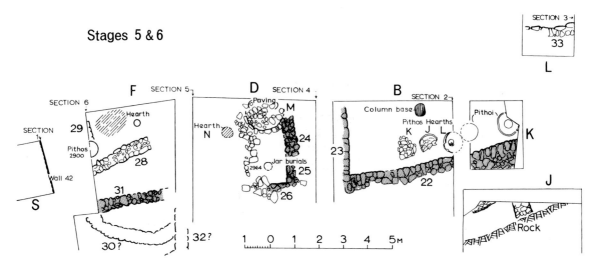

FIG. 88. Area F. Stages 5 and 6 (Middle and Late Bronze Age) (trenches J, K, L, B, D, F, S).

successively used as hearths. Possibly they were put to this use after the pithoi had been broken by accident. The pithos-hearth (J), which seems to have been the earliest, was apparently associated with the lower floor (stage 6A); but the other two hearths (K, L) evidently belonged with the later floor (stage 6B) (FIG. 91: Section 2). When the base of pithos K was sunk into the floor, stones had been packed in a ring for two-thirds of the way round it. After this pithos-hearth (K) went out of use it was covered with a large slab (0.90 m long by 0.60 m wide). It was evidently replaced by the third pithos-hearth (L) which shows in Section 2 (FIG. 91). Hearth L seems to have been in use at the time the building represented by walls 22 and 23 was destroyed or abandoned. In it were found the crushed remains of a jug of plain ware (2826) which may have been standing there at the time (PLATE 27 (*f*)).

A flat-topped stone roughly pentagonal in shape (0.37 × 0.30 m across) and 0.30 m high on the northern edge of trench B may have served as the base of a wooden post or column. The top of this stone showed above the level of the later floor, but could have been in use in connection with the lower one (stage 6A) as well.

A scrap of wall (33) in trench L, and others in trenches J, D and F, on more or less the same alignment as walls 22 and 23 of stage 6 in trench B may be of the same horizon. But it was difficult to relate the confused stratigraphy in these adjacent areas to that in trench B. The sequence of levels in trenches D and F, for instance, could have been somewhat different from what it was in trench B, since wall 23 appears to have been built against an earlier fill on the west.

Structure M in trench D seemed to be the remains of an oven like ones that appear at Troy for the first time in Troy IV. It was set against wall 24 of which the base appeared to overlap its edge and which may have been of one construction with it. A similar arrangement with a very comparable oven next to the wall is found at Troy (e.g. *Troy* ii fig. 300, Troy IV c). What was left of the oven consisted of a curved area of paving only a few centimetres above the floor of stage 4. The paving was bounded on the south by a ring of stones with their tops 0.05–0.10 m above its surface; the ring would have made a circle *c.* 1.50 m in diameter. A fill of ash in the northern section of trench D seemed to be associated with the oven. Hearth N, to the west of the oven (M) and on a level with the tops of the stones which formed its surviving edge, appeared to be contemporary with it.

Wall 25 was evidently a continuation of wall 24 to the south. These walls were *c.* 0.50 m wide and preserved to a maximum height of 0.40–0.45 m with two or three courses. Wall 26, which made a corner with 25, was much destroyed; it had been constructed against an earlier fill on the south.

A jar (2964) with two infant burials in it was found lodged in the top of wall 16 of stage 4. This had evidently been sunk from a higher level, and may have been buried beneath the floor bounded by walls 24–26. One of the two infant skeletons in the jar was lying on its back with arms and legs folded on top of it; the bones of the second infant were below it in some disorder. Underneath the burials was a small slab of stone, roughly circular and measuring 0.20–0.24 m across. In the bottom of the jar below this slab was earth with some traces of carbonised wood.

The stratigraphic situation in trench F was also somewhat obscure. Unfortunately no section was drawn of the Bronze Age levels, but a schematic reconstruction of the crucial western section has been made from the excavation records (FIG. 95: Section 6). As in trench D excavation in trench F was only carried down to the well-marked floors (1) of stage 4 (Period I) which lay nearly a metre below the bottom of a Roman partition wall exposed in the western section. Three successive floor levels (2, 3, 4) were distinguished above the stage 4 floors here.

The earliest of these (floor 2) was *c.* 0.30 m above the stage 4 floor 1 in the western section and seemed assignable to stage 6. Sunk into it was the bottom of a pithos (2900) reminiscent of the pithoi sunk in the floors of stages 6A and B in trench B. To the north of the pithos was a fire-place (hearth O). This floor (2) evidently belonged with wall 31, running from west to east below a Roman partition wall at the southern end of the trench. Wall 31 was about 0.45 m wide and preserved to a height of not much more than 0.35 m. Its top lay immediately underneath the Roman wall which followed the same alignment. At the back on the south it had evidently been built against debris filling room V of stage 4.

Wall 28 was built on top of the destroyed wall 21 of stage 4 and followed the same alignment. A deposit of F level 3 seemed to be traceable running below it. In that case it must have been constructed later in stage 6 in association with floor 3. It was preserved to a maximum height of 0.65 m with three courses. A stretch of wall (29) exposed in the west section of trench F running northwards from wall 28 for a distance of about 1.60 m similarly appeared to be associated with floor 3 and to overrun level 3. This wall survived to a maximum height of 0.33 m. Wall 42 visible in the eastern side of trench S (FIG. 90: Section 1) immediately to the west of trench F also appeared to belong to stage 6.

Another short stretch of wall (32) standing to a maximum height of 0.65 m with four courses at the south end of trench F may have belonged to stage 6, although it was at a higher level than the stage 6 walls and floors further north in the trench. Wall 32 seemed to overlap a stretch of curving wall (30). Wall 30 was between 0.50–0.60 m wide, built with smallish stones, and preserved to a height of three courses on the northern side. On the south it appeared to have been constructed against earlier fill. No floor was identified to go with wall 30; but the stones on top of the surviving part of the stage 41 wall 19, which lay just inside the curve of it, were noticeably worn as if they had been exposed for a time in a floor level. The worn top of wall 19 was at about the same level as the floor or surface which evidently went with walls 34 and 35 in the south-west corner of trench F.

At the time of the excavation this curving wall 30 was therefore interpreted by Michael Ventris and myself as an apse in association with walls 34 and 35 of stage 7 (Mycenaean III C) as shown on the plan, FIG. 89. One or two sherds that it was thought might be assignable to stage 6 were recovered from wall 30 when it was removed to explore the deposits below it. But the mass of the sherds were earlier, and included some wheelmade fragments of Period I. Moreover wall

30 does not seem to make a very good apse when linked to walls 34 and 35: such an apse would have been rather shallow, less than 2 m deep in relation to a width of 5 or 6 m. Wall 30 may therefore have belonged to an apsidal building of some earlier period, which must be after stage 4 (Period I), since it overlies the stage 4 wall 19, but perhaps before the time of floors 2 and 3 assignable to stage 6 further north in trench F.

Stage 7 (Mycenaean) (Plan, FIG. 89)

The walls of this stage were on an entirely different alignment from those of the previous stage 6. Sections of walling which evidently belonged to two different houses were preserved in trench F and in trenches B, J, K. Only part of one side or end (walls 34, 35) had survived of the house in trench F. Wall 34 ran across the top of wall 31. It was 0.60 m wide, and was found standing to a maximum height of 0.65 m with five courses. Wall 35 continued the line of wall 34, and there appears to have been a doorway in the gap between them. The earth floors that went with these two walls were c. 0.20–0.30 m above the latest ones of stage 6 in trench F (FIG. 95).

The house in trenches B, J, K (walls 36, 37, 40) was rather better preserved, and several complete or restorable vases were recovered from it, including the hydria 2833 and the amphora 2838. The space between walls 36 and 40 was about 5 m. Wall 36 was c. 0.60 m wide, standing to a maximum height of 0.58 m with five courses (PLATE 28 (b)) looking from the north, with wall 22 below on the right and a pithos associated with it in the foreground). It was built of roughly coursed rubble with some use of flat slab-like stones, especially at the corner with wall 37 (PLATE 28 (c)). A wall (38), of which only traces were left running parallel to wall 36 on the north, may have been part of another house. But apart from this no walls assignable to stage 7 were noted in trenches B or D. All remains of such, if they had ever existed, may have been removed by erosion during the space of 1,500 years separating the end of the Mycenaean from the beginning of the Late Roman occupation of the hill. At the same time a good deal of Mycenaean III C pottery was recovered from trench D, including the virtually complete kalathos 2757.

Wall 39 in trench L was on the same alignment as wall 38 in trench B, and may have

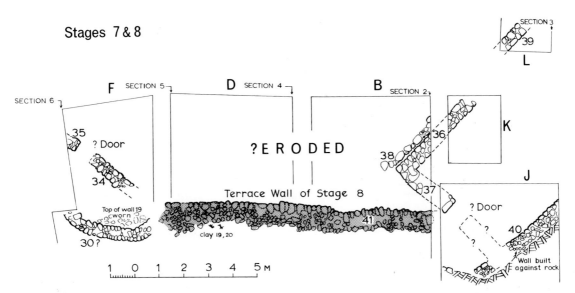

FIG. 89. Area F. Stages 7 (Mycenaean) and 8 (post-Bronze Age) (trenches J, K, L, B, D, F).

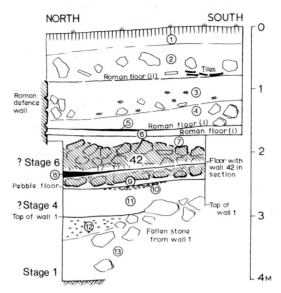

FIG. 90. Area F. Section 1: trench S (east side). Levels: (1) Light brown disturbed by cultivation; (2) Dark brown with large stones and tiles; (3) Hard light brown with stones and fragments of cement; (4) Light brown; (5) Thin layer of charcoal above floor; (6) Reddish brown; (7) Hard dark brown. Gritty with many small pebbles; (8) Patch of black ash above floor; (9) Light brown; (10) Pebble floor; (11) Brown with small pebbles; (12) Pebbly; (13) Soft blackish with large stones fallen from wall 1.

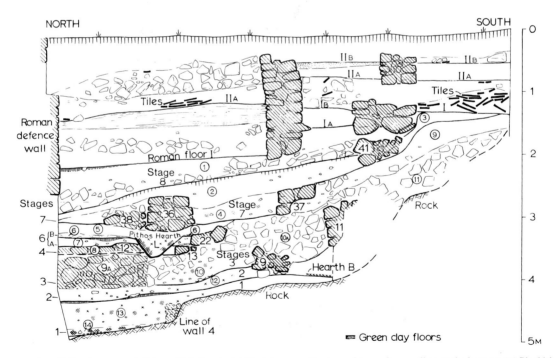

FIG. 91. Area F. Section 2: trench B (east side). Levels: (1) Dark brown with strew of stones from wall 41 at the bottom; (2) Blackish; (3) Blackish. Perhaps the same as 2; (4) Reddish brown; (5) Brown-grey ashy; (6) Grey ash above floor of stage 6 B; (7) Ashy brown above floor of stage 6 A; (8) Deposit with many vases above floor of stage 4; (9) Greyish brown with pebbles and stones; (10) Brown with reddish patches and pebbles and small stones; (10A) Fallen stone from wall 11; (11) Large stones; (12) Dark brown with charcoal above floor of stage 2; (13) Brown with red patches, small pebbles and charcoal; (14) Black ash on floor of yellow clay with small pebbles immediately above rock.

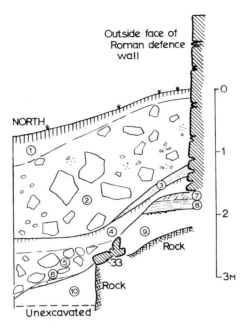

FIG. 92. Area F. Section 3: trench L (east side). Levels: (1) Surface; (2) Large stones, fallen from Roman defence wall; (3) White with grit; (4) Hard gritty brown; (5) Large stones; (6) Grey ashy above floor; (7) Red clay; (8) Grey ashy above pebble floor; (9) Light yellowish brown; (10) Light brown.

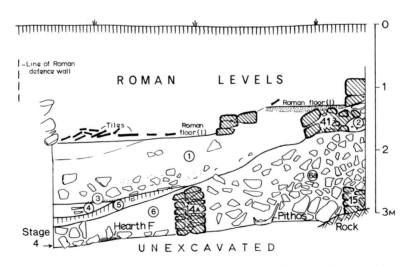

FIG. 93. Area F. Section 4: trench D (east side). Levels: (1) Dark brown; (2) Hard light brown with sherds, below wall 41 and above 6A; (3) Patch of reddish above 4 (FIG. 94, Section 5, Level 2?); (4) Light brown; (5) Blackish; (6) Hard light brown with much fallen stone; (6A) Fallen stones from walls.

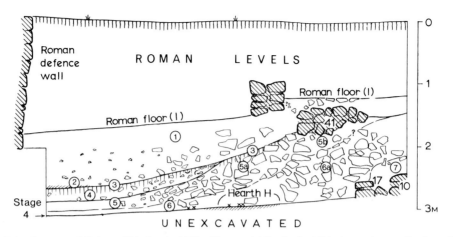

FIG. 94. Area F. Section 5: trench D (west side). Levels: (1) Hard brown; (2) Patch of reddish above 3 (FIG. 93, Section 4, level 3 ?); (3) Old surface (?) as above level 5 in Section 4; (4) Hard blackish brown with some stones; (5) Black; (5A) Black with stones; (5B) Loose black with stones; (6) Light brown with some charcoal; (6A) Fallen stones from wall 17; (7) Light brown above wall 10.

belonged to the same period; but it can hardly have been connected with the same building as it was at a much lower level.

Stage 8 (Plan, FIG. 89)

After the end of the Bronze Age there seems to have been little or no occupation on the Acropolis hill until Late Roman times in the sixth and seventh centuries A.D. Much of the Bronze Age deposit had evidently washed away down the steep slopes of the hill before then. But this process of erosion may have been delayed to some extent by the building of terrace walls of the kind that ring the slopes here today. Wall 41 (PLATE 28 (*d*)) appeared to be the remains of such a wall dating from later Greek times when the Acropolis may have been under cultivation. One or two Archaic Greek sherds were recovered from the wall itself and from a level of hill-wash which seemed to run below it and over the top of the eroded Mycenaean deposits.

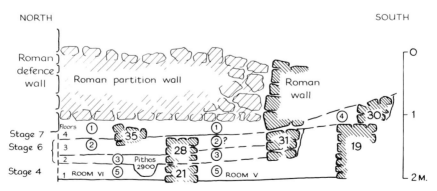

FIG. 95. Area F. Section 6: schematic reconstruction of trench F (west side). Levels: (1) Stage 7 (floor 4); (2) Stage 6: later phase (floor 3); (3) Stage 6: earlier phase (floor 2); (4) Stage 5 (?) or 7 (?); (5) Stage 4 (floor 1).

3. THE POTTERY

(1) Introduction

A rough count was kept of the amount of prehistoric pottery recovered (FIG. 96). This was estimated in terms of the baskets used to collect it, as was done in the American excavations at Troy. The baskets were the standard two-handled zembils, which it was calculated at Troy when full held about one bushel (*Troy* i 26 note 5). It will be seen from FIG. 96 that a large proportion, over one-quarter, of all the prehistoric pottery recovered came from the horizon of Period II in Area A. Relatively little was obtained from levels of the early periods (X, IX) or from Late Bronze Age or Mycenaean deposits. The figure for Period IV in Area A is a good deal smaller than it ought to be owing to the very large number of complete or restorable vases which were collected from the site separately and not incorporated in the count of baskets.

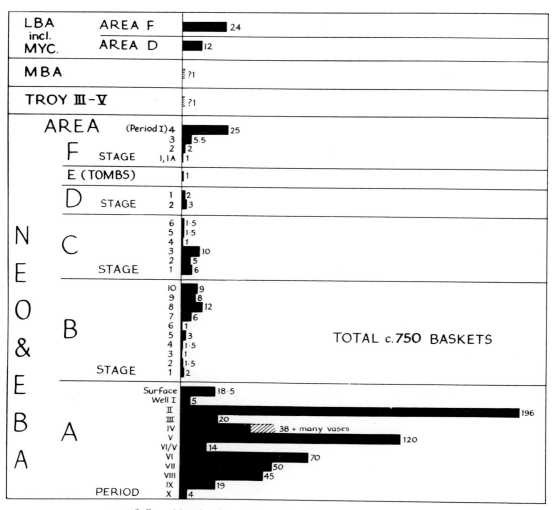

FIG. 96. Quantities of prehistoric pottery from Emporio (numbers of baskets).

(2) **Neolithic to the beginning of the Early Bronze Age (Troy I–II)**

(a) Fabric

Summary of wares

(A) *Native wares*	*Periods*
General local wares	X–I
Mottled Ware	VIII, VII–VI
Fine Black Burnished Ware	IX, VIII, VII–VI
Light Brown Burnished Ware	VIII, VII–VI
Red or Light Brown Washed Ware	VIII, VII–VI
Light Plain Ware	IX, VIII, VII–VI
White Slipped Ware	IX–IV
White Burnished Ware	II, I
Silvery Grey Ware	VIII, VI, V–IV
Cooking Pot Ware	X–I
Baking Pan Ware	X–VI or V/IV
(B) *Foreign imported wares*	
Micaceous Wares	X–II
Obsidian Ware	VII–IV, II
Fine Light Grey Burnished Ware	X–VIII, VII, V, II
White Coated Ware	II
Wheelmade wares	I

Wares by periods

NOTE. The wares marked with an asterisk (*) are described in detail under the heading of *Fabric* for the periods concerned.

Periods X–VIII
  *General local wares
  Mottled Ware (only from VIII)
  Fine Black Burnished Ware (IX and VIII)
  Light Brown Burnished Ware (only from VIII)
  Red or Light Brown Washed Ware (only from VIII)
  Light Plain Ware (IX and VIII)
  *White Slipped Ware (IX and VIII)
  Silvery Grey Ware (only from VIII)
  *Cooking Pot Ware
  *Baking Pan Ware

  Foreign fabrics (see Imports). Include:
    *Micaceous Wares
    *Fine Light Grey Burnished Ware

Periods VII–VI
  *General local wares
  *Mottled Ware
  *Fine Black Burnished Ware

*Light Brown Burnished Ware
*Red or Light Brown Washed Ware
*Light Plain Ware
White Slipped Ware
Silvery Grey Ware
*Cooking Pot Ware
Baking Pan Ware

Foreign fabrics (see Imports). Include:
   Micaceous Wares
   Obsidian Ware
   Fine Light Grey Burnished Ware

Periods V–IV
   *General local wares
   *Silvery Grey Ware
   *Cooking Pot Ware

Foreign fabrics (see Imports). Include:
   *Micaceous Wares
   *Obsidian Ware
   Fine Light Grey Burnished Ware
   White Slipped Ware

Period II
   *General local wares
   *White Burnished Ware
   *Cooking Pot Ware

Foreign fabrics (see Imports). Include:
   Micaceous wares:
     *(a) Standard Micaceous Wares
     *(b) Black Burnished Micaceous Ware
   Obsidian Ware
   *Fine Light Grey Burnished Ware
   *White Coated Ware

Period I
   *General local wares
   *White Burnished Ware
   *Wheelmade wares

All of the pottery used at Emporio was handmade until Period I, when some wheelmade vases appeared alongside those made by hand. The earliest handmade vases were very imperfectly fired and their fabric tended to be soft. But firing gradually improved, although it still remained relatively poor as late as Periods V–IV: hard well-fired pottery was not much in evidence before Period II. Grit and straw combined were used as tempering. The straw temper was more obvious in the pottery of Periods X–VI, but was still apparent in that of II. A notable feature in the local pottery of all periods at Emporio was the absence of mica: but mica was present in the clay of a large proportion of what were evidently imported vases.

From the first the bulk of the pottery was dark-surfaced. The predominance of dark surfaces was especially noticeable on the pottery of the earliest periods X–VIII, although some light brown and red surfaces occurred even then. Dark surfaces, shades of grey-brown to black, continued to predominate as late as Period II, but light-coloured ones were by that time more in evidence, and in Period I light brown and red ones were dominant. The eventual predominance of light-coloured surfaces may be an aspect of marked improvements in firing in the handmade pottery of Period I.

The surfaces of vases throughout the Neolithic and the earlier part of the Bronze Age at Emporio were normally burnished. But the proportion of unburnished pottery tended to increase with time. At first (Periods X–VIII) there was no clear distinction between fine and coarse wares: some large vases had a very fine burnish, while small vases with a careful burnish might be of very coarse fabric. By Periods VII–VI a considerable degree of differentiation had been achieved, however, and specialized wares had been developed in connection with specific types of vase. Thus bowls of Periods VII–VI tended to be of *Mottled Ware* with variegated surfaces, shades of red and light brown to black; while small jugs were of *Fine Black Burnished Ware* and larger ones of *Light Brown Burnished Ware*. Some large jugs, and many storage jars of various kinds, were made of *Light Plain Ware*. This distinctive ware, with the light surface plain and unburnished, appears before the end of Period VIII but seems to be especially characteristic of VII.

Even in Periods X and IX some vases had a red wash applied to them, and by VIII if not earlier these red-washed surfaces were occasionally left unburnished. The burnished vases of VII–VI had normally been given a wash which was light brown or red in colour when it was applied; but in the case of jugs of *Fine Black Burnished Ware* the red wash was deliberately transformed to black in the firing. While most of the vases with a red or light brown wash from the horizon of VII–VI were burnished, some had unburnished surfaces.

Many of the vases with a red wash in Periods V–IV and later had their surfaces fired to a different colour, notably to a distinctive purple-tinged black which was very characteristic of the finest burnished ware of II. Most vases in the horizon of V–II were still burnished, but there was a considerable range in the quality of the burnishing: in Period II especially the finest burnish often had the character of a high polish, while a summary 'stroke' burnish was the rule for the coarser wares. Some Period II vases, apparently of local fabric rather than imported, seem to have had a slightly lustrous red or black wash.

A variety of coarse ware used largely for cooking vessels could be distinguished as early as Periods X–VIII. In VII–VI and V–IV vases of *Cooking Pot Ware* were often burnished, but sometimes they had an unburnished red wash. Unburnished *Cooking Pot Ware* was in common use by Period II. The distinctive *Baking Pan Ware* with rough unburnished surfaces appears to have been employed for cooking vessels of some kind: it was especially characteristic of the early periods X–VIII, and may not have been made at Emporio as late as V–IV.

White Slipped Ware, attested in levels of all periods from X–VIII to V–IV, appears to have been of local manufacture like the *White Burnished Ware* of II–I. *Silvery Grey Ware*, which seems to be characteristic of Period V although attested in VIII and VI, may reflect a deliberate attempt to reproduce the effects of silver plate. It has interesting analogies in the Late Neolithic of the Greek mainland.

Foreign Wares. What seemed to be foreign or imported wares fell into three main classes: (1) *Micaceous Wares*. Fragments of vases of sandy clay with shiny particles of mica in it came from levels of all periods from X–II. A special variety of micaceous ware, labelled *Obsidian Ware* from the distinctive hard shiny black particles in the clay, was found in levels of VII–II. (2) *Fine Light*

Grey Burnished Ware. This was not as common as the *Micaceous Wares*, but fragments of it were recovered from levels of most periods between X and II. (3) *White Coated Ware.* The few fragments of this came from deposits of II and I. All or most of these foreign wares may derive from neighbouring islands like Samos or from the Cyclades.

The wheelmade vases from the horizon of Period I may also have been imported in spite of their number. The clay of these tended to be sandy, sometimes micaceous; and the vases were in general less well fired than the local handmade wares. Most of the wheelmade vases from levels of I had been given a red wash, which may have been slightly lustrous, although this was difficult to ascertain owing to the smoothing or burnishing of the surfaces.

(b) Types
(FIG. 97)

The classification by types follows the system adopted by the American excavators for the pottery from Troy. That is to say, the table ware, consisting of vases used (A) for eating and drinking and (B) for pouring, is considered first before (C) vessels used for storage and (F) covers and lids.

A: BOWLS / B: JUGS / G / H

	1	2	3	4	5	6	7	8	9	10	11	12	13	14	15	16	17	18	20	21	22	23A	23B	23C	24A	24B	25A	25B	26	27	G: MIN. VASES	H: PERIOD I TYPES
I	1	1		15	45	40	60		75				15	15			1	1					X		1		X		1	⊗		70 4
II		1	3	10	70	8	4	1	200			3	80	45		15		1		X		X			1		X			⊗		71 3
III			1	2	10	7	3		20	2		2	6	5	1	1														X		72 7
IV			2	25	70	3	6	2	80	5		8	20	10	1	30							10	1		5	2	4	1	⊗		73 2
V		22	55	100	29	43	10	175	12	4	15	35	60	5	10		1						1		X		1		X	⊗	3	74 2
VI–V			1	15	5	5	10	1	20	3	1	1										X	?		?				X			75 15
VI			26	25	70	25	35	30	15	40	20	5	3	20							⊛		?		X				X		1	76 1
VII			19	20	20	7	15	10	3	45	70	2	1	10							⊗		?		X				1	?		77 9
VIII	3	4	50	30	50		50	35	3	7	2	1		8					30												?	
IX	2	2	40	20	65		40		10	2	1								6									?				
X	3	1	5	5	14		15		3	5									3									?				

C: JARS / D: MISC / E PITHOI / F: LIDS & COVERS

	30	31	32	33	34	35	36	37	38	39	40	41	42	43	44	45	46	47A	47B	47C	50	51	E PITHOI	60	61	62	63A	63B	63C	63D	63E	64A	64B
I									X	X	X						X	1					X	⊗			1	1				3	3
II									X	X	X				X						1	2	X	⊛		2	2	6		14	5	22	2
III											X												X				1			1	1		
IV				⊗					X	X	X			1	⊗	2	1	2	2	5			X				1	1			1	1 2	
V				⊗					X	X	X					⊗	1					1	X										
VI–V	?								1														X									?	
VI	?	?	X	?	X	?			?					X	X								X										
VII	X	?	X	X	X	?			?					X	X								X										
VIII	X	X	X	?	X	X	1	1	?					⊛	⊛								X										
IX	X	X	?	?	X	X			?					⊗	⊗								X										
X	?	?			X	X			?					⊗	⊗								X										

KEY: ?   May occur   ⊗   Common   Approximate numbers in italics.   Complete or restored vases only count as one unit.
     X   Occur   ⊛   Very common

FIG. 97. Distribution of Neolithic and Early Bronze Age pottery types.

(A) Bowls (types 1–18) probably include most of the vessels out of which people ate and drank. (B) Jugs and other vessels with spouts (types 20–27) were clearly used for pouring liquids. Tripod cooking pots (type 27) have been grouped with jugs because they often have spouts. (C) Jars used for storage or cooking are in general of coarser fabric and taller in relation to the width of their mouths than (A) bowls. But in the earlier periods (A) bowls tended to merge into (C) jars. In recognition of this several of the early types classified under (C) have been called bowl-jars. The smaller of these bowl-jars at any rate were almost certainly used as table ware.

In the earlier periods vases for drinking (cups and goblets) were not obviously differentiated from ones employed for holding more solid foods. But the Dipper Cups (type 16) of Periods V–IV may have been specialised drinking vessels. In Period I, the horizon of Troy II, various types of drinking vessels were in evidence.

(A) Bowls (types 1–18)

1. Plates
2. Dishes with short outward-leaning or upright sides
3. Baking pans
4. Open bowls with straight or slightly curving sides: A. Deep, B. Medium, C. Shallow
5. Open bowls with curving sides: A. Deep, more or less hemispherical, B. Medium, C. Shallow
6. Bowls with inward-leaning rims
7. Bowls with inward-leaning rims and high shoulders
8. Bowls with carinated shoulders and tall rims
9. Carinated bowls: A. Rims at open angles, B. Rims at sharp angles, C. Rims concave on the outside, D. Short bevelled rims, on (1) deep bowls, (2) shallow bowls
10. Bowls with short, S-shaped, usually thickened club-like rims: A. Deep, B. Shallow
11. Bowls with inward curving rims, internally differentiated and usually thickened: A. Deep, B. Shallow
12. Bowls with straight rims, thickened and usually differentiated on the inside: A. Deep, B. Shallow
13. Bowls with outward curving rims, internally differentiated and thickened: A. Deep, B. Medium, C. Small and shallow
14. Bowls with outward curving rims, not internally differentiated, but sometimes thickened: A. Deep, B. Medium, C. Shallow, D. Dish-like
15. Carinated bowls with outward-spreading rims: A. Straight, B. Concave on the outside
16. Dipper cups: A. As type 5, B. As type 13, C. As type 14, D. As types 9 and 15
17. Bowls with a ledge round the inside
18. Bowls with a ledge below the rim outside

(B) Jugs, theriomorphic vases, and tripod cooking pots (types 20–27)

20. Jugs with straight necks and flat mouths
21. Small jugs with short straight necks, wide flat mouths and tripod feet
22. Jugs with curving necks and wide flat mouths
23. Jugs with sloping mouths and pointed spouts: A. Standard type, B. Tall, with differentiated neck and high knobbed handle, C. Double-mouthed
24. Jugs with cutaway spouts: A. Standard type, B. With tall slender neck
25. Theriomorphic vases: A. Bird-vases (askoi), B. Other animal-shaped vases
26. Cooking jugs: A. With handle to rim, B. With small handle set below rim
27. Tripod cooking pots

(C) Jars (types 30–47)

30. Squat bowl-jars with simple inward-curving rims (class A I)
31. As 30, but with ogival rims (class A II)
32. As 30, but with outward-curving rims (class A III)
33. Squat bowl-jars with low shoulders
34. Jars with simple incurving rims (class A I)
35. Large jars with simple incurving rims (class A I), low shoulders, and vertical handles
36. Bowl-jars with wide mouths, tall outward-curving rims (class A III), and low shoulders
37. Tall jars with narrow mouths, outward-curving rims (class A III), and low shoulders
38. Large tall storage jars with simple incurving rims (class A I) and vertical handles on the shoulder
39. As 38, but with ogival rims (class A II)
40. As 38, but with outward-curving rims (class A III)
41. Globular jars with collar necks (class B I) and a pair of small vertical handles joining neck to shoulder
42. Small pyxis-like jars with wide mouths, low collar necks, and a pair of handles joining neck to shoulder
43. Large jars with collar necks and four vertically perforated lugs on the swelling.
44. Small jars (pyxides) with short collar necks and handles or lugs on the swelling
45. Large globular jars with short upright collar necks and horizontal side handles on the swelling
46. Jars with tall slightly differentiated necks and outward-curving rims (class B III)
47. Globular jars with tall necks and upright or outward-leaning rims

(D) Miscellaneous (types 50–51)

50. Bottles
51. Double vases

(E) Pithoi

(F) Lids and covers (types 60–64)

60. Flat lids
61. Flat lids with handles
62. Flanged covers
63. Covers with handles or lugs on top: A. With central handle, B. With central handle and four smaller ones round edge, C. With central handle and four warts round edge, D. With central wart and four perforated lugs round edge, E. With central wart and four warts or solid lugs round edge
64. Flanged covers with flat tops and handles: A. With handles round edge, B. with 'crown' handles

(G) Miniature vases

(H) Bowls and drinking vessels of types not attested before period I (types 70–77)

70. Shallow bowls with internally differentiated rims
71. Deep bowls with inward-curving, internally differentiated rims
72. Bowls with inward-curving, S-shaped or bead rims

73. Carinated bowls with outward-spreading bead rims
74. Miscellaneous bowls with outward-curving and thickened rims
75. Shallow bowls with more or less well marked bead rims
76. Tall goblet with solid foot
77. Tankards

i. *(A) Bowls* (types 1–18) (FIG. 98)

Type 1. Plates

These were flat-bottomed with low outward-leaning or upright rims *c.* 30–50 in diameter. Large plates of this kind, usually circular although in one case (4) rectangular, made in coarse burnished ware, seemed to be virtually confined to the earliest periods X–VIII. But one fragment (2432) was recovered from a level assignable to Period I.

Low-rimmed circular plates are attested at Çatal Hüyük (*AS* xii (1962) 53 fig. 9: 6) and in Early Neolithic deposits on the Greek mainland and in Crete. Rectangular plates like 4 occur in Early Neolithic I at Knossos (*BSA* lix (1964) 175 fig. 28: 24, from Stratum VIII). Stone plates including a rectangular one were found in the earliest horizon (A) of Neolithic at Nea Makri in Attica (*AM* lxxi (1956) 24 f. fig. 46 pl. 16). But a rectangular 'tray' on four feet from Çatal Hüyük is thought to reflect wooden prototypes (*AS* xii (1962) 55, 53 fig. 9: 3).

Type 2. Dishes with short outward-leaning or upright sides

These resemble plates of type 1, but the sides are taller. Rim diameters range from *c.* 25 to 45. Like plates of type 1 dishes seem to have been characteristic of the earliest periods X–VIII at Emporio, occurring both in fine and coarse burnished ware, and in coarse unburnished Baking Pan Ware like that of which baking pans of type 3 were normally made. Fragments (including a rim of fine ware (1950)) from stage 8 in Area B assignable to Period II may be earlier strays; but a rim of coarse burnished ware (2433) came from a level of Period I in Area F.

Tigani 147 and 145, F. 41: coarse ware dish, appears to be of this type. Dishes closely resembling those from the early levels at Emporio in shape and fabric were at home at Kum Tepe in Phase I A (*Kum Tepe* 322 nos. 136–7; 326 no. 235). Rims that look very similar are illustrated from Ras Shamra V A (Late Neolithic) and IV (*Urgaritica* iv 282 f. pl. x: 26, 27; 278 f. pl. viii: 29).

Type 3. Baking pans

Under this heading are grouped the fragments of a number of vases of a distinctive coarse fabric (Baking Pan Ware) with a row of holes below the rim. The fabric, and the holes made while the clay was soft before firing, are essential features of the type. These holes range from 2 or 3 to nearly 10 mm in diameter. No complete examples of baking pans were recovered, but most of them appear to have been varieties of large dishes like those of type 2, although one at least (21 from IX Q level 158) resembled a plate of type 1. Some of the rims grouped under this type were evidently inward-leaning like those of bowls of type 6, while others may have come from jar-like vessels. Dish-like rims seem to range in diameter from *c.* 30–40 or more; but some of the inward leaning rims have a diameter of *c.* 20 or less.

Some baking pans were evidently equipped with handles set on top of the rim or below it on the outside. A few rims from levels of VI –V with perforations like baking pans had lugs on the outside. But large horizontal tongue-shaped ledge-lugs set just below the rim on the inside were more characteristic of the type. One or two of these internal lugs from levels of IX–VIII had several perforations through them. Internal lugs of this kind could have supported lids, but they

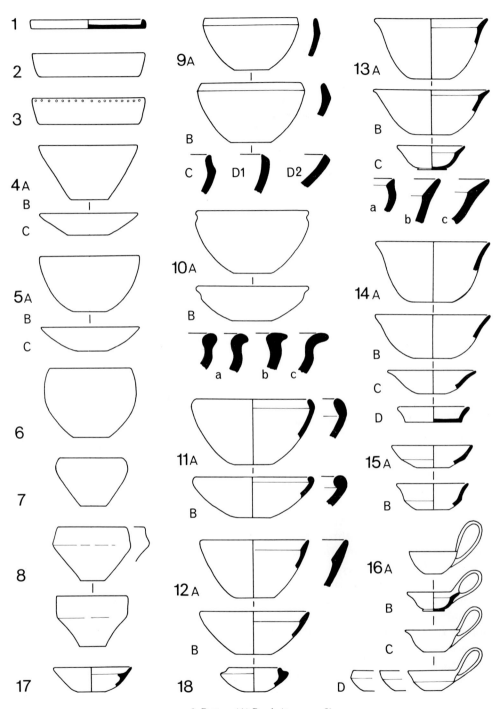

FIG. 98. Pottery (A) Bowls (types 1–18).

might have been developed to simplify lifting the vessels from the fire if, as seems highly probable, they were used for some form of cooking. Over half of a baking pan was found lying on top of an ash layer of a hearth in the new excavations at Tigani (*Samos* xiv 132). The type is so distinctive as to suggest that it was evolved for a specific purpose. Heidenreich, *Tigani* 139 ff., and others since have suggested that this might have been cheese-making. The holes around the rim look as if they were intended for string, perhaps to keep a cover in place.

Rims with holes assignable to this type occurred in levels of X and were very abundant in those of IX and VIII. Baking pans were evidently still being made and used at Emporio in Periods VII–VI and perhaps into V; but the few scraps of them from levels of IV–II could all be earlier strays. Remains of baking pans were recovered from the upper levels of the Upper Cave at Ayio Gala (AG 91–93). It is an interesting fact, however, that no traces of them were apparently recognised at Troy, Poliochni, or Thermi. In contrast to this baking pans appear to have been at home in various parts of the Aegean area during the Late Neolithic and Early Bronze Ages: they have been recorded from many of the islands and from a number of sites on the Greek mainland.

For the type see A. Furness, *PPS* xxii (1956) 182 (7) *Cooking-pan.* E.g. Kalymnos, Vathy Bay cave, ibid. 189 pl. xviii: 2. Samos: *Tigani* 139 ff. pl. 34: 6. *Samos* i 81 pl. 35: 74, Heraion (E. B. A.). Cos: *Aspripetra* 294 f. fig. 82. *Saliagos* fig. 40: 14, 18 (inward-leaning rims). Mykonos: *AJA* lxviii (1964) 398 f. pl. 127: 9. Phylakopi (Melos) and Grotta (Naxos): Renfrew, *Emergence* 155 f. fig. 10. 2: 5, 11. Kea, assigned to the Late Neolithic: *AJA* lxxviii (1974) 336: many fragments from Kephala (*Kephala* 17 f. pls. 37, 84). Cf. *Hesperia* xli (1972) 360 pl. 76: A 17–25, from the horizon of earliest pottery at Ayia Irini; ibid. 358 fig. 1 pl. 76: P 3–7, S 1–2, from Paoura and Sykamias. *Athenian Agora* xiii 15 pl. 12 nos. 185–8. Asea 55 fig. 57: c. Baking pans of this type also occur in the Early Bronze Ages of Thessaly and Macedonia (e.g. Milojcic, *Ergebnisse* 28 fig. 23: 2. *PMac* 8 fig. 8; 170 f. figs. 44 and 45: h. *Servia* 224, occasionally with internal ledge-lugs. *Argissa* iii 197 pl. 70: 17, from Kritsana I/II; 202 pl. 76: 4, Beil. 31 B: 27, from Ayios Mamas; 205 pl. 87: 11, from Saratse). At Argissa they appear to be characteristic of the latest phase of the local Early Bronze Age (*Argissa* iii pls. 37; 44: 6; 45: 1: form G 3). A rim fragment from Argissa has an internal lug like some from Emporio (*Argissa* iii pl. 37: 10).

These Aegean baking pans all seem to come from contexts assignable to the Late Neolithic or Early Bronze Ages. The situation is exactly the opposite at Emporio, where baking pans were characteristic of the earliest levels and may not have been any longer current in the developed Early Bronze Age of Periods IV–I on the analogy of their absence from contemporary deposits at Troy, Poliochni, and Thermi. At Troy it is true vessels which appear to have been of comparable shape and fabric occurred throughout Troy I–II; but these did not it seems have the characteristic holes round the rim (*Troy* i 75 shape D 23).

Standard baking pans of type 3 with holes through the rim are attested, however, in much earlier times in some parts of south-western Anatolia. Such baking pans are reported from the Elmali region near Karataş from an assemblage which has been tentatively assigned to the Middle Chalcolithic (Eslick 1980, 10, 9 ill. 3: 14). They are also said to occur in association with Beycesultan Late Chalcolithic 1 types at Boztepe in the same area (ibid. 13). What may be prototypes for our baking pans are to be found long before this in the Levant. Thus vessels like baking pans of type 3 with holes though the rim were at home in the earliest pottery horizon (V B) of the Neolithic at Ras Shamra on the Syrian coast, although these are thought to have been merely dried in the sun, not hardened by firing (*Ugaritica* iv 261, 286 f. pl. xii: 4, 5). There is also a fragment of what might be a baking pan of Coarse Red-slipped Ware from Judeideh Phase B, but it is illustrated as a high drum base (*Judeideh* 70 f. fig. 41: 13). Nothing comparable, however, appears to have been found at Byblos, or at Mersin or Tarsus in Cilicia.

Type 4. Open bowls with straight or slightly curving sides: A. Deep, B. Medium, C. Shallow

This type shades into type 5. The shallower varieties (C) appear to be most at home in the earlier periods (X–VI). But a number of rims of Period II and later also belonged to shallow bowls of this type. Shallow wheelmade bowls of type 4 occurred alongside handmade ones in levels assignable to Period I.

Type 5. Open bowls with curving sides: A. Deep, more or less hemispherical, B. Medium, C. Shallow

These were common in levels of all periods. As in the case of bowls of type 4 the shallow varieties (C) appear to have been more characteristic of the early periods (X–VI). A number of complete examples of bowls of varieties A and B were recovered from destruction levels of Period IV.

Type 6. Bowls with inward leaning rims

Bowls of this type merge into jars assignable to type 30 or allied types. It was often uncertain to which category fragments of rim should be assigned. This difficulty was particularly acute in regard to rims from the earlier levels (Periods X–VI). Many of those classified as jar rims of class A I might have belonged to bowls of this type in view of their fine burnished fabric.

Cf. Troy shape A 16 (*Troy* i 62 fig. 263).

Type 7. Bowls with inward leaning rims and high shoulders

These shade into bowls of type 6 and jars with rims of class A. I. Some thickened club-like rims grouped here are closely related to the internally differentiated rims of type 11 and like them appear to have been at home in the horizon of Period VII–VI. A variety of short thick rim with pointed top common in levels of V–IV is virtually a form of the following type 8, but with the carination rounded. In the case of some bowls, parts of the rim were assignable to type 7, while other parts were carinated as type 8.

Type 8. Bowls with carinated shoulders and tall rims

This type of bowl was especially characteristic of the earlier periods from X to VI at Emporio, being very well represented in VIII and again in VI. Comparatively few rims, and those not very typical ones, were recovered from levels of V–IV. Type 8 seems to be in effect the earlier equivalent of type 9 with short carinated rim, dominant from Period V onwards.

Rims assignable to type 8 ranged in diameter from *c.* 10 to 40 or more, but mostly seemed to lie between 15–30. The rims above the carination might be straight, convex or concave. The outsides of the rims in Period VIII were often decorated with pattern burnish. The carination was sometimes quite sharp, but more usually rounded. The sides below the carination often had a marked inward curve. Bases as far as it was possible to judge tended to be more or less sharply defined, and were often sunk, sometimes markedly sunk.

Bowls of type 8 occurred at Tigani on Samos (*Tigani* 133, F 11–14, 16. Cf. *PPS* xxii (1956) 180 fig. 8: 8–10). The new excavations suggest that they were common and characteristic in an early, but not in the earliest, phase of occupation there (*Samos* xiv 131, 132). They do not, however, appear to have been in evidence in the early periods at Poliochni. Similarly at Saliagos comparable bowls were extremely rare and only represented from the later Strata 2 and 3 (*Saliagos* 37, 83 f. fig. 35: 15, 17). On the other hand type 8 rims seem to have been at home on the Kephala site on Kea assigned to a rather later phase of the Late Neolithic than Saliagos (*Kephala* 14 pl. 29: B–D, F, H). Some Middle and Late Neolithic vases from Knossos are not unlike type 8 bowls in shape (e.g. *BSA* lix (1964) 199 fig. 40 (4), Stratum III. Cf. ibid. 187 fig. 34: 19–22; 193 fig. 37: 14, 15, Strata III and II. *BSA* xlviii (1953) 110 fig. 6: 41, 42).

On the Greek mainland this is 'a very common shape in Neolithic pottery' according to Weinberg, *Hesperia* vi (1937) 502. Ibid. 503 fig. 15 illustrates two rims of Neolithic 'Urfirnis' from Corinth which closely resemble type 8 ones from Emporio. Cf. *Hesperia* xlvii (1978) 436 ff. nos. 21, 22, Corinth: Forum West area, Late Neolithic. Bowls of this shape along with ones of Emporio type 11 are characteristic of the black burnished ware of transitional Middle to Late Neolithic in the Franchthi cave (*Hesperia* xlii (1973) 267 fig. 5: 1–5). Cf. *Athenian Agora* xiii 9, 31 no. 77, assigned by Immerwahr to 'Middle to Late Neolithic'. Cf. Kitsos cave: *BCH* xcvi (1972) 830 fig. 20, Late Neolithic, with a lug characteristically placed below the carination. Lerna: *Hesperia* xxvii (1958) 137 pl. 37: a–c; xxviii (1959) 205 pl. 41: d, Late Neolithic. *Prosymna* 369 pl. 621: 3. *Elateia* 181 ff. fig. 8: 9, 10. Varka (Euboia): *AE* 1975 Parart. 74 fig. 8, Late Neolithic. But rims assignable to type 8 also occur in Early Neolithic contexts on the Greek mainland (e.g. *Nemea* 262 fig. 3: b. *Otzaki-magula* Kat. I no. 19, pl. ii: 21, Protosesklo).

Bowls with rims of this kind were at home in the Late Chalcolithic of western Anatolia (e.g. *Beycesultan* i 89 fig. P. 8: 6, 7, 11; 93 fig. P. 9: 16–20). The type was evidently current in Anatolia from much earlier times, however, and many bowls which approximate to it were recovered from Hacilar and from the settlement at Çatal Hüyük West (*Hacilar* passim. *AS* xi (1961) 179 f. figs. 11, 12). Bowls of this type with sharp carinations are illustrated from Can Hasan level 2 B (*AS* xii (1962) 39 fig. 9: 3, 4, 6). There is a rim of this type, with the stump of a handle rising from it like the large bowl handles from the earliest levels at Emporio, illustrated from the Karain cave in the Antalya region and assigned to the Chalcolithic (*Belleten* xix (1955) 286 pl. iii).

At Byblos on the coast of Syria bowls with carinated bodies and type 8 rims were already present in the Early Neolithic (*Byblos* v 48 fig. 16: 24464, pl. lv). Bowls assignable to type 8 were found alongside jars akin to type 41 in the lowest levels at Hassuna in Mesopotamia (*JNES* iv (1945) fig. 7: 1–2); and they occurred with Halaf painted decoration at Arpachiyah and Chagar Bazar (e.g. *Iraq* ii (1935) fig. 60: 3, 5; iii (1936) fig. 22: 8).

Type 9. Carinated bowls: A. Rims at open angles, B. Rims at sharp angles, C. Rims concave on the outside, D. Short bevelled rims, on (1) deep bowls, (2) shallow bowls

This type seems to replace type 8, although it may not have evolved from it, or at any rate not in the Aegean area. The carination is in general sharper than is normal in type 8, and the rim above the carination is lower. A number of rims from the earlier periods X–VI have been classified as belonging to type 9, but this type was really characteristic of Periods V–IV when it became by far the commonest type of bowl. Carinated bowls of type 9 continued to predominate in Period II, and they were still fashionable in I.

The earlier series of rims of this type at Emporio may not have any connection with the later ones. They could be considered as merely low-rimmed varieties of type 8 rather than as ancestors of the later type 9 rims. Similar bowl rims are attested in early horizons elsewhere in the Aegean area and also in Syria. They occur for instance at the beginning of the Early Neolithic at Knossos and continue into the Middle Neolithic there (*BSA* xlviii (1953) 112 f. fig. 7: 5, 9; 121 f. fig. 11: 14. Cf. *BSA* lix (1964) 163 fig. 22: 12; 165 fig. 23: 6, 37, for other possible examples from levels of E.N.I.). A number of such rims was recovered from the upper Neolithic levels (N 3–1) at Tell Sukas on the Syrian coast (*Sukas* iii 66 fig. 162; 75 figs. 187–8, 192; 82 fig. 213. Cf. *Judeideh* 73 f. fig. 43: 12–14; 139 f. fig. 105: 9, in Dark-faced Burnished Ware from Phases B and C).

The later series of type 9 bowls at Emporio corresponds to Troy shape A 12, which was the commonest shape of bowl in the Early and Middle Subperiods of Troy I, but which became rare by the end of the Late Subperiod (*Troy* i 60 f.). It still occurred, however, in Troy II, and although not reported from Troy III, was fairly common in Troy IV and V (*Troy* i 226; ii 124, 239 f.). The early Trojan varieties of this shape as found in Troy I do not have any handles, but tubular or trumpet lugs appear on some of them. Handles like those of type 9 bowls from Emporio V–IV occur on shape A 12 bowls of Troy II and IV–V. Type 9 bowls with vertical handles like 1019 of Period IV were exceptional at Emporio, and correspond to the rare Trojan Shape A 15, of which only one example was recovered, from the end of the Early Subperiod of Troy I (*Troy* i 61 f. fig. 266: 1).

Bowls with carinated rims of this type were very common at Thermi, especially in the early periods (shapes A 1–4, and B 4, which reappears in Class C); but there were examples of every period (Towns I–V) (*Thermi* 75 fig. 26, Class A Shapes 1–4; 80 fig. 28, Class B Shapes 2, 4; 81 fig. 29, Class C Shape 3 (some!). Cat. nos. 2, 4, 56, 93, 159, 191, 230–1, 322, 491, 495, 567. Illustrated on pls. x–xi, xxxv–xxxvii. One from Town V has a handle on the rim like several from Emporio (*Thermi* 128 pl. xxxvii no. 495). The shape occurs, but is very rare, at Poliochni, most of the few examples coming from levels of the evolved Blue period (*Poliochni* i 563 f., pls. xxvi: k, l; xxviii: f; lxxiv: c (evolved Blue); pl. cxxi: i (Green)).

Type 9 bowl rims are abundantly represented on sites in the hinterland of north-west Anatolia (D.H. French, *AS* xvii (1967) 49 ff., 72 fig. 9: 25–35, and many others, some wheelmade; *AS* xix (1969) 60 ff., 77 ff. figs. 8–12). Such rims were found at the Late Chalcolithic site of Büyük Güllücek (*Belleten* xlvi (1948) pl. ciii fig. 43: top left), and in both the Chalcolithic and the Copper Age horizons at Alishar, those of the Chalcolithic apparently being more numerous and typical (*Alishar* 1930–32 i figs. 81, 175). One or two short carinated rims akin to type 9 are attested alongside rims of type 8 from the Late Chalcolithic at Beycesultan (*Beycesultan* i 87 fig. P. 7: 1, level XXX; 100 fig. P. 12: 44, level XX); but such rims were first well represented there in E.B. I (ibid. 121 type 5), while by E.B. II bowls with type 9 rims were by far the commonest bowl shape, and were provided with handles or lugs of one kind or another (ibid. 141 type 2). Rims like type 9 are attested further east in Anatolia, round Malatya at the beginning of local E.B. II, and in the neighbouring Elazığ region in E.B. III (*AS* viii (1958) 170, 194, 199 f. nos. 214–5, 235–6). But they do not seem to occur in northern Anatolia (C.A. Burney, *AS* vi (1956) 179–203); and they appear to be absent from the material assigned to the E.B. 1–2 horizon of the Konya plain which includes rims of type 11 (J. Mellaart, *AS* xiii (1963) 199 ff.). One, however, is illustrated from the Late Chalcolithic layer I at Can Hasan (*AS* xiii (1963) 38 fig. 5: 14).

The Anatolian versions of this type of rim may have derived their ultimate inspiration from the 'metallic' bowl rims of the Uruk-Jemdet Nasr (Protoliterate) horizon in Mesopotamia as reflected in Syria and Palestine in the Late Chalcolithic and E.B. I periods there. Potential ancestors of type 9 bowls abound in Palestinian E.B. I before the Dynastic period in Egypt, and are also at home in Palestinian E.B. II which overlaps with the earliest Egyptian dynasties (e.g. Amiran, *APHL* pls. 9: 7; 11: 3; 13: 4 (E.B. I); pl. 15: 4 (E.B. II). *Byblos* v 271 fig. 149; 274 f. figs. 152–3. Hennessy, *Foreign Relations* 63 pl. xlix. Cf. *AS* i (1951) 127 type 4). Bowls with short carinated rims like type 9 are still found later in the Bronze Age in Palestine (e.g. Hennessy, *Foreign Relations* pl. viii: 78, Jericho E.B. III A. *Hama* ii. 1, 53 fig. 58, Hama J). Rims from the E.B. II horizon in Cilicia (*Tarsus* ii pl. 347: AA–HH) are very comparable with type 9 rims from Emporio V–IV and might indicate the route by which the fashion for this kind of bowl rim spread from the east to Chios and the Troad, if the equation of Cilician E.B. II with Troy I is accepted (e.g. M.J. Mellink, 'Anatolian Chronology', in R.W. Ehrich, *Chronologies in Old World Archaeology* (Chicago and London, 1965) 101 ff.).

Bowls with type 9 rims were at home in Early Helladic II on the Greek mainland (e.g. Lerna: *Hesperia* xxix (1960) 291 fig. 1: C–E. *Zygouries* fig. 90: 107. *Eutresis* fig. 128: 3–5. *Asine* 233 f. figs. 163: top centre, 164: 1, 2, called E.H. III, but from a horizon comparable with Lerna E.H. II). But such bowls had already made their appearance in Early Helladic I (e.g. plain burnished wares assigned to E.H. I from Eutresis: *Hesperia* xxix (1960) 146 fig. 7: V. 2–3. Cf. Perachora Phase Y: *BSA* lxiv (1969) 63 fig. 5: 11). They are also attested in the Late Neolithic of southern Greece (e.g. Varka (Euboia): *AE* 1975 Parart. 74 fig. 8. *Thorikos* iii 16 fig. 26. Franchthi cave: *Hesperia* xlii (1973) 271 fig. 7: 19–20, matt-painted ware. *Elateia* 182 f. fig. 8: 4, 5. Cf. Kea, Ayia Irini, in Phase A assigned to the end of the Neolithic: *Hesperia* xli (1972) 360 fig. 2: A 7, A 8).

There are many comparable rims from the earliest (Black) period at Poliochni, and some
Bowls with rims of this type are also found in the Late Neolithic and Early Bronze Ages of Thessaly and Macedonia (e.g. eastern Macedonia: Doxat-Tepe: *ADelt* xxx (1975) 215 fig. 5: 21, and Paradimi: *JRGZMainz* x (1963) 2, 16 fig. 1, assigned to L.N. Western Macedonia: Kritsana: *PMac* 158 no. 134, and *Argissa* iii 197 pl. 70: 8, assigned to L.N. Thessaly: *Ayia Sofia Magula* 7 f. pl. 6: 14, with a wart on the carination, assignable to the Arapi or Otzaki phase of Dhimini). Type 9 rims occur sporadically at Early Bronze Age sites in western Macedonia (e.g. *Argissa* iii pls. 77: 4, 6; 79: 1, 2, 8 (Ayios Mamas); pls. 81: 1; 82: 2; 83: 9, 12, 13; 84: 5 (Vardaroftsa); pls. 86: 8; 87: 16; 88: 1 (Saratse)). They seem to be well represented throughout all phases of the Thessalian Early Bronze Age at Argissa (*Argissa* iii pls. 8: 1–4; 11: 7; 32: F Thess I–III, but more especially in F Thess II and III. Cf. Milojcic, *Ergebnisse* 27 fig. 22: 7. *AA* 1956, 155 fig. 10: 1, 2).

A few type 9 bowls appear alongside ones with rims of types 11 and 12 at sites in Romania (Berciu, *Contributii* 256 fig. 89: 20, Sǎlcuţa I; 441 fig. 217: 2, Gumelniţa I c).

Type 10. Bowls with short, S-shaped, usually thickened club-like rims: A. Deep, B. Shallow

Bowls of this type occurred in Period VIII but were characteristic of VII—VI. Some rims assignable to the type were recovered from levels of V; these and a few from later levels may be earlier strays. Rims of type 10 shade into those of other types, notably 13 and 14. Some of the bowls with type 10 rims were evidently deep (type 10 A), but most seem to have been more or less shallow as type 10 B. The bowls tended to be large, and some may have measured as much as 40 or 50 in diameter. They regularly appear to have had trumpet lugs set on the outside. Rims of this type occurred in Fine Black Burnished Ware and in Light Brown Burnished Ware and Red Burnished Ware. Many were of the distinctive Mottled Ware characteristic of Period VII.

This type was evidently at home in the Late Chalcolithic of north-west Anatolia. It is not in evidence at Troy, for instance, although characteristic examples are illustrated from Kum Tepe I B 2 and 3 (*Kum Tepe* 330 fig. 13: 409; 332 fig. 14: 518–9, 521; 337 fig. 15: 547). A rim from Kum Tepe I A 2 is drawn as if belonging to type 10 by Renfrew, *Emergence* 74 fig. 5. 3: 1, but has a much less distinctive profile in the final report (*Kum Tepe* 325 fig. 11: 227).

There are many comparable rims from the earliest (Black) period at Poliochni, and some from the evolved Blue (*Poliochni* i 540 pls. v–viii; 554 pl. x: p–t; 563 pl. xxvii: d. Renfrew, *Emergence* 74 fig. 5. 3: 14). A narrow trumpet-shaped lug below a rim assignable to this type is illustrated from Thermi as 'common in Town I, already rare in Town II' (*Thermi* pl. xxxi: 6). This suggests the possibility that some at any rate of the rims of this type from levels of Emporio V–IV might be of contemporary date.

Type 10 rims from sites in north-west Anatolia are grouped by French as (3) (b) 'Kum Tepe I b' along with rims of type 11 (*AS* xix (1969) 59, 77 fig. 8: 7, 4, 6). Some rims of his groups (5) Red burnished and (6) Grey/Black burnished of the Troy I horizon from the Akhisar/Manisa area are comparable with Emporio rims assigned to types 10 and 11, although most are akin to type 9 (ibid. 60 ff.). Some rims of his 'Beycesultan' type black burnished ware which may be contemporary with Beycesultan Late Chalcolithic are also rather like some type 10 rims (*AS* xvii (1967) 57, 75 fig. 12: 18, 19). A few Late Chalcolithic bowl rims from Beycesultan itself look similar (e.g. *Beycesultan* i 80 type 3, of L.C. 1, and some of type 19 of L.C. 3, ibid. 93 esp. 89 fig. P. 8: 1). An incipient form of this type of rim seems to be attested in Hacilar VIII (*Hacilar* ii 246 f. fig. 48: 28).

A number of rims of Weinberg's 'Gray Monochrome Ware' characteristic of the Late Neolithic at Corinth (e.g. *Hesperia* vi (1937) 509 fig. 24) resemble type 10 rims like 543 and 558, although the fabric seems entirely different. Some rims from the deepest level at Koufovouno in Thessaly, classified as Γ 1 α 1 or 2 ware and assignable to the very end of the Middle or beginning of the Late Neolithic, appear to be similar (*Thessalika* i (1958) 7 f. figs. 5, 6). Two rims from the grotto above the Asklepieion at Athens, associated with rims of type 11 and trumpet lugs and assigned to Late Neolithic or Early Helladic I, might be classified as of this type and are not unlike 527 of Period VII (*Annuario* xiii–xiv (1930–31) 475 figs. 58: f, 59: n). A rim with trumpet lug from the Late Neolithic at Vardina in Macedonia looks like a variety of type 10 (*PMac* 76, 153 no. 118). Rims akin to type 10 are also found on Early Cycladic marble bowls (e.g. *AA* 1969, 240 f. fig. 8).

Some rims from Sălcuţa in Romania contemporary with rims of types 11 and 12 could be derivatives of this type (e.g. Berciu, *Contributii* 251 fig. 85: 5, 11; 256 fig. 89: 23).

Type 11. Bowls with inward curving rims, internally differentiated and usually thickened: A. Deep, B. Shallow

This type was virtually confined to Periods VII–VI. It was especially characteristic of VII where it was the commonest type of bowl. But type 11 rims were still well represented in VI, although overshadowed there by ones of type 10 in the proportion of 2:1. Type 11 rims seem to merge into those of the following type 12, which may have developed from them: a certain number of internally differentiated rims from levels of VII–VI are embryonic versions of type 12 and have been classified as such. The thickened incurving rim was probably devised in the first instance to prevent the liquid contents of bowls splashing out of them.

Bowls with anti-splash rims of this kind were typical of phase I B at Kum Tepe in the Troad, and they were evidently characteristic of the pre-Trojan horizon in that part of western Anatolia (*Kum Tepe* 327, 330, 332. French, 'Late Chalcolithic Pottery in North-West Turkey and the Aegean', *AS* xi (1961) 99–141; 'Additional Notes', *AS* xiv (1964) 134–7. *AS* xix (1969) 59, 77 fig. 8: 3, 5, 8–13. Hanay Tepe: W. Lamb, *PZ* xxiii (1932) 115 fig. 2: 1–3. Renfrew, *Emergence* 72 ff. figs. 5. 2: 8–9 (Emporio VII), 5. 3: 4 (Kum Tepe IA), 6, 9 (Kum Tepe IB); ibid. 123, 162). Thus, while a few such rims are reported from Thermi (*Thermi* pl. xxxiii: 1. *AS* xiv (1964) 136 f. fig. 9: 9), they are not in evidence at Troy itself and in general the fashion for them appears to have died out before the beginning of Troy I in the Trojan area. At Poliochni, however, where the pottery of the earlier periods seems to show a development largely independent of the Trojan culture area, comparable rims are attested in the Black period (*Poliochni* i 541 pls. iv: s; vii: i), but seem to be more in evidence in the evolved Blue and Green (ibid. 554 ff. pls. xiv–xvi; 614 ff. pls. cx and cxi). Brea (ibid. 614 ff.) compared the type 11 rims of the Green period with those of Kum Tepe and made them one basis for equating the early part of his Green period with Kum Tepe IA and IB. But while some of the Green period bowls with these rims were provided with trumpet lugs, others only had unperforated and atrophied versions of them.

While such bowl rims are at home at Emporio and in the Trojan region of north-west Anatolia in the period before Troy I, they do not seem to be much in evidence in the more or less contemporary Late Chalcolithic of sites in the interior. The most characteristic example from Beycesultan appears to be a scrap of rim from Level XXXIX assigned to L.C. 1 (*Beycesultan* i 73, 79 fig. P. 1: 39, grouped with shape 1). But an isolated rim from Level XXX (L.C. 2) is also vaguely comparable with some Emporio rims assigned to type 11 (*Beycesultan* i 87 fig. P. 7: 1, classified as an aberrant form of shape 4); while the shallow bowls of black burnished ware with flat-topped short rims found at the beginning of E.B. 1 (Levels XIX, XVIII) might be considered as late and not very typical versions of type 11 bowls (*Beycesultan* i 119 shape 1, fig. P. 14: 2, 7). Bowls with rims of this type, however, appear to have been at home in the Konya plain at the beginning of the local Early Bronze Age (E.B. 1–2) (*AS* xiii (1963) 217 fig. 9: 13–15, 18–21).

Bowls with such rims were being made of marble as well as clay in the Cyclades by the beginning of the Early Bronze Age if not earlier (Renfrew, *Emergence* 152 ff. figs. 10. 1: 2–16; 10. 2: 6, 12 (marble). *AS* xi (1961) 111 fig. 15: 21–23. Paros: *AM* xlii (1917) 51 fig. 55, with a horizontally perforated lug below the rim, and traces of white painted decoration on the lug. Melos: *Phylakopi* 83 no. 4 may refer to such bowls among the Earliest Pottery. Kea, Paoura: *Hesperia* xli (1972) 358 f. fig. 1: P 1–2, assigned to the Late Neolithic). These bowls from the islands with their long horizontally perforated lugs are very comparable with Emporio type 11 bowls and their equivalents from north-west Anatolia.

Bowls with rims of this type, sometimes at any rate with long tubular lugs, and upon occasion apparently of a fabric akin to Emporio Mottled Ware, were also at home in different parts of the Greek mainland in the Late Neolithic, which appears to overlap with Early Cycladic I (Doxat-Tepe (East Macedonia): *ADelt* xxx (1975) 211, 215 fig. 5: 1. Kritsana I/II: *Argissa* iii 197 pl. 70: 8. Athens: *Annuario* xiii–xiv (1930–31) 467 fig. 50: u, v; 475 fig. 58: b, d. *Hesperia* vi (1937) 540 fig. 1: c, d; 541 fig. 2: a, b, d (two of these (fig. 2: a, b) have long tubular lugs below the rim, and one (fig. 2: a) is mottled red and black with red dominant, which sounds comparable with Emporio Mottled Ware). Cf. *AS* xiv (1964) 136 f. fig. 9: 1–3. *Athenian Agora* xiii 9, 32 no. 81. Cf. *AS* xi (1961) 111 fig. 15: 24. Kitsos Cave: *BCH* xcv (1971) 711 fig. 22, of red ware with pattern burnish inside; xcvi (1972) 830 fig. 21, for a typical complete bowl with vertically perforated lug, which from the description sounds as if it might be of fabric corresponding to Emporio Mottled Ware. Corinth, Forum West area: *Hesperia* xlvii (1978) 438 no. 25. Lerna II: Renfrew, *Emergence* 74 fig. 5. 3: 12, 13. Diros cave (Alepotrypa): *AA* 1971, 360 fig. 54: c, d. Possibly *Orchomenos* ii 29 f. fig. 27, class D. *Kephala* 14 pl. 29: K).

Comparable anti-splash rims, but none of them necessarily from bowls with long perforated lugs like those of Emporio type 11, are attested on the Greek mainland from the beginning of the Late Neolithic or end of the Middle Neolithic (e.g. *Prosymna* 369 pl. 621: 5. Franchthi Cave: *Hesperia* xlii (1973) 269, 267 fig. 5: 6–10, assigned to the transition from Middle to Late Neolithic. *Elateia* 183 fig. 8: 10, and 189 pl. 61 c: 2, from the Bothros in Trench 3, assigned to the end of the Middle Neolithic which seems to correspond to Franchthi transitional Middle to Late Neolithic).

Anti-splash rims akin to type 11 occur on bowls of crusted ware assignable to the Rakhmani horizon in Thessaly (*DS* 247 figs. 147, 149. *PThess* 18). But similar rims are also it seems attested in the Thessalian Early Bronze Age (D. French, *AS* xiv (1964) 135, in reference to *AS* xi (1961) 140 fig. 15: 13) and in Early Helladic I and II (French, *Pottery Groups* 18 fig. 21: 7, from Kastron (Topolia) Magoula. *Berbati* 147 fig. 112: 6).

Bowls with comparable anti-splash rims are found in the Balkans. Their importance was first recognised by J. Mellaart, *Antiquity* xxxiv (1960) 270 ff., who used them as an argument for equating the beginning of the Gumelniţa culture with the early stages of Troy I. This idea was developed by D. French, *AS* xi (1961) 99 ff., who suggested that the beginnings of Gumelniţa might have to be placed back in the Late Chalcolithic of western Anatolia, contemporary with Beycesultan L.C. 3 and 4 or earlier (ibid. 121); but it seems more likely that the Balkan rims of this type were copied from Troadic or Aegean prototypes. Rims akin to our type 11 were apparently found at Sitagroi (Fotolivos) in levels of the earliest Period I there well before the appearance of Gumelniţa type wares in Period III (e.g. *PPS* xxxvi (1970) 229 fig. 6: top). It is true that in western Anatolia this type of rim goes out of fashion at the beginning of the Early Bronze Age (Troy I). In the Balkans, however, as at Poliochni, it appears to survive alongside shapes inspired by Trojan prototypes of Early Bronze Age date (e.g. Berciu, *Contributii* 256 fig. 89: 5, Sălcuţa I, and many other examples illustrated from later phases at Sălcuţa; ibid. 457 fig. 234, ranging from Boian V to Gumelniţa IV at Tangîru).

On the southern side of the Aegean in Crete there is a similar late survival of a fashion for anti-splash rims of this kind. These appear towards the end of Early Minoan I, but are characteristic on bowls of the Early Minoan II period in the Knossos area and in eastern Crete (S. Hood, *The Minoans* (London, 1971) 37. *Myrtos* 100, 155 fig. 39, P 24–28, of Period I).

Anti-splash rims of this type are found on bowls in Syria and further east somewhat earlier it seems than their appearance in Anatolia or the Aegean area. At Geoy Tepe in north-western Iran such rims were at home in Period M (T. Burton-Brown, *Excavations in Azarbaijan, 1948* (London, 1951) 25 figs. 5 and 6, esp. fig. 5 pl. iii no. 46. Cf. Burton-Brown 1970: 42, 49, 58). At Judeideh in Syria they are characteristic of Phase G, but continue into H (e.g. *Judeideh* 265 fig. 202; 352 f. fig. 269: 8; 354 fig. 271: 1. Cf. *Hama* ii. 1, 35 fig. 37; 42 fig. 49 (Hama K); 53 fig. 58 (Hama J)). In Palestine they seem to appear in E.B. II which overlaps with the First Dynasty in Egypt (Amiran, *APHL pl.* 15: 5, 6). In Cilicia they are attested at Tarsus in E.B. I which appears to correspond to Judeideh Phase G (*Tarsus* ii 101 fig. 242: 97, 98 d). If Tarsus E.B. I is substantially earlier than the beginning of Troy I the fashion for such rims might have spread from Syria or Cilicia coastwise to the Aegean and north-western Anatolia. Some rims from the Konya region grouped by Mellaart as E.B. 1 or 2 look very comparable (e.g. *AS* xiii (1963) 217 fig. 9: 13, 15, 18, 21) Anti-splash rims of this type also occur on Egyptian stone bowls of late Predynastic and Protodynastic date (Burton-Brown 1970, 90).

It is just conceivable that this distinctive type of rim was first adopted on stone bowls and afterwards transferred to clay ones. But some vases of fine grey or grey-black burnished ware with small rims of this type in the Late Neolithic of the Greek mainland and in Cretan Early Minoan I B–II A look as if they could have been inspired by metal vases (e.g. *Annuario* xiii–xiv (1930–31) 430, 437 fig. 23: h. *Myrtos* 155 fig. 39, P 23, of Period I). Rims of this type in Black Ware from the Greek mainland are assigned by Phelps, *Thesis* to his Period III of Late Neolithic, while rims of the standard Kum Tepe I B–Early Cycladic I type (as type 11) are placed by him late in Period IV (Final Neolithic).

There is also a late version of this type of rim, assignable to the Middle and Late Bronze Ages in Anatolia (e.g. *Troy* iii pls. 359: 11; 369: 9, 10, early in Troy VI. *AS* vi (1956) 200 f. nos. 139–47, from north-western Anatolia. *Archaeologia* lxxxvi (1936) 25 fig. 9: 7, Kusura C. K. Bittel, *Boğazköy: die Kleinfunde der Grabungen 1906–12* (Leipzig, 1937) pl. 37: 2–6, 8. F. Fischer, *Die Hethitische Keramik von Boğazköy* (Berlin, 1963) pls. 91–96. *Tarsus* ii pls. 316–8, 384, L.B. II). These later varieties of anti-splash rim bowls do not appear to have anything to do with the earlier Chalcolithic series, and are comparable with Syrian bowls of the same general horizon like *Alalakh* pl. cix types 2a and 5, much at home in Period V there. Cf. Ras Shamra: *Syria* xvii (1936) 127 fig. 16: S, U; 131 fig. 18: E; xix (1938) 237 fig. 31: K.

Type 12. Bowls with straight rims, thickened and usually differentiated on the inside: A. Deep, B. Shallow

At Emporio this was in effect a later version of type 11, being well represented in Periods V–IV, although a number of rims classifiable as type 12 were recovered from levels of VII–VI. Rims of types 11 and 12 merge into each other, and French, *Pottery Groups*, Notes on Table Fig. 18 p. 2, considers the types as one. Type 12 bowls correspond to Trojan shape A 6, attested in all phases of Troy I, but not recognised from levels of Troy II during the latest excavations (*Troy* i 58 f. pl. 224: 33.167, Early Subperiod; pls. 253–5. Cf. *Kum Tepe* 346 fig. 23: 705; 351, from I C 1 and 2). Bowls with such rims also occurred at Thermi, where they seem to have been at home in Towns I–III but not later (*Thermi* fig. 26, Class A form 5; 77 fig. 27: 4–6, Towns I–III; fig. 28, Class B forms 5, 6; 108 no. 160, Town II or III; pl. xxxii: 3–5, Town III). A few rims of this type are illustrated from the Black and evolved Blue periods at Poliochni (*Poliochni* i 541 pls. iv: g, v: k (Black); 564 pls. xxviii: 1 (might be our Type 13), m; xxxix: h (evolved Blue)).

There are somewhat comparable rims from the Macedonian Late Neolithic, which may overlap with Troy I (*PMac* 153 no. 118, 158 no. 135, from Vardina and Kritsana. Cf. *AS* xi (1961) 108, 136 fig. 13: 28, from Drama (Gioumenitsa). *PZ* xlii (1964) 43 fig. 8: 13, 14, graphite-decorated ware, from Sitagroi (Fotolivos)). But rims of this type are also found at various stages of the Neolithic in the rest of the Aegean area, in the Early Neolithic of Crete, for instance, and on the Greek mainland (J.D. Evans, *BSA* lix (1964) 214, 179 fig. 30: 10, 11 (E.N. II). Cf. ibid. 165 fig. 23: 8 (E.N. I); *BSA* lxiii (1968) 274. *Prosymna* 368 f. fig. 620: 1. Athens: *Annuario* xiii–xiv (1930–31) 475 fig. 58: a. Other examples from Corinth and Gonia illustrated by Phelps, *Thesis* 223 fig. 31: 7; 291 fig. 49: 14). A rim of this type from Kastron (Topolia) Magoula in Central Greece is assigned by French, *Pottery Groups* 18 fig. 21: 10, to Early Helladic I. Another from Euboia has also been placed in Early Helladic (*BSA* lxi (1966) 88 fig. 19: 1).

Rims assignable to type 12 appear sporadically in the Chalcolithic and Early Bronze Age in parts of Anatolia outside the Troad. *Hacilar* ii 251 fig. 50: 13 from Level VI (end of the Late Neolithic) appears to be of this type. Some rims of painted ware from Çatal Hüyük assigned to the Early Chalcolithic look closer to rims of type 12 than to ones of type 11 (J. Mellaart, *AS* xi (1961) 183 fig. 14: 6, 9). For other possible type 12 rims from the Anatolian Chalcolithic, e.g. *AS* viii (1958) 162 f. no. 34; xvii (1967) 58, 74 fig. 11: 41. *AS* xix (1969) 60, 70 fig. 8: 37, 38, may be imports from the Troad according to D. French.

Rims of this type are found in Romania alongside those of type 11 (e.g. Berciu, *Contributii* 256 fig. 89: 1, 260 fig. 93: 10–12, 276 fig. 107: 3, 319 fig. 142: 6, 7, from Sălcuţa I, IIa, IIc, IV; 457 fig. 234: 14, 19, 26). They occur at Anzabegovo in southern Yugoslavia in Phase IV assigned to early Vinča (M. Gimbutas, *JFA* i (1974) 57 fig. 26: b. *Anza* 129 fig. 79).

Type 13. Bowls with outward-curving rims, internally differentiated and thickened: A. Deep, B. Medium, C. Small and shallow

This type was represented by a few rims from levels of VII and VI, but only became common in Period V at Emporio. It was still very much at home in Period II, but afterwards appears to have gone out of fashion. Some rims of this type were recovered from the lower levels of the Upper Cave at Ayio Gala (AG 54, 55).

Two rims of coarse ware from Kum Tepe I B 3 have profiles classifiable as type 13 (*Kum Tepe* 333 fig. 18: 532–3). At Troy type 13 rims are included along with those of type 12 in Trojan shape A 6, which was at home in Troy I but does not seem to be recorded from later deposits in the recent American excavations. Cf. *SS* 1 no. 13, Troy I. While rims of type 12 were quite well represented at Thermi, none of those published appear to correspond to our type 13. A few rims of the evolved Blue period at Poliochni, however, are akin to this type (*Poliochni* i 564 f. pls. xxxix: i, xli: b). There is a bowl rim of this type from a latish Bronze Age context at Tigani (*Tigani* 191 fig. 5: 6), but such rims are not in evidence at the Heraion site on Samos.

Rims like this are well attested in the Early Neolithic III Preseklo phase in Thessaly and are found on bowls of the succeeding Sesklo phase there (e.g. *Otzaki-magula* 35, 42, 52 f., 149 pls. xvii: 6, 7; xxi: 5–17; xxv: 16, 17; 4: 1–12. *Ergon* 1965, 7 fig. 2. Cf. *PAE* 1965 pl. 1). They also occur in the Late Neolithic of Macedonia (*PMac* 147 no. 72 and perhaps 158 no. 135). A stray rim of this type from Euboia has been assigned to Early Helladic I (*BSA* lxi (1966) 87 f. fig. 19: 6. *Argissa* iii beil. 29: 35).

At Beycesultan in Anatolia such rims appear to be much in evidence from the very beginning of the Late Chalcolithic (e.g. *Beycesultan* i 80 fig. P. 1: 2, 5). Possibly rims of this kind had their ultimate origin in the Halafian pottery of the Levant. Rims of a rather comparable shape are standard on Halaf and other contemporary wares of the Amuq (e.g. *Judeideh* 144 fig. 113, 149 fig. 166, Phase C). A rim of this type is illustrated from the Late Neolithic at Byblos (*Byblos* v 141 fig. 82). But such rims were also current in Predynastic Egypt (Petrie, *Corpus* pl. xlvi: type 26 a, SD 46–72; pl. xlv: type 8, SD 65–78).

There is a rim of this type from an early Starcevo context at Anzabegovo in Jugoslavia (*Anza* 53 fig. 30: 4). For possible derivatives of the type in the western Mediterranean (Malta: Tarxien cemetery and Sicily: Castelluccio) see J.D. Evans, *PPS* xxii (1956) 97 f. fig. 6.

Type 14. Bowls with outward-curving rims, not internally differentiated, but sometimes thickened: A. Deep, B. Medium, C. Shallow, D. Dish-like

Bowls of this type were first recognised in levels of VIII from which came the complete example 156. But they only began to be common in Periods VII–VI, and were very much at home throughout V–II at Emporio.

Rims of this shape are not conspicuous among the handmade wares of Troy I–II, nor do they seem in evidence at Thermi. But rims from Poliochni, mostly of the evolved Blue period, are of this type (*Poliochni* i 540 pl. v: t (Black), not very typical; 560, 564 f., pls. xxviii: d, xxxi, xxxiv, xxxv (Blue); 617 pl. cxxi: h (Green)). At Beycesultan, however, the type is very much at home in the Late Chalcolithic but not in the succeeding Early Bronze Age. Dish-like versions (type 14 D) seem best attested in the earliest levels there assigned to Late Chalcolithic 1 (*Beycesultan* i 79 fig. P. 1: 36–7, 42–3).

Type 14 rims are found in other parts of Anatolia during the Chalcolithic if not earlier. One from the Karain cave near Antalya with painted decoration is assigned to the Neolithic (*Belleten* vii (1963) 86 fig. 9 b). They also occur in the Late Neolithic (Levels IX–VI) at Hacilar (e.g. *Hacilar* ii pl. li figs. 45: 1, 21; 50: 10). There is a characteristic bowl of this type from the Early Chalcolithic Level V (*Hacilar* ii 272 fig. 60: 6). Another comes from the Middle Chalcolithic Layer 2 A at Can Hasan (*AS* xiii (1963) 39 fig. 6: 14). Bowls with this type of rim seem at home in the Late Chalcolithic of the Konya plain, and are very characteristic of Mersin XII A which is related to it (*AS* xiii (1963) 203 fig. 3: 14–19. *Mersin* 184 f. fig. 118). Such rims also occur in the Chalcolithic of eastern Anatolia (*AS* viii (1958) 162 f. nos. 13, 15).

Flaring-rim bowls, some of which correspond to our type 14, are very characteristic of Saliagos, although they appear to decline in popularity in the later Strata 2 and 3 (*Saliagos* 37 fig. 35: 11, 12, 19 and many of the pedestal bowls). In the Franchthi cave it was noted that towards the end of the Middle Neolithic there was a tendency towards slightly more graceful shapes, e.g. bowls with a gentle S-curve profile like our type 14 (*Hesperia* xxxviii (1969) 367, 364 fig. 6: 2). Such rims were also at home in the Late Neolithic at Franchthi (*Hesperia* xlii (1973) 270 fig. 7:

13–15), and at Corinth (*Hesperia* xlvii (1978) 443 ff. no. 49; 445 no. 52). They occur in Phase B at Nea Makri (*AM* lxxi (1956) 19 fig. 35, 22 fig. 40), and are attested at Kephala on Kea (*Kephala* 14 pl. 30: B). But incipient type 14 rims seem to come in the Early Neolithic Phase 1 at Elateia (*Elateia* 169 fig. 5: 8), and there are bowls with comparable rims in Phase I a at Achilleion near Pharsala assigned to the Early Pottery stage (E.N. I) of the Thessalian Neolithic (*Achilleion* 292 fig. 15). Similar bowls are also attested in the Presesklo phase (E.N. III) at Otzaki (Milojcic, *Ergebnisse* 38 fig. 8: 13, 17. *Otzaki-magula* pls. 9, 10, 12). Type 14 rims are common in the Middle Neolithic Sesklo horizon of Thessaly, and they are found in early Starcevo contexts at Anzabegovo in Jugoslavia (*Anza* 49 fig. 26: 1, 2).

Rims of type 14 abound in the Halaf culture, and they are found on Late Neolithic bowls at Byblos (*Byblos* v pl. lxxxiii). But dishes akin to our type 14 D are already seen in the Middle Neolithic there (*Byblos* v 104 fig. 57. Cf. ibid. pl. lxxxii and 141 fig. 82, Late Neolithic). Such dishes also occur in the Halafian horizon at the beginning of the Middle Chalcolithic (level XIX) at Mersin (*Mersin* 114 f. fig. 72: 2, 118 f. fig. 74: 6).

Type 15. Carinated bowls with outward-spreading rims: A. Straight, B. Concave on the outside

A few atypical rims, mostly from levels of Period V, are grouped here. Some or all of these may have belonged to dipper cups of type 16.

Type 16. Dipper cups: A. As type 5, B. As type 13, C. As type 14, D. As types 9 and 15

A number of small bowls with high-swung handles from levels of V–II have been placed together here. The handles were large in relation to the size of the bowls, which were often of very fine fabric and elegant in shape. They were presumably drinking cups. Rims were mostly classifiable under type 5, although some were more akin to type 4. A few were as types 9, 14 and 15. A group of these cups from levels of Period II had rims like bowls of type 13.

Shallow dipper cups akin to those of Emporio with type 14 rims are attested at Thermi (*Thermi* 80 fig. 28: cups B 4. Cf. ibid. 114 no. 257 pls. viii, xxxvi). But most of the cups with high-swung handles there appear to be deep like Trojan shape A 31 (*Troy* i 63, from Troy I. Cf. *Troy* ii 125 shape A 28, from Troy IV). The very few vases from Troy that are at all comparable with our dipper cups are assignable to Troy II or later (*Troy* i 317 fig. 414: 17. *SS* 13 no. 285, 27 no. 540). A dipper cup, however, like a crude version of 1140 of Period IV/III is assigned to the evolved Blue period at Poliochni (*Poliochni* i 565 pl. xl: b); and handles which might have belonged to such cups occurred in the Blue and were relatively common in the Black period there, although many of these might have come from two-handled varieties (*Poliochni* i 543, 565 pls. vi: f, vii: f, viii: a–c, xl: e–g, and pls. iii: a, vii: r, for the two-handled version). A dipper cup with type 14 rim from Kos is illustrated by Buchholz and Karageorghis 64 no. 805. Another from Kos with type 5 rim has a rounded base and thick-sectioned handle (*Boll. d'Arte* xxxv (1950) 325, 323 fig. 98).

Although they are not much in evidence at Troy, dipper cups akin to those of Emporio seem to be at home in the Copper and Early Bronze Ages elsewhere in Anatolia including the Trojan hinterland. There are many for instance from the Iznik region of north-west Anatolia assignable to the horizon of Troy I or later (*AS* xvii (1967) 49 ff. figs. 7: 39, 10: 21, 13: 47, 14: 23–26, 17: 22, 24, 18: 2, 19: 20, 46). For examples from other sites, e.g. Asarcik Hüyük (Ilica) west of Ankara: *Ist. Mitt.* xvi (1966) 63 fig. 3: 3–6, 9–10, with rounded or flat bases, assigned to E.B. 2–3. Polatli, most of groups 5 and 7: *AS* i (1951) 38 f., 33 fig. 5. Alaca Hüyük: *AJA* li (1947) 153 fig. 1, top left. *Beycesultan* i 143, pl. xxi: 19, Sheet 4, E.B. 2 type 6. Karataş-Semayük: *AJA* lxx (1966) 249 pl. 60

fig. 23, from level I (E.B. II). Dipper cups with rounded or flat bases are found in the region of the Konya plain (*AS* xiii (1963) 214, 223 fig. 12: 4–8). An embryonic version with a rather small handle level with the rim is illustrated from the Early Bronze Age settlement at Müskebi on the coast of Caria (*Archaeology* xvii (1964) 248).

A fragment with handle, apparently from another somewhat embryonic cup of this type, is assigned to E.B. I at Tarsus, but more characteristic examples occurred there in E.B. III (*Tarsus* ii 103 no. 138 fig. 346; 135, 161 nos. 705, 707 figs. 283, 354). A flat-bottomed cup with high-swung handle and painted decoration comes from the latest Middle Chalcolithic level XVI at Mersin (*Mersin* 150 f. fig. 93: 3). Ladles with rounded bottoms and high-swung handles occur in the Cypriote Early Bronze Age in Red Polished III ware (*SCE* iv Pt. 1 A fig. cxlix: 10–12).

Dipper cups were found at Eutresis in Groups III–V assigned to Early Helladic I (*Hesperia* xxix (1960) 140, 144, 146, 164 (IV. 8–12) with references to Anatolian Copper Age examples. Cf. *Eutresis* 86 fig. 106). Cups of a somewhat comparable shape, but often with rounded or pointed bases, are at home at the beginning of the Bronze Age in Thessaly and eastern Macedonia (Milojcic, *Ergebnisse* 26 fig. 21: 11–13. Cf. *AA* 1956, 155 fig. 12. *Argissa* iii pls. ii: 1–3, 5; 8: 1–4: F Thess I. Dikilitash: *BCH* xcii (1968) 1063 fig. 4. Sitagroi: C. Renfrew, *Baden Symposium* 430 fig. 1. Cf. *PPS* xxxvi (1970) pl. xli). Some of those from Sitagroi with flat bases are reminiscent of Middle Helladic cups like *Eutresis* 177 fig. 255: 1, 2.

Type 17. Bowls with a ledge round the inside
The only rim assignable to this type (2505) came from a level of Period I. It may have been from a lid rather than a bowl, but some rims from Troy I assigned to bowl shape A 14 are similar (*Troy* i 61, 131, pl. 262: 2, 3).

Type 18. Bowls with a ledge below the rim outside
The three rims assignable to this type came from levels of V, II and I. It corresponds to Trojan shape A 14 which apparently occurred only in the Early Subperiod of Troy I and in Fine Polished Ware (*Troy* i 61 pl. 262: 1–12. *SS* 4 nos. 112–4). A fragment of a bowl of this distinctive Trojan shape has been recognised from Koiladha, a Late Neolithic site in western Macedonia (D.H. French, 'Some Problems in Macedonian Prehistory', *Balkan Studies* vii (1966) 107 f. fig. 2: 2).

ii. (B) *Jugs, theriomorphic vases, and tripod cooking pots* (types 20–27) (FIG. 99)

Types 20–24. Jugs
Jugs of type 20 with flat mouths and strap handles rising above the rim occurred in the earliest levels (e.g. 161) and were evidently characteristic of Periods X–VIII. A carinated jug with sloping mouth (164) like type 23A was allegedly found in the same deposit of Period X as 161, but the context seems highly improbable and doubtless reflects some confusion in the excavation records.

Jugs of type 20 appear to have been in use in the Karain cave near Antalya alongside bowls with large handles rising above the rim like those current in Emporio X–VIII (*Belleten* xix (1955) 288 pl. iii, assigned to the Chalcolithic). The restored drawing of such a jug from the Karain cave is a more elegant version of 161 from Emporio X. But there is nothing similar to Emporio type 20 from Hacilar, and the flat-mouthed jugs of the Late Chalcolithic at Beycesultan with their outward-curving rims appear to be closer in shape to some of those of Emporio VII–VI described below.

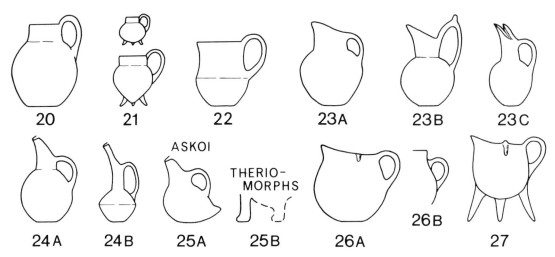

FIG. 99. Pottery (B) Jugs, theriomorphic vases and tripod cooking pots (types 20–27).

Jugs of type 20 were still it seems in evidence in the later horizon (upper levels of the Upper cave) at Ayio Gala (AG 167–71). But the Ayio Gala jugs of this type look more evolved in character than the early Emporio ones like 161, and they may have remained in use alongside jugs of type 23 as found in levels of Emporio VII–VI (e.g. AG 172–3).

The jugs of which large numbers of fragments were recovered from levels of Periods VII–VI at Emporio seem in general to have approximated to type 23A common in Emporio V–IV. But the mouths of jugs of Emporio VII–VI tended to be wider and straighter, either flat or sloping at a less steep angle than was usual later. Most of these jugs of Periods VII–VI were of Light Brown Burnished Ware, or, in the case of many of the smaller examples, of Fine Black Burnished Ware often decorated in white.

Some jugs with wide slightly sloping mouths from the cemetery at Kusura resemble in shape ones of Light Brown Burnished Ware from Emporio (*Archaeologia* lxxxvi (1936) 54 ff. pl. x). The cemetery appears to be assignable to Kusura A which may go back into the late Chalcolithic (ibid. 16, 59). Flat-mouthed jugs of a comparable type were at home in the Late Chalcolithic of Cilicia (*Tarsus* ii 90 pls. 231–2, 343 nos. 25, 27), and also in that of western Anatolia. Such jugs occurred in all phases of the Late Chalcolithic at Beycesultan: some of these were decorated in white in a manner reminiscent of jugs of Fine Black Burnished Ware from levels of Emporio VII–VI (e.g. *Beycesultan* i 92 fig. P. 9: 4, 22). Flat-mouthed jugs, some decorated in white, were also found in the Iasos cemetery, where the latest elements probably date from late Troy I or early II (*Iasos* i 564 fig. 97: 11; ii 529 fig. 163: left. J. Coleman, *AJA* lxxviii (1974) 33, for the date).

Similar jugs were evidently at home at Kum Tepe in Phase I B and earlier (*Kum Tepe* 332 fig. 14: 522–3). A fragment of one from Kum Tepe I A 2 has white-painted decoration like that which appears on jugs of Fine Black Burnished Ware from Emporio (*Kum Tepe* 325 fig. 9 pl. 73: 222a). But the closest parallels for the jugs of Emporio VII–VI come from the islands of Lemnos and Samos to north and south. Black burnished jugs with sloping mouths and decoration in white exactly like Emporio ones of Fine Black Burnished Ware occurred in the Black period at Poliochni, where they continued into the Blue period, although rare by the evolved phase of it (*Poliochni* i 543 f., 568 f. pls. i: d–f; xlviii: b, d—o). A complete jug from Tigani looks very much like a flat-mouthed variety of a Light Brown Burnished Ware jug from Emporio (*Tigani* 146 pl. 37: 1. Cf. ibid. 145 F 35, 39, 40). The new excavations at Tigani suggest that jugs like those of Emporio VII–VI were very characteristic of the latest occupation deposits before the abandonment of the site at the beginning of the Early Bronze Age (*Samos* xiv 133).

The Light Brown Burnished Ware of the majority of the jugs from Emporio VII–VI appears to be related to the Urfirnis ware of the Middle and Late Neolithic on the Greek mainland. Some Urfirnis jugs from Corinth may have been akin to those of Emporio VII–VI in shape (S. Weinberg, *Hesperia* vi (1937) 502). The handles are not illustrated, but Weinberg describes them as 'usually broad ribbon handles extending from the lip to the shoulder' (cf. Lavezzi, *Hesperia* xlvii (1978) 407). But a vase of Middle Neolithic Urfirnis ware with handle to rim from the Franchthi cave has a carinated body and is restored as an askos (*Hesperia* xlii (1973) 265 fig. 4). In view of the rounded bases of the Emporio jugs of Light Brown Burnished Ware it is interesting that none of the fragments of Urfirnis ware from Varka in Euboia came from bases, although rims were much in evidence; but nothing is said about handles, and there is no suggestion that jugs were among the shapes represented (*AE* 1975 Parart. 68).

The jugs of Periods V–IV were dominantly of type 23A, but mouths tended to be narrower and more sloping than was normal earlier, while spouts might be distinctly pointed (e.g. 1151) instead of rounded as was usual in VII–VI. Most of the jugs of type 23A from the Period IV destruction level correspond to Trojan shape B 13, which was the commonest shape of jug in Troy I but was not attested in Troy II (*Troy* i 66 fig. 228). But some of the Emporio jugs of this shape are distinctly more elegant than any of those preserved from Troy. The profile of 1151 with neat pointed spout and backward sloping neck is somewhat reminiscent of jugs from the Cyclades. Jugs with exceptionally low swellings like 1149 and 1150 of Period IV are illustrated from the Early Bronze Age settlement of Müskebi on the coast of Caria (*Archaeology* xvii (1964) 247 f.).

Jugs with sloping mouths akin to type 23A are attested in Cilicia from the beginning of the Bronze Age (E.B. I) onwards. But even the earliest examples assigned to E.B. I are relatively narrow-necked (*Tarsus* ii 99 ff. figs. 237, 241–3, 345 nos. 53–6, 102–5, 129). Varieties of jug akin to Trojan shape B 13 and Emporio type 23A also appear from the beginning of the local Early Bronze Age in other parts of western Anatolia (e.g. *Beycesultan* i 125 shapes 14 and 16. *Iasos* ii 534 fig. 167: 3).

On the Greek mainland such jugs are at home in Early Helladic II (e.g. *Eutresis* 104 fig. 137. Cf. *Hesperia* xxix (1960) 155 pl. 51: VIII. 28. *Asine* 209 fig. 156).

Jugs of type 23A also occur in Romania alongside bowls with rims of types 11 and 12 (e.g. Berciu, *Contribuţii* 302 fig. 127: 1 (303 fig. 128), from Sălcuţa IIc).

Jugs with clearly defined cutaway spouts as type 24A were first attested in Period VII (640, 641) and continued into I. A number of complete examples were recovered from the Period IV destruction level. These correspond to Trojan shape B 15 which, although never common, occurred throughout the Early Subperiod of Troy I and rarely in the Middle and Late Subperiods (*Troy* i 67 fig. 227: 35.649). The cutaway spouted jug first appears in the Konya plain in E.B. 3 and is evidently of West Anatolian origin according to J. Mellaart, *AS* xiii (1963) 220. But such spouts seem to be attested on jugs as early as E.B. II in Cilicia (e.g. *Tarsus* ii fig. 262 no. 356).

The exceptional jugs, 1158 of type 23B and 1168–9 of type 24B, have no close parallels at Troy. But two decorated jugs from Thermi resemble 1158 in shape although without its elegance (*Thermi* pl. viii: 207, 253, from Town III). Rather similar but squatter jugs were recovered from levels of the Blue period at Poliochni (e.g. *Poliochni* i pl. xlii). The tall narrow necks of 1168–9 are matched on the Trojan shape B 19, but this had the handle set below the rim (*Troy* i 68. Cf. K. Bittel, *Prähistorische Forschung in Kleinasien* (Istanbul, 1934) 30 f., 133 pl. iii: 2).

The two examples of double-spouted jugs of type 23C (2392, 2540) came from levels of II and I. The type is almost certainly Anatolian. There are several examples from Troy (e.g. *Ilios* 553 nos. 1174–5 from City IV. Cf. *Beycesultan* i fig. P. 67 no. 14, pl. xxvii: 4, E.B. 3. *Ist. Mitt.* xvi (1966) 8 f. fig. 4: 26). An example with three spouts was recovered from Karataş-Semayük (*AJA* lxxiii (1969) 321 pl. 73 fig. 10, Tomb 273).

In the earlier periods at Emporio the handles of jugs were almost invariably set to the top of the rim. This was still the rule during periods V–IV, but a few jug handles assignable to IV were attached below the rim. The setting of the handle below the rim became standard practice in Emporio II. Most jugs in Troy I similarly had the handles set to the rim, and although some types with handles below the rim (shapes B 3, B 17, B 18) are attested in Troy I, they are more characteristic of Troy II, while types which appear for the first time in Troy II or later at Troy seem to have their handles below the rim (e.g. *Troy* i fig. 130, shapes B 7, B 20–24). Jugs with handles set below the rim seem to be distinctly less in evidence than ones with handles to the rim at Thermi. Similarly jugs assignable to E.B. 1–2 on the Konya plain tend to have the handles to the rim (J. Mellaart, *AS* xiii (1963) 220).

A new feature which appears on a number of jugs of Emporio II is a sharp ridge or carination down the throat (e.g. 1575). The throat of a jug from Beycesultan level XV of E.B. 2 has a similar carination (*Beycesultan* i 160 f. fig. P 31: 11).

Type 25. Theriomorphic vases: A. Bird-vases (askoi), B. Other animal-shaped vases

Three fragments that may have belonged to vases in the shape of animals or birds were recovered from levels of Periods X, IX and VII (167–8, 652). But the few relatively complete examples of bird-vases of type 25A (1170–3) all came from the Period IV destruction level.

Bird-shaped as well as other animal-shaped vases are attested in Anatolia from very early times (e.g. *Hacilar* i 107; ii 267 fig. 57: 14, from Hacilar VI assigned to the end of the Late Neolithic). There are many Anatolian bird-vases of Bronze Age date (e.g. *Beycesultan* i 242 fig. P. 67: 12 pl. xxx: 3, E.B. 3 *b*. Karataş-Semayük: *AJA* lxxi (1967) 253 pl. 76 fig. 10. *BSA* xix (1912–13) 56 f. fig. 4: a). They were common in the Yortan culture of north-west Anatolia (*BMA* 6, A 32–33. *Ist. Mitt.* xvi (1966) 21 ff. fig. 9: 75–78). But theriomorphic vases from Troy are like animals, not birds (*Ilios* nos. 160, 333–9. *SS* nos. 607–8, 1481). Vases that are even more obviously bird-like than Anatolian examples were made in Crete during the earlier part of the Bronze Age there (e.g. *VTM* 41 no. 4121. Cf. *PM* i 115 ff. fig. 85, 146 fig. 107). Some from the palace at Phaistos assigned to Phase I b (M.M. II A?) are not at all unlike 1171 in shape (D. Levi, *Festòs e la Civiltà minoica* (Rome, 1976) pl. 148: a, e).

The legless askoi and askoid jugs made on the Greek mainland in Early Helladic II (e.g. *Eutresis* 104. Lerna: *Hesperia* xxv (1956) 169 pl. 46: e; xxviii (1959) 204 pl. 41: e. Dörpfeld, *Alt-Ithaka* 303 pls. 64: 5, 65: 3) are not bird-like and may stem from a different and very old tradition, since an Early Neolithic prototype is attested from the Peloponnese (*Nemea* 265 pl. 63). Vases of comparable shape from the Early Neolithic settlement of Nea Nikomedeia in Macedonia are handleless like one of Middle Neolithic date from Lianokladi I (*ILN* 11 April 1964, 566 fig. 9; 18 April 1964, 606 fig. 13. Cf. *PThess* 175 fig. 119: *b*). Such vases may be derived from gourd prototypes. Handled askoi of this non-theriomorphic class occur in the Thessalian Late Neolithic and in the Macedonian Early Bronze Age (*AM* lvii (1932) 114 f. pl. xxviii. *PMac* 82). An askos of the early Blue period at Poliochni may have been of this kind rather than theriomorphic (*Poliochni* i 569 f. pl. xliii: a). Early Balkan askoi also appear to belong in the same tradition (Gaul, *Neolithic Bulgaria* pl. lv: 4–9. Berciu, *Contributii* 278 fig. 109: 3).

Type 26. Cooking jugs: A. With handle to rim, B. With small handle set below rim

One complete vase (1174) and fragments of others from levels of V–IV were assignable to this type. A number of rims from deposits ranging from V–II may have belonged to vases of this kind, but could not be distinguished from those of other types, notably tripod cooking pots (type 27).

Some vases from Thermi seem comparable (*Thermi* fig. 26, Class A cups 1; pl. viii nos. 25, 73, from Town I).

Type 27. Tripod cooking pots

Tripod cooking vessels of all shapes have been grouped under this heading. Such vessels were first well attested in Period V, although three cooking pot feet were allegedly found in levels of VI, and one (654) in a deposit of VII. Several complete or restorable examples were recovered from the Period IV destruction level (1178–1182 and 2329). Tripod cooking pots remained common in Period II, from deposits of which 927 feet were counted, an average of 4 or 5 a basket. More than 65 feet were assignable to Period I making an average of nearly 3 a basket.

The standard type of tripod cooking pot in Periods V–IV was evidently jug-like with a single vertical handle to the rim and sometimes with an open spout opposite the handle. Cooking vessels of this kind were in effect tripod versions of type 26. Some, however, appear to have been shallower, resembling large tripod dishes. In Period I it seems that tripod cooking vessels of a different type with a pair of vertical handles like 2543 were current.

Tripod cooking pots were at home at Thermi and also at Troy from the time of Troy I onwards. Our cooking pots from the Period IV destruction level correspond to Trojan shape D 24, common in Troy I and still found in Troy II but rare it seems later (*Troy* i 75 f., 240; ii 33 f., 248 f.). The fragment illustrated from Troy III has the handle set below the rim like our 2543 of Period I (*Troy* ii fig. 74: 35.516). Cooking pots from Thermi, especially those of Class A Cooking Cup 2 (*Thermi* fig. 26), appear to be even more closely comparable with ones from Emporio. Compare our 1181 of Period IV with *Thermi* no. 26 from Town I, and 1180 with no. 210 from Town III. *Thermi* no. 440 from Town IV (illustrated with nos. 26 and 210 on *Thermi* pl. ix) resembles Emporio 2543 of Period I but has only one handle.

Tripod cooking pots are not attested at Poliochni in the Black period which corresponds to Emporio VII–VI, and those of the Blue period and later with their elegant legs and neat lunate-sectioned handles are not strictly comparable with the types found at Troy, Thermi and Emporio. But a type with a single handle to the rim which was current in the Blue and Green periods at Poliochni seems to be replaced in the Red by one with two handles set below the rim (*Poliochni* i 578 ff., 624, 643 f. pls. lxx–lxxiii, cxxxii, cxlii, cliv-clvii). This change corresponds to what can be observed at Emporio, and also perhaps at Thermi and Troy.

At Beycesultan tripod cooking pots are not attested in the Late Chalcolithic, but are relatively common in E.B. 1 and continue in E.B. 2 and 3 (*Beycesultan* i shape 28 of E.B. 1, shapes 20 and 23 of E.B. 2, shape 31 of E.B. 3). The E.B. 1 cooking pots with handles to rim are reminiscent of those from the Period IV destruction levels at Emporio, while Emporio 2543 of Period I with handles below the rim is more akin to Beycesultan shape 20 of E.B. 2. Tripod cooking pots are not mentioned from Kusura Phase A, but occurred in B and C (*Archaeologia* lxxxvi (1937) 19 ff. fig. 7: 2, 26 f. fig. 10: 11).

Tripod cooking pots do not seem to occur in Cilicia, nor in the central and eastern regions of Anatolia (cf. B. Brea, *Poliochni* i 580). They are only common in the western part of Anatolia and there only from the beginning of the Bronze Age. In Crete they appear for the first time in Early Minoan II (e.g. *Myrtos* 123 ff., 179 f. figs. 62–3), but remain one of the standard types in use throughout the island during the rest of the Bronze Age and into the Early Iron Age. In the Cyclades, however, and on the Greek mainland tripod cooking pots were evidently not at home, and their sporadic appearance there may reflect Anatolian or Cretan influence (e.g. G.E. Mylonas, *Προϊστορικὴ Ἐλευσίς* (Athens, 1932) 84 f. fig. 62: 1–3: fragments of handmade cooking vases said to have three or four feet and assigned to Middle Helladic. *Thera* iv pl. 101: a, right). The ones found in the Late Neolithic settlement at Olynthus in western Macedonia (*Olynthus* i 22, 1: d fig. 22: 1) may have been inspired by examples further east, assuming that the Macedonian Late Neolithic overlaps with the horizon of Troy I. Cooking pots on four instead of three legs occurred at Tsangli in Periods V and VI assignable to the Thessalian Late Neolithic (*PThess* 113, 108 fig. 58: b): these are reminiscent of the bowls on four legs from the Gumelniţa horizon in Romania (e.g. Sultana: *Dacia* i (1924) 80 ff. fig. 12 pl. xviii: 2. Pietrele: *Mat. si Cercetari* ii (1956) 532 fig. 51: 2).

The idea of the tripod cooking vessel may have originated in the Levant and spread westwards from there. Large tripod vases with everted rims and circular-sectioned feet were in general use at Byblos in the Late Aeneolithic, although there was no evidence that they had been set over fires (*Byblos* v 300 fig. 161 pl. cl).

iii. (C) Jars (types 30–47) (FIGS. 100, 101)

Few jars apart from those from the Period IV destruction levels were sufficiently well preserved for it to be possible to distinguish their types when complete. The great mass of jar rims could not be assigned with confidence to one type of vessel rather than to another. The rims have therefore been divided into two groups according to whether or not they came from vases with clearly differentiated necks; where the neck did not seem to be differentiated from the body the rim was grouped as class A, where the rim sprang from a more or less clearly differentiated neck it was placed in class B. Class A rims tended to belong to comparatively wide-mouthed jars, while many of those of class B were from narrower mouthed vessels. Within each of these two main classes A and B three categories of rim have been distinguished: I, inward-leaning; II, ogival; and III, outward-curving.

In the earlier periods X–VIII bowl–jars of various kinds, including simple hole-mouthed jars with rims of class A I, were much in evidence (FIG. 100). The term bowl-jar has been used for these early vessels because it is often difficult in practice to decide whether they should be classified as jars or bowls. There was evidently a range of vessels of the same general type shading from what were clearly jars at one end of the scale to bowls at the other. J. Mellaart has drawn attention to a similar feature in the earliest pottery from Hacilar levels IX–VI. 'Very typical of this early pottery is a graduation in size of the vessels as well as in shape, so that it is often purely arbitrary to regard a vessel as a bowl or a jar' (*Hacilar* i 102). While hole-mouthed jars with rims of class A I (types 30, 34, 35) were characteristic of the early levels, such jars (e.g. types 34, 38) remained current at Emporio into the Early Bronze Age.

Bowl-jars resembling those from the early levels at Emporio and from the earlier horizon distinguishable at Ayio Gala are standard at Hacilar in the Late Neolithic levels IX–VI, but the vase shapes from Hacilar V onwards are not so comparable. Hacilar may not lie in the direct route of ancestry for the pottery of the earliest Periods X–IX at Emporio, although it appears to do so for the earlier horizon of red-surfaced pottery from Ayio Gala through the intermediary of sites like Morali inland from Smyrna.

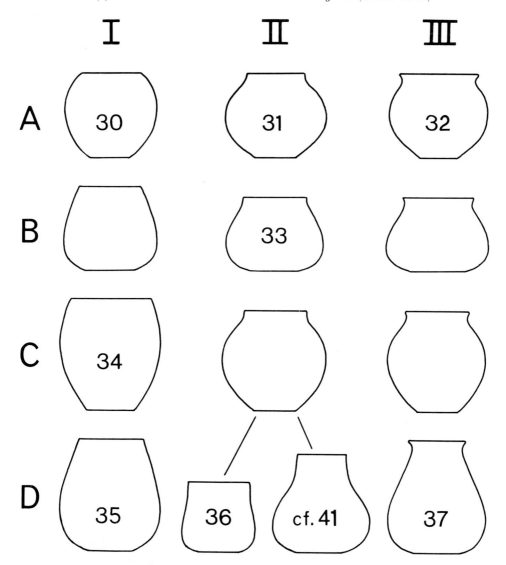

FIG. 100. Potential range of jar and bowl-jar shapes of Periods X–VI.

The earliest Neolithic pottery of Cilicia (Mersin levels XXXII–XXVI) includes shapes that might be ancestral to the bowl-jars of Emporio and Hacilar alongside prototypes of jars of Emporio type 41 (*Mersin* 20 f. fig. 11). Some vessels from Mersin XXXII–XXVI have simple inward-leaning rims of class A I, while others display ogival or outward-curving ones (as classes A II and III).

Bowl-jars similar in a general way to those from the early levels at Emporio were evidently at home on the Greek mainland from the beginning of the Neolithic there (e.g. *Nea Makri* 5 figs. 1, 3. *Nemea* 264 fig. 5: g. *Orchomenos* ii 36 fig. 34. French, *Pottery Groups* 4 fig. 20: 1–7, from Souvala in Central Greece). Such bowl-jars, including some with distinctive rims of class A III as found on early ones from Emporio, are a feature of the Early Neolithic of Thessaly from the Early Pottery

(Achilleion Culture) phase onwards through Protosesklo (E.N. II) and Presesklo (E.N. III) (Milojcic, *Ergebnisse* figs. 5–8. *Otzaki-magula* pls. 7–9, beil. 5, rim form V. 1–4. *Achilleion* figs. 15–18). Similar bowl-jars were recovered from the Early Neolithic settlement at Nea Nikomedeia in western Macedonia (*ILN* 11 April 1964, 564 ff. figs. 4–6). Bowl-jars in shape like those of Emporio from Ayios Petros off Kira-Panayia in the Sporades have painted decoration which Theochares compared with Early Neolithic Protosesklo and Chaeronea wares on the one hand and Anatolian Early Chalcolithic ones on the other (*ADelt* xxv (1970) Chron. 274 ff. figs. 3–5; xxvi (1971) Chron. 296).

Bowl-jars of shapes very comparable to those of Emporio VIII occur in Middle Neolithic patterned Urfirnis ware from Corinth (*Hesperia* xlvii (1978) 435 f. nos. 13, 14, 19; 434 fig. 3). But the vase shapes of the Thessalian Middle Neolithic Sesklo Culture, like those of Hacilar from level V onwards, do not appear to offer such good parallels for the bowl-jars from the early levels at Emporio (e.g. Milojcic, *Ergebnisse* figs. 9–12. *Achilleion* figs. 20–21).

Type 30. Squat bowl-jars with simple inward-curving rims (class A I)
This and the following types 31 and 32 might be classified as bowls of type 6. They were common in the earliest periods X–VIII, when they were characteristic of fine fabric with the outside surfaces well burnished and often elaborately decorated with incision.

Bowl-jars of type 30 might have a pair of small vertical handles or vertically perforated lugs on the shoulders. This type was attested from levels of X–VIII (e.g. 169, 170) and from those of VII and perhaps VI.

Type 31. Squat bowl-jars as type 30, but with ogival rims (class A II)
This is an early type, attested in Periods IX and VIII (171–2), and perhaps in VII–VI. Bowl-jars of this type might have small vertical handles on the shoulders.

Type 32. Squat bowl-jars as type 30, but with outward-curving rims (class A III)
Bowl-jars of this type like those of type 31 might have small vertical handles on the shoulders. The only restorable example (173) came from a level of VIII: it was decorated with incision in the manner characteristic of that period.

Type 33. Squat bowl-jars with low shoulders
The only certain example of this type (656) may be an import, since it has unique features, such as the little horizontal strap-handle inside the rim and the elaborate curvilinear decoration combining alternate swags of encrusted red paint and jab-like incisions.

Type 34. Jars with simple incurving rims (class A I)
These may have small vertical handles (like 174) or vertically perforated lugs (657) on the shoulder. Jars of this type were at home in Periods X–VI, but were still common in V–IV. Some of the later jars may have had only one handle (e.g. 1194). A one-handled jar like this would correspond to Trojan shape A 25, not common, but occurring throughout Troy I (*Troy* i 63). But most of the jars of this type from levels of V–IV including 1194 may have had two handles, like the round-bottomed amphoroid cooking pot 1 of *Thermi* figs. 28, 29a: Classes B and C.

The shape appears to be at home in the earliest horizon of Neolithic pottery in Anatolia (e.g. Mellaart, *Çatal Hüyük* pl. 110. *ILN* 9 Feb. 1963, 196, 198 fig. 14). It is evidently derived from the hole-mouthed bowl which was the standard shape in the earliest Neolithic of Cilicia (*Mersin* 19 note 2, fig. 10).

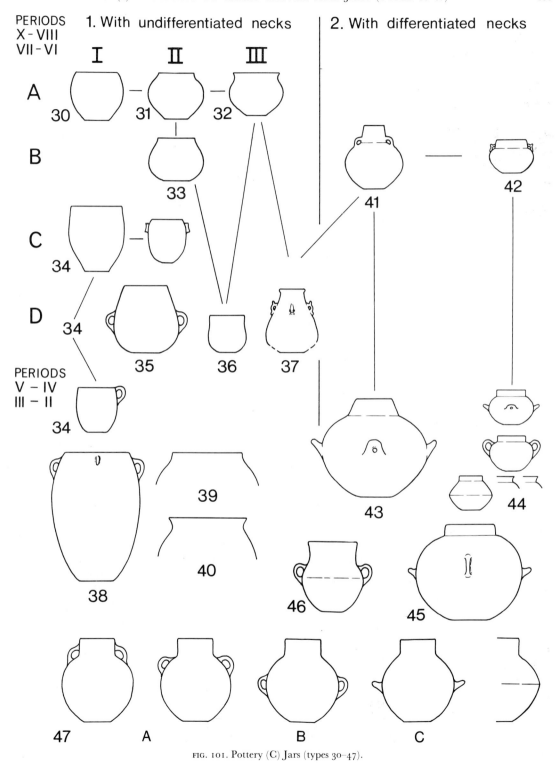

FIG. 101. Pottery (C) Jars (types 30–47).

Type 35. Large jars with simple incurving rims (class A I), low shoulders, and vertical handles

The two fragmentary examples assignable to this type (175–6) came from levels of IX and VIII. But the type was evidently in use in Period X, and perhaps later in VII and VI. Jars of this general shape with low shoulders appear to have been in use at Çatal Hüyük (e.g. *ILN* 9 Feb. 1963, 196, 198 fig. 11, with basket handle).

Type 36. Bowl-jars with wide mouths, tall outward-curving rims (class A III), and low shoulders

The only example (177) from a level of VIII is of very fine fabric with a red surface and elaborate pattern burnish. It may be an import.

Type 37. Tall jars with narrow mouths, outward-curving rims and low shoulders

The only example of this type (178), which appeared to belong in Period VIII, has been somewhat conjecturally restored. It is of very fine fabric with a red surface and elaborate pattern burnish reminiscent of 177 of type 36. It may also be an import.

Type 38. Large tall storage jars with simple incurving rims (class A I) and vertical handles on the shoulder

This is in effect a large version of type 34. One complete example (1184) and fragments of others were recovered from the Period IV destruction level. But jars of this general type may have been in use in earlier periods from X onwards.

The complete 1184 is comparable with Trojan shape C 17, common in the Early and Middle Subperiods but less frequent in the late Subperiod of Troy I (*Troy* i 70 pl. 229: 35.543), and with large examples of Amphora Cooking Pots 2 of *Thermi* fig. 29a, Class C, like ibid. pl. xxxvii: 519 from Town V.

Type 39. Large tall storage jars as type 38, but with ogival rims (class A II)

This variety of type 38 was only represented by fragments from levels of Period IV and later.

Type 40. Large tall storage jars as type 38, but with outward-curving rims (class A III)

In this variety of type 38 the mouth is wider owing to the way in which the rim curves outwards. Fragments assignable to this type were recovered from levels of Periods V–I.

The type corresponds to Trojan shape C 16, common in Troy I but occurring in Troy II (*Troy* i 70, 235 pl. 229: 36.736). Compare *Thermi* fig. 28, Class B Amphoroid Cooking Pot 2, and ibid. 117 pl. xxxvi no. 311. *PMac* 174 f. nos. 203, 205, of the Macedonian E.B.A.

Type 41. Globular jars with collar necks (class B I) and a pair of small vertical handles joining neck to shoulder

This type was common in the earlier levels from Period X onwards, being especially well represented in those of VIII, although still present in those of VII–VI. There was no evidence for its survival into Period V, and the unique 1231 with a rim of this kind from the Period IV destruction level has been classified as a separate type 43 in virtue of the character and position of the four vertically perforated lugs on the belly. The handles on the smaller vases assignable to type 41 tended to be miniature, resembling horizontally perforated lugs. Many of the handles, especially the smaller ones, were surmounted by warts.

Jars from Tigani which may have been very similar in appearance to those of Emporio type 41 had the same handles joining neck to shoulder, and in some cases at least these were surmounted by warts (*Tigani* 144, 140 F 25–27. *Samos* xiv 131 f.: Amphoren). One of these jars bears incised decoration of the kind typical of Emporio VIII: it is interesting that this was regarded by Heidenreich as an import (*Tigani* 135, 157 F 73, pl. 34: 1, 2).

Jars of type 41 are found at a very early stage in the Levant, and may have been inspired by Mesopotamian jars of comparable shape like those with relatively narrow upright necks and no handles recovered from the lowest levels I and II at Hassuna (*JNES* iv (1945) fig. 7). Jars closely resembling Emporio type 41 with handles joining neck and shoulder are already present in the earliest Pottery Neolithic (PNA) of Palestine (Amiran, *APHL* 18 f. Photo 1, with a style of decoration closely related to Hassuna). Such jars also occur in the Early and Middle Neolithic at Byblos (*Byblos* v 57 fig. 26. Cf. ibid. pls. lxxiii, lxxvi); while comparable jar rims appear in the Late Neolithic (Level VA or V.3) at Ras Shamra and are still current there in Level III (*Ugaritica* iv 165 fig. 6: 6, 12; 282 f. pl. x: 10; 487 fig. 6: C). There are a number of such jar rims from the Neolithic levels at Sukas (*Sukas* iii 41 fig. 97; 46 figs. 113–5; 57 figs. 132–3; 69 fig. 164). They are also found at Judeideh in Phase B (*Judeideh* 75 fig. 47: 10; 79 fig. 52: 14). A Neolithic jar from Mersin is similar to type 41 in shape, but has a wide mouth and no handles (*Mersin* 20 f. fig. 11: 7). Jars with type 41 rims, upright or sloping, and sometimes clearly differentiated at the join with the shoulder, were evidently much at home at Mersin in the Early Chalcolithic (Levels XXIII–XX) (e.g. *Mersin* 86 f. fig. 52: 1, 3, 4, 11, 15; 90 f. fig. 54: 8, 12, 16, from Level XXIII, and others from Levels XXII–XX on figs. 55–58). Similar rims, but narrower, were still in evidence in the Middle Chalcolithic (Levels XIX–XVII) there (*Mersin* 122 f. fig. 76: 1, 3).

The inspiration for this type as for the type 3 baking pan may have reached Emporio coastwise from the Levant rather than overland through Anatolia. The type has not been illustrated from Çatal Hüyük, and at Hacilar jars with necks of this kind do not appear to be attested before Level VII (*AS* viii (1958) 151, 142 fig. 7:17. *Hacilar* ii 248 f. fig. 49: 11); but rims like this neatly differentiated at the join with the shoulder occur in VI (e.g. *Hacilar* ii 258 f. fig. 54: 2), and after V they are common. Some jars from Hacilar with rims assignable to type 41, especially ones from the later levels, boast lugs or small handles set high on the shoulder or even in the angle between the shoulder and the base of the neck, as *Hacilar* ii 293 fig. 70: 28, 347 fig. 98: 2, 349 fig. 99: 5.

Straight upright rims, with a clear differentiation between neck and shoulder, and sometimes it seems with small handles joining them, occurred at Saliagos but were not common there (*Saliagos* 37 fig. 53: 4, 8). Similar well differentiated upright rims are found, however, in the earliest Neolithic of the Greek mainland and of Crete. Thus at Elateia jars with rims of this kind were one of the two predominating shapes of the earliest Phase 1 of the Early Neolithic (*Elateia* 169 f. pl. 52: e. Cf. *Nemea* 266, 264 fig. 5: h. *Prosymna* 368 f. fig. 620: 5, 6). Straight upright rims of this kind are also attested in the Early Pottery phase (E.N.I) of the Thessalian Early Neolithic (Milojcic, *Ergebnisse* fig. 5: 15). An example from a level of Early Neolithic I at Knossos in Crete has a small but wide handle joining neck and shoulder (*BSA* lix (1964) 169 fig. 25: 4). This is in harmony with the early appearance of jars with rims of this class at Emporio and in the Levant.

Rims of type 41 from relatively narrow-mouthed vases occur in the Middle Neolithic of the Greek mainland (e.g. Milojcic, *Ergebnisse* fig. 9: 10, 13, of the Thessalian Sesklo Culture. Walker Kosmopoulos, *Corinth* pl. ii: a, assigned to Period II). But jars with rims of type 41 were also at home in Thessaly and other parts of Greece in the Late Neolithic (e.g. *PThess* 31 fig. 11. Milojcic, *Ergebnisse* figs. 16: 21 (pl. 4: 1), 17: 6, 7. *Arapi-magula* pl. 23: 8 and beil. 4, types 41–42, 53, of the Arapi phase (Dhimini 2). Athens: *ADelt* xxi (1966) Chron. 42 f. pl. 63, called Subneolithic. Cf.

Kea, Kephala: *Hesperia* xxxiii (1964) 316 pl. 46: h). Rims assignable to type 41 are even found it seems in the Late Neolithic of Crete (e.g. *BSA* lix (1964) 193 fig. 37: 26, 195 fig. 38: 9).

A jar rim of the evolved Blue period at Poliochni has a pair of handles joining neck to shoulder after the manner of type 41 jars from Emporio (*Poliochni* i 571 pl. liv: d). Some jars with rims of this type assignable to the Late Neolithic on the Greek mainland similarly have a pair of handles joining neck to shoulder (e.g. *AA* 1971, 355 figs. 47, 48; 360 fig. 54: b, from the Diros cave (Alepotrypa) in the Mani). But often the Late Neolithic jars of this shape on the mainland are given a pair of vertical handles set on the shoulder or the swelling of the body, like the type 41 jar AG 205 from the later horizon at Ayio Gala (e.g. *AA* 1971, 356 fig. 49, from the Diros cave: another has four such handles on the swelling (*ADelt* xxvii (1972) Chron. pl. 192). The situation of these handles corresponds to that of the lugs on the unique 1231 of type 43 from the Period IV destruction level at Emporio. These mainland Late Neolithic jars with type 41 rims closely resemble in shape a type of jar with handles on the shoulder or belly very prominent at Mersin at the beginning of the Late Chalcolithic (Level XVI) there (*Mersin* 146 ff. figs. 91–92; 152 f. fig. 94: 13).

Some large jars, notably ones of shape C 10, from Troy II, and others from the archaic Blue and the Yellow periods at Poliochni, and from later levels at Thermi, are in effect similar (e.g. *Troy* i 233 f. pls. 390: 35.490; 394: 35.535, 35.775. *Poliochni* i 571 pl. liii: b; ii 266 ff. pls. ccxvi: a, ccxxiv: c. *Thermi* 82 fig. 29 *a*: Class C Amphora 1).

Jars with type 41 rims and handles on the belly in this manner occur in the later Neolithic of the Balkans (e.g. Berciu, *Contributii* 267 fig. 98: 1 (fig. 106: 2), Sălcuţa III). They are also found in Liguria in the local Middle Neolithic (*Arene Candide* ii 68 fig. 2 pl. xiii). A rather tall handleless jar of this type is illustrated from the pre-Starcevo level I B at Anzabegovo in Jugoslav Macedonia (*Anza* 44 fig. 20: 4).

Jars with type 41 rims, but with perforated lugs, or without lugs or handles of any kind, were at home at the beginning of the Early Bronze Age in the Cyclades (e.g. Renfrew, *Emergence* 160 fig. 10. 3), and have been found at Early Bronze Age sites on the mainland like Ayios Kosmas where Cycladic influence was strong (*Ayios Kosmas* 85 f. pl. 147 nos. 191, 194, 196). Jar rims of this type have also been recovered at Perachora in Phase X assigned to Early Helladic I (*BSA* lxiv (1969) 56 fig. 2: 13, 14), and in the Rakhmani horizon in Thessaly (Milocjic, *Ergebnisse* fig. 20: 7).

Jars with similar rims and lug-handles are found in Crete at the beginning of the Early Bronze Age, but these Early Minoan jars often at any rate had lids which fitted over the rims (e.g. *PM* i 61 fig. 24). Some Early Minoan jars with rims of this kind had shoulders flattened as if to receive a lid (*PM* i 61 fig. 20). Similar flattened shoulders are a feature of some jars with type 41 rims assignable to the Late Neolithic on the Greek mainland (e.g. *Orchomenos* ii 12 fig. 9).

Type 42. Small pyxis-like jars with wide mouths, low collar necks, and a pair of handles joining neck to shoulder

Jars of this type were in effect small wide-mouthed versions of type 41, and like type 41 jars were characteristic of the earlier periods (X–VIII) at Emporio, although still occurring in Emporio VII–VI. Such jars were no doubt used for the same kind of purposes as the type 44 pyxides which were at home in the succeeding Periods V–II, and may have been their ancestors. Small jars of comparable type are attested at Hacilar by Level VI there (e.g. *Hacilar* ii 258 f. fig. 54: 11, 12).

Type 43. Large jars with collar necks and four vertically perforated lugs on the swelling

One complete example (1231) was recovered from the Period IV destruction level. This unique vase may be a variant of a type of jar of similar shape, but with vertical handles on the swelling instead of lugs, found in the Late Neolithic of the Greek mainland as noted under type 41.

Type 44. Small jars (pyxides) with short collar necks and handles or lugs on the swelling

The rim may be conical, upright, or everted. The body is sometimes carinated. A pair of vertical handles, or two or four vertically perforated lugs, are set on or just above the swelling. Bases were normally it seems flat, but some jars of this type may have had ring bases or short tripod feet. A fragment (1891) from Area B stage 5, apparently of Period IV, comes from a jar of comparable shape, but with horizontal side handles on the belly and perhaps a spout.

Type 44 jars were common and characteristic in Periods V–IV, but still attested in II. They tended to be of fine fabric, with the surfaces well burnished and usually decorated with more or less elaborate incised designs. But a number of small jars assignable to this type of which fragments were recovered from levels of II had the surfaces plain with a very high burnish.

The type corresponds to Trojan shape C 27 with flat base (as 1232), or to C 31 or C 34 with a ring base or three short feet, all attested from the Early Subperiod of Troy I (*Troy* i 71 f.). Comparable pyxides were common at Thermi in levels of Towns I–III (*Thermi* 75 fig. 28 Class A, Pyxis 1; 99 ff. nos. 9–11, 98, 112–14, 127, 196–201, 249, 250, 565). The type is at home in the Yortan culture of north-western Anatolia (e.g. *Ist. Mitt.* xvi (1966) 16 nos. 57–59).

Comparable pyxides with a pair of perforated lugs are found in the Early Bronze Age in the Cyclades and in Crete (e.g. Syros: *AE* 1899 pl. 8: 8. Miamou: *AJA* i (1897) 290 fig. 3, 303 fig. 15).

Type 45. Large globular jars with short upright necks and horizontal side handles on the swelling

Two examples of such jars (1233–4) were recovered from levels of Period IV. One of these (1233) has small subsidiary handles on the shoulder, the other (1234) a pair of vertical handles on the shoulder in the spaces between the horizontal ones. The first of these jars (1233) at any rate may be an import.

There seems to be nothing exactly comparable from Troy, but the Trojan shape C 4 comes nearest (*Troy* i 69 fig. 131a: C 4). Large jars from the Red period at Poliochni with similar rims and with handles set high on the shoulders are taller and more evolved in appearance (*Poliochni* i 648 pl. clxii: c, d). A large store jar from the Mt. Kynthos settlement on Delos, however, is exactly comparable in shape, with a very low rim and four small handles on the shoulder: the handles on the swelling appear to be slashed like those on 1233 (*Delos* xi 40 f. fig. 38. MacGillivray 1979, 31 f. fig. 15 no. 392). A fine Early Bronze Age amphora from Thessaly with subsidiary handles is not unlike 1233 but has an everted rim (*AA* 1956, 149 f. fig. 6). The exceptionally large jar from the lowest stratum at Vasiliki, assignable to the end of Early Minoan I or beginning of Early Minoan II, may have been rather similar (*PM* i 60 f. fig. 22).

Type 46. Jars with tall slightly differentiated necks and outward-curving rims (class B III)

This is in effect a wide-mouthed variety of type 47. The only certain example of the type (1235) came from the Period IV destruction level. It has a pair of vertical handles set low on the shoulder with pairs of warts in the spaces between them.

Comparable in size and rather similar in shape, but with handles joining neck and shoulder, is the vase of shape A 42 from a level of Troy I (*Troy* i 64, 137 fig. 267: 35.542).

Type 47. Globular jars with tall necks and upright or outward-leaning rims

This type seems to be characteristic of Periods V–IV, but is attested later. Several complete or largely complete examples were recovered from floors of the Period IV destruction. The belly was normally rounded (e.g. 1240–2), but might be carinated (e.g. 1237, 1239). The standard type with rounded body was more or less globular in shape, but the most elegant examples had rather high perked-up shoulders. The type may be subdivided into three groups according to the arrangement of the handles: A, with two or four vertical handles on the shoulder (e.g. 1236); B, with a pair of vertical handles set on the belly (e.g. 1239); and C, with a pair of horizontal side handles on the belly (e.g. 1241–2). A greaty variety of rims seemed assignable to jars of this type.

Jars of Group A are comparable with Trojan shape C 3 which seems confined to Troy I (*Troy* i 69. Cf. *Thermi* figs. 26 and 29a, Classes A and C, Amphorae 2).

Group B jars recall one from a deposit of the end of the Blue period at Poliochni (*Poliochni* i 571 pl. liii: b).

Group C jars bear some resemblance to ones of Trojan shape C 15, which appears to have been developed in the late phases of Troy II, not being certainly attested before II f (*Troy* i 235 esp. pl. 390: 35. 431); but these are mostly taller and more evolved-looking then the complete examples from levels of Emporio IV. Compare with the Trojan jars, *Poliochni* i 623 pl. cxxiv: d, e of the Green, and 641 pl. clxii: a of the Red period, which Brea links to a standard type of Early Helladic jar. Some of these Early Helladic jars with globular bodies are not unlike the ones from Emporio in shape (e.g. *Asea* 79 fig. 81: a. *Asine* 213 fig. 158: 5. *Ayios Kosmas* fig. 54, shape S–16. *Eutresis* 118 fig. 157. Lerna: *Hesperia* xxv (1956) 168 pl. 46: j, of an early phase of E.H. II).

iv. (D) Miscellaneous (types 50–51)

Type 50. Bottles

The only fragments assignable to this shape (2095) came from Area B, stage 9, dating from a mature phase of Period II.

Wheelmade alabastron-shaped bottles derived from Syria were at home in E.B. III at Tarsus (*Tarsus* ii 131, 154 pl. 268 nos. 614–7), and occurred in Troy III (*Troy* ii 27 shape B 5, pl. 70: 34.750). Rare handmade bottles are attested at Beycesultan in Level XII of the beginning of E.B. 3 there (*Beycesultan* i 205 fig. P. 48: 16).

Type 51. Double vases

A few fragments of such vases were recovered, mostly from levels of Period II, but one (1280) which may have been an import from a deposit of V.

Multiple vases are attested at Troy as early as the beginning of Troy I, but not it seems in Troy II or later (*Troy* i 76 shape D 31). They are represented among Yortan vases (*BMA* 11, A 62–63 pl. ii), and occurred at Beycesultan in E.B. 1 (*Beycesultan* i 127 shape 22). There is one from Level V at Karataş-Semayük (*AJA* lxx (1966) 252 pl. 61 fig. 30). Several E.B. II examples were recovered at Tarsus, but others, some of them wheelmade, came from levels of E.B. III there (*Tarsus* ii 129 pl. 260 no. 360; 154 f. fig. 278). Such vases are found in the Cyclades in the Early Bronze Age and later (e.g. Paros: *AM* xlii (1917) 27 fig. 21. *Phylakopi* 87, 102, 104, 153 figs. 135–6 pls. iv: 2, xi: 12). There is a double pyxis from Ayios Kosmas (*Ayios Kosmas* 90 no. 209).

Double and even triple vases with connecting holes were in use at Byblos in the Late Chalcolithic there (*Byblos* v 300, 284 fig. 162). Twin vessels occur in Palestine in E.B. I and II (Amiran, *APHL* 58).

v. (E) Pithoi

Fragments of large storage vessels classifiable as pithoi were recovered from levels of all periods at Emporio. Those of the earlier periods (X–VIII and VII–VI) tended to have simple flat-topped or rounded and thickened rims. Large vertical handles of oval section were already in use on pithoi as early as Period X. The bases of these early pithoi appear to have been flat and more or less clearly differentiated. The pithoi were sometimes decorated with relief ornament which might be quite elaborate.

The occurrence of such large storage vessels in the earliest levels at Emporio may appear surprising. But simple round-topped rims as large as or larger than any pithos rims from Emporio X–VIII are illustrated from the Neolithic levels at Tell Sukas on the Syrian coast (*Sukas* iii 41 fig. 104; 46 fig. 119). A large flat-topped rim in profile like early pithos rims from Emporio, and with a horizontal rib it seems below it, comes from the Late Neolithic (V A) at Ras Shamra (*Ugaritica* iv 165 fig. 6: 9).

The fabric of pithoi from all levels of the Neolithic and Early Bronze Age at Emporio, especially of ones from levels of the earlier periods X–VIII, tended to be noticeably harder than the fabric of the mass of the pottery, implying a higher firing temperature. A similar observation was made about the firing of the large orange-ware pithoi of Period II at Anzabegovo in Yugoslav Macedonia, assigned to early Starcevo: these, it was noted, were very highly fired, unlike the other contemporary wares from the site (*Anza* 172). In the case of the large storage vessels of Emporio it is tempting to wonder if these might not have been made by itinerant craftsmen, who specialised in their manufacture, as was the system in Crete into recent times.

The pithoi of Periods V–IV were entirely different in fabric and in details of shape and decoration from the earlier ones. An important series of complete pithoi and large fragments of others came from the Period IV destruction levels. The necks and rims of these were in many cases just enlarged versions of those on contemporary jars, but their bases seem to have been relatively small, often more or less pointed, apparently to facilitate sinking them for some distance into the ground. The standard pithoi of this period had pairs of handles joining neck and shoulder, with one or two more pairs of handles on the body below them. Round the base of the neck there was often a band in relief with incised decoration on it imitating rope-work. Other parts of the vessel might be adorned with similar relief ornament or with bold incised decoration on the flat surface.

Pithoi existed at Troy in the time of Troy I, but shapes could not be reconstructed (*Troy* i 72 f.). Rims of pithoi resembling those of Emporio V–IV are illustrated from the evolved Blue period at Poliochni (*Poliochni* i, 582 pl. lxxvii). Pithoi at Thermi seem to have been not unlike those of Emporio V–IV with small bases (*Thermi* 92 f.). Some Early Helladic pithoi were similar in shape (e.g. *Zygouries* 118 ff. figs. 111, 112).

A few pithoi from Emporio assignable to Period IV (1283, 1287, 2332) had a hole for a bung or spout cut low in the side just above the base, suggesting that they had been used for storage of liquid of some kind; although such holes might have been made simply to facilitate rinsing the insides of the vessels with water to cleanse them. Similar holes are recorded on Early Bronze Age pithoi found in Anatolia (e.g. Karataş-Semayük: *AJA* lxx (1966) 245). Short tubular spouts occur just above the bottoms of some Early Helladic pithoi (e.g. Levkas, R graves: Dörpfeld, *Alt-Ithaka* pl. 67a: 9, b: 4, 5). Grape pips were recovered from a pithos at Ayios Kosmas with a pointed base and tubular spout of this kind (*Ayios Kosmas* 39 f. fig. 132: 50).

vi. (F) Lids and covers (types 60–64) (FIG. 102)

There was no evidence for the existence of pottery lids at Emporio before Period VI, and the only possible fragment of a lid (754) from a level of VI was assignable to type 62. Lids were still relatively uncommon at the time of the Period IV destruction. But many lid fragments were recovered from deposits of Emporio II. The Period II lids were mostly covers of type 63. Covers of the elaborate 'crown' type 64B seem to have been characteristic of I, although already attested in II.

Type 60. Flat lids

The lids of this type might have solid lugs rising from the top surface. Flat lids were common in Period II, but at least one fragment of such a lid (1850) came from a deposit with material assignable to Period V or earlier.

Flat lids (shape D 14) were much in evidence at Troy from the beginning of Troy I and into Troy II–III (*Troy* i 74, 239; ii 33). They are also attested in all five Towns at Thermi, and in the

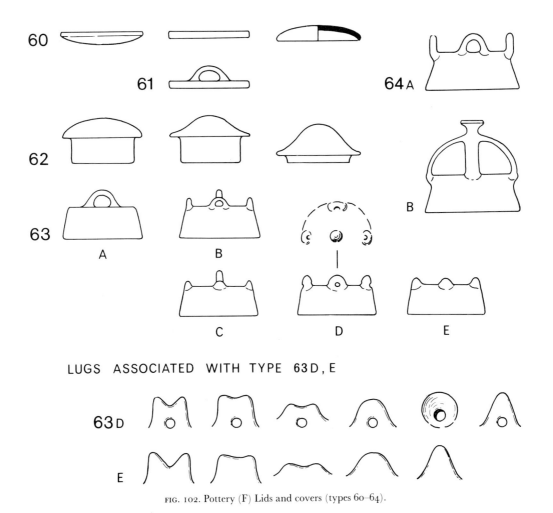

FIG. 102. Pottery (F) Lids and covers (types 60–64).

Blue period at Poliochni (*Thermi* pl. xxxviii lid type I. *Poliochni* i 576 f. pl. lxv: b, d). They occurred at Beycesultan in E.B. 1 but were not common (*Beycesultan* i 129 shape 24). There is a flat lid from a level of E.B. II at Tarsus, and one is illustrated from the Middle Chalcolithic Level XVI at Mersin (*Tarsus* ii 125 fig. 250 no. 307. *Mersin* 150 f. fig. 93: 16). Two from the Konya plain are assigned by Mellaart to the Late Chalcolithic (*AS* xiii (1963) 199, 204, fig. 3: 23, 24).

Type 61. Flat lids with handles

This type seems to have been rare at Emporio. The only complete example (1296) came from the Period IV destruction level and apparently belonged with the jar 1236. The two other fragments assignable to this type were recovered from levels of II. But some of the fragments grouped under type 60 may have belonged to lids of this kind.

There are no lids from Troy exactly corresponding to this type, but a flat lid of the Late Subperiod of Troy I has a 'crown' handle (*Troy* i 75 shape D 18). Lids akin to type 61 are attested at Thermi, however, in Towns II/III–V, and in the Blue period at Poliochni (*Thermi* pl. xxxix lid type VII. *Poliochni* i 580 pls. lxxi: c, lxxv: a–g). There is a lid closely resembling Emporio 1296 from a level of E.B. II at Tarsus (*Tarsus* ii 124 f. fig. 251 no. 306).

A lid of this type occurs among bowl-shaped lids with handles inside them from the Late Chalcolithic at Byblos (*Byblos* v fig. 168: 21880).

Type 62. Flanged covers

These were flat or rounded on top and might have string-holes through the flanges. Such string-holes evidently fulfilled the function of the perforated lugs on some type 63 lids. Type 62 was not well represented at Emporio. The complete 1297 belonged with the pyxis 1232 from the Period IV destruction level. Two other fragments of small flanged covers were found in deposits of II. The fragment 754 with a slight flange and string-holes through it apparently came from a cover of this type; it was obtained from the fill of the Period VI wall 20.

The intact cover 1297 fitted inside the neck of 1232. But the other lids assigned to this type may have been made to enclose the necks of vases. Some if not most of the corresponding Trojan shape D 1, occurring throughout Troy I and into Troy V, were evidently meant to fit over collar-like necks (*Troy* i 73, 238). But at least one lid from Troy II (*Troy* i pl. 404: 35. 437) looks as if it may have been intended to fit inside a neck like 1297.

Lids of this kind are at home in the Early Bronze Age in the Cyclades and in Crete (e.g. *Phylakopi* 88 fig. 72). A pyxis lid from Syros closely resembles 1297 in shape but has painted decoration (*AE* 1899, 109 pl. 8: 11a). Type 62 lids do not appear to be well represented, however, in the Early Helladic of the Greek mainland; but while clay lids of any kind are distinctly rare on the mainland during the Neolithic, a few akin to this type are attested (e.g. *Nea Makri* 15 f. fig. 26, assigned to the end of A II. Phelps, *Thesis* 209 fig. 28: 10, and 280 fig. 45: 12, from Corinth, assigned to the Late Neolithic).

Simple covers were at home in the Halafian pottery of Syria; and some of these appear to have been flanged like our type 62 (e.g. M.F. von Oppenheim, *Tell Halaf* i (Berlin, 1943) pl. xxiv: 13).

Type 63. Covers with handles or lugs on top

Several varieties of these could be recognised: A. With central handle, B. With central handle and four smaller ones round the edge, C. With central handle and four warts round the edge, D. With central wart and four perforated lugs round the edge, E. With central wart and four warts or solid lugs round the edge.

Some examples of type 63 covers were found in the Period IV destruction levels. But they became extremely common in Period II when they were evidently in general use. Many of these Period II covers were of the finest fabric with elaborate incised decoration no doubt matching that on the vases to which they belonged. There was a great range in size. A series of very large lids apparently came from the massive jars of fine burnished ware decorated with white-filled incision which were such a distinctive feature of Period II. The smaller lids evidently fitted pyxis-like jars of various kinds.

Comparable lids seem to be early at Troy and Thermi, where they were virtually confined to Troy I and Thermi Towns I–III. At Poliochni covers of this general type were common in the Blue period and continued into the Green but not into the Red (*Poliochni* i 645 pls. lxiv-lxviii). Comparisons for the different varieties of type 63 are listed below.

Type 63A. There seems to be nothing which exactly corresponds to this variety at Troy or Thermi.

Type 63B (e.g. 1298). Trojan shape D 9 is very similar, but has a central wart in place of the handle (*Troy* i 73 pl. 231: 35.647, 35.642). This shape occurred throughout Troy I, being especially well represented in the Early Subperiod, but was not it seems attested in Troy II or later.

Type 63C (e.g. 1299). There seem to be no exact parallels for this variety from Troy or Thermi.

Type 63D. This corresponds to Trojan shape D 11 only found in the Early Subperiod of Troy I (*Troy* i 74), and to Thermi lid type XIV a and b with rounded or flat tops (*Thermi* pl. xl). Some lids from Troy I closely resembling ones of this type from Emporio are described and illustrated in *SS* 7 nos. 188–195. The variety with rounded top (type XIVa) was only represented by a single example from Thermi Town III, but flat-topped lids of type XIVb were very common and virtually confined to the early Towns I–III. A number of the lids of this type from Thermi had incised decoration. A miniature lid from Romania is somewhat comparable with type 63D (Berciu, *Contributii* 326 fig. 149: 2, Sǎlçuta I).

Type 63E. This variety also seems without any precise parallels at Troy or Thermi.

Type 64. Flanged covers with flat tops and handles

Two varieties were recognised: A. With handles set round the edge, B. With 'crown' handles.

A number of fragments of lids of this general type were recovered from levels of Period I (Troy II). Some fragments from Area B at Emporio came from levels of stages 9 and 10 assignable to Period II, but none were noted in the main Period II deposits in Area A.

Flanged covers akin to type 64A were already it seems at home at Poliochni by the evolved Blue period there (*Poliochni* i 575 pls. lxiv: e, f; lxv: a).

A flat lid with simple four-armed 'crown' handle was recovered from the Late Subperiod of Troy I (*Troy* i 75 fig. 231: 37.978). But type 64 b corresponds to Trojan shapes D 7 (with three arms) and D 8 (with four arms) which first occurred in Troy II and continued through III–IV into V (*Troy* i 239 fig. 405: 35.859; ii 32, 135f., 247 f.). At Thermi 'crown' lids akin to type 64B are attested from Towns IV and V but not earlier (*Thermi* pl. xl lid type XIIa). At Poliochni such lids may have begun in the Green period, but are first certainly recorded from the Red, becoming very widespread in the Yellow (*Poliochni* i 645; ii 255 f.). They are also found on Samos (*Samos* i pl. 17: 1–3 (43: 2, 10, 13)).

While 'crown' lids of this kind appear to be characteristic of western Anatolia, they occur at Beycesultan, but not before the beginning of E.B. 3. Then, however, they are represented in most levels (*Beycesultan* i Sheet 6, type 20). There is one from Karataş-Semayük, and others were apparently found at Karahüyük near Konya (*AJA* lxx (1966) 254 pl. 60 fig. 24).

vii. (*G*) *Miniature vases*

A number of bowls from levels of Periods X–VIII were very small and of miniature size (e.g. 82). Apart from these bowls miniature vases were comparatively rare in the Neolithic and Early Bronze Age levels at Emporio. Only six examples were noted, one each from levels of IX or VIII (308) and VI (755), and three assignable to V (1303–5).

Miniature vases have been made as toys in many different parts of the world at different times. Such 'children's vases' have been recovered from Early Neolithic Protosesklo deposits in Thessaly (*Otzaki-magula* 26. Cf. *Nea Nikomedeia* 281 fig. 9: P2. *ILN* 11 April 1964, 565 f. fig. 2). At Hacilar miniature vases that may have been used as drinking cups are said to be typical of Level IV and subsequent levels, but it is not entirely clear how miniature these are (*Hacilar* i 112). Miniature vases were not uncommon in Level V at Karataş-Semayük (*AJA* lxx (1966) 252). A large number were recovered from levels of all five Towns at Thermi (*Thermi* pls. xli–xliii).

viii. (*H*) *Bowls and drinking vessels of types not attested before Period I* (types 70–77)

These are discussed in Volume ii after (A) Bowls under Period I.

ix. (*I*) *Handles and lugs*

These are considered in detail under the various groups of periods. A summary by periods is given below.

Vertical handles are those with the ends set one above the other in relation to the vase when standing upright on its base.

Horizontal handles are ones which have the ends more or less on the same level in relation to the vase, although the handles themselves may not be horizontal, but may slope or curve upwards from the points of attachment, or may even stand upright like some of the handles on bowl rims characteristic of the earliest levels (Periods X–IX).

The term strap-handle is reserved for handles with a thin strap-like cross-section.

Periods X–VIII (FIGS. 103–105)

There was a remarkable variety and flamboyance in the handles and lugs set on vases of these earliest periods at Emporio.

A striking series of handles of the horizontal class, most if not all of them from bowls, was recovered in levels assigned to Periods X and IX (309–324) (FIG. 103). These handles were of an impressive size, some of them being truly gigantic, and they had usually it seems been shaped and finished with great care; some had neat triangular or rectangular sections, others were twisted. But the handles in spite of their sophisticated elegance had been affixed in a thoroughly primitive manner on top of the vase rims without being keyed into them.

Horizontal handles of a more usual kind also occurred on the sides of bowls, e.g. 92 from a

BOWL HANDLES :

		X			IX		VIII		VII	VI
PERIOD / AREA		G	Q	H	G	Q	G	Q		
(A) VERTICAL (93, 156, 437)						1 *93*		3 *143 156*	R *437*	R *631*
(B) HORIZONTAL ON TOP OF RIM: SECTIONS										
1	Circular			3	4	21	26	7	c.8	S
2	Oval	1	2		1			2	2	
3	Oval with sharp edges					3	5	1		2
A	Triangular			1	4	18	7	2	2	1
4 B	Thin triangular				1	1		3	1	1 *757*
C	Triangular with groove at base					1				
5	Rectangular						1	2		
6	Twisted		2					2 *321*	1 *758*	
	STUMP OF HANDLE ON TOP OF RIM				5	7	8	6	2	c.1 *756*
TOTAL		1	4	4	15	51	51	21	c.16	5+
(C) HORIZONTAL BELOW RIM					1 *92*					22 *480*

R : Rare   S : Several

FIG. 103. Periods X–VI. Bowl handles. Distribution (catalogue numbers in italics).

level of IX. This handle makes a relatively 'late' impression, as does the unique vertical handle 93 with kidney-shaped section from a level of IX, and the fragment of what must have been a triple handle (338) from one of X.

The earlier levels also produced a number of large and elaborate lug-handles. Most of these at any rate evidently came from bowls like the giant horizontal handles. Among them were many tab-handles (326–334) (FIG. 105: 5–11); several of these were horned (e.g. 331–2, 334) (FIG. 105:

5, 8, 9). Tab-handles, although not of exactly comparable types, were also in evidence in the upper levels of the Upper Cave at Ayio Gala (AG 250–2), and they reappear at Emporio in the Early Bronze Age from Period V onwards. The large lug-handle 325 from a bowl rim appears to have been horned in shape like some of the tab-handles (FIG. 105: 1). Vertically perforated lug-handles rising above bowl rims (113, 327) seem characteristic of Period X (FIG. 105: 32). Vertical tubular lugs with projections on top from levels of VIII might be regarded as devolved versions of these earlier lug-handles (e.g. 361, 357) (FIG. 105: 33).

Vertical handles occurred on jugs and jars from the earliest levels of X onwards. Some of the early vertical handles were adorned with large and often elegant horns (e.g. 335, 337). But the multi-horned handles flanking the bowl 156 of Period VIII were unique. Warts appeared on some vertical handles as early as Period X, and were extremely common on the small handles which were a feature of VIII. A few large jar handles from levels of IX and VIII had a conspicuous hole made before firing near the top end (e.g. 347); but this feature, intended perhaps to help in fastening a lid, was more in evidence in VII–VI.

Most of the early vertical handles from jugs or jars were thick or thin oval in section. Some, however, from levels of IX–VIII were more elaborate, being circular in section at the lower end but changing through thick oval to thin oval at the top where they joined the rim of the vase (e.g. 162). Handles of semi-circular section already occurred in levels of X, but ones of lunate or kidney-shaped section were first noted in Period IX.

Elongated lugs with horizontal perforations reminiscent of the heads of animals were characteristic of VIII and do not appear to be attested earlier at Emporio (172, 178, 366–8) (FIG. 105: 13–16). Similar lugs are first recorded at Hacilar in Level VIII there, but only become common from Level V onwards. What seems to be an evolved version of the type, often very elongated like an elephant's head with trunk, is at home in the Late Neolithic of the western Aegean, at Kephala on Kea and in Attica.

Both vertical and horizontal tubular lugs were recovered from these early levels (355–6, 362). Some horizontal tubular lugs were slightly trumpet-shaped (e.g. 363–4) (FIG. 105: 20); but distinctive trumpet lugs of the kind abounding in Periods VII–VI (FIG. 105: 21–23) were not attested in X–VIII. The solid trumpet-shaped lug 129 (FIG. 105: 24) may come from a level of VIII.

Upturned lugs with vertical perforations like 351–3 (FIG. 105: 26) from levels of X can be paralleled in the earliest Pottery Neolithic (PNA) of Palestine (Amiran, *APHL* 21 pl. 1:2), as well as in the Early Neolithic of southern Anatolia. But the closest parallels for the tailed lugs (e.g. 228, 358, 360) (FIG. 105: 34) characteristic of Period VIII are to be found in the Late Neolithic of the western Aegean and the Greek mainland. The single-tailed lugs on vases from the Lower Cave at Ayio Gala (AG 11, 17, 18) may be related to these. A few small vertical handles assignable to Period VIII also have tails (e.g. 172, 276). One horizontally perforated lug of the animal-head type (365) might be grouped with these (FIG. 105: 15). Tailed lugs of the kind found at Emporio could represent a development from perforated crescentic lugs. No examples of these were recovered from early levels at Emporio, however, although unperforated crescentic lugs occurred on bowls of Periods IX and VIII (58, 79, 128).

Large solid tongue-shaped lugs were placed on the insides and perhaps on the outsides of baking pans of type 3 (e.g. 20, 24, 25). Lugs of this kind are found on the outsides of vases from the earliest Phases A and B at Judeideh (*Judeideh* 48 fig. 21: 13; 50 fig. 22: 18–22; 70 f. fig. 40: 17, 19).

Periods VII–VI (FIGS. 103–105)
The variety of handles and lugs was much less marked than in Periods X–VIII.

JUG & JAR HANDLES:	X			IX		VIII		VII	VI
(A) VERTICAL HANDLES	G	Q	H	G	Q	G	Q		
TOTAL NUMBER OF FRAGMENTS	16	30	22	82	218	160	372	2060	3244
SECTIONS:									
1 Circular	1			c.3		2		S	
2 Oval	9		1	M	M	M	M	S	S
3 Thin oval	2	7	2	c.12	M	S	S	S	M
4 Semi-circular	1	1			1		S	S	S
5 Lunate				1	1	4	S	S	S
6 Kidney-shaped				1	c.2 *348*		c.4	S	S
7 Sub-rectangular	1					1	1	S	c.2
8 Rectangular								1	1
9 Ribbed oval									c.2
10 Ribbed ogival									c.3
HORNED HANDLES	2 *335*	3 *336-7*	1		3		1	1	1
HANDLES WITH WARTS									
Single		2		4	20	20	c.100	10	14
Double		1 *338*				1 *341*	2	1	2
At base					1	3	c.2 *344-5*		1
Each side of base						1 *346*	2		1
Hole at top of handle				1	1	1 *347*	4	c.20	6
(B) HORIZONTAL SIDE HANDLES									c.27

S : *Several*   M: *Many*

FIG. 104. Periods X–VI. Jug and jar handles. Distribution (catalogue numbers in italics).

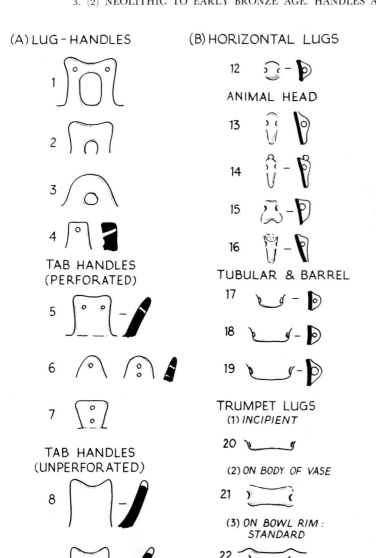
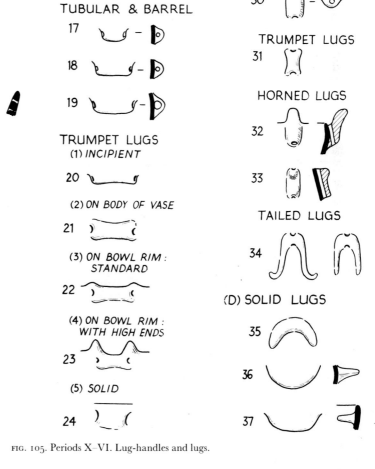

FIG. 105. Periods X–VI. Lug-handles and lugs.

Large horizontal bowl handles were still in evidence, especially in levels of VII; but some of these might have been earlier strays. A few examples of horizontal handles set on the outsides of bowls as commonly in Periods V–IV were recovered from levels of VII–VI (e.g. 480). Two examples of handles of the pointed shape (FIG. 107: 2) much at home on bowls of Periods V–IV were obtained from VI (759).

Vertical handles from bowls were only attested by two possible examples (437, 631). But vertical handles from jugs and jars were extremely abundant. Most of these were oval or thin oval in section; but semi-circular, lunate and kidney-shaped sections were now in evidence. A few handles, mostly from levels of VI, had sharp rectangular, ribbed oval, or ribbed ogival sections.

Some of the finer jug handles were tapered, or had a waisted hour-glass shape (FIG. 152, taper 1 and 2). Handles of hour-glass shape are very characteristic of the Late Neolithic on the Greek mainland (Phelps, *Thesis* 262 f. Cf. Franchthi cave: *Hesperia* xxxviii (1969) 368 pl. 98: a, on cups of matt-painted ware from the beginning of the Late Neolithic. *Elateia* 186 fig. 10 pl. 60, on bowls from the Bothros horizon assigned to the end of Middle or beginning of Late Neolithic. Tsangli: *PThess* 102 fig. 55 a, apparently from a jug. Dikili Tash in eastern Macedonia: *BCH* xcii (1968) 1074 f. fig. 22, on bowls of the Middle Neolithic which overlaps with Thessalian Late Neolithic). But what appears to be a fragment of such a handle, evidently from an imported vase, comes from the top of the Protosesklo (E.N. II) layer at Otzaki (*Otzaki-magula* 73 pl. xix: 34).

Handles surmounted by warts, abundant in Period VIII, were still not uncommon in VII–VI. A number of handles, apparently from large jars, had a conspicuous hole made before firing near the top end, intended perhaps to help in fastening a lid. The unique angled handled 845 with a perforation through it from R ?83 may be of Period VI rather than later.

Horizontal side-handles of the type usual on jars of Periods V–IV were quite numerous in levels of VI. Slashed handles of Cycladic type were represented by a single example each from VII and VI (761–2). The bowl-jar 656 assignable to VIII or VII was unique in having a little horizontal handle set inside the rim. The earliest example of a true 'pushed through' handle came from VII.

Tab-handles and animal head lugs of the kind at home in X–VIII were scarcely attested from levels of VII–VI. The only animal head lug (768) from VII is not very typical of the class. Trumpet lugs, however, were now much at home and occurred in a variety of forms which ranged from incipient to highly flamboyant examples with horn-like ends. Most of these trumpet lugs had been set horizontally on or below the rims of bowls, notably ones of the characteristic Period VII–VI types 10 and 11. But vertical trumpet lugs were also recovered, nearly all of them from levels of VII (e.g. 657). Large tubular lugs with big perforations, set vertically (e.g. 483, 486) or horizontally (e.g. 767), were also in evidence.

Small vertically perforated lugs include a single example of the horned shape common in Periods V–IV (771) (FIG. 105: 27). A lug set to the rim of a bowl of type 14 had a double perforation (632) (FIG. 105: 28). One or two double lugs were recovered from levels of VI (e.g. 484). Large solid tongue-shaped lugs occurred on the outsides of some vases.

Periods V–IV (FIGS. 106–108)

The variety of handles and lugs rivalled if it did not surpass that of the earliest periods X–VIII.

In several cases bowls had vertical handles to the rim (FIG. 106: 1). Small bowls with large handles of this kind rising above the rim formed a distinctive class (type 16: dipper cups). Vertical handles were also found on the sides of bowls below the rim (FIG. 106: 3).

Horizontal handles were more common on bowls than vertical ones. These handles were normally rounded in shape (FIG. 107: 1); but varieties of pointed (2, 3) and nicked handles (4) were not uncommon. A wider horned shape of nicked handle also occurred (FIG. 107: 5). These horizontal side handles were normally set to the rim or just below it, but in a few instances they were on top of the rim. Two bowls with rounded handles on the tops of their rims were assigned to Troy I by Schliemann, *Troja* 35 nos. 6, 7. Horizontal side handles were also common on jars, especially on those of type 47 C. A few such handles were slashed in the Cycladic manner (e.g. 1233).

A variety of lug-handle in the form of a projection rising from the rim with a large circular opening through it (FIG. 106: 8) appears to be attested on bowls for the first time now, although it was more characteristic of Period II, under which it is discussed. The projections of these lug-handles were normally at any rate horned in shape as FIG. 106: 8b. Tab-handles reminiscent of those from the earliest levels (X–VIII) occurred but were rare (FIG. 106: 9–11). A comparable tab-handle with a single perforation through it rises above the rim of a cup-like bowl assigned to Troy I by Schliemann, *Troja* 35 f. no. 8.

Vertical handles of jugs and jars were more varied in character than they had been in any earlier period. Horned handles (FIG. 106: 4a) were not rare in levels of V, from which several elbow-handles as FIG. 106: 4b were also recovered (e.g. 1317). Elbow-handles occurred on the rims of jugs or bowls in the Early Subperiod of Troy I, although they were more frequent it seems in the Late Subperiod (*Troy* i 65 figs. 227: 37.1026; 235: 14, 15; 236: 22, 23). Such handles were also at home in the Blue period and later at Poliochni (*Poliochni* i 568, 620 pls. xlvii: b–d, i–m; cxxiii: o). Some vertical handles from levels of V and a number from those of IV were surmounted by warts. Sections of vertical handles included thin strap and hollow strap, as well as neat sharply defined triangular, rectangular, hollow rectangular, and ribbed rectangular varieties (FIG. 108). Ribbed handles were at home in Troy I from as early as Troy I a (*Troy* i figs. 235: 16, 17; 236: 15, 16, 21; 245: 1; 247: 28–31. Cf. *Thermi* pl. xxxiv: 6).

Lugs, mostly at any rate from bowls, were of many different kinds. Horizontal trumpet lugs, which may all have belonged to bowls, were still in evidence, although not as much as they had been in Periods VII–VI. Some trumpet lugs were encircled by a central rib as FIG. 106: 14, or occasionally by a number of ribs as FIG. 106: 21 (e.g. 1028). One trumpet lug was surmounted by a wart as FIG. 106: 15. Trumpet lugs with single or multiple ribs were very much at home in Troy I (*Troy* i 78 figs. 235: 3; 239: 13; 243: 31; 244: 7, 8; 246: 21, 22; 260: 16; 261: 10, 17. Cf. *Thermi* pls. xvi: 1; xxxi: 1, 2. *Poliochni* i 558 ff., 615 pl. xx: a, Blue period. *PMac* 166 no. 163 fig. 37: d (*Argissa* iii 197 pl. 70: 15), beginning of E.B.A. at Kritsana). The horizontal trumpet lugs of Emporio V–IV might be set on the rim of the bowl or on its side below the rim. Tubular lugs of one kind or another set horizontally on (912) or below the rim (913) also occurred. Vertically perforated tubular lugs were still attested in levels of V (e.g. 916).

In several cases (859, 1073, 1081) the rim of a bowl was raised in a projection above the spot where a horizontal lug, usually trumpet-shaped, was set. This projection might be horned as FIG. 106: 16, and in two instances (859) the top was serrated as FIG. 106: 17. Such projections occasionally appeared above lugs of other shapes or above handles (e.g. 1118) (FIG. 106: 26). Some triangular and horned rim projections on bowls akin to Emporio types 12–14 from levels of Troy I surmount vertically perforated lugs: several of the triangular projections on bowls of Trojan shape A 6, which embraces Emporio types 12 and 13, have faces incised on the inside (*Troy* i figs. 253, 257). On bowls from Thermi horned projections like those of Troy I also surmount vertically perforated lugs, and in one instance at any rate a horizontal trumpet lug (*Thermi* pl. xxxii). Projections occur above horizontal lugs on bowls from the Kephala site on Kea assigned to the Late Neolithic (*Kephala* pls. 28: 104; 29: N, P. *Hesperia* xxxiii (1964) 316 pl.

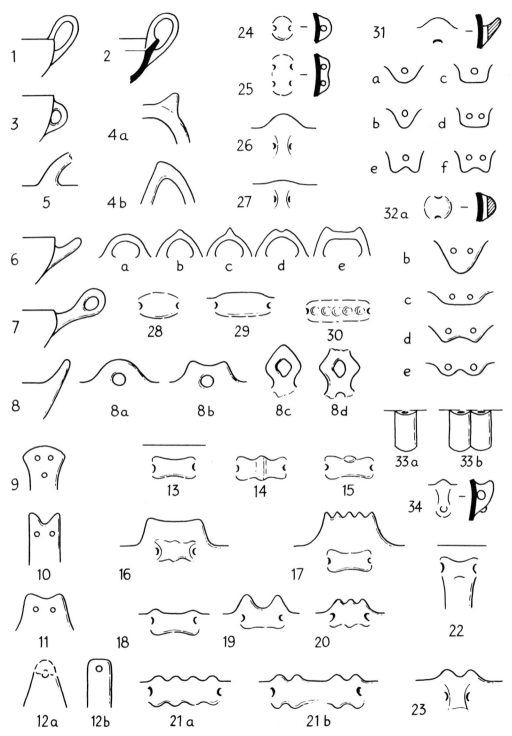

FIG. 106.

FIG. 106. Periods V–I. Handles and lugs.

	VI	V	IV	III	II	I
1		S incl. 931 970 937	S incl. 1017 1019 1051 1018 1076		c. 12 incl. 1566	
2					1537–8 1567	2503
3		908 934 928 995	907			
4a		c. 80	S	6	c. 12	
4b		c. 6 incl. 1317	1069?			
5		852 1009 1117				1
6a		S incl. 909 954 1007 911 984 1078 933	S incl. 910 1005 1038 925 1026 1046 927 1029 1050 993 1032 1071 1072		M incl. 1439 1500 1453	S incl. 2444
6b, c		c. 10	M incl. 1041 1049 1047	1	c. 45 incl. 1440 1697–1701	2489
6d		c. 9	S incl. 924 1033 1043	2	c. 12 incl. 1704	2
6e		1037	S incl 927			
7					1437	
8a					1540	
8b		1 ?			c. 15 incl. 1706	c. 5
8 c, d					1702 1703	
9		1308	1116 ?			
10			1083			
11	1122		1315	1410		
12a					1707 1709	
12b					1710	
13		c. 5 incl. 1120 1074 1119		1408	c. 7 incl. 1441 1520	
14		1	c. 5			
15		1				
16			1073			

FIG. 106 (cont.).

	VI	V	IV	III	II	I
17			859			
18		c. 7	c. 3 incl. 1021	2 incl. 1370	c. 5 incl. 1505	1
19			1081			
20		1				
21a. b		1309	1028			
22		1310				
23		1020				
24		c. 3 incl. 1319		1409	1442 1723–4	
25	1314					
26		1118				
27			1313			
28	1022	1312	938		1420 1721–2	1
29		4 incl. 912				
30		913				
31a, b		S incl. 1320–1	1 ?		S incl. 1727	
31c		c. 2 incl. 1323	9 incl. 1231–2 1322			
31d			1326			
31e		2	12 incl. 1300 1302 1324		S incl. 1732	2 incl. 2594
31f		1325			1443	
32a		S incl. 917	1082 (pair)		1725–6	3 incl. 2504 2506
32b		914				
32c		1067				
32d		S incl. 960 1121 915 1315				
32e		2 ?			1729	4 incl. 2460 2465
33a		916				
33b					1730	
34		1318				

M = Many, S = Several.

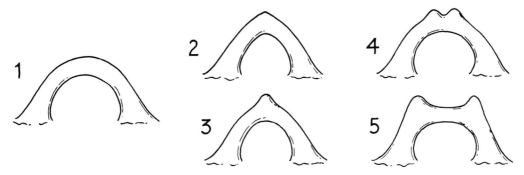

FIG. 107. Periods V–II. Bowl handles: 1. rounded; 2. Pointed; 3. Ogival; 4. Nicked; 5. Horned.

47: f). A similar rim projection, but without a lug beneath it, appears on a bowl akin to Emporio type 14 from Eutresis stage II assigned to the latest Neolithic immediately preceding E.H. I (*Hesperia* xxix (1960) 134 f., 161 pl. 46: II. 28).

Other varieties of lugs, horizontally or vertically perforated, include a number with a pair of perforations and some double ones. Upturned lugs as FIG. 106: 31, semi-circular, triangular, square, or horned in shape, and with single or double perforations, evidently came from jars, mostly from small pyxides of type 44. Similar lugs but unperforated were also in evidence.

Periods III–II (FIG. 106)
Handles and lugs from levels of III and II were basically of similar types to those of Periods V–IV.

Additions to the repertory of V–IV include the unique bowl handle 1437 (FIG. 106: 7). Tab-handles of a kind still occurred (e.g. 1410, 1707, 1709) (FIG. 106: 12). Lug-handles in the form of horned projections rising above the level of the rim with a large circular hole through

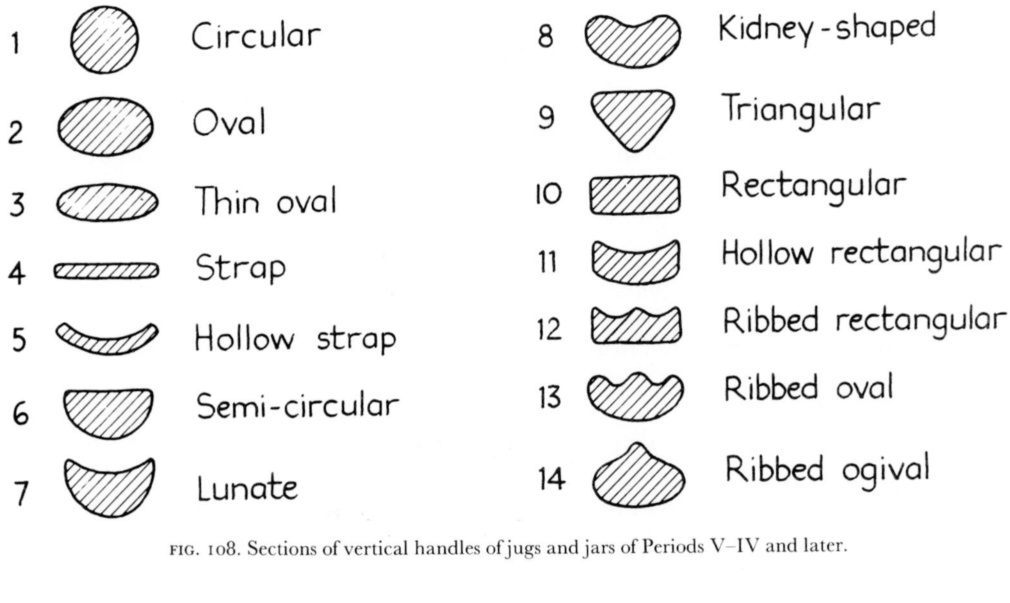

1		Circular	8		Kidney-shaped
2		Oval	9		Triangular
3		Thin oval	10		Rectangular
4		Strap	11		Hollow rectangular
5		Hollow strap	12		Ribbed rectangular
6		Semi-circular	13		Ribbed oval
7		Lunate	14		Ribbed ogival

FIG. 108. Sections of vertical handles of jugs and jars of Periods V–IV and later.

them, as FIG. 106: 8b, were apparently first attested in levels of V–IV, but only became common in Period II: in at least one case (1540) the projection was of a simple rounded shape instead of horned (FIG. 106: 8a). The fragments 1702–3 may be from elaborate versions of such lug-handles (FIG. 106: 8c, d).

Lug-handles, both perforated like FIG. 106: 8a, b, and unperforated, appear on 'degenerate' late forms of Trojan shape A 6 bowls which correspond to Emporio types 12 and 13 (*Troy* i 59). The rims of these are usually undecorated. A complete example, assigned by Schmidt, *SS* 18 no. 396, to an early phase of Troy II, has the lug-handle as FIG. 106: 8a; but some fragments from the Middle and Late Subperiods of Troy I evidently belonged to horned lug-handles like 8b (*Troy* i 133, 139 fig. 246: 6–8; 164, 168, 174 f. fig. 249: 1–8). Horned lug-handles like 8b also occurred at Poliochni in the Blue period, and perhaps in the Green; while ones as 8a are attested from the Green and Red periods there (*Poliochni* i 564 pl. xxxix: c; 618 pl. cxvi: e, f, g; 636 pl. clii: d (cliii: e)). What seems to be a simple rounded lug-handle as 8a appears on a bowl from Tigani (*AA* 1928, 626 fig. 21). Lug-handles as FIG. 106: 8a were evidently at home in Cilicia in E.B. II there (*Tarsus* ii 127 f. fig. 260: 345–8).

Vertical handles from jugs or jars included the twisted 1711. The ends of jug handles were 'pushed through' in a number of cases. Among the many horizontal side handles from jars were several of the slashed Cycladic type which may come from imported vases (1717–19).

Horizontal tubular lugs (e.g. 1420, 1721–2) including trumpet lugs as FIG. 106: 13 and 18 (1441, 1505, 1520) still occurred on bowls. One or two horizontally perforated lugs (e.g. 1723–4) were somewhat elongated, reminiscent of the animal head lugs at home in Period VIII. Upturned vertically perforated lugs of simple (e.g. 1727) or horned shape (e.g. 1443, 1732) from pyxides of type 44 were not uncommon (FIG. 106: 31a, b, e, f). A pair of close-set vertical tubular lugs (1730) evidently came from a pyxis (FIG. 106: 33b).

Upturned vertically perforated lugs like FIG. 106: 31 seem to be characteristic of Complexes I and II of E.B. III at Aphrodisias (*AJA* lxxiii (1969) 58). Such lugs are in evidence at Troy from at least as early as Troy II (e.g. *Troy* i fig. 414: 38). They also appear to be a feature of the earliest Bronze Age pottery of Ezero in Bulgaria, where both simple and horned varieties as found at Emporio are attested (*Baden Symposium* 234 fig. 14: 2, 4, 6).

Period I

Handles and lugs were less varied than they had been in earlier periods.

Some bowls were still provided with handles, which might be pointed or horned in shape as FIG. 107: 2, 5. But the new wheelmade bowls tended to be handleless, apart from tankards of type 77. Horned lug-handles (FIG. 106: 8b) of the kind at home in Period II still occurred.

Horizontal tubular lugs were extremely rare, and only one example of a trumpet lug on a bowl rim as FIG. 106: 18 was assignable to Period I.

Small lugs from pyxides might be of simple shape with single vertical perforations like FIG. 106: 32a. But horned lugs with single or double vertical perforations also occurred (e.g. 2460, 2465).

The fish-tailed lug-handle 1823 from the well in the main Area A is reminiscent of AG 256.

Handles with warts

Vertical handles surmounted by warts occurred in Period IX, becoming very prominent in VIII, and remaining in evidence as late as V–IV.

Such handles appear to be a feature of the Late Neolithic in the western Aegean and on the Greek mainland. Phelps, *Thesis* 321, 325, regards them as most characteristic of the early part of his Phase IV of Final Neolithic, citing examples from the Athenian agora and from Kephala in Kea. Several handles from the agora with warts are reminiscent of ones from Emporio (*Athenian Agora* xiii 45 f. pl. 13: 189, 191, 194, 196, 205. Cf. *Kephala* pls. 84–5. *Hesperia* xli (1972) 358 pl. 76, P. 15, from Paoura on Kea. *BSA* lxi (1966) 84 pl. 19 b: top left, from Euboia). Two handles with warts like these are illustrated from Period IV at Anzabegovo in Jugoslav Macedonia, assignable to early Vinca (*Anza* 124 fig. 73).

Handles and lugs flanked by warts, or with a row of warts down the centre, were found at Saliagos; but ones surmounted by a single wart, as was most common in the early levels at Emporio, do not seem to be attested there (*Saliagos* 39).

While they seem to have flourished in a relatively late horizon in the Cyclades and on the Greek mainland, handles surmounted by warts comparable with those from early levels at Emporio were much older in south-western Anatolia. Some are attested from a complex in the Elmali region which has been tentatively assigned to the Middle Chalcolithic there (Eslick 1980, 8, 9 ill. 2: 2). Wart-surmounted handles were also at home in the Late Chalcolithic at Beycesultan (e.g. *Beycesultan* i 74 fig. P. 2: 33, 76 fig. P. 3: 14, 82 fig. P. 5: 24, from Levels XXXVIII, XXXVI, XXXV of Late Chalcolithic 1). Handles with warts at the base, as known from levels of Emporio IX–VI (FIG. 104) as well as from ones of V–IV, appear in the complex tentatively assigned to the Middle Chalcolithic in the Elmali region (Eslick, 1980, 9 ill. 2: 11); and in Level IV at Hacilar (*Hacilar* ii 280 f. fig. 64: 38–42, interpreted as versions of animal head handles).

Twisted handles

There are said to be many twisted rope-like handles from Troy II (*Troy* i 242 pl. 413: 17); but they do not appear to be in evidence in Troy I. A solitary twisted handle to the rim of a jug comes from the Yellow period at Poliochni corresponding to Troy II (*Poliochni* ii 264 f. pl. ccix: m). At Thermi twisted handles increase in number in the later Towns (*Thermi* 83 f. fig. 30; 90 fig. 32. Cf. Burton-Brown 1970, 78 f.). There are a number from the Heraion site on Samos (*Samos* i pls. 37: 59, 60; 49: 24–6).

Both vertical and horizontal versions of twisted handles were very much at home at Beycesultan in E.B. 2–3, but not it seems in E.B. 1. For examples of such handles to the rims of jugs from the Iznik area of north-west Anatolia see *AS* xvii (1967) 49 ff. figs. 14: 28; 18: 22.

Horizontal slashed handles

Handles of this type appear to be derived from rope-work or basketry. The few recovered at Emporio evidently came from imported vases or from imitations of them (e.g. 1233): most were found in levels of Periods V–IV, but there was one from VI and one from VII.

Such handles were at home in the Cyclades during the earlier part of the Bronze Age there. Many were recovered at Phylakopi, where most are said to have borne traces of a coat of black glaze (*Phylakopi* 86. Cf. *AE* 1898 pl. ix: 37; 1899. 122, from the Kastri settlement at Chalandriani on Syros. *Delos* xi 35 fig. 34, from the Mt Kynthos settlement, exactly like ones from Emporio. Cf. MacGillivray 1979, 32 f. pl. 11 nos. 408–9, noting that no. 409 is coated with a black wash. *ADelt* xx (1965) 46 pl. 33, from Naxos: Korfi t' Aroniou. Doumas, *Burial Habits* 118 no. 35 pl. xliv: e, from Naxos: Ayioi Anaryiroi).

Handles of this type have also been recovered from surrounding regions including Anatolia (e.g. *AS* xvii (1967) 76 fig. 13: 23, from the Iznik area of north-western Anatolia. *Samos* i pls. 40: 16, 17; 48: 33. Kea, Ayia Irini: *Hesperia* xli (1972) 366 pl. 79, B 44). A possible imitation comes from the Early Subperiod of Troy I (*Troy* i 99 fig. 236: 27). There is one from Deposit Alpha dated Early Helladic I–II in *Kythera* pl. 17: 55. Phelps, *Thesis* 48, refers to comparable handles from Koufovouno near Sparta and assigns them to Early Helladic I. I have seen a handle of this type from Kastritsa in Epirus in Ioannina Museum.

Pushed-through handles

Pushed-through or 'thrust' handles reflect a stage when the handle of a vase was keyed into the body by pushing it through a hole made in the side while the clay was still soft. The inside end of the handle might then be smoothed over and integrated with the inside wall of the vase; but in the case of closed vases with necks too narrow for the potter to reach the projecting end of the handle, it was left.

The idea of fixing a handle by inserting the end of it through a hole in the wall of the vase is already attested before the end of the Early Neolithic at Elateia on the Greek mainland (*Elateia* 174 f. pl. 62, b: 1); but in this case the end of the handle was smoothed over. Handles with the ends left projecting on the inside because they come from vases, especially jugs, with relatively narrow necks, occur in the Bronze Age in Anatolia and throughout the Aegean area. Good examples assigned to E.B. 1–2 are illustrated from the Konya plain (*AS* xiii (1963) 220 fig. 11: 13–15, 28, 29). Such handles are attested at Troy from the middle of the Early Subperiod of Troy I onwards, and at Thermi on jugs of Class B ware (*Troy* i 65. *Thermi* 79). They occur in the Bronze Age in the Cyclades (e.g. *Phylakopi* 94), and in Crete (e.g. *BSA* x (1903–4) 200. *AS* xxii (1972) 120 fig. 6), as well as on the Greek mainland (e.g. *Ayios Kosmas* 126) including Macedonia (*PMac* 198 no. 370). At Eutresis such handles were noted towards the end of Early Helladic II, and they were common there in Early Helladic III, continuing into Middle Helladic (*Eutresis* 120 fig. 164).

At Emporio true pushed-through handles were only common in Period II; but one was recorded from VII, two from V, four from IV, and one or two from I.

String-holes

Holes made through the rim or body of the vase after firing are a regular feature of early pottery in the Aegean area as elsewhere. Such holes usually at any rate seem to have been intended to facilitate repairs to the vase with string or cord.

A good many repair holes of this kind were noted on fragments of vases from the Upper Cave at Ayio Gala, where they seemed to be more in evidence in the upper levels. But such holes were also attested on pottery from the Lower Cave.

On the Greek mainland repair holes appear to be especially prominent on some varieties of pottery of the Middle and Late Neolithic (e.g. Corinth: *Hesperia* xlvii (1978) 419, 438 f. nos. 25–28, on L.N. black burnished ware. Eutresis: *Hesperia* xxix (1960) 131, on vases of thin black burnished ware of Group I. *Elateia* 190 pl. 62, b: very frequent on Grey-Black Burnished Ware of the Bothros horizon and later. *Orchomenos* ii 35, 21 pl. viii: 1 c, on vases of Urfirnis and Black Polished Ware. *PThess* 111 fig. 57: c, on Grey-on-Grey Ware from Tsangli. *PMac* 141 fig. 10: a, on Grey-on-Grey Ware from Servia. *Olynthus* i 35, on Black Burnished Ware. *Kephala* 10).

x. (*J*) *Spouts*

A wide cutaway mouth of Period VIII appears to have belonged to a jug (165). But opposed pairs of spouts of a similar kind occur at Elateia on eccentric bowls found in conjunction with white-slipped ware in Early Neolithic 2 there (*Elateia* 172 pl. 55: b). A comparable system of spout-like excrescences is found on an Early Neolithic bowl from Knossos (*BSA* lix (1964) 197 fig.

39 (4), from Stratum VIII). No other certain examples of spouts were recognised from levels of X–VIII at Emporio. But cutaway spouts were represented by several examples from VII (e.g. 640–1), and they were common on jugs and askoi in V–IV when open trough-like spouts akin to them also occurred on bowls.

Nozzle spouts were not attested at Emporio before VI/V–IV (e.g. 1327–9). But one is illustrated from the end of Early Neolithic I at Knossos (*BSA* lix (1964) 210, 175 fig. 28: 27, from Stratum V), and there are a number from Saliagos (*Saliagos* 40 fig. 59: 13–19). Phelps, *Thesis* 330, assigns one or two from the Greek mainland to the early phase of his Final Neolithic (Period IV). At Byblos such spouts occurred in the Early Aeneolithic (*Byblos* v 195 fig. 123). In three instances Emporio nozzle spouts had a small handle on top joining them to the rim or side of the vase. Two of these (1329, 1193) were from levels of VI/V and V/IV, one from stage 3 in Area F assignable to classic Period II. This curious arrangement can be paralleled from Anatolia and by Early Helladic examples from the Greek mainland (e.g. Buchholz and Karageorghis no. 795. *Orchomenos* iii 10, 48 no. 30 pl. xv: 1, from Bothros 11 which is a closed deposit, perhaps E.H. III). A handled spout from Troy I is very like 1329 (*Troy* i 158 fig. 245: 24).

xi. (*K*) *Bases* (FIGS. 109, 110)

These have been described in detail under the various groups of periods. A summary by periods is given below with an account of the various classes of base recognised after it.

Periods X–VIII

Bases from these early levels were in general confined to varieties of the simple flat or sunk classes 6 and 5. A few jar bases from Period X onwards were of the flat splayed class 7A. Bases of these classes were still in evidence at Emporio in Periods VII–VI and even later.

Some pedestal feet (class 2 A) were recovered from levels of VIII. A few bases which had belonged to small vases of fine burnished ware from levels of VIII were incipient ring bases as class 5 D.

Mat-impressed bases were not much in evidence. Only three examples were found at Emporio: one from level 158 of Period IX in Area A, and two (1860, 1942) from levels of V and II in Area B. Similarly at Ayio Gala only one base with a mat impression was noted (AG 40, from the Lower Cave).

A few possible tripod feet (class 9) were assignable to Period VIII.

Periods VII–VI

Bases were largely of the classes already at home in Periods X–VIII. But ring feet of classes 3 A and 4 A were now attested for the first time. Tripod cooking pot feet (class 9) were not represented in deposits of VII, but several were recovered from levels of VI.

Periods V–IV

Pedestal feet (class 2) although first recognised in levels of VIII did not become common until Period V. High pedestal bases (class 1) occurred for the first time at Emporio in V–IV but were rare. A couple of bowls (1107, 1116) from levels of IV had a wide ring bases.

Tripod cooking pot feet (class 9) although already attested in VI if not back in VIII did not become really common until V.

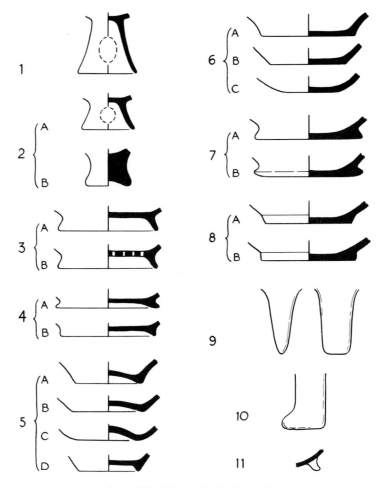

FIG. 109. Bases of Neolithic and Early Bronze Age classes.

Periods III–II

Enormous numbers of tripod cooking pot feet (class 9) were counted from levels of II, when pedestal and high ring feet (classes 2 A and 3 A) were also much in evidence. The ring foot 1743 (class 3 B) was perforated like a strainer. Low ring feet as class 4 B and flat differentiated bases (classes 8 A and B) appear to have been characteristic on large bowls of fine burnished ware in Period II.

Short feet of class 11 were noted for the first time at Emporio in deposits of II. These evidently belonged to small pyxis-like jars akin to type 44 or to jugs of type 21 like 1570.

Period I

Pedestal feet and high ring feet of classes 2 A and 3 A continued to be at home in Period I.

1. *Pedestals*

High pedestals were not much in evidence at Emporio. The earliest certain examples were on bowls of Period IV (859). A couple of fragments of pedestals from levels of II had openings in

Type		X	IX	VIII	VII	VI	V	IV	III	II	I
1	Pedestal						F	F		F	
2A	Pedestal foot			4		5	S	S	2	M	S
2B	Pedestal foot: solid						2	1			
3A	High ring foot					6	6		4	M	S
3B	High ring foot: strainer									1	
4A	Low ring foot: splayed				1	1			1	6	1
4B	Low ring foot: straight						1			2	2
5A	Sunk		S	S	F	F					
5B		4	S	S	F	F	S	S		1	
5C		3	S	S	S		S	S			F
5D				S	2		1			1	
6A	Flat	S	S	S	S	S	S	S			
6B		S	S	S	S	S	S	S			
6C		S	S	S			S	S		S	
7A	Flat splayed	3	S	S		3	1			2	
7B	Flat splayed, with rounded edge									1	
8A	Flat differentiated									1	
8B						1		1		S	F
9	Tripod foot			3		8	M	M	S	M	M
10	Theriomorphic foot		1								
11	Short tripod foot									4	

F = Few   S = Several   M = Many

FIG. 110. Distribution of bases of Neolithic and Early Bronze Age classes.

their sides (2036, 2167); but one of these (2167) at any rate may have been an earlier stray if it did not belong to an imported vase.

High pedestals were much at home at Poliochni where they occurred as early as the Black period overlapping with Emporio VII–VI (*Poliochni* i 541 f. pl. i: a, b). They were also standard during the Late Neolithic on the Greek mainland, especially in Thessaly and Macedonia, and at Saliagos (*Saliagos* 38 figs. 31–32). Bell-shaped pedestals like some from Saliagos appear to be attested at Knossos from Early Neolithic I onwards (BSA xlviii (1953) 130 ff. fig. 15: 10).

2. *Pedestal feet*

These first occurred in levels of VIII, but only became common from Period V onwards. One or two from levels of V and later were more or less solid as class 2 B. A remarkable fragment (1331) from a level of V has a silvery burnished surface and a profile like a Mycenaean kylix stem.

Pedestal feet appear to be at home at Judeideh in Syria by Phase B if not already in Phase A (*Judeideh* 48 fig. 21: 17; 70 f. fig. 41: 31, 32). They are attested in the Early Neolithic of Crete (*BSA* xlviii (1953) 130 ff. fig. 13: 3, 6); and they were also at home in that of the Greek mainland, occurring from the earliest phase at Elateia and in the Protosesklo and Presesklo (E.N. II–III) horizons in Thessaly (*Elateia* 170, 174 fig. 7: 5. Milojcic, *Ergebnisse* 36 fig. 6: 6. *Otzaki-magula* pl. xix: 1; pl. 13: 1–6; beil. 7: Bodenform I, 1).

In the Troad pedestal feet were found at Kum Tepe from Phase I A onwards (*Kum Tepe* 325 f. fig. 11 no. 230; 337 fig. 15 nos. 548–551; 348). Typical pedestal bases of class 2 A appear alongside high pedestals of class 1 at Poliochni as early as the end of the Black period which overlaps with Kum Tepe I B and Emporio VII–VI (*Poliochni* i 557 pl. iv: k). Pedestal feet were common at Troy from the beginning of Troy I, and occurred in Troy II, but do not seem to have been so much in evidence then (*Troy* i 59, 61 shapes A 7, A 13; 228 shape A 26). A number of Troy I pedestal feet had openings in them. Pedestal feet are attested from Tigani on Samos (*AA* 1928, 626 fig. 21).

Some rather wide pedestal bases approximating to Emporio class 3, but with circular openings in them, are illustrated from level IV and later at Hacilar (e.g. *Hacilar* i 112; ii 281 fig. 64: 9; i 112; ii 331 fig. 90: 33). There is a fragment of a pedestal base from a level of Late Chalcolithic 1 at Beycesultan (*Beycesultan* i 74 f. fig. P. 2: 36. Cf. *Alishar* 1930–32 i 76 fig. 84 no. 23 (e 2106) etc.). None is illustrated from E.B. 1 levels at Beycesultan, although varieties of them are well represented in E.B. 2–3 there.

3. *High ring feet*

These shade into pedestal feet of class 2. At Emporio high ring feet were first noted in Period VI, and occurred in V–IV, but only became common in II. One (1743) from a level of II was pierced with holes as a strainer (class 3 B).

Such feet are known from Çatal Hüyük and from the Early Neolithic of the Greek mainland (*AS* xiv (1964) 82. *Elateia* 174 fig. 7: 6). They were characteristic of the pottery from Skyros compared by Theochares with Thessalian A 1 (*AE* 1945–47 Arch. Chron. 3 fig. 4).

4. *Low ring feet*

Bases assignable to this class were relatively uncommon. The splayed variety (class 4 A) was first attested from Period VII and by several examples from levels of II. The straight variety (class 4 B) was even less in evidence than class 4 A.

5. *Sunk bases*

Varieties of these were at home in all periods at Emporio. They were fairly well represented in levels of X–VIII.

6. *Flat bases*

Like bases of class 5 these were at home in all periods including X–VIII.

7. *Flat splayed bases*
These were characteristic of the earliest levels (Periods X–VIII). But isolated examples of bases assignable to this class occurred later from Period VI until II.

An Early Neolithic jar base from Elateia is comparable with class 7 B (*Elateia* 170, 174 fig. 7: 3).

8. *Flat differentiated bases*
A few bases of this class were recovered from levels of VII–IV, but it was really characteristic of Period II.

9. *Tripod feet*
Feet that might have come from tripod vases were attested by a few examples from levels of VIII. But tripod cooking pots of type 27 did not begin to be at home at Emporio until Period VI, and only became common in V. Vast numbers of feet from such cooking pots were recovered from levels of II.

Tripod cooking pots were common at Troy from the time of Troy I onwards, as noted under type 27. Legs of tripod cooking pots were not much in evidence at Kum Tepe before Phase I C 1 contemporary with Troy I (*Kum Tepe* 349, 354): but there was a wide flat leg of rectangular shape from Phase I B 3, while legs of fine burnished ware from levels of I A 1 and 2 resembled in shape those of later tripod cooking pots (ibid. 337 no. 558; 320 no. 116 and 325 nos. 218–220).

Tripod cooking pot legs are already attested in the Late Chalcolithic it seems at Aphrodisias (Pekmez level VII d) (*AJA* lxxv (1971) 127 f. pl. 27 fig. 15).

10. *Feet of theriomorphic vases (type 25)*
The foot of such a vase (168) was recovered from a level of IX. An isolated foot (652) from VII might have belonged to a theriomorphic vase, but could have come from some variety of tripod vessel.

The foot 168 is not unlike one from Saliagos which may be anthropomorphic (*Saliagos* 40, 87 figs. 59: 22; 77: 3).

11. *Short tripod feet*
A few feet of this class from small jars were recovered from levels of II.

(c) Decoration

Decoration on vases of the Neolithic and Early Bronze Age at Emporio included (1) Pattern burnish, (2) Paint (white and occasionally red) on dark burnished surfaces, (3) Incision, with or without a fill of white paste, and (4) Relief (ribs and warts).

(1) Pattern burnish
This distinctive type of decoration was made by intensive selective rubbing with the burnishing tool on a smoothed or less well burnished surface in such a way as to effect patterns.

No examples of pattern burnish were noted from levels of X, and only a few scraps from doubtful contexts of IX. The flourishing time for it at Emporio was Period VIII, from levels of which some 50 fragments were recovered. Even in Period VIII, however, pattern burnish was not the standard system of decoration, being far less common than incision. It occurred on the rims and bodies of jars, especially on those of small ones of types 41–42 (265–270), and on the outsides of bowl rims, notably of type 8 (138, 140–1). Alternate groups of diagonal stripes were the standard design on bowl rims, and they were also usual on jars. But some jars had other designs such as vertical rows of multiple chevrons (178).

About six fragments with comparable pattern burnish were recovered from levels of VII and a dozen from those of VI. Some of these at any rate may have been strays of Period VIII. But the number of fragments with pattern burnish from VI is impressive. Moreover the burnishing tool was evidently used with an eye to decorative effect on jugs of Light Brown Burnished Ware in VII–VI, and occasionally patterns of rough lattice were made with it. The half-dozen scraps with pattern burnish from levels of V, however, all looked as if they might have been earlier strays. But some examples of true pattern burnish were assignable to Period II (e.g. 1544, 1758, 1761), and a bowl rim (2481) with distinctive pattern burnish from a level of Period I appeared to be of contemporary date.

An uncommon but distinctive form of decoration characteristic of Period II and perhaps still current in I combined incision in areas of fine burnish with contrasting areas left unburnished. This kind of decoration seems to have been most at home on small bowls of type 13 (e.g. 1545, 1987–8, 2369); but it appears on a few bowls of other types, like 1518 of type 9 and 2503 of type 14, as well as on fragments of jugs or jars (2106, 2298, 2422, 2431) and on lids (e.g. 1659). Sometimes on these vases the white-filled incised decoration was combined with areas of matt red paint to create a polychrome effect (e.g. 2298). In one instance at least, on a bowl (1759) of type 5, the decoration combining white-filled incision and areas of red paint was confined to the unburnished parts of the vase.

Pattern burnish comparable with that from Emporio VIII is found in very early contexts in Syria. It occurs in levels of the Early and Middle Neolithic at Byblos (*Byblos* v 49 f. fig. 18 (T. 1016) 25481 bis, pl. lxix). At Judeideh it first appears in Phase B and continues into C (*Judeideh* 77 fig. 51; 109 ff. figs. 79, 81; 141 f. fig. 110). As in Emporio VIII it is attested there on red surfaces as well as on black ones (ibid. 73, 77, 109. Cf. J. Mellaart, *Iraq* xl (1978) 124, 128 f. fig. 4: 28, 30, 31). The designs in Phase C at Judeideh include alternate groups of diagonal stripes of the kind standard in Emporio VIII, and these may have been already current in Phase B to judge from *Judeideh* 78 fig. 51: 5. Pattern burnish was also at home in the Late Neolithic horizon (V Phase 3) at Ras Shamra (*Ugaritica* iv 503 f. figs. 26, 27); and it adorned many bowls of the earliest (Chalcolithic) Periods I–III at Sakce Gözü (*Iraq* xii (1950) 84, 90). Mellaart, *Iraq* xl (1978) 128, has reasonably suggested that the idea of pattern burnish may have developed in Syria during the Amuq B phase, inspired perhaps by metope patterns on Early Halaf painted bowls in Assyria. But the fashion for pattern burnish never appears to have taken root in Cilicia: none is reported from Mersin. Five sherds of grey pattern burnished ware recovered at Tarsus were assigned to the Late Chalcolithic or Early Bronze I, but actually came from later contexts (*Tarsus* ii 89 f. pl. 230: c, d).

Pattern burnish has been regarded as typical of Period I A at Kum Tepe, although it was in fact distinctly rare there. Only five sherds were found in stratified deposits, three in ones of I A 1, and one each in those of I A 2 and I B 1 (*Kum Tepe* 316 note 7, pl. 72 nos. 101, 112, 113 a; 325 pl. 73 no. 223). On the other hand pattern burnished ware with surfaces 'black, brown, or most commonly, red-brown, the colour of a horse-chestnut' appears to abound at Beşik Tepe on the coast south of Kum Tepe and south-west of Troy (W. Lamb, *PZ* xxiii (1932) 126 ff. fig. 13. Cf. *Ilios* 667 f. *Tu I* 546 fig. 467). It looks as if this pattern burnish horizon at Beşik Tepe may belong to a period earlier than Kum Tepe I A (cf. D. French, *AS* xix (1969) 60). The total absence of spindle whorls and tripod vessels which Schliemann, *Ilios* 668, noted as 'astonishing' at Beşik Tepe is in itself suggestive of a rather early date in this part of the world.

Pattern burnish was evidently not much at home in the interior of Anatolia in early times. It occurs in the hinterland of the Troad, but does not seem to be common there (*AS* xix (1969) 59 f. Group 3 (c) 'Besika'. Cf. A. Furness, *PPS* xxii (1956) 208. F. Fischer, *Ist. Mitt.* xvii (1967) 22 ff., but the p. b. ware from sites 8 and 9 is buff burnished of the 2nd millennium!). Two sherds were found at Beycesultan in levels (XXXIII and XXXI or XXXII) of Late Chalcolithic 2, while a third from Level XIII was regarded as an earlier stray (*Beycesultan* i 91, chart on 112, 84 f. fig. P. 6: 6, 10). Both in the Troad and in other parts of Anatolia, however, there are sporadic examples of pattern burnish from Early Bronze Age contexts. It is found alongside incised decoration at the beginning of the Early Bronze Age (E.B. I–II) at Ikiztepe on the Black Sea coast of northern Anatolia (Y. Yakar, *Tel Aviv* ii (1975) 138. Cf. *AS* xxix (1979) 54). A theriomorphic vase from the Mound of Protesilaos from a horizon with depades assignable to Troy II is decorated with wide bands of pattern burnish (*Protesilaos* 61 figs. 76: 7, and 79). Simple pattern burnish like that on 2481 of Period I occurs at Alishar in a Copper Age stratum contemporary with Troy II (*Alishar* 1930–32 i fig. 161: 7). Fragments with pattern burnish from the Heraion site on Samos appear to belong to the horizon of Troy II–III (*Samos* i 43 pls. 28: 1–5; 48: 5–20). Some Early and Middle Bronze Age wheelmade pottery from north-western Anatolia (French's 'Inegöl' Grey ware related to the grey ware of Troy V, and Orange-buff burnished ware) is commonly decorated with pattern burnish (*AS* xvii (1967) 49 ff., 61 f., 64. Cf. J. Mellaart, *Ist. Mitt.* vi (1955) 66 figs. 58–60; 85 fig. 66; 86 figs. 74, 87).

Tigani on Samos is another early site in the eastern Aegean besides Emporio and Beşik Tepe where pattern burnish was at home (*Tigani* 128 ff., 156 ff. A. Furness, *PPS* xxii (1956) 187). Here, as at Emporio, pattern burnish does not seem to be attested in the earliest deposits, and it was apparently out of fashion by the time of the latest occupation (*Samos* xiv 131, 133). In some respects the Tigani pattern burnish is comparable with that of Emporio VIII. Thus the surfaces of the pattern burnished vases are dominantly grey-black rather than reddish in colour. But, unlike what is found at Emporio, pattern burnish at Tigani is largely confined to the inside surfaces of bowls and only occasionally appears on the outside of the rim as well (*Tigani* pl. 61). Moreover the pattern burnish designs at Tigani are more elaborate and varied than are those of Emporio VIII. The Tigani pattern burnish has indeed many points of comparison with that of Early Minoan I in Crete.

The fashion for decorating the insides of bowls with pattern burnish, not it seems attested at Emporio, recalls the earlier pattern burnished ware of Sakce Gözü in Anatolia (*Iraq* xii (1950) 84). But the practice was also at home at Kephala on Kea, and in the Late Neolithic on the Greek mainland: at Corinth, for instance, the pattern burnish on bowls of black burnished ware was mostly it seems on the insides (*Hesperia* xlvii (1978) 440 under no. 31). Possibly therefore the bulk at any rate of the Tigani pattern burnished ware belongs to a later period than Emporio VIII, and is contemporary with Emporio VII–VI. Heidenreich in fact assigned the pattern burnished ware to the later of the two periods into which he attempted to divide the Tigani material. It may be significant in this connection that distinctive Kum Tepe I B features like the type 11 bowls dominant at Emporio in VII–VI appear to be missing at Tigani and at the Heraion site on Samos. For some reason perhaps the new fashions which appear at Emporio in Period VII did not spread to Samos, where pattern burnish may have continued in favour after it was abandoned in Chios.

Pattern burnish never appears to have been popular in the Cyclades. At Saliagos it was very rare, and was sometimes combined with white paint: the examples of it are not easily paralleled at Emporio or Tigani (*Saliagos* 44 fig. 56: 14–18). An isolated sherd with pattern burnish has been reported from Paros (Schachermeyr, *Ältesten Kulturen* 138, 140 fig. 35: 4); but Renfrew,

Emergence 509, doubts if it was pattern burnished. At Kephala in Kea, however, pattern burnish was very much at home (*Kephala* 11 f. Cf. J.E. Coleman, *AJA* lxxviii (1974) 336 f.). This Kephala pattern burnish is dominantly on red surfaces and, as at Tigani, is most commonly found on the insides of bowls. The usually broad lines of the burnish and the more flexible character of the designs serve to distinguish it from the pattern burnish of Emporio VIII and suggest that it belongs to a later period. There is a fashion for comparable red pattern burnished ware in some neighbouring parts of the Greek mainland, notably Attica, and on the island of Aigina about the same time (e.g. *Thorikos* iii 25 fig. 21–22. Kitsos cave: *BCH* xciii (1969) 962. 965 fig. 17; xciv (1970) 758; xcv (1971) 711 fig. 22, including bowl rims of the Kum Tepe I B type 11. *Athenian Agora* xiii 5, 7. Athens Acropolis: *ADelt* xix (1964) Chron. 27 pl. 15: b, called Subneolithic. *Prosymna* 375 f. fig. 635. Aigina: *AA* lii (1937) 19 ff. figs. 1–6. G. Welter, *Aigina* (Berlin, 1938) 7 ff. figs. 2–7). Pattern burnish of a rather similar kind with broad stripes on a red surface is attested in the Cypriote Early Bronze Age (*SCE* iv Pt. 1 A fig. cli: 1–4, Red Polished I, on the outsides of bowls).

This horizon of red-surfaced pattern burnish ware in Greece also seems to be relatively late. At Corinth, where both black- and red- or brown-surfaced ware with pattern burnish was recovered, the latter appeared to belong to a late phase of the Late Neolithic (*Hesperia* xxix (1960) 250 pl. 63: b). But grey-black burnished ware with pattern burnish was already at home in the Bothros horizon at Elateia assigned to the end of Middle or beginning of Late Neolithic (*Elateia* 188. Cf. French, *Pottery Groups* 10 fig. 20: 19, from Amouri II, assigned to the Bothros phase). Dark surfaced pattern burnish ware has been found in many parts of the Greek mainland in Late Neolithic contexts (e.g. Corinth: *Hesperia* vi (1937) 512 fig. 29: *c–e*; xlvii (1978) 440 under no. 31, mostly it seems on the insides of bowls as at Tigani. *Eutresis* 76 f. fig. 92. Cf. *Hesperia* xxix (1960) 131 f. pl. 43. *Orchomenos* ii 18 f. pls. I: 1; IX: 2, 3; X: 1. Perhaps the Franchthi cave: *Hesperia* xxxviii (1969) 367, 370, pl. 98: a, bottom left). The pattern burnish ware of the latest phase (B II) at Nea Makri in Attica appears to have been dark surfaced (*Nea Makri* 18: only one example reported from the earlier horizon B I). Black burnished ware with pattern burnish from Varka in Euboia and isolated fragments from other Euboian sites are assigned to the Late Neolithic (*AE* 1975 Parart. 75. *BSA* lxi (1966) 84 fig. 18: 26, 27. *Ist. Mitt.* xvii (1967) 27 no. 27. Cf. *Kephala* 102 note 19). In Crete pattern burnish appears in the Late Neolithic but is rare then and only becomes a dominant fashion in decoration at the beginning of the Cretan Bronze Age in Early Minoan I (*BSA* xlviii (1953) 132; lix (1964) 229). The surfaces of Early Minoan pattern burnish ware are normally grey-black but sometimes red or brown.

In Thessaly dark-surfaced pattern burnish ware was at home during the Tsangli and Arapi (Dhimini 1 and 2) phases of the Late Neolithic. Sherds of grey-black pattern burnish ware from Tsangli itself have alternate groups of diagonal lines resembling those of Emporio VIII pattern burnish (*PThess* 105 fig. 55: n–p). But in general the designs of this Thessalian Late Neolithic pattern burnish look elaborate and more comparable with those of the red-surfaced pattern burnish wares of the latest Neolithic in southern Greece (e.g. *Arapi* 23 f., 56 ff. Cf. *AA* 1955, 188 ff. fig. 2: 9–12: Dhimini 1. Milojcic, *Ergebnisse* 14 fig. 13: 15, 17–19, 24–26: Dhimini 1). Pattern burnish is also found in the Late Neolithic of Macedonia, but appears to be rare (*Ist. Mitt.* xvii (1967) 29. *PMac* 71).

There is some evidence, however, for the use of pattern burnish already in the Early Neolithic of Greece. At Knossos in Crete one example of pattern burnish was probably although not certainly Early Neolithic (*BSA* xlviii (1953) 132). A certain amount of pattern burnish of a simple kind occurs in the Presesklo (E.N. III) phase of Early Neolithic in Thessaly (*Otzaki-magula* 32, 35, 50 pls. xiii: 26; xiv: 11, 31, 32; xv: 8; xvii: 15; xviii: 6; xx: 23; xxi: 19; xxii:

10). An isolated fragment from the top of the Protosesklo (E.N. II) deposit at Otzaki has alternate hatching comparable with the alternate groups of diagonal lines on Emporio VIII pattern burnish (ibid. 26 pl. x: 21). This taken in conjunction with the very early appearance of pattern burnish in the Levant suggests that the horizon of pattern burnish at Beşik Tepe in the Troad and at Emporio in Periods IX–VIII may be a good deal older than the Late Neolithic manifestations of it in the Aegean and on the Greek mainland.

(2) Paint

Painted decoration when it occurred at Emporio was normally in white; but some instances of red painted decoration were recorded from the earlier levels.

(a) *White paint.*

Groups of white diagonal stripes were noted on four fragments of type 41 jars from levels of X (244–5, 377). White painted decoration, sometimes at any rate encrusted, that is, applied after the burnishing and firing of the vase, was better attested in Periods IX (10 fragments) and VIII (some 40 fragments). A number of jugs of Period VIII (e.g. 165) had white painted decoration of this kind, and jugs of Fine Black Burnished Ware from levels of VII–VI were regularly adorned with designs in white paint. It was in these Periods VII–VI that white painted decoration most flourished at Emporio. In V it was superseded by white-filled incision, which achieved the same effects of contrast between dark burnished surfaces and designs in white but in a more efficient and enduring manner (cf. J. Mellaart, *AS* iv (1954) 207). The relatively few fragments with white painted decoration from levels of periods after VI (some 10 from V, but only 3 from IV, and one or two from II) may have come from imported vases (cf. *Troy* i 79).

The situation at Tigani in Samos appears to be comparable to that at Emporio. There decoration in matt white paint occurs, but is rare, in the earliest phase of occupation revealed by the new excavations. It seems to be more common, however, in the latest deposits, when it is found on jugs comparable with ones from Emporio VII–VI (*Samos* xiv 130, 133).

Vases with a red slip were being decorated with designs in white paint in the Naqāda I (Amratian) stage in Predynastic Egypt (E.J. Baumgartel, *CAH*³ i Pt. 1, 477).

A bowl rim from Akrata in Achaia with multiple chevrons in white reminiscent of the groups of diagonal stripes on the necks of jars from the lowest levels at Emporio is assigned to the Early Neolithic by Phelps, *Thesis* 106 fig. 10: 29. At Ayios Petros (Kira-Panayia) in the Sporades Theochares noted a small amount of white painted alongside the dark-on-light painted ware akin to Protosesklo (E.N. II) and Chaeronea Early Neolithic wares (*ADelt* xxvi (1971) Chron. 296). But white painted decoration first began to become fashionable on the Greek mainland in the Middle Neolithic (Sesklo) period on red-surfaced (A 3) ware (J.E. Coleman, *AJA* lxxviii (1974) 334. *PThess* 14). Designs then included multiple chevrons comparable with those on jugs of Fine Black Burnished Ware of Emporio VII–VI (e.g. *Ergon* 1968, 33 fig. 35. Theochares, *Neolithic Greece* pl. 5).

In the Bothros horizon at Elateia, assigned by Weinberg to the end of the Middle Neolithic, but regarded by others as early in the Late Neolithic, white painted decoration occurred on grey-black burnished ware which sounds comparable in fabric with Emporio Fine Black Burnished Ware (*Elateia* 188, 190 pl. 62: a). In any case the fashion for this kind of white painted decoration on black burnished surfaces continued into the Late Neolithic on the Greek mainland (S. Weinberg, *Hesperia* vi (1937) 512 fig. 29: f–h, from Corinth. *PAE* 1951, 100 f., fig. 6, from Palaia Kokkinia. Holmberg, *Neolithic Pottery* 25 f.). White painted decoration is found in the Tsangli and Arapi (Dhimini 1 and 2) phases of the Thessalian Late Neolithic, although it is less common than pattern burnish (*Arapi* 25, 58. Cf. *PThess* 17, 105 fig. 55). But the designs of this Late Neolithic white painted decoration of the Greek mainland appear to be more varied and elaborate than those of Emporio VII–VI.

A variety of white painted ware with elaborate thick-lined designs was at home at the very end of the Late Neolithic in some parts of the Greek mainland (e.g. Zervos, *Nais* 497 figs. 828–9, from the Cave of Pan at Marathon. *BCH* c (1976) 756 fig. 11, from Argos: Aspis). A similarly elaborate and varied style of white painted decoration also flourished, however, in the Cyclades at Saliagos, where it was most characteristic of the earliest phase 1, declining in popularity in phases 2 and 3 (*Saliagos* 40 f., 82).

White painted decoration was at home on black burnished ware of the Late Chalcolithic in many parts of Anatolia (e.g. *Beycesultan* i 71 ff. Aphrodisias: *AJA* lxxv (1971) 128 f., 140 pl. 27 figs. 15, 16. Cf. A.S. Burney, *AS* vi (1956) 182, 194 f. nos. 3–6. D. French, *AS* xi (1961) 122 f. figs. 4, 5). It occurs in Period A at Kusura (*Archaeologia* lxxxvi (1936) 15 fig. 6: 12, 13), and is represented in level 1 at Can Hasan (*AS* xiii (1963) 37 f. fig. 5: 11; xv (1965) 88). The horizon of related black burnished ware with white painted decoration at Mersin in Cilicia is assigned to Level XII A which may overlap with E.B. I at Tarsus (*Mersin* 182 ff. fig. 118).

The pottery of this Anatolian Late Chalcolithic horizon and the style of its white painted decoration have affinities with Emporio VII–VI. But in Anatolia as in Greece there is some evidence for the sporadic use of white paint to decorate vases in earlier times. White painted decoration occurs although rare at Hacilar in the Late Neolithic level VI and again in I (*Hacilar* i 108, 141 f.). A bowl from Hacilar VI is decorated with parallel diagonal stripes (*Hacilar* ii 271 fig. 59: 2).

The fashion for white painted decoration does not appear to have taken root in all parts of Anatolia during the Late Chalcolithic. It is not much in evidence in the Troad. Thus at Kum Tepe it was extremely rare in the pre-Troy I levels which may overlap with Emporio VII–VI; two sherds with white painted decoration were recovered from Kum Tepe I A 2, and a third from I B 4 contemporary with Troy I (*Kum Tepe* 324 note 12). The 24 fragments with white painted decoration from levels of Troy I itself may have come from imported vases (*Troy* i 79).

The fashion for decorating the burnished surfaces of vases with white paint survived in many parts of Anatolia into the Bronze Age, as emphasised by D. Levi, *Iasos* iv 532. White painted decoration occurs in western Anatolia on vases of the Yortan culture, mostly on jugs but also on small jars, assignable to the time of Troy I or later (*Ist. Mitt.* xvi (1966) 1 ff., 26. Cf. ibid. 68 fig. 8: 4, 5, from Asarcik Hüyük near Ilica west of Ankara, level V (E.B. 2–3). Cf. *Iasos* ii 539; iv 530 ff. Karataş-Semayük: *AJA* lxx (1966) 252 pls. 58–9 (E.B. II). J. Mellaart, *AS* iv (1954) 194 ff., 202 ff. A. Furness, *PPS* xxii (1956) 204 f. Schachermeyr, *Ältesten Kulturen* 280 S. 131).

(b) *Red paint.*

Although red painted decoration was very rare at Emporio it occurred in the earliest levels. Thus diagonal stripes in red instead of in the more usual white paint are found on two fragments (249, 387) from levels of Period IX.

Decoration in red paint also occurs at Tigani in Samos, although it is rare and appears to be a feature of an advanced stage in the occupation of the settlement (*Tigani* 151 ff. *Samos* xiv 131).

It is interesting that red paint was occasionally used for decorating pottery in the Neolithic of southern Turkey, although there seems to be some doubt as to whether the few examples of red painted decoration are to be assigned to the early Neolithic Kizilkaya Culture or to Late Neolithic (*AS* xi (1961) 172, 171 fig. 6: 19).

The use of red instead of white paint to decorate a dark burnished surface is similarly not unparalleled in early contexts in the Aegean. Pottery from the lowest levels (17–15) at Paradimi in eastern Macedonia is reported to include black and brown surfaced fragments of biconical bowls with encrusted decoration in white or red (Hauptman, *AA* 1971, 380). None of this early pottery from Paradimi is illustrated: it is said to be like the Maritsa pottery of Bulgaria; but this horizon (levels 17–15) is well below that (level 9 upwards) from which material comparable with that of Sitagroi I and Karanovo III is reported. At Saliagos encrusted red was also used alongside or in place of the more usual white paint for vase decoration (*Saliagos* 36, 84). At Knossos in Crete the earliest (E.N. I) incised decoration was very occasionally filled with red instead of with the normal white paste (*BSA* lxiii (1968) 271).

Encrusted red, applied after the burnishing and firing of the vase, is combined with incision on 396 from Emporio VIII and on 656 from a level of VIII or early VII. The latter at any rate may be an import, and a similar combination of rows of triangular jabs with red painted decoration is attested on vases assigned to the early part of the Middle Neolithic Sesklo horizon in Thessaly. But red paint is already found in combination with incised decoration in the Protochalcolithic level XXIV at Mersin (*Mersin* 62 fig. 137). The incised lines enclosing red triangles on trichrome ware from level XV of the later Chalcolithic there are somewhat reminiscent of 396 (*Mersin* 159 fig. 101). The same system of decoration appears on Halaf ware from Ras Shamra (*Ugaritica* iv 245 f. pl. i: 6, 9).

No example of red painted decoration was attested from levels of Emporio V–IV, when the use of white paint was excessively rare. But in Period II matt red paint, usually applied after the surface had been burnished, was sometimes employed in conjunction with white-filled incisions to decorate vases (1759, 1762–4). It was even it seems used at times on its own for decoration: the rim 2260 of a type 9 bowl of Period II was hatched in matt red. Some jars assignable to Periods II and I had a thick coat of red paint on the inside (2399, 2426, 2584); but this might be the remains of their original contents. A similar coating of red paint, however, was noted on the inside of a Period II lid (1659).

Decoration in red and white (and in red alone) on dark burnished surfaces is a feature of a late variety of Neolithic pottery in Crete (L. Vagnetti, *Annuario* l–li (1972–73) 68 ff., 80 class (C)). A similar use of encrusted red paint is also found on pottery of the Rakhmani horizon in Thessaly.

(3) Incision

Incised decoration was fashionable at Emporio in two separate horizons, which appear to reflect two different traditions, although these may have had a common ancestor at long remove. The earlier horizon of incised decoration with its zenith in Period VIII is characterised by rather simple linear designs and the virtually complete absence of white fill in the incisions. In the later horizon, covering the Early Bronze Age (Periods V–I), the incisions were normally filled with white, and the designs, although still essentially linear, were more varied, while areas of punctuation (pointillé) hardly attested in Period VIII were not uncommon.

Periods X–VIII (FIGS. 111–112)

The very few fragments with incised decoration assigned to Period X were from an uncertain context and might have strayed from IX or VIII (379–381) (FIG. 111 no. 1: a, b = 381). But three fragments with incised decoration (388–390) came from safe contexts of Period IX (FIG. 111 nos. 2 = 389; 3a, b = 390). All these were remarkable: 388 in having the incisions made after firing; 389 in the curving band reserved against a background of close-set jabs; and 390 in its bands of fine multiple incisions. The last two (389, 390) were unique at Emporio, and nothing that might

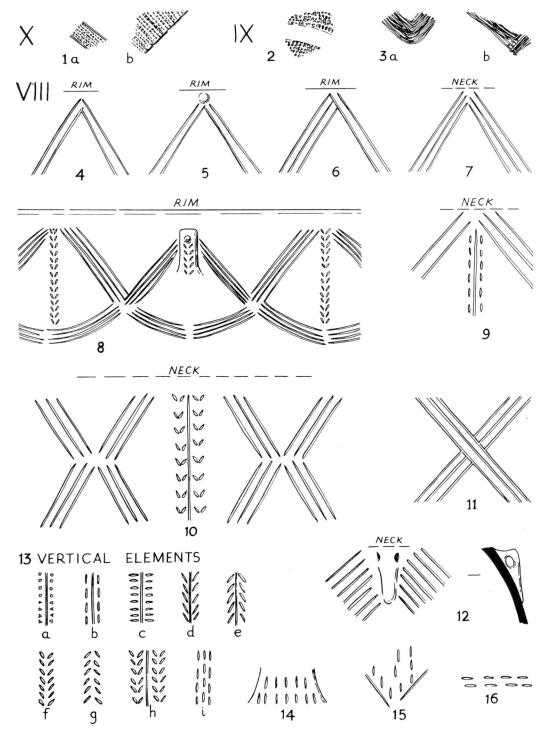

FIG. 111. Incised decoration of Periods X–VIII (catalogue numbers in parentheses): X. 1 a, b (381); IX. 2 (389); 3 a, b (390); VIII. 4 (170); 7 (172); 8 (173); 9 (397); 10 (398); 11 (399); 12 (367); 13 e (264); 13 h (398); 13 i (400); 14 (402); 15 (403); 16 (401). See also PLATES 33 (a) no. 3 for VIII. 6; 33 (a) no. 5 and 40 (a) no. 4 for VIII. 13 c; 41 (a) no. 3 for VIII. 13 g.

be regarded as continuing their tradition was recovered from levels of the succeeding Period VIII. This suggests that they may have belonged to imported vases, although their fabric gave no indication of a foreign origin.

Incision was by far the commonest form of decoration in Period VIII, but was virtually confined to jars (FIGS. 111, 112). In general at any rate the incised designs were not filled with white paste. The basic scheme of decoration consisted of groups of diagonal lines, which might intersect to form net patterns, or could be organised in bands of chevrons (FIG. 112 nos. 17–20). Panels filled with horizontal rows of smaller chevrons also occurred (FIG. 112 nos. 21–23). Groups of concentric lozenges were another characteristic motif (FIG. 112 nos. 34, 35). Rows of dots or dashes were used in various combinations, often flanking or flanked by incised lines. But dot-filled (pointillé) panels were rare, and the dot-filled strips found in later periods from VI onwards were not attested in VIII.

As might be expected there are close parallels for the incised decoration of Emporio VIII from Tigani on Samos (*Tigani* 134 ff.). Heidenreich assigned this incised ware to his Period I and the pattern burnished ware of Tigani to his later Period II. A fragmentary jar of type 41, thought to be an import, and another fragment with rows of incised chevrons like FIG. 112 no. 21, would have been at home in Emporio VIII (*Tigani* 135, 157 F. 73, pl. 34: 1, 2; pl. 30: 6). But pointillé decoration, often with a fill of white paste, was very much more in evidence at Tigani. Much of the Tigani incised ware like the pattern burnished ware may therefore date from a period contemporary with Emporio VII–VI if not later. Incised concentric lozenges reminiscent of the design on FIG. 112 no. 35, but filled with white paste, appear on fragments assigned to the Neolithic from the Santa Barbara cave on Kalymnos (*Clara Rhodos* i 108 fig. 88. Cf. Furness, *PPS* xxii (1956) 188).

Nea Makri on the east coast of Attica is virtually the only site on the Greek mainland that has produced a comparable class of incised ware (*Nea Makri* 10 ff. pls. 4–7). This was characteristic of the earliest phase A I at Nea Makri, although it continued into A II. The commonest motifs were multiple chevrons, usually horizontal, but often vertical. Concentric lozenges like those of FIG. 112 nos. 34 and 35 were also typical. Pointillé occurred, but was evidently rare. In sharp contrast to the situation in Emporio VIII, however, nearly all the Nea Makri incised vases were open bowls, and the incisions were normally at any rate filled with white paste.

This kind of incised decoration, which was almost unique on the Greek mainland at the time that Theochares found it, was named by him the Nea Makri Style. He considered it to be contemporary with the Protosesklo (E.N. II) and Presesklo (E.N. III) horizons of the Early Neolithic in Thessaly, and noted comparable Early Neolithic incised ware from Nemea. A bowl from Nemea is in fact decorated with a row of incised concentric lozenges (*Nemea* 267 pl. 65: 1. Cf. *Nea Makri* pl. 7). It is interesting that at Nemea as in Emporio VIII white filling does not appear to have been used to emphasize the incised patterns. A sherd from the lowest level of the Early Neolithic at Lerna is decorated with bold grooves which similarly appear to have no white fill (Vitelli 1977, 20 f. fig. 7). The absence of white fill is also a feature of the earliest incised ware of the Cyclades assignable to Early Cycladic I in contrast to that of Early Cycladic II, as noted by Edgar, *Phylakopi* 87.

A marble idol, allegedly from Sparta and perhaps from the Koufovouno site near there, is incised with multiple chevrons and concentric lozenges like those on pottery of Emporio VIII and Nea Makri A (*AM* xvi (1891) 52 f. fig. 1. Zervos, *Naïs* 170 f. figs. 113–14). The idol is assigned by Milojčić, *Otzaki-magula* 90 f., 152, to the end of the Protosesklo horizon of the Early Neolithic in Thessalian terms. Titov quoted by Milojčić also dates the idol in the Early Neolithic.

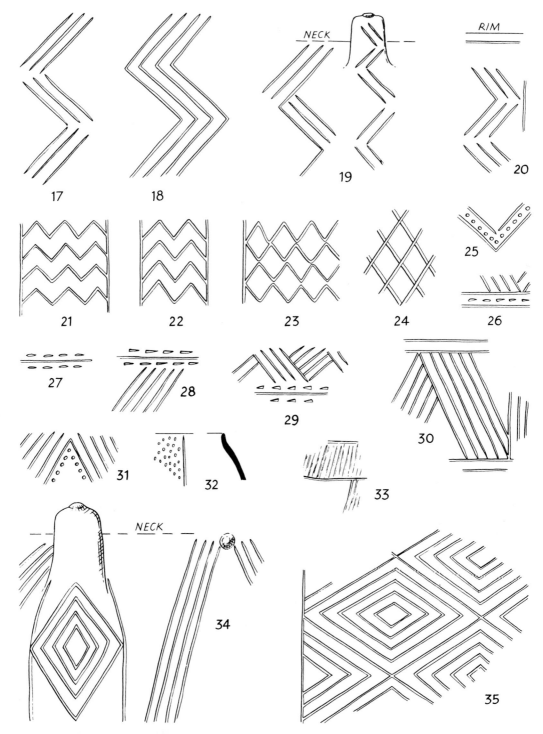

FIG. 112. Incised decoration of Period VIII (catalogue numbers in parentheses): VIII. 17 (404); 18 (405); 19 (407); 20 (406); 24 (408); 25 (409); 26 (410); 28 (411); 29 (412); 30 (413); 31 (414); 32 (415); 33 (416); 35 (417). See also PLATES 33 (a) nos. 6, 8 and 41 (a) no. 2 for VIII. 21, 23, 22.

The closest parallels for the incised decoration of Emporio VIII therefore appear to be forthcoming from the Early Neolithic of the Greek mainland. But this kind of incised decoration seems to be rooted in a tradition at home on the coasts of the Levant and well represented in the Early Neolithic of Byblos. The Byblos Early Neolithic is certainly much older than the beginning of Emporio X, but many of the motifs of the incised ware of Emporio VIII are present there in embryo. Compare for instance the rows of chevrons and dashes of FIG. 111 no. 13: f, g, i, with *Byblos* v 48 ff. figs. 16–20. Even the hatched band of FIG. 112 no. 33 has a parallel in Early Neolithic Byblos (*Byblos* v fig. 23: 33061). Like the incised ware of Emporio VIII and Nemea, that of Early Neolithic Byblos is innocent of white fill: there is also as in Emporio VIII a great variation in the size of the incisions, which range from bold grooves to fine scratches. White fill is similarly absent from incised decoration on Neolithic pottery from Palestine (Amiran, *APHL* 17 ff.). Bands of concentric lozenges, like those incised round Early Neolithic bowls from Nea Makri and Nemea (*Nea Makri* pl. 7: top. *Nemea* pl. 65: 1), appear in paint on ones of Samarran ware from Hassuna and others of the Philia Culture in Cyprus (*JNES* iv (1945) fig. 1: 9. Cf. *JNES* xi (1952) fig. 14: 1, from Matarrah. Mellaart, *Neolithic Near East* 133 fig. 78).

The more immediate ancestors of the incised ware from early levels at Emporio and Nea Makri are to be found perhaps in southern Anatolia. The scanty incised decoration of an early horizon of pottery in the Elmali region, tentatively assigned to the Middle Chalcolithic, looks as if it might be comparable with that of Emporio VIII and is without white filling (Eslick 1980, 10 f., 9 ill. 3: 18–20). An absence of white fill similarly appears to be a feature of the earliest incised ware of this region as known from Mersin and Çatal Hüyük (e.g. *AS* xi (1961) 167 fig. 4). Theochares noted, although he later rejected the idea, a parallelism between the earliest occupation at Nea Makri and the latest Neolithic and earliest Chalcolithic at Mersin (*Nea Makri* 28. Cf. Weinberg, *CAH* 587. *Hesperia* xxxi (1962) 208 note 99). Groups of multiple chevrons were a standard motif of decoration on the Early Chalcolithic incised ware of Cilicia (*Mersin* 59 ff. pl. xi b); but the incisions on this were normally at any rate filled with white paste as at Nea Makri. Groups of chevrons were also characteristic of the Early Chalcolithic painted ware of Mersin, and might be set vertically, as in FIG. 112 nos. 17–20, as well as horizontally (e.g. *Mersin* 86 f. fig. 52). It is interesting that horizontal multiple chevrons were the commonest motif on the Early Neolithic painted ware of Nemea.

But some of the motifs found on the early incised ware of Emporio are more easily paralleled on incised ware of a later horizon in Cilicia. Thus motifs like FIG. 111 no. 13: a, f and g, and FIG. 112 no. 25 appear at Tarsus on incised ware of E.B. I date (*Tarsus* ii pl. 242: 118, 120–1). Motifs as FIG. 111 no. 13: a–c are similarly not uncommon on the Late Neolithic pottery of Knossos (*BSA* xlviii (1953) pl. 32 (a): 13; 32 (b) 15. *BSA* lix (1964) 195 fig. 28: 25, pls. 52 (2): 11; 53 (2): 7; 53 (3): 5). A design resembling FIG. 112 no. 31 appears on a fragment of an imported vase found at Orchomenos (*Orchomenos* ii 21 pl. vi. 1: e).

The early incised ware of Can Hasan near the southern edge of the Konya plain is also reminiscent of that of Emporio VIII. Incised decoration is already attested in Can Hasan 3, and is very characteristic of 2 B (equated with the Early Chalcolithic at Mersin), but rare in 2 A (thought to overlap with Mersin Middle Chalcolithic) (*AS* xii (1962) 32; xviii (1968) 49). In Can Hasan 2 B at any rate the incisions were almost invariably filled with white. The designs illustrated from Can Hasan 3 and 2 B include groups of dashes reminiscent of FIG. 111 nos. 14 and 15 (e.g. *AS* xii (1962) 32 pl. i (b), (c); 39 fig. 9: 2, 3; xviii (1968) 49 fig. 2: 6). A bowl akin to Emporio type 8 from 2 A is covered with an incised design which appears to be based upon multiple concentric lozenges like FIG. 112 no. 35 (*AS* xii (1962) 35 fig. 5: 13). Concentric lozenges are among the motifs on painted ware of Can Hasan 2 B (*AS* xii (1962) 37 fig. 7: 4); and they also occur among painted designs on Early Chalcolithic pottery from Çatal Hüyük West and Mersin (*AS* xi (1961) 178 fig. 12: 11. *Mersin* 88 f. fig. 53: 7).

D. French, *AS* xii (1962) 32 note 13, has indicated that the origins of the Late Chalcolithic incised ware of the Halys region of northern Anatolia (Alaca Hüyük and Büyük Güllücek) may have to be sought in the Konya plain in the light of resemblances between it and the earlier incised ware of Can Hasan. This Late Chalcolithic incised ware of northern Anatolia is also reminiscent of that from Emporio VIII, as if it derived from the same tradition (*AJA* li (1947) 152 ff. pl. xxxiv. *Belleten* xii (1948) 471 ff. pls. lxxxix–xcv, cv–cviii). But the incisions are sometimes at any rate filled with white paste, and the designs are in general more elaborate and evolved, suggesting that they belong to a considerably later period of time: some of the motifs, including groups of multiple chevrons, appear on Late Neolithic incised ware of the Greek mainland (e.g. Corinth: *Hesperia* xxix (1960) 249 f. pl. 63: a. *Elateia* 198 pl. 62, d; 7, 8. *Orchomenos* ii pl. v: 1). There is also a fair amount of pointillé decoration on this northern Anatolian Late Chalcolithic incised ware.

Moving westwards to Hacilar, a unique bowl, thought to have been an import, from the earliest Late Neolithic level IX has incised decoration on the inside, including multiple chevrons and rows of dashes flanked by lines (*Hacilar* 103 fig. 47: 28): the motifs are very comparable with those of Emporio VIII incised ware, but at Emporio incised decoration is not attested on the insides of bowls. Two fragments with areas of dashes flanked by incised lines like FIG. 111 no. 15 from the Karain cave near Antalya have been assigned to the Neolithic (*Belleten* vii (1963) 85 fig. 9 a: top).

The concentric lozenges or diamonds which are such a distinctive motif on the incised ware of Emporio VIII and Nea Makri, and which can be paralleled on early incised and painted wares from Anatolia and elsewhere in the Near East, are not uncommon in paint at Saliagos, and occur once in a very crude form in the rare incised decoration there (*Saliagos* 43 fig. 36: 10). The motif is also found on the Urfirnis patterned ware of the Middle Neolithic on the Greek mainland (Holmberg, *Neolithic Pottery* 20), and in a more elaborate version on the more or less contemporary Sesklo painted ware of Thessaly (e.g. *AM* lvii (1932) pl. xxi: 7. *Achilleion* 297 fig. 22: Phase III b). *PThess* 105 fig. 55: b, in white paint on Late Neolithic Γ 1 α 1 ware from Thessaly, may be this design according to Coleman, *AJA* lxxviii (1974) 333, comparing it with *Saliagos* fig. 39: 4.

In its simplest form with two lozenges or diamonds one inside the other the motif appears incised and painted on Late Neolithic pottery from Corinth (*Hesperia* vi (1937) 510 fig. 27: a. Phelps, *Thesis* 232, 269 fig. 43: 55): but there is also an elaborate version in pattern burnish (*Hesperia* xlvii (1978) 419, 440 pl. 108: 32). Concentric lozenges still occur as a motif of decoration in the Bronze Age of the Aegean area (e.g. *ADelt* xvii (1961–62) 117 EM 8808 pl. 49, on an Early Cycladic jug from the Spedo cemetery on Naxos). Incised designs on pottery from the Neolithic site of Matera in southern Italy include multiple concentric lozenges (M. Mayer, *Molfetta und Matera* (Leipzig, 1924) pl. xxi: 2, 3).

Pointillé decoration hardly occurs at Emporio in Period VIII. But very bold pointillé, sometimes in areas bounded by curving instead of straight lines, was already at home in the Early and Middle Neolithic at Byblos (*Byblos* v 105 fig. 58 pls. lv, lviii, lix). Pointillé is also attested in the earliest Chalcolithic of Cilicia (*Mersin* 59 ff. fig. 36: 49, 50), and at the beginning of the Early Neolithic at Knossos in Crete (e.g. *BSA* lix (1964) 210, 216, 173 fig. 27, pl. 46 (3), (4). Cf. *Mersin* 60 f. fig. 36: 49, from Level XXIV. In the hinterland of Anatolia it appears in the Chalcolithic of the Konya plain, in Can Hasan 2 B, and on jars of grey burnished ware of Early Chalcolithic II at Çatal Hüyük West (*AS* xii (1962) 32, 39 fig. 9: 2, 3; xv (1965) 153).

Periods VII–VI (FIG. 113)

Incised decoration is much less common than in Periods VIII or V–IV. Some incised decoration from upper levels of VI is akin to that characteristic of V. But most of the incised ware from the horizon of VII—VI appears to be similar to that of Period VIII with a tendency perhaps to the disintegration of traditional motifs. The incised decoration on fragments from E.B. I levels at Tarsus looks rather similar (*Tarsus* ii 95 f. pls. 240, 242). The incisions on the carination of 569 of Period VI can be paralleled from the Agora wells (*Athenian Agora* xiii 39 no. 140). The incised decoration of Emporio VII–VI like that of Period VIII was hardly if ever filled with white paste.

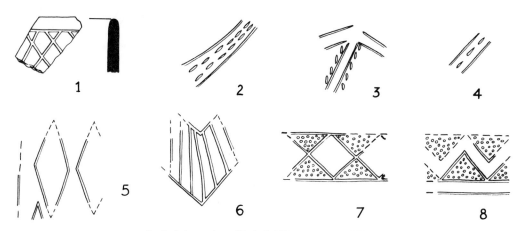

FIG. 113. Incised decoration of Periods VII (nos. 1–3) and VI (nos. 4–8).

Periods V–IV (FIGS. 114–16)

Incision once again becomes the favourite method of decorating clay vases as it was in Period VIII. It occurs on jugs, and on jars of various shapes and sizes and on their lids; but on bowls it is virtually confined to types 13 and 14 (FIG. 114). The incised designs were normally at any rate filled with white paste. As in earlier times the decorative motifs are almost invariably linear, and some recall those of Period VIII. But strips and panels and areas of various shapes filled with pointillé are now common.

The incised decoration of Emporio V–IV corresponds to that of Troy I, and especially to that illustrated from the early levels (Troy I a–c), when decoration of any kind was commoner than it was later (*Troy* i 77). Incised bowl rims of Trojan shape A 6 (which includes Emporio type 13) were in particular characteristic of this Early Subperiod of Troy I; but many of the motifs found on them (*Troy* i fig. 256) are not attested on Emporio bowl rims, while FIG. 114 no. 7 does not appear to occur on a Trojan one. The eyes on the necks of the jugs 1168–9 from the Period IV destruction level (FIG. 115 no. 39) are reminiscent of the face-lugs on some Troy I bowls, but the outlines of the eyes on these are normally rounded. Handles with incised decoration which are a marked feature of Periods V–II at Emporio (FIGS. 115, 116) are not well represented at Troy, but are more in evidence at Thermi.

Pontillé decoration with areas filled with dots or jabs has been fashionable in many different parts of the world at different times (references for its occurrence in the Aegean area and further afield, e.g. *Orchomenos* ii 19. *PPS* xxii (1956) 186. *BSA* lxiii (1968) 273 f. *Saliagos* 84). At Mersin in Cilicia it appears at the beginning of the Early Chalcolithic, but is again at home at the end of the Middle and in the Late Chalcolithic (*Mersin* 59 ff. fig. 36: 49, 50 (Level XXIV); 90 f. fig. 54: 9

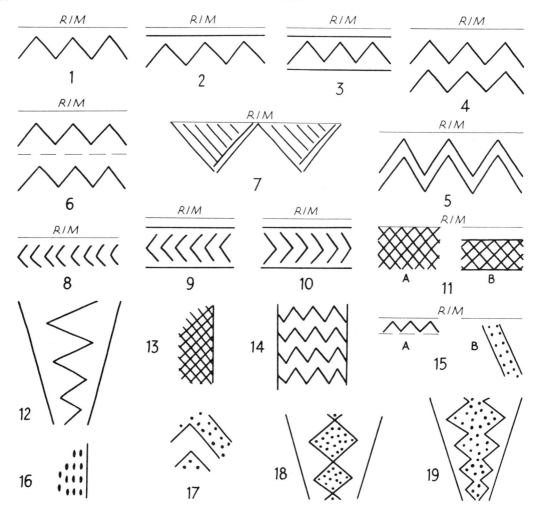

FIG. 114. Incised decoration on bowls, mostly type 13, of Periods V–IV: 1. 1077, 1079, 1083, 1090, 1116; 3. 1081, 1314, PLATE 65 (*a*) Nos. 2, 4; 5. 1079, 1081; 6. 1025; 7. 1082; 10. 1086, PLATE 65 (*a*) No. 3; 11 A. 1073, 1091; 11 B. 1091; 14. 1079; 15 A, B. 1092; 18. 1314; 19. 1077.

(Level XXIII); 142, 150 f. fig. 93: 8, 19 (Level XVI); 166 figs. 104–5 (Levels XIV, XIII). At Tarsus it is found in E.B. II (*Tarsus* ii 126 figs. 257–8 nos. 327, 330–1). At Troy it is most in evidence in Troy I, although it occurs sporadically in Troy III and into Troy V and VI (*Troy* ii fig. 78: 34.289; 250, 276 figs. 245: 7, 249: 4–6. *Troy* iii fig. 370: 19).

The pointillé decoration of Emporio V–IV corresponds to that of Troy I, where motifs like FIG. 115 no. 35 can be paralleled (e.g. *Troy* i figs. 230: 33.159 (Early Subperiod); 244: 30; 265: 16). Areas of pontillé with curved boundaries like FIG. 115 no. 36 occur in the earliest levels of Troy I and at Thermi (*Troy* i figs. 235: 18 (Ia); 236: 20 (Ib). *Thermi* pl. xv: 2). Pointillé decoration sharing motifs with Emporio V–IV and Troy I is at home in parts of the Greek mainland at the end of the Neolithic there (*Gonia* 68 f. Phelps, *Thesis* 294. *Hesperia* xxxviii (1969) 368. Zervos, *Naïs* figs. 838, 841–2. *DS* 202 figs. 113–4. *PThess* 106 fig. 56. Milojcic, *Ergebnisse* fig. 16: 15. *ADelt* xxvii (1972) Chron. 329 f. pl. 281, from Rakhes near Melitaia. *ADelt* xxvi (1971) Chron. 293, 295 fig 3,

FIG. 115. Incised decoration on jugs and jars of Periods V–IV: 1. 1232; 2. PLATE 75 (*b*) No. 2. Cf. No. 15 and 1301; 3. PLATE 75 (*b*) No. 7. Cf. 1237; 4. 1161. Cf. 1166, 1302; 5. 1231. Cf. PLATE 75 (*b*) No. 9; 6. 1165; 7. 1302; 8. 1144; 9. 1297, 1300, 1338; 10. PLATE 75 (*b*) No. 11. Cf. 1233; 11. 1239; 12. 1282; 13. 1171, 1238, 1280; 16. PLATE 75 (*b*) No. 6. Cf. 1168; 17. 1145; 18. 1146; 19. PLATE 79 (*b*) No. 3; 21. 1161, 1165, 1233, 1350; 22. 1165, 1237; 23. 1239; 24. 1300; 25. PLATE 75 (*b*) Nos. 8, 13; 26. 1171. Cf. 1239 (on handle), 1339; 31. 1337. Cf. 1340, PLATE 79 (*b*) No. 10; 32. 1341; 33. 1342; 34. 1352; 35. 1171. Cf. 1343; 36. 1351; 37. 1300; 38 A, B. 1344. Cf. 1338; 39. 1168, 1169.

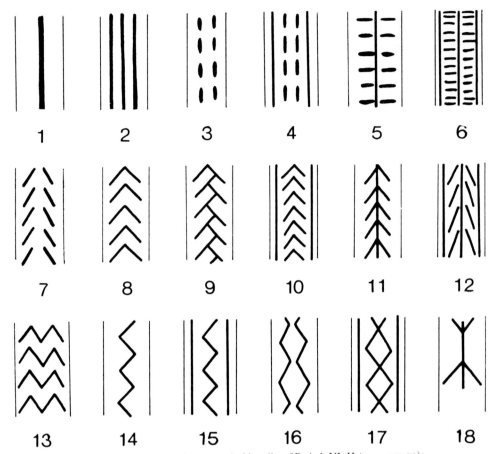

FIG. 116. Incised decoration on vertical handles of Periods VI–II (see PLATE 79):

Number of examples

	VI	V	IV	III	II
1	1	4			1
2	1	6	1		
3		1	1 +		
4		1			
5		3			
6		1			
7		2		1	
8		25	4	4	3
9		1		1	
10		6	c. 5 +	1	c. 6
11	2	4		1	1
12		1			
13		9	1 +		1
14		2			1
15	1	3			1
16		1			
17			1		
18		1			

from Ayios Petros off Kira-Panayia in the Sporades). Vases from the Kitsos cave in Attica have designs like FIG. 115 nos. 34, 35 (*BCH* xciii (1969) 964 fig. 14; xcv (1971) 713 figs. 26, 27; xcvi (1972) 821, 827 fig. 13: 2). The lid of a jar from the Cave of Pan at Marathon containing a necklace with beads of blue glass-paste and rock-crystal is decorated with pointillé-filled circles reminiscent of FIG. 115 no. 36 (Zervos, *Naïs* 501 fig. 841). Pointillé, sometimes in curving bands, occurred at Saliagos in both Strata 1 and 2, but was rare (*Saliagos* 43 f., 84 fig. 56: 9–13 pl. xxv).

Reed-impressed circles were used to decorate two vases (1239, 1300) from levels of IV, but only became common at Emporio in Period II. Such circles appear on a number of vessels of E.B. II date at Tarsus in Cilicia (*Tarsus* ii pls. 257–8; 320–2, 324), and are attested on pottery from the earliest levels of Troy I (*Troy* i figs. 235: 19 (Ia); 238: 16 (Ic); 247: 9 (Middle Subperiod). In one instance at Thermi a circle of this kind has a short incised line attached to it like FIG. 115 no. 23 (*Thermi* pl. xv: 1).

Period II (FIG. 117)

Incision filled with white paste was still the dominant type of decoration, although it was not as much in evidence as it had been in Period IV. This situation is paralleled at Troy, where it was noted that decoration of any kinds was more in evidence at the beginning of Troy I than later. Incised decoration in Emporio II was mostly confined to bowls of types 13 and 14, and to jars, large and small, and their lids. Motifs were similar to those current in V–IV, but more varied.

The incised decoration of Period II at Emporio seems to be much richer than that of any phase of Troy I or Thermi. But some of the motifs that occur at Emporio for the first time in Period II are best paralleled in Troy I. Compare for instance the neat multiple chevrons of PLATE 85 nos. 4, 5, 9, with *Troy* i fig. 244: 21; or the handle design, FIG. 117 no. 5, with *Troy* i fig. 245: 8.

The incised decoration on some fragments of Early Helladic A II ware with a burnished red

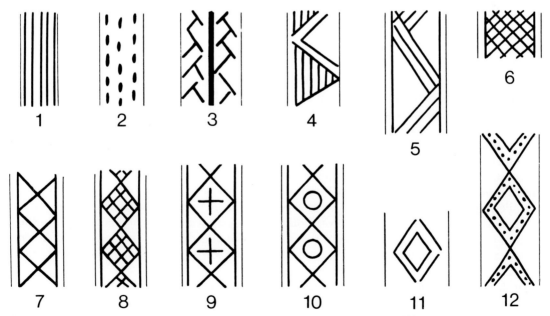

FIG. 117. Incised decoration on vertical handles of Period II, in addition to FIG. 116 Nos. 1, 8, 10, 11, 13–15.

slip from Zygouries is reminiscent of that on the large and richly decorated jars characteristic of Emporio II (*Zygouries* 77 f. pl. vi). Rims with fingernail impressions along the top like 1430 seem to be at home in the Late Neolithic and Early Bronze Age of the Greek mainland.

The system of decoration combining areas of fine burnish with incision and contrasting unburnished areas, peculiar to Period II at Emporio, has already been noted under *(1) Pattern burnish.*

Period I

Incision remained the commonest form of decoration, but some at any rate of the fragments with it may have been strays of Period II. The rim 2536, however, with boldly incised or reed-impressed circles, is certainly of Period I date.

(4) Relief

Warts and ribs in relief appeared on pottery of every period at Emporio from X to I. In the earlier periods X–XVIII elaborate relief decoration was characteristic of pithoi and large jars. In V–IV the ribs on pithoi were often adorned with incision.

Periods X–VIII

Pithoi and large jars were habitually decorated with ribs. These might be triangular or rounded in section (FIG. 137). The fashion for decorating with ribs in relief is a feature of the Early Neolithic both in Crete and on the Greek mainland, as noted under AG 87–89. The relief decoration on fragments from E.N. I levels at Knossos is in many ways comparable with that from early levels at Emporio (compare *BSA* lix (1964) 171 fig. 26 and pl. 49 (2): 1, 2, with examples on PLATE 36).

Several fragments from the lower levels of the Upper Cave at Ayio Gala (AG 87–89) had curving ribs. The pithos fragment 297 from a level of Emporio X boasts a snake-like squiggle in relief on it. It is interesting that the only examples of relief decoration on the Early Neolithic pottery of Byblos were in the shape of wriggling serpents (*Byblos* v 45). Wavy or zigzag lines in relief are a feature of the earliest Neolithic of the Greek mainland according to Holmberg, *Neolithic Pottery* 9.

Horsehose-shaped lugs appear on some bowls from levels of IX (58, 78, 128). These can be paralleled from the earliest Phases A and B at Judeideh in Syria (*Judeideh* 53 fig. 27: 48; 71 fig. 40: 18). In Period VIII a class of vertically perforated lugs had relief tails (358–360); but apart from these decoration in relief was virtually confined to pithoi in VIII.

Warts of different sizes with varying profiles were applied to vases (FIG. 138). Flat-topped discs and discs with sunk tops (382) were recovered from levels of X (FIG. 138: 4, 5). Both varieties are attested as early as Phase A at Judeideh (*Judeideh* 48 fig. 21: 18; 51 fig. 25: 2). Disc-shaped warts are already found in the Early Neolithic of the Greek mainland (e.g. *Nemea* 271 pl. 68: 5, 6). In Period VIII at Emporio warts were very common on handles, especially on those of jars of fine burnished ware with incised decoration, and they appeared on the bodies or shoulders of jugs and jars; sometimes they formed a row around the outside of the rim (e.g. 206). A vertical row of warts is attested on a few jars of coarse burnished ware from a high level of VIII (e.g. 420 on PLATE 38).

In these early periods at Emporio the warts were normally applied to the surfaces of vases, not bonded with them. But a fragment, apparently from an early level of VIII, had a wart formed by pushing the clay through from the inside of the vase.

Periods VII–VI
Large jars and pithoi were sometimes decorated with ribs as in X–VIII. The arrangement with a horizontal rib on the rim and a vertical one descending from it as found on 749 can be paralleled from the Athenian agora assigned to the Late Neolithic, as well as from the Early Neolithic Protosesklo horizon of Thessaly. One jar (726) appears to have had a rib around the base of the neck. Relief decoration is also attested on some fragments of smaller jars from levels of VI. One or two bowls seem to have had curving ribs on the inside (e.g. 444). The handles of some jugs of Fine Black Burnished Ware had one or more ribs down the length. The deep flutes on 812 can be paralleled in the Late Neolithic of the Greek mainland.

Warts were often pointed in cross-section instead of rounded. They occurred on some handles and on the bodies of a few jugs and jars. As in X–VIII they were usually applied to the surface, not bonded with it; but a few low warts were made by pushing through the clay from the inside. Pairs of circular warts appeared on the bodies of some jugs and jars and on a few handles. Bold vertical warts like those which were at home in the succeeding periods V–IV are already found on rims of cooking jars from levels of VI (e.g. 711).

Periods V–IV
Ribs were only in evidence on pithoi and jugs, and perhaps on a few small jars akin to type 44. Those on pithoi were often decorated with incisions. On vases of other types apart from pithoi the ribs normally at any rate seem to have been vertical, and they might be combined with incised decoration as on 1146. On the shoulder of another jug (1147) three vertical ribs met together in a wart. Some fragments, mostly perhaps from bowls, had relief horseshoes reminiscent of the horseshoe-shaped lugs on bowls of X–VIII.

Circular warts of many different kinds abounded in Periods V–IV on vases of every type including bowls, jugs and jars. Jugs in particular normally had three warts set at intervals on the swelling. Warts were sometimes grouped in pairs or in threes. Oval warts were common on bowls; and more elongated horizontal and vertical warts occurred on vases of all kinds. Vertical warts sometimes projected above the level of the rim on bowls, and often on cooking vessels.

Period II
Ribs occurred and were now often curving. Horseshoes in relief are found on the bodies of jugs and jars. Circles in relief might have a wart in the centre (1803–4). Warts, and large solid lugs which merged into them, were common, especially on bowls of the standard type 9.

Period I
Relief decoration of any kind was uncommon. Warts were less in evidence than they had been in Period II, but occurred on some type 9 bowl rims.

(d) Imports

The presence of mica in the clay or other unusual or unique features were taken to be signs of a possible foreign origin.

Mica seems to be absent from the local wares at Emporio. This is in contrast to many of the surrounding areas. Thus mica is present in the pottery from the Lower Cave at Ayio Gala. It appears to be a regular ingredient in the early pottery of western Anatolia (D.H. French, *London Institute of Archaeology Bulletin* v (1965) 18. Cf. *AS* xix (1969) 41 ff. passim). It occurs in some of the standard Fine Polished Ware of Troy I, and is a feature of some of the Fine Gray and Red

Polished wares of Troy II–III (*Troy* i 52, 220 f.; ii 19). A fair amount is reported in the clay of vases at Saliagos (*Saliagos* 34). When noted in the early pottery of southern Greece it is usually taken to be a Cycladic or Eastern phenomenon and sign of an import (W.R. Biers, *Hesperia* xxxviii (1969) 456. Cf. *Zygouries* 94, 212). But it is in fact often noticeable in the clay used for vases in early periods on the Greek mainland. It was abundant in some of the Early Neolithic pottery from Nea makri in Attica (*PAE* 1954, 116. *Nea Makri* 10). It was also observed in much of the pottery of all Neolithic periods from Corinth (*Hesperia* xlvii (1978) 433, 436, 438 ff.). The clay used for pottery in the Neolithic and Early Bronze Age at Servia in western Macedonia is said to be always micaceous (*Servia* 191). The presence of mica has been noted as very characteristic of all types of Middle Neolithic pottery at Dikili Tash in eastern Macedonia (*BCH* xcii (1968) 1076). There was mica in the clay of Early Bronze Age pottery from Ayios Kosmas, especially it seems in vases from the cemetery (*Ayios Kosmas* 14, 122).

Micaceous wares of one kind or another were attested at Emporio in levels of every period from X to II. Other fabrics which were taken to be exotic included the micaceous Obsidian Ware (VII–V and II), Fine Light Grey Burnished Ware (X–VII, V and II), White Slipped Ware (IV), White Coated Ware (II), and the wheelmade wares of Period I.

A relatively large number of imported vases may have reached Emporio in view of its position by the sea on an excellent harbour. Well over 70 fragments of handmade vases identified as imports were recovered from levels of X–I: 4 from XI, 6 from IX, 20 from VIII, 10 from VII, 9 from VI, more than 11 from V–IV, 11 from II, and 2 from I (apart from the wheelmade vases).

(e) Pottery from Area A

i. Periods X–VIII

GENERAL

The pottery from the levels assignable to these periods is considered together. There are many general similarities, and features such as the virtual absence of bowls of type 10 distinguish X–VIII from the succeeding Periods VII–VI. At the same time some differences can be noted within these periods. Incised decoration, uncommon in levels of X–IX, is abundant in Period VIII. Similarly pattern burnish, which is well represented in VIII, hardly occurs in IX and no examples of it were recognised from X. But these differences may in part at least reflect such factors as the extraordinary preponderance of jars with incised decoration in levels of VIII, and the very small amount of material recovered from those of X, being less than one-third the amount from IX, which in turn was only about half of that from VIII (see FIG. 96).

The material assigned to Periods X–VIII came from three separate areas (A, B, and C). These were never linked together stratigraphically during the course of the excavations. The best sequence was obtained in area A in the southern corner of trench G where in a depth of some 3 m of deposit six or more successive occupation levels of Periods X–VIII were identified.

In all three areas (A, B, and C) the levels assignable to Period X seem to have been associated with houses. But occupation levels in association with houses assignable to IX or VIII were only recognised in area A: in B the deposits of IX and VIII appeared to consist of ruin debris from the great walls 4 and 10 which seem to have successively encircled the spring or well to the west.

Period X

Pottery assigned to X was recovered from all three areas A, B and C. The surface of the pottery from the lower part of the deposit in C (trench H) was much worn by water action.

Bowls mostly had incurving rims of one kind or another (types 6–8), but some were open (types 4–5). Large fish-tailed and related types of lug-handles, together with elaborate vertically perforated lugs like that on 113, seem to be characteristic of X. But giant handles springing from the tops of bowl rims as found in Periods IX–VIII are also attested. Bowl bases were flat or sunk.

Bodies of jars and jugs were normally it seems more or less rounded. But there was some evidence for carinated shapes, and the exceptional jug (164), if it is truly of this period, which seems highly improbable, has a carinated body and pointed spout. Normally, however, jugs were flat-mouthed with high-swung handles set to the rim (type 20). Such jugs were in effect one-handled versions of jars of the standard type 41. Characteristic horned handles like 337 may come from jars of this or related types.

Large pithoi were already in use, and may have been manufactured by specialist travelling potters. Pithoi are characteristically decorated with ribs in relief. Decoration in white paint or with incision is attested on smaller vases. No example of pattern burnish was recognised from levels of X.

Period IX

The material assigned to this period came from the two adjacent but stratigraphically disconnected areas A and B in trenches G and Q.

A large number of bowls (types 6–8) had incurving rims as in X. But deep open bowls with curving sides as type 5A seem to have been more common. There were also many straight-sided bowls (type 6). Lug-handles and elaborate vertically perforated lugs like those of Period X were most prominent in the lowest levels of IX. Giant handles springing from the tops of bowl rims seem to be more at home in IX than they were earlier.

Jugs were still flat-mouthed with high swung handles (type 20), and jars of type 41 continued to be very common.

Pithoi may have elaborate relief decoration. Some smaller vases it seems were also decorated in relief, and solid lunate lugs are found on bowls of type 5. But incision was the commonest form of decoration, although simple linear designs in white, or occasionally red paint, are also attested. A very few examples of true pattern burnish were noted from the upper levels of IX.

Period VIII

The material of this period like that assigned to IX came from the two adjacent areas A and B in trenches G and Q. Fragments of bowls were much less in evidence in area B, but remains of jars, especially of jars of type 41, abounded there. These jars may have been used in connection with rites at the spring or well, as appears to have been the case with the jugs of the following periods.

Bowls of type 8 were more at home in VIII than in X–IX, and may be considered as characteristic of this horizon: some 20 per cent of all bowl rims recovered from levels of VIII were assignable to type 8, a number of them being decorated with pattern burnish. Bowl handles normally spring from the tops of rims as in Period IX.

Jugs of type 20 appear to have continued in use, but others akin to type 23 which was common in the succeeding Periods VII–VI are also attested.

The commonest shape of jar is still type 41, but bowl-jars like type 32 with rims as class A III are characteristic of VIII. These and the jars of type 41 may be elaborately decorated.

Incised decoration with a wide variety of simple linear designs is extremely common on jars of Period VIII. But a good deal of pattern burnish is found on jars and on bowls of type 8. White paint is largely confined to jugs as in Periods VII–VI.

Pithoi are still adorned with ribs like those of Periods X–IX. Some of the smaller vases, usually bowl-jars of one kind or another, have lugs with tails in relief.

FABRIC

The great mass of the pottery assignable to Periods X–VIII was dark-surfaced, and almost all of it was burnished. Vases ranged in size from large pithoi downwards; but fragments of very small thin-walled vessels were only conspicuous in levels of X–IX. There was no sharp distinction between fine and coarse ware, and vases of quite coarse fabric might be given a high burnish. The larger jars, however, tended to be of coarser fabric and more roughly made in comparison with smaller vessels, while their surfaces often had a poor burnish or sometimes none at all. The finer vases were carefully finished and their surfaces were smooth, but even they were apt to be irregular in shape and lop-sided with uneven rims (e.g. 112).

The firing was less good than it became in later times, and the fabric was therefore in general softer; although there seems to have been a gradual improvement in the firing between Period X and the end of VIII. The clay was tempered with straw, and straw impressions are normally visible in the surfaces of vases. While straw impressions are especially prominent in the coarser wares, they also tend to be conspicuous in fine burnished surfaces, except perhaps in those of some of the most carefully finished bowls of IX and VIII. There is also usually grit, often large lumps of it, in the clay together with the straw even in the case of small vases with a high burnish. The grit does not appear to be the residue of original impurities in the clay, but to have been added as temper like the straw.

The clay is normally black at the centre of the break, but may shade to light brown or brick-red at the outer edges: sometimes it is fired an even light brown or brick-red colour throughout. Surfaces are usually shades of grey, grey-brown, or greyish black; less commonly light brown or red. The surfaces of the shallower varieties of bowls of types 4 and 5 in Period VIII tend to be light brown or dark crimson red in colour; and some of the finest of the contemporary jars, like 177 and 178, have bright red surfaces which appear to be due to the application of a red wash. These two jars may have been imports, but the sporadic use of a red wash was clearly attested on some unburnished surfaces of Period VIII as well as on some burnished ware of IX and to a more limited extent on some of X. Red-washed wares are found alongside Monochrome or Dark-faced Burnished Ware in the earliest pottery of Syria (Amuq A) (J. Mellaart, *Iraq* xl (1978) 124, 126). A thin red wash has similarly been observed on some of the earliest Neolithic pottery of Thessaly assigned to the Early Pottery (Achilleion or E.N. I) phase there (*Otzaki-magula* 139). But at Sesklo the use of a slip, usually red, is apparently first attested in Early Neolithic II (*Servia* 194).

In general, however, the vases of Emporio X–VIII must have presented a sombre appearance in contrast to the reds and light browns which were prominent alongside the fine black burnished surfaces of the succeeding Periods VII–VI. At the same time the vase surfaces of X–VIII often shaded from one colour to another, ranging from black or a dark shade of grey or brown to lighter grey or brown and reddish. Multi-coloured surfaces of this kind recall the Variegated or Rainbow Ware of the Early Neolithic on the Greek mainland. Such variegation may be due to the haphazard nature of the firing, effected perhaps in an open fire-place rather than in an oven or kiln; although it has been suggested that the variegated or rainbow surfaces of the mainland Neolithic pottery might have been deliberately induced (e.g. Blegen, *Nemea* 261). The aggressive mottling of the *Mottled Ware* of Periods VII–VI was almost certainly deliberate, and some Emporio vase surfaces were apparently being mottled in this way before the end of VIII. Remains of vases with fine black or light brown burnished surfaces indistinguishable in fabric from the *Fine Black* and *Light Brown Burnished Wares* of VII–VI were similarly recovered from levels of VIII and even from those of IX. The distinctive *Light Plain Ware*, which was most at home in Period VII, also appears to be attested in VIII if not earlier.

As in later periods, bowls tended to have a better finish than jars. The surfaces of most bowls, and those of many jars, had been well smoothed or burnished. Sometimes the burnish was very fine, the surface having a soapy feel, with the marks of the burnishing tool hardly if at all visible. But on the whole surfaces lack the high polish-like gloss of the finest burnished wares of later periods, and characteristically appear dull shades of dark grey, grey-brown or black. The dull surfaces of these early levels may be due to some extent, however, to the softness of the fabric leading to rapid wear which has impaired the original gloss of the burnish. Moreover the surfaces in the case of much of the pottery from the lowest deposits of X–IX had clearly been affected by water action.

Various fabrics were distinctive enough to be separated from the general mass.

Mottled Ware. A very few fragments from levels of VIII (e.g. the rim 109 from a bowl of type 6) had mottled surfaces reminiscent of this ware characteristic of Periods VII–VI under which it is described.

Fine Black Burnished Ware. Some fragments of jugs and some of small jars of types 41–42 with finely burnished surfaces were indistinguishable in fabric and finish from the *Fine Black Burnished Ware* of periods VII–VI under which it is described. Such fragments were not uncommon in the upper levels of VIII and occurred even in deposits of IX.

Light Brown Burnished Ware. This distinctive ware, used mostly for jugs in Periods VII–VI under which it is described, appears to have affinities with the Neolithic Urfirnis ware of the Greek mainland. Some jug fragments from upper levels of VIII were of this ware, but they mostly came from ones such as 145 and 144 in area B (trench Q) suspect of some degree of contamination with later material.

Red or Light Brown Washed Ware. From the same levels of VIII as the fragments of *Light Brown Burnished Ware* came fragments with unburnished red washes, including at least five rims, apparently from jugs, in fabric indistinguishable from the *Red* or *Light Brown Washed Ware* of Periods VII–VI.

Light Plain Ware. Like *Fine Black Burnished Ware* and *Light Brown Burnished Ware* this fabric is characteristic of Periods VII–VI under which it is described. But it seems to be attested as early as IX (e.g. 285). A rim of this fabric with a high-swung handle, apparently from a jug of type 20, came from VIII Q level 145, and fragments of jars of it were recovered from upper levels of VIII.

White Slipped Ware. One or two fragments from levels of IX and VIII had white or creamy white burnished surfaces. The surface colour appears to have been deliberate and due to the application of a white slip. In the case of small vases this might be a conscious imitation of marble. The shapes of much of the white-slipped pottery from Otzaki-magula in Thessaly were clearly derived from stone vases, and a fragment of a white marble vase was recovered from a level of Emporio VIII (STONE No. 1). But most of the fragments of *White Slipped Ware* from levels of Emporio X–VIII like the jar rim 203 appeared to come from large vases or even from pithoi (e.g. 304).

A distinctive white plaster ware (white ware or vaiselle blanche) is a feature of the Early Neolithic of Syria, where it begins in Prepottery Neolithic B (Mellaart, *Neolithic Near East* 62 f., 227 f. *Sukas* iii 19, 26 f. *AASyr* xiv (1964) 127 f. *Archaeology* xxiv (1971) 282 f.). A fragment of an imported vessel said to be of this ware was recovered from level VI B at Çatal Hüyük (*Iraq* xl (1978) 126, with reference to *AS* xvi (1966) 170 pl. xlix (*b*), described as having a cream slip with decoration in red and black).

Varieties of white-slipped ware are attested from the beginning of the Neolithic on the Greek mainland (Holmberg, *Neolithic Pottery* 9). White-slipped ware occurred, although it was not common, among the Early Neolithic wares at Corinth (*Hesperia* vi (1937) 493, 495 fig. 4). Only one sherd with a fugitive white slip was recognised, however, from Phlius (*Hesperia* xxxviii (1969) 450). A small amount of white-slipped ware as found at Corinth was noted even in the lowest metre of deposit (E.N. I) at Elateia, but it increased in popularity during the succeeding E.N. II period there (*Elateia* 168, 172). Weinberg observes that on some of the earliest pieces of E.N. II date at Elateia the slip was cream-coloured and highly polished, although it was more often dull white and powdery. Plain white-slipped ware continues to occur in the Middle Neolithic in central Greece and the Peloponnese (Holmberg, *Neolithic Pottery* 19).

The monochrome A 4 ware with cream-coloured clay and well burnished surface is the Thessalian counterpart of the early white-slipped wares of central and southern Greece. There were a few white 'china' sherds, presumably of this fabric, from the Early Neolithic at Servia, but they were extremely rare there (*Servia* 193 f.). A very few sherds of white ware described as A 4 were recognised as probably coming from the earlier level of the Early Neolithic (Period A) at Nea Makri in Attica, but such sherds also occurred in the later level of A there (*PAE* 1954, 117 f. *Nea Makri* 10, 14 ff.). The clay in the case of some of the sherds of white-surfaced vases from Nea Makri was reddish like that of Emporio *White Slipped Ware* (*Nea Makri* 16). A considerable number of fragments of A 4 ware from Rakhmani similarly had a red biscuit (*PThess* 28).

A 4 ware is much in evidence in the earliest Thessalian Neolithic. Wace and Thompson reported it from Rakhmani I (*PThess* 25, 27 f.). K. Grundmann recovered a number of sherds with a whitish yellow slip and fine burnish from the deepest level at Magula Hadzimissiotiki in Lake Karla (Boibe) and noted the occurrence of such A 4 ware at other sites in north-east Thessaly (*AM* lxii (1937) 63 f. Cf. Milojčić, *JdI* lxv-lxvi (1950–51) 52). At Achilleion near Pharsala a burnished white kaolin slip is already attested in the Early Pottery phase I a (*Achilleion* 283). What seems to have been A 4 ware was observed in the lowest part (A) but not in the upper (B) of Layer I at Pyrasos (*Thessalika* ii (1959) 43 f.). Theochares remarks that similar fine white ware occurs in Layer I at Sesklo. White-slipped ware was at home in the Protosesklo and Preseklo (E.N. II–III) phases at Otzaki, where vases of all sizes, including large ones, were made of it (*Otzaki-magula* 33, 36 f., 41, 55, 69 ff., 116: Kat. VI, Gelbe bis cremefarbige/weisse Keramik, identified with the A 4 ware of Rakhmani). Milojčić notes that some of the shapes strongly suggest a deliberate imitation of marble vases. Vases of white marble were numerous in Protosesklo levels at Argissa (Milojcic, *Ergebnisse* 9).

Silvery Grey Ware. This rare but distinctive fabric, which may represent a deliberate attempt to imitate the appearance of silver, is described under Periods V–IV. It seems to be attested at Emporio as early as Period VIII, and fragments of at least two vases of it (261) were recovered from VIII Q level 146.

Cooking Pot Ware. Jars of type 34 like 175 often have dusky surfaces suggestive of use over a fire. Such jars may have been employed for cooking, and their fabric approximates to a variety of cooking pot ware, the clay being somewhat grittier and harder than usual. The surfaces of these jars tend to have abundant straw impressions showing in them: they may be given a poor burnish, or be roughly smoothed or left untreated.

Baking Pan Ware. This distinctive variety of coarse ware was most at home at Emporio in X–VIII: it was indeed a characteristic feature of these early periods there. The clay is very coarse, occasionally sandy, but usually full of grit, with an abundance of straw of which impressions show everywhere in the surface. Surface colours range from red through various shades of brown to dusky. This fabric was virtually confined in later periods to baking pans of type 3 with holes round the rim. But during X–VIII other types of bowls and jars, as well as baking pans and the large type 2 dishes which resemble them, were evidently made of this ware.

Foreign Fabrics (see also under 'Imports'). Thirty or more fragments, some two-thirds of them from levels of VIII, appeared to belong to imported vases. Over half of these were classifiable as *Micaceous Wares*, a few as *Fine Light Grey Burnished Ware*.

(1) **Micaceous Wares.** Traces of shining particles (mica) were noted in some fifteen or more sherds from levels of X–VIII. The clay of these was often distinctly sandy: this might suggest that the particles were in sand mixed with the local clay to temper it, but since the fragments in question tended to be exceptional in other ways—in shape, surface finish, or decoration—it seems likely that they came from imports.

(2) **Fine Light Grey Burnished Ware.** Two fragments of vases from levels of X (247) and IX (424) were made of very fine clay fired an even light grey colour throughout. The clay did not have any visible trace of mica particles in it, and the fabric was reminiscent of that which distinguishes a class of vases found in Early Minoan Crete, but the Early Minoan vases in question normally have elaborate incised decoration. Some other fragments, however, assignable to this fabric (e.g. 246, 428, 429) from levels of IX and VIII had silvery mica-like particles showing in the clay. All of this fine grey pottery appears to have been imported: it is quite different in character from the hard *Silvery Grey Ware*, which may be of local manufacture.

SHAPES

(A) BOWLS

Baking pans of type 3 with their distinctive coarse fabric are extremely characteristic of these early periods. A number of rims of similar fabric came from large open dishes (type 2).

In general the rims of bowls in Period X tended to be sharp and pointed; but in IX they were sometimes flattened on top. Bases of bowls throughout Periods X–VIII were usually flat, but often had a slight sinking to help the vase stand better.

In Period X most of the bowls appear to have had inward leaning rims like types 6 and 7. But some of the rims assigned to these types may have come from jars. It is difficult to distinguish jar rims of class A I from those of bowls of types 6 and 7 except on grounds of fabric, and bowls of these types may in fact have merged into jars without any strict line of division between them. In Periods IX and VIII inward leaning rims assignable to bowls of types 6 and 7 were still common, but the standard bowl shape was hemispherical as type 5.

Bowls of type 8 with high carinated rims appear to have been very characteristic of Period VIII, when rims assignable to this type account for some 20 per cent of all bowl rims; but the type seems to have been rare in IX, and is only represented by a few atypical rims in X. Some short carinated rims like 144–5 from levels of X are virtually indistinguishable in shape from rims of type 9 common in Periods V–II.

Large handles, some of them of truly gigantic size, rising from the tops of bowl rims, were characteristic of Periods X–VIII, but were especially well represented in the material assignable

to IX. These handles, which were normally of very fine burnished ware, may all have belonged
to open bowls of types 4 and 5. In view of the fragmentary character of most of the material,
however, it is always possible that some were really basket handles set across the mouths of jars as
at Çatal Hüyük in Anatolia.

Imposing lug-handles are also found in connection with bowls of Periods X–VIII. These
were either set on top of the rim or applied to the outside of the vase just below it.

1. *Plates* 1–6 (FIG. 118)

These were evidently not uncommon. Most of the seven fragments of profiles from levels of
Periods X–VIII assignable to this type belonged to large circular plates between *c.* 30 and as
much as 40 or 50 in diameter. But rectangular plates or trays like 4 also existed. Similar plates
and trays were at home in the Early Chalcolithic of Cilicia, and they are found in early Neolithic
contexts on the Greek mainland. Plates of Periods X–VIII at Emporio had upright or outward

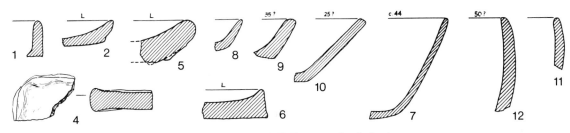

FIG. 118. Periods X–VIII. Types 1 and 2. Scale 1/3.

leaning rims. They were in general roughly made, and of coarse fabric. The inside surfaces were
normally smoothed or burnished; but the underneaths, which were more or less flat, were left
rough, and often had straw impressions showing in them. In the case of 2, however, the
underneath had been smoothed or burnished as well as the inside.

1. (X Q 166) Profile. Angle of rim uncertain. Possibly from a rectangular tray like 4. Gritty grey-brown clay.
   Surface light brown to reddish, burnished.
2. (VIII H 150) Profile. Grey to red-brown clay with fine grit including mica. Surface now worn, but it may have
   been burnished, both inside and on the underneath which is still smooth. The micaceous clay suggests an
   import.
3. (IX H 161) Profile as 2. Grey clay with abundant straw. Inside surface light brown to red, burnished.
4. (IX Q 156) Corner of rectangular tray. Coarse orange clay. Surface light brown; rough and irregular, but more
   or less smoothed.
5. (VIII Q 145) Profile. Coarse fabric. Inside surface light brown, burnished. The underneath very rough with
   straw impressions.
   Cf. Milojcic, *Ergebnisse* 11 fig. 9: 1. *Otzaki-magula* ii 24 f. no. 241 (Presesklo).
6. (VIII Q 145) Profile as 5, but with the inside surface light brown shading to red and dusky, burnished. A
   fragment from VIII G level 139 with the inside light brown, burnished, may come from the same plate.

2. *Dishes* 7–13 (FIG. 118)

The shallower dishes 8–10 are of more or less fine burnished ware. But 7 is of Baking Pan Ware,
and exactly like some baking pans of type 3 except that it has no holes round the rim. It is just
possible that this and similar rims came from the lids of baking pans. One such vessel (13), of
which many fragments were recovered but which defied restoration, had possible traces of a red
wash. Its rim may have been incurving like 11 and 12, which in view of their large diameter
appear to have belonged to dishes rather than to deep bowls or jars.

7. (IX G 154) Profile and other fragments of a large dish. Baking Pan Ware. Grey-brown clay. Surface rough and wiped; smoky black outside as if used over a fire, lightish brown to salmon pink inside. About four other similar rims noted from levels of IX A.

8. (VIII G 142) Rim. Angle not entirely certain, and perhaps from some other type of vase. Surface shades of grey-brown to deep reddish with very fine burnish.

9. (VIII G 139) Rim. Black to brown, shading to light brown round the rim, burnished.

10. (VIII Q 145) Profile. Shades of lightish brown, burnished.

11. (X Q 167) Rim. Baking Pan Ware. Coarse grey-brown clay. Surface shades of light to darker brown, rough outside, smoothed inside.

12. (VIII H 150) Rim as 11. Coarse light greenish clay. Surface light brown to dusky, full of straw impressions, and without any trace of burnish. One of two similar rims from the same deposit was dusky on the outside as if from use over a fire.

13. (IX Q 156 and 159) Fragments of large dish, including much of flat base and one piece of rim. Angle of rim and height uncertain. Baking Pan Ware; coarse, soft crumbly grey to light brown clay. Outside surface rough, but much flaked, dark purplish brown in colour. Inside light purplish brown shading to dusky greyish in the base. Superficial burnish round inside of rim. Underneath of base grey-brown, very rough, and impressed with straw marks which have traces of red colour in them. The outside of the vase may have once been coated with a red wash.

3. *Baking pans* 14–31 (FIG. 119)

These vessels, of distinctive Baking Pan Ware, with a row of perforations around the rim, were much in evidence in the earliest levels at Emporio like the plates and dishes of the related types 1 and 2. Remains of such baking pans occurred in levels of Period X, but they were especially abundant in those of IX and VIII. In profile 21 resembles a plate of type 1; but other profiles are like those of large dishes of type 2, and most of the vessels classifiable as baking pans would appear to have resembled large shallow dishes of this type with rim diameters of *c.* 30–40 or more. Inward leaning rims such as 17, 22, 24 with diameters of *c.* 20 or less may come from deep bowls or jar-like vessels.

Some baking pans appear to have been provided with handles. Three typical perforated rims from levels of IX Q had what seemed to be the stumps of circular-sectioned handles set on top of

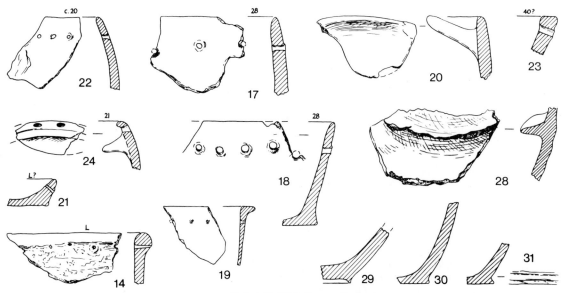

FIG. 119. Periods X–VIII. Type 3. Scale 1/3.

the rim or horizontally just below it on the outside of the vase. But large tongue-shaped horizontal ledge-lugs (20, 29) were more common than handles. These lugs occurred in levels of all phases of X–VIII, and were normally at any rate placed on the inside of the vase below the rim. It has been suggested that internal lugs of this kind might have supported lids, and rims like 7 assigned to type 2 could have belonged to lids of baking pans rather than to dishes. Possibly, however, the same vases served both as dishes and as baking pan lids. Internal lugs may also have facilitated handling, if, as seems probable, baking pans were used in cooking over open fires. Most of these baking pan lugs were solid. A few perforated lugs may have been set on the outsides of vessels rather than on the insides like the solid ledge-lugs. A couple of lugs from levels of IX had traces of at least three perforations made before firing like the holes in baking pan rims. These and some of the other lugs and bases grouped under type 3 may in fact come from vases of different types which were made of Baking Pan Ware.

Bases were normally flat, and often it seems had the edges splayed like 18. This and 30–31 are reminiscent of the splayed bases of pans of Kum Tepe I A, which appear to be comparable in fabric but lack perforations around the rim (*Kum Tepe* 322 fig. 10: 136–7; 326 fig. 11: 235). The underneaths of many bases, and the outside surfaces of a few rims like 14 and 19, were very rough, as if the wet clay had been applied to something like basketry. In these cases the clay may have formed an inner lining to a vessel made of some more perishable material.

Baking Pan Ware has been described under fabric. The abundant straw temper characteristically shows in the surfaces of the vases which are apt to be irregular. There is a great variety in surface colour, ranging from red through shades of brown. Outsides are often dusky as if the vessels had been used for cooking over fires. In line with this inside surfaces normally appear to have been given a better finish than outsides: outsides were for the most part left rough, while insides were sometimes treated to a superficial burnish; but there are cases where the outside surface has a poor burnish while the inside is rough.

14. (X Q 166) (PLATE 38) Rim, possibly from a dish of sub-rectangular shape. Coarse grey-brown clay. Outside below the rim dusky, and rough as if applied as an inner lining to a vessel of some other material (cf. 19). Inside light brown to reddish, wiped.
15. (IX G 154) (PLATE 30) Rim.
16. (IX G 155) (PLATE 30) Base with short rim.
17. (VIII G 141) Rim. Coarse grey-brown clay. Outside rough, dusky, but reddish round the rim. Inside light brown with poor burnish.
18. (VIII G 141 and 142) Profile cf. type 2. Coarse grey-brown clay with abundant straw impressions in surface, which is dusky brown, rough, outside; light brown to salmon pink, roughly smoothed, inside.
19. (IX G 158). Rim. Grey-brown clay. Outside darkish brown, and rough as if applied as the lining to a vessel of some other material (cf. 14). Inside light brown to reddish smoothed, but with abundant straw impressions showing in it.
20. (IX Q 156). Rim with internal lug. Coarse grey-brown clay. Surface rough; dark brown outside, light brown inside.
21. (IX Q 158) Profile cf. type 1. Coarse grey-brown clay. Surface light brown, unburnished. Underneath of base greyish, and very rough, as if applied to basketry or material of a similar kind (cf. 29).
22. (VIII G 140) Rim. Coarse grey-brown clay with abundant straw and large grit showing in surface, which is rough; dark brown outside, light brown to salmon pink inside.
23. (VIII G 140) Rim. Coarse grey clay with large grit. Surface light brown with a reddish tinge, rough and unburnished.
24. (VIII G wall 16) (PLATE 30, showing inside) Rim with internal lug. Coarse grey clay. Outside surface dusky to black with poor burnish, inside light orange-brown.
25-27. (VIII G 139, Q 146/7, Q 144) (PLATE 30) Rims.
28. (VIII Q 145) (PLATE 30, showing inside) Large internal lug. Coarse grey-brown clay with abundant straw impressions showing in surface; outside with wide shallow corrugations, black, smoothed or with a poor burnish; inside rough, light brown to salmon pink.

Bases of baking-pan ware

29. (X G 164) Coarse grey-brown clay. Outside rough, dusky black. Inside lightish brown to reddish, smoothed. Underneath of base very rough, as if applied to something like basketry (cf. 21).
30. (X Q 167) Coarse grey-brown clay. Outside rough, dusky. Inside light brown to reddish, smoothed.
31. (X Q 158) Coarse grey-brown clay. Outside rough, dark brown. Inside light reddish brown, smoothed. A horizontal impression *c*. 0.7 wide round the foot looks as if it had been made by a withe or cord of some kind.

4. *Open bowls with straight or slightly curving sides* 32–55 (Fig. 120)

These were not uncommon, and two complete profiles were recovered together with a number of rims. Most of the rims appeared to belong to rather shallow bowls. The bowls were evidently of all sizes, some being as much as 35 or more in diameter. But two rims of very small bowls with diameters of only 7 were found in levels of Period X: one of these (32) was exceptional in having steep bucket-like sides, the other (43) was unusually shallow..

Many of the rims from X–VIII assigned to this type were of fine burnished ware, and a number of them had outstandingly fine burnished surfaces. But a few, notably rims of large shallow bowls like 48, were of very coarse fabric akin to Baking Pan Ware with a poor burnish or even none at all.

Rims were usually rounded, but in a number of cases they had been flattened. The unique and atypical rim 47 may come from an imported vase.

One rim of Period VIII appears to have had a large vertical strap handle set below it on the outside. The outsides of a couple of other rims from VIII were decorated with pattern burnish (42).

A, B. Deep and medium

32. (X Q 166) Profile. Grey-brown clay; surface irregular, shades of light and dark brown with a poor burnish.
33. (IX G 154) Rim. Grey-brown to black, burnished. Three others similar.
34. (IX Q 156) Rim. Grey-brown, finely burnished. Three others similar.
35. (IX Q 156) Rim. Light brown, burnished.
36. (VIII G wall 16) Rim. Grey-brown to black with a reddish tinge, very finely burnished. Two others similar: one from IX Q level 156, grey-brown; the other from VIII Q level 146, brick-red, burnished.
37. (VIII G 140) Rim. Shades of light and dark brown, burnished.

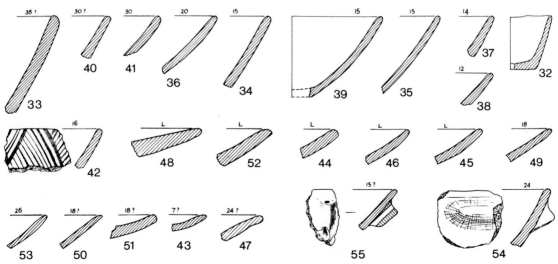

FIG. 120. Periods X–VIII. Type 4. Scale 1/3.

38. (VIII G 139) Rim. Grey-brown, burnished. Another similar.
39. (VIII Q 145) Profile, Grey-brown, burnished.
40. (VIII Q 145) Rim. Surface grey-brown, even and finely burnished, without any trace of the burnishing instrument.
41. (VIII Q 145) Rim. Grey clay; surface worn, but with traces of a burnished red wash.
42. (VIII Q 145) Rim with pattern burnish on outside. Light brown to red-brown, burnished. Another similar.

C. Shallow

43. (X Q 168) Rim. Grey-brown with a poor burnish.
44. (IX G 155) Rim. Coarse fabric. Outside surface irregular, smoothed or with a poor burnish, and black, apparently from use over a fire. Inside light brown (salmon pink) with a poor burnish.
45. (VIII G 141) Rim. Angle not certain. Surface finely burnished, dark grey-brown outside, reddish inside.
46. (VIII G 141-2) Rim. Angle not certain. Roughly made; surface shades of light brown to reddish, wiped rather than burnished.
47. (IX Q 159) (PLATE 30) Rim. Sandy orange clay, soft, but fired an even colour throughout, with some specks of silvery mica. Surface very worn, but traces of a red wash. Probably an import.
48. (IX Q 156) Rim. Angle not certain. Fabric akin to Baking Pan Ware. Coarse grey-brown clay; surface rough, full of straw impressions; dusky outside as if from use over a fire, light brown inside. Another similar.
49. (IX Q 156) Rim. Grey-brown, finely burnished. Another similar, but red inside.
50. (IX Q 158) Rim. Outside grey-brown, finely burnished. Inside dark purple-brown with superficial stroke burnish.
51. (IX Q 158) Rim. Coarse grey-brown clay; surface rough, unburnished, dark purple-brown outside, light brown inside.
52. (VIII Q 145) Rim. Light brown to red, finely burnished. Another (IX Q level 156) similar, but with tip of rim flattened and surface grey-brown.
53. (VIII Q 145) Rim. Dark brown to black; very fine burnish.

Some rims with lugs below them appear to come from bowls of this type rather than from those of type 5.

54. (IX Q 156) Rim with horizontal lug. Grey-brown, burnished.
55. (VIII G 139) Rim with vertically perforated tubular lug. Gritty reddish clay; surface shades of red-brown and dark and light brown, burnished.

5. *Open bowls with curving sides* 56–93 (FIG. 121)

Bowls of this type were very common in Periods X-VIII like the bowls of type 4 into which they merge and from which in practice they may have been indistinguishable. They ranged in diameter from under 10 to 40 or more: a number of rims evidently came from small bowls with diameters of less than 15 to as little as 6. Many of the rims were thickened: elegantly pointed and thickened rims like 66, 70 and 72, were characteristic and occurred on bowls of very fine burnished ware. A number of rims were flat-topped as 61, 64. The only complete profile that could be restored was 77.

Several bowls (e.g. 76) appear to have had large handles set on top of the rim and rising above it. But smaller handles are also attested. The handle on 92 is unusual in being set horizontally below the rim as was common later in Periods V-IV. One rim (93), apparently from a level of IX Q, has a small vertical strap handle. Some of the fish-tailed lugs characteristic of Periods X–IX may have come from deep bowls (class A) of type 5. A number of bowls of this type seem to have had large horse-shoe shaped or crescentic lugs set just below the rim on the outside as 58 and 78. Six examples of these lugs, associated with rims of open bowls of type 5 or perhaps in some cases of type 4, were recovered from levels of IX Q.

The bowls of type 5 like those of the related type 4 tended to be of fine burnished ware, and some, especially of the smaller bowls, were given an exceptionally fine burnish. But as in the case

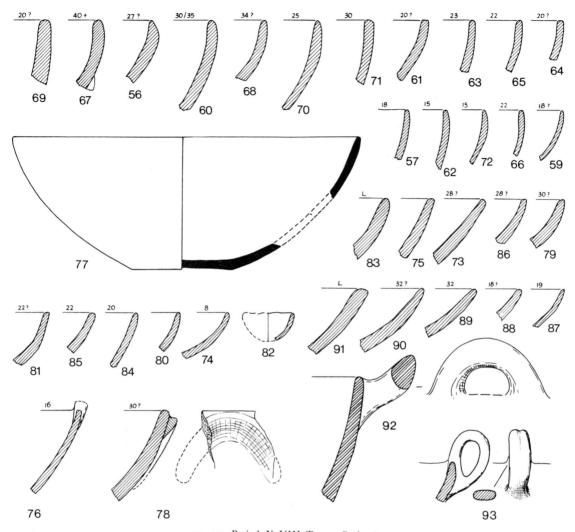

FIG. 121. Periods X–VIII. Type 5. Scale 1/3.

of type 4 bowls, a few of type 5 were of coarser fabric with only a poor burnish, and one rim (73) had no trace of burnish at all. The small rim 87 of class C may come from an imported vase.

A. Deep, more or less hemispherical

56. (X G 163) Rim. Grey-brown, burnished.
    For the rim shape cf. *Sukas* iii 46 figs. 110-2; 66 fig. 155 (from N 7 & 3).
57. (IX H 161) Rim. Irregular. Soft fabric; clay grey, light brown at edges. Traces of light brown burnished surface with straw impressions showing in it.
58. (IX/VIII H 150) (PLATE 30) Large rim with bold crescentic lug like 78. Surface worn, but once apparently light brown, burnished.
59. (IX G 155) Rim. Shades of light and dark brown, finely burnished.
60. (VIII G 142) Rim. Shades of light and dark brown, burnished. Five others similar.
61. (VIII G 142) Rim with flattened top. Lightish grey-brown; fine burnish. Two others similar with burnished surfaces light brown to dark grey-brown and shades of light and dark brown to reddish.

62. (VIII G 142) Rim. Outside light brown, inside shades of light brown to dusky, burnished. Two others similar.
63. (VIII G 141) Rim. Grey-brown clay with some large grit; surface with minute straw impressions showing in it, dark grey-brown outside, light brown inside, burnished. About ten similar, all with finely burnished surfaces.
64. (VIII G 141) Rim with flattened top. Grey-brown, burnished.
65. (IX Q 156) Rim. Outside light to dark brown, finely burnished; inside grey-brown.
66. (IX Q 156) Rim. Light brown to red; fine burnish.
67. (IX/VIII Q ?158) Rim. Coarse fabric. Outside grey-brown to black, burnished. Inside irregular, and perhaps worn by use, with traces of a burnished red wash.
68. (IX/VIII Q ?158) Rim. Dark grey-brown, burnished.
69. (VIII G ?141) Rim. Gritty clay; surface shades of brown, burnished.
70. (VIII G ?140) Rim, pointed and thickened. Grey-brown; fine burnish. Six similar, all with very fine burnished surfaces, grey-brown to black, light brown or reddish.
71. (VIII G 140) Rim. Light brown, burnished. Another similar, but with the burnished surface grey-brown to reddish.

B. Medium

73. (IX G 154) Rim. Angle not certain. Coarse clay with grit; surface unburnished, shades of light to dark brown with a reddish or purple tinge.
74. (IX G 154) Rim. Surface with rather poor burnish and worn, shades of light and dark brown. Another similar from X Q level 167, grey-brown, burnished.
75. (VIII G 142) Rim. Grey-brown, burnished.
76. (VIII G 141) Rim with stump of thick handle rising from it. Grey clay; surface shades of dark and light brown to reddish, burnished but worn.
77. (IX/VIII Q 159, 156, 148) Fragments, including seven from rim and part of base, apparently all from same vase. Surface dark red; fine burnish.
78. (IX Q 159) Rim with bold crescentic lug like 58. Light brown, finely burnished. Five other rims with similar lugs from IX Q levels 159, 158, 156 (two) and VIII Q level 148, apparently all from bowls of type 5; their surfaces finely burnished, shades of light and dark brown to reddish.
79. (IX Q 156) Rim. Outside light brown, finely burnished; inside darker brown. Four others similar with finely burnished surfaces, one from level 158 light brown to red, the rest dark brown.
80. (IX Q 156) Rim. Surface light brownish grey, pitted, with traces of original burnish but much worn.
81. (VIII Q 148) Rim. Grey-brown; fine burnish. Another similar from IX Q level 156, light brown with a fine burnish.
82. (VIII Q 148) Rim of miniature bowl. Very irregular. Surface dusky grey-brown, rough and without burnish.
83. (VIII Q 147) Rim. Angle not certain. Shades of dark and light brown to black; very fine burnish.
84. (VIII Q 147) Rim. Dark brown outside, light brown to dusky inside; very fine burnish.
85. (VIII Q 146) Rim. Light reddish brown; very fine burnish. Another similar, dark brown to black.
86. (VIII Q 144) Rim, flat-topped and irregular. Coarse clay with grit; surface shades of lightish to dark brown with poor burnish.

C. Shallow

87. (X Q 166) (PLATE 30) Rim. Thin-walled and of very fine fabric; well levigated clay, grey throughout the break, with silvery mica showing in it. Surface with a flaky black slip, well burnished. Possibly an import.
88. (IX Q 148) Rim. Brownish grey clay; surface lightish brown to grey, rough and without burnish.
89. (IX/VIII Q ?158) Rim. Surface with a very fine burnish, dark red outside, light brown inside. Another similar apparently from a bowl of type 5 from IX Q level 156; coarse grey-brown clay; surface light brown to dusky, rough, without burnish, and full of straw impressions.
90. (IX/VIII Q ?158) Rim. Very finely burnished, light brown outside, dark red inside.
91. (VIII Q 144) Rim. Outside light brown to reddish, rather rough with a poor burnish; inside light greyish.

Two rims with handles evidently come from bowls of type 5.

92. (IX G 154) (PLATE 35) Rim with horizontal handle below it. Shades of light brown to dusky, burnished.
    Handles of this type set below the rims of bowls appear to be a feature of the earliest Phase I A at Kum Tepe (*Kum Tepe* 316 f. fig. 8. no. 115; 324, 319 fig. 9 nos. 201, 202, 215, 216).
93. (IX Q 158) (PLATE 30) Rim with vertical handle rising above it. Angle uncertain. Coarse grey-brown clay; surface light brown, originally perhaps with a poor burnish.

Cf. AG 135 from the very top level in the Upper Cave at Ayio Gala, and the handles 348–9 from levels of Emporio VIII with similar kidney-shaped sections. There is a vertical handle with kidney-shaped section like 93 from level XXXVIII of Late Chalcolithic 1 at Beycesultan (*Beycesultan* i 74 fig. P. 2: 31). For other vertical handles rising above rims from Anatolian Late Chalcolithic contexts see *Beycesultan* i 84 fig. P. 6: 7, 25, 26, L.C. 2. Cf. *AS* xv (1965) 88, 94 fig. 5: 7, from Can Hasan. A bowl with handle rising above the rim comes from the Middle Chalcolithic level XVI at Mersin (*Mersin* 150 f. fig. 93: 3). Bowls of the Middle Neolithic period from Byblos also have vertical handles rising above the rim like this (*Byblos* v 106 fig. 59). Some Byblite handles of this period were divided by a bold groove down the centre (e.g. *Byblos* v figs. 60: 23162; 63: 23161).

6. *Bowls with inward-leaning rims* 94–111 (FIG. 122)

These bowls merge into ones of types 7 and 8 and into jars of type 35 with rims of class A I. The allotment of rims as between these types is therefore somewhat arbitrary. As a rule finely burnished rims and rims with large diameters have been assigned to type 6. Bowls of this type seem to range in diameter from about 10, like 101, to 30 or 40 or more. A good many rims assigned to this type were thickened, and among these were some with carefully flattened tops. A few bead rims and incipient bead rims appear to come from bowls of this type rather than from those of type 8 or from bowl-jars of type 32: one such rim (110) had the stump of a lug or handle below it. The rim 111 grouped here preserves a vertical tubular lug like 483 of period VII.

The surfaces of type 6 bowls were normally it seems given a fine burnish. Rims of coarser fabric like 96, with surfaces less well burnished or altogether unburnished, may come from jars akin to type 35 rather than from bowls.

94. (X G hearth in 163) Rim. Grey-brown; fine burnish.
95. (X G 163) Rim. Grey-brown clay; surface probably once burnished, but worn. Two others similar with traces of a red wash, smoothed or burnished.
96. (IX G 154) Rim with bead. Gritty grey clay; surface shades of light to darker brown and reddish, wiped or smoothed.
97. (IX G 154) Rim. Surface well burnished, light brown to reddish and dusky outside, light brown inside. Another similar.
98. (VIII G 152) Rim. Outside light brown to red, inside dark brown, burnished.
99. (IX Q 156) Rim. Grey-brown; fine burnish. Others similar.
100. (IX/VIII Q ?158) Flat-topped rim. Grey-brown to black; fine burnish.
101. (IX/VIII Q ?158) Rim. Grey-brown; fine burnish.
102. (VIII G 140) Rim. Shades of light and dark brown, reddish round the top, burnished. Two others similar, including one from IX Q level 159, shades of light brown to red, burnished.
103. (VIII G 140) Rim with bead. Outside surface light brown, inside dark brown, well burnished.
104. (VIII G wall 16) Rim with incipient bead. Shades of dark and light brown to red, burnished.
105. (VIII G wall 16) Rim. Light brown; fine burnish.
106. (VIII G 139) Rim. Shades of grey-brown to light brown with slight reddish tinge round the top, burnished.
107. (VIII G wall 16) Thickened rim. Outside shades of greyish brown, burnished; inside straw-wiped, less well burnished.
108. (VIII Q 145) Flat-topped rim. Outside lightish brown, well burnished; inside wiped. Another similar.
109. (VIII Q 145) Rim. Fabric akin to Mottled Ware characteristic of VII-VI. Surface with very fine burnish rendering marks of burnishing instrument invisible; shades of light brown to dusky and red outside, light brown to red inside. Possibly a stray of Period VII.
110. (VIII Q 144) Rim with incipient bead and stump of lug or handle. Gritty grey clay; surface dark brown inside, lighter brown outside, well burnished.
111. (VIII G 140) (PLATE 38) Rim with vertically perforated lug as 483 of Period VII. Outside surface light brown, inside reddish, smoothed or with dull burnish.

7. *Bowls with inward-leaning rims and high shoulders* 112–129 (FIG. 122)

One complete bowl (112) and another virtually complete (113) from the deepest level of X in area B (trench Q) are assignable to this type. Rims which may be grouped here were extremely

FIG. 122. Periods X–VIII. Types 6–9. Scale 1/3.

common, but there is no sharp line of division between them and rims of types 5, 6, 8 and 9. Sections of rim from the same bowl may be classifiable under different types within this range. Thus parts of the rim of 112 are akin to rims of type 5.

A number of rims (e.g. 126-8) grouped here were distinctly thickened. Several of these closely approximated to rims of type 11, which is in effect a variety of type 7. The rim 128 has a bold crescentic lug like 78 of type 5. Rim 129 with a solid tubular lug could be a stray of Period VII. Similarly 124 from a very large bowl with an unburnished red wash may be a later stray.

112. (X Q 167) (PLATE 31) Bowl with large solid lug-handle rising above rim. Broken, but nearly complete. Ht. to rim 11. Max. diam. 15. Thick-walled, roughly made and irregular, with uneven rim. Orange to red-brown clay, sandy with abundant fine grit (grey, red, and some white) and straw. Surface burnished, but much perished and worn owing to water action; shades of dark brown and red with patches of black.

Two small holes in the upper surface of the lug-handle, made before firing but not carried through to the other side, may have contained some kind of inlay, perhaps decorative wooden studs. An identical lug with similar holes was recovered from IX Q level 159: cf. 331 from level 158. But most lugs of this or comparable shapes have the holes carried through as perforations (e.g. 333).

113. (X Q 167) (PLATE 31) Bowl with vertically perforated lug-handle cf. 327, 361. Broken, and large parts missing, including a section of rim which may have had a similar lug-handle. Ht. to rim 11. Max. diam. 15. Grey to orange clay, sandy with grit (much of it red, but some grey and white). Surface black to dark brown, burnished.

114. (X G 163) Rim. Grey-brown; fine burnish.

115. (X G 163) Rim. Outside light brown to red, fine burnish; inside dark grey-brown, burnished.

116. (X G 163) Rim. Grey-brown; fine burnish.

117. (X Q 168). Rim. Light brown to reddish; fine burnish.

118. (IX Q 159) Rim. Grey-brown; fine burnish. Another similar.

119. (IX Q 156) Rim. Grey-brown; fine burnish.

120. (VIII Q 148) Rim. Grey-brown; fine burnish.

121. (VIII G 140) Rim. Light brown; very fine burnish. Groups of diagonal lines in pattern burnish round outside.

122. (VIII G 140) Rim. Light greyish brown, burnished.

123. (VIII Q 146) Rim. Grey-brown; very fine burnish.

124. (VIII Q 145) Rim. Coarse grey-brown clay. Surface rough and unburnished, with a red wash shading to dull purple on the inside. Perhaps a later stray.

Rims with marked thickening

125. (X G 163) Rim. Light shading to dark brown; fine burnish. Another similar, grey-brown to reddish, burnished.

126. (VIII Q 146) Rim. Grey-brown; fine burnish.

127. (VIII Q 146) Rim. Grey-brown to lighter reddish brown; very fine burnish.

Rims with lugs

128. (IX Q 156) (PLATE 37) Rim with crescentic lug cf. 58, 78. Grey-brown; fine burnish.

129. (?VIII Q ?145) Rim with solid trumpet-shaped lug set diagonally below it. Context not entirely certain, and perhaps from a level of Period VII. Coarse clay with large grey and white grits. Grit and straw impressions showing in surface, which is light brown with rough stroke burnish.

Solid trumpet-shaped lugs are attested from Kum Tepe Phase I B, the Late Subperiod of Troy I, and the Blue period at Poliochni (*Kum Tepe* 332 pl. 75 no. 510. *Troy* i 78, 164 fig. 249: 20. *Poliochni* i 558 pl. xxix: b, c). One very like 129 comes from the earliest phase (B) at Hanay Tepe in the Troad, assignable to the Kum Tepe I B horizon (W. Lamb, *PZ* xxiii (1932) 117 fig. 4: 4). Solid versions of trumpet lugs were common, however, at the beginning of the Neolithic (E.N. I-II) at Knossos although rare it seems there later (*BSA* lix (1964) 208, 214 figs. 25: 6-9; 31: 13; and 37: 47 from LN Stratum II).

8. *Bowls with carinated shoulders and tall rims* 130–143 (FIG. 122)

This was a common and very characteristic shape in Period VIII, but it also occurred in IX, and was represented by a few rather atypical rims of small bowls from X. The carination was not very pronounced until an ogival profile for the lower part of the body came into fashion (e.g. 142): no example of an ogival profile was recognised for certain before Period VIII. The fragment 143 which may come from a bowl of this type appears to have had a vertical handle joining carination and rim. A number of rims of bowls of type 8 from levels of VIII have traces of pattern burnish on the outside. This normally consists of alternate groups of diagonal stripes which may form hatched triangles.

130. (X Q 167) Rim. Coarse orange clay; surface shades of light and dark brown to reddish, originally perhaps burnished, but worn by water action.
131. (IX Q 167) Rim. Coarse grey-brown clay with large lumps of grit; surface shades of light and dark brown to black, burnished.
132. (X Q 166) Rim. Outside shades of dark and light reddish brown, inside grey-brown, burnished.
133. (IX Q 156) Rim. Grey-brown; fine burnish.
134. (IX Q 158) Rim. Light brown to dark brown and black, burnished. Two others similar; surfaces light brown, and dark brown to red.
135. (VIII G 140) Rim. Grey-brown; fine burnish.
136. (VIII G 139) Rim. Light brownish grey surface, very well burnished, but worn.
137. (VIII G 139) Rim with bead. Shades of dark and light brown, burnished.
138. (VIII Q 145) Rim. Grey-brown, burnished. Bold pattern burnish (groups of diagonal stripes) outside.
139. (VIII Q 145) Rim. Gritty clay, grey to brick red, shading to light brown at the edges. Surface light brown with fine burnish, more thorough outside than inside.
140. (VIII Q 145) Rim. Grey-brown to black, burnished. Pattern burnish (groups of diagonal stripes) outside. Inside less well burnished with marks of the burnishing instrument clearly visible.
141. (VIII Q 145) Rim. Grey-brown, burnished. Pattern burnish (groups of diagonal stripes) outside.
142. (VIII Q 146) Carinated shoulder. Outside light brown, burnished. Inside light brownish grey, less well burnished.
143. (VIII Q 145) Carinated shoulder with stump of vertical handle. Grey, with fine burnish outside and inside.

9. *Carinated bowls* 144–149 (FIG. 122)

A few rims from levels of X–VIII were classifiable as being of this type rather than of type 8. Some of the earliest of these (e.g. 144 and 145) were in fact indistinguishable in profile from type 9 rims of much later periods. This is surprising; but comparable rims occur in Early Neolithic I at Knossos in Crete (e.g. *BSA* lix (1964) 165 fig. 23: 6, 35 both from Stratum V).

144. (X G 163 hearth) Rim. Irregular in shape. Gritty grey-brown clay; surface uneven, but well burnished, shading from grey-brown to lightish brown, with a reddish tinge in one place.
145. (X Q 167) Rim. Gritty grey-brown clay; surface shades of dark and light brown to reddish, burnished. In fabric and appearance hardly distinguishable from some rims of Periods V–IV (e.g. 988).
146. (IX Q 158) Rim. Grey mottling to light brown; fine burnish.
147 (VIII G 139) Rim. Black to brown, shading to lighter brown round the rim, burnished.

Two very large rims of distinctive type were recovered from X H, and may have belonged to the same vase. One of them (149) came from a level with an admixture of Periods VII–VI. This rim in particular is closely paralleled by *Asea* 37 fig. 34: b, Neolithic Coarse Burnished Ware, and *Kephala* pl. 45: H. Some rims from Erimi in Cyprus are not dissimilar (*SCE* iv Pt. 1A, 120 fig. 59).

148. (X H 161) Grey-brown clay, shading to light brown at the edges, tempered with straw and fine grit. Straw impressions showing in surface, which is worn, but may have been burnished.
149. (X H 149) Angle not certain. Fabric as 148.

10. *Bowls with short, S-shaped, usually thickened club-like rims* 150–154 (FIG. 123)

This type was characteristic of Periods VII–VI. The few rims from levels of X–VIII which may be grouped here were either atypical, or came from upper deposits of VIII which might have been contaminated with later material. Two rims with trumpet lugs from VIII Q level 144 may have belonged to bowls of this type, since trumpet lugs are commonly found on such bowls in Periods VII-VI.

150. (IX Q 156) (PLATE 30) Rim. Grey clay, light brown at edges. Traces of smoothing or burnishing on outside, not so much inside. Possibly an import, in view of the unique shape.

   Somewhat reminiscent of early Late Chalcolithic rims from Beycesultan, like 154 below. Compare also Cretan Neolithic rims from Knossos, *BSA* lix (1964) 179 fig. 30: 22, Stratum IV (E.N. II); xlviii (1953) 124 fig. 12: 14, 15, assigned to Middle Neolithic.

151. (VIII Q 146) Rim. Brown to black; outside with a fine burnish, with a soapy feel; inside less well burnished.

   Cf. Cretan Neolithic rims from Knossos, *BSA* lix (1964) 179 fig. 30: 7, Stratum IV (E.N. II); xlviii 1953) 124 fig. 12: 26, 27, assigned to Middle Neolithic. *Kephala* pl. 28: K is similar.

152. (VIII Q 145) Rim. Well made; shades of dull brown and red with traces of burnish.

153. (VIII Q 145) Rim. Fabric cf. Light Brown Burnished Ware. Grey clay; surface light brown, burnished but much worn.

   Cf. *BSA* lix (1964) 179 fig. 30: 20, from Stratum IV (E.N. II) at Knossos.

154. (?VIII Q ?145) Rim. Context not certain, but apparently of Period VIII. Unusually elegant, and sharply differentiated on inside. Light brown to light greyish brown, burnished.

   Not altogether unlike some early Late Chalcolithic rims from Beycesultan (e.g. *Beycesultan* i fig. P. 1: 7–9).

11. *Bowls with inward-curving rims, internally differentiated and usually thickened* 155

This type, an early version it seems of type 12 into which it merges, was characteristic of Periods VII–VI. Only two rims assignable to it were recovered from earlier levels, and both of these came from upper deposits of VIII suspect of some degree of contamination with later material.

155. (VIII Q 144) Rim, like 592 of Period VII. Shades of dark and light brown, burnished.

12. *Bowls with straight rims, thickened and usually differentiated on the inside*

This type was characteristic of Periods V–IV, and only a few rims which could be ascribed to it were recovered from earlier levels. A single rim of grey-brown burnished ware from the top level 144 of VIII in trench Q was somewhat like 1072 of Period IV.

14. *Bowls with outward-curving rims, not internally differentiated, but sometimes thickened* 156–160 (FIG. 123)

The comparatively few pieces that could be assigned to this type all came from high levels of VIII. But they included the complete vase 156 of which the stratified position was certain. Bowls of type 14 clearly shade into bowl-jars of type 32. The rim 160 from a doubtful context, but apparently of Period VIII, has a vertically perforated lug set just below it. One or two other rims of this type from levels of VIII in area A (trench G), roughly made and of coarse fabric, may have

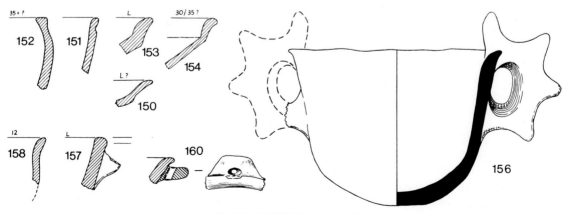

FIG. 123. Periods X–VIII. Types 10–14. Scale 1/3.

belonged to cooking bowls of some kind; one from an uncertain context, but perhaps from level 140, of gritty grey-brown clay, the surface grey-brown to reddish with a poor burnish, had a thin strap handle rising from its top.

156. (VIII G 139) (PLATE 31) Vase with pair of multi-horned handles. Complete and unbroken, except for one handle missing. Ht. to rim. *c.* 13. Diam. 16.5-18. Thick-walled, crudely made and irregular in shape. Base roughly flat. Dark grey clay with large greyish grit and straw; surface dirty grey-brown shading to orange with rather poor burnish outside and in.

   From the situation in which it was found it seems likely that this was a ritual vase. The multi-horned handles are unique at Emporio. The profile of a bowl handle from the earliest horizon A at Kusura looks somewhat similar (*Archaeologia* lxxxvi (1936) 15 fig. 5:1). Ribbed handles which present a modified version of this profile occur in Troy I-II and at Thermi (*Troy* i 99 fig. 236: 25; 106 fig. 240: 9, 10; 242, 274 fig. 371: 6. *Thermi* 83 fig. 30: 2, 3), and at Beycesultan in E.B. 2 there (*Beycesultan* i 148 Fig. P. 25: 3). Cf. K. Bittel and H. Otto, *Demirci-Hüyük* (Berlin, 1939) 20 pl. 8: 5 (on dipper cups). K. Bittel, *Prähistorische Forschung in Kleinasien* (Istanbul, 1934) pl. vi: 2, 3, on jugs from Ahlatlibel. *AM* xxv (1899) pl. iii: 26, from Boshüyük. The multiple warts on the handle of a jug from Karataş-Semayük (*AJA* lxviii (1964) 276 pl. 78 fig. 7. Cf. *Troy* i 78 pl. 245: 16, from Troy I), and on bowl handles from Lianokladhi I (*PThess* 176 f. fig. 121), are not so comparable.

157. (VIII G 140) Rim, with stump of handle or lug. Light and dark brown to red, burnished.

158. (VIII G 139) Rim. Perhaps better classified as a variety of bowl-jar of type 32. Grey-black clay, light brown at edges; surface light brown, well burnished outside and in.

159. (VIII G 139) Everted rim, like 615 from level 119 of Period VIII. Light brown to red surface, burnished but worn.

160. (?VIII Q ?145) Rim, with vertically perforated lug. Context not entirely certain, and perhaps of Periods VII-VI. Soft fabric; surface grey-brown, burnished, with straw impressions showing in it.

(B) JUGS AND THERIOMORPHIC VASES 161-166 (FIG. 124)

Jugs were not as much in evidence as they were in the succeeding Periods VII-VI and later. The comparatively low proportion of jugs in relation to vases of other types from levels of X-VIII may reflect the fact that these early deposits consisted to a large extent of occupation debris associated with houses. The high proportion of jug fragments in levels of later periods seems explicable in terms of rites of breakage of vessels used for containing water around the spring or well. If such rites were practised earlier, vases of other shapes, such as jars of type 41, much in evidence in levels of VIII, may have been used instead of one-handled jugs.

The upper part of a jug like 161 of type 20 was virtually indistinguishable from that of a jar of type 41 apart from the handles. It is therefore highly probable that some of the large number of rims grouped under type 41 really belonged to jugs of type 20. Some twenty or more rims with high-swung handles from levels covering most phases of X–VIII probably ought to be assigned to this type. Some at least of the many strap handles recorded from levels of X–VIII presumably came from jugs of one kind or another.

The high-swung handles on rims assignable to jugs of type 20 were for the most part of normal thick or thin oval section. At one extreme were rims with grey-brown surfaces very finely burnished, at the other ones of coarse unburnished ware; one from level 145 of VIII in trench Q was of Light Plain Ware. A number of high-swung handles which may have come from jugs found in levels of IX-VIII were circular in section at the lower end, changing through thick oval to thin oval at the top where they joined the rim (e.g. 162). The rim 163 is unique in having a large hole made before firing just below the point where the handle joins it. The handle with an oval wart (340) may have belonged to a jug of type 20.

The label with them indicated that the fragments of the jug 164 came from the same level 167 of Period X as 161 of type 20. But 164 has a carinated body, sloping mouth and pointed spout, reminiscent of jugs of Periods V–IV. The presence of such a jug in this early horizon is surprising,

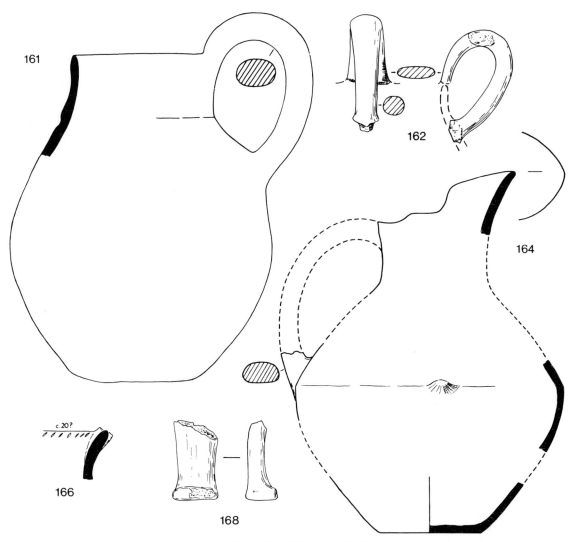

FIG. 124. Periods X–VIII. Jugs etc. Scale 1/3.

and suggests that the label must have been misplaced. But there was no obvious explanation as to how this could have happened, and the jug has therefore been described and illustrated here.

One or two other carinated fragments from the bodies of jugs or jars appear to have been found in levels of Period X. There was no evidence, however, for the existence of jugs with sloping mouths as early as X apart from 164. But fragments of jugs of Fine Black Burnished Ware with sloping mouths resembling those common in Period VII were recovered from levels of VIII, and a few scraps of these came from early levels of the period. Thus two fragments from level 142 in trench G—a rim with a group of five stripes in white below it, and a handle of lunate section (FIG. 104, class 5)—may have belonged to a jug of Fine Black Burnished Ware of the type standard in Period VII. Two other jugs rims of the same type and fabric, one with three, the other with four stripes painted in white below it, were recovered from levels 146 and 147 in area B (trench Q). The rim 383 with five stripes appears to come from level 142 of VIII in trench G rather than from one of Period IX.

Fragments of such jugs were not rare in upper levels of VIII; they included a dozen or more rims of Fine Black Burnished Ware with stripes in white paint, and a few handles of neat lunate and semi-circular section (FIG. 104, classes 4 and 5). Four of these rims came from the top level 139 of VIII G together with a hollow base of the same fabric; one of the rims had three broad horizontal stripes, another four thin lines, below it, while the base was decorated with groups of three vertical lines radiating from it. Another fragment of a jug body from the same level had traces of a group of vertical lines in white, and two others displayed groups of four or five diagonal stripes. The large vase 165 appears to have been a jug with a wide open spout of the cutaway type, but no other example of a cutaway spout was recognized from deposits of X–VIII.

Fragments of jugs of the Light Brown Burnished Ware typical of VII–VI were recovered from upper levels of VIII, but mostly from ones such as 145 and 144 in area B (trench Q) suspect of some degree of contamination with later material. Fragments of red burnished jugs were also found in these levels, together with at least five rims which appear to have belonged to jugs with unburnished red washes. The outward curving rim 166 with the stump of a handle which rose above it and unique incised decoration round the inside may have belonged to a jug of some kind.

Handles of jugs in these early periods were invariably set to the rim as they continued to be throughout VII–VI and later. The one possible exception was a fragment of rim from level 139 of Period VIII in trench G with a small strap handle set just below it but rising above it. The surface of this, however, was light brown, without any burnish, and it may have come from a jar of some kind.

161. (X Q 167) (PLATE 31) Jug with collar neck and handle of thick oval section rising above rim. Broken, but virtually complete. Ht. to rim 26. Diam. of rim c. 11. Roughly made, of rather coarse fabric. Grey-brown clay; outside surface uneven, with fine straw marks and some grit showing all over it, dominantly dusky brown, aggressively mottling to light brown and red with splodges of black; smoothed, or with a poor burnish.

162. (IX G 154) Handle with join to rim. Grey-brown and black to reddish; fine burnish.

163 (VIII G 153) Rim of jug or jar with stump of handle rising above it. A large hole made before firing below rim at point where handle joins it. Outside dark to light brown, burnished; inside dark brown, smoothed.

164. (X Q 167) (FIG. 124 with restored drawing. PLATE 32). Fragments of jug, including base, most of rim, and parts of carinated body. Warts on each side of rim and on carination. Thick-walled. Soft, crumbly fabric. Coarse clay, grey-brown at centre of break, with very large grit showing on inside surface which is rough, wiped, purplish in colour. Outside, together with inside of rim, grey-brown to dark brown and reddish, finely burnished. Probably Period V–IV.

165. (VIII G 139) (PLATE 32) Four fragments of large jug, including part of wide cutaway mouth. Light grey clay. Inside light grey, unburnished. Outside light greyish brown to darker brown with high burnish, polish-like and soapy to feel. Decoration in white: three horizontal stripes below mouth; band of lattice at base of neck; groups of four or five diagonal stripes on body.

166. (VIII G 139) Rim with stump of handle rising above it. Coarse grey-brown clay; surface lightish brown with poor burnish. Inside of rim decorated with a row of diagonal incisions.

Incised lines along or (as on 166) across the rim are said to be new and characteristic in Level IV at Hacilar (*Hacilar* i 112; ii 281 fig. 64: 10). Similar short lines were cut on the outer edges of bowl rims in the second phase of the Early Neolithic at Elateia in Central Greece (*Elateia* 175 pl. 54, d: 3-5, 7, 8). They also occur on rims of Early Neolithic I at Knossos (*BSA* lix (1964) 171 fig. 26, Stratum VI), and on some rims from Saliagos (*Saliagos* fig. 40: 17).

25. *Theriomorphic vases* 167-168 (FIG. 124)

One or two fragments of fine burnished ware may have come from vases in the shapes of animals or birds.

167. (X Q 164) Fragment. Grey-brown clay. Outside pale greyish brown to pinkish, very well burnished and soapy to feel. Inside pale greyish brown, smoothed.

168. (IX Q 156) (PLATE 30) Foot. Shades of light and dark brown; fine burnish.

    Cf. *Saliagos* fig. 77: 3. But 168 may not be from a theriomorphic vase! A rectangular box from Tsangli assigned to the Thessalian Middle Neolithic has four rather similar legs (Theochares, *Neolithic Greece* col. pl. 13 opp. 46).

(c) jars 169-293 (figs. 125-132)

Two basic shapes of jar were standard throughout these early periods: one bag-like, akin to types 34–35, with a hole-mouth, the other combining a more or less globular body with a collar neck as types 41-42.

Jars resembling types 41–42 occurred in a wide range of sizes, and might be of very fine fabric with elaborate decoration: normally in pattern burnish or incision in Period VIII, but sometimes in white or occasionally red paint in X–IX. Some of the larger jars of this kind were of comparatively coarse fabric, their surfaces with a poor burnish or even altogether unburnished.

Jars akin to types 34–35 were normally of coarse fabric, and were often it seems used as cooking vessels. But a number of rims, assignable to hole-mouthed jars of this kind rather than to bowls, were of fine burnished ware, and some of these had elaborate incised decoration.

Small bowl-like jars with S-shaped rims, akin to type 32 but with many variations (e.g. types 31, 36, 37), were very characteristic of Period VIII; but no fragments of them were recognised from pure deposits of X–IX.

Period X. Only a few remains of jars were recovered from levels of X, and these came almost entirely from area B (trench Q).

Rims of class A I appear to belong to jars akin to types 34-35. Out of eleven rims of this class from levels of X four were thick-walled as 179, while the others were thinner and came from smaller vases (e.g. 180). Most of these rims were of coarse cooking-pot type ware, made of gritty grey-brown clay, with surfaces shades of light and dark brown (once red) shading to dusky in colour, usually rough or roughly smoothed rather than burnished. Three of the rims (e.g. 180) had warts set below them; one being oblong and set more or less vertically as on 189 from level 158 of Period IX, the other two circular as on 180. Two rims (195, 196) were of class A II, the thinner of them (195) being of cooking-pot type ware like the rims of class A I.

Jars akin to types 41-42 were evidently common even in Period X. Five out of the twenty odd rims assignable to such jars from levels of X had remains of handles joining neck to shoulder. The surfaces of these rims were dominantly grey-brown in colour, sometimes light brown or red, with a fine burnish, or poorly burnished, or even upon occasion altogether unburnished. Remains of decoration in white paint consisting of groups of diagonal stripes were noted on three fragments, a rim (245), a shoulder with the stump of a handle (377), and the base 244 which may come from a jar of type 41. Some jars of this type appear to have been decorated with incision.

Several shoulders of grey-brown burnished ware with the join to the base of the neck distinctly marked probably came from jars of type 41. But a fragment from level 166 of X in area B (trench Q) with the neck flowing into the shoulder evidently belonged to a thick-walled vase resembling the large jars of Light Plain Ware characteristic of Periods VIII and VII–VI. This was of grey-brown clay shading to light brown at the outer, brick-red at the inner, edge, the surface with abundant straw impressions in it being light brown outside, reddish inside, smoothed but not burnished.

The exceptional rim 282 from X Q level 166 is like one from the Lower Cave at Ayio Gala

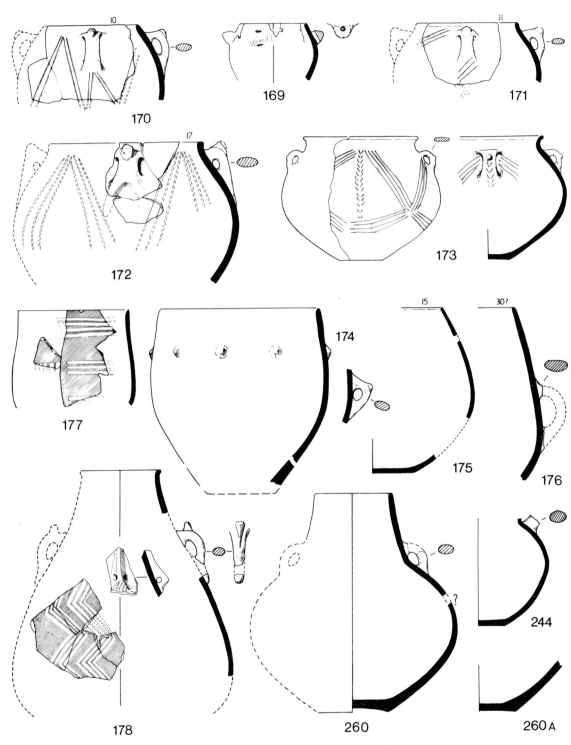

FIG. 125. Periods X–VIII. Jars. Scale 1/4, except 176 (1/8).

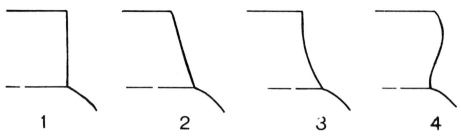

FIG. 126. Periods X–VIII. Rim varieties of type 41 jars: 1. straight and upright; 2. straight and sloping; 3. concave; 4. convex.

(AG 77) and can be paralleled from early contexts in the Aegean and the Near East. Other unique rims were 281 from level 164 in trench G and 283; but 283 from level 150 in area C (trench H) may belong to Period VIII rather than to X.

There is some evidence for the existence of carinated shapes in Period X, apart from the somewhat improbable jug 164. The fragment of a carinated body belonging to a small jug or jar was recovered from level 168 of X in area B (trench Q). The surface of this was grey-brown, burnished outside, rough inside. Another fragment (from level 166 in area B (trench Q)) from the lower part of a jar, or perhaps from a bowl of type 8, had an ogival profile like 142. The outside of this was light brown to dusky, well smoothed or burnished, the inside being only roughly smoothed. Carinated jar bodies are already attested in the Neolithic of Syria (e.g. *Sukas* iii 57 fig. 134 (from N 5). *Ugaritica* iv 504 fig. 27: 1 (Ras Shamra V A). *Judeideh* 76 fig. 48: 2–4 (Phase B)).

Period IX. Rims of class A I were common. More than half of the rims of class A I from levels of IX appeared to come from cooking jars of coarse ware. The surfaces of these ranged in colour from black through dusky brown and lighter brown to reddish, and they had a very poor burnish, or showed signs of being roughly smoothed or wiped. The surfaces of some other rims of class A I, especially those of some of the larger ones, were dominantly a lighter shade of brown to reddish, and a few of these light-coloured rims were fairly well burnished. Nine class A I rims, mostly of coarse cooking-pot type ware, had stumps of vertical handles. The handles usually seem to have been set on the shoulder of the vase not far below the rim (e.g. 187, 191); but on the large fragment 176 of type 35 the handle is on the swelling, which in this case is nearer to the base than to the rim. Once at least (184) a handle is surmounted by a wart.

One rim (188) of class A I, apparently from a large cooking jar, has the stump of a handle which rose vertically above it. This is interesting for comparison with a certain type of handled jar found in the Late Chalcolithic of Beycesultan in south-western Anatolia. Another rim (190) of this class with a vertically perforated lug below it can also be paralleled at Beycesultan in the Late Chalcolithic. A similar lug appears on the little squat bowl-like jar 169 of type 30. One rim (205) of this class reveals a pair of V-shaped string-holes made after firing, either for repairs, or perhaps for fastening a lid in place.

Warts seem to be common on these rims of class A I. Three rims have small vertical warts set below them, as on 189; two others (e.g. 186) boast circular warts. A pair of circular warts evidently flanked the lower end of the vertical strap handle on 187. The very large rim 182 has an irregular lump instead of a wart. Great interest attaches to the rim 422 of this class with elegant seed-shaped warts irregularly placed on the outside. These warts are closely paralleled in the Presesklo (E.N. III) horizon in Thessaly, and comparable wart-studded vases are typical of the early Neolithic levels at Nea Makri on the eastern coast of Attica. The Emporio rim may come from an import.

Rims assignable to class A II were not nearly as common as those of class A I in levels of IX. Some of these A II rims were from thick-walled, others from thin-walled vases; but like the A I rims they largely appear to have belonged to cooking jars. At least one rim of class A II had the stump of a vertical handle below it, like many A I rims (e.g. 187). The rim 199 with an unburnished red wash may be from an imported vase.

Two class A II rims (171, 172) with fine burnished surfaces evidently came from squat jars as type 31. Both have elaborate incised decoration, and handles surmounted by warts; the handle on 172 being provided with relief tails. These rims were from a deposit of level 158 in area B (trench Q) with some admixture of material from an early phase of Period VIII, to which they are perhaps to be assigned. But the small rim 198 evidently belonged to a similar bowl-like jar. At the same time, three other rims from the mixed deposit of level 158 in trench Q (230-2) are of class A III and come from bowls akin to type 32 characteristic of Period VIII. The rim 216 grouped under class A II has a groove round the base of the undifferentiated neck, making it like a class B II rim from a jar of types 41–42.

Jars akin to types 41–42 appear to have been the commonest shape of vase in use in Period IX, from levels of which large numbers of rims and fragments assignable to them were recovered. But some of the rims grouped here may have belonged to jugs of type 20 or to jars of other unidentified shapes, while some may have come from jars of similar shapes but without a sharp differentiation between neck and shoulder. These rims are sometimes straight, either upright (FIG. 126: 1), or sloping (2); sometimes concave (3), occasionally it seems convex (4). Three upright rims (286–8) with slight beads described under class B III may come from jars of types 41–42.

Jars of these types evidently varied much in size and fabric, the smaller tending to have the outside surfaces well burnished, and black, or light brown shading to red, in colour. Some of the larger jars also had well burnished surfaces, shades of black, often varying to grey, dark reddish, and light and dark brown, the dark brown sometimes having a tinge of purple in it. But the surfaces in the case of a good many of these larger jars were a nondescript shade of grey-brown with a poor burnish, and several of them were unburnished. Some of the jars had evidently been coated with a red wash, of which traces could be distinguished on burnished as well as on unburnished surfaces. One or two rims had a thin dark matt wash on the outside, ranging in colour from dusky through dark purplish brown to light brown. Some jars, especially those with unburnished surfaces, were made of very coarse clay with large lumps of grit in it. Jars like these tended to be rough and irregular in shape and finish. But many of the ones with a fine burnish appear to have been well and evenly made.

Some eight fragments of necks of jars of types 41–42 with handles attached to them were recovered from the mixed deposit of level 158 in trench Q, and all of these handles were surmounted by warts; some came from small jars with incised decoration, but others were from large ones of coarse ware. The setting of warts on the handles of jars of these types may be a fashion which began at the end of Period IX or in VIII. There is certainly no suggestion of a preponderance of wart-surmounted handles on jars of these shapes from earlier levels of IX. The three complete handles from such jars from pure levels of IX in trench Q do not have warts, and it is significant that one of them is the exceptionally neat and elegant 250 from a small finely burnished jar of type 42.

Two or three rims of jars of types 41–42 from levels of IX had traces of painted decoration, consisting of groups of diagonal lines, either in white as on 247, or once at least (249) in red. But incised decoration may have been more usual on jars of these shapes to judge from fragments of them from level 158 in area B (trench Q). The rim 246 in shape and fabric like 247 from a level of X may come from a jar akin to type 41 imported from one of the Cyclades.

Period VIII. Rims of class A I were common as in levels of IX, and at least half of them appear to have belonged to cooking jars. The complete profile of one cooking jar (174) with a rim of this class was restorable. These cooking jar rims were normally rather pointed (e.g. 210), and might be thickened like 214; but some were flattened as on 174. In the case of 211, however, the flattened rim merges into one of the more usual pointed variety. The large fragment 174 has a row of warts below the rim, like 206; another rim of a cooking jar from wall 16 in area A (trench G) has an oblong wart set horizontally below it.

These jars were of coarse ware, the surfaces being sombre in colour, shades of dark grey-brown to black with a suggestion of lighter brown and reddish patches, and having a poor burnish or none at all. But a number of class A I rims came from jars of noticeably finer fabric, which appear to have been rather squatter in shape, with markedly less upright rims, than most of the cooking jars with rims of this class. They approximate to type 30 (e.g. 170), and merge into type 31 with rims of class A II.

Class A II rims are more prominent than they were in levels of X–IX, and they mostly come from jars of finer ware, although some may have belonged to cooking jars. Some rims assignable to this class (e.g. 223) evidently come from narrow-mouthed jars, akin to type 41, but without any differentiation between neck and shoulder.

Jars akin to types 30–31 had more or less well burnished surfaces ranging in colour from light brown through reddish to dark grey-brown and black. They were quite often decorated with incision (e.g. 170). Vertical handles, usually set on the shoulder (e.g. 170, 212), but once at least (225) on the rim, were normally it seems surmounted by warts. Wart-surmounted handles also occurred, however, on jars of coarse fabric reminiscent of cooking jars (e.g. 226). Some of the jars of fine burnished ware evidently had a pair of elaborately tailed lugs, as seen on 228, in place of handles. One or two rims belonging to such jars preserved V-shaped string-holes made after firing, whether for repairs or to help keep a lid in place (215, 221A).

The smaller examples of these jars like 220 merge into little jars with out-turned rims of class A III. These seem to have been characteristic of Period VIII; they were not recognised from any pure levels of X–IX, and were rare in the succeeding Period VII. The only complete profile recovered (173) is assignable to type 32; but there was evidently a great variety in the shapes of small jars with rims of this class, and they appear to have ranged from squat bowl-like vases of type 32, to deep narrow-mouthed vessels like the unique 178 of type 37. At one end of the scale jars of type 32 merge into bowls of type 14 with outward curving rims, while at the other end of it narrow-mouthed jars like 178 shade into ones with differentiated necks of type 41.

On 178 the swelling was low down on the body just above the base, and some of the squat wide-mouthed jars with rims of class A III may have had the swelling set low down in this manner (cf. type 33, with rim of class A II). But the complete profile 173 has the swelling about half way between rim and base, and this may have been more usual.

Some of these little jars were of Fine Black Burnished Ware; others had dark brown surfaces with a fine burnish. But in general surfaces were not well burnished, and ranged in colour from dusky shades of grey-brown to light brown and occasionally red. One or two rims of coarse ware with unburnished surfaces may have come from varieties of cooking jars, akin to types 34-35 but with rims of class A III.

A number of the little wart-surmounted handles common in Period VIII evidently belonged to small jars of this kind (e.g. 173). But some jars had vertically perforated lugs in place of handles (e.g. 234). Such lugs might have tails in relief, straight or ending in curls, as on 228 with a rim of class A II.

Most of the small jars with rims of class A III were plain and undecorated. Some evidently had warts on their shoulders, like 239. The large rim 236 boasted elaborate decoration in pattern burnish; but when decoration occurred it was normally incised, as on 173.

It was noticeable that the larger jars of fine burnished ware or with incised decoration tended to have rims of classes A I–II, while the smaller ones had rims of class A III; but some A III rims like 233 evidently came from large jars.

Jars of types 41–42 continued to be very common as in Periods X–IX. Over 250 rim fragments assignable to such jars were recovered from levels of VIII. Jars of these types have necks more or less clearly differentiated from their bodies; but they merge into jars of similar shapes with no clearly marked differentiation at the base of the neck, which flows in an even S-curve into the shoulder as in the case of 223.

The outsides of these jars of types 41–42 in Period VIII were almost invariably it seems more or less well burnished, the surfaces ranging in colour from black (with a fine burnish, especially in the case of small jars, such as 265 of type 42), through grey and shades of grey-brown, purplish red-brown and red. Red surfaces at any rate evidently reflect the application of a red wash. The insides of necks, and even of bodies, were often more or less well burnished, but might be left rough. There was a considerable range in the size of these jars. The rims were upright or inward leaning; some were thickened (e.g. 279). A number of rims, apparently from jars of these types, had beads (277, 291, 292). A few short differentiated rims of small jars are grouped here (237, 238): one of them (278) may come from an import.

A considerable number, although by no means all, of the handles belonging to such jars were now surmounted by warts. Some of these handles, including many of those with warts, were very small, like horizontally perforated lugs. These lug-handles tended to come from the smaller jars of fine burnished ware. One handle (272) from a jar of type 41 has tails in relief. Some vertically perforated lugs with similar relief tails may come from such jars, but others were certainly from bowl-like jars of types 30–32. Warts were sometimes placed on the shoulder just below the bottom of the neck. A handle with a wart at its base came from a deposit of level 145 in area B (trench Q) which may have included material of Period VII. Another handle from the same deposit was evidently flanked by warts.

Several especially of the smaller jars of types 41-42 were decorated with pattern burnish or incision. Incision when it occurs is often elaborate, and may cover most of the body, but it hardly if ever encroaches on the neck. Pattern burnish on the other hand is regularly found on the neck and rim, and may spread over the body of the jar as well, as seen on 265. Vases with pattern burnish were normally of fine grey-black burnished ware; but sometimes had light brown or red surfaces. Incised vases might be of any colour, including black, shades of grey-brown, light brown, and red.

In the upper levels of VIII were found a number of fragments of large jars with outward curving rims. Some at any rate of these jars had the neck sharply differentiated from the shoulder, so that the rims are assignable to class B. Many, if not most, appear to have been fitted with vertical strap handles set on or below the rim. These large jars were characteristically of Light Plain Ware, with surfaces unburnished or showing traces of a very superficial 'stroke' burnish. Sometimes the surface had a white slip, once at any rate (293) with a tinge of green in it. Some jar rims of comparable shapes had an unburnished red, or occasionally light brown, wash.

A. *Jars with rims of class A undifferentiated from the rest of the body*

(1) **Types 30-37. Vases of which the shapes could be restored** (FIG. 125)

30. *Squat bowl-jars with simple incurving rims (class A I) (*FIG. 125)

169. (IX G 154) Small jar; about a third of rim with one of pair (?) of vertically perforated lugs on shoulder. One string-hole apparently made before firing preserved just to right of lug. Grey-brown, burnished; less well burnished inside.

170. (VIII Q 146, 145) (PLATE 32) Rim, with one of pair (?) of small vertical strap handles on shoulder. Handle surmounted by wart. Light to dark brown, well burnished outside, less well inside. Bold incised decoration (diagonal lines).

31. *Squat bowl-jars with ogival rims (class A II)* (FIG. 125)

171. (IX/VIII Q 158?, 146) (PLATE 32) Probably Period VIII. Rim, with one of pair (?) of small vertical strap handles on shoulder. Handle surmounted by wart. Outside red to dark brown with fine burnish; inside dark grey-brown, less well burnished. Incised decoration.

172. (IX/VIII Q 158?, 148, 146, 145) (PLATE 32) Probably Period VIII. Rim, with one of pair (?) of small vertical strap handles on shoulder. Ribs in relief splaying like tails from bottom of handle, which surmounted by wart. Light grey to light brown clay; surface shades of lighter and darker brown to grey, well burnished outside, smoothed rather than burnished inside. Incised decoration.

32. *Squat bowl-jars with outward-curving rims (class A III)*

173. (VIII Q 146) (FIG. 125. PLATE 31) Profile, with one of pair of small vertical strap handles on shoulder. Ht. 13.3. Diam. of rim 12.5, of body 17. Handle with small wart. Base sunk. Thin-walled. Fairly well fired. Grey-brown clay with fine grit; surface mottled, shades of dark grey and grey-brown, burnished. Incised decoration; diagonal lines with vertical chevrons on handles and on shoulders each side between them.

34. *Jars with simple incurving rims (class A I)*

A large number of rims of class A I evidently belonged to jars of this or allied types like 35.

174. (VIII Q 147) (FIG. 125. PLATE 32) Rim and most of profile. Ht. preserved 16. Diam. *c.* 15. Row of warts below rim. A small vertical strap handle surmounted by a wart from VIII Q 145 may be one of a pair from this vase. Grey-brown clay with abundant straw. Surface shades of dark to lighter brown and dusky with abundant straw impressions; outside wiped, inside smoothed, rather than burnished.

35. *Large jars with simple incurving rims (class A I), low shoulders, and vertical handles (*FIG. 125)

175. (IX G 154) Profile, restored. Part of base, fragments of body, and one scrap of rim preserved. Diam. of rim *c.* 16, of body *c.* 22, of base 9. Thin-walled; rather coarse clay, straw impressions showing in surface. Inside grey-brown, to dusky (especially in bottom of base), rather well burnished. Outside reddish brown mottling to dusky, less well burnished.

176. (VIII G 141) Rim and fragments with stump of strap handle. Ht. of largest fragment 38. Gritty clay, grey-black at core shading to red-brown at edges; surface dominantly dark brown shading to light brown and dusky with reddish splodges. Outside with poor stroke burnish, inside smoothed.

36. *Bowl-jars with wide mouths, tall outward-curving rims (class A III), and low shoulders*

177. (VIII Q 146, 145) (FIG. 125. PLATE 33) Fragment of rim and scraps. Ht. preserved 10. Diam. estimated *c.* 12. Fabric cf. 178. Greyish brown clay. Outside crimson red with small dusky patches, decorated with pattern burnish incorporating groups of vertical and horizontal lines; inside orange, smoothed.

37. *Tall jars with narrow mouths, outward-curving rims (class A III), and low shoulders*

The restored vase 178 was the only example of this type noted. Its shape has been inferred from the few pieces of it recovered. While most of these came from a deposit of level 145 with some possible admixture of Period VII, one fragment was from a pure deposit of VIII. In some respects, notably in the colour of the inside surface, this unique vase is reminiscent of the micaceous wares, apparently imports, found in levels of VIII in the same area B (trench Q). It and 177, which is of comparable fabric, may therefore have been imported from some other centre.

178. (VIII Q 146?, 145) (FIG. 125. PLATE 33) Two scraps of rim, one small vertical strap handle, one horizontally perforated lug (probably upside down in drawing and photo), and body fragments with pattern burnish. Greyish brown clay. Inside orange, well smoothed rather than burnished. Outside red shading to light brown with dusky patches; fine pattern burnish incorporating vertical chevrons with two groups of three thin lines separated by a thick one: there may have been a vertical strip of this decoration below the lug, or two or more strips of it in intervals between lug or lugs and handles. The lug appears to be an elaborate version of the animal head type as found at Hacilar, like 365–368.

These two pattern burnished vases (177, 178) with their red surfaces are reminiscent of the red pattern burnish ware at home towards the end of the Late Neolithic on the western side of the Aegean (*Kephala* 11 f.). *Athenian Agora* xiii 27 no. 35 pls. 4, 69, in particular has a design very like that on 177. But in general this western Late Neolithic pattern burnish seems coarser, and it may belong to a later horizon in time, even if it is in some way related. The pattern burnish of Beşik Tepe in the Troad, for instance, is said to be most commonly red-brown surfaced (*PZ* xxiii (1932) 126 ff.). This horizon at Beşik Tepe is probably contemporary with Emporio VIII, and if 177 and 178 are imports they may have come from that region.

(2) **Undifferentiated jar rims: class A I** (FIGS. 127, 128)
Rims of this class were common in levels of all the early periods from X onwards. The tops tend to be rather pointed, but some (174, 182, 185, 211) are flattened; the rim may change from pointed

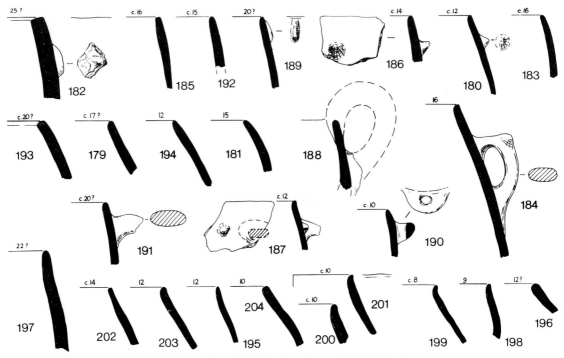

FIG. 127. Periods X–IX. Jar rims: classes A I–II. Scale 1/3.

to flattened on the same vase (e.g. 211). Similar flattened rims appear on vases of shapes like 174 at Çatal Hüyük and in the Kizilkaya Culture of southern Anatolia (*AS* xi (1961) 162 fig. 1: 6-9, 23; 166 ff. figs. 4; 5: 3, 7). Some thickened rims of Neolithic hole-mouth jars from Mersin are flattened in a comparable manner.

A number of class A I rims had vertical handles set below them. One exceptional handle rising from the top of the rim (188) is interesting for comparison with a type common in the Late Chalcolithic of Beycesultan. Conical warts, more or less circular, are not infrequent on these rims; and on the jar 174 of type 34 with a rim of this class there was a row of such warts. Short

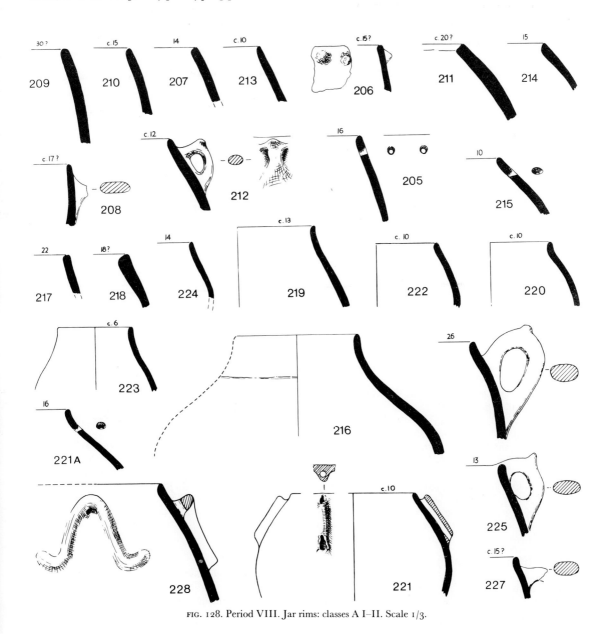

FIG. 128. Period VIII. Jar rims: classes A I–II. Scale 1/3.

vertical oblong warts are also found on such rims as early as Period X (e.g. 189 cf. 206). There is a long horizontal wart on the shoulder of 217 from level 140 of VIII.

A majority of the rims of this class are from cooking jars of coarse ware akin to types 34 and 35. The surfaces of these cooking jar rims tend to be sombre, ranging in colour from black through dusky brown and lighter brown to reddish, and are either altogether unburnished, or have been only slightly smoothed, or given a very superficial burnish. Some unburnished rims from the later levels of Period VIII in trench G have an obvious red wash, and traces of a red wash could be detected on some earlier rims (e.g. 182). The reddish or purple tinge noticeable in the dark surfaces of many other rims suggest that the application of such a wash was usual.

Some of the rims from larger jars have a light brown to reddish surface, which upon occasion has been given a fairly good burnish on the outside. Such rims presumably came, not from cooking vessels, but from storage jars, which may have been akin to type 38 in shape. Rims of small size with finely burnished surfaces grouped here may come from bowl-jars of type 30, if not from bowls of type 6.

179. (X Q 165) Cooking pot type ware; coarse grey-brown clay; surface shades of light and dark brown to dusky, roughly smoothed.
180. (X Q 166) (PLATE 38) Conical wart below rim. Fabric as 179.
181. (IX G 155) Grey-brown; fine burnish. Two others similar: one light brown with fine burnish; the other unburnished, blackish outside, purple-brown inside.
182. (IX G 155) Large rim with irregular wart. Greyish brown to brick-red clay. Outside light brown to reddish, well smoothed or burnished; inside red, roughly smoothed.
183. (IX G 154) Shades of reddish to dusky and light brown; rather poor burnish.
184. (VIII Q 146) Small vertical strap handle surmounted by wart on shoulder. Outside dusky purple grey-brown, with coarse burnish; inside less well burnished.
185. (IX Q 159) Cooking pot ware; coarse grey-black clay; surface dusky brown, wiped or smoothed outside and in.
186. (IX Q 159) (PLATE 33) Conical wart below rim. Cooking pot ware; coarse light greyish clay; surface light brown to dusky and reddish, unburnished.
187. (IX Q 156) Stump of vertical strap handle with conical wart beside it. Cooking pot ware; coarse grey-brown clay; surface unburnished.
188. (IX Q 158) Stump of vertical handle rising above rim. Cooking pot ware; coarse grey-brown clay; surface dusky to purple-brown, unburnished. One or two others similar.
   Cf. *Beycesultan* i 85 f., 89 shape 13: Late Chalcolithic 2. Not common, but typical of L.C. 2, from Level XXXIII onwards. A large vertical handle of circular section rises from the top of the rim of a ladle or cup from Sesklo assigned to the 'monochrome phase' of the Thessalian Early Neolithic (E.N.I) (Theochares, *Neolithic Greece* fig. 213: b).
189. (IX Q 158) (PLATE 33) Small vertical wart. Coarse grey-black clay; surface dusky to reddish brown with tinge of purple, unburnished.
190. (IX Q 158) (PLATE 33) Vertically perforated lug. Cooking pot ware; coarse grey-brown clay; surface light brown to dusky, unburnished.
   For similar lugs cf. *Beycesultan* i 84 Fig. P. 6: 3, and 90 shape 12 (not of this shape, but with similar lugs). Lugs of this type occur from Levels XXXV-XXXIII (end of L.C. 1 and early part of L.C. 2).
191. (VIII Q 148) Stump of vertical strap handle. Cooking pot ware; coarse grey-brown clay; surface unburnished.
192. (IX Q 158) Cooking pot type ware; coarse grey-black clay; surface dusky to light brown, unburnished.
193. (IX Q 158) Coarse clay; outside dark brown with poor burnish; inside dark purple-brown, wiped.
194. (IX Q 158) Cooking pot type ware; coarse grey-brown clay; abundant straw impressions showing in surface, which dusky to dark and light brown with slight traces of smoothing or poor burnish.

(3) Undifferentiated jar rims: class A II (FIGS. 127, 128)

195. (X Q 168) (PLATE 38) Cooking pot type ware; surface shades of light and dark to dusky brown, smoothed outside and in.
196. (X Q 166) Grey clay; outside light brown, smoothed rather than burnished; inside pale brown, roughly smoothed.

197. (IX G 154) Gritty clay, brick-red in break; surface light brown to reddish, smoothed but not burnished.

198. (IX G 153) Gritty clay, grey at centre of break, light brown at edges; surface irregular, light brown, with poor burnish.

199. (IX Q 156) Thin-walled; but fabric coarse, and surface irregular. Greyish clay, with large grit and straw impressions together with some specks of silvery mica showing in surface. Outside with red wash, unburnished. Possibly an import.

200. (IX Q 159) Coarse sandy orange clay with thin pale wash, unburnished. Another similar from IX Q level 156 with traces of red wash, unburnished, inside.

201. (IX Q 158) Coarse greyish clay; surface light brown to reddish, apparently unburnished.

202. (IX Q 158) Coarse clay with straw impressions in surface. Outside shades of light and dark brown to reddish, well burnished; inside greyish, wiped.

203. (IX Q 158) White Slipped Ware (?). Coarse clay; surface dirty whitish, perhaps owing to slip, smoothed but not burnished.

204. (IX Q 158) Outside light brown with fine burnish; inside greyish, wiped.

205. (IX Q 158) Holes made after firing cf. 215, 221A. Outside light reddish brown mottling to darker brown and dusky, unburnished; inside dark grey, roughly smoothed.

206. (VIII G ?141) Conical warts. Light greyish brown clay; surface rough, unburnished.

207. (VIII G 140) Greyish brown with poor burnish outside and in.

208. (VIII G wall 16) Stump of vertical strap handle. Gritty clay; surface smoothed rather than burnished, dusky brown outside, light (salmon pink) brown inside.

209. (VIII G 139) Gritty grey-brown clay; surface smoothed, dusky outside, dull lightish (salmon pink) brown inside. Another similar: outside surface variegated, shades of grey, light brown and red, with poor burnish; inside grey-brown.

210. (VIII Q 146) Cooking pot type ware; surface wiped, dusky brown outside, lightish brown inside. Several others similar.

211. (VIII Q 147) Coarse grey-brown clay; surface light reddish brown, smoothed but not burnished.

212. (VIII Q 146) Small vertical strap handle surmounted by wart. Outside light brown with fine burnish; inside less well burnished.

213. (VIII Q 146) Cooking pot type ware. Outside dark brown mottling to lighter brown and reddish, smoothed but not burnished; inside dusky black, smoothed.

214. (VIII Q 145) Coarse grey clay; surface dusky grey-black, smoothed but not burnished, outside and in.

215. (VIII Q 145) V-shaped hole made after firing cf. 221A. Coarse grey clay. Outside light brown, well burnished; inside darker, wiped.

216. (IX Q 158) (PLATE 34) Fragments, including part of rim with rough groove round base of neck. Vase apparently over-fired at time of manufacture. Grey-brown clay. Outside surface badly cracked by heat, red mottling to light and dark purplish brown and dusky, unburnished; inside red of various shades, roughly smoothed.

217. (VIII G 140) Greyish brown, wiped outside and in.

218. (VIII G wall 16) Angle of rim uncertain. Gritty clay. Outside reddish with poor burnish; inside orange, rough.

219. (VIII Q 146) Gritty grey clay. Outside with light brown to red wash, apparently burnished, but worn; inside grey-brown, smoothed.

220. (VIII Q 146) Outside grey-black with fine burnish; inside roughly smoothed. Another similar.

221A. (VIII Q 145) V-shaped hole made after firing cf. 215. Light brown to dusky, well burnished outside, wiped inside.

221-223. (VIII Q 145) Typical rims of Period VIII.

224. (VIII Q 145) Coarse greyish clay; surface grey-brown to black with poor burnish.

225. (VIII Q 145) Vertical strap handle surmounted by wart and set to rim. Coarse clay; surface grey-brown to dusky, burnished.

226. (VIII Q 145) Handle as 225, but set below rim. Coarse grey-black clay; surface smoothed but not burnished, light reddish brown to dusky grey outside, grey inside.

227. (VIII Q 145) Stump of strap handle set below rim. Grey-black clay shading to light brown at edges; outside with burnished red to light brown wash continuing red around inside of rim.

228. (VIII Q 145) Rim, and non-joining fragment apparently from same vase, with vertically perforated lug with curly ended tails in relief. Rather coarse grey clay; surface grey-brown to black. Outside with fine polish-like burnish; inside rough, with superficial burnish.

(4) Undifferentiated jar rims: class A III (FIG. 129)

The rims studied and drawn here were almost all from levels of Period VIII; two (230, 231) came from level 158 which was of Period IX, but had an admixture of material from an early deposit of VIII; none were certainly from pure levels of X or IX. Several of these rims had belonged to vases with finely burnished surfaces, some of which may have been in fact bowls. The rim 243 appears to come from a handled jug cf. type 20.

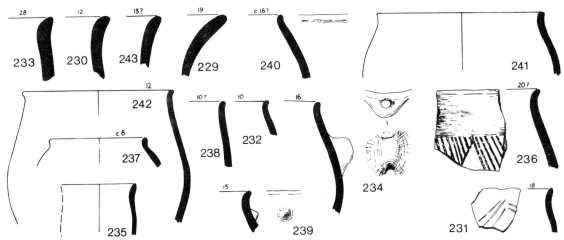

FIG. 129. Period VIII. Jar rims: class A III. Scale 1/3.

229. (VIII Q 148) Red, shading to light brown around rim; very fine 'stroke' burnish.
230. (IX/VIII Q 158) Light brownish grey; very fine burnish.
231. (IX/VIII Q 158) Roughly made; soft fabric. Grey-black clay; surface black, with abundant straw impressions, burnished outside, less well inside. Incised decoration.
232. (IX/VIII Q 158) Sandy red-brown clay; surface brownish grey-black with fine burnish.
233. (VIII G 140) Grey-brown clay; outside well burnished, inside less well.
234. (VIII Q 146) Small horizontal strap handle low on shoulder. Rather coarse fabric; surface light brown to dusky with poor burnish outside and in.
235. (VIII Q 146) Thin-walled, but of rather coarse fabric with irregular surface. Grey-brown to black clay. Outside burnished, inside rough, unburnished.
236. (VIII Q 146) Grey-black, burnished outside and in. Pattern burnish (hatched triangles ?).
237. (VIII Q 146) Fine light brownish grey clay; surface smoothed or burnished, but worn.
238. (VIII Q 146) Grey-brown to black. Outside with rather superficial burnish, inside wiped.
239. (VIII Q 146) Conical wart. Grey-black; very fine burnish.
240. (VIII Q 146) Rough groove on outside below rim, as if some kind of cord or withe impressed into clay while still wet. Outside grey-brown shading to light brown, burnished; inside grey-brown with superficial burnish.
241, 242. (VIII Q 145, and 145 with possible admixture of VII). Typical rims.
243. (VIII Q 145) Light grey-brown; fine burnish. Possibly from jug cf. type 20.

B. *Jars with necks or rims of class B more or less clearly differentiated from rest of body* (FIGS. 130-132)

(1) Types 41 and 42. Restorable shapes and rims of class B I-II (FIGS. 130, 131)

41. *Globular jars with collar necks (class B I) and a pair of small vertical handles joining neck to shoulder*

42. *Small pyxis-like jars with wide mouths, low collar necks, and a pair of handles joining neck to shoulder*

The shape of vase of which types 41 and 42 were varieties appears to have been the one that was in most common use in the early Periods X–VIII. Some 20 rims assignable to jars of this shape

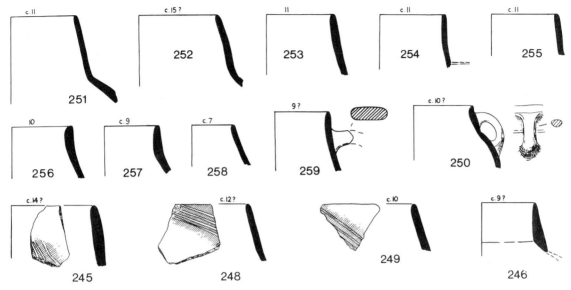

FIG. 130. Periods X–IX. Jar rims: classes B I–II. Scale 1/3.

were recognised from levels of X, over 150 from those of IX, and over 250 from those of VIII. But some of these rims may have belonged to jugs of type 20, or to other types of which the shapes were not detected.

The only jar of type 41 of which the complete shape could be restored was 261 from level 146 of VIII; and the fragmentary small jar 265 of type 42 came from the same deposit. There was evidently a great variation in the sizes of jars of these shapes, and in the relationships between the diameter of rims and bodies and height. Bodies as far as could be ascertained were basically globular, necks being more or less clearly differentiated from shoulders. Rims normally sloped inwards or stood upright; but one rim had a bulging profile as FIG. 126: 4, like rims of comparable jars from Chalcolithic Palestine. A number of rims were thickened, e.g. 279 from a high level of VIII. Sometimes, as in the case of 277 from level 145 of VIII, the thickening formed a bead on the outside of the rim.

There were normally two handles joining neck and shoulder and set on opposite sides of the vase; no evidence was forthcoming for the existence of more than two handles. In the case of the smaller jars of this shape in Period VIII the handles tended to be diminutive in size, resembling horizontally perforated lugs. Virtually all of these lug-handles from small jars and many of the others were surmounted by warts. The elegant horned handles, of which numbers were recovered from these early levels, may well have come from large jars of this shape. Some jars appear to have been fitted with vertically perforated lugs. Warts are attested on their shoulders in some instances.

Fabric. There was a considerable variety in fabric corresponding to the range in size. Some of the smallest jars had black surfaces with very fine burnish, soapy to the feel (Fine Black Burnished Ware); while others boasted finely burnished light brown or red surfaces. In the case of the larger jars the outside surface might be well burnished, and variegated, shades of black or grey-brown, to grey, dark brown with a purplish tinge, dark reddish and light brown. But a good many of the larger jars had surfaces nondescript shades of grey-brown with a poor burnish, or, in

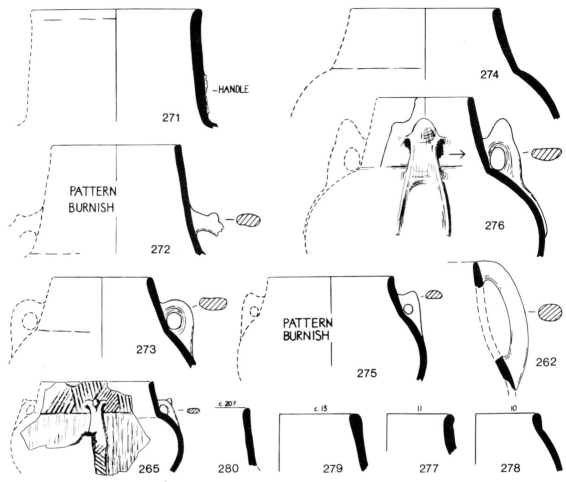

FIG. 131. Period VIII. Jar rims: class B II. Scale 1/3.

some cases, none at all. Some of the unburnished jars, and a number of the burnished ones, showed clear traces of a red wash. In one or two cases where the surfaces of the vases had been left unburnished it was possible to detect a thin matt wash ranging from dusky through dark purplish brown to light brown in colour. Most, if not all, of the more numerous jars of burnished ware may have been coated with a wash, basically red or light brown in colour when it was applied; but the burnishing of the surface had usually made it difficult to be certain about this. In the case of the jars of burnished ware the inside of the neck was often smoothed or burnished like the outside surface. Sometimes, however, when the inside of the neck was left unburnished, it preserved clear traces of a wash.

Many of the jars of fine burnished ware seem to have been well and evenly made. But some, especially of the unburnished ones, were of very coarse fabric with large lumps of grit in the clay, several of them being irregular in shape with surfaces carelessly finished.

Decoration. A good many of the smaller jars of fine burnished ware were decorated with pattern burnish, their surfaces being normally black, but sometimes light brown to reddish: others, especially those of the earliest periods X/IX, had decoration in white paint (e.g. 247,

249). But in Period VIII if not earlier the commonest type of decoration found on vases of this shape whatever their size was incision. This incised decoration in Period VIII might be very elaborate even on large vases (e.g. PLATE 34).

A few rims had small V-shaped holes bored after firing through them. In several cases these were in pairs, normally set just below the rim (e.g. 260); but in one instance at least such holes occur at the base of the neck. The holes were evidently meant for string, but are unlikely to have been made for string handles, since jars of these types are regularly supplied with handles or string-hole lugs. If they were made for tying lids in place it is curious that no certain examples of clay lids were recovered from levels of Periods X–VIII. In two or three cases pairs of holes were irregularly spaced on jar necks, and once as many as three irregularly spaced holes of this kind occur on the neck near the stump of a handle. In these instances, and when such holes occur on fragments from the bodies of jars, it seems clear that they were made to hold string used to strengthen the vase or repair cracks in it; and all such holes, wherever they occur, may have served this function. Rivet holes of this type are common on the early pottery of the Levant.

One or two jars assignable to these types but of exotic fabric may be imports, perhaps from the Cyclades, where similar jars were at home (e.g. 246, 262, 278). The two rims 246, 246A, of Fine Light Grey Burnished Ware from levels of IX and X are of particular interest in this connection.

244. (X Q 167) Base and large parts of body, apparently from a jar of type 41. Ht. preserved *c.* 11. Diam. of body *c.* 16. Grey-brown to black clay; surface grey-brown to black with fine burnish outside, less well burnished inside. Traces of decoration in white paint (groups of three thin diagonal lines).

245. (X Q 168, 165) Rim. Angle not certain. Grey-brown with fine burnish. Traces of decoration in white paint (group of diagonal lines).

246. (IX Q 156) (PLATE 35) Rim. Fine Light Grey Burnished Ware. Very fine clay, brownish grey, with silvery mica showing in surface. Inside of rim well smoothed, but outside worn. Fine lattice impressions on inside of body, as if vase formed round a basketry core. Probably an import cf. 424.

247. (X G 163) (PLATE 35) Neck of similar profile to 246 and of comparable fabric, but without any trace of mica. Battleship grey clay; surface well smoothed outside and in. Probably an import like 246.

248. (IX Q 156) Rim. Surface dark brown outside shading to light brown inside with fine burnish. Traces of decoration in white paint (four thin diagonal stripes).

249. (IX Q 156) Rim. Grey-brown with fine burnish. Decoration in red paint (group of diagonal stripes).

250. (VIII Q 148) (PLATE 33) Rim with handle. Grey-brown with fine burnish outside, wiped inside.

251–259. (IX/VIII Q 158) Typical rims.

260. (IX/VIII Q 158) (PLATE 34) Rim with horned handles and rivet holes. Coarse ware.

261. (VIII Q 146) (PLATE 32) Neck and two bases, one of which may belong with it. Silvery Grey Ware. Very fine hard fabric. Surface even without any sign of grit or straw impressions, shades of dark grey to light brownish grey, burnished. Metallic in appearance, and perhaps a deliberate imitation of silver.

262. (VIII Q 146) (PLATE 35) Rim with large handle to it. Micaceous Ware. Sandy greyish brown to brick red clay; surface red, with sand and abundant silvery mica showing in it, smoothed rather than burnished. Fragment of base of similar fabric may come from same vase. Probably imported.

263. (VIII Q 146) (PLATE 34) Rim and part of body with handle surmounted by wart. Light brown to dusky, burnished. Bold incised decoration, including multiple chevrons, and concentric lozenges below handle.

264. (VIII Q 146) (PLATE 34) Rim with handle surmounted by wart, and fragment of body apparently from same vase. Surface dusky to light brown in places, burnished. Body fragment with bold incised decoration (multiple chevrons).

265. (VIII Q 146) (PLATE 35) Part of rim and body with handle surmounted by wart from small jar of type 42. Ht. preserved 7.4. Diam. of rim *c.* 9. Soft fabric; dark reddish brown clay with grit and straw. Surface black, finely burnished outside, less well inside. Elaborate pattern burnish decoration.

266. (VIII Q 146) (PLATE 34) Fragment of body with pattern burnish.

267–270. (VIII Q 145) (PLATE 34) Rims with pattern burnish.

271–276. (VIII Q 145 with possible admixture of material from VII) (PLATE 35) Typical rims.

277. (VIII/VII Q 145) Rim with slight bead. Coarse grey clay; surface light brown, well burnished outside, smoothed or with a poor burnish inside.

278. (VIII/VII Q 145) (PLATE 35) Rim. Surface light brownish grey, burnished but worn, with some straw impressions showing in it. Possibly an import.

279. (VIII G 139) Rim. Reddish brown; outside with fine burnish, inside less well burnished.

280. (VIII Q 144) Rim. Coarse grey clay. Inside light brownish grey; outside with burnished red wash.

(2) Differentiated jar rims: class B III (FIG. 132)

Some of these (e.g. 290–2) may come from jars of types 41-42. Sharply differentiated jar rims like 282 of Period X occur from the beginning of the Neolithic in Crete and on the Greek mainland (cf. AG 77 with references).

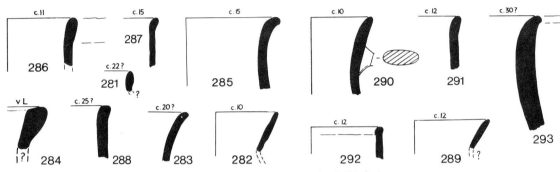

FIG. 132. Periods X–VIII. Jar rims: class B III. Scale 1/3.

281. (X G 164) Orange clay, fired an even colour throughout, with fine white, black, and red grit; surface with thin slip of paler colour, smooth but not burnished.
    For the rim shape cf. *Sukas* iii 41 f. fig. 99 (from N 8) of Dark-Faced Burnished Ware.

282. (X Q 166) Grey-brown clay. Outside with light brown to red wash, burnished; inside dark brown, burnished.
    For this type of rim cf. AG 77, with references to early examples from elsewhere in the Aegean and the Near East.

283. (VIII H 150) Grey-brown clay; surface lightish brown, wiped.

284. (VIII G 141) Hard fabric; gritty grey clay; surface light reddish brown with poor burnish.

285. (IX Q 156) Light Plain Ware. Pale greyish clay shading to light brown at edges; surface with traces of paler brown slip, smoothed but not burnished.

286. (IX Q 158) Coarse greyish clay shading to light brown at edges; surface with thin dull purplish to dusky wash, unburnished, outside and in.

287. (IX Q 158) Surface pale brown, irregular, but smoothed.

288. (IX Q 158) Coarse light brown clay; outside surface smoothed.

289. (VIII G 140) Gritty grey-brown clay. Outside dark reddish, well burnished; inside less well burnished or worn.

290. (VIII Q 146) Stump of strap handle. Gritty grey clay, light brown at surface, which has grit and straw impressions showing in it. Surface not smoothed or burnished, but covered with a thin reddish brown shading to purplish wash, apparently slightly lustrous. Possibly an import.

291. (VIII Q 146) Red-brown clay; surface red, burnished outside, smoothed or with poor burnish inside.

292. (VIII Q 146) Fine light brownish grey clay; surface smoothed or burnished, but worn.

293. (VIII Q 144) Coarse grey clay. Outside with thick rather greenish white slip, smoothed or with poor burnish; inside light brown, rough.

(E) PITHOI 294–307 (FIG. 133)

Remains of jars of exceptional size which qualify for the name of pithoi were found even in the lowest levels reached. The fabric of these vases, and the way in which they were regularly decorated with bands in relief, were also distinctive. Rims were simple, usually more or less flat-topped, but once at least (304) rounded like 746 of Period VI. Large vertical strap handles of oval section from pithoi were already attested in levels of X. Bases seem to have been flat, and more or less clearly differentiated from the body.

The fabric is in general hard as the result of exceptionally thorough firing, so that the clay, even in the case of thick-walled fragments, may be an even reddish colour throughout. The clay is sandy or gritty, but often has abundant straw in it as well; straw impressions show in the surfaces, which range in colour from black through shades of dark and light brown to reddish, and are more or less well smoothed or burnished. Some fragments from levels 154 and 142 of IX and VIII in area A (trench G) had bright red burnished surfaces; others from level 142 of VIII were black with a very high burnish; while fragments from X G level 163 and IX Q level 156 were black outside, red inside, well smoothed. In the case of some fragments from levels of IX and VIII it was clear that the surface, although afterwards well smoothed or burnished, had been coated with a light-coloured slip (White Slipped Ware): thick cream (IX G level 155, VIII G

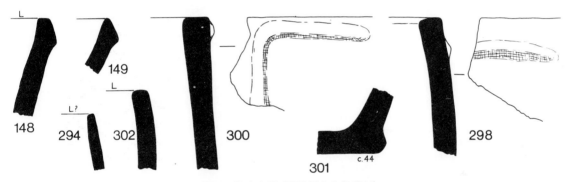

FIG. 133. Periods X–VIII. Pithoi. Scale 1/4.

level 140), dusky white (IX G level 155), white (304 from wall 16 of VIII), yellowish (IX G level 155), or occasionally pale greenish (VIII G levels 142, 141). A slip or wash, normally perhaps red in colour (e.g. 301), may have been usual.

Decoration was characteristically in relief and might consist of simple horizontal bands set below the rim (306), or round the body as on 296, which has a vertical handle springing from two of the bands. Pithoi with horizontal bands and handles similarly placed have been found at Byblos in the Aeneolithic and in Crete dating from Early Minoan I. But on the early pithoi from Emporio the relief bands often it seems ran vertically as well as horizontally (300, 305); and there is a hint of elaborate designs which might include curvilinear motifs, as on the fragment 303 from IX Q level 156. A fragment (297) from X Q level 167, one of the lowest levels excavated, has a wavy relief band like a snake. The relief bands are usually rounded but sometimes sharply triangular in section (FIG. 137: 1, 2), and once as FIG. 137: 3. In a few cases it seems relief bands were decorated with finger-tip impressions, but only two examples were noted, both from an upper level 145 of VIII in area B (trench Q) (e.g. 307). Some of these early pithoi may have had channelled or grooved decoration, to judge from a fragment from IX Q level 156 with part of a broad shallow channel c. 1.6 wide on it. But, apart from this, pithoi with channelled, grooved, or incised decoration were not attested.

These great vases must have been comparatively difficult to make, and were perhaps the work of specialist potters, if not of itinerant craftsmen like those who travel round Crete to this day. The quality of the firing and the distinctive relief ornament, which at Emporio is virtually confined to pithoi, are in harmony with the idea of a specialized industry of some kind.

Several fragments including 294–297 were recovered from level 167 of X in area B (trench Q):

294. Rim, which may belong with 296. Grey clay; surface smoothed, or with poor burnish.
295. (PLATE 36) Rim with horizontal rib below it.
296. (PLATE 36) Large fragment with horizontal ribs and vertical strap handle. Perhaps from same vase as rim 294. Outside light brown, smoothed or with poor burnish.
297. (PLATE 36) Fragment with relief decoration including 'snake'. Stump of possible handle at top left. Light brown to red, smoothed or burnished.

The fragments 298–307 were from levels of IX–VIII:

298. (VIII G 142) Rim with relief ornament. Corase clay, grey-brown to brick red, fired brick red throughout in places, tempered with grit and straw which shows in surface. Much of surface flaked away; well burnished, light brown to red outside, dark brown inside.
299. (VIII G 142) (PLATE 36) Fragment with ribs crossing at right angles.
300. (VIII G 141) (PLATE 36) Rim with relief decoration. Gritty brown clay; surface light brown shading to darker brown and dusky, burnished outside and in.
301. (VIII G 141) Base. Gritty brownish grey clay; surface well smoothed or burnished with traces of red wash outside and in.
302. (IX Q 156) Rim. Angle not certain. Gritty grey-brown clay; surface shades of light and reddish brown, well burnished outside and in.
303. (IX Q 156) (PLATE 36) Rim with curving rib and wart. Light brown to reddish, burnished.
      Some rims from Stratum VI of the earliest Cretan Neolithic (E.N. I) at Knossos have a closely similar system of ribbed decoration (*BSA* lix (1964) 171 fig. 26: 19, 22).
304. (VIII G wall 16) Rim with rounded top like 746 of Period VII. White Slipped Ware. Gritty clay fired an even colour throughout. Outside with thick white slip, inside brown; smoothed outside and in.
305. (VIII G wall 16) (PLATE 36) Fragment with ribs meeting at right angles.
306. (VIII Q 146) (PLATE 36) Rim with horizontal rib below it.
307. (VIII Q 145) (PLATE 36) Fragment with relief band with finger-tip impressions. Light brown, burnished. Another fragment with similar finger-tip impressed decoration from the same level.
      Hatched relief bands are already present in the Early Neolithic of the Greek mainland (e.g. *Nemea* pl. 68: 4). They are also found on Middle and Late Neolithic vases from Byblos (*Byblos* v pl. lxx, and pl. lxxx: 26998, running below the rim).

(G) MINIATURE VASES 308 (FIG. 134)

Small thin-walled vessels were conspicuous in levels of X–IX. A number of very small bowls (e.g. 82) and the jar 305 below qualify as true miniature vases.

308. (IX/VIII Q 158) (PLATE 33) Complete and unbroken. Ht. 4.8. Diam. of body 4.5. Probably meant to represent a jar of type 41. Rim irregular. Deep incision round bottom of neck. Base sunk. Dark brown clay. Outside brownish grey with fine burnish; inside brown, rough.

(I) HANDLES AND LUGS

(1) *Bowl handles and lugs* 309–334 (FIG 134. PLATES 35–37)

One of the most striking features in the pottery of these early periods at Emporio was the occurrence of surprisingly large handles on bowls. These handles were set on the tops of bowl rims and rose from them. Large bowl handles of this type were apparently most at home during Period IX, but many fragments of them were recovered from levels of VIII, and some from pure deposits of X. In addition some 12 fragments of rims with stumps of handles of this type rising

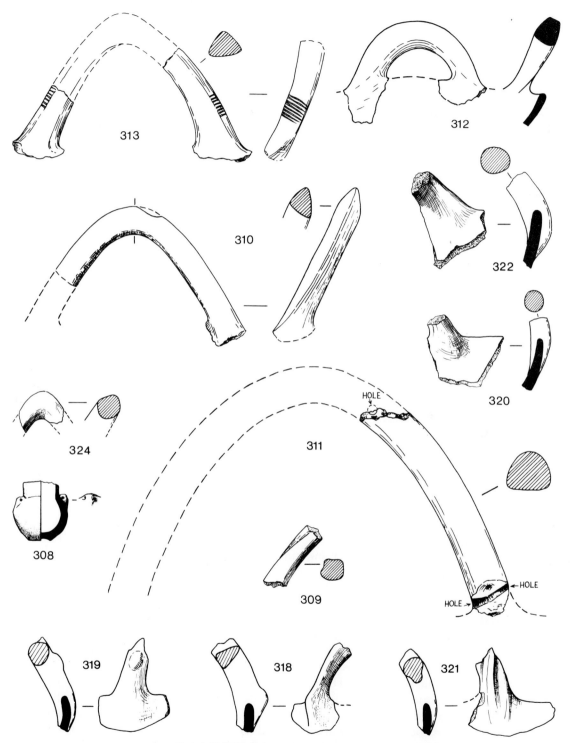

FIG. 134. Periods X–VIII. Bowl handles and miniature vases. Scale 1/3.

from them (as 312, 322) were recovered from levels of IX, and 11 from those of VIII. These bowl handles were characteristically large, and some were truly gigantic in size (e.g. 310, 313) (PLATE 36); but smaller handles of the same type were also in evidence. The large handles were almost all carefully shaped and finished, and they displayed a great variety in cross-section, ranging from circular, through thick oval, to thin oval with sharp edges; while a number were more or less triangular in section, usually with rounded, but sometimes with sharp angles (e.g. 310, 313, 323), or less commonly rectangular, like the small handle 312 from VIII G level 142. A few twisted handles, including two (309) from levels of X, appear to have belonged to bowls. These handles characteristically had projections at the point where they joined the bowl rim (PLATE 37).

The larger handles mostly seemed to come from vases of the finest burnished ware; but the smaller ones like 312 were not always of such good fabric. The handles for the most part at any rate belonged to open bowls of type 5, although some may be from bowls of the allied type 4. Some of the large handles appear to have stood more or less upright above the rim, if they did not actually curve inwards over the bowl.

In spite of their size these handles were not made in one piece with the bowl, and there was no attempt to key them into the rim; they were simply applied to the top of the rim after the vase was made, so that in many instances the shape of the rim is preserved at the base of the handle which has come away from it. In the case of 311 string-holes had been made after firing at the base of the handle; these may have been repair holes, but it is possible that string was regularly wrapped round the base of such handles to strengthen them at the point where they joined the rim: the thin white stripes at the base of the large handle 313 might represent a painted imitation of string.

Large handles of a similar type were at home at Tigani on Samos, but the shapes of the vases from which they came remained uncertain (*Tigani* 163 pl. 47). Some of these Tigani handles had projections or warts like ones from Emporio, and some were twisted.

Large handles rising from the tops of rims in this way do not appear to be attested in the Trojan area, but they are a distinctive feature of the earliest pottery of southern Anatolia, occurring in numbers at Çatal Hüyük from Level VI onwards into Early Chalcolithic I, after which they seem to have disappeared (*AS* xiv (1964) 82; xv (1965) 152). But these are basket-handles spanning the tops of jars with incurving rims, and some of the Chalcolithic examples at any rate seem to be in the nature of strap handles (*AS* xi (1961) 183 fig. 14: 1–3), although others have relatively thick triangular sections like several of the comparable ones from Emporio (e.g. *AS* xv (1965) 148 fig. 11: 17). One over the mouth of a jar from level VI at Çatal Hüyük has projections at the point of junction with the rim like some of the Emporio bowl handles (*ILN* 9 February 1963, 196, 198 fig. 11). A little basket-handled jar was recovered from a child's grave in level XXIII (Early Chalcolithic) at Mersin (*Mersin* 72 fig. 42: 3). A small handle rising from the top of a rim in the manner of the early Emporio bowl handles from Erimi is assigned to the Cypriot Early Chalcolithic (*SCE* iv Pt. 1 A, 120 fig. 59).

A jar with a basket-handle of thick oval section came from the earliest ceramic level IX at Hacilar, but was exceptional there (*Hacilar* i 104; ii 244 f. fig. 47: 39). Mellaart lists *bowls* with basket-handles as among characteristic Early Neolithic shapes which had become rarities and were evidently on their way out by Hacilar IX (*Hacilar* i 103). Bowl rims with the stumps of handles from the Karain cave in the region of Antalya closely resemble examples from Tigani and from the early levels at Emporio (*Belleten* xix (1955) 288 pls. ii: 7 and iii: bottom right). The handles in these cases appear to have curved inwards over the bowls like some of the comparable Emporio handles. These fragments come from the layer 0.90–1.10 m thick with pottery assigned

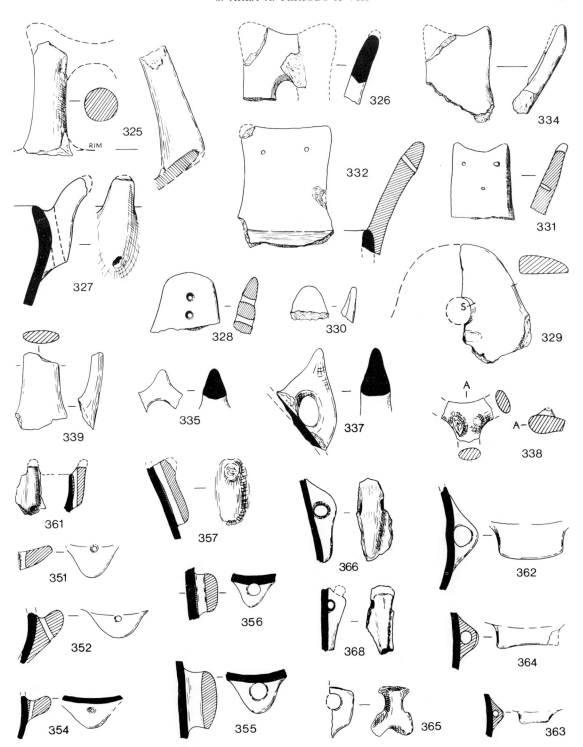

FIG. 135. Periods X–VIII. Miscellaneous handles and lugs. Scale 1/3.

to the Copper Age, Chalcolithic and Neolithic: they are dated to the Copper Age and Chalcolithic, but on what grounds is not clear.

Large handles like those from Emporio and Tigani also occur in the earlier Neolithic of the Greek mainland. Such handles springing from the rims of bowls of Thessalian A 1 ware are assignable to the Early or Middle Neolithic (*PThess* 90 fig. 40: d, Tsangli; 135 fig. 82: e, Tsani; 172, 177 fig. 121, Lianokladhi). From the lowest metre of deposit at Elateia, equated by Weinberg with the Early Pottery and Protosesklo (E.N. I and II) phases in Thessaly and with the earliest phase of Early Neolithic in Attica and the Peloponnese, comes 'one fragment that seems to be from a loop or basket handle off the rim of an open bowl' (*Elateia* 171 pl. 52: d, 9); this sounds very comparable with the early Emporio handles. A Neolithic bowl rim from Asea has the stump of a handle rising from the top with a wart beside it like some of those from the early levels at Emporio (*Asea* 39 fig. 37: m).

Handles of this general type are also found in later contexts. The handles of four-legged cult vases from the Bothros horizon at Elateia, assigned to the end of Middle or beginning of Late Neolithic, look rather similar and include examples with triangular cross-sections; but they do not spring from the tops of rims (*Elateia* 190 ff. figs. 12, 13 pl. 64: a). More comparable with the early Emporio handles are some large handles rising from the tops of rims of the evolved Blue and the Red periods at Poliochni (*Poliochni* i 566 pls. lxii: a–d, lxiii: b (evolved Blue); 636 pl. cliii: a (clii: b) (Red)).

A very few vertical cup-handles, set at right angles to the bowl and rising above its rim, were recognised from levels of IX and VIII (see under 93 for references). They included 93 of type 5 from IX Q level 158 with a handle kidney-shaped in section. The rim 143 of type 8 from VIII Q level 145 may have had a vertical handle rising above it. The unique bowl 156 of type 14 with a pair of multi-horned handles should also be cited here.

309. (X Q 166) Section of twisted handle, apparently from a bowl. Grey-brown; very fine burnish. Another similar but smaller from X Q level 167; light brown, with very fine burnish.
310. (IX G 154) (PLATE 36) Bowl handle. Grey-brown; very fine burnish.
311. (IX G 154) (PLATE 36) Bowl handle. Traces of hole of hour-glass section bored from opposite sides apparently after firing. Shades of brown to dusky and red; very fine burnish.
312. (VIII G 142) Bowl handle. Coarse fabric; surface red mottling to dark and light brown and dusky.
313. (VIII G 141) (PLATE 36) Giant bowl handle (two fragments). Grey-brown; fine burnish. Decoration in white paint (group of thin parallel stripes at base of handle each side).
314–317. (IX Q 159 (2), 158; VIII Q 148) (PLATE 37) Fragments of large bowl handles.
318. (IX Q 158) (PLATE 35) Stump of bowl handle with projection at base.
319. (IX/VIII Q 158) (PLATE 35) Stump of bowl handle with projection at base.
320. (VIII G ?141) Bowl handle. Dark brown to red; very fine burnish. Another similar.
321. (VIII G 140) (PLATE 35) Stump of twisted bowl handle.
322. (VIII Q 147) (PLATE 37) Bowl handle. Grey-brown to black with reddish tinge; fine burnish.
323. (VIII Q 147) (PLATE 37) Bowl handle with projection at base. Grey-brown; fine burnish. Several others similar.
324. (VIII Q 145) ? Bowl handle. Grey-brown clay; surface shades of dark and light brown to red, burnished but worn.

The fragment 325 seems to come from a large handle which may have ended in a pair of horns. This and 326 are interesting as possible relatives for a type of handle of comparable, although not identical, horned shape that was very much at home in the earliest Cretan Neolithic (E.N. I) at Knossos (*BSA* lix (1964) 169 fig. 25: 14–17 and Chart, ibid. 204 fig. 45). Some of these Knossian Early Neolithic handles were apparently quite large like 325.

Tab handles, basically of the same horned shape, appear to have been at home on bowls of these early periods, but they also occur in Emporio V–IV and later. Some of these early horned tab handles are perforated, as 326 and 332, while others are solid (331, 334). The horned tab handles are related to the ones of rounded outline set on or just below the rims of bowls of types 5–7 (e.g. 112).

Tab handles were also very much at home in the latest horizon at Ayio Gala (e.g. AG 129, 148, 252). But these Ayio Gala tab handles seem to have been more evolved in character than the early series from Emporio. Tab handles with flat or horned tops were evidently common at Tigani (*Tigani* 161 f. figs. 3, 4. *PPS* xxii (1956) 183 f., 181 fig. 9). Ones of various shapes, occasionally horned, occur at Saliagos, but they seem in general smaller than examples from Emporio (*Saliagos* 39 fig. 58: 3–10, pl. xxxi, *a*).

A tab handle with rounded top was found in the Neolithic layer B in the Beldibi cave in the region of Antalya (*Anatolia* iv (1959) 146, 167 pl. iv: 9). One with a horned top like 332 of Period IX from the Karain cave in that area is also assigned to the Neolithic (*Belleten* xix (1955) 284 ff. pl. iv: 12, upside down). Elaborate tab handles, in shape rather like that on the bowl 112 of Period X, but associated with horizontally perforated lugs, appear at Mersin in level XVI (end of the Middle Chalcolithic) (*Mersin* 150 f. fig. 93: 7, 8, 11, 12). What seems to be a tab handle with rounded top, however, is illustrated from the earliest Chalcolithic level XXIV (*Mersin* 56 f. fig. 34: 33). Tab handles are at home at Erimi assigned to the beginning of the Cypriot Chalcolithic (*SCE* iv Pt. 1 A, 120 fig. 59).

Large solid lugs project horizontally from the rims of some Early Neolithic bowls from Byblos, and in one case at any rate what appears to be a lug of this shape stands upright on top of the rim like the early tab handles and related lugs from Emporio (*Byblos* v 48 fig. 16: 34239, 21190; pl. lxiv: 25479).

A few simple horizontally perforated lugs from levels of Emporio VIII appear to have come from bowls. One from VIII G level 140 with a light brown burnished surface seems to have been set on the carination of a bowl of type 8 like 507 of Period VII or later.

Vertically perforated tubular lugs set on or just below the rim were also it seems not uncommon in the early periods X–VIII at Emporio, and some may have come from bowls (e.g. 111). Lugs akin to 221 occur in the early Neolithic Kízílkaya Culture of southern Turkey (e.g. *AS* xi (1961) 170 fig. 6: 36), and abound on vases of Hacilar IX–VI.

A vertically perforated lug from a high level 139 of VIII in trench G is markedly trumpet-shaped. The solid lug set at an angle below the type 7 rim 129 of Period VIII is also reminiscent of a trumpet lug. But trumpet lugs are not really at home on bowls or jars until the succeeding Period VII.

Solid horizontal tongue-shaped lugs, which appear to have served as handles or to hold lids, are found on the insides of baking pans (e.g. 20, 28).

325. (VIII Q 146) (PLATE 37) Fragment of large handle, apparently with a pair of horns. Evidently from a bowl, with the mark of the rim to which it was applied clearly visible as in the case of other large bowl handles. Grey-brown clay with fine silvery mica; surface grey-brown to black with very fine polish-like burnish. Possibly an import in view of the unique shape and mica.
326. (IX Q 156) (PLATE 37) Fragment of lug-handle, apparently with a pair of horns. Light brown to dusky, burnished.
327. (X Q 167) (PLATE 37) Lug-handle with horn-like projection as on 113, but more elegant. Cf. 361. Surface grey-brown, burnished but worn.
328. (IX G 154) Tab handle with a pair of holes through it. Light brown to dusky; fine burnish.
329. (IX G 154) Flat lug-handle, perhaps from a plate or dish (types 1, 2). Coarse gritty grey-brown clay. The rounded upper side lightish brown, burnished. The lower side dark brown, rough, with grit and straw impressions showing in it, as if the lug had been moulded on a flat surface. A fragment of a very coarse irregular rim from the same level might belong with it.
330. (VIII G 142) Solid tab handle. Red to light brown; fine burnish.

331. (IX Q 158) (PLATE 37) Solid tab handle with pair of horns. Three small holes in upper surface, but not carried
      through to other side, cf. 112. Grey-brown clay; surface shades of light and dark brown and reddish,
      unburnished but even.
332. (IX Q 156) Tab handle with pair of horns and two holes through it. Grey-brown clay; surface shades of light
      and dark brown, unburnished but even.
333. (VIII Q 146) (PLATE 37) Tab handle with two holes through it. Grey-brown mottling to red, burnished.
334. (VIII Q 144) Solid horned tab handle cf. 331. Dark brown to reddish with a deep purple tinge, well burnished.

(2) *Jar etc. handles* 335–350 (FIGS 104, 135. PLATES 37, 38)

Handles belonging to jugs or jars were common. Over 60 were recovered from levels of X, about
300 from those of IX, and 530 from those of VIII. As far as could be judged these handles were all
vertical; there was no evidence for the existence of handles set horizontally on the bodies of jugs
or jars: the large horizontal handles already discussed all appear to come from the rims of bowls.

The vertical handles assignable to jugs or jars from levels of X–VIII were normally oval,
sometimes thin oval in section, or occasionally more or less circular (FIG 104: 1–3). A few,
including two from levels of X, were semi-circular (as 4), while some were lunate (as 5). Lunate
handles mostly came from levels of VIII, but there were two from IX; they may have belonged to
jugs, since one at least was set to the rim of a jug of Fine Black Burnished Ware. Some vertical
handles from VIII, but including at least one from IX, had kidney-shaped sections (e.g. 348–9)
like the handle of the bowl 93; but these may have belonged to jars resembling 188. Some very
elegant handles from levels of IX (e.g. 162) were thin oval in section at the lower end, but
narrowed and thickened until they became circular at the top where they joined the rim. A
number of other handles appear to have been attached like these to the rims of jugs or jars; and
some jars may have had a pair of handles to the rim in this manner. But most of the vertical
handles recovered had evidently been placed on the shoulders or bodies of vases.

A few handles (2 from IX and 5 from VIII) which appear to have been set to the rims of jugs
or jars had a hole made before firing at the top near the point of junction with the rim (347).
These holes may have been for string to fasten lids, although no clay lids were recognised from
levels of X–VIII. In the case of 163 a hole had been made before firing through the neck of the
vase below the handle.

At first vertical handles of all kinds may have been simply applied to the surface of the vase as
is clear in the case of 339. But one or two 'thrust' or pushed-through handles (anchored by
pushing one or both ends through the wall of the vase) were noted in levels of VIII. One handle
pushed through the wall of a jar with a red wash from VIII G level 140 had a short 'tail' left on
the inside; but there were no examples from these early levels of the long tails which are a feature
of later pushed-through handles. This absence of tails may simply reflect the fact that the mouths
of jugs or jars from the early levels were rarely if ever too narrow for the potter to reach inside and
smooth away the pushed-through end of the handle.

Horned handles. Elegant horned handles like 335 and 337 may have belonged to large jars akin
to type 41. Such handles were characteristic of the two earliest periods (X–IX) at Emporio
(PLATE 37). Ten handles of this distinctive type were recovered from levels of X–VIII, and of
these six came from ones of X, three from those of IX. A handle from VIII Q level 145 with an
exceptionally large wart is in effect one of this type. The Period VIII bowl 156, which may have
been a ritual vase of some kind, boasted a pair of unique multi-horned handles.

Vertical handles with single horns have a wide distribution in time and place. They occurred
in both the earlier and the later horizons distinguishable at Ayio Gala (AG 83, 140, 257–8).
Furness, *PPS* xxii (1956) 199, 204, 209, cites parallels for these from Tigani, Kalimnos, Crete

(dating from the end of the Neolithic or beginning of Early Minoan), Thessaly, Macedonia, and sites in the Troad; but notes that they are absent from Troy itself and from Thermi: nor do they seem to be in evidence at Poliochni. One of those from Tigani of fine black burnished ware is exceedingly elegant like Emporio 337 (*Tigani* 164 pls. 44: 2, 48: 6). At Saliagos such handles were relatively rare, and they appeared to the excavators to be chiefly characteristic of the latest phases of the settlement (*Saliagos* 39 pl. xxxii: 7, 8).

In the Troad at any rate horned handles belong to a relatively early phase and seem to have gone out of fashion by the beginning of the Bronze Age (Troy I). There is a horned handle of fine burnished ware from the lowest level (I A 1) at Kum Tepe (*Kum Tepe* 316, 318 no. 114), and two each are recorded from Hanay Tepe and Beşik Tepe, assignable to Kum Tepe I B and earlier (W. Lamb, *PZ* xxiii (1932) 115 ff. figs. 2: 17, 5: 7; 127 f. fig. 14: 3). The material from Beşik Tepe, which includes abundant pattern burnish, appears to overlap with Kum Tepe I A and with Emporio VIII.

Examples of horned handles from the Iznik region of north-west Anatolia have been assigned to the Late Chalcolithic (*AS* xvii (1967) 58, 75 fig. 12: 25, 26). They occur at Büyük Güllücek (*Belleten* xii (1948) pl. cvii), and in the Late Chalcolithic or earliest Bronze Age (E.B. I–II) at Ikiztepe on the Black Sea coast (Y. Yakar, *Tel Aviv* ii (1975) 138, 142. Cf. *AS* xxix (1979) 54: called animal handles, because thought to represent schematized animals. Yakar believes they were adopted from south-east Europe, citing examples from Karanovo III).

Horned handles are reported from the Late Chalcolithic layer 1 at Can Hasan (*AS* xv (1965) 88, 91 fig. 5: 4). But Mellaart notes that, while horned handles are frequently a feature of the Late Chalcolithic, they may well have survived in the coarse ware of the Konya plain (*AS* xiii (1963) 216 fig. 9: 34). A characteristic example was recovered from a level of E.B. III at Tarsus, although it was regarded as an intrusion there (*Tarsus* ii 140 no. 457 fig. 280). Horned handles are similarly attested from the Early Bronze Age in Cyprus (*SCE* iv Pt. 1 A fig. cxi).

Such handles were at home in the Middle Neolithic at Dikilitash and Sitagroi in eastern Macedonia, and in the Late Neolithic of western Macedonia, as well as in the Arapi and Otzaki (Dhimini 2 and 3) phases of the Late Neolithic of Thessaly (*BCH* xcii (1968) 1074 f. fig. 22. *Archaeology* xxv (1972) 204 f. *PPS* xxxvi (1970) 299 fig. 6, from Sitagroi I. *PZ* xlii (1964) 41 fig. 7: 1–3, from Mylopotamos. *PMac* 72, 153 fig. 19: a–c, from Vardina and Kritsana. *Arapi* pl. vi: 7, 8 (pls. 17: 4, 11: 9). *Ayia Sofia Magula* 10 f. pls. 7: 12, 11: 14, 14: 19, 17: 4). Horned handles are also a feature of the latest Cretan Neolithic at Phaistos, which may overlap with Early Minoan I (*Festos* i 107 figs. 44, 47. Cf. J.D. Evans, *BSA* lxiii (1964) 276). They occur in Late Vinca contexts in Jugoslavia (e.g. *BRGK* 43–44 (1962–63) 23 pl. 14: 6, from Zelenikovo).

At Byblos in Syria horned handles are found in the Early Aeneolithic and to some extent in the Late Neolithic (*Byblos* v 195 fig. 123: 27248, pls. lxxxiii, cxlvi); but according to Braidwood's chart in Ehrich, *Chronologies* (1965) 82, this is a relatively late horizon, contemporary with Judeideh E and F and Merson XV–XIII (Late Chalcolithic).

Small vertical handles, which often approximated in shape and size to horizontally perforated lugs, were very common and characteristic in Period VIII at Emporio. These seemed to come from bowl-jars akin to types 30–32, and from small jars of types 41–42. Many were surmounted by warts (e.g. 263–4, 341–2): the wart sometimes made the handle resemble a miniature one of the horned type. While handles with warts occurred in levels of Periods X–IX they were somewhat rare there, the average being less than 1 : 20 in deposits of X and 1 : 15 in those of IX. In deposits of VIII on the other hand about one handle in every four was surmounted by a wart.

In a very few instances handles from levels of VIII had a pair of warts set along the length of the handle (e.g. 343). From X Q level 166 came the unique fragment 338, apparently the meeting place of three handles, surmounted by a pair of warts (PLATE 38). Warts are occasionally found set at the base of handles (344), or underneath them (345), sometimes in conjunction with a second wart on top in the ordinary manner; one example of a wart at the base of a handle was noted from a level of IX, but none from X.

Some handles from deposits of VIII had a pair of ribs descending from the bottom and continuing the line of the lower edges (350) in the manner of the tailed lugs of the period.

335–337. (X G 165; Q 165, 167) (PLATE 37) Horned handles from levels of X. Grey-brown with fine burnish (335, 337). On the less elegant 336 of coarser fabric the horn approximates to a large wart.

338. (X Q 166) (PLATE 38) Fragment with point of junction of three handles, surmounted by a pair of warts. Possibly from a bowl. Grey-brown, burnished.

There are examples of three-armed handles from the Late Neolithic of the Greek mainland (Phelps, *Thesis* 230 fig. 34: 47, in Grey Ware of his Period III from Corinth. *Arapi* 59, 62 pl. 23: 1, 2, of the Arapi (Dhimini 2) horizon. Cf. *JdI* lxviii (1953) 35, 33 fig. 37). Ones like this also occur on bowls from Vinca (*Vinca* iv 94 figs. 153, 154 nos. 1055–6. Cf. A. Cermanović, *Ziva Antica* 9 (1959) 248 fig. 6). A fragment with four arms was recovered from the Kephala settlement on Kea (*Kephala* 18 pl. 37: c). But there is some evidence to suggest that handles of this type may have existed earlier in Greece. An example of a three-armed handle cited by Hauptmann, *Arapi* 59, 62, comes from Stratum I at Rakhmani with material of the Sesklo (Middle Neolithic) and perhaps earlier (E.N.II–III) periods (*PThess* 28 fig. 26: c). A fragment like 338 might conceivably be from a scoop of the kind found at Kephala; one Kephala scoop handle does in fact have a pair of warts on it (*Kephala* pl. 36: A).

339. (X/VIII H 150) Vertical handle; thin oval section. Applied to outside surface of vase, not bonded with it. Fine fabric; lightish grey clay; surface light greyish brown, burnished but worn.

340. (IX/VIII Q 158) (PLATE 37) Handle with oval wart across it.

341, 342. (VIII G ?140, 139) Small handles surmounted by warts.

343. (VIII G ?139) Small handle surmounted by a pair of warts.

344. (VIII G 140) Stump of lower end of handle with wart at base.

345. (VIII G 139) Stump of lower end of handle with wart below it.

346. (VIII G 140) Small handle with wart each side of lower end.

347. (VIII G 140) Top of large handle with hole made before firing through it.

348, 349. (VIII G 139, ?140) Large handles with kidney-shaped sections. Cf. 93 of Period IX, with references.

350. (VIII Q 146) (PLATE 37) Lower end of strap handle with ribs descending from it on each side.

(3) *Miscellaneous lugs* 351–368 (FIG. 135. PLATES 38, 39)

Lugs attached to bowls have already been discussed, but some of the lugs described below may have come from bowls rather than from jars or other types of closed vase. Lugs whether from bowls or closed vases might be perforated horizontally or vertically. Both horizontally and vertically perforated lugs are attested in the earliest Neolithic pottery of Thessaly (*Otzaki-magula* i 26. *Thessalika* iv (1962) 80 pl. viii: 3).

A number of lugs, both horizontal and vertical, were tubular, and a few were trumpet-shaped. Trumpet-shaped lugs which shade into handles were at home in the Cretan Early Neolithic I pottery of Knossos (e.g. *BSA* lix (1964) 167 fig. 24: 22; 169 fig. 25: 5–7, 11). Two distinctly trumpet-shaped lugs (363–4) came from a level of Period IX, and others were recovered from ones of VIII; but none was recognised from those of X. The perforations in lugs of all kinds from these early levels tend to be larger than is usual in succeeding periods, so that lugs blend into handles (e.g. 362). Vertical tubular lugs are apt to be somewhat triangular instead of semi-circular in cross-section. Some vertical lugs from the Lower Cave at Ayio Gala were similarly triangular in section. A vertical lug with triangular section from the Neolithic hut on the Acropolis at Athens could be of Middle Neolithic date (*Annuario* xiii–xiv (1930–31) 450, 447 fig. 32: p). A number of vertically perforated lugs, mostly if not all from bowls, have a horn-like projection rising from the top (113, 327, 361). The lug 357 from an early level of VIII is in effect a stunted variety of this class.

Simple upturned vertically perforated lugs were not rare (e.g. 351–4). Upturned lugs of this kind are found on the Early Neolithic pottery of Çatal Hüyük and Alan Hüyük in Anatolia (*AS* xi (1961) 165 fig. 3: 16; 168 fig. 5: 18). A small lug from the latest level 139 of VIII in trench G had a vertical hole in the top which was not carried through to the other side. Similar incomplete perforations occurred on a few large lug-handles from bowls (112, 331).

Tailed lugs. A number of vertically perforated lugs from levels of Emporio VIII, and one or two doubtfully from ones of IX, had relief tails, straight or curling at the ends (172, 228, 358–360). Some of these tailed lugs were from bowl-jars akin to types 30–32, but 358 belonged to a jar of type 41.

Similar tailed lugs occurred at Tigani in black burnished ware of class C 2 assigned to the later of the two horizons of material distinguished there (*Tigani* 164 pl. 46: 2). Two fragments from Kephala on Kea with opposed curling ribs might come from similar lugs (*Kephala* 12 f. pls. 46: 8; 89: AS, AT); but the only tailed lugs preserved complete were double with straight tails (ibid. 19 pls. 39: D, E; 84: BO–BR, BT, BU). A fragment of what might be the upper part of a tailed lug comparable with those from Emporio is illustrated from the Skoteini cave in Euboia (*AAA* ix (1976) 47 fig. 2, assigned by Sampson, ibid. 50, to the Late Neolithic).

The tailed lugs of Emporio and Tigani seem to be related to the single-tailed Ayio Gala lugs found on vases from the Lower Cave there (e.g. AG 11, 17, 18). Some parallels for these are forthcoming in the material from the Athenian agora assigned to the Late Neolithic. One form of tailed lug from the Athenian agora appears to be really a perforated version of a crescentic lug, and is dated by Phelps, *Thesis* 325, to the early part of his Final Neolithic Period IV, citing parallels from Corinth and from Kephala on Kea. A jar with long-tailed versions of such lugs from the Iasos cemetery is compared with Early Cycladic I examples by Renfrew, *Emergence* 166, 164 fig. 10: 5. Perforated crescentic lugs from Thessaly were assigned to the Bronze Age by Tsountas, *DS* 264 f. figs. 172, 175; one with curling ends (*DS* 264 fig. 173) is reminiscent of some from Emporio, but this may be accidental.

Tailed lugs of a kind are attested at Hacilar (*Hacilar* i 107; ii 262 f. fig. 56: 3, 292 f. fig. 70: 6, from Levels VI and II B). These are not very comparable with the Chian examples, but appear to be if anything closer to the tailed lugs of Emporio VIII than to the single-tailed Ayio Gala lugs.

Tailed lugs of the type at home in Period VIII at Emporio may have developed from perforated crescentic lugs. None of these was identified from levels of the early periods at Emporio, but unperforated crescentic lugs occurred on bowls assigned to type 5 from levels of IX and VIII (e.g. 58, 78).

There is a perforated crescentic lug (AG 266) unstratified from the Upper Cave at Ayio Gala. An incomplete perforated lug from Tigani might have been crescentic or tailed (*Tigani* pl. 46: 1). At Saliagos both perforated and unperforated crescentic lugs were recovered (*Saliagos* 39, 83 fig. 47 pl. xxxi (*b*)).

Unperforated crescentic lugs are already attested in the Early Neolithic on the Greek mainland (e.g. *Nemea* 267 pl. 64: 11, 28), but continue in the Late Neolithic there (e.g. *Athenian Agora* xiii 42 no. 163 pl. 11. Corinth, Forum West area: *Hesperia* xlvii (1978) 439 no. 28). They are also found in the Early Neolithic of Anatolia at Çatal Hüyük (*AS* xi (1961) 164 f. fig. 3: 1), and alongside occasional perforated examples in the Early Chalcolithic of Çatal Hüyük West (*AS* xv (1965) 148, 151 f. fig. 11: 20, 21). But such lugs are virtually timeless, occurring for example throughout the Early Bronze Age at Troy (e.g. *Troy* i figs. 248: 12, 403: 35.486; ii figs. 170: 16, 243: 36.867.)

Animal head lugs. Lugs resembling the stylized heads of animals (365–8) do not seem to be attested before Period VIII at Emporio. The lug associated with 178 was apparently of this type, being shown upside down in the drawing and photo. A jar from Tigani in Samos has four animal head lugs on the shoulder comparable with ones from Emporio VIII (*AA* 1928, 625 fig. 20).

Similar animal head lugs first occur at Hacilar in Level VIII, but only become common there from V onwards, continuing until the end of II (*Hacilar* i 104, 109 f.). Ones illustrated from Hacilar VIII resemble 366 (*Hacilar* ii 246 f. fig. 48: 25, 26). For later examples, e.g. *Hacilar* ii 292 f. fig. 70: 7; 302 f. fig. 75: 10, 13, 14, 16. A lug of this kind, not unlike 365 as viewed in profile, was found in the Karain cave in the region of Antalya and assigned to the Neolithic (*Belleten* vii (1963) 85 fig. 9 a). What might be an animal head lug is illustrated from the Early Chalcolithic Level XXII at Mersin (*Mersin* 94 f. fig. 56: 25). Rather comparable lugs were at home in the late Proto-literate (Jamdat Nasr) period in Mesopotamia and in Amuq Phase G (*Judeideh* 272 fig. 213).

An evolved version of the type, usually elongated like an elephant's head with trunk, is found in the Late Neolithic of the western Aegean and the Greek mainland (Phelps, *Thesis* 325. Kea, Kephala: *Hesperia* xxxiii (1964) 316 pl. 47: a–e. *Thorikos* iii 26 fig. 23. Phlius: *Hesperia* xxxviii (1969) 451 f. fig. 3 pl. 115: 36. Rini: *PThess* 131 fig. 79: l, o. *Argissa* iii 145 for other examples from Thessaly, including some from the earlier of two Rakhmani period building levels at Pevkakia). A comparable lug appears on a sherd with incised decoration from Phaistos assigned to the Cretan Neolithic and probably dating from a very late phase of it (D. Levi, *Festòs e la Civiltà minoica* (Rome, 1976) pl. 9: b, top).

Fragments of vases, both jars and bowls, with V-shaped or hour-glass perforations made after firing, were recovered from levels of all phases of X–VIII. These may have been rivet-holes for string to mend or strengthen cracked vases; but in some instances they could have been for string handles, or even for tying lids in place, as suggested in the case of the holes made before firing in the top of a few jug or jar handles.

Vertically perforated lugs are described first, afterwards those with horizontal perforations through them. But it was often not certain how the lug was set, and whether the perforation was horizontal or vertical.

351, 352. (X G 164) (PLATE 38) Vertically perforated lugs. Grey-brown, burnished.

353. (X Q 168) (PLATE 38) Small vertically perforated lug cf. 351-2.

354. (VIII Q 146) Vertically perforated lug. Outside light red-brown to dark brown; inside of vase grey-brown to black; burnished outside and in.

355. (IX Q 158) Vertical tubular lug. Coarse grey-brown clay. Outside shades of light and dark brown to reddish, without any trace of burnish; inside of vase roughly burnished.

356. (VIII Q 146) Vertical lug, triangular in section. Coarse fabric. Outside light brown, burnished; inside of vase rough.
     Vertical tubular lugs with a rather triangular cross-section and large string holes occur on Early Neolithic pottery from Çatal Hüyük (*AS* xi (1961) 165 fig. 3: 11).

357. (VIII Q 146) Vertical tubular lug with projection at top. Outside shades of light and dark brown, burnished; inside of vase dark brown, less well burnished.

358, 359. (VIII Q 146) (PLATE 39) Ends of tails, curly (358) and straight (359), of lugs akin to 360.

360. (VIII Q 145) (PLATE 37) Lug with curly tails in relief.

361. (VIII Q 145) Long vertical lug-handle rising above rim in a horn, cf. 113, 327. Perhaps from a bowl of types 5 or 6. Surface with a wash, red shading to dark brown, burnished.

362. (VIII Q 148) Tubular lug. Perhaps vertical rather than horizontal as drawn. Perforation very large, making

the lug approximate to a wide strap handle. Red-brown to grey clay; surface pale brown outside, reddish inside, unburnished.

363. (IX Q 156) Incipient trumpet lug. Perhaps vertical rather than horizontal. Soft fabric. Grey-black, burnished.

364. (IX Q 156) Incipient trumpet lug. Perhaps vertical rather than horizontal cf. 363. Outside light brown with very fine burnish; inside with poor burnish or smoothed.

365. (VIII Q 146) Horizontally perforated 'animal head' lug. Coarse fabric. Light brown, burnished.

366. (VIII Q 145) Horizontally perforated 'animal head' lug, apparently from a jar. Rather coarse clay. Outside with traces of burnished red wash; inside dark brown, roughly smoothed or wiped.

367. (VIII G 139) (PLATE 40) Fragment with 'animal head' lug, apparently from a jar. Grey-brown; outside with poor burnish and bold incised decoration.

368. (VIII Q 145) Horizontally perforated 'animal head' lug surmounted by wart. Rather coarse clay. Outside shades of dark and light brown with traces of a red wash, burnished; inside rough, dark purple-brown.

Cf. *Athenian Agora* xiii 45 no. 196 pls. 13, 69, assigned to the Late Neolithic. The fabric, gritty grey clay with traces of a red slip, also sounds comparable.

(K) BASES 369–376 (FIG. 136)

Even in the earliest levels of X bases of bowls and jars were normally it seems flat (class 6), and often sunk (class 5); the sinking appears to have been deliberate to help the vases stand where the surface was uneven. One or two sunk bases of a peculiar type like incipient ring bases (class 5D)

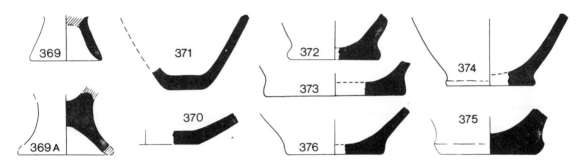

FIG. 136. Periods X–VIII. Bases. Scale 1/3.

were noted in upper levels of VIII in area B, but not in levels of X–IX; these seemed to belong to small vases of fine burnished ware.

Some jar bases from Period X onwards were markedly splayed as class 7A (372–4). The only fragment of a jar base with a mat impression came from level 158 of IX. Four pedestal feet (class 2 A), all from upper levels of VIII, may have belonged to bowls. Tripod feet (class 9), common later in the Bronze Age, were virtually absent from these early levels: three feet which might have belonged to tripod vases were recovered from levels 147, 145 and 140 of VIII, but the one from level 145 had a red wash and may have been a stray of Period II.

369, 369A. (VIII Q 145) Two fragments of pedestal feet (class 2A), apparently from different vases. Grey-brown, burnished.

370. (VIII Q 145) Base (class 6B) of bowl. Fine sandy brownish grey clay with some large grit and small particles of silvery mica showing abundantly in surface. Outside shades of dark and light brown, inside dark reddish, very well burnished. Probably an import, in light of fabric and apparent absence of other clearly differentiated bowl bases of this type from levels of X–VIII.

371. (IX Q 158) Small base (class 6C), apparently from bowl. Greyish brown clay; surface shades of red mottling to dark brown, well burnished outside and in.

372. (VIII G 140) Jar base (class 7A). Coarse gritty grey-brown clay; surface dusky brown, rough and unburnished.
373, 374. (IX Q 159, 156) Jar bases (classes 7A and 7A/B).
375. (VIII G 141) Jar base (class 7B). Very coarse grey-black clay with grit and straw; surface roughly smoothed.
376. (IX Q 159) Jar base (class 6A).

DECORATION

Period X 377–382

Decoration was not much in evidence on pottery from levels of X, but what there was does not appear to have differed in character from that current in Period IX.

Pattern burnish. No example was noted from X, but in view of the small amount of material recovered and the worn condition of the sherds it is not impossible that it existed. There was no safe evidence for it, however, even in Period IX.

Paint. Four fragments, all apparently from jars of type 41, had groups of diagonal lines in white (244, 245, 377). On some of these the painted decoration may have been applied (encrusted) after the vase was burnished and fired, as it appears to have been in a number of instances from IX. But on 377, where the original burnished surface had been worn away exposing the body clay, the painted decoration had survived. This suggests that the paint had been applied before the vase was fired, if not before the surface was burnished.

377. (X G Hearth in 163) (PLATE 38) Shoulder with stump of handle, apparently from jar of type 41. Lightish brown clay; traces of original dark grey-brown burnished surface, much worn. Decoration in white (groups of three diagonal lines).
378. (X Q 168) (PLATE 38) Shoulder with part of neck and stump of handle, apparently from jar of type 41. Grey-brown; fine burnish. Decoration in white (group of three or four diagonal lines).

Incision. The very few fragments with incised decoration all came from the same level 166 at the top of the deposit of X in area B (trench Q). There is some possibility of an admixture of material here from levels of IX or even from the bottom of VIII. Four of these fragments may have belonged to jars of type 41: they show simple linear designs indistinguishable from those current in IX–VIII, including pairs of diagonal lines (379), and a panel of multiple chevrons (380) like FIG. 112 No. 21. In addition to these four fragments there were three scraps, apparently from the same vase, with bands of pointillé made with a comb (381).

379. (X Q 166) (PLATE 38) Fragment of shoulder with join to neck, apparently from jar of type 41. Grey-brown clay; surface lightish brown, burnished. Pairs of diagonal lines.
380. (X Q 166) (PLATE 38) Shoulder with base of neck, apparently from jar of type 41. Sandy grey-brown clay. Vertical group of multiple chevrons, cf. FIG. 112 No. 22.
381. (X Q 166) (FIG. 111: 1. PLATE 40) Three fragments apparently from the same vase. Coarse grey-brown clay; inside rough, as if from a jug or jar; outside with a light brown to reddish wash, smoothed rather than burnished. Bands of pointillé outlined with incisions. The pointillé appears to have been made with a comb or Cardium shell; the lines of it run, some of them parallel with, others at right angles to the edges of the bands. Possibly from an imported vase.
　　Another fragment (808) with similar decoration was recovered from a level of Period VI.

In a very general way the comb decoration on these fragments is reminiscent of that on some of the so-called Cardium decorated ware of the Presesklo (E.N. III) phase of the Early Neolithic in Thessaly (e.g. *Otzaki-magula* ii pl. P). But this is not so close-set and it is not outlined with incisions. Moreoever it belongs to a phase in Presesklo after barbotine ware like 418 of Period VIII.

Close-set comb decoration more like that on 381 but without incised outlines occurs on some Neolithic pottery from Cilicia (e.g. *Tarsus* ii 67 figs. 216, 338: on Black, Beige, or Red Polished Ware). What looks as if it might be a similar type of combed decoration is illustrated in drawings of E.N. I pottery from Knossos (*BSA* lix (1964) 175 fig. 28: 13, 14).

Incised outlines appear to be exceptional on the Cardium decorated ware of the Levant, but they occur on a fragment of black burnished ware with decoration reminiscent of 381 from level 15 on virgin soil at Chagar Bazar (*Iraq* iii (1936) 53 pl. iii: 12).

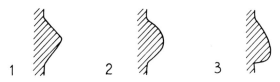

FIG. 137. Periods X–VIII. Sections of relief ribs on pithoi.

Relief. Pithoi and large jars were decorated with ribs in relief, as commonly in Periods IX–VIII (FIG. 137). The pithos fragment 297 from X Q level 167 had a snake-like squiggle on it. Circular warts were evidently common on vases of all kinds, but especially on jars. They varied a good deal in size and profile (FIG. 138); some were distinctly large. Warts like FIG. 138 No. 1 are

FIG. 138. Period X. Varieties of warts.

found below rims of jars akin to types 34–35 (e.g. 180). A large wart as No. 2 comes on a fragment of a jar with smoothed dusky grey-brown surface from X Q level 166, and a very large one as No. 3 on another jar fragment from the same level with the surface shades of light to dark brown, smoothed. The flat disc-shaped wart No. 4 was on a jar fragment with a poorly burnished grey-brown surface from X Q level 167. The wart with a sunk top (No. 5) is 382 below.

382. (X Q 166) (PLATE 38) Jar fragment with large wart with sunk top. Grey-brown, smoothed.

Period IX 383–392

Decoration of any kind was still comparatively rare. The most common method seems to have been incision. Painted decoration, when it occurs, is normally white; but in two instances it seems red paint was employed (e.g. 387). The evidence for the use of pattern burnish is ambiguous.

Pattern burnish. If this existed at all it was extremely rare. The three fragments with it that might have belonged to Period IX all came from doubtful contexts. One was the rim 393, and the other two were scraps from levels in trench G suspected of contamination with material of VIII.

Paint (FIG. 139) Some ten fragments had traces of decoration in white. One was the large bowl handle 313, while the rest, including the handle 386, appeared to come from jugs, or from jars akin to type 41 like the rim 248. The designs were entirely linear, and similar in character it

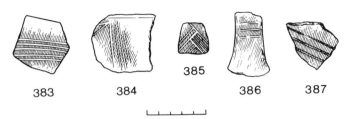

383   384   385   386   387

FIG. 139. White, and red (387), painted decoration of Periods IX–VIII.

seems to those from levels of Periods VIII–VI. Groups of lines run horizontally, vertically, or diagonally, and the designs composed on this basis may be quite elaborate (e.g. 385). In some cases the decoration seems to have been applied (encrusted) after the vase had been burnished and fired. Two fragments are exceptional in having decoration in red paint instead of the usual white. One (249) is the rim of a jar of type 41, the other (387) the shoulder of a jug or jar. The rim 383 described below appears to come from level 142 of Period VIII in trench G. The other fragments (384–7) are all from level 154 of IX in the same trench.

383. Rim of jug. Probably in fact of Period VIII. Fine Black Burnished Ware. Group of five horizontal stripes in white.
384. Shoulder of a jug or jar. Hard gritty clay, grey-black at core; surface black with fine burnish. Group of four vertical stripes and two diagonals in white.
385. Fragment of jug or jar. Grey-brown, burnished. Groups of intersecting diagonal stripes in white.
386. Handle, perhaps from a jug of type 20. Oval section. Grey-brown, burnished. Three thin stripes across in white.
387. Shoulder of jug or jar. Grey-brown; fine burnish. Three diagonal stripes in red.

Incision. This may have been more common than painted decoration, but less than twenty fragments with incision were recovered from levels of IX, and most of these—largely belonging to jars of type 41 and bowl-jars of types 30–32—came from deposits of levels 148 and 158 in area B (trench Q) which seemed to belong to Period VIII or had some admixture of material from VIII. The style of the decoration on these fragments was indistinguishable from that characteristic of VIII; the designs were linear, and more or less boldly incised as in VIII. As then and later the incisions were made while the clay was still damp before the vase was fired. While some of these fragments might be strays of Period VIII, the three described below (388–390) came from safe contexts of IX. One (388) is the rim of a large bowl with groups of diagonal lines scratched on the outside after firing; the other two groups of fragments (389, 390) have incised decoration of an exceptional character and may be imports.

388. (IX G 154) (PLATE 40) Rim of large bowl with stump of handle on top. Grey-brown to black, burnished. Groups of diagonal lines, roughly incised after firing, radiate from base of handle.
389. (IX G 154) (FIG. 111: 2. PLATE 42) Fragment, apparently from a bowl. Reddish clay with grit, some large. Surface burnished, reddish brown inside, grey-brown outside, which has a curving band reserved against a background of rows of close-set jabs.
    No very close parallels appear to be forthcoming for the system of decoration on this fragment, which is unique at Emporio. Some pointillé decoration from Saliagos looks as if it were jabbed (*Saliagos* pl. xxv, *a*). Areas of similar jabbing, although with cruder jabs and always it seems contrasting with areas or bands of red paint, are found on fragments from Mersin assigned to the Early and Middle Chalcolithic there (*Mersin* pl. x, a: 1, left; 2, second from left). Jab-like pointillé also occurs as filling of linear motifs on some incised ware from Can Hasan 3, 2A and 2B, which appear to overlap with the Early and Middle Chalcolithic of Mersin (*AS* xii (1962) 35 fig. 5: 13, 39 fig. 9: 2–4; xviii (1968) 49 fig. 2: 6).
390. (IX Q 156) (FIG. 111: 3. PLATE 41) Three fragments, all perhaps from same vase, which was evidently large but quite thin-walled. Fairly coarse grey-brown clay. Inside well smoothed; outside ranging from black through

dark brown to light brown and reddish, with very fine burnish; decorated with diagonal bands consisting of fine close-set multiple incisions, which make a continuous curve or meet at an angle.

At first sight this looks very much like the crowded incision found at the end of the Late Neolithic on the Greek mainland. Walker Kosmopoulos, *Corinth* 55 fig. 34, in particular is closely comparable: assigned to her Period IV, which is latest Neolithic or Early Bronze Age, immediately preceding Period V (Early Helladic II). Cf. *Hesperia* vi (1937) 512 fig. 29: i–k. Lerna: *Hesperia* xxvii (1958) 137 pl. 36: a–c. *Elateia* 198 f. pl. 62: d. *Orchomenos* ii pl. vi: 1 a, e. Phelps, *Thesis* 213 f., calls this ware Scratch Crusted, noting that the incision is really made as a key for white crusted paint, which has sometimes survived.

The Emporio fragments had no traces of paint, however, and must in any case be earlier. Some of the Cardium decorated ware found at Byblos from the Early Neolithic onwards looks comparable (e.g. *Byblos* v pl. xlix: Early Neolithic, and pl. lxxx, top left: Late Neolithic). Even closer is a fragment of Early Chalcolithic incised ware from Mersin (*Mersin* pl. x, *a*: 2, second from right: Levels XXIV–XIX). But similar ware is also illustrated from the Middle Chalcolithic there (ibid. pl. x, *a*: 1, and p. 116 f. fig. 73: 50–53).

Relief. Pithoi and large jars might be adorned with ribs as earlier in Period X and later in VIII–VI. There were at least seven examples of horseshoe-shaped or crescentic lugs on the outsides of bowls which appear to have been for the most part akin to type 5 (e.g. 78), but some may have had straight sides as type 4, and 128 h as an incurved rim (type 7). As in Period X, warts varied a good deal in size and character, and were evidently common on jars. They were normally applied to the surface of the vase like contemporary handles. The repoussé wart 392 described below comes from an early level of VIII rather than from IX.

391. (IX Q 156) Bowl rim of uncertain type with large horseshoe-shaped lug or rib.
392. (VIII Q 148) Fragment of jug or jar with wart in repoussé made by pushing wall of vase outwards from inside. Fine Black Burnished Ware.

Period VIII 393–423

Four different methods of decoration were in contemporary use during this period at Emporio. Incision was easily the most popular, but pattern burnish was not uncommon, and paint, although not as much in evidence as pattern burnish, was by no means rare. Decoration in relief, however, was largely confined to pithoi.

Whatever the method of decoration the motifs are still basically linear. True curvilinear designs, involving arcs or loops or spiraliform elements, do not seem to occur. The commonest element of decoration consists of groups of parallel lines, arranged vertically or horizontally, or most characteristically in diagonals, when they often form chevrons. The designs which occur in pattern burnish, white paint and incision, although clearly related, tend to be somewhat different. Vertical chevrons, for instance, are found in incision and occur in pattern burnish, but were not identified, although they may have existed, in paint. The greatest variety of design is found naturally enough in incision, which was the commonest method of decoration; the most limited repertory perhaps in pattern burnish, with decoration virtually confined to groups of diagonal lines, although vertical chevrons like those occurring in incision appear on the remarkable bowl-jar 178, which, however, may be an import.

There seems to have been no strict rule about the type of decoration to be used on each shape of vase. Jars of the standard types 41–42 for instance may be decorated with incision, or pattern burnish, or white paint. Bowl-jars of types 30–32 are normally incised; but the fine vases 177, 178, of the allied types 36–37 have pattern burnish. When decoration occurs on jugs, however, it always seems to be in white paint. Bowls were normally plain; but when they did have decoration it was usually in pattern burnish, which was especially prominent on rims of the characteristic type 8.

Little or no attempt seems to have been made to combine different methods of decoration on the same vase. The one exception is the fragment 396 decorated with incision and encrusted with red paint. This, and the unique, presumably imported bowl-jar 656 described under Period VII, were the only two examples where such a combination of paint (in each case red) and incision was noted.

Pattern burnish. Some fifty fragments with this type of decoration were recovered from levels of VIII, and twenty or more of these came from levels 144 and 145 in area B (trench Q). Pattern burnish occurred on the rims and bodies of a select number of jars, especially small jars of types 41–42 (265–270), and on a few rims of bowls assignable to types 4–7 (e.g. 42), but most characteristically it seems on rims of bowls of type 8 like 138, 140, 141. Pattern burnish on jars tended to be more elaborate and less stereotyped than it was on bowls. On small jars like 265 it might cover the whole of the body, while in the case of bowls it seems to have been confined to a zone around the rim, where it normally consisted of alternating groups of diagonal hatching, areas of such hatching being occasionally separated by double lines as on 393. Hatching of this kind also appears on rims of jars of types 41–42, and vertical zones of it are found on the bodies of some of the smaller ones like 265. But other motifs besides this also occur on jars: there is a row of inverted hatched triangles on the rim 236 of a jar of type 32, and a vertical zone of multiple chevrons on 178 of type 37, while groups of vertical and horizontal bands adorned the bowl-jar 177 of type 36. These two exceptional vases, 177 and 178, and a few other fragments with pattern burnish, had red surfaces, and the red might shade to light brown; in a few cases indeed it seems that the surface was dominantly light brown. But normally it was a shade of dark grey or grey-brown, the burnished patterns standing out in a darker tone, often black, against the lighter greyish background.

393. (IX/VIII Q 158) (PLATE 33) Rim, apparently from a bowl of type 8. Areas of diagonal hatching separated by a pair of vertical lines of pattern burnish.
394. (VIII G wall 16) Rim of bowl-jar. Diagonal strokes of pattern burnish.

Paint. Decoration in white paint occurred, but was rather less in evidence than pattern burnish. As in the case of pattern burnish, the designs were invariably linear, consisting of horizontal, vertical or diagonal groups of parallel lines, usually three or four together, varying in thickness, but normally quite thin. The fashion for painted decoration appears to have been on the increase towards the end of VIII, foreshadowing Periods VII–VI when it was more common than incision. Thus out of some forty fragments with white painted decoration from VIII, only 4 or 5 (1 in 8) were found in the earlier levels, 141–3 in trench G and 146, 147, in Q; while three quarters of the fragments (24 out of some 35) from the later levels actually came from VIII Q 144 and 145, both suspect of some degree of contamination with material of VII–VI. But jugs akin to those abundant in Periods VII–VI were evidently in use at the beginning of VIII, if not earlier in IX, and some of these had painted decoration, as described under JUGS. Three of the fragments of 165 were decorated with a band of lattice, and lattice as FIG. 154 No. 14 also appears on a handle of neat lunate section apparently from a jug from VIII Q 145, and on two or three other jug handles of black burnished ware from upper levels of Period VIII.

But decoration in white was not confined to jugs. It also appears on jars of various sizes, some if not most of them akin to types 41–42. The shoulders of a large jar (395) apparently of type 41 displays a row of bold quadruple chevrons. The unique fragment 396 has traces of encrusted red paint combined with incised decoration. While decoration in red was noted on two fragments (249, 387) from levels of IX, this combination of red paint with incision was only matched at Emporio on the bowl-jar 656 assigned to Period VII.

395. (VIII Q 146) (PLATE 40) Fragments of large closed vase, probably jar of type 41. Rather coarse fabric. Outside grey-brown, with dull burnish; inside dark red-brown, wiped. Shoulder with row of quadruple chevrons in white.

    Groups of four isolated chevrons in white paint like these, but divided by a group of vertical lines, appear on a fragment from Layer 1 assigned to Late Chalcolithic at Can Hasan (*AS* xiii (1963) 38 fig. 5: 11).

396. (VIII Q 146) (FIG. 140. PLATE 37) Shoulder with beginning of neck from large jar, apparently of type 41. Outside grey-brown, burnished, with bold incised decoration. Traces of encrusted red paint round base of neck and flanking incisions. Cf. Bowl-jar 656 of type 33 from VII.

    For a similar scheme of incised lines with bands of red paint, see *Mersin* 114 f. fig. 72: 12, and 159 fig. 101, from Middle and Late Chalcolithic Levels XIX and XV. But the combination of red paint and incision is already attested in the Protochalcolithic Level XXIV there (ibid. 62 fig. 137), and at Hassuna in Mesopotamia in the pre-Halaf levels IV–V (*JNES* iv (1945) figs. 13–14).

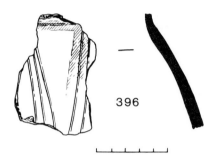

FIG. 140. Combined incision and red paint on 396 of Period VIII.

Incision (FIGS. 111, 112. PLATES 33, 34, 39–42). This was by far the commonest type of decoration. About 600 fragments with incised ornament were recovered from deposits of VIII, and of these some 250 came from VIII Q levels 146 and 147 alone. In these two levels incised fragments averaged nearly 28 per basket, but in the upper levels 144 and 145 of VIII Q the average had fallen to *c.* 8. In levels of VIII in area A (trench G), however, the average number of incised sherds per basket was only just over 6 in the lower levels 140–3, falling to *c.* 6 in the top level 139. The levels in area A (trench G) were not stratigraphically connected with those in area B (trench Q), and the smaller proportion of incised ware in deposits of area A might suggest that they were somewhat later in date than those in area B. But the bulk of the pottery from area B (trench Q) consisted of the remains of jars, which may have been used in connection with rites at the spring or well; and incised decoration in Period VIII was virtually confined to jars, and hardly occurred at all on jugs, or on bowls, which were well represented in the occupation levels of area A (trench G). In any case the proportion of incised ware in deposits of VIII in area A (trench G) was considerably higher than it had been in any of the levels of X–IX, where the average was only about one sherd per basket.

    The incised decoration of Period VIII was in general bold, and rather clumsy in its execution. Where the designs were at all complicated, like the concentric lozenges on FIG. 112 Nos. 34, 35, they were often bungled. The incisions varied in character, ranging from thin scratches to massive grooves which might be as much as 5 mm in width and depth. They were invariably made before firing, and were not as a rule filled with colouring material: traces of possible white fill were only noted in the case of one or two fragments from the top level 139 in trench G.

    Fragments with incised decoration appeared to come almost exclusively from jars akin to types 30–32 and 41–42. The decoration might cover the whole of the outside surface of the body of the vase, the most elaborate designs being found on jars of type 41; but their necks it seems were rarely if ever decorated with incision, although 401, 402 may be exceptions to this rule. The basic element in most schemes of decoration consists of groups of diagonal lines, which may intersect or form chevrons, horizontal or often vertical. The lines sometimes bend owing to the exigencies of the design or following the curve of the vase (e.g. 264. PLATE 34); but true curvilinear motifs, as seen for instance on 656 of Period VII, do not seem to occur. In its remote origins this linear decoration may be skeuomorphic, deriving from the string nets in which the ancestors of such vases whether made of clay or of some other material (e.g. gourds) were slung.

The range of motifs is given in FIGS. 111 and 112. Nos. 4–6 represent the basic scheme of decoration as found on many jars akin to types 30–32 (e.g. PLATES 33 (a) upper row, 3rd from l.; 39 (b) upper r.); but the same design appears on the bodies of jars of type 41 (e.g. FIG. 111, No. 7, where the dotted line represents the join between body and neck, cf. 264 (PLATE 34)). Sometimes the diagonals meet at a wart, set just below the rim in the case of jars akin to types 30–32 (No. 5. Cf. PLATE 39 (b) upper l.), or below the base of the neck on jars of type 41; or they may splay from a lug (No. 12) as on 367 (PLATE 40). No. 8 shows a more elaborate scheme of decoration as seen on the bowl-jar 173 from VIII Q level 146 (PLATE 31). Nos. 9 and 10 are on fragments of jars of type 41 (397, 398). Once on a bowl-jar of type 32 (399) groups of diagonal lines cross in the way shown in No. 11, but this appears to be exceptional. No. 13 shows varieties of the vertical elements which appear incorporated in designs such as Nos. 8–10 (PLATES 33 (a) top r.; 34: 264; 40 (a) upper r. and bottom l.; 41 (a)). Most of these occur more than once; but vertical rows of short upright strokes as No. 13, i, were only found on 400 which may be from the neck of a jar of type 41: the horizontal version of this design (No. 16) is from the base of the neck of such a jar (401). Short upright strokes appear in rows as No. 14 at the base of a handle (402), and as a fill it seems in a panel on 403.

FIG. 112 Nos. 17–20 from 404–7 illustrate varieties of vertical chevrons. No. 19 shows the way in which a pair of vertical chevrons are combined on the body of a jar of type 41 (407). Multiple chevrons, usually if not always in vertical bands outlined with incision as Nos. 21, 22, were not uncommon (PLATES 33 (a) mid. row; 41 (a) upper centre). A fragment with multiple chevrons of this kind (380) was recovered from a level of Period X. The variety FIG. 112 No. 23 (PLATE 41 (a) lower 3rd from l.) approximates to lattice, and true lattice made by crossing diagonal lines as No. 24 was recognised on some fragments from VIII Q level 146 (e.g. 408).

Lines flanking or flanked by rows of dots were not uncommon (FIGS 111 Nos. 9; 13a, b; 112 Nos. 25–29. PLATES 39 (a), (b) lower l.; 41 (a) lower r.). The dots were normally more or less circular in shape, sometimes triangular, once at least square, depending upon the instrument which made them. This was usually no doubt a stick, but in the case of 414 the circular impressions suggest the bone of a small animal or bird. The alternate groups of incised lines on FIG. 112 Nos. 29, 30 (412, 413) are reminiscent of the groups of stripes which represent the most characteristic motif of decoration in pattern burnish. No. 31 (414) shows rows of dots flanking groups of parallel lines, a motif with a long history in the Balkans and still found on the Knobbed Ware of Troy VII B.

Panels filled with dots as seen on FIG. 112 No. 32 (415) appear to have been rare in Period VIII, although fields of dots and strips filled with dots occur in VI and are not uncommon in V–IV. No. 33 (416) is the only certain example of a hatched band: the fine close-set hatching differentiates it from those which occur, although they are not common, in levels of VII–VI. A possible example of a hatched band of this later type was noted on a scrap from the top level 139 in trench G. The incisions on this showed possible traces of white fill.

The concentric lozenges of FIG. 112 Nos. 34 and 35 (263, 417) are interesting for comparison with similar designs in the Neolithic of the Greek mainland. A rim (166) apparently from a jug from the top level 139 of VIII G had short diagonal incisions like stitches round the inside edge. The finger nail impressions on 418 from an early level of VIII Q are important for their similarity to the so-called 'barbotine' ornament of the Preseklo phase in Thessaly.

397. (VIII Q 146) (FIG. 111 No. 9) Jar, apparently of type 41. Surface brownish grey, presumably once burnished, but worn.

398. (VIII Q 146) (FIG. 111 No. 10. PLATE 41) Jar of type 41. Black, burnished. Bold incision.

399. (VIII Q 145 or 144) (FIG. 111 No. 11) Jar, apparently of type 32. Grey-brown to black, burnished.

400. (VIII Q 145) (FIG. 111 No. 13, i) Neck of jar, apparently of type 41. Outside light grey-brown, burnished; inside rough.

401. (IX/VIII Q 147) (FIG. 111 No. 16. PLATE 39) Base of neck of jar of type 41.

402. (VIII Q 146) (FIG. 111 No. 14) Base of handle of large jar. Light reddish brown, burnished. Fine incision.

403. (VIII G 140) (FIG. 111 No. 15. PLATE 42) Jar. Inside rough, reddish; outside greyish brown, burnished.

404. (VIII Q 146) (FIG. 112 No. 17) Jar, apparently of type 41. Sandy red-brown to red, burnished.

405, 406. (VIII Q 145) (FIG. 112 Nos. 18, 20) Jars, apparently of type 31. Light grey or grey-brown, burnished.

407. (VIII Q 145) (FIG. 112 No. 19) Jar of type 41. Light brown, burnished. For the chevrons on the handle cf. PLATE 33 (a) upper row, 2nd from l.

408. (VIII Q 146) (FIG. 112 No. 24. PLATE 41) Jar. Brownish grey, burnished. Bold incision.

409. (VIII Q 146) (FIG. 112 No. 25. PLATE 39) Jar of type 41. Outside with a red wash, burnished.

410. (VIII Q 146) (FIG. 112 No. 26. PLATE 39) Jar. Light brown, burnished.

411. (VIII Q 144) (FIG. 112 No. 28) Shoulder of small jar. Light brown, burnished.

412. (VIII Q 145) (FIG. 112 No. 29) Shoulder of small jar. Fine Black Burnished Ware.

413. (VIII Q 145) (FIG 112 No. 30) Shoulder of jar. Sandy grey-brown clay; surface dark brownish grey, burnished. Incised decoration exceptionally careful.

414. (VIII Q 145) (FIG. 112 No. 31) Large jar. Grey-brown, burnished. Holes of decoration large, roughly circular, apparently made with bone of small animal or bird.

415 (VIII Q ?145) (FIG. 112 No. 32) Rim of unusually small jar of type 31. Grey-brown, burnished. Panel of dots (pointillé).

416. (VIII G 140) (FIG. 112 No. 33. PLATE 42) Fragment of bowl-jar or bowl. Grey-brown with very fine burnish outside and in. Outside with closely hatched incised bands; the area of the bands apparently reserved, without burnish.

417. (VIII Q 145) (FIG. 112 No. 35) Jar. Shades of light to dark brown; fine burnish.

418. (VIII Q 146) (PLATE 42) Four fragments, apparently from a large jar, perhaps akin to type 41. Sandy brownish grey-black clay with occasional large lumps of grit; silvery mica showing in surface. Inside dark grey, smoothed; outside dark brownish grey with traces of red wash, smoothed but not it seems burnished. Rows of semicircular impressions apparently made with fingernail. Probably imported, perhaps from Thessaly, where this type of decoration is characteristic of the Preseklo horizon.

The original object in roughening the surface of vases by covering them with fingernail impressions in this manner may have been the practical one of helping to prevent them slipping from wet hands (L. Scott, in Singer, *History of Technology* i (Oxford, 1954) 401 f.).

Fingernail impressed ware of one kind or another was very much at home in some parts of Thessaly in the Early Neolithic III Preseklo period. Sometimes fingernail impressions exactly like those on 418 occur in similar lines (e.g. *Otzaki-magula* ii 50 Kat. viii b no. 10, pl. M: 10. Cf. Milojcic, *Ergebnisse* 10 pl. 2: 4, 7. *AM* lvii (1932) 104 Beil. xx: 4. *Thessalika* i (1958) 47 f., 41 fig. 2, from Magoulitsa). *AAA* iv (1971) 168 fig. 7 from Prodromos II has similar impressions, but they are very close-set. A fragment from Elateia, apparently assignable to the later phase 2 of the Early Neolithic there, also looks very comparable with 418 (*Elateia* pl. 54, d: 1).

A fragment with typical fingernail impressions is illustrated as from Neolithic deposit at Phaistos in Crete by A. Mosso, *The Dawn of Mediterranean Civilization* (London, 1910) 82 fig. 47. Cf. Schachermeyr, *Ältesten Kulturen* 59 fig. 5: 4. This and other examples of fingertip and fingernail impressed ware found outside Thessaly may be later in date.

Fingernail impressed ware with the impressions in orderly rows as on 418 has been recovered from Kastritsa near Ioannina in Epirus (*PAE* 1951, 177 f. fig. 2: 2), from Sidari on Corfu (*AA* 1971, 363 fig. 55 a, c), and from the Choirospilia cave on Levkas (Dörpfeld, *Alt-Ithaka* 335 f. pl. 83: b). The Kastritsa fragment is referred by Dakaris to Thessalian Early Neolithic A 2 ware. But the bulk at any rate of the associated material from Choirospilia appears to be Late Neolithic. The impressions are perhaps rather neater in character than was usual on Thessalian Presesklo wares.

Even in Thessaly this type of decoration seems to continue after the Early Neolithic. Thus surface finds from Rakhes in the region of Domokos in southern Thessaly assigned to the Late Neolithic include fragments with decoration of this kind (*ADelt* xxvii (1972) Chron. 329 f. pl. 281). One or two sherds from wells in the Athenian agora classed as Late Neolithic have fingertip impressions like those on 418, but they are not set in rows (*Athenian Agora* xiii 14 pl. x nos. 143, 147).

Fingertip and fingernail impressed ware akin to that of Thessalian Presesklo is found in the Early Neolithic of western Macedonia (Servia: *PMac* 63 f., 138 fig. 5. Nea Nikomedeia: *PPS* xxviii (1962) 284 pl. xl). Such impressed ware also occurs in the Early Neolithic (Starčevo etc.) of the Balkans (e.g. *Glasnik Sarajevo* NS xii (1957) pls. v–viii, xii; xiii (1958) pls. vii, ix esp. ix: 5, from Crvena Stijena (Red Cave), Stratum III. Ibid. xii (1957) 73 figs. 1–2, 75 fig. 2, pls. v–x, from Zelina Pécina (Green Cave), Stratum III. Berciu, *Contributii* 22 fig. 2: 2). It is similarly present in the Early Neolithic of southern Italy (e.g. M. Mayer, *Molfetta und Matera* (Leipzig, 1924) pl. iv).

This type of decoration is still found in some parts of the Balkans in later times. Some later fragments from Romania have fingernail impressions in rows as on 418 (Berciu, *Contributii* 253 fig. 86: 7; 274 fig. 105: 4, 5; 313 fig. 135: 10, from Sălcuţa I, II and IV). A vase with this type of decoration from Alaca in Anatolia is assigned to the Copper Age (*Alaca 1937–39*, 145 pl. C fig. 1: b. 417. Cf. F. Schachermeyr, *Das ägäische Neolithikum* (SIMA vi) (Lund, 1964) 6).

It has been suggested that this type of decoration must have reached western Macedonia and Thessaly from the direction of Yugoslavia (e.g. *Otzaki-magula* 137. Weinberg, *CAH* 585 f. Holmberg, *Neolithic Pottery* 13 f. Hammond, *Migrations* 88 f.). But it occurs alongside incised decoration in the Neolithic of Syria (e.g. *Judeideh* 77 fig. 50: 7, Phase B. *Byblos* v pl. lxvii, Middle Neolithic). Light cuts made with the fingernail are also found on Neolithic pottery from Cilicia, and F. Schachermeyr, *Ägäis und Orient* (Vienna, 1967) 16, has suggested that the idea of decorating pottery with fingernail impressions was brought from that region to Thessaly and the Balkans.

Relief. Pithoi and large jars were decorated with ribs in relief as in Periods X–IX and later in VII–VI. A class of vertically perforated lugs on jars of fine burnished ware have relief 'tails' which may be straight at the ends like 359 (PLATE 39), or curved as in the case of 358 and 360 (PLATES 39, 37).

Warts occur on the bodies or shoulders of jugs and jars: they are set below the rims of jars akin to types 34 and 35 (e.g. 419 on PLATE 38), and sometimes there is a row of them round the outside of the rim as on 206. In two or three instances (all from VIII G level 140) a vertical row of at least three warts appears on the shoulder of a jar of coarse burnished ware (e.g. 420 on PLATE 38). As already noted under *Handles and lugs* (2) *Jar etc. handles*, these were commonly surmounted by warts, especially when they belonged to jars of fine burnished ware with incised decoration.

In view of their fabric or the unique character of their decoration the sherds 421–3 below with varieties of warts are likely to be from imported vases, which may have been brought from Thessaly or from some region of central Greece. Two of these (421, 422) are from a level of IX with an admixture of VIII, and are more likely perhaps to belong to IX; but 423 comes from the latest level 139 of VIII in trench G with a fragment from level 119 of VII. The warts on 421 are so closely packed as to amount to a form of barbotine.

421. (IX/VIII Q 158) (PLATE 41) Fragment, apparently from a jar. Sandy brownish grey clay with a few specks of silvery mica showing in surface. Inside rough; outside with barbotine. The barbotine seems to have been applied to the surface of the vase.

This fragment was unique at Emporio, and the fabric suggested an import. A fragment from the second (A II) phase of the Early Neolithic at Nea Makri in Attica looks rather similar (*Nea Makri* pl. 8: 2).

Somewhat comparable but more densely packed barbotine occurred on five fragments from Saliagos (*Saliagos* 43 fig. 43: 15 pl. xxviii, b, bottom r.). Another example of this denser barbotine is illustrated from the lower part of Stratum IV of E.N. II at Knossos in Crete (*BSA* lix (1964) 214 pl. 47 (3): 6). *BSA* xlviii (1953) 115 pl. 30, a: 10. 11, assigned to E.N. I, look similar, but may be more akin to a type of barbotine decoration found in the Neolithic of Cilicia (*Tarsus* ii 66 fig. 315, 1: g, i). The decoration in this case is not applied, but made by pushing up the clay to give an embossed effect. But some fragments with dense barbotine applied to the vase surface are illustrated from Judeideh Phase C (*Judeideh* 148 f. fig. 117: 5 pl. 17: 16, 17).

422. (IX/VIII Q 158) (PLATE 41) Jar rim of class A I. Cooking pot type ware. Two neat seed-shaped warts set diagonally on outside.

Seed-shaped or oval warts are a feature of the earliest Neolithic pottery on the Greek mainland (Corinth: *Hesperia* vi (1937) 493, 496 fig. 29: a, b. *Elateia* 171, 175 pl. 53: c, d. *Orchomenos* ii 16 pl. vi: 2, Class A: Black Burnished Ware; 29 pl. xiii: 2 esp. *a*, of Class D: Red Burnished Ware). In a number of cases from Nemea such warts appear set diagonally like those on 422 (*Nemea* pls. 60: N 9; 61, 62: N 3. Cf. *Nea Makri* 10 fig. 20 pl. 8, top (A I and II)). An Early Neolithic vase from Lerna has many oval and irregular warts set diagonally in this manner (Vitelli 1977, 20 fig. 6); but it sound as if our fragment might be most easily paralleled from the E.N.–M.N. transition at Lerna (ibid. 21).

Bean-shaped warts are said to be at home in the Protosesklo (E.N. II) phase of the Thessalian Early Neolithic (*Otzaki-magula* 31 pls. iii: 8, 9; vi: 24; xii: 7; xvi: 13, 14). The closest parallel for the shape of the warts on 422 is ibid. pls. ii: 11; 8: 20, from the early Protosesklo house in A and B 17 of Fläche III. But some of the warts on a jar from Tirnavo: Ayia Anna (Megali Vrysi) assigned by Theochares to an advanced phase of the Early Neolithic are exactly comparable to those of 422 (Theochares, *Neolithic Greece* 40 col. pl. 26). Compare *ADelt* xix (1964) Chron. 262 pl. 304 from Tirnavo: Ayios Athanasios Magoula, also assigned by Theochares to an advanced phase of Early Neolithic. A pair of thin oval warts set diagonally in the manner of those on 422 is illustrated by Milojcic, *Ergebnisse* fig. 9: 11, as from the beginnning of the Middle Neolithic Sesklo period.

Plastic decoration in general is characteristic of the beginning of the Neolithic (E.N. I) at Knossos in Crete, and some fragments have irregularly placed warts, both circular and oval, like those found in the Early Neolithic of the Greek mainland (*BSA* lix (1964) 210 pl. 46 (2): 2).

423. (VIII G 139, VI G 119) (PLATE 42) Two fragments, apparently from the same vase, evidently a jug or jar. Very sandy grey-brown clay. Inside rough, wiped; outside grey with fine burnish, except in area of strips with raised pellets which left unburnished.

Rows of circular warts set vertically or diagonally are a feature of the later part (Phase 2) of the Early Neolithic at Elateia (Drakhmani) in central Greece (*Elateia* 175 pl. 53 (d): 1. Cf. *PThess* 15, 202 f. fig. 142: e, classified as A 5 γ ware (*AM* xxx (1905) 137 fig. 8. *Orchomenos* ii 16 and pl. vi, 2: d, on Class A: Black Burnished Ware).

A fragment from Mesiani Magoula illustrated in *DS* 239 fig. 137 and assigned there to the Early Bronze Age has a row of warts similar in appearance to those on 423; but these are much smaller, only about 3 mm as opposed to 7 mm in diameter. *PThess* 55 tentatively groups this fragment with Γ 1 α 2 ware.

IMPORTS 424–430

Fragments of vases which from their unusual fabric, shape, or method of decoration, seemed likely to be imports from elsewhere were fairly numerous in levels of X–VIII. In most cases the clay of these was micaceous, and mica is not apparent in the ordinary run of local wares at Emporio. But assuming that these micaceous fragments were imported, they were not necessarily brought from any great distance. Mica for instance is in evidence in the local pottery of more or less contemporary date at Ayio Gala in the north-western corner of Chios. At the same time Emporio is a harbour, and clay vases are easily transported by sea. Even at the time of our excavations boats from the neighbouring island of Samos used to bring stocks of clay pots for sale in the villages of the interior, in spite of the existence of local potteries nearby at Armolia.

Period X. Four fragments may have belonged to imports: a plate (2) and bowl rim (87) of micaceous ware, the neck of a jar of type 41 of Fine Light Grey Burnished Ware (247), and the scrap (381) with comb or Cardium shell imprints.

Period IX. Out of some six fragments of vases which might have been imported, three (47, 150, 199) were in varieties of micaceous ware, two of them (47, 199) having clear traces of a red wash. The jar rim 246 is of Fine Light Grey Burnished Ware like 424 below.

424. (IX G 154) Fragment of jug or jar. Fine Light Grey Burnished Ware. Sandy light grey clay fired an even colour throughout. Outside burnished, but worn. A base of similar fabric, but with traces of a red wash, might come from the same vase.
425. (IX G 154) Fragment, apparently of a jar. Clay shades of orange, brick-red and greyish, with abundant grit, some large. Outside with a thick pale greenish slip, smoothed but not burnished; inside orange brown with grit showing in surface.

Period VIII. Some twenty or more fragments might have belonged to imports. About half of these, all of micaceous ware, came from the lower levels 147, 146, of VIII in trench Q, several being from the same vase or vases, mostly at any rate with a red slip or wash, smoothed or burnished. The clay of these micaceous wares was normally greyish brown to brick-red; the surface brick-red shading to light brown, sometimes dark purplish brown or dusky black, with abundant silvery mica showing in it together with sand. With these red-surfaced vases of micaceous ware may be grouped the pattern burnish jars 177 and 178, although no traces of mica were noted in them. The two fragments 428, 429, apparently from jars of type 41, are in a variety of Fine Light Grey Burnished Ware. The fabric of 430 with a black lustrous wash was unique. Potential imports from levels of VIII already described apart from 177 and 178 include the jar rims 262, 278, 290; the bowl handle 325 and base 370, together with the unusual decorated fragments, 418, 421–423.

426. (VIII G ?140) (PLATE 42) Rim of jar of type 41 with stump of handle. Grey clay with silvery mica.
427. (VIII Q 146) (PLATE 34) Fragment of small strap handle surmounted by wart. Fabric cf. 262.
428. (VIII G ?140) Neck of small jar of type 41 with stump of handle. Fabric akin to Fine Light Grey Burnished Ware. Grey-black clay, fired an even colour throughout; surface light grey, well smoothed or burnished, with silvery mica showing in it.
429. (VIII G 140) (PLATE 42) Small neat strap handle, apparently from jar akin to type 41. Fabric akin to Fine Light Grey Burnished Ware. Brownish grey clay with silvery mica showing in surface. Outside lightish brown, smoothed or burnished; inside light grey, roughly wiped.
430. (VIII G 140) (PLATE 42) Fragment, apparently from shoulder of jug or jar with pair of warts set vertically on it. Thin-walled. Hard fabric; brick-red clay fired an even colour throughout, with some large grit. Surface regular, but not absolutely even. Outside with a thick black unburnished lustrous wash on a base which seems to be whitish; inside now bright red, but this appears to be merely the base of the black wash, which has worn away.

ii. Periods VII-VI

GENERAL

A much larger area of Periods VII–VI was opened than of X–VIII.

The pottery of VII differed in character from that of VI. It seems in the main to represent ordinary occupation debris from houses, whereas that of VI was largely composed of fragments of jugs which may have been broken in connection with rites at the well. Thus while fragments of bowls were abundantly represented in levels of VII, there were comparatively few of them in those of VI. The pottery of VI from trench G in particular consisted of small scraps, apparently thrown away over wall 20.

FABRIC

The bulk of the pottery was burnished as in Periods X–VIII. But the firing appears to have somewhat improved, at any rate in the case of bowls; although jugs tended to be of very soft clay, and sherds from them were easy to break in the hand. When the vases were dark-surfaced the clay was apt to be grey-black, and even in the case of light-surfaced vases it might be black in the centre of the break, shading to light brown near the edges; but some light surfaced vases were fired a light brown to brick-red colour throughout.

There was no clear line of demarcation separating fine from coarse wares, and no simple relationship between fineness of fabric and finish. The clay was often fairly refined, but some vases with carefully burnished surfaces were made of quite coarse clay with large lumps of grit and straw in it. It is possible that the grit sometimes reflected natural impurities in the clay rather than tempering, although in the case of *Cooking Pot Ware* at least it had clearly been deliberately added. The proportion of straw to grit in the clay, however, was in general noticeably greater than it was in the succeeding periods from V onwards. Straw appears to have been favoured as tempering for the finer burnished wares, especially for the jugs of *Fine Black* and *Light Brown Burnished Ware* described below: straw impressions were apt to be prominent in the break, and often showed in the surfaces of vases except when the burnish had been unusually thorough and had survived unworn.

The surface treatment varied a good deal, and distinct classes of ware could be distinguished on the basis of it: *Mottled Ware, Fine Black Burnished Ware , Light Brown Burnished Ware*, and *Light Plain Ware*. Each of these wares was favoured for certain types of vase: *Mottled Ware* for bowls, especially for those of type 10 characteristic of this horizon; *Fine Black Burnished Ware* for small jugs with white-painted decoration; *Light Brown Burnished Ware* for larger jugs; *Light Plain Ware* for some large jugs and for jars. This implies a deliberate choice of surface colour and a considerable degree of control over the firing. The mottled or variegated surfaces characteristic of many of the bowls and found on some of the jugs and jars, and more especially on those from levels of VII, were therefore clearly intentional and not the result of chance: some of the vases with mottled surfaces from Emporio VII–VI are of the finest burnished ware. The proportion of light brown and red surfaced sherds from bowls (as apart from jugs and jars) appeared to be greater in deposits of VII than in those of VI. In Period VI shades of grey-brown or black distinctly predominated, as they had in the earliest periods (X–IX) and were to do in V–IV.

The range of fabrics that are widely different in appearance, but all contemporary and all apparently of local manufacture, is a striking feature of Emporio VII–VI. A comparable phenomenon is observable in the Late Neolithic of the Greek mainland, which should overlap with Periods VII–VI at Emporio in time: J. Lavezzi, *Hesperia* xlvii (1978) 418, has drawn attention to the 'remarkably wide range of fabrics plainly in contemporaneous use' in the Late Neolithic of Corinth.

The finer vases were normally it seems coated with a slip or wash before they were burnished and fired. But, where the surfaces had been well burnished, this could not be detected, except when the slip or wash had splashed or overlapped onto the untreated parts of the insides of closed vessels like jugs. The slip or wash when applied seems to have been red or light brown in colour. Traces of a red wash could be distinguished on some of the coarser pottery, mostly jars, which had only a superficial burnish or none at all. But it seems clear from the splashes of it on their insides that even the small jugs of *Fine Black Burnished Ware* were coated with a red wash which was deliberately transformed to black in the firing. The wash on jugs of *Light Brown Burnished Ware*, however, appears to have been light brown from the start, and a few vases had an unburnished light brown wash. Sometimes unburnished surfaces had been wiped with a bunch of twigs or brushwood or a cloth. Bowls tended to have a better finish than jars used for storage, but the small jugs of *Fine Black Burnished Ware* rivalled any of the bowls in fineness of fabric and care of finish. The very finest burnished surfaces, whether of bowls or jugs, were as if polished and had a distinct soapy feel; but the marks of the burnishing implement could almost always be detected except where the surfaces had become worn.

Mottled Ware. Many bowls, especially those of the distinctive type 10 peculiar to Periods VII–VI, were of this ware. These bowls tended to be irregular in shape with uneven surfaces in spite of the normally fine burnish. The marks of the burnishing instrument were usually quite visible, but sometimes the burnish was so thorough that they could hardly be distinguished. The clay was apt to be relatively well levigated, but the firing was patchy; thus the clay appeared shades of orange, and grey and black, in the break. The surfaces were strikingly variegated: light brown, red, dark brown, deep purple brown, greyish brown, and black, all mottling and shading into one another. The variegated surfaces of this ware appear to have been deliberately produced, even if they had an ultimate origin in a lack of control over the firing. It seems that *Mottled Ware* was virtually confined to bowls, and the variegated surfaces of these bowls must have formed a striking contrast to the more or less uniform blacks and light browns of the jugs of *Fine Black* and *Light Brown Burnished Ware*. *Mottled Ware* was more at home in Period VII than in VI, and less in evidence in the latest deposits of VI than in the earlier ones.

Blegen, *Nemea* 261, suggested that the mottled and variegated surfaces of the Variegated and Rainbow Ware of the Early Neolithic on the Greek mainland might have been deliberately induced. Ridley and Wardle have formed the same impression in regard to the mottled ware common in the Early Neolithic of Servia in western Macedonia (*Servia* 193): this and the related Buntpoliert ware of Thessaly appear to be the equivalent of the Rainbow or Variegated ware of the southern Greek Neolithic (Milojcic, *Ergebnisse* 9). Buntpoliert ware is first attested at Sesklo it seems in Early Neolithic III (*Servia* 194). The fashion for this type of ware may have spread owing to southern influence as far as Thessaly in the course of Early Neolithic II and III (Protosesklo and Preseklo) there (*Otzaki-magula* i 28, 71 ff.). This Early Neolithic Variegated (Rainbow or Buntpoliert) ware of the Greek mainland in general appears to have a smoother finish than the Mottled Ware of Emporio VII–VI. It is more comparable perhaps with the pottery of Periods X–VIII at Emporio and with the red-surfaced vases from the Lower Cave at Ayio Gala. When the surfaces of these Ayio Gala vases are mottled, they recall those of the Variegated or Rainbow Ware of the Greek mainland.

At the same time there seem to be later parallels on the mainland for Emporio Mottled Ware. J. Lavezzi, *Hesperia* xlvii (1978) 417, has noted 'variegated ware (like that customarily considered Early Neolithic)' from Middle Neolithic contexts in the Forum West area at Corinth together with a dozen examples from Late Neolithic ones (ibid. 418, 428). H. Hansen, *Hesperia* vi (1937) 541f., commented on the mottling of the surfaces of some sherds with Kum Tepe I B affinities from the Late Neolithic horizon on the north slope of the Acropolis at Athens. Cf. *Athenian Agora* xiii 4 for mottling on some vases of the standard red burnished ware from the

Agora wells assigned to the Late Neolithic: in one case at least S. Immerwahr, ibid. 4, 23 no. 5, thought that the mottling had been deliberately produced by the application of coals.

Fine Black Burnished Ware. This was the standard ware for the small jugs with white-painted decoration of which many hundreds of fragments were recovered especially from levels of VI. The fabric of these jugs was in general extremely soft: sherds from them, even if thick, being easily broken or crumbled in the hand. The softness of the fabric presumably reflects a low firing temperature; but some fragments were of harder fabric, implying that the degree of firing varied. The clay in the break was normally black or grey-black throughout.

The inside surfaces of the jugs of *Fine Black Burnished Ware* were usually left rough, and were normally grey, but sometimes orange or brown, in colour. Their outsides were very well burnished; the burnish sometimes amounted to a polish, the surface being soapy to feel with the marks of the burnishing instrument hardly visible. The outside surfaces had evidently been coated with a wash before burnishing, and this appears to have been red when it was applied, altering to black with the firing; some fragments of jugs of *Fine Black Burnished Ware* had splashes of red paint on the inside. A few bowls, notably ones of type 14 (e.g. 629), with black surfaces very finely burnished, were also assignable to this fabric.

Some of the black burnished ware from levels of Emporio IX and VIII was virtually indistinguishable from the *Fine Black Burnished Ware* characteristic of Periods VII–VI. Black burnished ware was similarly at home from the beginning of the Neolithic on the Greek mainland (e.g. Lerna: *Hesperia* xxvi (1957) 160; xxvii (1958) 143. Corinth: Walker Kosmopoulos 1953, 4. *Nemea* 261). Some sporadic black burnished ware of very fine fabric comparable with Thessalian A 5 γ ware is recorded by Theochares from the lowest of the two levels of Early Neolithic at Nea Makri (*PAE* 1954, 116). The black burnished ware that appears at Elateia soon after the painted ware marking the start of Period 2 of the Early Neolithic there sounds very much like Emporio *Fine Black Burnished Ware* as regards the fabric (*Elateia* 172). But the *Fine Black Burnished Ware* with painted decoration in white characteristic of Emporio VII–VI appears to correspond to the Grey-black Burnished Ware of the Bothros horizon at Elateia assigned by Weinberg to the end of the Middle Neolithic although by some others to the beginning of the Late Neolithic there (*Elateia* 186 ff.). This was associated with Urfirnis, which may correspond to the *Light Brown Burnished Ware* of Emporio. Hour-glass handles comparable with those found on jugs of Emporio VII–VI were at home on bowls of the Elateia Bothros horizon.

The Elateia Gray-Black Burnished Ware seems to be the equivalent of Weinberg's later Neolithic Black Monochrome Ware (class II D) found at Corinth but thought by him to have been imported there (*Hesperia* vi (1937) 511 f.). Lavezzi, however, notes that in what appear to be transitional or mixed Middle/Late Neolithic contexts in the Forum West area at Corinth the Late Neolithic pottery is overwhelmingly black burnished ware, and black burnished ware continues to form over 30 per cent of the pottery in pure Late Neolithic deposits (*Hesperia* xlvii (1978) 417 f.). In the Franchthi cave a ware comparable to the Elateia Gray-Black Burnished and Corinthian Black Monochrome seems to appear in a horizon corresponding to that of the Elateia bothros, slightly before the occurrence of matt-painted ware which defines the beginning of the Late Neolithic (*Hesperia* xxxviii (1969) 368). Black burnished ware is much in evidence in the Late Neolithic at Varka in Euboia, but it is not recorded from the Middle Neolithic there (*AE* 1975 Parart. 75 f.).

The account by Walker Kosmopoulos, *Corinth* 30 note 55, of the 'Black Ware with Red Paint', which occurs most commonly in her Period III (Late Neolithic) there, appears to be describing a phenomenon like the splashes of red paint found on the insides of some jugs of *Fine*

Black Burnished Ware from Emporio. Blotches of lustreless red paint have also been noted on the insides of Middle Neolithic vases from the Franchthi cave (*Hesperia* xxxviii (1969) 366).

At Servia in western Macedonia the first really fine black burnished ware did not appear until the middle phase of the local Middle Neolithic (*Servia* 210). At Sesklo, however, in Thessaly fine black burnished pottery is said to occur, although rare, in Early Neolithic II (*Servia* 194). Fine black burnished ware is certainly attested in the Thessalian Middle Neolithic. In the case of the A 5 α Monochrome Black Ware of Rakhmani I it was noted that the deep black colour seemed to be 'due to the application of some pigment' (*PThess* 15). More comparable perhaps with the *Fine Black Burnished Ware* of Emporio, however, is the A 5 γ ware typical of the First Stratum at Orchomenos and other sites in Phocis where it occurs with A 3 β Sesklo-type painted ware (*PThess* 15); but the Γ 1 α 1 white-painted ware with ashy grey biscuit is an even more obvious equivalent for it (*PThess* 17). This is characteristic of Tsangli V, identified with the earliest (Tsangli or Dhimini I) phase of the Thessalian Late Neolithic. The painted designs on this look a good deal more evolved, however, and may be later in date than the white-painted decoration of Periods VII–VI at Emporio (e.g. *PThess* 105 fig. 55: a–l).

Weinberg has noted that the black burnished wares of the Middle and Late Neolithic in Greece are likely to derive from the Late Chalcolithic black wares of Anatolia (*CAH*[3] i Part 1, 599. Cf. *Hesperia* xxix (1960) 249). Walker Kosmopoulos (1953) ingeniously argued that details of the Corinthian Black Polished Ware of her Period III (Late Neolithic) might reflect a tradition of making utensils of birch-bark, suggesting an origin for it in the highlands of Anatolia where birch trees grew. The close relationship between the Late Chalcolithic black wares of Anatolia and the *Fine Black Burnished Ware* of Emporio VII–VI seems obvious.

It is interesting to note that the fine black burnished ware from the pre-Starcevo horizon of Period I at Anzabegovo in Jugoslav Macedonia appears to have been coated with a paint fired black like that of Emporio. The description of the very finest of this ware from the succeeding early Starcevo horizon, Anza II, with no stroke marks of the burnishing implement visible, is reminiscent of the best of the *Fine Black Burnished Ware* from levels of Emporio VII–VI (*Anza* 171 f.).

Light Brown Burnished Ware (PLATE 43). This distinctive ware appears to have been used for most of the larger varieties of jugs; these, unlike the small jugs of *Fine Black Burnished Ware*, were normally plain without any white-painted decoration. A few bowls and some jars were also made in this ware, which as regards the fabric was basically the same as *Fine Black Burnished Ware*, with the difference that the clay, although grey-black at the centre of the break, shaded to light brown at the edges. The inside surfaces of the jugs made of this ware were normally left untreated, and were light brown in colour; but the surfaces which were to be burnished were first coated with a light brown or less commonly with a red wash. This wash sometimes extended to the insides of jugs, where it was left unburnished. The burnished surfaces usually stayed light brown after firing, but might shade from light brown to red or dusky in patches; and red was evidently in some cases the dominant colour.

Most of the bowls and some of the jugs and jars of this ware had finely burnished surfaces. But many of the jugs and jars were only given a rather superficial scribble burnish, the stroke marks being very prominent and separated by unburnished areas. The effect of this superficial burnish is striking, and it may have been meant to be ornamental, a simple variety of 'pattern burnish' (PLATE 43).

The shapes of the jugs, which were the commonest type of vase made in this ware, taken in conjunction with their dominantly light brown surface colour, might suggest that they were copies of jugs made from gourds. The distinctive light brown surfaces could in that case have been evolved to reproduce the yellowish colour of original gourd vessels.

Light Brown Burnished Ware first makes its appearance in levels of Period VIII at Emporio. It seems to correspond to some at any rate of what is classified as Neolithic Urfirnis on the Greek mainland. Neolithic Urfirnis was first distinguished as a class by Kunze, *Orchomenos* ii 31–5: Class E. Kunze was inclined to set it at the end of the Neolithic, since he regarded it as ancestral to the Urfirnis ware of the Early Bronze Age (*Orchomenos* ii 47). He thought that it might have been produced in Central Greece, but could find no evidence for its existence in Thessaly, although a few sherds from the Choirospilia Cave on Levkas were similar.

Weinberg, *Hesperia* vi (1937) 500 ff., described Neolithic Urfirnis ware from Corinth, where numerous fragments of jugs with high necks, either vertical or splayed, were recognised in that fabric. These evidently had broad ribbon handles extending from lip to shoulder like the jugs of *Light Brown Burnished Ware* characteristic of Emporio VII–VI. Some of the fragments of Corinthian Neolithic Urfirnis closely resemble some *Light Brown Burnished Ware* from Emporio (ibid. 499 fig. 8, confirmed by inspection of selected examples in Corinth Museum). The insides of closed vases of Urfirnis ware illustrated by Kunze, *Orchomenos* ii 32 f. figs. 29, 30: A, similarly look very much like the insides of Emporio jugs of *Light Brown Burnished Ware*.

From the description of it Weinberg's Class A: Red Monochrome Ware from Corinth, equated with Thessalian A 1 ware, might correspond to some of what has been classified as *Light Brown Burnished Ware* at Emporio (*Hesperia* vi (1937) 498 ff.). None of this is illustrated, but 'fragments of globular jugs with high cylindrical necks sometimes sharply set off from the body' are reported to be most common (ibid. 500). Weinberg like Kunze has argued that Neolithic Urfirnis was simply a later development of this Red Monochrome Ware, citing stratified evidence from Ayioryitika in Arcadia (*Hesperia* vi (1937) 500. Cf. ibid. xxix (1960) 249). At the same time he has emphasised a close relationship between the Neolithic Urfirnis of Greece and the early type of Halaf ware of the Near East, especially that of Syria and Cilicia, in fabric, shape, glaze-paint and decoration (*CAH³* i Part 1, 596. Cf. *AJA* lxii (1958) 225. *Elateia* 208): 'decoration' here refers to vases with designs in lustrous paint of the kind used to coat Urfirnis ware; nothing comparable with this Neolithic Urfirnis patterned ware of the Greek mainland was recognised at Emporio.

Blegen called Neolithic Urfirnis from Prosymna 'Monochrome Brownish Black Ware', and noted that vast quantities of it were found in the upper strata at Ayioryitika (*Prosymna* i 371; ii 153 fig. 624). At Lerna Urfirnis was at home in Period II of the Neolithic there (*Hesperia* xxvi (1957) 159). From the upper Neolithic levels in Pit BD (Square E) at Lerna a large amount of red-brown glazed ware was recovered together with a smaller amount of red slipped ware, which occurred mainly but not exclusively in the earlier phases (*Hesperia* xxvii (1958) 137).

On the basis of the evidence from Corinth and Ayioryitika Weinberg assigned Neolithic Urfirnis to the Middle Neolithic, and defined the beginning of the Middle Neolithic period in the Peloponnese in terms of the first appearance of this ware there. Walker Kosmopoulos, *Corinth* i ff., 43 f., observed that Neolithic Urfirnis (called by her Corinthian Brown) already occurred at Corinth in her Period I, although typical of Period II (Middle Neolithic) and still in use to some extent at the beginning of Period III (Late Neolithic). She believed it to be a development of her 'Rainbow Ware' (Walker Kosmopoulos 1953, 2 and note 7), and stated that it was earlier at Corinth than at sites further south like Asea and Ayioryitika (ibid. 5). The most recent Neolithic excavations at Corinth suggest that the first Urfirnis appears there in a context assignable to the transition from Early Neolithic to Middle Neolithic alongside red-on-buff patterned ware and red-slip ware (J. Lavezzi, *Hesperia* xlvii (1978) 406).

In the Franchthi cave the beginning of the Middle Neolithic is marked by the emergence of 'a monochrome slipped ware which certainly anticipates (and is probably related to) the characteristic M.N. "glazed" ware (Urfirnis)' (*Hesperia* xxxviii (1969) 363). From its description this sounds more like Emporio *Light Brown Burnished Ware* than does the standard monochrome Neolithic Urfirnis which evolved from it. It is said that although the slip 'on occasion has what appears to be a natural sheen, most often it is thin and dull and gives the appearance of having been swabbed on the vessel with a cloth.' The clay generally ranges in colour between buff and orange-red throughout. The interiors of closed shapes frequently show signs of scraping. The slip is usually orange to red, but it may be darker (brown to black) and may vary from red to black on the same vase.

At the same time it is stated that at Franchthi the inner surfaces of many large vases, apparently of standard Middle Neolithic Urfirnis Ware, 'bear large spots or blotches of lusterless red paint . . . which may be accidental'. Lavezzi has called examples of this from Corinth 'dappled Urfirnis', noting its occurrence at Asea as well as in the Franchthi and Kefalari caves (*Hesperia* xlvii (1978) 407 and note 16; 417). Similar splashes of paint were noted on the insides of jugs of *Fine Black* and *Light Brown Burnished Ware* from Emporio. Moreover the 'Burnished Urfirnis' of the latter part of the Middle Neolithic in the Franchthi Cave looks very much like some Emporio *Light Brown Burnished Ware* (*Hesperia* xxxviii (1969) 366 f. pl. 97: c). This Burnished Urfirnis appears to continue into the Late Neolithic at Franchthi, and the standard Middle Neolithic Monochrome Urfirnis was also produced in substantial quantities throughout much of the Late Neolithic there. Finally Jacobsen notes that 'the quality of the L.N. "glaze" is generally inferior to that of the best M.N. Urfirnis, and in that sense it is somewhat reminiscent of the thin slipped ware which introduces the M.N. period' (ibid. 370). Similarly Lavezzi notes that some 7 per cent of the pottery from Late Neolithic deposits in the Forum West area at Corinth was monochrome Urfirnis ware (*Hesperia* xlvii (1978) 418, 423, 429). He remarks that there seems to be little to distinguish this Late Neolithic from Middle Neolithic Urfirnis, with the suspected exception of a greater use of pattern burnishing in the Late Neolithic.

Weinberg, *Hesperia* vi (1937) 502, implies that some of the burnishing on Neolithic Urfirnis ware from Corinth was deliberate for decorative effect. But Lavezzi, *Hesperia* xlvii (1978) 407, observes that there was only a small amount of scribble-burnished Urfirnis and no true pattern burnishing from the Middle Neolithic deposits in his soundings in the Babbius area at Corinth. He is inclined to assign this material, however, to a relatively early phase of the local Middle Neolithic. A few sherds of scribble-burnished Urfirnis occurred in the Forum West area, mostly in mixed or transitional Middle/Late Neolithic contexts (ibid. 417).

The Urfirnis with burnished decoration of the 'Streifig polierte' class described by Felsch from the Kefalari Cave in the Argolid looks exactly like much of the Emporio *Light Brown Burnished Ware* (*AM* lxxxvi (1971) 5 pl. 3: 4-11). Felsch notes that the finest of this is reminiscent of the veining in wood. Some of the fragments included in his Urfirnis with regular pattern burnish can also be matched at Emporio (e.g. the rough lattice on *AM* lxxxvi (1971) pl. 2: 15. Cf. *Hesperia* xxxviii (1969) pl. 97: c, top right, from the Franchthi Cave). Felsch argues that this kind of Urfirnis with burnished decoration is something peculiar to the north-east Peloponnese, and he distinguishes it from the Monochrome Urfirnis Ware (*AM* lxxxvi (1971) 9). The Stroke-firnis from Koufovouno near Sparta assigned by Phelps to his Period II (Middle Neolithic) similarly looks indistinguishable from the Emporio variety of *Light Brown Burnished Ware* with the stroke marks visible (Phelps, *Thesis* figs. 71: 1; 77: 10, 15).

Neolithic Urfirnis Ware seems to have been at home in Attica and Euboia as well as in the Peloponnese. At Nea Makri on the eastern coast of Attica it appeared before the end of Period A II, but was especially characteristic of the succeeding periods B I and II, although it still occurred in B III (*PAE* 1954, 118 f. *Nea Makri* 20, 28 note 33). Theochares noted that at first the

Urfirnis at Nea Makri was usually monochrome, although Urfirnis patterned ware occurred immediately afterwards (*PAE* 1954, 118 f.). It is interesting that the incised ware comparable with that of Emporio VIII belonged to an earlier horizon at Nea Makri.

Urfirnis Ware was one of the best represented classes of Neolithic pottery observed in survey work in Euboia (*BSA* lxi (1966) 84). There appears to be only a limited amount of it, however, in the Skoteini cave near Tharounia (*AAA* ix (1976) 51). It was similarly scarce it seems at the important settlement of Varka, although it was found there in the lowest layer together with red monochrome ware assignable to the Middle Neolithic. The description of the Varka Urfirnis sounds very much like Emporio *Light Brown Burnished Ware* (Sampson, *AE* 1975 Parart. 68 f.).

Neolithic Urfirnis Ware does not appear to have been so common in the north of Greece despite its first recognition by Kunze at Orchomenos. There was very little at Elateia, and most of this was found scattered in bits in the uppermost mixed levels, except for 'one large group of it, or a variant of it' recovered from the Bothros in trench 3 assigned by Weinberg to the end of the Middle Neolithic (*Elateia* 179 ff.). It never seems to have become a feature of the Neolithic in Thessaly. But fragments of a bowl of decorated Urfirnis Ware, evidently an import, were recovered from a late context of the Middle Neolithic at Pyrasos (*Thessalika* ii (1959) 52 ff.). Urfirnis ware has also been recognised at Otzaki from pits and ditches cut into Middle Neolithic levels, and therefore presumably of Late Neolithic date (Milojcic, *Ergebnisse* 16).

The evidence for a connection between the *Light Brown Burnished Ware* of Emporio and varieties of the Neolithic Urfirnis of the Greek mainland seems overwhelmingly strong. The association of this ware with gourd-like jugs at Emporio suggests that it may have been developed in an attempt to reproduce the yellowish brown surfaces of original vessels made from gourds. But a theory of gourd-imitation does not exclude the possibility of development from earlier red-surfaced wares on the technical side, nor even that of Halafian influence from the east. It might, however, indicate that Emporio was nearer than the Greek mainland to the source of origin of this distinctive ware.

There is a hint that at Nea Makri on the eastern coast of Attica the earliest Urfirnis was monochrome (*PAE* 1954, 118 f.). Perhaps the idea of patterned Urfirnis was developed on the Greek mainland on the basis of an original monochrome variety under the influence of the painted patterned ware at home in the Early Neolithic there.

Red or Light Brown Washed Ware (PLATE 52(*a*)). A number of jars, and some larger jugs, had an unburnished wash, usually red, but sometimes (in the case of jugs at least) light brown in colour.

Light Plain Ware (PLATE 52 (*b*)). This distinctive ware was already it seems current during Period VIII if not earlier, and it appears to have been more at home in Period VII than in VI. Some small thin-walled vases were evidently made in this ware, but it was characteristically used for large thick-walled jugs and for large jars with differentiated shoulders and wide mouths. The fabric was normally rather coarse, tempered with grit and some straw, impressions of straw and grit being often very prominent in the surfaces of vases. The clay was dark—black or grey-black—in the centre of the break, but light brown towards the edges. Surfaces were usually whitish, and often at least the whiteness appears to have been enhanced by the application of a thin slip or wash. But sometimes the surface was orange, pale brown, or reddish; occasionally a darker shade of brown. Surfaces might be wiped or smoothed, or given a very superficial burnish.

The Coarse Ware of the Early Neolithic at Nemea on the Greek mainland sounds rather comparable (*Nemea* 268 f.). Cf. *Prosymna* i 370, from the area about the graves, assigned to the earlier Neolithic, under A I (c): 'Another type of coarse ware is pink or buff in colour, with clay fired to gray at the core'.

White Slipped Ware. This is discussed under Periods X–VIII. One or two sherds from levels of VII–VI were coated with a thick white slip which was in most cases burnished. But a fragment from G level 119 of Period VII had an unburnished white slip on what appeared to be the inside surface.

Silvery Grey Ware. This is described under Periods V–IV, but it seems to be attested as early as VIII. A few sherds from grey-surfaced bowls found in upper levels of VI (e.g. 512, 513 of type 8) were of a hard fabric which approximated to this ware.

Cooking Pot Ware. This was characteristically used for large jars, many of which were probably in fact cooking pots. The clay had a good deal of grit in it and was often fired quite hard. In many cases, if not as a normal rule, the vases of this ware were coated with a red wash but were left unburnished.

Baking Pan Ware, of the kind at home in Periods X–VIII, was still used for making baking pans of type 3.

Foreign fabrics (see also under 'Imports'). Some twenty fragments of what appear to have been imported vases were recovered from levels of VII and VI. But very few of these were of distinctive fabrics.

(1) **Micaceous Wares**, identified by the presence of shining mica-like particles in the clay, as noted in levels of Periods X–VIII, were not much in evidence, apart from the *Obsidian Ware* noted below.

(2) **Obsidian Ware**. This variety of *Micaceous Ware*, which is described in detail under Periods V–IV, is distinguished by its hard fabric and the presence of shiny black angular particles resembling specks of obsidian. Two pithos rims from levels of VII (742) and VI (746) were assignable to this ware.

(3) **Fine Light Grey Burnished Ware**. The handle 818 is of a fabric akin to this ware, of which fragments were recovered from levels of X and IX.

SHAPES

(A) BOWLS

Bowls tended to be large, and some were evidently very large in size, notably those of type 11 which appeared to have diameters of as much as 50 or more, while the small, almost miniature and very thin-walled bowls, of which fragments were noticed in deposits of the earliest periods X–IX, were no longer in evidence. The finest bowls might be of the standard *Fine Black Burnished* or *Light Brown Burnished Ware*, and especially in Period VII of *Mottled Ware*; but well burnished surfaces shades of brown, grey-brown, and red also occurred.

Bowls with inward leaning rims tended to be high-shouldered as type 7, rather than like type 6, and merged into type 8. But rims assignable to type 8, which formed about a fifth (20 per cent) of all bowl rims in Period VIII, accounted for less than 5 per cent of them in VII and some 8 per cent in VI. Over one-third (c. 35 per cent) of the bowl rims from VII were of the distinctive type

11, and more than one-fifth (over 20 per cent) were of type 10, as against 14 per cent of type 10 and only 6 per cent of type 11 from VI. Thus type 11, virtually unrepresented in VIII and less common in VI than in VII, may be regarded as the hallmark of Period VII, while type 10 serves to distinguish VII and VI as a whole.

In Period VI simple rims, whether open or inward-curving, as found on types 4–7, appear to account for nearly one half (at least 44 per cent) of all those from bowls; but in VII such rims only formed some 22 per cent of the total. In VI as well as in VII carinated bowls of type 9 were distinctly rare, and some or all of the few rims assigned to this type may be freaks or later strays; over one half (seven out of twelve) were of the somewhat atypical class D.

3. *Baking pans* 431–435 (FIG. 141)

Fragments of baking pans were still common in levels of VII–VI, although vases of this type were clearly not as abundant as they had been earlier in X–VIII. There were no examples of rims with large tongue-shaped lugs on the inside such as were met in X–VIII; but 434 from a deposit with

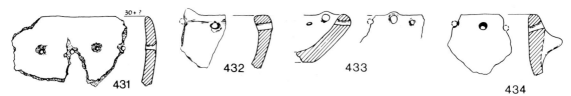

FIG. 141. Periods VII–VI. Type 3. Scale 1/3.

some admixture of Period V has a small lug of this class on the outside, and the strainer spout on the outside of 435, which to judge from its fabric may come from a baking pan, could in fact be a lug like that which appears on the inside of 28 from VIII Q 145.

431. (VI G 93) Rim. Sandy greyish clay; surface dusky orange, unburnished.
432. (VI G ?103/93) Rim. Soft fabric. Lightish grey clay; surface possibly light brown to red, burnished but worn.
433. (VI G 93) Profile. Outside grey-brown, rough; inside light brown, burnished.
434. (VI/V H ?103) Rim with small tongue-shaped lug on outside. Coarse grey clay; outside surface light brown, rough.
435. (VI/V Q ?75) (PLATE 53) Strainer spout, or rim of baking pan with crescentic lug cf. 28 (VIII Q 145) but on outside. Very coarse baking pan type fabric. Outside light brown, inside dark grey.

4. *Open bowls with straight or slightly curving sides* 436–453 (FIG. 142)

These still seem to have been common as in X–VIII. A number of rims assignable to such bowls are markedly thickened (e.g. 439). The thickened rim 441 seems to have belonged to a small deep bowl of flower-pot shape. Some of these bowls evidently had vertical handles (437, 440) or horizontally perforated lugs (446) set immediately below the rim on the outside. But 445 apparently had a lug or handle on the inside, while a curving rib in relief graces the inside of 444. A number of rims (447–452) evidently came from shallow plate-like bowls (type 4 C), and these more than the others tended to be of exceptionally fine fabric with a high polish-like burnish.

A, B. Deep and medium
436. (VII G 119) Light brown; fine burnish.
437. (VII G 119) Stump of small vertical handle. Angle possibly wrong, and perhaps from a jar not a bowl. Coarse gritty clay, grey at core; surface orange, with poor burnish outside, inside unburnished.
438. (VII G 122) Mottled Ware; abundant grit showing in surface, which pitted, light brown to dusky, burnished.

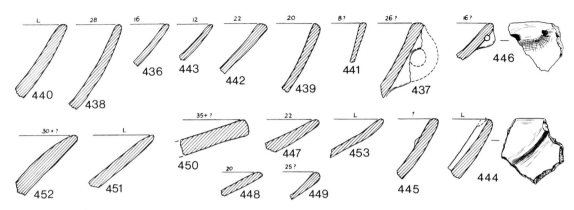

FIG. 142. Periods VII–VI. Type 4. Scale 1/3.

439. (VII G 115) Mottled Ware; shades of dark and light brown to red, burnished.
440. (VI G wall 20) Shades of dark to light brown and red outside, red to light brown inside, burnished. Similar rim from VIII/VII Q 145 with stump of vertical handle. Coarse gritty clay; surface light brown to reddish, somewhat pitted with poor burnish outside and in.
440A. (VII G 122) (PLATE 46) cf. 440. Orange clay with grey and white grit; surface with whitish slip. Possibly an import.
441. (VI G 103) Outside dark brown, inside lightish brown, burnished.
442. (VI G ?103/93) Mottled Ware: light brown mottling to black; very fine burnish.
443. (VI G 93) Outside red, inside light brown, burnished.
444. (VI G ?103/93) Rib in relief on inside. Outside light brown, inside red; very fine burnish.
445. (VI H ?106) Stump of possible lug or handle on inside. Straw impressions showing in surface, which light brown with fine burnish but worn.
446. (VII G 130) Horizontally perforated lug. Soft fabric; straw impressions showing in surface, which grey-brown, burnished.

C. Shallow

447. (VII G 122) Mottled Ware; dark brown to black, shading to deep reddish, burnished. Two others similar, including one (VII G 115) of very coarse cooking pot type fabric; dusky grey-brown clay with large grit, unburnished.
448. (VII G 122) (PLATE 44) Mottled Ware; shades of dark and light brown to reddish; very fine burnish. Another similar from VI G level 103.
449. (VI G/H 109/89) Thickened, club-like. Grey-brown, burnished.
450. (VI G 103) Soft fabric; light greyish brown clay; surface much pitted, shades of dark to light brown, well burnished inside; outside unburnished.
451. (VI G 93) Surface deep purple shading to red, burnished. Another similar from VI H level ?106.
452. (VI G 93) Grey-brown to black with poor burnish.
453. (VII Q ?129) Mottled Ware; shades of light and dark brown to red; fine burnish.

5. *Open bowls with curving sides* 454–479 (FIG. 143)

A. Deep, more or less hemispherical

The thickening, already in evidence on rims assignable to bowls of this shape from levels of X–VIII, was if anything a more prominent feature in VII–VI. Some of these thickened rims were flat-topped. But unthickened rims with rounded or flattened tops continued to occur (e.g. 462, 463.). The rim 459 has a vertically perforated trumpet-like lug rising above it, and there was evidence for the presence of a horizontal trumpet lug below at least one other rim. Some rims (e.g. 456, 457) were of exceptionally fine fabric with a high burnish, and simple rims from small

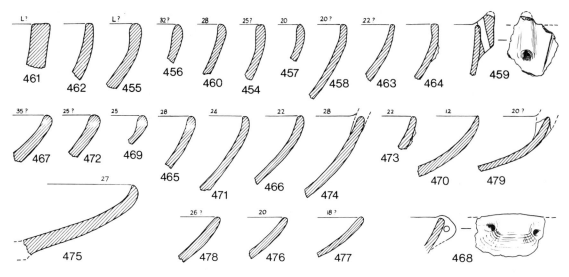

FIG. 143. Periods VII–VI. Type 5. Scale 1/3.

bowls with a diameter of less than 15 of which a number were recovered were mostly of fine burnished ware, although one of grey clay from VI G/H level ?109 was exceptional in having an orange surface, rough, wiped and unburnished. Two very large rims (461) were of coarse unburnished ware, reminiscent of jars rather than bowls.

454. (VII G 119) Angle not certain. Black, burnished. Another similar and apparently from the same vase, light brown to reddish.
455. (VII G 121) Surface dark shading to light brown with fine burnish, worn. Two others similar from VII G levels 122, 119.
456. (VII G 122) Dark brown to deep purplish red-brown; very fine burnish.
457. (VII G 122) Dark brown to black; very fine burnish.
458. (VI G wall 20) Shades of light and dark purplish brown; fine burnish.
459. (VI/V Q ?108) Rim with vertically perforated trumpet-like lug rising above it. Grey-brown; fine burnish.
460. (VI G ?103/93) Dark brown to black; very fine polish-like burnish.
461. (VI G ?103/93) Large, flat-topped rim. Cooking pot ware; surface purple-brown, burnished.
462. (VI H 106) Hard fabric; surface light reddish brown, burnished.
463. (VI H ?106) Light brown to red; fine burnish.
464. (VI H ?103) Stump of lug or handle. Surface rough and pitted, light brown inside, shades of grey and light brown outside, with coarse burnish.

B. Medium

A number of rims appeared to come from bowls assignable to this shape. They ranged in diameter from 12 to 30 or more. A good many were more or less markedly thickened (e.g. 465, 466, 469, 472), and one was flat-topped. One (474) had the stump of a lug or handle rising from it, and another (473) the remains of a horizontally perforated lug.

465. (VII G 122) Mottled Ware; dark red shading to dark brown and dusky, burnished.
466. (VII G 122) Light brown to dark brown and dusky; fine burnish.
467. (VI G wall 20) Grey-brown to reddish; fine burnish.
468. (VI G/Q 88) (PLATE 45) Horizontally preforated lug. Soft fabric; abundant straw impressions in surface, which grey-brown to light brown and reddish, burnished.

469. (VI G 103) Mottled Ware; grey-brown to black, except along top of rim which light brown; fine burnish.
470. (VI G 103) (PLATE 44) Mottled Ware; light brown mottling to reddish and black in patches; fine polish-like burnish. Two or three others from similar small bowls with surfaces grey-brown, burnished.
471. (VI G ?103/93) Grey-brown to black; top of rim tinged with dark reddish brown. Very fine burnish outside; inside dull as if worn by use. Four others similar, shades of light and dark brown, burnished.
472. (VI H ?106) Dark purplish brown to black, burnished but much worn. Another similar from VI R level ? 95 of soft fabric, with a red wash, burnished but worn.
473. (VII/VI H 117/105) Stump of horizontally perforated lug. Light to dark brown and black, burnished but much worn.
474. (VII Q ?129) Stump of handle rising from rim. Dark grey-brown clay; surface with a wash, deep purple-red, well burnished. Two others similar, grey-brown, burnished.

C. Shallow

The rims grouped here, mostly from levels of VII, belong to shallow bowls of fine burnished ware with a diameter of *c.* 20-30. One (479) has the stump of a handle rising above it.

475. (VII G 122) Mottled Ware; light brown to red and dusky black; fine burnish. Two others similar, one with the inside unburnished.
476. (VI G 93) Light brown; fine burnish. Another similar from G level ?103, light grey brown with fine burnish.
477. (VII Q 130) Angle not certain. Grey-brown shading to dark red; very fine burnish.
478. (VII Q ?129) Light greyish brown, burnished. Another similar, red, with fine burnish.
479. (VII Q ?129) Stump of handle rising above rim. Outside dusky grey-brown, inside lighter brown, well burnished. Two others similar.

6. *Bowls with inward-leaning rims* 480–487 (FIG. 144)

Bowl rims of this type are similar in profile to jar rims of class A I, and some of the rims grouped here, notably those with handles and lugs (483, 484, 486), might come from jars akin to type 35. A number of large rims of coarse fabric had clear traces of a red wash, but others came from bowls with fine burnished surfaces, grey-brown, light brown, or mottled. These last were indistinguishable in shape from later rims like 935 (V G level 54) and 1449 (II X level 7).

480. (VII G 122 with fragment of rim from VI G 103) (PLATE 46) Profile of large bowl with one or more horizontal strap handles. Very coarse fabric. Clay dark grey in break, light brown at edges, with straw and abundant grit, including lumps measuring up to 2 in length. Straw impressions and grit showing everywhere in surface, which has a thick red wash, burnished but worn.
481. (VII G 122) (PLATE 46) Several fragments of large bowl. Coarse gritty grey clay; surface pitted, with grit showing in it, and coated with a thick red wash, burnished outside and in. Another similar, light brown outside, red to light brown and dusky inside, well burnished.
482. (VII G 122) Rim. Coarse fabric. Grey clay with large grit showing in surface, which light brown with a slight reddish tinge, perhaps due to a red wash; traces of very slight, poor burnish. Another similar with a thick red wash and slight burnish.
483. (VII G 119) Rim with vertically perforated lug. Fine Black Burnished Ware.
484. (VI G wall 20) Rim with stump of lug, perhaps double as 1729 of Period II. Light greyish brown; outside with poor burnish and incised decoration, inside smoothed but not burnished.
485. (VI G 103) Rim, as 939 from IV G level 25. Light brown to red; fine burnish. Several others from levels of VI similar, shades of grey-brown, light brown and red, burnished.
486. (VI H 94 (PLATE 54) Rim with vertically perforated lug. Very rough and irregular. Well fired; clay grey at core, brick-red at edges. Outside with a red wash mottling to light brown and dusky, inside light brownish grey; very poor burnish.
487. (VII Q ?129) Rim. Grey-brown to light brown; fine burnish.

7. *Bowls with inward leaning rims and high shoulders* 488–506 (FIG. 144)

Rims which may be grouped here were extremely common as earlier in X–VIII. Some were simple, like rims of this type current in V–IV (e.g. 940 from IV H level 35); but they were

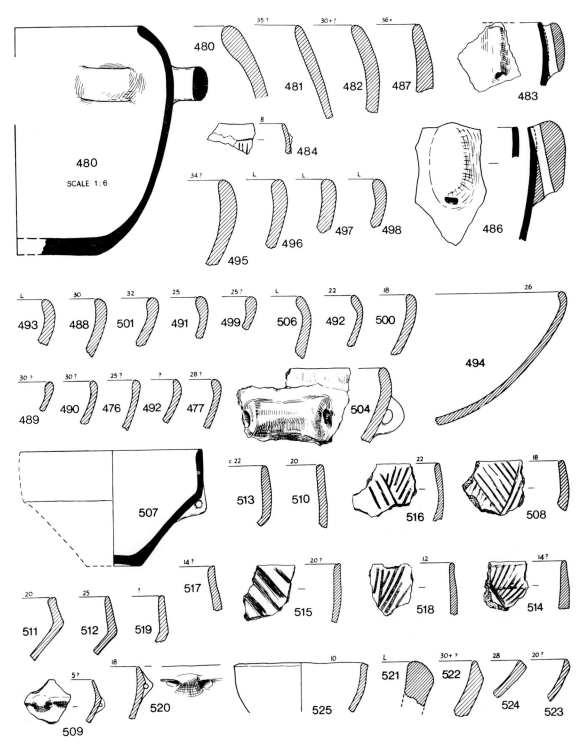

FIG. 144. Periods VII–VI. Types 6–9. Scale 1/3.

normally thickened and often club-like. Club rims indeed seem to be very characteristic of VII–VI, and merge into the rims of type 11 with a sharp internal differentiation, which are also characteristic of this horizon. Some type 7 bowls had horizontally perforated lugs, simple or trumpet shaped, set low on the side below the swelling. Rims assignable to this type tend to have a very fine burnish, many being of Mottled Ware; but 496 and the somewhat atypical 506 are unburnished.

488. (VII G ?132) Mottled Ware; shades of dark and light brown and red, well burnished.
489. (VII G 122) Grey-brown shading to deep reddish at the rim; very fine burnish.
490. (VII G 122) Mottle Ware; shades of light and dark brown and reddish, burnished. Four others similar.
491. (VI G wall 20) Grey-brown shading to reddish and light brown; very fine burnish. Another similar from VII G level 120, grey-brown, burnished.
492. (VI G wall 20) Outside shades of dark and light brown to red, inside dark brown; very fine polish-like burnish. Three others similar from VII G level 122, of Mottled Ware, surfaces dominantly light brown shading to red and dusky, with fine burnish.
493. (VI R ?137/?114/110/89) Hard fabric; surface red to light brown; fine burnish.
494. (VI G 103) Mottled Ware, shades of light and reddish brown mottling to dark brown and black; very fine burnish. Two others similar from VI G level 111, one with a simple horizontally perforated lug below the swelling. Mottled Ware; grey-brown shading to lighter brown and reddish, and light brown to darker brown and black; very fine burnish.
495. (VI G 103) Grey clay orange at surface, which has traces of a red wash; poor burnish outside and in.
496. (VI G 103) Grey clay orange at surface, which has traces of an unburnished red wash.
497. (VI G ?103/93) Grey-brown; fine burnish.
498. (VI G ?103/93) Outside light brown, inside red, burnished. One or two others similar; red, burnished.
499. (VI G 93) Light brown to red; fine burnish.
500. (VI G 93) Light brown to dusky; fine burnish.
501. (VI H ?106) Light brown to red, burnished. Two others similar.
502. (VI H ?106) Light brown to dark brown and black, burnished.
503. (VI H ?106) Black, burnished but worn.
504. (VI H ?106) Horizontal trumpet lug below rim. Light brown shading to dusky, burnished.
505. (VII Q 130) Grey-brown, burnished but worn. Two others similar.
506. (VII Q ?129) Angle not certain. Grey clay; surface red to light brown, unburnished.

8. *Bowls with carinated shoulders and tall rims* 507–519 (FIG. 144)

Bowls of this type were evidently still in common use. The only complete profile recovered (507) was not unfortunately from a very good context, but it may be of Period VII rather than later. This and several rims assignable to type 8 (including the miniature 509) had a simple horizontally perforated lug, perhaps one of a pair, set just below the carination. Small sunk bases of similar fabric to the rims may come from type 8 bowls.

These bowls were usually it seems dark-surfaced, shades of grey or grey-brown, but sometimes light brown or red. They might be well burnished, but did not as a rule have the highly polished surfaces found on many bowls of types 10 and 11. As in Period VIII they were characteristically decorated with pattern burnish, consisting of a frieze round the rim, normally of alternate hatched triangles (e.g. 508).

507. (VII/V Q ?127) (PLATE 46) Profile, with about a quarter of rim and one horizontally perforated lug below carination. Ht. 9. Diam. *c.* 15. Grey-brown clay with grit, some very large, and straw; surface dark brownish grey, rather uneven and with straw impressions showing in it, but well stroke burnished outside and in.
508. (VII G 119) Rim. Grey-brown; pattern burnish (alternate hatched triangles).
509. (VII G 119) (PLATE 45) Rim of exceptionally small bowl with horizontally perforated lug below carination. Brownish grey; fine burnish outside and in.
510. (VIII/VII Q ?127) Rim. Outside light brown to dusky, inside grey-brown, well burnished.
511. (VI G 108) Rim. Surface with a wash, red to light brown, unburnished.

512. (VI G 93) Rim. Hard fabric akin to Silvery Grey Ware. Grey, with a brownish tinge, burnished. One or two others similar in shape and fabric.

    Cf. *Kephala* pl. 29: B–D for comparable rims.

513. (VI G 93) Rim. Fabric as 512. Two or three others similar in shape and fabric.
514. (VI G 93) Rim. Grey clay; surface grey to chestnut brown; pattern burnish as 508.
515. (VI G 93) Rim. Chestnut brown; pattern burnish (wide diagonal bands).
516. (VI H ?106) Rim. Fine Black Burnished Ware; surface worn, but traces of pattern burnish as 508.
517. (VI Q ?100) Rim. Dark grey; fine burnish. Another similar from VII Q level 130 with pattern burnish as 508.
518. (VI/V Q ?75) Rim. Grey-brown; traces of pattern burnish as 508.
519. (VI/V Q ?75) Rim. Shades of light and dark brown; fine burnish.

9. *Carinated bowls* 520–526 (Fig. 144)

As in X–VIII rims of this type were rare, and mostly assignable to class D; although several from levels of VI were like rims 975 and 1000 of Period V with warts on the carination, but some at any rate of these might be later strays. A few rims assignable to type 9, however, came from deposits of VII (e.g. 520, 526). All the pieces described are rims.

520. (VII G 123) As 975 from V R level 50. Grey-brown to light brown and reddish, burnished.
521. (VI G ?103/93) Angle not certain. Hard fabric. Grey clay; surface shades of light brown to dusky; fine polish-like burnish.
522. (VI G ?103/93) With stump of side handle. Grey clay; surface shades of light brown to dusky; fine polish-like burnish.
523. (VI G ?103/93) Surface irregular, shades of brown mottling to black, well burnished.
524. (VI G 93) Light grey; surface worn, without any trace of burnish.

    For the rim shape (but not the fabric) compare *Elateia* 183 fig. 8: 5, from the Bothros in trench 3, assigned to the end of Middle Neolithic or beginning of Late Neolithic.

525. (VII Q ?129) Irregular and uneven. Outside with a red wash shading to light brown, inside dark brownish grey, well burnished.
526. (VI/V G ?93/54) Horizontally perforated lug. Dark brown to black; fine polish-like burnish.

10. *Bowls with short, S-shaped, usually thickened club-like rims* 527–569 (Figs. 145-147)

Bowls with rims of this type were evidently much at home in Period VII, and continued to be so in VI. The rims were normally more or less carinated, and often, although not invariably, thickened at the ends, which were usually rounded and club-like, but in about 25 per cent of the examples, sharp and pointed (fig. 146). The bowls were often rather crudely made and irregular in shape, so that different sections of rim from the same vase may have varied considerably in profile. The rims grouped here shade into those of other types, and a good many might be classified under types 13 or 14.

No complete profile was recovered, but the bowls from which these rims came appear to have been for the most part large and relatively shallow. Since they were so unevenly made and irregular in shape, it is difficult to be certain about the diameters of fragments of rim; but rims 30 or more in diameter were evidently not uncommon, and some of the bowls of this type may have been half a metre or more across. At the same time some diameters of 20 or less, and one (558) of as little as 10, were also recorded.

Several rims assignable to this type have remains of horizontal trumpet lugs, either set on the rim with the ends rising above it (fig. 147 class 1, e.g. 564–6), or below the rim as fig. 147 class 2. The lugs may have been in pairs, one on each side of the bowl, but there was no evidence about this.

It was noted that the fabric of bowls of type 10 tended to be rather soft in comparison with that of bowls of fine burnished ware of the other characteristic type 11. At the same time bowls of type 10 were normally well burnished inside and out, in spite of the often rather coarse clay, with

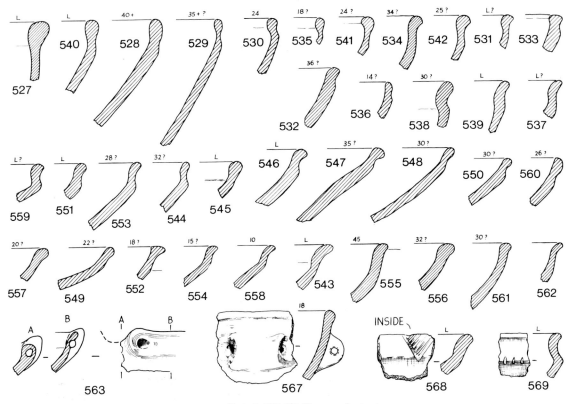

FIG. 145. Periods VII–VI. Type 10. Scale 1/3.

large lumps of grit and straw impressions showing in the surfaces, which were apt to be irregular and uneven. There was a considerable variety in surface colour, but many of the bowls were of the distinctive Mottled Ware, shading or mottling in splodges from red or light brown to dark brown and black. Some type 10 bowls, however, appear to have been more or less uniform in colour, with surfaces black (Fine Black Burnished Ware), light brown (akin to Light Brown Burnished Ware), or red. The bowls with red or light brown surfaces at any rate were evidently coated with a wash, of which the traces were clear in the few instances where the bowls had been left unburnished (e.g. 533, 534).

The mottling of the surface, which appears to have been especially favoured for the bowls of

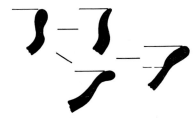

FIG. 146. Periods VII–VI. Rim variations of type 10 bowls.

this type, may have been deliberate and decorative in intention; but apart from this bowls of type 10 were normally it seems left undecorated. The somewhat atypical rim 568 was exceptional in having a hatched triangle in white on the inside. Another atypical rim (569) from a level of VI boasts a row of vertical incisions on the carination.

The rims have been divided into groups, according to whether they seem to come from (A) deep or (B) shallower varieties of bowl.

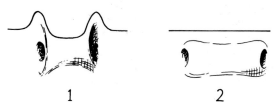

FIG. 147. Periods VII–VI. Trumpet lugs on type 10 bowls.

A. Deep

527. (VII G 122) Light brown to red, burnished. Two other rims from the same or a similar bowl from levels 123 and 122.
  Cf. *Poliochni* i pl. iv: e, Black period.
528. (VII G 122 and 115) Somewhat irregular. Outside dark brown shading to reddish brown round rim, inside dark purplish brown, well burnished.
529. (VII G 122) Mottled Ware; outside red to light brown mottling to black, inside shades of brown and dusky black, well burnished.
530. (VII G 122) Dark grey, burnished. Three other similar rims; one from VI G level 93 with a trumpet lug of FIG. 147: class 1, surface grey-brown with fine burnish.
531. (VII G 122) Light brown; fine burnish.
532. (VII G 122) Outside dark brown, inside dark purple-brown to black, burnished.
  Cf. *Poliochni* i pl. v: e, Black period.
535. (VII G 115) Grey clay, orange at surface, which has a red to light brown wash, unburnished.
534. (VII G 122) Fabric as 533, with an unburnished red wash.
535. (VI G 108) Light brown; fine burnish. Another similar from VII G/Q wall 19 with remains of a trumpet lug; dark brown to red, burnished.
536. (VI G 108) Light brown, fine burnish.
537. (VI G/H 109/89) Fine greyish clay; surface light greyish, burnished but worn.
538. (VI G 103) Irregular. Shades of dark brown; high polish-like burnish. Three others similar.
539. (VI G 103) Grey clay. Outside red-brown mottling to dusky purplish, inside light brown; fine burnish.
540. (VI G ?103/93) Irregular. Coarse fabric, with large grit. Outside red, inside black to light brown, well burnished. Eight or nine similar rims from levels of VII-VI with burnished surfaces varying from red to light brown, dark brown, and black. One from VII G/Q level 131 of Mottled Ware with an elegant trumpet lug of FIG. 147: class 1.
  Cf. *Poliochni* i pl. v: s, Black period.
541. (VI G ?103/93) Grey-brown to black; fine burnish.
542. (VI/V H cleaning wall 20) Dark brown to reddish, well burnished.

B. Shallow

543. (VII G 119) Outside light brown, inside reddish to purple-brown, burnished. Possibly from the same bowl as 563.
544. (VII G 122) Outside reddish to light brown, inside light brown mottling to dusky black, burnished.
545. (VII G 122) Fine Black Burnished Ware.
546. (VII G 122) (PLATE 44) Mottled Ware; outside light brown to dusky, inside darker brown, burnished.

547. (VII G 122) (PLATE 45) Very irregular. Mottled Ware; outside lightish brown with superficial stroke burnish, inside deep purple-brown; light brown to reddish round rim.

548. (VII G 122) (PLATE 44) Irregular. Large grit showing in surface. Outside light to dark brown and black; inside black, well burnished.

549. (VII G 122) Light brown; fine burnish.

550. (VII G 115) Irregular. Light mottling to darker brown, burnished. Another similar from VI G level 122; outside light brown, inside red, burnished.

551. (VII G 123) Light brown, shading to dusky inside; fine burnish.

552. (VII G 123) Light brown, fine burnish.

553. (VII G 122) Very irregular. Soft fabric. Outside reddish to light brown, inside dark brown, burnished.

554. (VII G 122) Soft fabric. Outside red to light brown, inside dark brown, burnished but worn.

555. (VII G 122) Grey clay, orange at surface. Outside red, inside light brown, with rough burnish.

556. (VII Q 131) Light brown; fine burnish.

557. (VI R ?137/?114/110/89) Lightish brown, burnished.

558. (VI G 103) Soft fabric. Grey clay; traces of original light brown surface, burnished but much worn. Another similar from VII G/Q 131/122; orange surface, rough and uneven, wiped but not burnished.

559. (VI G ?103/93) Soft fabric; dark grey to black clay. Outside light brown, inside grey; poor burnish, much worn.

560. (VI G 93) (PLATE 44) Light Brown Burnished Ware; dark grey to black clay; surface light brown with straw impressions showing in it, well burnished.
    Cf. *Poliochni* i pl. v: d, Black period.

561. (VI H 106) Soft fabric; surface light brown to red, burnished but much worn.
    Cf. *Kum Tepe* 334 fig. 14: 519, Phase I B 3.

562. (VI/V H ?103) Shades of dark to light brown; fine burnish.

Rims with lugs or decoration

563. (VII G 122) With part of trumpet lug of FIG. 147: class 1. Fine Black Burnished Ware. Possibly from same bowl as 543.

564-566 (VII G 122, 120, 122) (PLATE 44) With trumpet lugs of class 1.

567. (VI G ?103/93) (PLATE 45) With trumpet lug of class 2. Irregular; dark brown mottling to light brown and dusky, burnished.

568. (VII G 123) Grey-brown; fine burnish. Inside of rim with painted decoration in white: inverted hatched triangle.
    Hatched triangles like this occur on the insides of rims of Late Chalcolithic (Kum Tepe I B) bowls from Kayişlar near Akhisar in the part of western Anatolia more or less opposite Chios (*AS* xi (1961) 124 f. fig. 5 esp. 9, on a bowl cf. type 10). The same design, but in dark paint on a light ground, is found on the inside of rims of vases of the Bothros horizon at Elateia, assigned to the end of Middle or beginning of Late Neolithic (*Elateia* 182 ff. fig. 9 pl. 59, f: 1).

569. (VI G/H 109/89) Light grey shading to light brown, burnished. Incisions on the carination.
    There are close parallels from Late Neolithic contexts on the Greek mainland, e.g. *Athenian Agora* xiii 39 no. 140 pls. 10. 69. *Arapi* pl. 20: 5. *Balkan Studies* v (1964) 116 pl. 6 B, from the Rhodokhori cave in western Macedonia.

11. *Bowls with inward-curving rims, internally differentiated and usually thickened* 570–606 (FIG. 148)

This type is in effect an early version of type 12, into which it merges. It appears to be peculiar to Periods VII–VI, and is especially characteristic of VII. Along with type 10 it was much the commonest variety of bowl in use in VII, and was still quite well represented in levels of VI. Bowls of this type were evidently more or less conical or hemispherical in shape, and varied a good deal in the proportions of height to diameter, the deeper examples tending to approximate to bowls of types 6 and 7, some of the shallower to those of type 5. Most were large, with diameters ranging from 25–50 or more; but one or two (e.g. 604, 606) were only *c*. 20 in diameter. Two of the smaller bowls (597, 606) were exceptionally open and shallow.

A number of bowls of type 11 had long horizontally perforated lugs, or pairs of lugs, set below the swelling. These lugs were normally, if not in every case, trumpet-shaped. Whether by

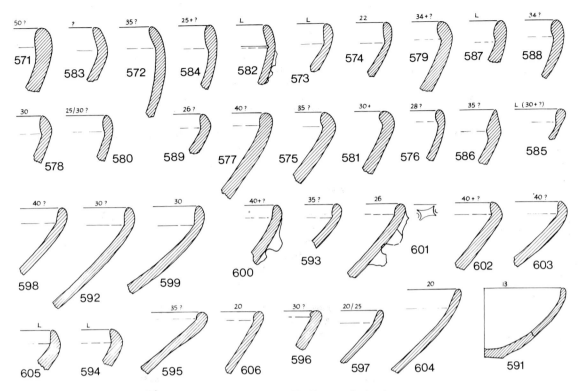

FIG. 148. Periods VII–VI. Type 11. Scale 1/3.

accident or design the trumpet lug on 601 was placed at an angle to the rim. Some type 11 bowls at least appear to have had flat or sunk bases, and these may have been comparatively small in relation to the diameter of the rim, if 595A really belongs to 595. The small bowl 591 has been reconstructed with a base which may go with it. It looks as if many of these bowls, especially the larger ones, were very irregular in shape. Nevertheless the fragments of them are almost invariably well burnished, and a number of them have a very high polish-like burnish, many being classifiable as of Fine Black Burnished or Mottled Ware. Indeed there was only one rim assignable to this type, in profile resembling 601, without any trace of burnish at all, and this had a lug attached, so that the surface of other parts of the bowl from which it came may have been burnished in the usual manner.

The rims have been divided into two groups, (A) coming from the deeper, (B) from the shallower varieties of bowls.

A. Deep

570. (VIII G 123, 122) (FIG. 150. PLATE 46). Large part of rim, and fragment of base which may belong with it. Gritty grey clay; surface much pitted, with straw impressions showing in it, dominantly light brown, shading to dark brown, dusky black and reddish, well burnished.
571. (VII G 122) Shades of light brown, burnished.
572. (VII G 122) Outside light brown, inside red, well burnished. Six others similar from VII G levels 122 and 120; Mottled Ware, with surfaces shades of dark brown, deep purple-brown, light brown and red, burnished.

573. (VII G 122) Light brown; very fine burnish. Four others similar; light brown and grey-brown to black, burnished.

574. (VII G 122) Mottled Ware; shades of dark and light brown to reddish; very fine burnish.
      Cf. *Kephala* pl. 29: K for a comparable rim.

575. (VII G 122) Mottled Ware; shades of light and dark purplish brown to dusky and reddish, burnished. Inside with rather scanty burnish; stroke marks clearly visible.

576. (VII G 122) Outside shades of light and dark brown, inside light brown; fine burnish.

577. (VII G 123, 122, 119) Rim and fragments of same bowl. Mottled Ware; orange to grey clay; surface dominantly red shading to light and dark brown, deep purple-brown and dusky, irregular and uneven but well burnished.

578. (VII G 123) Outside light brown, inside dark brown; fine burnish. Another similar from VII G level ?122.

579. (VII G/Q 131) Dark brown mottling to lighter brown, burnished.

580. (VII G/Q 131) Lightish brown, burnished.

581. (VII Q 127) Light brown; very fine burnish.

582. (VI G wall 20) With stump of long horizontal (?trumpet) lug. Dark grey-brown to light brown and reddish, burnished.

583. (VI G/Q 111/108) Angle not certain. Grey-brown; fine burnish.

584. (VI G/Q 111/108) Light brown mottling to dark brown and black; fine burnish. Three others similar: one from VII G/Q level 131, grey-brown to black, deep reddish at rim, burnished; two from VI G level 111, light brown, and light brown to red, burnished.

585. (VI G/H 109/89) Dark brown mottling to reddish and lighter shades of brown, burnished.

586. (VI H 103) Grey clay; outside light brown and reddish mottling to black at rim, inside dark brown to black, burnished.

587. (VI G 103) Grey clay; surface shades of dark and light brown; fine polish-like burnish.

588. (VIII/VI H ?149) Light brown to reddish, burnished.

589. (VIII/VI H 149, 117/105) Dark brown to black, burnished.

B. Shallow

590. (VII G 122) (FIG. 150. PLATE 47) Large fragment of rim with horizontal trumpet lug below swelling (FIG. 147: class 2). Hole bored after firing through side. Fine Black Burnished Ware; surface black to shades of dark brown. Two others similar of Mottled Ware; light brown with a reddish tinge and dusky patches, well burnished.

591. (VII G 119) Rim, and base which may belong with it. Dark brown to black; very fine burnish.

592. (VII G 122) Three rims, all perhaps from the same bowl. Mottled Ware; dominantly light brown to reddish, with dark brown and dusky black patches, well burnished. For the shape cf. 155 from VIII B level 144.

593. (VII G 122) Mottled Ware; shades of light and reddish brown to deep purple, burnished.

594. (VII G 122) Shades of light and dark brown to reddish, burnished.

595. (VII G 122) (PLATE 44) The sunk base 595A may belong with this rim. Light brown; fine burnish.

596. (VII G ?122) Black, burnished but worn.

597. (VII G 122) Fine Black Burnished Ware; outside dark brown with a slight reddish tinge, inside black. Three or four others similar; Fine Black Burnished Ware and Mottled Ware.

598. (VII G 122) Mottled Ware; shades of light and dark brown to black, burnished.

599. (VII G 122) Mottled Ware; outside shades of light and dark brown, inside light brown, burnished. Three others similar.

600 (VII G 122) With stump of long horizontal (?trumpet) lug. Mottled Ware; outside dark brown to black with a tinge of reddish, inside black, burnished. Another similar from VII Q level 130/129; red, burnished but much worn.

601. (VII G 122) With stump of large, elegant trumpet lug, set at angle. Outside dark brown, inside deep purple-brown burnished. Another similar with trumpet lug has the surface light brown to reddish, unburnished.

602. (VII G 122) Mottled Ware; dominantly dark brown, burnished.

603. (VII G 122) Mottled Ware; shades of dark and light brown to reddish, burnished.

604. (VII G 122) Fine Black Burnished Ware; dark brown to black. Another similar; Mottled Ware, dominantly light brown, burnished.

605. (VI G 103) Grey clay, orange at surface, with a whitish slip, burnished.

606. (VI G 93) Light brown mottling to dusky black; fine burnish.

12. *Bowls with straight rims, thickened and usually differentiated on the inside* 607–610 (FIG. 149)

Bowls with rims like this appear to be later versions of type 11. They were evidently rare in VII–VI; but a few rims which may be grouped here were recovered from levels of VI, and one or two from VII.

607. (VII G 122) Fine Black Burnished Ware.
608. (VI G 93) Mottled Ware; light brown to reddish mottling to black; fine burnish. Two others similar: one from VII G level 119, grey-brown, burnished; the other from VI G level 93, Fine Black Burnished Ware.
609. (VI G 93) With bold horizontal groove outside. Dark grey clay; surface light grey, either very worn or unburnished.
610. (VI R ?95) Fine Light Brown Burnished Ware.

13. *Bowls with outward-curving rims, internally differentiated and thickened* 611–614 (FIG. 149)

None of the few rims classified under this heading are very typical. Some might be considered as varieties of type 10, others could be assigned to type 14.

611. (VII G 123) Mottled Ware; shades of light brown and red, burnished.
612. (VI G ?103/93) Irregular in shape. Deep reddish to dusky brown, burnished.
      Cf. *Kum Tepe* 333 fig. 18: 533, Phase I B 3.
613. (VI G 93) Grey to light brown; poor burnish.
614. (VII/Q ?129) Light brown to red, burnished but worn.

14. *Bowls with outward-curving rims, not internally differentiated, but sometimes thickened* 615–636 (FIG. 149)

Bowls of this type were already at home in Period VIII, and were evidently not uncommon in VII–VI. The rims may be divided according to whether they appear to come from (A) deep,

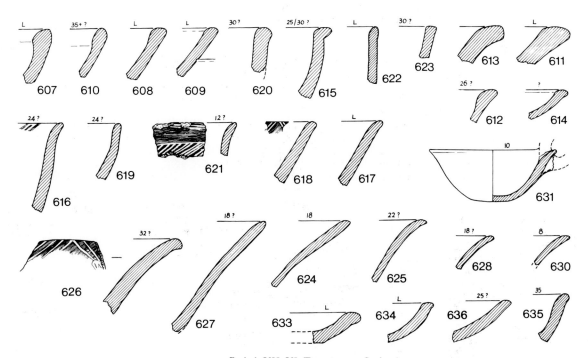

FIG. 149. Periods VII–VI. Types 12–14. Scale 1/3.

(B) medium, (C) shallow, or (D) dish-like varieties of bowl. Some, especially those of the widely splayed type grouped under C, have finely burnished surfaces, either black (Fine Black Burnished Ware), or variegated, shades of brown, black and red (Mottled Ware). The rim 615 grouped under class A is unusual. Dishes like 633 are interesting for comparisons with the Anatolian Late Chalcolithic.

Most of the bowls of this type appear to have been handleless, although a few had lugs. The profile 631 is unique in its vertical strap handle rising from the rim; it is also unusual by reason of its small size and lack of burnish: it appears to be the earliest example of a class of small handled bowls (Dipper cups of type 16) which are a feature of subsequent periods from V–II. The rim 632 from the upper part of VI has a lug with double vertical perforations.

Four rims preserved traces of white-painted decoration, once (621) on the outside, but in the other three cases (616, 618, 626) round the inside of the rim.

A. Deep

615. (VII G 119) Grey-brown, apparently with a rather poor burnish, but worn. For the shape cf. 159 from VIII G level 139.

616 (VII G 121) Mottled Ware; shades of dark and light brown to reddish, burnished but worn. Inside with traces of white-painted decoration (three diagonal stripes cf. 626).

617. (VII G 122) Grey-brown, burnished. Two others similar: one from VII G level 119, Mottled Ware, shades of light and dark brown to red, burnished; the other from VII Q 130, soft fabric, light brown to red, burnished but worn.

618. (VII Q 131) Mottled Ware; dark brown to red, worn. Inside with traces of white-painted decoration (groups of fine diagonal lines).

619. (VII G/H 113) Light brown to reddish and dusky, burnished.

620. (VI G 103) Grey clay, orange at surface, which is full of straw impressions without any trace of burnish.

621. (VI G ?103/93) Dark brown to black; very fine polish-like burnish. White-painted decoration on outside.

622. (VI H 106) Light brown; very fine burnish.

623. (VI/V Q ?75) Grey-brown, burnished.

B. Medium

624. (VII G 122) Mottled Ware; shades of dark and light brown; very fine burnish.

625. (VII G 120) Mottled Ware; red to shades of dark and light brown; exceptionally fine burnish, with stroke marks hardly if at all visible. Another similar from VII G level 122; red to light brown, burnished.

626. (VI G wall 20) Light Brown Burnished Ware. Inside with painted decoration in white (alternate groups of diagonal stripes cf. 616).

Rims of Late Chalcolithic bowls of various types from Beycesultan and other sites in western Anatolia are regularly painted in white on the inside. Some rims of this type have designs like 626 (*Beycesultan* i 74 FIG. P. 2: 18, 86 fig. P. 7: 3, 5, of L. C. 1 and 2).

627. (VI G/H 109/89) Grey-brown; fine polish-like burnish.

628. (VI G 103) Grey clay; surface mottled, shades of light and dark brown to red; very fine burnish, but much worn.

C. Shallow

629. (VII/VI G 115, 93) (FIG. 150. PLATE 47) About half rim and other fragments. Diam. *c.* 19. Fine Black Burnished Ware; soft grey clay; surface jet black with very high polish-like burnish, soapy to feel, but with stroke-marks of burnishing implement clearly visible.

630. (VI G 93) Grey-brown, burnished.

631. (VI G ?103/93) (PLATE 45) Profile, with stump of vertical handle rising from rim. Ht. 4. Diam. 11. Grey clay; surface light brown mottling to reddish and dusky black, unburnished.

632. (VI G 93) (FIG. 150. PLATE 45) With large vertically perforated lug. Soft fabric; dark grey clay with white grit. Surface apparently with a light brown to red wash, burnished but much worn.

Compare 914 of Period V and examples from Troy I (*Troy* i figs. 237: 30; 241: 31, 32; 246: 26). Cf. *Saliagos* fig. 46: 6. *Beycesultan* i 100 fig. P. 12: 11, level XX of L. C. 4. *BRGK* xliii-xliv (1962-63) 20 pl. 14: 2, Starčevo Culture, from Zelenikovo in Jugoslav Macedonia.

D. Dish-like
633. (VII G 122) Profile. Rough and irregular. Outside red, inside light brown, burnished.
634. (VII G 123) Light brownish grey, burnished.
635. (VI G wall 20) Rough and irregular. Light brown to red; poor superficial burnish.
636. (VII/VI R ?137/?114/110/89) Outside grey-brown, inside light brown, burnished.

(B) JUGS, THERIOMORPHIC VASES, AND TRIPOD COOKING POTS

Jugs 637–651 (FIGS. 150–153)

Fragments of jugs were common, especially in levels of Period VI. Their abundance in deposits of VI may be due to the fact that jugs were used and broken in connection with rites of some kind at the well. From the layers of pebbles (levels 111-108, 89-87) forming the roadway down to the well and the platform round it some comparatively large fragments of jugs were recovered, but none was complete.

Most of the jugs represented by these fragments were of a distinctive fabric: either Light Brown Burnished Ware, or, in the case of many of the smaller jugs, Fine Black Burnished Ware. The outsides of the jugs were coated with a wash, which, in the case of those of Light Brown Burnished Ware was light brown or reddish in colour. While most of these Light Brown Burnished jugs were of that colour, their surfaces often shaded to reddish, and in some cases it seems the whole surface was red. The wash coating jugs of Fine Black Burnished Ware may have been the same as that used for ones of Light Brown and Red Burnished Ware, the difference in surface colour being deliberately induced by a different technique of firing. The wash normally extended fairly deep round the inside of the jug rim, and splashes of it on the inside surfaces of the bodies often escaped burnishing. Unburnished areas of wash on the insides of jugs of Fine Black Burnished Ware were apt to be a shade of dark purple which might have a reddish tinge. In some cases it seems the outside surface of a jug was shades of dusky brown or brown to black, intermediary between the colours of the Fine Black and Light Brown Burnished Wares. But in general the two fabrics were quite distinct, and it seems to have been the intention of the potters to make the surface either black or light brown. In addition there were evidently some jugs of a very different, coarse, gritty fabric, with burnished surfaces shades of grey or grey-brown. A number of fragments of these were recovered, notably from the upper levels of VI, but they do not appear to have been common.

The burnish, especially in the case of jugs of Fine Black Burnished Ware, was often very fine, like a polish, leaving the surface smooth and even, although the strokes of the burnishing implement can normally be detected. Jugs of Fine Black Burnished Ware were evidently much less numerous, and on the whole distinctly smaller, than those of Light Brown Burnished Ware. The burnish on jugs of Light Brown Burnished Ware might be very fine and thorough, as in the case of 645; but it normally tended to be rather superficial, and was often just a partial 'stroke' burnish, the lines of it standing out against the unburnished parts with an effect, which, although not strictly 'pattern burnish', may have been to some extent consciously decorative (PLATE 43). A number of jugs, most of them it seems relatively large, had the outsides coated with a matt wash, light brown or more often red in colour, which was left unburnished (Red or Light Brown Washed Ware).

The material, although abundant, was so fragmentary that it was only possible to reconstruct complete shapes in a very few instances. Jugs evidently varied a great deal in size, ranging from ones which were virtually miniatures less than 0.10 m high (like 639) to very large examples of which fragments were noted. Mouths were commonly wide, with the rims either flat

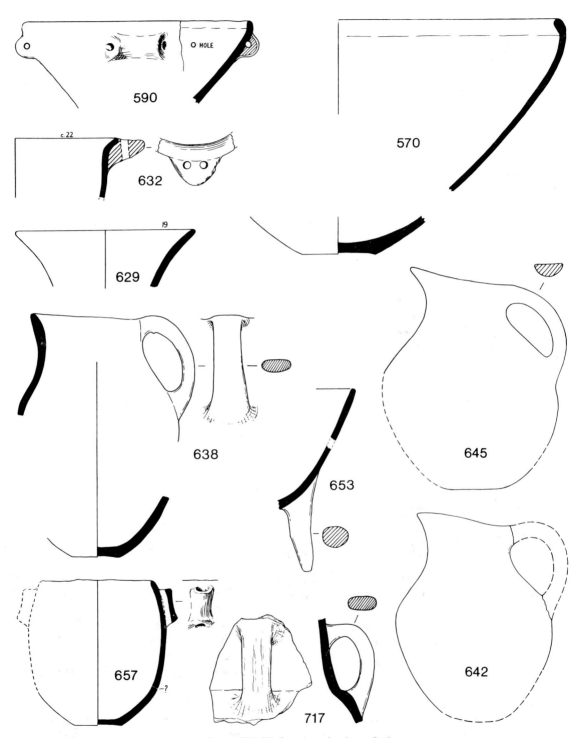

FIG. 150. Periods VII–VI. Jugs, large bowls etc. Scale 1/4.

(as 1 on FIG. 151), or more usually sloping (as 2). A number of small jugs with rims of class 1 may have been virtually handled bowls; some of Fine Black Burnished Ware were evidently burnished for a considerable distance below the rim, while some of the (usually larger) jars of Light Brown Burnished Ware appear to have had a red wash covering the inside: this was normally unburnished, but upon occasion it seems the whole of the inside of the vase was smoothed or given a superficial burnish.

Some jugs of Fine Black Burnished Ware were narrow-mouthed with more sharply sloping rims as 3 on FIG. 151: the one on PLATE 51 (*c*) from VI G/H level 109/89 is an example. One in particular (648 from VII G level 122) has an excessively steep slope. A very few fragments suggest the possible existence of jug rims with angular profiles (as 4 on FIG. 151), and of forms of cutaway spouts (as 5). Four or five of the cutaway spouts were recovered from level 122 of Period VII (e.g. 640, 641); a fragment from VI G level 93 may belong to one similar.

Jug necks were normally not well differentiated from bodies, into which they flowed with an

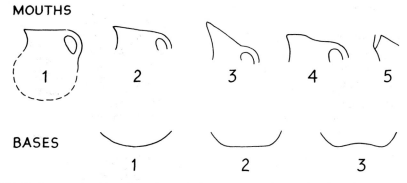

FIG. 151. Periods VII–VI. Jug variations. Mouths: 1. flat; 2. sloping; 3. steep sloping (rare); 4. irregular; 5. cutaway spout. Bases: 1. rounded; 2. flat; 3. sunk.

even curve. But some jugs of Fine Black Burnished Ware had necks more or less sharply differentiated at the base, like 646. Handles it seems were invariably to the rim: there appear to be no examples of handles with the top set distinctly below the rim, as was common later. The handles, especially those of the smaller jugs, were often elegantly tapered, narrowing towards the top where they joined the rim, or hour-glass shaped, as FIG. 152, taper 1 and 2. Handles like these might have a neat semicircular or lunate section; but the handles of many of the less finely made jugs of Light Brown Burnished Ware were oval or thin oval: a few appear to have been circular (FIG. 152) Rare examples of ribbed handles also occurred; the rib was usually single, as on 650, but once at least double (649). Some handles from levels of VI with three grooves down the length may be crude versions of multi-ribbed handles, but these were more at home in Periods V–IV and later. The lower end of the handle was normally it seems keyed into the jug by being stuck through a hole in its side, instead of being merely applied to the surface as was usual in Periods X–VIII; but the pushed-through end was afterwards flattened and smoothed so as to be inconspicuous. In later periods, when the mouths of jugs tended to be narrower, it was no longer possible for the potter to get his hand down through the neck in order to smooth away the projecting end, and handles of the blatantly 'pushed-through' type are therefore more common. But one handle from VII G/Q level 131 approximates to the complete 'pushed-through' type.

Bodies of jugs were more or less globular, sometimes with a slight angle at the belly; but

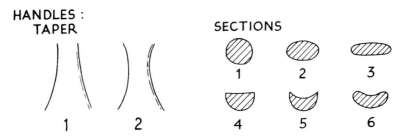

FIG. 152. Periods VII–VI. Jug handles: taper and sections. Sections: 1. circular; 2. oval; 3. thin oval; 4. semi-circular; 5. lunate; 6. kidney-shaped.

sharply carinated forms appear to have been exceptional: no fragments of carinated jug bodies were recognised from levels of VII, although there were a very few from deposits of VI, mostly from the latest ones. One of these (651A), from an exceptionally small jug of Fine Black Burnished Ware, has a double wart on the carination and remains of white-painted decoration on the body above it. Bases were not in general sharply differentiated; they might be more or less rounded or vaguely flat, or might have a sinking to make the vase more stable (FIG. 151).

In their shapes these jugs of Periods VII–VI are reminiscent of gourd vessels, and were perhaps inspired by them. The standard light brown surface colour of the great majority of the jugs may originate from a deliberate imitation of the yellow surfaces of gourds. Similarly in Crete jugs of Ayios Onouphrios Ware of the Early Minoan I period seem to copy gourds both in shape and surface colour; but the surfaces are yellowish, not light brown, and have painted decoration in shades of brown, black or red.

Decoration. Virtually all the jugs of Light Brown Burnished Ware and many of those of Fine Black Burnished Ware were plain and undecorated. But a large number of the latter, and a very few of the more finely burnished of the former, had painted decoration in white (PLATES 48, 49). There was usually a group of three—sometimes four, five or six—stripes below the rim; once or twice only a pair of stripes was painted here. The neck was left plain, except for a group of three stripes at the base of it; these might be surmounted by a wavy stripe, and sometimes a wavy stripe occurred alone at the base of the neck. Even in the case of jugs with painted decoration handles were usually plain, but some were adorned with simple linear designs in white (FIG. 154. PLATE 50 (a)). Thus about 15 out of 120 (just over 12 per cent) of jug handles of Fine Black Burnished Ware from levels of VII, and some 37 out of 350 (around 10 per cent) of those from ones of VI, had traces of white-painted decoration.

The commonest design in white paint on handles from levels of VII was lattice as FIG. 154 No. 14. Lattice decoration like this was already attested on three or four handles of black burnished ware from upper levels of Period VIII, and there were some half a dozen examples of it on handles from levels of VII. Other motifs occurring on handles from levels of VII were FIG. 154. Nos. 2, 6–8, 12 and 17: of these Nos. 8, 12 and 17 were not recorded from deposits of VI. FIG. 154 Nos. 7 and 14 were the commonest motifs of white-painted decoration on handles in Period VI as well as in VII.

When decoration occurred on the body of a jug in Period VI it was usually confined to the upper part of it, and consisted of triple, less commonly double or quadruple chevrons (PLATE 49). Sometimes, however, but more often it would seem in VII than in VI, the whole body of the jug was covered with groups of interlacing diagonals which crossed on the swelling (FIG. 153. PLATE 49: 647); or alternatively with groups of vertical stripes, usually three or four but occasionally more in each group, which crossed underneath the base. This system of decoration embracing the whole body of the jug appears to have been commoner during Period VII than the chevrons confined to the upper part of the body which were standard in VI. Indeed the white-painted decoration on jugs in VII (PLATE 48) seems to have been on the whole a shade less stereotyped than it was to become in VI (PLATE 49). But in both periods, although more often perhaps in VII, wide bands are sometimes found instead of narrow stripes.

Warts, both single and double, occurred on the swelling in the case of some jugs of Fine Black

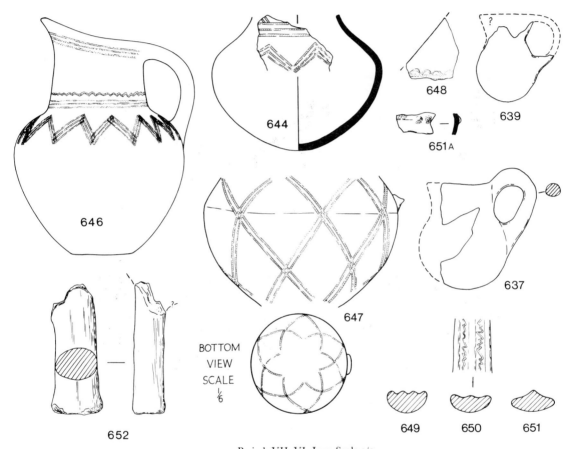

FIG. 153. Periods VII–VI. Jugs. Scale 1/3.

Burnished Ware (e.g. 651A on FIG. 153); there were some 9 examples of single and 12 of double warts. But warts were not as common as they were to be on jugs of the following periods V–IV. Two fragments of jug bellies from VII G level 122 had a group of four vertical white stripes flanked by warts. On another fragment from VI G level 108 the warts flanked a pair of vertical stripes enclosing a wavy one.

String- or rivet-holes bored after firing were preserved on a fragment of a jug of Light Brown Burnished Ware from VI G level 93.

637. (VII G 122) (FIG. 153. PLATE 56) Miniature jug. About half preserved. Ht. to rim 9. Light Plain Ware. Grey clay, dusky at core, with straw; surface light brown to orange and dusky, unburnished.

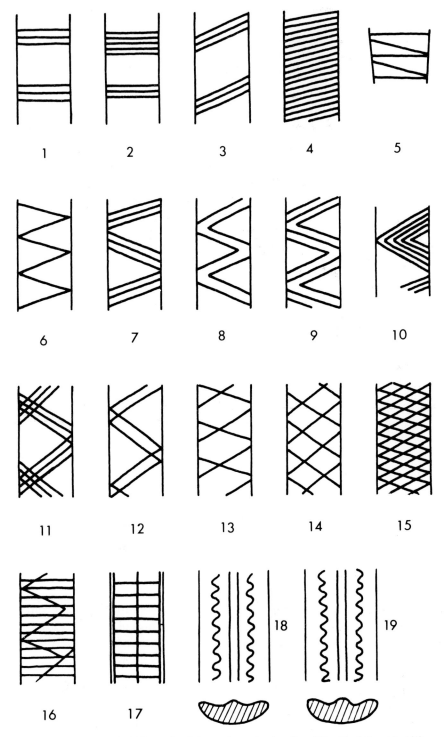

FIG. 154. Periods VII–VI. White-painted decoration on jug handles of Fine Black Burnished Ware.

638. (VII G 122) (FIG. 150. PLATE 51) Rim with handle, and base which may belong with it. Outside red to light brown; very poor burnish.

639. (VII G 122) (FIG. 153) Miniature jug. Rim and handle missing. Ht. as preserved 6.4. Coarse grey-brown, burnished.

640. (VII G 122) (PLATE 51) Cutaway spout. Fine Black Burnished Ware. Another, apparently similar, grey-brown with fine burnish.

641. (VII G 122) (PLATE 51) Cutaway spout. Dark brown to red; fine burnish.

642. (VI G 111) (FIG. 150. PLATE 51) Large parts, including base and handle, missing. Ht. preserved c. 21. Diam. of body c. 16. Light Brown Burnished Ware. Soft grey clay without grit, but with straw. Abundant straw impressions in surface. Outside with light brown shading to darker brown wash, well burnished. Wash covers most of inside, which rough, unburnished.

643. (VI G 93) (PLATE 44) Side of wide cutaway spout (?). Fine Light Brown Burnished Ware.

644. (VI G ?103/93) (FIG. 153. PLATE 49) About two-thirds of body; neck and rim missing. Ht. preserved c. 10.5. Diam. of body 14. Base rounded. Grey clay, pinkish at surface. Inside rough; outside shades of dark brown mottling in patches to black and reddish with very fine burnish. White-painted decoration, triple chevrons on upper part of body, a group of three horizontal stripes below neck.

645. (VI G 93) (FIG. 150. PLATE 51) Restored from large parts, including most of rim and handle, with base which does not join. Ht. estimated c. 22. Diam. of body 20. W. of rim c. 9. Light Brown Burnished Ware. Inside dusky light brown, rough; outside light brown, shading in places to reddish or dusky black, with exceptionally fine burnish although stroke marks visible.

646. (VI G 93) (FIG. 153). Base and rim missing. Ht. preserved c. 11. Diam. of body c. 15. Fine Black Burnished Ware. Grey clay. Inside rough; outside dark brown to black with fine burnish. White-painted decoration, triple chevrons on upper part of body, a group of three stripes below a wavy one at base of neck.

647. (VII G/H 113) (FIG. 153. PLATE 49) Fragments of body. Fine Black Burnished Ware. White-painted decoration, crossing pairs of diagonal stripes.

648. (VI G 122) Rim, apparently of jug. Fine Black Burnished Ware.

649–651. (VI G/Q 88, R 95, G/Q 111/108/88) (FIG. 153. PLATE 50) Ribbed handles, apparently from jugs. Fine Black Burnished Ware.

651A. (VI G/H 109/89) (FIG. 153) Fragment of carinated body with pair of warts. Fine Black Burnished Ware; decoration in white.

25. *Theriomorphic vases*

The large foot 652 may come from an animal-shaped vase, unless it belonged to some variety of tripod vase akin to type 27.

652. (VII G 115) (FIG. 153. PLATE 44) Coarse grey-brown clay; surface with slight traces of an unburnished red wash.

27. *Tripod cooking pots* 653–655 (FIG. 150)

These do not seem to have existed in Periods X–VIII, and appear to have been unusual in VII–VI. But one typical foot (654) was apparently recovered from a level of VII. This has a flat oval section, like the three feet from the mixed deposit in R described below, and some early tripod feet in Crete (e.g. *Myrtos* 179 fig. 63: 2).

653. (VI G 93) Tripod foot and part of rim evidently from same vase. Shades of dark and light reddish brown with stroke burnish outside and in.

654. (VII Q 130/?129) (PLATE 46) Tripod foot. Flat oval section.

655. (VI G/H 109/89) (PLATE 46) Tripod foot. Oval section.

(c) JARS

No complete profiles of jars were recovered from levels of VII–VI.

A number of rims and fragments are assignable to small bowl-jars of types 30–33. Some of these had incised decoration (e.g. 665), while others, mostly from the larger varieties of such jars, carried ornament in relief. But 656, the only vase of this group of which the shape could be substantially restored, was unique in several respects, and may have been imported. One fragment of it apparently came from a level of VIII, and it ought perhaps to be assigned to that period rather than to VII.

Many of the rims grouped under A I–III are of coarse gritty fabric, or cooking pot ware. The larger no doubt belonged to storage vessels, the smaller almost certainly to vases used for cooking. Jars of types 41 and 42 with rims of class B I–II were still in evidence in VII, but less so in VI.

Characteristic of this horizon, and especially common it seems in VII, were large jars with everted rims (class A/B III). These rims were often thickened. A number were of coarse cooking pot ware, the surface at times having an unburnished red wash (PLATE 52(a)); others were of Light Brown Burnished Ware; but many were of Light Plain Ware (PLATES 52 (b); 53 (a)). A number of fragments which evidently belonged to such jars preserved a well differentiated shoulder (making the rims class B III). Most of these shoulder fragments were of Light Plain Ware; but while the majority of the fifteen recognised from levels of VII were of this fabric, one had an unburnished red wash: in four instances there was a wart on the shoulder below the base of the neck (PLATE 52 (b)). None of these shoulder fragments could be joined to a rim, but 717 was associated with a vertical strap handle, and a number of everted rims with stumps of similar handles were of the same fabric (Light Plain Ware) and may have come from jars with differentiated necks. The top of a handle associated with an everted rim from VII G level 119 (PLATE 52 (b)) had a string-hole made before firing through it. The jars to which these rims and fragments belonged may have boasted a pair of vertical handles, making them in effect early versions of the collar-necked jars of type 47 which are characteristic of the succeeding periods V–IV.

Period VII. Jars with simple incurving rims of class A I (as 657, 659) and of the allied class A II (as 663) appear to have been somewhat rare by contrast both with Periods X–VIII and with Period VI and later. But among them is the substantial fragment 657 with a pair of vertical trumpet lugs on the shoulder. A similar rim (660) also had a trumpet lug, but other vases with such rims were evidently provided with vertical strap handles set on the shoulder as in the case of 663. The unique rim 664 of class A II has a rib (or ledge for a lid?) round the outside.

It seems that jar rims during this period were dominantly everted, either as class A III, or with the base of the neck differentiated from the shoulder (class B III). Jars with the necks differentiated in this way appear to have been for the most part large, and made of Light Plain Ware; but some (e.g. 722) had a red wash, and the red-washed surface might be burnished as in the case of 718. Many rims of class A III come from large jars of coarse gritty fabric, the surface either unburnished or with a poor burnish, and often showing traces of a red wash. Some of these red-washed jars of coarse ware may have been used as cooking pots. The unique 725 from a level mixed with VIII had a light brown surface well burnished inside and out. One A III rim from a small jar had a strap handle; several others (692, 693) preserved characteristic vertical trumpet lugs which projected above the rim line.

A number of rims of classes A II-III (665-670, 694-7) evidently belonged to small bowl-jars (types 31–32 etc.) like those characteristic in Period VIII. These mostly came from lower levels of VII which may have had some material of VIII in them. About one-third (four out of twelve) of these rims bore traces of incised decoration (e.g. 665, 668). Two rims (668 with incised decoration and 669) preserved small lug-like handles surmounted by warts which gave them a triangular profile as common in Period VIII; but one (670) had a vertical trumpet lug of the kind at home in VII–VI. Two other rims had warts on the shoulder, another a V-shaped perforation (rivet-hole) made through it after firing. The unique 656 of type 33 with its combination of incised and painted decoration may be an import; most of it came from level 119 of VII, but one fragment was from a somewhat doubtful context of VIII.

Rims assignable to jars of type 41 or the allied type 42 were not uncommon in levels of VII, but about three quarters of them (25 out of a total of some 32) came from VII G level 119 which may have had some material of VIII in it. One or two of these rims preserve the stumps of handles joining necks to shoulders. The surfaces of the rims were mostly burnished, ranging in colour from grey-black, grey (especially in the case of the smaller examples of fine burnished ware), through shades of dark and light brown to reddish. One rim which may be from a jar of type 41 had clear traces of an unburnished red wash outside and in. A small rim from VII G level 119 assignable to a jar of type 42 had a grey surface with traces of pattern burnish (groups of diagonal lines).

Period VI. Rims were akin to those of VII. Elements reminiscent of V in the upper levels of VI may in some cases at any rate reflect later intrusions, but large collar-necked jars of type 47 characteristic of Periods V–IV were nowhere in evidence. As in Period VII, large jars with outward curving rims of class A III, or in some cases with differentiated necks and rims of class B III, are found in place of them. Jars of the traditional type 41 characteristic of Periods X–VIII were not as well represented as in levels of VII, but were more in evidence than later in V–IV.

About ten rims of class A I (e.g. 662) and a few of class A II (671–673) evidently belonged to large storage jars like type 38, the surfaces dusky shades of dark and light brown and reddish, mostly with a poor burnish, but in one or two cases unburnished (e.g. 662). Most of the rims of classes A I–III, however, belonged to smaller jars with surfaces shades of grey, dark and light brown, and reddish (the red sometimes at any rate due to a wash), usually with a poor burnish, once or twice with a fine burnish, but in some cases unburnished. A few of these rims had the stumps of handles which had been set vertically on the shoulder, as found on some of the larger jars akin to type 38. The rim 661 appears to have had a vertical trumpet lug like similar rims of Period VII (e.g. 657, 660).

Some eighteen rims were assignable to jars of type 41, but several of them, notably a group of seven from uncertain deposits in trench Q, may be earlier strays. One or two had stumps of vertical handles joining neck and shoulder. These rims were of fine light grey, light brown, or red burnished ware: none appeared to have a dark brown or black burnished surface.

Large jars with everted rims of classes A III and B III were common as in Period VII. One or two such rims had stumps of vertical strap handles set below them (e.g. 735). These jars it seems were normally of coarse ware, with much straw showing in the surfaces, which were mostly unburnished, shades of light brown or red due to a wash.

Cooking pots may have rims as FIG. 180, class A III a. The surface is characteristically dusky grey-brown, either burnished, or without any burnish. One or two cooking pot rims from upper levels of VI have bold vertical warts of a kind more at home in V–IV (e.g. 711).

About fifteen differentiated necks belonging to jugs or jars were recovered. These were of various sizes and fabrics, ranging from 717 and 728 of Light Plain Ware to 730 of Fine Black Burnished Ware.

The little pyxis rim 741 appears to belong to an imported vase.

A. Jars with rims of class A undifferentiated from the rest of the body

(1) Types 33, 34. Vases of which the shapes could be restored

33. *Squat bowl-jar with low shoulder*

656. (VIII G ?140, VII G 119, VI G 93) (FIG. 155. PLATE 54) Large fragment with small internal handle. Ht. preserved 10. Diam. of rim. *c.* 11. Dark grey clay; surface brownish grey, burnished outside, very roughly wiped inside. Small horizontal strap handle on inside of rim, one end of it being opposite a small wart on the outside. From this wart as a centre radiate swags of triangular or wedge-shaped jabs made with a sharp pointed instrument. There are twelve rows of these on the part of the vase preserved. Further decoration was added in red paint, apparently after the vase had been burnished and fired (encrusted), consisting of bands round the outside and inside of the rim, a solid semi-circle on the wart, and concentric swags alternating with the swags of jabs. The use of encrusted red paint is exceptional at Emporio, as is the combination of painted and incised decoration; but a comparable instance is the fragment 396 from VIII Q level 146. Since one piece of 656 was recovered from a somewhat doubtful level of VIII, and the bulk of it from an early one of VII, it may also be of Period VIII.

    Small internal handles or lugs of this kind are found on some vases from Hacilar (e.g. *Hacilar* ii 244 f. fig. 47: 30, from Level IX).

    A similar combination of triangular jabs with red paint appears on pottery assigned to the early part of the Middle Neolithic Sesklo period in Thessaly (e.g. Milojcic, *Ergebnisse* 13 fig. 11: 3, 4, 8. Cf. *PThess* 14, under A 2: incised ware. *AM* lvii (1932) 104 Beil. xx: 14. Buchholz and Karageorghis nos. 762-4). The combination of cardial decoration with red paint is said to be a new feature at Servia in western Macedonia in the Early phase of the local Middle Neolithic (*Servia* 210). But no examples of curvilinear decoration appear to be attested in this incised and painted ware of the Thessalian and west Macedonian Middle Neolithic.

    The idea of combining red paint with jabs or pointillé may have been derived from Syria or Cilicia. Such a combination is found on some pottery from Mersin assigned to the Late Chalcolithic (*Mersin* 159 fig. 101). The designs here are linear, but concentric swags are at home on painted ware of this horizon at Mersin. Closer, however, to 656 is the combination of red paint with triangular jabs on a fragment from Ras Shamra V Phase 3 (Late Neolithic) (*Ugaritica* iv 504 fig. 26, bottom left).

    Concentric swags or loops are a characteristic Ubaid motif adopted on Middle and Late Halaf pottery in Syria (e.g. Mellaart, *Neolithic Near East* 163 fig. 98: bottom left; 168 fig. 103: centre right. *Iraq* ii (1935) pl. xxii: 3 (A 738). There is a close parallel for the painted swags of 656 from the Çarkin cave near Antalya assigned to the Neolithic (U. Esin and P. Benedict, *Current Anthropology* iv (1963) 341, citing *TAD* viii. 2 (1959) Lev. xv Res. 6). But the swags on a fragment of S-shaped rim of painted ware in the Hacilar tradition from Demircihuyuk are even more comparable (*Ist. Mitt.* xxvii-xxviii (1977-78) 19 f. fig. 7: 5).

    Concentric swags are painted hanging from the insides of bowl rims from Çatal Hüyük West and Can Hasan Level 2A (*AS* xv (1965) 140 fig. 4: 4; 142 fig. 6: 1-6, 9; xii (1962) 35 fig. 5: 6, 7). Incised decoration on other vases from Can Hasan 2 A includes pointillé composed of wedge-shaped marks like those on 656 (*AS* xii (1962) 35 fig. 5: 13).

34. *Jar with simple incurving rim (class A I)*

657. (VII G 122) (FIG. 150. PLATE 47) Three rim fragments and a base which may belong with them. A pair (?) of vertical trumpet lugs on shoulder. Ht. estimated *c.* 15. Diam. of rim 12. Good fabric, thin-walled. Grey-brown, well burnished outside and in.

(2) Undifferentiated jar rims: class A I
From levels of VII (FIG. 155)

658. (VII G 122) (PLATE 46) Coarse gritty grey clay; surface pitted with grit and straw impressions showing in it; wiped with straw outside and in. Three more similar: one (Q 131) red, burnished outside and in; the others (G 122), one with an unburnished reddish to light brown wash outside, the other of cooking pot type ware with poor burnish outside and in.

659. (VII G 123) Hard fabric; sandy clay with straw. Outside black, inside dull mushroom brown, burnished.

660. (VII G 122) With stump of vertical trumpet lug cf. 657. Grey-brown to black, shading to deep purplish red; fine burnish.

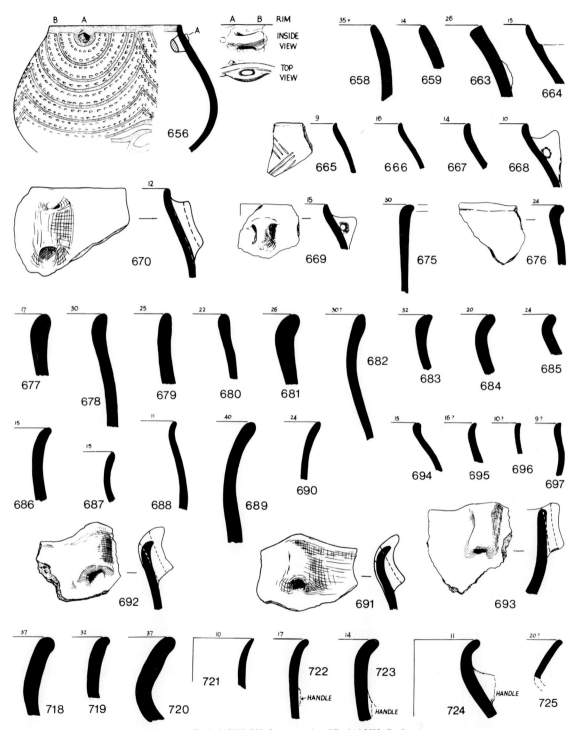

FIG. 155. Periods VII–VI. Jars, mostly of Period VII. Scale 1/3.

From levels of VI (FIG. 156)

661. (VI G wall 20) With stump of trumpet (?) lug. Inside light brown, outside dull purple brown, burnished but worn.
662. (VI/V Q ?75) Surface with a wash, light brown to dusky, unburnished.

(3) Undifferentiated jar rims: class A II
From levels of VII (FIG. 155)

663. (VII G 119) With stump of vertical handle. Surface much worn; traces of possible red wash, unburnished.
664. (VII G 122) (PLATE 56) With ridge (for lid?) outside. Rather sandy grey clay with grit, some showing in surface. Outside with a red wash, well burnished; traces of a similar wash, unburnished, inside.
        For the shape cf. 815, which appears to be imported.
665–667. (VII G 119) Rims, perhaps from bowl-jars of type 31. Grey-brown; fine burnish. One (665) with incised decoration.
668. (VII G 119) (PLATE 45) With small vertical horned handle. Fine grey clay; surface shades of grey and lightish brown, burnished. Decorated with incised lines and triangular punctuations.
669. (VII G 119) With small vertical lug-handle. Dark grey-brown; fine burnish.
670. (VII G 119) (PLATE 45) With vertical trumpet lug. Soft black clay. Outside black, burnished but worn; inside rough.

From levels of VI (FIG. 156)

671. (VI G wall 20) Shades of light and dark purplish brown; stroke burnish outside and in.
672. (VI G wall 20) Angle not certain. Shades of dark and light brown to dusky and reddish; stroke burnish outside and in.
673. (VI Q 87) Clay fired reddish throughout; surface pitted, with straw impressions, but much worn. Outside with traces of a purplish red wash, which may have been smoothed or burnished.
674. (VI G 93) Soft grey clay; surface pitted; red wash outside and in, smoothed rather than burnished.

(4) Undifferentiated jar rims: class A III
From levels of VII (FIG. 155)

Variation 1
675. (VII G 122) Cooking Pot Ware; hard gritty clay, grey at core. Surface outside and in with a dark purplish brown to red wash, wiped; marks of wiping very visible. Others similar.
676. (VII G 122) Angle very uncertain. Cooking Pot Ware; gritty grey clay. Surface probably with a wash, light brown to dull purplish, wiped inside; outside worn.

Variation 2
677. (VII G 122) Cooking Pot Ware; hard gritty clay, grey at core. Surface with a wash, light purplish brown to dull red, unburnished. Others similar.
678. (VII G/Q 131) Very coarse grey-brown clay; surface shades of dark brown to dusky outside, lighter brown to reddish inside, wiped rather than burnished.
679. (VII G 119) Cooking Pot Ware; hard gritty clay, grey at core; surface dull purple-brown, with poor burnish outside, roughly wiped inside.
680. (VII G 119) Cooking Pot Ware; hard gritty clay; surface with straw impressions. Outside dusky to dark brown with poor burnish; inside red, burnished.

Variation 3
681. (VII G/Q 131) Fabric akin to Cooking Pot Ware; hard gritty grey clay, brown at core. Outside purple-brown, inside reddish, smoothed or with poor burnish.
682. (VII G 122) Cooking Pot Ware; corase gritty clay. Outside light brown to reddish, inside purple-brown unburnished. Several others similar.
683. (VII G 119) Cooking Pot Ware; gritty clay, grey-black at core, light brown at edges; surface much worn.
684. (VII G 120) Cooking Pot Ware; coarse gritty clay, grey at core. Surface with a wash, dark purple-brown to red, apparently with poor burnish, but worn.

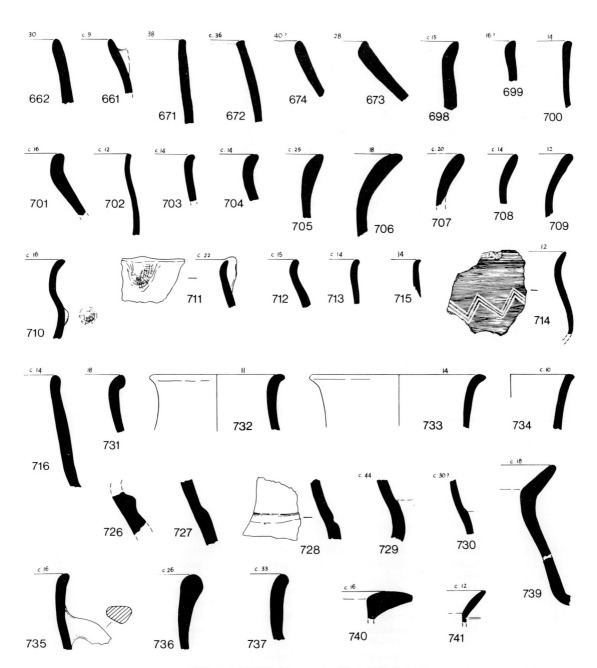

FIG. 156. Periods VII–VI. Jars, mostly of Period VI. Scale 1/3.

685. (VII G 119) Fabric akin to Light Plain Ware. Outside orange, inside buff, unburnished.
686. (VII G 119) Cooking Pot Ware; hard gritty clay, grey at core. Surface irregular, with straw impressions, dusky grey-brown; poor burnish. Others similar.
687. (VII G 112) Fabric akin to Cooking Pot Ware; coarse, gritty clay, grey-black at core. Surface much pitted, warm pale brown; poor burnish outside and in. Others similar.
688. (VII G 122) Fabric akin to Cooking Pot Ware; rather gritty clay, grey-black at core. Outside with a red wash, unburnished; inside dusky to dark purple-brown, smoothed but not burnished. Others similar.
689. (VII G 122) Cooking Pot Ware; hard gritty clay, grey at core, light brown at edges. Surface with a wash, red shading to brown, unburnished. Others similar.
690. (VII G 122) Cooking Pot Ware; coarse gritty clay, dark grey at core; surface much pitted. Outside light brown to dusky, wiped; inside with traces of a red wash. Others similar.
691. (VII G 119) With vertical trumpet lug. Coarse grey clay with grit. Surface irregular, with straw impressions, light brown to red shading to dusky in places; very poor superficial burnish.
692. (VII G 122) (PLATE 45) With vertical trumpet lug. Soft fabric; rather coarse grey-black clay; surface rough inside, black with superficial burnish outside.

    The lugs on this and 691 closely resemble those on the rims of two jars, said to have been found in a tomb in the region of Nero on Kato Koufonisi near Naxos, and assigned to Early Cycladic (*ADelt* xxv (1970) Chron. 429 pl. 373).

693. (VII G 119) (PLATE 45) With vertical trumpet lug. Grey-brown, burnished outside; superficial burnish inside.

Finely burnished rims from small jars cf. type 32 (FIG. 155)

694. (VII G 120) Grey-brown clay. Outside dark red with fine burnish; inside grey-brown, less well burnished.
695. (VII G 119) Irregular. Soft fabric; surface red, burnished but worn.
696. (VII G 119) Light grey-brown; fine burnish. Another similar; dark grey to black with fine burnish.
697. (VII G 122) Mottled Ware. Outside light brown, inside red, burnished. Another similar; light greyish brown with very fine burnish.

Rims mostly from levels of VI (FIG. 156)

698. (VI G 108) Hard grey clay, light brown at edges; surface with a red wash, unburnished.
699. (VI G 103) Outside shades of light and dark brown tinged with reddish, with fine stroke burnish; inside similar but darker, less well burnished.
700. (VII Q 130/?129) (PLATE 55) Thin-walled; fabric cf. 726. Orange clay, fired an even colour throughout. Large grit showing in surface, which smoothed rather than burnished outside and in. Possibly an import.
701. (VII/VI R ?137/?114/110/89) (PLATE 54) Red with traces of red wash shading to light brown; fine burnish outside and round inside of rim.
702. (as 701) Coarse greyish brown clay with large grit; surface pitted, smooth but not burnished. Four others similar from levels of VI; shades of light and dark brown, grey-brown and red, usually burnished.
703. (VII Q 130) Soft fabric; grey-brown clay. Surface with straw impressions; little or no trace of burnish.
704. (VI G wall 20) Surface pitted; outside shades of light brown to dusky, well stroke burnished; inside dusky, with less good burnish.
705. (VI G wall 20) Coarse clay; surface with a red wash; slight traces of smoothing or burnishing outside and in.
706. (VI H ?106) Surface with straw impressions; red wash, well burnished but worn. Two others similar; surfaces red or light brown, burnished.
707. (as 701) Clay black at core, light greyish brown at surface, which much worn. Another similar (VI G 103) of coarse grey-brown clay; surface shades of purple-brown and red, unburnished.
708. (VI G 93) Coarse clay; surface with abundant straw impressions; red wash outside and in. Two others similar.
709. (VII G/H 113) Coarse clay; surface with abundant straw impressions; red wash, unburnished, outside and in.
710. (VI G 103) With wart on shoulder. Clay grey-black at core; surface with straw impressions. Outside black with poor burnish; inside dark brown with reddish tinge, unburnished.
711. (VI G 103) With vertical wart. Outside dusky black, inside dark red, unburnished.

Finely burnished rims from small jars cf. type 32 (FIG. 156)

712. (VI G wall 20) Outside black shading to dark brown round top of rim with very fine burnish; inside dark brown to black, wiped with fingers of which marks visible.
713. (VI/V Q ?75) Outside light greyish brown with fine burnish; inside darker grey, less well burnished.

714. (VI G 93) Fine Black Burnished Ware; surface dark brown to black with fine polish-like burnish outside and in. Traces of white-painted decoration (group of three thin stripes below rim and triple chevrons on shoulder).

715. (VII Q ?129) Light grey to greyish brown; fine burnish outside and in.

B. *Jars with necks or rims of class B more or less clearly differentiated from the rest of the body*

(1) **Differentiated jar rims: classes B I and II**

About thirty rims of these classes, assignable to jars of type 41, were recovered from deposits of VII, mostly from G level 119. Surfaces ranged in colour from grey-black and grey (especially in the case of the smaller jars of finer fabric) through shades of dark and light brown to reddish, and were normally more or less well burnished, but in one or two cases unburnished. One small rim, evidently from a jar of type 42, had a grey surface with pattern burnish.

716. (VII Q?129) (FIG. 156. PLATE 54) Hard fabric. Outside red to purplish, well burnished; inside shades of darkish brown, less well burnished.

(2) **Differentiated jar rims: class B III**

A number of differentiated necks, mostly from large jars of Light Plain Ware or allied fabrics, were recovered from levels of VII (717, 726) and VI (727–730). None of these had survived with a rim, but rims of similar fabric like 718–721, 731–4, may have belonged with differentiated necks of this kind. The rims 733, 734, with fine burnished surfaces, may come from small bowls of type 14 rather than from jars.

From levels of VII (FIG. 155, except 717, 726)

717. (VII G 122) (FIG. 150. PLATE 46) Shoulder with vertical handle. Light Plain Ware; clay grey-black at core with abundant straw. Outside pale brown to orange with poor stroke burnish; inside brown, rough.

718. (VII G 122) Fabric akin to Light Brown Burnished Ware; clay grey-black at core. Surface with a red wash, burnished inside, but no trace of burnish left on outside. Others similar.

719. (VII G 122) Cooking Pot Ware; hard fabric. Clay grey at core, light brown at edges; inside surface with fine straw impressions, and an overall wash, dull purplish red outside, darkish brown inside, smoothed or with poor burnish. Others similar.

720. (VII G 122) Cooking Pot Ware; coarse clay with abundant grit, much of it large; clay grey-black at core, light brown at edges; traces of wash, light brown and originally perhaps red, but much worn. Others similar.

721. (VII Q 127) Possibly from a jug of type 20. Fine grey clay; surface light brown to dusky, burnished.

722. (VII G 119) Clay grey at core, light brown at edges. Surface with straw impressions and red wash, unburnished.

723. (VII G 119) (PLATE 56) Fabric akin to Light Plain Ware; clay grey at core, with straw. Outside pale brown to orange mottling to dusky, with poor burnish; inside light brown to reddish. Several others similar.

724. (VII G 122) (PLATE 56) Light Plain Ware; grey clay with some grit and straw; surface with straw impressions, pale orange, unburnished.

725. (VIII/VII G wall 16A and 119) Angle not certain. Greyish clay; surface lightish brown, well burnished outside and in.

726. (VII Q 130) (FIG. 156) Shoulder with rib round base of neck. Fabric cf. 700. Gritty orange clay, fired an even colour throughout. Possible traces of a red wash. Perhaps an import.

From levels of VI (FIG. 156)

727. (VI G 103) Shoulder. Gritty clay; surface light brown, worn.

728. (VI G 93) (PLATE 56) Shoulder. Light Plain Ware; surface light brown with faint reddish tinge, unburnished. For the groove at the base of the neck cf. *Hesperia* xlvii (1978) 439 no. 30, Corinth: Forum West area, from a context of mixed or transitional Middle/Late Neolithic.

729. (VI R ?95) (PLATE 56) Shoulder. Coarse gritty clay; surface with abundant straw impressions, light brown outside, red inside, unburnished.

730. (VI G 103) Shoulder. Fine Black Burnished Ware.

For the differentiated shoulders of 729, 730, compare Eslick 1980, 10 ill. 4: 3, from a horizon in the Elmali region of south-western Anatolia assigned to the Middle Chalcolithic. Cf. *Beycesultan* i 72 fig. P. 1: 24, 74 fig. P. 2: 28, from Levels XXXIX, XXXVIII, of Late Chalcolithic 1. *Kum Tepe* 320, 317 fig. 8: 124, from Kum Tepe I A 1. *Hesperia* xlvii (1978) 443 no. 45, on a jar of L.N. matt-painted ware from Corinth: Forum West area.

731. (VI G/H 109/89) Coarse clay; surface with straw impressions and large grit, pale light brown, unburnished. Two others similar: one (VI G 103) with a red wash; the other (VI G wall 20) with surface full of straw impressions, light purple-brown, unburnished.

732. (VII Q ?129) Coarse fabric; surface with abundant straw impressions, pale buff outside, orange inside, unburnished. Another similar; surface brick-red, unburnished.

733. (VI G 103) Possibly from a small bowl of type 14. Grey clay. Outside shades of light and dark brown to red, inside light brown mottling to red, with fine polish-like burnish. Several others similar; surfaces grey, grey-brown, light brown, red, and light brown to whitish, all with very fine burnish.

734. (VI G 103) Possibly like 733 from a small bowl of type 14. Surface very pale light brown shading to dusky white, irregular but with fine polish-like burnish. Another similar (VII Q 130/?129); dark purple-brown with rough burnish outside and in.

735. (VI G wall 20) With stump of vertical handle. Coarse clay; surface light brown, smoothed but not burnished.

736. (VI G 103) Outside with a red wash, inside light brown; unburnished.

737. (VI G 103) Coarse clay. Outside with an unburnished red wash; inside dark purple-brown to light brown with slight traces of smoothing or burnishing.

738. (VI R ?95) As 1260 from V H level 76. Soft grey clay, light brown at edges; surface pitted, but worn. Another similar (VI G 103) with possible traces of a red wash.

739. (VII Q ?129) Drawing reconstructed from two non-joining fragments. Hard fabric; coarse clay. Surface purple-red with abundant straw impressions; poor burnish outside and round inside of rim.
   Cf. 1258 from a level of Period IV with parallels from contexts assigned to Early Helladic I at Eutresis and Vouliagmeni.

740. (VI G/H 109/89) Soft grey-brown clay; surface pitted, with traces of a burnished red wash outside and in.

741. (VI G/H 109/89) Evidently from a small jar (pyxis) akin to type 44. Reddish brown clay, fired an even colour throughout; surface originally dark purple-brown, burnished. Incised line at base of rim. Probably an import.

(E) PITHOI 742–753 (FIG. 157)

Some of these were evidently very large. Rims were mostly simple, with flat or rounded tops, resembling those of pithoi from levels of IX–VIII. Only one scrap (747) from an upper level of

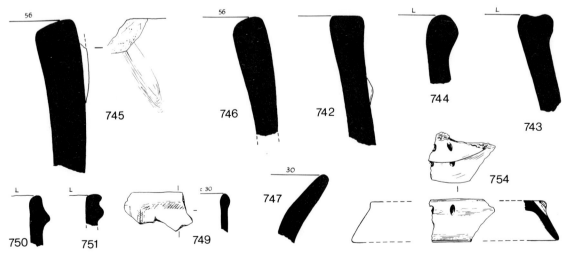

FIG. 157. Periods VII–VI. Pithoi and lid. Scale 1/3.

VI looks as if it might have come from the splayed rim of a collar-neck of the type standard on pithoi of the succeeding periods V–VI.

Decoration when it occurred was in relief (e.g. 745). Smaller rims, shaped like those of pithoi and with similar relief decoration, evidently came from large pithoid jars. One of these (749) had a combination of horizontal and vertical ribs, another (748) a curving rib, on the outside. Among other fragments of such jars was 752 which had remains of elaborate relief decoration with curving elements.

As noted in the case of pithoi from levels of X–VIII the firing tends to be superior to that of the mass of pottery, and this taken in conjunction with the relief ornament of a type rarely found on small vases suggests the possibility that the pithoi were made by specialists who travelled from place to place and used local clay beds as is still done in Crete and other parts of Greece.

Some pithoi, however, might have been imported by sea. The fragment of a large jar with relief decoration (752) may be an import; and the fabric of two pithos rims (742, 746) approximated to obsidian ware like that of a number of apparent imports from levels of V–II, although in shape, surface colour, and the sandy character of the clay fired an even colour throughout, the rims were indistinguishable from the others of this horizon.

Two handles appeared to come from pithoi; one from VI G level 93 was a large strap-handle, flattened oval in section, the other from a mixed deposit (VIII/VII H 149) was circular.

742. (VIII/VII G wall 16A and 119) Rim, with rib in relief. Hard fabric akin to Obsidian Ware cf. 746. Very sandy orange clay, fired an even colour throughout; mica, and shiny black particles, together with fine straw impressions, showing in surface, which well smoothed or burnished outside and in.

743. (VII G 122) Rim. Very hard fabric. Clay grey at core; surface light brown to red mottling to dark purple-brown and dusky, with poor burnish outside and in.

744. (VIII/VI H 149) Rim. Angle not certain. Hard gritty grey-brown clay; surface with an unburnished red wash.

745. (VIII/VI H 149) Rim, with rib in relief. Gritty light reddish brown clay, fired an even colour throughout; surface with straw impressions. Inside reddish, left rough; outside light brown, burnished.

746. (VI G 93) Rim. Very hard fabric akin to Obsidian Ware cf. 742; many shiny black particles showing in surface. Sandy light reddish brown clay, fired an even colour throughout; straw temper (some impressions in surface), but apparently no large grit. Outside light brown, burnished; inside light reddish brown, smoothed. Probably an import; but a rim of similar shape from VIII A wall 16 appeared to be of ordinary local fabric.

747. (VI G 93) Rim, apparently from collar neck of type standard on pithoi of Periods V–IV. Hard gritty grey clay; surface reddish to light brown outside, reddish inside, well smoothed or burnished.

Rims (748–751) and fragments (752, 753) of large jars resembling pithoi and with similar relief decoration (748–753):

748. (VII G 119) (PLATE 56) Rim, with curving rib in relief. Clay grey at core; surface light brown with poor burnish.

749. (VII G 122) Rim, with horizontal rib outside and vertical one descending from it. Fabric akin to Light Brown Burnished Ware; clay grey at core, light brown at edges; surface with thick red wash, unburnished.
    Cf. *Athenian Agora* xiii 6 nos. 33, 34. *Otzaki-magula* pls. C: 3, vii: 12 (8: 23). Milojcic, *Ergebnisse* 8 fig. 8: 4.

750. (VI H ?94) (PLATE 53) Rim as 749 with horizontal rib below it. Coarse greyish clay. Outside with traces of a light brown to reddish wash, which seems to have been unburnished.

751. (VI H ?106) Rim as 749. Coarse greyish brown clay; surface apparently unburnished.

752. (VII Q 130) Fragment with elaborate relief decoration. Gritty black clay. Outside black with very fine burnish; inside sandy, light brown, smoothed but not burnished. Possibly an import.

753. (VI R ?95) (PLATE 53) Fragment with notched horizontal rib. Hard fabric; surface light reddish brown outside, darker brown inside, burnished.
    Ribs with comparable widely spaced impressions are much in evidence at Kephala on Kea (e.g. *Kephala* pls. 35, 79: 146, 170). They also occur in Troy I (e.g. *Troy* i fig. 242: 3). Similar ribs have appeared on pithoi in Palestine by the Chalcolithic there (Amiran, *APHL* 25, 27 pl. 3: 4, from Ghassul).

(F) LIDS 754

Only one fragment that might come from a lid was recognised from the horizon of VII–VI.

754. (VI G wall 20) (FIG. 157. PLATE 45) Fragment apparently from lid of type 62 with pair of string-holes through edge. Grey-brown; fine burnish.

(G) MINIATURE VASES 755

A base from VI evidently belonged to a true miniature vase.

755. (VI R ?95) Max. diam. of body 4.5. Light brownish grey, roughly smoothed.

(I) HANDLES AND LUGS

(1) *Bowl handles* 756–759 (FIG. 158)

Handles were not common on bowls. Bowls with large handles rising from the tops of the rims may have continued in use (e.g. 474, 757, and PLATES 44 (*a*) lower centre, from VII G 119; 45 (*b*) lower 2nd from l., from VIII/VI G wall 16A and 119); but only some 20 fragments of such handles were recognised from levels of VII–VI as compared with nearly 70 from those of VIII and about 65 from ones of IX. Some at least of those from levels of VII-VI may therefore be earlier strays.

Side handles set below the rim were common on bowls of the succeeding periods V–IV, and some examples of such handles were recognised from levels of VII–VI. Thus the large bowl 480 of type 6 had one or more horizontal strap handles, while the stump of a side handle was noted on a fragment of a baking pan of type 3 from VI Q level 88/87, and on the type 9 bowl rim 522. Two or three handles of grey-brown burnished ware from levels of VI (e.g. 759) were of the pointed shape (FIG. 107 No. 2) common on bowls in Periods V–IV and later, but already attested as early as Phase I A at Kum Tepe. A fragment from VI G level 93 might have come from a nicked handle of the type also found on bowls in V–IV, as FIG. 107 No. 4.

Vertical handles occurred on some bowls in VII–VI, but were distinctly rare. A few rims with small vertical handles set below them (e.g. 437) were assignable to bowls of types 4–6, unless these really came from jars, and the rim of the little bowl 631 of type 14 has the stump of a vertical strap handle rising from it, making it in effect an early example of type 16, which was at home during the succeeding periods V–II.

756. (VI G wall 20) As 320 from VIII G level ?141. Soft fabric; light brownish grey clay; surface with straw impressions.
757. (VI H 106) Fragment of large handle with thin triangular section. Grey-brown with reddish tinge, burnished but much worn.
758. (VIII/VII G wall 16A and 119) (PLATE 44) Fragment of twisted handle. Mottled Ware; surface dominantly light brown shading to darker brown and red, burnished.
759. (VI G 108) Pointed handle, apparently from a bowl. Grey-brown, burnished. Another similar from VI G level 93.
    Side handles of pointed shape with more or less triangular sections are attested on bowls at Kum Tepe as early as Phase I A (*Kum Tepe* 324 fig. 9 pl. 73 nos. 215, 216).

(2) *Handles of jugs and jars* 760–762 (FIGS. 104, 152, 158)

Vast numbers of vertical handles were recovered. These had evidently belonged to jugs or jars. Over 2,000 fragments of them were counted from levels of VII, and over 3,200 from those of VI—an average of about 41 and 47 per zembil. Most of the handles were strap-like and more or less flattened oval in section as FIG. 152: 3; occasionally thicker oval or circular, sometimes kidney-shaped. A very few handles (one from VII Q level 130, another from VI G level 93 surmounted by a wart) had rectangular cross-sections. The majority of these vertical handles appear to have come from the jugs of Light Brown Burnished and Fine Black Burnished Ware of which fragments were so abundant in the deposits round the well. The handles assignable to these ubiquitous jugs were often neat, and might be elegantly tapered, semi-circular or lunate in section, occasionally ribbed (FIGS. 104, 152. PLATE 50 (*a*) right).

A number of handles (some 20 from levels of VII, 6 from ones of VI) had holes made before firing through the top end. Nearly all these perforated handles came from vases of Light Plain Ware, and therefore probably from jars of some kind. The holes may have been for string to fasten lids—of wood, presumably, as clay ones are hardly attested in VII-VI.

Two horned handles (from VII Q level 130 and VI G level 93) resembled those characteristic of the earliest periods X–IX. Some 10 handles from levels of VII, and 14 from those of VI, were surmounted by warts (e.g. 668, 669, 760). In one case at least (from VII G level 119) the wart resembled a metal rivet, but the resemblance may have been accidental. Three handles (one from VII, two from VI) had double warts. The stump of a vertical strap handle from VI G level 93 had a wart at the base, and the base of another, from VI G level 103, was flanked by a wart each side.

The little horizontal strap handle on the inside of the rim of the bowl-jar 656 was unique, and the vase may have been imported. But some half a dozen small horizontal side handles and fifteen large ones, all apparently from jars, were counted from levels of VI. These were more or less circular, verging sometimes to triangular in section, like those of Periods V–IV.

One example of the slashed type of handle (761) was apparently found in a context of VII, and another (762) came from an upper level of VI. They provide the earliest evidence for this distinctive type of jar-handle at Emporio. These and other early examples may have belonged to imported vases, probably from the Cyclades, where handles of this kind were at home. Eventually, however, such handles appear to have been copied by local potters. A number of slashed handles were recovered from levels of V–II.

One handle of the true 'pushed-through' type was noted. It came from VII G/Q level 131, and had evidently belonged to a jug of Fine Black Burnished Ware.

760. (VI G/H ?103/?102) Small handle surmounted by wart. Hard fabric. Grey, burnished.
761. (VII G 123) Horizontal slashed handle as 1717 of Period II. From a thin-walled vase. Hard, gritty grey-brown clay; surface with abundant grit showing in it. Thick red wash outside and in. Presumably from an import.
762. (VI G/Q 88) Fragment of a small handle as 761. Gritty greyish brown clay; surface with pin pricks showing in it, light orange-brown with a spot of red wash, unburnished. Presumably from an import.

(3) *Lugs* 763–774 (FIG. 158)

Perforated lugs seem to have been more common than handles on bowls, and they also occurred on a number of jugs and jars.

A. Trumpet lugs (FIG. 105). Incipient waisted or trumpet lugs were recovered from levels of Period VIII and even from those of IX (e.g. 363-4). But developed lugs of this type were not in evidence at Emporio until Periods VII–VI when they were common. None of the many trumpet lugs from this horizon, however, were ribbed like some of those from levels of V–IV and ones from comparable Early Bronze Age sites such as Thermi.

(1) *Horizontal trumpet lugs* (PLATES 44 (*a*), 45 (*a*)). These were by far the most common type of lug found on bowls, and the 80 or more horizontal trumpet lugs recognised from levels of VII–VI all

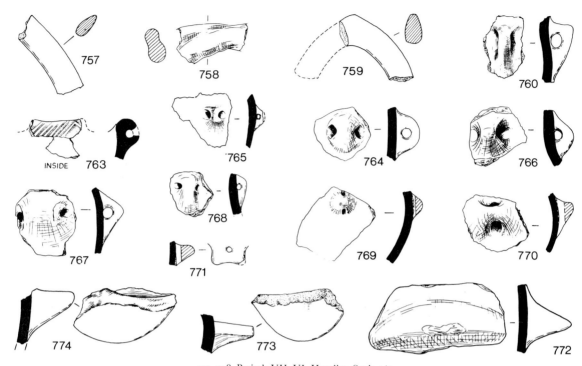

FIG. 158. Periods VII–VI. Handles. Scale 1/3.

appeared to come from bowls rather than from jars, most of them being from ones of the characteristic types 10 and 11; but they were also attested on bowls of types 5 and 7 (e.g. 504). These lugs varied a good deal in size, some being very large and measuring over 7 across from one string-hole to the other. There was also a considerable range in shape. At one end of the scale a trumpet lug as FIG. 105 No. 20, with the waist nearly as thick as the expanded ends, hardly differed from an ordinary tubular lug (e.g. 567 and PLATE 45 (a) second row, left, from VI G level 103).

At the other extreme are the elegant lugs as FIG. 105 No. 23 with their ends rising like horns above the rim (e.g. 565, 566 and PLATE 45 (a) upper row, left, from VI G level 103); most if not all the lugs of this class may come from bowls of the characteristic type 10. More commonly when trumpet lugs were set on the rims of bowls in this way the expanded ends only projected slightly above the level of the rim as FIG. 105 No. 22. The majority of horizontal trumpet lugs, however, appear to have been set on the outside of the vase below the rim in Periods VII–VI. The trumpet lug 763 as FIG. 105 No. 22 from the rim of a bowl of uncertain type had remains of white-painted decoration on the inner side.

Horizontal lugs of this distinctive shape have a wide distribution in time and place, and the story of their development may differ from one area to another. Contrast, for instance, the development in Troy I with that in Early Bronze Age Kritsana (*Troy* i 60. *PMac* 80 note 7). A variety of trumpet lug is found as early as the beginning of the Neolithic (E.N. I) at Knossos in Crete (*BSA* lix (1964) 169 fig. 25: 5; lxiii (1968) 273).

Trumpet lugs set on or below rims and reminiscent of those from Emporio VII–VI were recovered from Kum Tepe I B (*Kum Tepe* 330 pl. 74: 402, 408–10; 337 pl. 76: 547; 339 pl. 75: 619.

Cf. W. Lamb, *PZ* xxiii (1932) 117 fig. 4: 1–3, from the earliest phase B at Hanay Tepe, assignable to Kum Tepe I B). Sperling, *Kum Tepe* 330 note 13, stresses the gap between the lugs of this type at Kum Tepe and the trumpet lugs which succeed the straight tubular ones in Troy I. But there seems to be no suggestion of a similar gap or break in the development of trumpet lugs at Emporio.

Trumpet lugs were at home on bowls of shape A 12 in Troy I, especially in the Middle and Late Subperiods (*Troy* i 60 figs. 243: 33; 244: 1–10; 246: 14–20). Such lugs also seem to be more in evidence in the later material than they are in the earlier at Thermi (*Thermi* 79 pl. xxxi). At Poliochni trumpet lugs do not appear to be attested before the Blue period, but fine and highly developed examples occur in the Green and Red (*Poliochni* i 558 pl. xxvii: c; 614 with references).

In the Konya plain trumpet lugs occur in the E.B. 1-2 horizon, but not apparently before that in the Late Chalcolithic (*AS* xiii (1963) 214, 216 f. fig. 9: 5, 10). They are still found in parts of Anatolia after the end of Troy I (e.g. *Ist. Mitt.* xvi (1966) 62 fig. 2: 1, from Asarcik Hüyük level V. Cf. *Thermi* 137 fig. 39: 5).

Trumpet (described as waisted) lugs appear to be attested in the Late Neolithic at Servia in western Macedonia (*Servia* 213). They were also characteristic of the earliest level (I) at Kritsana, appearing there on vases of types apparently derived from north-west Anatolia. Such lugs still occurred in later levels at Kritsana, and they are attested sporadically throughout Macedonia in Early Bronze Age contexts (*PMac* 118, 166 nos. 162-3 fig. 37; 183 no. 252 fig. 56: d. *Argissa* iii 197 pl. 70: 12, 16. Cf. surface finds by D. French in eastern Macedonia, *PZ* xlii (1964) 32 fig. 2: 10, Galepsos; 41 fig. 7: 30, Phanarion; 43 fig. 8: 29, 30, Sitagroi (Fotolivos)).

In the Cyclades trumpet lugs are found at Saliagos and in the Early Bronze Age settlement on Mt. Kynthos on Delos (*Saliagos* figs. 44: 6, 57: 14, 15. *Delos* xi 37 fig. 35, 39 fig. 37, on storage jars. Cf. *PMac* 88 note 7 for Naxos). But they do not seem to be a feature of pottery from the Kephala settlement on Kea. Trumpet lugs, however, from a Late Neolithic horizon at Thorikos, which appears to be contemporary with Kephala, look very comparable with ones from Emporio VII–VI (*Thorikos* iii 26 figs. 23 and 25). An incipient trumpet lug from the grotto above the Asklepieion at Athens also seems to be Late Neolithic (*Annuario* xiii–xiv (1930-31) 465 fig. 49: d). A squat jar assigned to the Late Neolithic from the Diros cave (Alepotrypa) in the Mani has horizontal trumpet lugs on the belly (*AA* 1971, 361 fig. 54: g). At Perachora horizontal trumpet lugs are in evidence in contexts assignable perhaps to Early Helladic I (*BSA* lxiv (1969) 58 fig. 3: 20, Phase X; 63 fig. 5: 15–17, 21, Phase Y).

(2) *Vertical trumpet lugs.* These were not nearly as common as horizontal trumpet lugs, and only some 10 of them were recognised as compared with over 80 horizontal ones; all except the doubtful example 661 came from levels of Period VII. Some of the inturned or incurving rims on which vertical trumpet lugs were found might have been from bowls akin to types 6–9; but most at any rate of these vertical trumpet lugs seem to have belonged to jars. The lugs were either set below the rim (e.g. 657, 660, 670), or on the rim with the top rising above the rim line (e.g. 691–693).

It is less easy to find parallels for vertical trumpet lugs than it is for horizontal ones. *Saliagos* fig. 57: 16 shows what appears to be a vertical trumpet lug set just below the rim like 691–3. A vertical trumpet lug from the Burghügel site on Paros is presumably of Bronze Age date (*AM* xlii (1917) 24 fig. 16). A slightly trumpet-shaped lug is set just below an incurving rim of the beginning of the Early Bronze Age (Phase 8) at Servia in western Macedonia (*Servia* 219 fig. 14: 73).

Two jars from Kato Koufonisi near Naxos with vertical trumpet lugs to the rim are very comparable to examples from Emporio, and the fabric of one from the illustration looks as if it might be akin to Emporio Light Plain Ware; they are classified as Early Cycladic (*ADelt* xxv (1970) Chron. 429 pl. 373). Fragments of a similar vase with rounded base and slightly trumpet-shaped lugs to the rim comes from a settlement with occupation from the Neolithic to Early Bronze Age near Ayia Marina on the south coast of Attica (*AAA* ix (1976) 174 f. fig. 6).

The fashion for such lugs may have spread from the Levant. In Palestine vertical trumpet lugs occur in Early Bronze II alongside bowls with type 11 rims (Amiran, *APHL* 59 Photo 53, 63 pl. 16: 4). Some Early Neolithic jars from Byblos have small handles which look very much like vertical trumpet lugs in profile (*Byblos* v figs. 23: 33061, 25: 25376, 27063 and 28616, pl. lxiii).

B. Other lugs

(1) *Horizontally perforated:*

(a) Short horizontally perforated lugs as FIG. 105 No. 12 seemed to be not uncommon on bowls of type 8, and four of the nine or ten examples from levels of VII–VI came from such bowls; a single lug it seems was often placed below the carination (e.g. 507, 509). Isolated lugs of this kind were also noted on bowls of type 7 (one as 494 from VI G level 111) and 9 (one from VI Q ?100).

(b) Tubular or barrel-shaped lugs occurred on a number of vases, including a bowl of type 4 (446). The example 767 from a jar has a triangular cross-section like some lugs in Periods X–VIII.

(c) An animal head lug (768) from VII resembles ones from levels of VIII.

763. (VII G 122) Horizontal trumpet lug (class II). Grey-brown, burnished. Inside of rim with white-painted decoration (groups of diagonal lines).
    Cf. *BCH* c (1976) 757, 756 fig. 11, for a tubular lug to the rim decorated with stripes in white, from Argos: Aspis, grouped with 'Heavy Burnished Ware' characteristic of the extreme end of the Neolithic.
764. (VIII/VII G wall 16A and 119) Short horizontal lug, from a bowl (?). Coarse grey-brown clay; surface smoothed or with poor burnish.
765. (VI H ?106) As 764. Light brownish grey; fine burnish.
766. (VI G 103) Short horizontal lug, from a jug or jar. Outside grey-brown, burnished; inside rough.
767. (VII G 122) Long horizontal lug with marked triangular section, from a jar. Fabric akin to Light Plain Ware; surface orange, rough inside; outside very worn with traces of possible red wash.
    The triangular section of this lug is reminiscent of some vertical lugs on vases from the Lower Cave at Ayio Gala.
768. (VII G 123) Horizontal lug resembling the stylised head of an animal, from a jar (?). Sandy grey-brown clay; outside surface orange, inside with traces of a dark red wash, burnished or smoothed.
    Cf. 365–8 of Period VIII, when animal head lugs of this type resembling ones from Hacilar appear to have been at home at Emporio.

(2) *Vertically perforated:*

(a) Short vertically perforated lugs occurred on some bowls, and also on closed vases (e.g. 769, 770).

(b) Tubular or barrel-shaped lugs appear set vertically below a few rims, classified as from bowls of type 6 (483, 486), but perhaps from jars like the rims with vertical trumpet lugs.

(c) Horned lugs as FIG. 105 No. 27 were not uncommon in levels of V–IV. The only example from this horizon (771) came from an upper level of VI.

(d) Tailed lugs as FIG. 105 No. 34 appear to have been characteristic of VIII; but a fragment of one was recovered from VI G level 111.

(e) Lugs with double perforations. The rim 632 from a bowl of type 14 has a large lug as FIG. 105 No. 28 with a pair of vertical holes (PLATE 45).

(f) Double lug. One of the few examples noted was set below the rim 484 of a small bowl of type 6. It may have resembled 1729 of Period II. Another, apparently similar, from VI G level ?103/93, came from a jug or jar of red burnished ware.

769. (VII G 122) Short vertical lug, from a jug or jar. Fine Black Burnished Ware; inside rough.
770. (VI R ?95) Short vertical lug, from a jug (?). Sandy clay, as on jugs of Period V; surface black with fine burnish.
771. (VI G 93) Horned lug, from a jar (?). Soft fabric; surface grey-brown, burnished.
        Cf. FIG. 106 No. 31: e. Perforated lugs of this type were at home at Emporio in Periods V–II. This is the only example noted from an earlier level.

(3) *Solid*. A number of tongue-shaped lugs were recovered, mostly large as 773, but some small like 434, which is from a baking pan of type 3; but such lugs evidently occurred on bowls of other types and on jars. One or two (e.g. 772) may come from imported vases, if the sandy character of the clay is a guide. No internal lugs of the kind found on baking pans of type 3 (as FIG. 105 No. 37) in X–VIII were recognised from VII–VI.

772. (VII G 122) Large tongue-shaped lug, possibly from a bowl of type 6. Very sandy clay, grey-black at core, light brown at edges. Outside red to dark brown with fine burnish; inside with traces of a red wash. Perhaps an import.
773. (VII G 122) (PLATE 46) Large tongue-shaped lug, from a bowl. Gritty dark grey clay; surface light brown, much pitted, with traces of a red wash. Two others similar: one rather coarser, the surface shades of brown with poor burnish. The other apparently from a jar, and perhaps an import; very sandy clay, dark grey-black at core and on inside surface, which rough; outside dusky pale brown, unburnished.
774. (VI G 103) Large tongue-shaped lug. Soft fabric; grey-brown clay; surface much worn, but traces of a red wash which may have been burnished. Another similar.

V-shaped rivet-holes made after firing for string to mend vases still occurred, but were not as common as in Periods X–VIII. About a dozen fragments with such holes were recovered from levels of VII, and one or two from ones of VI. A section of a thin strap handle of fine grey burnished ware from VII had a pair of such holes.

(J) SPOUTS

The strainer spout 435 (PLATE 53) may be the rim of a baking pan of type 3 with a lunate-shaped lug cf. 28 of Period VIII. No other example of a strainer spout, and no nozzle spouts, were recognised from VII-VI.

(K) BASES 775–790 (FIGS. 109, 159)

Relatively few bases could be assigned with certainty to bowls, but they included about ten flat bases from levels of VII—nearly all of them large and mostly of class 6 B, although one was assignable to class 6 A—and some ten others sunk as classes 5 A and 5 B; the base which may go with 591 of type 11 is a small example of class 5 B. One or two small sunk bases of the elegant class 5 D from VII might belong to bowls, or to jugs or jars (e.g. 785). A few small flat bases of hard grey burnished ware from levels of VI, some flat, others sunk as classes 5 A and 5 B, appear to come from bowls of type 8.

    A number of pedestal and ring feet (classes 2 A and 3 A) were recovered, and evidently belonged to vases of various different types, including bowls as well as jugs or jars. These feet were normally quite small in diameter, but a fragment from VII G level 123 may have belonged to a wide ring base of the type characteristic of the Sesklo (Middle Neolithic) horizon in Thessaly; it had a light greyish brown burnished surface.

    Bases of jugs and jars were normally it seems flat as classes 6 B and 6 C (e.g. 787), or sunk

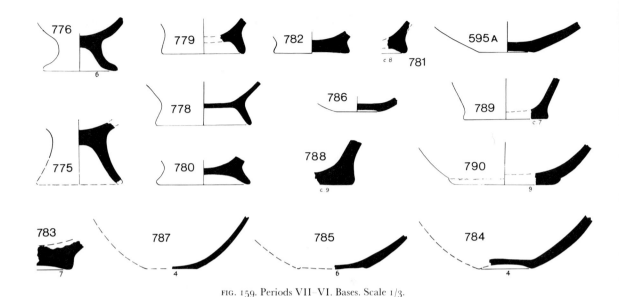

FIG. 159. Periods VII–VI. Bases. Scale 1/3.

(classes 5 A–C) (e.g. 784). One or two splayed bases (class 7 A) were noted; when sunk such bases approximate to low ring feet of class 4 A (e.g. 781–3).

775. (VI R ?95) Pedestal foot (class 2 A). Soft fabric; surface grey-brown with very fine burnish, worn.
776. (VI G 103) As 775. From a bowl. Soft fabric; outside light brown mottling to black, inside grey-brown to black, burnished.
777. (VI G 111) High ring foot (class 3 A) as 1333. Grey-brown, burnished. Another similar from VI G level 103 may come from a jar; surface grey-brown, unburnished.
778. (VIII/VI H 149) High ring foot (class 3 A). Very soft fabric; surface with pin-holes and abundant straw impressions, shades of dark and light brown, burnished.
779. (VI R ?95) As 778. Soft fabric; surface pitted and with straw impressions, greyish brown, with poor burnish.
780. (VI G 93) As 778. Greyish clay; surface much pitted. Outside shades of light to dark brown, burnished; inside red. Another similar from VI G level ?103/93; grey-brown, burnished.
781. (VII Q 131) Low ring foot (class 4 A). From a jug or jar. Soft fabric; grey-brown clay. Outside with traces of a red wash, burnished.
782. (VI Q 111/108) As 781. Soft fabric; surface pitted, light brown mottling to darker brown and reddish, burnished, but very worn.
783–785, 787. Bases of jars (classes 4 B, 5 A, 5 D, 6 B), from VII G.
786. (VII G 122) Sunk base (class 5 D). From a small jug or bowl. Light Brown Burnished Ware.
788. (VII/VI H 117/105) Splayed base (class 7 A). Grey clay; surface with straw impressions, grey inside, light orange-brown outside; poor stroke burnish.
789. (VIII/VII/VI H 149) Splayed base (class 7 A). Clay grey to shades of brown with straw and fine grit; surface shades of light brown, presumably once burnished, but worn.
790. (VIII/VII/VI H 118) Differentiated base cf. class 8. Soft fabric; grey clay with some fine grit and straw. Outside grey, inside reddish brown; probably once burnished, but much worn.

DECORATION 791–812

There was no obvious difference in the character of vase decoration between VII and VI. The decoration of both periods is therefore considered together here.

Pattern burnish

True pattern burnish was much less in evidence than it had been in VIII. About half a dozen fragments with pattern burnish were recovered from VII (e.g. PLATE 55 (*c*)), and rather more—a dozen in all—from VI. These fragments were almost entirely it seems from vases of types common in Period VIII: most of them were from rims of bowls of type 8, and some came from jars of types 41–42. The designs, as far as it was possible to judge, consisted of groups of alternate diagonal hatching as was usual in VIII, and as in VIII the surfaces with pattern burnish were normally a shade of grey-black or grey, sometimes light brown. Many of the fragments were mere scraps, and all might have been earlier strays.

The vertical stroke burnishing found on a number of jugs of Light Brown Burnished Ware characteristic of VII–VI could have been decorative in intention, but hardly qualifies as pattern burnish, except perhaps in the few instances where the strokes are diagonal and cross to form a rough lattice.

Paint

(1) **Light on dark.** White paint seems to have been the method of decoration most in vogue during VII–VI, but this impression may be exaggerated by the fact that it was usual on the small jugs of Fine Black Burnished Ware of which a disproportionately large number of fragments was recovered from this horizon (PLATES 48, 49 (*a*), 50 (*a*)). The scheme of decoration on these has been described under JUGS. A similar scheme of decoration (three stripes below the rim and triple chevrons on the shoulder) appears on the fragment 714 of identical black burnished ware, but apparently not from a jug but from a jar of some kind.

Bowls in Periods VII–VI were normally plain without any form of decoration. But a certain number, especially ones of type 14, had designs in white paint consisting of alternate groups of diagonal lines round the inside of the rim (e.g. 616, 618, 626, 763). An inverted hatched triangle had been painted on the inside of 568 from a bowl of type 10. In one case at least white painted decoration appears on the outside of a bowl (621 of type 14). A fragment from VII Q wall 21 which also seemed to come from a bowl had four diagonal lines in white (or just possibly red) paint on the outside. The only example of decoration in red paint apart from this was on 656 which was unique in several respects and apparently an import: here it was combined with incision, as in the case of 396 of Period VIII.

(2) **Dark on light.** This only occurred on the scrap 791, evidently an import, perhaps from the Greek mainland.

791. (VI Q ?100) (PLATE 55) Fragment, apparently from upper part of jug with stump of handle. Soft fabric; grey clay with large grit, some showing together with straw impressions in surface. Outside deep yellow buff, burnished; inside very pale buff, smoothed but not burnished. Decoration in matt black paint (group of four thin diagonal stripes).

This may be from a vase of Late Neolithic matt-painted ware from the Greek mainland (Weinberg, *CAH* 601 ff. Holmberg, *Neolithic Pottery* 28 f. Cf. *Hesperia* vi (1937) 513 f. *Elateia* 197 f. *Nea Makri* 22. Varka: *AE* 1975 Parart. 70 ff.).

Incision (FIG. 113)

Some fifty fragments of vases with incised decoration were recovered from levels of VII. This represents an average of only about one a basket as opposed to six or more a basket from the upper levels of Period VIII. Incised decoration was if anything even less well represented in VI. As in Period VIII, most of the incised fragments from VII (and some of those from VI) appeared to belong to small bowl-jars (e.g. 665, 668) or jars of types 41-42; but some fragments from VI evidently came from large thick-walled vases (e.g. 805), although others were from jugs or jars of smaller size.

While bowls rarely had decoration of any kind, the rim 484 with incised decoration appears to come from a small bowl of type 6, and 609 of type 12 has a bold horizontal groove below it. A rim of lightish grey-brown burnished ware from VII G level 115 with bold lattice incised on the outside may be from a bowl of some kind if it is not from a jar of type 41 (FIG. 113 No. 1). The carination of the unusual rim 569 assigned to type 10 had incised notches on it.

In its general character and in the motifs used most of the incised decoration from levels of VII, and much of that from VI, is hardly distinguishable from what was current in Period VIII. Indeed many of the fragments found in levels of VII, and some of those from ones of VI, may be earlier strays, including 665 and 668 from VII G level 119. Another fragment from VII G level 119 has a vertical zone of multiple chevrons like FIG. 112 No. 21. At the same time a certain tendency towards the disintegration of traditional schemes of decoration and elements of design is perhaps to be discerned in Periods VII–VI, although with such fragmentary material it is difficult to be certain about this. The decoration on 799 and 800 from levels of VI is reminiscent of that on fragments of one-handled cups from the E.B. I horizon at Tarsus which may be of about the same date (*Tarsus* ii 101 fig. 240: 88-91).

One or two of the motifs of incised decoration from VII (e.g. 793, 794) were not recognised in VIII, but this may be fortuitous and does not necessarily mean that the motifs were unknown then. At the same time some of the incised decoration from upper levels of VI is reminiscent of that characteristic in Period V. A few strap handles for instance have incised decoration exactly like ones from V (e.g. 809–811); the motifs on such handles resemble FIG. 116: 1, 2, 11 (two examples), and 15, of Periods V–IV. Similarly a number of fragments from levels of VI had remains of hatched bands, as FIG. 113 no. 6, which are hardly if at all represented in the great mass of incised pottery from VIII, and are not certainly attested in VII, but occur in V–IV; while panels filled with dots (pointillé), as FIG. 113 Nos. 7, 8, excessively rare in VIII, and not found in the meagre quantity of incised decoration from VII, are no longer exceptional in VI (e.g. 805-7).

The fragments 808 from VI H level ?103 has fine comb-ornament like that of the so-called Cardium ware characteristic of the Presesklo phase (E.N. III) in Thessaly. This may be an earlier stray, since three fragments of similarly decorated ware (381) were recovered from X Q level 166.

As in Period VIII, and in marked contrast to the fashion in V–IV, it seems that incisions were rarely filled with white paste: a single fragment from VII (G level 119), and one or two more (e.g. 809) from VI, retained possible traces of a deliberate fill of white.

792. (VII G) Rim of bowl or jar of type 41. Lightish grey-brown, burnished. Decoration as FIG. 113 No. 1.

793. (VII G) (PLATE 41) Grey; fine burnish. Two rows of jabs flanked by incised lines, as FIG. 113 No. 2.

794. (VII G) Grey; fine burnish. Two incised lines flanked by jabs, as FIG. 113 No. 3.

795. (VI G 93) Fragment, apparently from a jug. Gritty clay, like jugs of Period VI. Surface black; fine burnish. Decoration as FIG. 113 no. 4.

796. (VI G/H 91) Fragment, apparently from a jar. Hard fabric; surface dark grey to black, burnished outside and in. Decoration as FIG. 113 No. 5.

797. (VI G 93) (PLATE 49) Fragment of small jar. Hard fabric; surface grey, burnished.

798. (VI H ?103) (PLATE 55) Fragment of jar. Hard fabric. Outside grey-brown, burnished; inside purple-brown, rough.

799. (VI G 103) (PLATE 55) Fragment of bowl or jar. Hard fabric; surface dark grey, burnished outside and in.

800. (VI G wall 20) (PLATE 55) Hard fabric. Outside grey-brown with poor burnish; inside rough, wiped.

801. (VI G/H 109/89) (PLATE 55) Fragment of small jar or jug. Hard sandy fabric like jugs of Period V. Outside black with very fine burnish; inside rough, wiped.

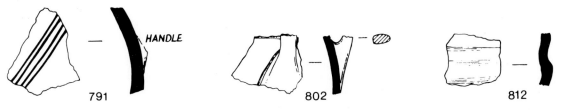

FIG. 160. Periods VII–VI. Decoration. Scale 1/2.

802. (VI G 103) (FIG. 160) Fragment of small jug, or jar of types 41–42, with stump of neat strap handle. Hard fabric; surface dark brownish grey, burnished outside and in. Base of neck differentiated by incised line.

803. (VII/VI Q ?129) (PLATE 49) Fragment of large jar. Outside red-brown, unburnished; inside rough. Wide hatched band, as FIG. 113 No. 6.

804. (VI G 93) (PLATE 49) Fragment of small jar. Hard fabric; surface grey, burnished.

805. (VI G ?103/93) (PLATE 49) Fragment of bowl or jar. Hard fabric; grey clay. Outside light brown, inside grey, burnished. Decorated with bold dots.

806. (VI G 93) (PLATE 55) Fragment of bowl or jar. Soft fabric; surface black, burnished outside and in. Band of opposed triangles filled with dots, as FIG. 113 No. 7.

807. (VI H 106) (PLATE 49) Fragment, apparently of a jar. Clay well fired an even orange colour throughout; surface once burnished, but worn. Chevron reserved against a background of triangles filled with dots, as FIG. 113 No. 8. Possible an import.

808. (VI H ?103) (PLATE 49) Fragment of a jar (?). Soft grey clay; surface light brown, apparently burnished outside, but not inside. Rows of fine comb or Cardium shell impressions. Cf. fragments with similar decoration (381) from X Q level 166. Possibly therefore an earlier stray. Probably imported.

809. (VI G wall 20) (PLATE 50) Strap handle. Surface grey-brown, burnished but worn. Zigzag flanked by lines; traces of white fill.

810. (VI G/H 109/89) (PLATE 50) Strap handle with rectangular section. Light brown, burnished. Single broad groove down centre.

811. (VI (G/H 109/89) (PLATE 50) Strap handle. Grey-brown, burnished but worn. Groove down centre flanked by diagonal dashes.

Relief

Circular warts occurred on some handles, and were common on the bodies of jugs and jars during VII–VI. They were usually applied to the surface, not bonded into it, and were often high and pointed in profile; but a few low warts made by pushing the clay outwards from the inside of the vase were also noted. Warts were normally placed on the belly or on the shoulder—on large jars of Light Plain Ware with rims of class A III sometimes high on the shoulder just below the point of junction with the neck. Circular warts occurred in pairs on the bodies of some jugs and jars and on a few handles. Bold vertical warts are found on the rims of one or two cooking jars from VI (e.g. 711), but are more at home in Period V and later.

Pithoi and large jars were sometimes adorned with ribs in relief as in Periods X–VIII. In one instance (726) there seems to have been a rib around the base of the neck of a large jar. But relief decoration was not entirely confined to large vases. One or two open bowls appear to have had curving ribs on the inside (e.g. 444 of type 4).

Some handles of jugs of Fine Black Burnished Ware had one or more ribs running down their length (PLATE 50 (*a*)). A fragment from the body of a jug or jar with a black burnished surface from VI H levels 104 or ?103 had a combination of horizontal and vertical ribs like the large jar rim 749, while another fragment from VI G level 111 seemed to preserve the tail of a vertically perforated lug akin to those from levels of VIII. The deep horizontal channels and ridges on 812 are reminiscent of fluted metal.

812. (VI H ?103) Small fragment, apparently from a jug. Fine Black Burnished Ware.

    The 'rippling' on fragments of jars from the Bothros horizon at Elateia assigned to the end of the Middle Neolithic or beginning of Late Neolithic looks very similar to fluting of the kind seen on 812 (*Elateia* 190 pl. 60, d: 3, 7). But in general such fluted ware appears to be at home on the Greek mainland at the very end of the Neolithic (e.g. *Athenian Agora* xiii 9 f., 30 f., pl. 6, on Grey or Black Burnished Ware assigned to the latest Neolithic: S. Immerwahr regards it as imported and as belonging to a Chalcolithic horizon with Anatolian affinities, citing black ribbed or rippled ware from Thermi I–II (e.g. *Thermi* pl. viii: 10 etc.). Cf. Kitsos cave: *BCH* xcviii (1974) 735 fig. 10. *Nea Makri* 18 pls. 10, 11: concentric fluting on bowls of the latest Neolithic Phase B III there. *PMac* 141 ff. nos. 19–36, Late Neolithic).

IMPORTS 813–818

Some twenty fragments equally divided between levels of VII and VI may have belonged to imported vases. From levels of VII come 440A, 656, 700, 726, 742, 752, 761, 772; from those of VI, 741, 762, 791, 807 and 808. To these must be added:

813. (VII G 122/115) Fragments from the body of a jug (?). Rather thick-walled. Very gritty grey to brick-red clay; surface grey. Broad vertical stripes in white paint, worn.

814. (VI G/H 109/89) (PLATE 56) Fragment from body of jug (?). Fabric akin to Light Brown Burnished Ware, but very thin-walled and with an exceptional finish. Soft grey clay. Inside surface pale, smoothed; outside wiped, and coated with a thin, lightish brown, apparently slightly lustrous wash. Possible traces of decoration in matt black paint around top edge of fragment.

815. (VI G wall 20) (PLATE 54) Rim of jar with ridge around outside cf. 664. Sandy grey-brown clay; surface dark purple-brown, smoothed but not burnished outside, rough inside.

816. (VI G 93) (PLATE 55) Fragment from belly of jug or jar. Hard fabric; gritty orange clay fired an even colour throughout; the grit sandy in character, all of the same size, and dominantly white. Outside well burnished, but a bit crackled; inside red, slightly pitted, unburnished but wiped.

817. (VI G/H 109/89) (PLATE 56) Two fragments, apparently from a jar. Light porous clay, tempered with fine sand, pale buff with a slight greenish tinge and a faint hint of orange; surface pale buff with a slight greenish tinge. The larger fragment with marks on the inside which might be from use of the fast wheel; the smaller with decorative grooves outside.

    The fabric and the possible use of the fast wheel suggest that this vase may have been imported from somewhere in the Near East. It is not entirely out of the question that a wheelmade vase from the Near East reached Emporio before the end of Period VI. Kühne has drawn attention to a wheelmade jar that could have been a Syrian import found by Schliemann at Troy apparently in a safe context of Troy I (*Ilios* 214 no. 23. H. Kühne, *Die Keramik vom Tell Chuëra* (Berlin, 1976) 49 f. pl. 40: 2).

818. (VII G/Q 135) (PLATE 42) Small handle with circular section. Fabric cf. Fine Light Grey Burnished Ware. Grey-brown clay fired an even colour throughout; surface light grey, perhaps smoothed or burnished, but much worn.

iii. Periods VI/V (R ?83)

GENERAL

This deposit in trench R produced fourteen baskets of fragments, all very much comminuted, with no complete or restorable vases. The pottery has features which link it both with Period V and with VII–VI, and the deposit may have consisted of rubbish dumped here at the beginning of V. But it is just possible that it reflects a phase intermediary in time between Periods VI and V.

    The high proportion of rims from carinated bowls of type 9 link the deposit with V. On the other hand the jugs of which fragments were recovered from it appear to have been like those from levels of VII–VI: jugs of Light Brown and Fine Black Burnished Ware characteristic of VII–VI were abundantly represented. The almost complete absence of incision, combined with the occurrence of a certain amount of white-painted decoration, also seems to reflect VI rather than V.

SHAPES

(A) BOWLS 819–839 (FIG. 161)

About sixty bowl rims were recovered, and over a third of these (some twenty-two in all) belonged to carinated bowls of type 9. Their rims tended to be concave, as type 9C. This concavity is a feature which appears to be more at home in Period V than in IV and later. One rim of type 9D had the stump of a side handle below the carination.

About sixteen incurving rims were assignable to bowls of types 6 and 7. Only one or two of these were of the thickened club shape at home in Periods VII–VI. Type 10 characteristic of Periods VII–VI was represented by three rims, which had the appearance of being earlier strays, and types 11 and 12 by one rim each. Only one atypical rim (830) was assignable to type 8.

4. Open bowls with straight or slightly curving sides

819. Irregular; surface light brown shading to dusky, burnished but much worn.
820. Surface pitted; light brownish grey, burnished.
821. Light brown to red, burnished but much worn.
822. (PLATE 45) Rim, with large solid lug below it. Grey-brown; fine burnish.

5. Open bowls with curving sides

823. Orange clay; traces of red surface, burnished but much worn.
824. Rim, with hour-glass perforation bored through it after firing. Soft fabric; surface dark brown to black, much worn.
825. Rim, with horizontally perforated lug on outside. Light brownish grey; fine burnish.

7. Bowls with inward-leaning rims and high shoulders

826. Light brown to reddish, burnished but much worn. Two or three others similar.
827. Surface rather irregular; dusky to shades of dark and light brown, burnished. Two others similar.
828. Irregular; surface grey-brown to dark reddish, burnished.
829. Rim with horizontal trumpet lug set below it. Surface very much pitted; dull light greyish brown, burnished.

8. Bowls with carinated shoulders and tall rims

830. Outside dark brown mottling to reddish and black, inside light brown to reddish; fine burnish.

9. Carinated bowls

831. Rim (class A) with oval wart on carination. Soft fabric; surface with straw impressions, light brown to reddish, burnished but much worn.
832. (Rim (class B). Irregular; surface light brown to reddish and dusky black, burnished.
833. (PLATE 45) Rim (class C) with wart on carination. Surface irregular; dark grey-brown to black, with fine burnish.
834. Rim (class B) with horizontal trumpet lug. Dark purple-brown to reddish, burnished.

10. Bowls with short, S-shaped, usually thickened club-like rims

There were only three rims assignable to this type, and all of these could have been earlier strays.

835. Soft greyish clay; surface light brown, burnished but much worn.
836. Soft fabric; surface light greyish brown to reddish, much worn.
837. (PLATE 44) Outside light brown mottling to dusky black, inside light brown to red; very fine burnish.

11. *Bowls with inward-curving rims, internally differentiated and usually thickened*

Only one rim was definitely assignable to this type, which was the commonest and most characteristic type of bowl in Period VII.

838. Light brown shading to reddish and darker brown; fine burnish.

12. *Bowls with straight rims, thickened and usually differentiated on the inside*

The only rim (839) grouped here is on the borders between this and type 11.

839. Light brown shading to reddish at rim; fine burnish.

(B) JUGS AND TRIPOD COOKING POTS

There were large numbers of fragments of jugs, mostly of Fine Black and Light Brown Burnished Ware, indistinguishable from those of VII–VI. A few fragments of Fine Black Burnished Ware, apparently from jugs, had remains of white-painted decoration.

Three feet of tripod cooking pots were recovered; one of them was large.

(C) JARS 840–843 (FIG. 162)

Jar rims were mostly comparable with ones from levels of V–IV. One rim was thickened and differentiated on the inside like 1228 of V. The rim of a large store jar akin to type 38 had a sharply flattened top like 1183 of V. The fragment 842 may come from an imported vase.

840. Rim (class A I). Surface with straw impressions; outside dull light brown, inside grey-brown; poor burnish.
841. Rim (class A III) with large wart on outside. Gritty greyish clay; surface with an unburnished wash, purplish to dusky outside, reddish brown to dusky inside.
842. Fragment of body of small jar with join of neck. Soft fabric; grey-brown clay, with fine sandy red and white grit. Inside well smoothed; outside black, burnished. Groove round base of neck, apparently caused by a band of cord or some other material applied while the clay was still wet and before the surface was burnished, cf. 1251, 1403, 2086, 2584. Possibly an import.
843. Rim, perhaps of class B III. Inside light brown, unburnished except round top of rim; outside darker brown to dusky, burnished.

(I) HANDLES AND LUGS

(1) *Bowl handles and lugs* 844 (FIG. 161)

As in VII–VI, and in contrast to the situation in V–IV, handles seemed to be rare on bowls. The stump of a side handle was noted below the carination of a rim of type 9D, and two fragments of side handles appeared to come from bowls of some kind rather than from jars. Three horizontal trumpet lugs included 829 on a bowl of type 7, and 823 on one of type 9. A small horizontally perforated lug was set below the rim 825 of type 5, and a solid lug below 822 of type 4. A lug of the same kind projects from the rim 844 of a bowl of uncertain type. An hour-glass perforation (rivet-hole) was bored after firing through 824 of type 5.

844. Rim, apparently from bowl, with solid lug projecting from it. Grey clay; surface light brown, unburnished.

(2) *Handles and lugs from jugs and jars* 845, 846 (FIG. 162)

Many fragments (about 550 in all) of strap handles were recovered from this deposit. In every case where it was possible to judge these handles had been set to the rims of vases, apparently jugs. A large proportion was of Light Brown Burnished Ware, and a considerable number (some

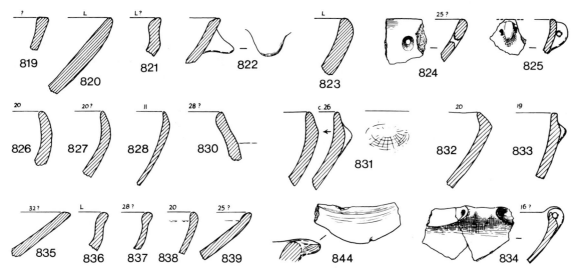

FIG. 161. Period VI/V, R ? 83. Bowls. Scale 1/3.

120 in all) was of Fine Black Burnished Ware, as in deposits of VII–VI. Some handles of Fine Black Burnished Ware had ribs down their length, normally single, but once at least double (PLATE 50: 845 A); and several of them were kidney-shaped in section. One or two were decorated with designs in white paint, including lattice.

The large fragment 845 appears to come from a handle of some exotic kind. The vertically perforated lug 846 may have belonged to a small jar (pyxis) akin to type 44.

845. (PLATE 53) Handle (?) with angled profile. Perforation made before firing. Soft gritty grey-brown clay, light brown at edges; surface with an unburnished red wash.

A fragment of a handle which looks similar but has no perforation through it is illustrated from Tarsus E.B. II (*Tarsus* ii 114 fig. 244: 152). Somewhat comparable elbow handles occur in Troy I (e.g. *Troy* i 124, 152 fig. 245: 19, 18).

846. Vertically perforated lug. Sandy clay; outside black with fine burnish, inside rough. Another similar with traces of a red wash.

(K) BASES 847 (FIG. 162)

These were mostly flat, and nearly all of class 6 B. But at least one bowl base was sunk as class 5 B, and another was assignable to class 8 B. There was a pedestal foot (class 2A), and the scrap 847 evidently comes from a high ring foot of class 3 A.

847. High ring foot (class 3 A). Surface pitted; grey-brown, burnished.

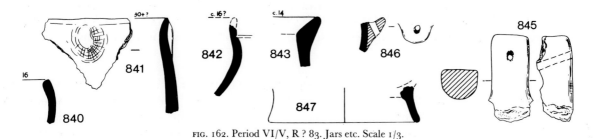

FIG. 162. Period VI/V, R ? 83. Jars etc. Scale 1/3.

DECORATION

This was not much in evidence in the deposit. A few sherds, and one or two strap handles of Fine Black Burnished Ware, all probably from jugs, had remains of white-painted decoration indistinguishable from that current in Periods VII–VI; but incised decoration, characteristic of V–IV, was very rare. The only examples of it were on two scraps, one (849) from the neck, the other (848) from the shoulder, of small closed vases, perhaps jars of the pyxis type 44 (PLATE 55). The shoulder fragment 848 with a black burnished surface has lattice incised on it, the neck 849 (of soft brown clay with the surface unburnished) has a row of dot-filled diamonds, a type of design characteristic of Periods V–IV; but panels filled with dots were already it seems at home at Emporio in Period VI, although not perhaps earlier.

IMPORTS

The fragment 842 with differentiated neck may come from an imported jar.

iv. Periods V–IV

GENERAL

The pottery of this horizon is comparable with that of Troy I. It is still handmade; there is no sign of the use of the fast wheel.

The increasing preponderance of carinated bowls of type 9 distinguishes this horizon from Period VI. Bowls of type 13 also become common, and are not infrequently decorated with incision. Incised decoration—often, although not it seems invariably, filled with white paste—supplants painted decoration in white.

The material from deposits of V has the same character as that from levels of VII–VI; that is to say, it is mostly rubbish, including many fragments of broken jugs. But Period IV ended with a conflagration, and numbers of complete vases were recovered from above the floors of the fire-destroyed houses which occupied this part of the site at the time. The largest group of vases came from House IV in trench H, with other groups from House VII in Q, and from House VIII and the area of open ground on the north side of it in G.

The vases from these three houses differ to some extent in character and in the range of types displayed. These differences might reflect the taste or inclination of the family concerned, or the uses to which the vases were being put. But none of the houses was completely excavated; relatively small areas of Houses VII and VIII were examined, and the southern end of House IV was never cleared. The vessels recovered from these houses do not therefore necessarily represent the complete range of what was in them at the time of their destruction. The vases of the finest fabric, exhibiting the most elaborate shapes and the richest incised decoration, mostly came from the cache on the floor of House VII in trench Q. Nearly all these vases from House VII were fine table ware; there were no large storage vessels among them like those found in Houses VI and VIII.

House IV. The remains of a great many vases, some sixty-two in all apart from pithoi, were recovered from above the floor of this large house. These had either been resting on the floor at the time the house was destroyed, or standing on shelves against the walls or on some kind of raised sleeping bench or platform which served as an upper floor. Twenty-six, that is nearly a half, were bowls: they included a pair with high pedestals as 859 assignable to type 4, a couple of hemispherical shape (type 5), and two dipper cups (type 16); but the vast majority were carinated bowls of type 9, mostly of medium size, but two of them large, and three others small, including one (1052) with an open trough spout. There were thirteen jugs, mostly assignable to type 23 A, but including one at least (1160) of type 24A with cutaway spout. The juglet 1157 of type 23 A is a miniature. An askos (1170) of type 25 and three tripod cooking pots (type 27) were also recovered.

One storage jar of type 38 could be restored, and remains of two or three others of this or the allied types 39–40 were noted. Other jars included an unique example (1231) of the archaic type 43, a pyxis (1232) of type 44 with its lid (1297), and two large jars of type 45 with low collar necks, one of which (1233) with slashed handles may be an import or a local imitation of one. There were at least seven jars of type 47 with high collar necks, including 1239 with elaborate incised decoration. Four lids were recovered: one (1296) of type 61 belonged to the jar 1236, another (1297) of type 62 to the pyxis 1232; two others were of type 63.

The base of a large pithos was found embedded in the floor in the north-east corner of the house. Rims of two pithoi (one of which may have belonged with this base) and pithos fragments with relief decoration were recovered from the destruction debris (level 26) in this area.

House VII. The vases above the floor here were found concentrated in a heap at the foot of wall 47, and may have fallen from a wooden shelf or platform built against it. Virtually all of them were of fine table ware: most (some forty-five out of a total of fifty-eight) being bowls of various types, but including six jugs and three askoi. Fragments of one or perhaps two coarse, thick-walled, tripod cooking pots (type 27), which appear to have belonged with this deposit, were also noted, but no jars of any kind, and no pithoi.

Small bowls were much in evidence, nearly half (twenty or more) of the forty-five bowls recovered being dipper cups of type 16, and eleven of them small varieties of type 5 with side handles (all except one of the horned class, as FIG. 106: No. 6 e). But there were at least three larger bowls of type 5 together with seven or eight of the standard carinated type 9, one of them (1050) having a pedestal foot; also a bowl of type 12 with a high pedestal foot, and three of type 13, each with a different variety of lug, but all with incised decoration.

The seven jugs included the elegant 1158 of type 23B, and the unique pair 1168–9 of type 24B with faces incised on their long necks. Two other jugs had cutaway spouts (type 24A); but jugs with simple beaked spouts (type 23A) common in House IV were curiously absent here. The three askoi included 1171 with elaborate incised decoration.

House VIII. The remains of about thirty-five more or less complete vases were recovered from both sides of wall 50. Some twenty-two, about two-thirds, were bowls; but they included jugs, tripod cooking pots, storage jars of various types, and a lid. It looks as if a number of the vases had fallen from a high platform or upper floor of some kind, since parts of at least one (1051) were recovered from both sides of wall 50, and several others, notably the little dipper cups of type 16, were found at a high level in the ruin debris. In addition there were fragments of several pithoi, mostly from inside the house on the south side of wall 50.

Only one of the twenty-two bowls was of type 5. Some eight were of the carinated type 9, four of them, including 1028 with a ribbed trumpet lug, being large. These large bowls of type 9 all tended to have reddish surfaces in contrast to the dark surfaces of the smaller ones. The four smaller type 9 bowls from House VIII included the unique 1051 with a wide trough spout, side handle, and pedestal foot. Two bowls were of type 13, one of type 14; all three of these had been decorated with incision. There seem to have been a good many, perhaps ten or a dozen, little dipper cups of type 16, but very few could be restored.

Remains of three jugs, one very small, were identified. The unusually large jug 1163 had lost its mouth, so that it was impossible to assign it as between types 23A and 24A. At least three tripod cooking pots (type 27) were identified, and parts of several storage jars of types 38–39. There were also remains of two or three large globular jars of type 47 with tall collar necks. The only lid (1300) was of type 63D with elaborate incised decoration.

FABRIC

The fabric of vases was in general soft; sherds were still easy to break in the hand. The softness of the fabric evidently reflected the continuation of imperfect methods of firing. The clay tended to be black at the core, light brown at the edges, and was normally tempered with grit and straw. The grit, dominantly white, was often large even in the case of the finest burnished ware, and huge lumps of it might occur in vases of coarse ware used for cooking or storage. Minute 'pin-holes', often apparent in the break of sherds, and pittings sometimes visible in their surfaces, may indicate the use of finely chopped straw as temper, unless they are due to the dissolution of particles of limestone grit in cleaning the pottery with the help of acid (T. Jacobsen, *Hesperia* xxxviii (1969) 362; xlii (1973) 264). This phenomenon of 'pin-holes' seems to correspond to the 'spongy appearance' noted in the case of the less well-fired of the Fine Polished Ware of Troy I (*Troy* i 52). A certain number of vases had thin walls, but most even of the smaller vases tended to be relatively thick-walled, as the coarseness of the clay and the imperfect nature of the firing would demand.

Black or shades of dark brown were the dominant surface colours in the case of the finer wares. The dark surfaces, however, were often tinged with red or shaded into patches of red. It seems clear that many vases at any rate had been coated with a red wash, which was normally transformed in the firing. Thus splashes of red paint occurred on the insides of jugs and jars whose outside surfaces had been fired black or dark brown. A number of vases, including several of the finest burnished ware, had surfaces dominantly light brown or red in colour.

Burnishing was general as in earlier periods. Bowls were normally well burnished, the surfaces as a rule shades of grey-brown and black, less often red, sometimes light brown, and even on occasion white (1006, 1078). The finest burnishing appears to have been reserved for some bowls of type 13 with incised decoration on the body as well as on the rim (e.g. 1077, 1079); the surfaces of these bowls were dominantly grey-brown, but shaded to delicate tints of pink and a distinctive olive-green. Even on the finest burnished surfaces the marks of the burnishing implement tended to remain visible, although they might be very faint. In the case of a few bowls the burnishing had been so thorough as to cause ripples, but there was no indication that this rippling of the surface was deliberate as on the Ripple Ware of the Cretan Middle Neolithic.

The surfaces of jugs and jars like those of contemporary bowls ranged in colour from black to brown, light brown, red and even white. Some relatively thin-walled jugs and small jars with surfaces usually black, sometimes brown, were given a very fine polish-like burnish. But the burnishing might be very poor and superficial on vases (mostly jars) of cooking pot or coarse ware: a good many fragments of dull reddish surfaced pottery, remains of storage jars and cooking vessels of various kinds, had little or no burnish. The insides of some closed vases from levels of V–IV appeared to have been wiped or scraped with a bunch of twigs or with something which gave a combed effect.

Silvery Grey Ware (PLATE 58 (*c*)). This distinctive ware was evidently at home in Period V at Emporio, although some fragments from levels of VIII (261) and from upper levels of VI (512, 513) appeared to be similar. The vases of this ware may have been of local manufacture rather than imported. The clay was rather coarse, with white grit, and was grey or black in the break like the local ware; although the fabric was exceptionally hard. The surface was normally burnished and was a distinctive silvery grey mottling to patches of light brown and black in colour.

Vases of various different shapes were evidently made in this ware. The fragments of it recovered from levels of V–IV came from bowls and from two or more jugs. The jugs may not have been of standard shapes; their necks do not appear to have been differentiated from their bodies, and their bases it seems were sharp and angular instead of being more or less rounded. A spout rising from a carination (1328) is another unusual feature which occurs in *Silvery Grey Ware*. This carination and the sharp angular bases are reminiscent of metal-work, and taken in conjunction with the colour suggest that *Silvery Grey Ware* may have been evolved, like the later Minyan which it somewhat resembles, in an attempt to reproduce in clay the effect of the silver vases which were becoming known in the Aegean at the time.

The *Silvery Grey Ware* of Emporio seems to be related to, if it is not identical with, the Gray Monochrome Ware recognised by Weinberg at Corinth and occurring in the Middle and Late Neolithic of the Greek mainland (*Hesperia* vi (1937) 503 ff. Cf. ibid. xlvii (1978) 418. *AJA* li (1937) 174 note 61; xliii (1939) 599. Holmberg, *Neolithic Pottery* 27 f.). Weinberg notes that 'The ware comes in varying shades of gray, but the most usual is a very light silvery gray tone' (*Hesperia* vi (1937) 504). Several of the published examples of this ware look very much like our *Silvery Grey Ware*.

A fine grey ware was also isolated by Walker Kosmopoulos at Corinth (Walker Kosmopoulos 1953, 2 note 10; *Corinth* 44, 47 f., 51, 53 pl. iii: a, e, f). She called it 'Proto-Minyan, and thought that it was non-Corinthian, perhaps even exotic to Greece. It occurred in roughly equal quantities in her Corinthian Periods II and III (Middle and Late Neolithic). Such a distribution might tally with that of *Silvery Grey Ware* with a range between Emporio VIII–V. But it is not clear that the Proto-Minyan of Walker Kosmopoulos exactly corresponds with Weinberg's Gray Monochrome Ware or Emporio *Silvery Grey Ware*, and more recent excavations at Corinth do not suggest a similar distribution of Gray Monochrome Ware in time. The Gray Ware noted by Lavezzi from the Forum West area at Corinth seems to correspond to Weinberg's Gray Monochrome: a few sherds (14 in all) were recovered from Late Neolithic contexts, but over 140 came from deposits which included examples of Gonia style polychrome ware and red-slipped and red burnished wares assignable perhaps to Early Helladic I (*Hesperia* xlvii (1978) 418, 423).

Both the fabric and the sharp carinations of the Grey Ware attributed by Phelps, *Thesis* fig. 90: 3–6, to his Period III (Late Neolithic) bring to mind Emporio *Silvery Grey Ware*. A small ribbon handle from the wells in the agora at Athens, assigned to the Middle Neolithic (?) and said to be reminiscent of the Neolithic Gray Ware class from Corinth, sounds as if it might be akin to *Silvery Grey Ware* in fabric (*Athenian Agora* xiii 9, 32 no. 79).

Gray Ware at Nea Makri identified with Weinberg's Gray Monochrome Ware occurred there in Period B, but was especially characteristic of the last phase, B III (*Nea Makri* 20 ff.). At Varka in Euboia a large quantity of pottery from the Late Neolithic horizon is said to be Grey Ware (described as Protominyan) comparable with Weinberg's Gray Monochrome (Sampson, *AE* 1975 Parart. 74 f.). This Grey Ware according to Sampson, ibid. 76, appears at Varka along with matt-painted and polychrome wares, and before black burnished ware.

'A few pieces of light silvery gray ware' occurred in the Bothros in trench 3 at Elateia assigned by Weinberg to the end of Middle but by others to the beginning of Late Neolithic (*Elateia* 196). A comparable fabric (Monochrome Grey Ware) seems to have been at home in the Late Neolithic of Thessaly. Some of this Monochrome Grey Ware from Arapi belonging to the earliest, Tsangli (Dhimini 1), phase of the Thessalian Late Neolithic looks very much like *Silvery Grey Ware* from levels of Emporio V (*Arapi* 20 pl. ii: 1).

Cooking Pot Ware. This was not as well differentiated from ordinary coarse domestic ware as it was to be in Period II. But it was distinguishable to some extent by its hard, brittle fabric; although this difference in the fabric might perhaps have been caused by the heat of fires over which cooking pots were used. Sometimes the clay was conspicuously sandy. The vessels of this ware might be coated with a red, occasionally with a brown, wash. Many of them had burnished surfaces, but some were left unburnished. The unburnished surfaces in particular were apt to be full of straw impressions.

Foreign Fabrics (see also under 'Imports'). Distinctive fabrics which appeared to be foreign in origin were:

(1) **Micaceous Wares.** Fragments of at least two vases (1364, 1365) of distinctly hard fabric, made of sandy clay with shining mica-like particles in it, were recovered from levels of V. The clay of one or two other fragments from levels of V (1360) and ?IV (1359) also had shining mica-like particles. The vases to which these belonged may have been imports from the Cyclades.

(2) **Obsidian Ware.** This distinctive ware is a variety of *Micaceous Ware*. It is of hard fabric, the clay being sandy with some mica and fine grit, including the distinctive shiny black angular particles which resemble, but are probably not in fact, obsidian. The only fragments certainly of this ware from levels of V–IV belonged to a large storage jar or pithos (1362) like the rims 742 and 746 of Periods VII–VI.

Obsidian Ware may correspond to the Scored Ware 'tempered with good-sized particles of blue-black stone', which was imported to Troy, being most at home in the Middle and Late Subperiods of Troy I but occurring, although not very abundant, in Troy II (*Troy* i 39, 53 f., 222). The centre of manufacture of this Trojan Scored Ware was probably further east in Anatolia. Scored Ware is said to be relatively abundant in E.B. 1–2 in the region of the Konya plain, where it had already appeared at Can Hasan in the Late Chalcolithic level 1 (*AS* xiii (1963) 224 ff., 234; xiv (1964) 126; xv (1965) 88). This may correspond to the Red Gritty Scored and Comb-incised Ware which occurred at Tarsus in Cilician E.B. I and was much at home in E.B. II (*Tarsus* ii 97, 108 f. Cf. Mellaart, *AS* xiii (1965) 224, citing *Tarsus* ii fig. 243: 125, 137, classified as varieties of Cooking Pot Ware, and fig. 252: 244, 245 a and b, of Red Gritty Combed Ware). A comparable and perhaps related 'wiped' ware makes its appearance in the Late Neolithic of Knossos in Crete (*BSA* lix (1964) 225), and is at home there in Early Minoan I and into Early Minoan II.

(3) **Fine Light Grey Burnished Ware.** The solitary fragment (1366) of this ware from a level of V may have strayed there from an earlier horizon.

(4) **White Slipped Ware.** A few fragments (e.g. 1363) found in levels of V and IV had a creamy white slip or wash on the outside. These fragments evidently came from closed vases like jugs or narrow-mouthed jars which may have been imported. White or creamy surfaced wares occur at the beginning of the Early Helladic period on the Greek mainland (e.g. *Eutresis* 83, assigned to Early Helladic I. Corinth: *Hesperia* xlvii (1978) 424, Early Helladic II). But possibly the *White Slipped Ware* of Emporio was of local manufacture, as the *White Slipped Ware* of periods

VII–VI appears to have been. In that case the fragments might have strayed from earlier levels, since the fabric was unusually soft and abundant straw impressions were normally visible in the surface. The base of a bowl with a white slip from V H level 49 certainly appeared to be of local manufacture, but the ware of this was anomalous: soft grey clay, with some grit dominantly red in colour; the inside surface a light battleship grey, stroke burnished; the outside, which was rather worn, having traces of a slip, whitish shading to reddish, with a smooth even burnish.

SHAPES

(A) BOWLS

3. *Baking pans* 850 (FIG. 163)

Only fragments of these were recovered, and they came almost entirely from levels of Period V; some if not all are therefore probably earlier strays. The rim 850 has the stump of a horizontal handle on the outside.

850. (VI/V Q 88) (PLATE 53) Very roughly made. Baking pan fabric. Inside black, outside dusky purple-brown, very rough.

4. *Open bowls with straight or slightly curving sides* 851–876 (FIGS. 163, 165)

These seem to be more in evidence in Period V than later in IV, when open bowls are normally akin to type 5. The very shallow varieties (type 4 C) are distinctly rare, the one or two rims of shallow bowls (e.g. 851) of this type coming from levels of VI/V or the early part of V. A group of small bowls with rims less than 15 in diameter merge with similar ones classifiable as type 5; some of the rims and profiles grouped here (871–6) may have belonged to dipper cups (type 16). A

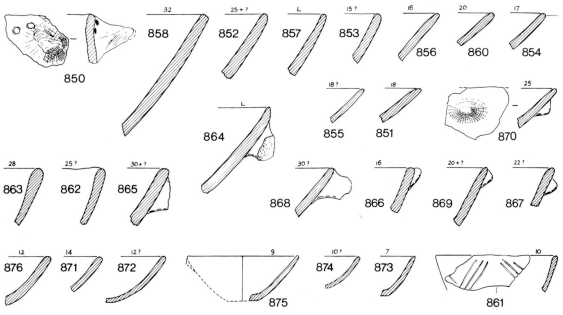

FIG. 163. Periods V–IV. Types 3 and 4. Scale 1/3.

number of rims were markedly thickened, as 862, 863; these resemble ones of type 12, but they are not differentiated on the inside.

The surfaces of type 4 bowls were invariably burnished, it seems. In one case (853) the traces of burnish were doubtful, but might have been removed by water action. Some of the smaller bowls, especially those with diameters of less than 15, had a very fine polish-like burnish. But surfaces were often irregular and uneven, and the burnish on the larger bowls of this type was apt to be rather poor.

One rim from G level 85 as 852 had the stump of a large handle rising from the top in the way that was characteristic on bowls of Periods X–VIII, although some examples were noted from levels of VII–VI. But bowls of type 4 in V–IV were normally it seems provided with a single horizontal side handle, like the complete bowls of the related type 5 recovered from the Period IV destruction level. This handle was set on the outside of the bowl just below the rim; a number of rims assignable to type 4 had the stumps of such handles. Warts were in evidence, as on bowls of type 5; these were normally circular, but in one instance at least oval.

A rim from R level 59 as 852 had a rough trumpet lug of class 1a (FIG. 191). Another rim which appeared to resemble 852 from the same level 59 in R was decorated with incision consisting of a simple zigzag round the inside edge as found on bowls of types 13 and 14; it may have come from a bowl of type 14 rather than type 4.

851. (VI/V H 92) Rim. Inside grey-brown, outside light chestnut brown, well burnished.
852. (V H 49) Rim. Grey clay; surface red to light and dark brown and black, well burnished.
    About a dozen similar rims from levels of V, mostly in G. In general somewhat roughly made, surfaces shades of grey-brown, light brown, or reddish, with a rather poor burnish. One (V G 85) of fine grey-brown burnished ware has the stump of a handle rising from the top as on bowls of Periods X–VIII; another of similar fabric (IV Q 32) a rough trumpet lug of class 1a (FIG. 191). Another (V R 59) of similar fabric and apparently of this type has a simple zigzag incised round the inside edge like some bowls of types 13 and 14.
853. (V H 49) Rim. Grey clay with white grit; surface dusky light brown with little or no trace of burnish.
854. (V R 59) Rim. Surface grey-brown outside, black inside, burnished.
855. (V R 59) Rim. Surface light brown to reddish with rather poor burnish.
856. (V R 50) Rim. Irregular. Soft fabric; surface pitted, red to light brown, burnished. Fragments of some eight others similar, mostly from V G; surfaces grey-brown, light brown, and reddish, burnished.
857. (V R 50) Rim. Grey clay; surface uneven, dull purplish brown to dusky, burnished.
858. (V X ?77/60) Rim. Light brown to reddish, burnished.
859. (IV R 26 House IV) (FIG. 165. PLATE 57) Bowl with high pedestal base (class 1); rim rising in a projection with serrated top above a horizontal, slightly trumpet-shaped lug. Broken, but complete except for small part of rim. Ht. to top of rim 13. Diam. of rim 16.5. Soft fabric; clay orange to grey; surface with minute pin-holes, light brown mottling to orange and red, dark brown, and black; well burnished, but with marks of burnishing instrument visible. Parts of another similar pedestal bowl with serrated lug-projection recovered from the same area in House IV.
    For similar projections rising above horizontally perforated lugs cf. 1073, 1081, and parallels cited under Handles and Lugs for Periods V–IV. There is a crude parallel for the serrated top on 859 in *Kephala* pl. 29: P. A bowl of shape A 6 from Troy I is described as having a scalloped projection rising above a vertically perforated lug (*Troy* i 58). The neat serrations of 859 are matched on a projection above a horizontally perforated lug on a bowl from Moravia assigned to the Baden horizon of which the pottery has many Anatolian affinities (*Baden Symposium* 387 pl. 6: 3).
860. (IV R Bin in 26 House IV) Rim: Light brown to red; fine burnish.
861. (IV/III no level) Rim, with incised decoration. Soft fabric; grey-brown clay; inside surface greyish, outside shades of dark and light brown to reddish; very fine polish-like burnish. The incisions, with traces of white fill in them, were evidently made *after* firing.

A number of thickened, somewhat club-like rims, may be grouped here rather than under type 12 as they are not obviously differentiated on the inside.

862. (V H 48) Rim. Angle not certain. Grey clay; surface uneven, lightish brown, burnished.

863. (V Q 85) Rim. Grey-brown with reddish tinge, burnished. About ten similar rims with an average diam. of *c.* 25 from levels of V mostly in G; rather irregular in shape, but surfaces well burnished, mostly grey-brown, with one or two shading to light brown.

Handles and lugs

864. (V H 49) Rim, with stump of handle. Black clay with large white and red grit, some showing in surface, which grey-black to dark brown, burnished.
865. (V R 59) Rim, with stump of handle. Dark grey-brown to reddish, burnished.
866. (V R wall 37) Rim, with wart set to it. Grey-brown to black; fine polish-like burnish. Two others similar from V H level 49; grey-brown, burnished.
867. (V R 50) Rim, with wart below it. Grey clay; inside surface pinkish light brown, outside dusky and shades of brown, burnished.
868. (IV G 26) Rim, with stump of handle. Grey-brown with reddish tinge, burnished.
869. (IV G/H 25) Rim, with wart set to it. Grey-brown with reddish tinge, burnished.
870. (IV R 26) Rim, with oval wart below it. Grey-brown clay; surface with reddish tinge, light brown outside, dark brown inside, burnished.

Small bowls (diameters less than 15)

871. (V H 49) Rim. Grey-brown to reddish; fine burnish.
872. (IV H 35) Profile. Surface grey-brown, slightly pitted, but with fine burnish. Some five others similar from levels of V mostly in G; surfaces grey-brown or light brown, sometimes shading to red, burnished.
873. (V R wall 44) Profile. Irregular. Grey clay with grit showing in surface, which pitted; light brownish grey, burnished.
874. (V G wall 51) Rim. Surface light mustard brown; very fine burnish. Another similar from V R level 59; surface grey-brown to black with very fine burnish.
875. (V R 59) Profile. Grey-black clay; surface black inside, lightish brown to dusky outside, with fine polish-like burnish. Three others similar from V G; surfaces grey-brown, or reddish to light brown and dusky, burnished.
876. (V R 50) Rim. Irregular. Shades of brown to dusky, burnished.

5. *Open bowls with curving sides* 877–927 (FIGS. 164, 165)

Bowls of type 5 seem to have been common and characteristic both in Period V and in IV; they merged into carinated bowls of type 9 which abounded in this horizon. Type 5 bowls of V–IV tended to be more definitely hemispherical and steep-sided (as type 5 A) than those of ealier periods which were apt to be more open as type 5 B. Diameters ranged from less than 10 to 40 or more. Fragments of some very large vases, apparently bowls of this type, were recovered from levels of V–IV (e.g. 878); but many bowls seem to have had a diameter of *c.* 20–25. Small bowls less than 15 in diameter were much in evidence (891–906); some of the rims grouped here may have belonged to dipper cups of type 16.

Many of the rims assignable to type 5 were flat-topped (884–6) One or two thickened club-like rims (883, 889) may be earlier strays. Shallow bowls of type 5 C, like those of the related type 4 C, appear to have been very rare, and the few rims grouped under this heading are anomalous: the massive rim 890 of type 5 C might in fact have belonged to a large dish of type 2.

Like bowls of type 4 those of type 5 in V–IV characteristically appear to have had a single more or less horizontal side handle set just below the rim. A number of complete vases of this type were recovered from the destruction levels of Period IV; these had a single horizontal side handle and three warts, one opposite the handle and one each side. Some rims which may be grouped here have small vertical handles set below them (e.g. 907, 908). Long tubular lugs are found on or just below some type 5 rims from levels of V (e.g. 912, 913). Vertically perforated lugs, single (916, 917) or double (914, 915), occur on or just below some rims that may have come from

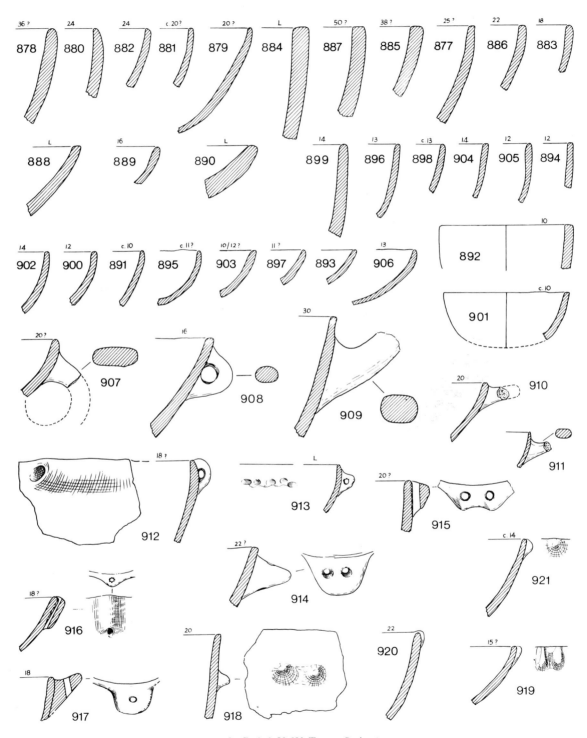

FIG. 164. Periods V–IV. Type 5. Scale 1/3.

bowls of this type. Warts frequently appear on or just below rims of type 5 bowls in V–IV; sometimes these are double (e.g. 918, 919).

Small bowls with rims less than 15 in diameter were evidently common. The handles of these were often of the horned class 4 (FIG. 107) to judge from the remains of small bowls found in the destruction levels of Period IV, notably in House VII (trench Q level 26). But the simple rounded handles of class 1 (FIG. 107), usual on the larger bowls of this shape, are also attested. Warts occur on small bowls (e.g. 921), but appear to be less common than on the larger ones. Small bowls with rims of type 5 and large vertical strap handles rising above them are listed as dipper cups (type 16).

The surfaces of bowls of type 5 tended to be dark, either black or a deep shade of grey-brown in colour; but light brown and occasionally red surfaces occurred. The bowls were almost invariably burnished, and some especially of the smaller ones had a very high polish-like burnish.

The rims 877–906 described below are grouped as from:

A. Deep, more or less hemispherical bowls

877. (VI/V H 92/78) Hard grey clay; surface grey shading to brown with rather superficial burnish, more thorough inside than out.
878. (IV H 37) Hard fabric; grey to brick-red clay; surface light brown mottling to reddish and dusky black, burnished. Another similar (V R ?50) with stump of side handle below it. Irregular; coarse grey-black clay; abundant straw impressions and grit showing in surface, which has a red wash, smoothed, but not burnished.
879. (IV H 35) Grey-brown, burnished. Some ten similar, several with stumps of side handles, and one (879 A) from V G wall 44 with a large oblong wart set horizontally below it (PLATE 58).
880. (V R 50) Grey-brown clay with abundant grit; surface lightish brown with rather dull burnish. Another similar (VI/V H 94) with surface much worn. Possibly strays of Periods VII–VI.
881. (V R ?73) Dark grey clay; surface rather rough, dark grey outside, light grey inside, burnished.
882. (V G 54) Grey-brown clay; surface lightish brown, burnished.
883. (VI/V Q 88) Thickened club-like. Dark brown to black; fine burnish. Possibly a stray of Periods VII–VI.
884. (V/IV X 60/40/25) Large, flat-topped. Light brown, outside with a reddish tinge, burnished.
885. (IV G 26) Flat-topped. Grey-brown with a reddish tinge, burnished. Four others similar from levels of V.
886. (IV G 26/25) Grey-brown, burnished. Many others similar from levels of V–IV; surfaces grey-brown, shades of light brown to red, burnished.
887. (IV R 26) Large, flat-topped. Hard fabric, well fired. Grey to light brown clay; surface light brown to reddish, burnished.

B. Medium depth bowls

888. (IV R 26) Flat-topped. Grey clay, light brown at edges; surface much pitted, pale light brown, burnished. Two others similar: one (V R 49) grey-brown to black, the other (IV Q 32) light brown with a reddish tinge, burnished.
889. (V G wall 23) Thickened club-like. Surface rather uneven, grey-brown, burnished but worn. Probably a stray of Periods VII–VI.

C. Shallow bowls

Shallow bowls with curving sides assignable to type 5 C were evidently rare, but a few rims including the large 890 may be grouped here.

890. (V R 59) Hard fabric; coarse gritty grey-brown clay. Inside yellowish brown, well burnished; outside reddish brown to dusky, less well burnished. Two others similar (V G ?70, Q 62) with surfaces well burnished inside, less well outside.

Small bowls (diameter less than 15)

891. (IV H 37) Dark grey-brown with a reddish tinge, burnished. Two others similar (VII/V H 117/47, V G 85) with surfaces grey-brown, and reddish to light brown, burnished.

892. (VI/V H 90) Hard fabric; grey clay; surface dark brown shading to dusky black, burnished.
893. (V H 76) Grey-brown, burnished.
894. (V H 49) Soft fabric; light grey clay; surface light brown to red with very fine burnish, but worn.
895. (V H 49) Surface irregular and pitted, grey-brown, burnished.
896. (V H 48) Surface even and regular, grey-brown to light brown and reddish, with fine burnish but worn.
897. (V G wall 51) Irregular. Grey-brown, burnished.
898. (V H wall 26) Grey-brown clay; surface light brown with fine burnish, but worn.
899. (V R ?50) Rough and irregular. Sandy grey-brown clay; surface orange, with no trace of smoothing or burnishing, but worn. Possibly from a jar cf. type 38.
900. (V G 85) Inside light to dark brown, outside light brown to red; fine burnish, but worn. Two others similar (V R 59, H 49).
901. (V R 86) Irregular. Outside light brown, inside dark grey-brown, burnished.
902. (V Q 62) Purplish brown, burnished.
903. (IV G 36) Grey-brown clay; surface rather irregular and pitted, lightish brown, burnished. Two others similar from V G level 54: one of soft fabric with large grit; surface purple-brown, burnished: the other light greyish, well burnished.
904. (IV G 25) Grey-brown; fine burnish.
905. (IV G 25) Grey-brown with a reddish tinge, burnished.
906. (IV G 25) Grey-brown clay. Outside light brown to reddish, inside dark brown; fine burnish. One or two others similar.

Handles and lugs

907. (IV G 25) Strap handle below rim. Grey-brown, burnished.
908. (V R ?73) (PLATE 58) Small lug-like strap handle below rim. Irregular. Coarse grey-brown clay; surface burnished.
909. (V R wall 37) Rim with stump of large side handle. Shades of light and dark brown to dusky and reddish, burnished.
910. (IV X ?26 south of wall 49) Side handle below rim. Shades of brown, well burnished.
911. (V R 59) Rim with neat side handle. Very fine fabric; surface grey-brown to black with high polish-like burnish.
912. (V R 50) Long tubular lug on rim. Grey-brown, burnished. Three others similar from V G level 85, and Q levels ?70, 62; surfaces grey-brown and light brown, burnished.
913. (V X 82/77/60) Long tubular lug set below rim; decorated with finger-tip impressions. Light brown, burnished.
914. (V R 59) (PLATE 58) Double vertically perforated lug below rim. Irregular. Outside grey-brown, inside grey; poor burnish.
    Cf. 632 of Period VI with references to examples from Troy I.
915. (V/IV H no level) (PLATE 58) Double vertically perforated lug, set to rim. Irregular. Shades of light and darker brown; poor burnish.
    Cf. *Troy* i 105 fig. 241: 31 (Troy I c) for this type of lug, which was common at Poliochni in the Blue period (e.g. *Poliochni* i pl. xxxii: g, h, k, l).
916. (V G 51) Long vertically perforated lug, set to rim. Grey clay; surface fairly even, grey outside, light brown to grey inside, burnished but worn.
    Cf. *Poliochni* i pl. xxviii: j (evolved Blue period) for a similar lug to a rim of this type.
917. (V H wall 40) Vertically perforated lug, set to rim. Grey-brown clay; surface black inside, grey-brown outside, slightly pitted but with high polish-like burnish.
918. (V H 49) Double wart set below rim. Grey clay, red-brown at edges; surface light brown with fine stroke burnish.
919. (V H wall 38) Pair of vertical warts set on rim. Grey-brown; very fine burnish.
920. (IV G 25) Wart on outside of rim. Grey-brown with a reddish tinge, burnished.
921. (V R wall 37) (PLATE 58) Wart set on outside of rim. Grey-brown, burnished.

Complete vases and large fragments from the Period IV destruction level 26 (FIG. 165)

922. (G House VIII) Side handle; three circular warts below rim. Broken, large parts missing. Ht. estimated *c.* 9.5. Diam. of rim *c.* 21. Dark grey clay; surface dark reddish brown with fine stroke burnish.

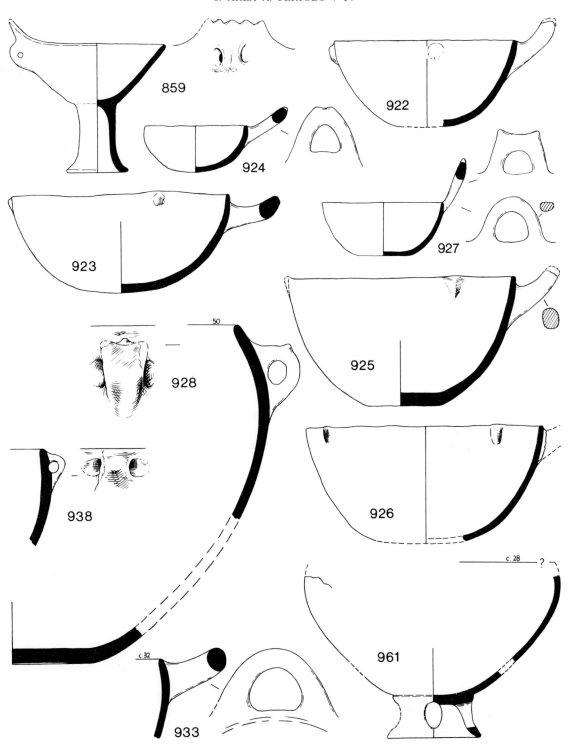

FIG. 165. Periods V–IV. Types 4–7. Scale 1/4.

923. (R House IV) (PLATE 57) Side handle; three circular warts below rim. Broken, but virtually complete. Ht. *c.* 10. Diam. of rim 24. Abundant grit, some very large, dominantly grey and white, showing in surface, which light brown to reddish with a dusky patch on inside, burnished but much worn.

924. (R House IV) (PLATE 57) Side handle of nicked class (FIG. 107 No. 4). Broken, but virtually complete. Ht. to rim 5. Diam. 11.4. Thick-walled; surface light brown to reddish, stroke burnished.

925. (Q House VII) (PLATE 57) Side handle; three small vertical warts on rim. Broken, parts of rim and most of handle missing. Ht. to rim 13. Diam. of rim *c.* 26. Orange clay; surface burnished, now mostly dark brown to black, but originally perhaps light brown to red but discoloured by fire.

Three similar rims from levels of V: one (V X 60) with a vertical wart as 925; surface red to shades of light and dark purple-brown, burnished.

926, 926A. (Q House VII) (PLATE 57) Side handle; three small vertical warts on rim cf. 925. Ht. *c.* 12. Diam. of rim 25.5. Clay with grit, including white, grey, and red; surface much pitted, black; strokes of burnishing implement clearly visible.

927. (Q House VII) (PLATE 57) Small bowl with side handle of horned class (FIG. 107 No. 5) rising from top of rim. Broken, parts of rim missing. Ht. to rim 5.5. Diam. 13.5. Fairly thin-walled. Rather fine clay, grey-brown in centre of break, brown or red-brown at edges, with some medium-sized grit, including grey and red; surface dark purplish brown to reddish with careful stroke burnish.

Parts of at least nine others similar (two reconstructed on PLATE 57 bottom) from the same deposit; mostly with handles of the horned class as 927, but one with a simple rounded handle of class 1 (FIG. 107).

6. *Bowls with inward-leaning rims* 928–939 (FIGS. 165, 166)

A number of rims were assignable to this type which merges into types 7, 8 and 9 as well as into jars with rims of class A 1. Some of these bowls may have been very large, having rims 40 or 50 or more in diameter (e.g. 928, 929); but small bowls with rim diameters of less than 15 are also attested (931, 936). Some rims were apparently flat-topped.

Small bowls with strap handles to their rims like 931 almost approximate to dipper cups of type 16. Strap handles are also found set vertically on the shoulder (as on the large bowl 928) or just below the rim (e.g. 934). Side handles as on bowls of type 5 are attested as well (e.g. 933, unless this is part of a carinated bowl of type 9). The rim 938 has a horizontally perforated lug on the outside.

It is curious that warts, which are such a regular feature on bowls of types 5 and 9, do not appear to occur on those of type 6.

928. (V X ?77/60) (FIG. 165) Fragments of large bowl. One strap handle of kidney-shaped section preserved on shoulder. A flat base (diam. 18) appears to belong. Shades of grey and light and dark brown, burnished.

929. (VI/V H 105/47) Rim of large bowl. Coarse grey clay with large grit and straw; surface orange, without any trace of burnish, but very much worn.

930. (IV H 37) Rim. Inside dark brown to black, outside lighter brown, well burnished. Others similar from levels of V.

931. (V R ?50) Rim, with stump of very thin-sectioned strap handle. Fabric cf. 1074. Grey clay, with grey and white grit showing in surface, which finely pitted, light buff-brown, well burnished. Outside with traces of thick red wash (or remains of decoration in red?) applied after burnishing.

932. (V R 50) Flat-topped rim, as 1448 from II R level 7a. Grey-brown, burnished. Five similar from levels of V, including one from VI/V G/H level 88 of hard Silvery Grey Ware.

933. (V R 50) (FIG. 165) Fragments of bowl, with large side handle set just below rim. Possibly part of a carinated bowl of type 9. Irregular; surface uneven. Grey clay; surface shades of light brown mottling to dusky and red-brown, stroke burnished.

934. (V R ?73) Rim, with stump of small strap handle below it. Grey clay; surface dark purple-brown, stroke burnished.

935. (V G 54) Rim. Shades of grey and dark brown mottling to black, well burnished.

936. (VI/V G/H 88) Rim. Light brown to reddish; fine burnish.

937. (VI/V R ?87) Rim, with small kidney-sectioned handle rising above it. Grey-brown, burnished.

938. (V/IV X 60/40/25) (FIG. 165) Rim, with horizontally perforated lug set just below it. Light grey-brown, burnished.

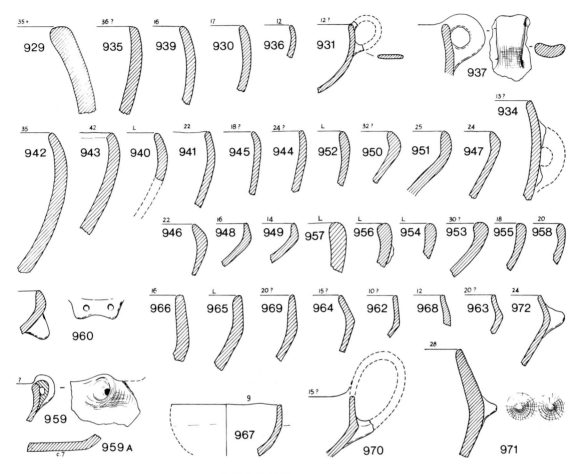

FIG. 166. Periods V–IV. Types 6–8. Scale 1/3.

939. (IV G 25) Rim. Grey-brown, burnished. Some ten others similar from levels of V: mostly grey-brown, but some partly light brown and red, burnished.

7. *Bowls with inward-leaning rims and high shoulders* 940–961 (FIGS. 165, 166)

These merge into bowls of types 8 and 9; and it is always possible for the rim of the same bowl to correspond to type 7 in one section and to type 9 in another. A number of rims grouped here are thickened, and some of these (946–952) have distinctively pointed tops, so that they could be regarded as varieties of type 9 rims with rounded carinations. Other thickened rims (953–8) have rounded club-like tops of the kind which were at home in levels of Periods VII–VI, from which some of them at least may be strays.

Some bowls assignable to type 7 appear to have had side handles (e.g. 944). One or two rims grouped here boast horizontal trumpet lugs set on them as 959. Short horizontally perforated lugs on the swelling (like 1409 from III R level 19) are also attested. The thickened and pointed rim 960 has a horned lug with double perforations below it. The absence of warts is noticeable as in the case of type 5 bowls.

The fragmentary bowl 961 with a high pedestal foot and unusually bold incised decoration is grouped here, but it may have been of some other type.

940. (IV H 35) Rim. Dark grey clay; surface light brown with fine polish-like burnish. Three or four others similar from levels of V; surfaces usually grey-brown, once light brown to red, burnished.
941. (V R 50) Rim. Surface rough and irregular, shades of dull purplish and light brown; rather poor burnish.
942. (V R 69) Rim. Soft fabric. Grey-brown clay; abundant straw impressions in surface, which appears to have had a light brown to reddish wash, unburnished.
943. (VI/V R ?87) Flat-topped rim. Hard fabric akin to Silvery Grey Ware. Outside dark brown to black, inside lighter brown, burnished.
944. (IV R 35) Rim, with stump of possible side handle on outside. Grey-brown; fine burnish. Eight others similar (diam c. 20) from levels of V–IV: two with side handles on the swelling.
945. (IV G 25) Rim. Outside light brown, inside grey-brown; fine burnish.

Pointed rims

946. (V H 49) Rim. Surface even and regular, grey-brown, with high stroke burnish.
947. (V R 50) Rim. Red to shades of light and dark brown, burnished.
948. (V R 50) Rim. Surface minutely pitted, grey-brown, with very fine burnish.
949. (V R wall 37) Rim. Dark brown to black shading to light brown, burnished but worn.
950. (V Q ?70) Rim. Dark brown with a reddish tinge in places, burnished. One similar (VI/V Q 88) with stump of lug or handle below swelling cf. 960; surface grey-brown, burnished.
951. (V R 86) Rim. Irregular. Shades of grey-brown to light brown and reddish, well burnished.
952. (V X 74) Rim. Red shading to light brown; fine burnish.

Club-like rims

953. (VI/V H 92) Rim. Incipient crackles in surface, which dark brown to black with slight purplish tinge; fine polish-like burnish. Fabric cf. Period V, although profile looks earlier.
954. (V H 76) Rim. Grey clay; surface light brown to reddish, burnished but much worn.
955. (VI/V H 117/47) Rim. Soft fabric. Abundant straw impressions showing in surface, which light to reddish brown and dusky; fine burnish.
956. (V G wall 50) Rim, with stump of handle, lug, or wart. Grey-brown; fine burnish.
957. (VI/V Q 88) Rim. Grey clay, orange at surface; traces of a red wash, which may have been burnished.
958. (V Q 85) Rim. Grey-brown; poor burnish. Two others similar from V/IV G 54/36.

Handles and lugs

959. (V H 76) Rim, with part of trumpet lug of class 3 a (FIG. 191) A flat base 959A from the same level may belong with it. Outside grey-brown, inside black, burnished.
      Two similar rims with trumpet lugs from V R level 59: one (959B) illustrated on PLATE 58 (a). The other seems to have had a pair of trumpet lugs side by side on it.
960. (V G/Q 85) Rim, thickened and pointed cf. 950–1, with vertically perforated lug below the swelling. Grey-brown, stroke burnished.
961. (V/IV X 60/40/25) (FIG. 165. PLATE 63) Fragments of bowl, apparently of type 7, with high pedestal foot (class 2A). Diam. of rim estimated c. 28; of base 10. Gritty grey-brown clay. Surface (of foot) red, shading elsewhere on body to dark reddish and deep purple-brown and light brown, with fine burnish; but in many places the surface has flaked away and perished. Decorated with very bold incision filled with white paste; apparently a single row of hatched diamonds.
      The design with bold white-filled channels is closely paralleled on material from the potter's kiln at Dhimini assignable to a late stage in the Thessalian Late Neolithic, although the shapes of this are different (Hourmouziadhes, *AAA* x (1977) 218, 220 fig. 20. Cf. *DS* 201 pl. 18: 3).

8. *Bowls with carinated shoulders and tall rims* 962–972 (FIG. 166)

This type seems to be less clearly defined than it was in Periods VII–VI, and rims assignable to it in general rise less high above the carination than they did earlier. But a certain number of tall carinated rims are better grouped here than under types 6, 7, or 9, which merge into it.

At least one of these rims is flat-topped (968). The rim 970 with the stump of a large strap handle might almost be classified as belonging to a dipper cup of type 16, and some small rims like 967 may have come from such cups. Some of the rims assignable to type 8 had warts on the carination like bowls of type 9. A scrap of rim from a bowl of type 8 or type 5 from V H level 49 had traces of pattern burnish; it was probably a stray of VII–VI.

962. (VI/V H 92) Light grey-brown, well burnished.
963. (V R 59) Purple-brown to reddish; very fine stroke burnish.
964. (V R 59) Grey-brown; fine stroke burnish.
965. (V R 50) Grey clay; surface light brown, originally with fine burnish, but worn.
966. (V R ?73) Hard fabric. Grey clay; surface light brown outside, grey-brown inside, burnished.
967. (V R ?73) Grey-brown; fine burnish. Inside with high polish-like burnish. Possibly from a dipper cup (type 16).
968. (V G 85) Shades of light and dark brown to reddish; very fine stroke burnish.
969. (IV G 36) Angle uncertain. Grey-black clay; surface black with fine burnish.
970. (VI/V G 88) Large strap handle rising above rim. Surface pitted, grey-brown, burnished. Possibly better classified as a dipper cup (type 16).
971. (V X 82/77/60) (PLATE 58 (a)) Pair of warts on carination. Shades of grey and brown, burnished.
972. (V/IV Q 62/32) Large wart on carination. Grey clay with grit (some large), dominantly white, showing in surface, which somewhat pitted, shades of light and dark brown and red, stroke burnished.

9. *Carinated bowls* 973–1052 (FIGS. 167–169)

These were very common both in V and IV in contrast to their rarity in earlier periods. Between a quarter and a third of all bowl rims from levels of V were carinated, and in IV it would seem that the proportion of carinated bowls was even higher. A considerable number of complete or nearly complete bowls of this type were recovered from the Period IV destruction levels. Most of the rims fall into classes A and B, but a certain number are of class D, and some with a hollow on the outside belong to class C: rims of class C were perhaps more in evidence in V than in IV. Type 9 bowls evidently ranged in size from miniatures with a diameter of less than 10 to very large examples 40 to 50 or more across. Large bowls with diameters of 40 to 50 or more do not appear to have been common, but are attested in V as well as in IV. The average diameter would seem to have been in the region of *c*. 20–25, although a considerable number of rims had a diameter of *c*. 15 or less.

Some large and medium-sized bowls like 1035 and 1043 had two side handles set opposite each other with two lugs or solid warts in the intervals between them. But more usual, and very characteristic on bowls of this type of all sizes, was a single side handle, rising from the carination, or occasionally from the top of the rim. The handle was often (but not invariably) accompanied by three warts set on the carination, one opposite it, and one in the middle of each side. These side handles were normally rounded or pointed (FIG. 107, classes 1 and 2), or ogival (class 3) (e.g. 1041, 1043, 1049). Handles of the horned class 5 were not so common. While side handles were a regular feature on carinated bowls of Period V, they were perhaps even more in evidence on those of IV. On the other hand, small vertical strap handles springing from rim and carination (e.g. 1018–1020) were better represented in V than in IV, although even in V they were not as common as side handles. Some of these small vertical strap handles are lug-like, and when kidney-sectioned approximate to short trumpet lugs (e.g. 1020). Small strap handles were also occasionally set on the side of the bowl below the carination instead of above it (e.g. 995).

Trumpet lugs occur on the rim above the carination as FIG. 191: 3 in IV (e.g. 1021) as well as in V. Some of these trumpet lugs are ribbed, as FIG. 191: 3, b, c (e.g. 1028). In addition small horizontally or vertically perforated lugs are found on or just below the carination of some bowls (e.g. 1022). Solid lugs at times take the place of warts on the carination, like the rectangular lug on 989, and the horned lug on 1034.

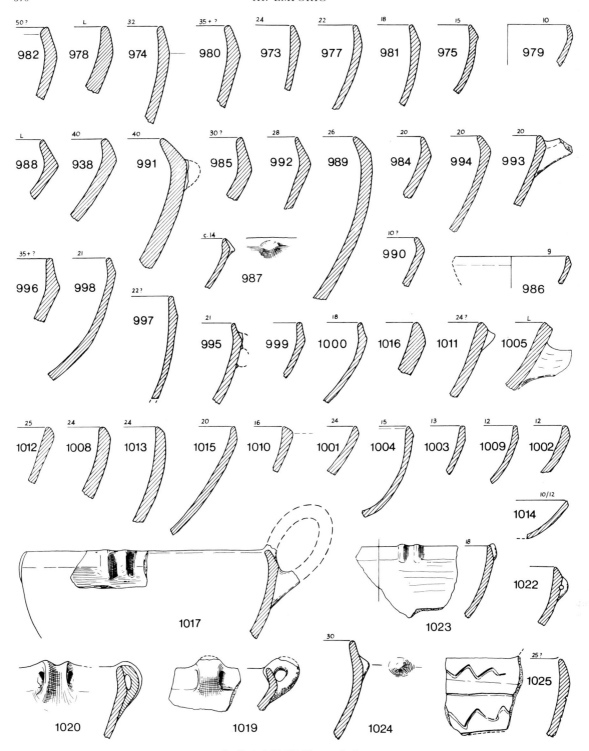

FIG. 167. Periods V–IV. Type 9. Scale 1/3.

Warts were commonly set on the carination or on the outside of the rim above it, but occasionally on the side of the bowl below the carination (e.g. 1045). These warts were normally circular, sometimes, when set on the carination, oblong or oval. Some of the warts on Period IV bowls, both large (e.g. 1026) and small (e.g. 1033), are upturned like those common in Period II. Vertical warts sometimes appear on the rims of type 9 bowls, and slightly project above rim level: five such warts (instead of the more usual three) are found on the rim of the pedestal bowl 1050 from IV Q level 26. Vertical warts may occur together in pairs (e.g. 1023).

Wide trough spouts occur on a few carinated bowls from Period IV destruction levels (e.g. 1051–2). One of these (1051) has a large wart-surmounted strap handle to one side of the spout and a solid pedestal foot (class 2B). Bases were normally flat or flattened, and often more or less sunk; but occasionally it seems rounded. The complete bowl 1050 has a high pedestal foot (class 2A) with two rows of holes through it, the spouted bowl 1051 a solid pedestal foot (class 2B) as already noted. Some of the other pedestal feet of class 2 from levels of V–IV no doubt belonged to carinated bowls.

Fabric. A few of the carinated bowls of V–IV were evidently of the hard Silvery Grey Ware, which may have originated from a desire to imitate the appearance of silver. But the majority were of standard local fabric, the clay grey-brown; the burnished surfaces in V dominantly shades of dark brown, sometimes light brown, often with a reddish tinge; in IV sometimes black, but normally shades of dark brown, light brown, or red, as in V. It was noticeable that the largest type 9 bowls tended to have red surfaces (e.g. 1026–7). Some carinated bowls, especially those with black surfaces from levels of IV, had a very fine polish-like burnish; but even in IV, and still more it seems in V, the burnishing might be comparatively poor and superficial, the vase being irregular and its surface uneven.

Occasionally type 9 bowls were of coarse ware with poor burnish, and one rim from V X level 77 was of cooking pot ware with traces of an original red wash with a very superficial burnish. In at least one instance (1008) the outside surface of the bowl appears to have been left unburnished. A number of bowls seem to have been black inside and a lighter shade of colour, sometimes light brown to red, outside. In the case of bowls from the Period IV destruction levels it is not always certain what the original surface colour was, owing to the chances of discoloration by the fire which destroyed this part of the settlement.

Decoration hardly occurs on carinated bowls of type 9 from levels of V–IV, except in the form of warts. But the rim 1025 from V G level 51 shows that such bowls might upon occasion be decorated with incision, while the thorough burnishing of the surface on 976 has given it a rippled look which may have been deliberate.

A. Rims at open angles
973. (V H 49) Stump of wart or side handle on carination. Surface grey inside, dark brown to reddish outside; irregular, but with high stroke burnish. Another similar (V G 51) but with surface a lighter brown.
974. (V R 50) Shades of dark and light greyish brown, burnished. Another similar (V G 54) with wart above carination; outside light brown, inside black, burnished.
975. (V R 50) Grey clay; surface light brown, burnished. Another similar (V R 86) with stump of side handle on carination; light brown to red wash, burnished.
976. (V G 54) Parts of rim cf. 1043 and of body including two warts on carination. Diam. of rim *c.* 24. Shades of dark brown and black to deep purplish with very fine polish-like burnish which has given the surface a rippled look.
977. (V G 54) Grey-brown; fine burnish.
978. (V G 85) Hard fabric. Grey clay; surface reddish purple-brown, burnished but much worn.

979. (V X 61) Light grey, shading to black on outside; fine burnish.
980. (IV G 36) Grey-brown clay. Outside dull brown, inside black; very fine polish-like burnish. Three others similar from levels of V: one (V R ?50) with bold oblong wart on carination; soft fabric, with surface dark purplish red to black, well burnished but worn.
981. (IV G 36) Grey-brown; high stroke burnish. Several others similar from levels of V: one (V G/Q 85) with stump of vertical strap handle below carination.
982. (III G 19) Probably of Period IV. Grey-brown with a reddish tinge, burnished. Three others similar from levels of V; surfaces grey-brown or lightish brown, burnished.

B. Rims at sharp angles

983. (V H 49/48) Surface pitted, lightish brown, burnished.
984. (V R 50) Soft fabric; surface deep purple-brown to reddish with high burnish, but worn. Several others similar from levels of V, including two with stumps of side handles. Surfaces mostly shades of grey-brown, but some light brown, burnished. One (V H ?50) of hard Silvery Grey Ware; surface silvery grey to dusky and light greyish brown, burnished.
985. (IV R 28) Grey clay; surface light brown to reddish with fine burnish, but worn. Several others similar from levels of V: one of hard Silvery Grey Ware.
986. (V R ?73) From small bowl. Grey clay; surface dark grey-brown to reddish, burnished. Another similar (V H 48) with oblong wart on carination; surface light brown to reddish with fine burnish.
987. (V G 54) Bold wart on carination. Outside light brown to red, inside dark grey to black; fine burnish.
988. (VI/V G/Q 87) Surface pitted, lightish brown, burnished.
989. (V/IV X no level) Grey-brown clay with large grit showing in surface, which red to light brown, well burnished. A fragment from this bowl or one similar (surface dark brown to red) has a bold rectangular lug on the carination.
990. (V/IV X ?41) Grey-brown, shading to reddish round rim; fine burnish.
991. (V/IV X 60/40/25) Stump of wart on carination. Coarse fabric; surface uneven and badly pocked, light brown to red outside, deep purple-red inside, burnished. Several others similar from levels of V.
992. (V/IV X 60/40/25) Light brown to reddish, burnished.
993. (IV Q 32) Stump of side handle on carination. Grey-brown to black; fine polish-like burnish.
994. (IV G 25) Dark brown to black; very fine polish-like burnish. Several others similar from levels of V and IV.

C. Rims concave on the outside

995. (V H 49) Stump of small vertical handle (?). Soft fabric; grey-brown clay, with very large soft white grit, some showing in surface, which dark grey-brown to reddish, apparently burnished, but worn.
    About ten or more similar from levels of V: one (V G 54) with stump of lug or handle (perhaps a strap handle cf. 1018) rising above rim; soft fabric with large white grit; surface purplish brown with traces of red wash, burnished. Another (V X 77/60) with side handle; surface grey-brown, burnished. Others with warts.
996. (V H 49) Very irregular; surface grey-brown with poor burnish. Another similar (V G 64) with wart on carination; surface shades of brown with poor burnish.
997. (V G 54) Soft fabric. Clay with large grit; surface with a red wash, well burnished but worn.
998. (IV G 26) Dark brown to black; very fine polish-like burnish. Several others similar from levels of V and IV.
999. (IV G 36) Fragments of bowl with side handle. Rough and irregular in shape; rim showing a considerable variety in profile. Grey-brown; very high stroke burnish.
1000. (IV R bin in 26, House IV) Stump of wart or side handle on carination. Shades of dark and light brown with a tinge of reddish; fine burnish. One or two others similar.

D. Short bevelled rims

Some rims of this class are from large bowls, and a number of them resemble ones like 1469, 1471, 1474, from levels of Period II. At the other extreme is a series of small bowls with diameters of less than 15. Several rims of these also resemble ones from levels of II (e.g. 1494–5, 1497, 1500).

1001. (VI/V H 92/78) Irregular. Grey-brown; poor burnish.
1002. (VI/V H 117/47) Light brown; very fine burnish. Others similar from levels of V and IV; shades of black, grey-brown, light brown, and red, burnished.

1003. (IV H 37) Grey-brown to black; fine burnish. Five others similar: one with large oval wart on carination; light brown to red, burnished.

1004. (V H 49) Grey clay; surface dark purplish grey-brown with fine burnish. One similar (V R 50); shades of brown to reddish with fine burnish.

1005. (V H 49) Wart below carination. Soft fabric. Pale grey-brown clay; surface light brown, burnished but worn. Three others similar; one (V R ?73) with trumpet lug surmounted by wart set below rim.

1006. (V H 49) Profile and fragments, including stump of side handle and wart on carination. Grey clay with grit and large pieces of straw; surface uneven, but with high stroke burnish; light brown mottling to red outside, pale grey inside. Fragments of this or of one or more similar bowls from the same deposit and from V G/Q 85 and IV G 36.

1007. (V R 50) (FIG. 169. PLATE 61) Fragments of bowl with side handle and warts on rim. Grey clay with abundant grit (some white) showing in surface, which pitted, brownish grey, stroke burnished.

1008. (V R 50) Coarse grey clay with large grit and abundant straw showing in surface, which shades of dark and light brown to reddish with rough stroke burnish inside, but unburnished outside.

1009. (V R 50) Stump of side handle (?) rising from rim. Soft fabric. Outside shades of brown to red, inside dark brown, burnished. Another similar (V/IV G 54/36) with wart on carination; surface grey-brown, burnished.

1010. (V R wall 37) Well and evenly made. Light brown; fine burnish.

1011. (V G/Q 70) Stump of large side handle below carination. Coarse grey clay; surface with a red wash, burnished.

1012. (V/IV X ?41) Irregular; surface uneven, but with high stroke burnish, dark brown to red outside, deep red inside.

1013. (IV X ?26 south of wall 49) Soft fabric. Light brown to red, burnished but worn.

1014. (IV G 25) Profile. Red shading to light brown; fine burnish. Another similar (VI/V R 105/47); light brown with very fine burnish.

1015. (IV G 25) Inside light brown, outside shades of darker brown with a reddish tinge, burnished. Three others similar: two from V H level 49; and 1015A (PLATE 45) from VI/V Q level 88 with vertical wart on carination.

1016. (IV R 26) Grey-brown, burnished but much worn. About five others similar from levels of V and IV.

Handles, lugs, and decoration

1017. (III wall 53 face 1) Probably of Period IV. Several rims from the same or possibly from two different bowls: one with stump of vertical handle rising above it, another with pair of vertical warts set on it. Soft fabric; dark grey clay, brown at edges, with grit including white prominent in surface, which very much pitted, shades of light and dark brown, burnished.

1018. (V/IV X no level) (FIG. 169) Kidney-sectioned strap handle rising from rim. Surface uneven, shades of brown to red, burnished. One or two others similar.

1019. (IV R 26) Small lug-like strap handle. Coarse, soft fabric; clay with large grit, including red and white; surface grey-brown, burnished but worn. Another (V R ?73) exactly similar in shape and fabric.

Cf. *Troy* i 61 f. fig. 266: 1, shape A 15, represented by only one example, from the end of the Early Subperiod of Troy I.

1020. (V G/Q 85) (PLATE 58) Small kidney-sectioned lug-like strap handle, as FIG. 106 No. 23. Light brown to red, burnished.

1021. (IV Q 26, House VII) (PLATE 70) Trumpet lug set on rim. Rather coarse fabric. Light to dark brown and dusky, burnished. Two others similar from V X level 77.

1022. (VI/V H 92/78) Stump of horizontally perforated lug set just below carination. Grey-brown, burnished.

1023. (IV R 35) (PLATE 70) Pair of vertical warts on rim. Gritty grey-brown clay, red-brown at edges; surface grey-brown, shading to light brown and reddish round outside of rim; high polish-like burnish.

1024. (IV G 25) Wart on carination. Dark brown to black; fine polish-like burnish.

1025. (V G 51) (PLATE 65) Bold incised decoration on outside of rim, which has stump of possible strap handle rising from top. Grey to light brown clay with grit including some large white; surface light brown shading to reddish; fine burnish.

Complete or nearly complete bowls from Period IV destruction levels: (1) Large, with rim diameters 25 or over; (2) Medium-sized, with rim diameters *c.* 20; (3) Small, with rim diameters 15 or less; (4) With pedestals or spouts.

(1) Large bowls with rim diameters 25 or over (FIG. 168)

1026. (G and G/H 26, 25, 19, House VIII and area to north) (PLATE 59) Only about half preserved, including one side handle (FIG. 107, class 1) and a large pointed lug on the carination. Rim class A. Diam. 42. Ht. 11.5. Grey-brown clay; surface dark to light brown and red, stroke burnished. Two rims of similar large bowls with side handles: one (diam. *c.* 40) from V X level 77 with surface shades of dark and light brown to red as 1026.

1027. (G 26, House VIII) Profile, with large oval wart on part of carination preserved. Rim class A. Diam. *c.* 28. Ht. 13.5. Surface dark reddish; fine stroke burnish.

Fragments of another similar (diam. *c.* 26) from III G ?19, north of House VIII, with side handle and three warts; inside dark brown, outside shades of dark and light brown and red, well burnished.

1028. (G 26, House VIII) (PLATE 59) Less than half preserved. Ribbed horizontal trumpet lug on rim of class A. Diam. 25. Ht. 13.5. Light grey-brown clay; surface dark red-brown, stroke burnished.

For trumpet lugs with multiple ribs cf. *Troy* i 78 figs. (235: 3; 239: 13; 260: 16; 261: 10, from early levels of Troy I including Troy I a.

1029. (R 26, House IV) (PLATE 59) Only about half preserved, including one side handle (FIG. 107, class 1). Rim cf. class A. Diam. *c.* 29. Ht. *c.* 12. Surface discoloured by fire which destroyed this part of settlement, leaving one fragment black, the other which joins it light brown (the original colour ?); fine burnish.

1030. (R 26, House IV) (PLATE 59) Only about half preserved, including one rounded side handle (FIG. 107, class 1) and one of a pair of solid horned lugs. Rim cf. class A. Diam. *c.* 27. Ht. *c.* 13. Burnished surface originally light brown to reddish, but much discoloured by fire.

1031. (R 26, House V) Fragment of rim (class A) with unusually large rounded side handle (FIG. 107, class 1). Possibly an intrusion of Period II in view of fabric which harder and better fired than normal in IV. Gritty grey-brown clay, light brown at edges; outside surface brown to reddish, well and evenly burnished; inside brown, burnished, but worn and rough below rim as if bowl used to grind or rub some kind of food in it.

1032. (Q 26, House VII) (PLATE 59) Broken, but nearly complete. Pointed side handle (FIG. 107, class 2) and three warts on carination. Rim cf. class D (2). Diam. 25. Ht. 13. Clay with grit, some large and dominantly grey it seems in colour; surface dark purplish brown to reddish; very fine stroke burnish inside and out.

1033. (Q 26, House VII) (PLATE 59) Broken, but nearly complete. Nicked side handle (FIG. 107, class 4) and three warts on carination. Rim class D (2). Diam. 25. Ht. 11.5. Outside brown to reddish, inside dark brown to blackish, well burnished.

1034. (X 40/25, House VI) (PLATE 59) Two opposite rounded side handles as FIG. 107, class 1, and two large warts in gaps between them. Broken, but virtually complete except for one handle missing. Rim cf. class A. Diam. *c.* 39. Ht. *c.* 26. Lopsided; more unevenly made and rougher in finish than 1026. Soft fabric; grey-brown clay with abundant straw and grit; surface light brown to dusky outside, darker brown to reddish inside, stroke burnished.

1035. (X ?26 south of wall 49) Most of rim missing. Two opposite side handles. Rim cf. class A. Diam. *c.* 35. Ht. 23. Coarse fabric; clay with large grit; surface shades of light to dark brown, irregular and uneven, but well burnished.

1036. (X 40/25 or ?26 south of wall 49) Part of rim cf. class A with large wart on carination, and section of base. Diam. *c.* 25. Surface uneven, red to light brown outside, dusky inside, burnished.

(2) Medium-sized bowls with rim diameters c. 20 (FIG. 169)

1037. (G 25 north of wall 50) Profile, with wart on carination. Rim class A. Diam. 22. Ht. 11.5. Grey clay with white grit prominent in surface, which shades of lightish and dark brown, well burnished.

1038. (H and H/R 26, House IV) (PLATE 60) Broken, but virtually complete. Rounded side handle (FIG. 107, class 1) and three warts on carination. Diam. 20. Ht. *c.* 10.5. Dark grey clay with whitish grit prominent in it; surface dark brown to black, burnished. Five others similar from the same area in House IV (diam. 19–23, ht. 10–11.5).

1039. (H and H/R 26, House IV) (PLATE 60) Parts including most of handle missing. As 1038. Diam. 20. Ht. *c.* 10. Lightish grey-brown, burnished.

1040. (H 26, House IV) (PLATE 60) Parts of body missing. As 1038. Diam. 22.5. Ht. *c.* 11.5. Grey clay with white grit prominent; surface light brown shading to dark brown and black, burnished.

1041. (H 26, House IV) (PLATE 60) Broken, parts missing. Slightly ogival handle and three warts on carination. Rim cf. class C. Diam. 21. Ht. *c.* 11.5. Light brown to red; fine burnish. Another very similar (diam. *c.* 19, ht. 11) from same area in House IV.

1042. (H 26, House IV) (PLATE 60) Large parts of rim together with handle and one wart missing. Originally with side handle and three large warts on carination. Rim class A. Diam. *c.* 20. Ht. *c.* 12.5. Grey-brown clay with

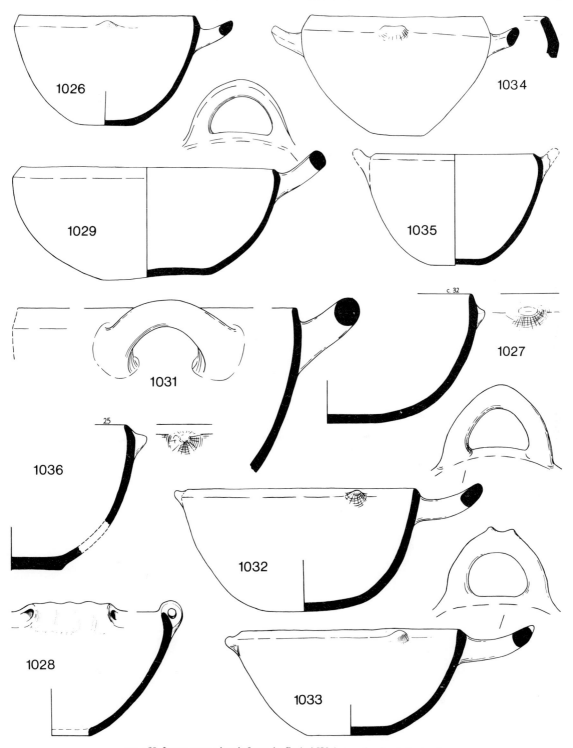

FIG. 168. Large type 9 bowls from the Period IV destruction level. Scale 1/4.

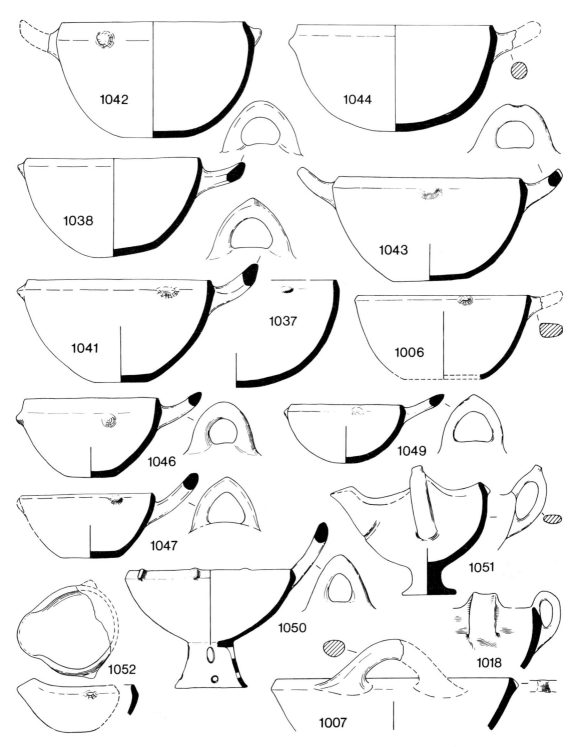

FIG. 169. Medium-sized and small type 9 bowls from the Period IV destruction level. Scale 1/4.

white grit prominent; surface dark brown to black, burnished. Parts of another similar (diam. *c.* 24, ht. 13.5) from same area in House IV.

1043. (R 26, House IV) (PLATE 60) Broken, parts of rim missing. Two opposite nicked side handles as FIG. 107, class 4, with two warts on carination in gaps between them. Rim class A. Diam. 20. Ht. 11. Soft fabric; grey clay, light brown at edges; surface light brown to red, burnished.

1044. (R 26, House IV) Only half preserved. Side handle, and single wart on carination opposite it. Diam. *c.* 22. Ht. *c.* 11. Grey clay with straw and white grit prominent; surface light brown to red with dusky areas, burnished.

1045. (Q 26, House VII) (PLATE 60) Broken and incomplete. Side handle; horned wart preserved on one side. Diam. 18.3. Ht. to rim 9.5. Burnished surface black, changing abruptly in places to light brown, owing to effects of fire which destroyed house. Several others similar from same deposit in House VII.

(3) Small bowls with rim diameters 15 or less (FIG. 169)

1046. (G 26, House VIII) (PLATE 60) Broken, but virtually complete. Rounded side handle (FIG. 107, class 1) and three warts on carination. Rim class A. Diam. *c.* 14.5. Ht. 9. Outside light brown except for dusky patches round top of rim, inside black; high burnish.

1047. (R 26, House IV) (PLATE 61) Slightly ogival side handle and three warts on carination. Part of rim including one wart missing. Rim class D (2). Diam. 15. Ht. 7. Light brown to red; fine burnish.

1048. (X 41/24 north of wall 49, with join from X II 15) (PLATE 62) As 1046, but handle missing. Diam. *c.* 14.5. Ht. 8.5. Hole (diam. 1.2–1.4) bored through bottom of base after firing. Inside black, outside brown mottling to red with patches of black around rim, well burnished.

1049. (Apparently from Q 26, House VII) (PLATE 61) Broken, parts missing. Ogival side handle (FIG. 107, class 3) and three warts on carination. Rim class A. Diam. 12.5. Ht. 6. Light grey-brown, burnished.

(4) Pedestal and spouted bowls

1050. (Q 26, House VII) (PLATE 61) Pedestal bowl, with pointed side handle (FIG. 107, class 2) rising from rim. Broken, but virtually complete. Five small vertical warts set on rim. Pedestal base with two rows of holes through it. Diam. 18. Ht. to rim 13. Shades of dark brown mottling to black and reddish; fine burnish.

1051. (G 25 north of wall 50, with join from III G 19) (PLATE 61) Bowl with solid pedestal foot, wide trough spout, and strap handle to one side. Large parts missing. Wart on carination opposite spout, and perhaps another opposite handle, which itself surmounted by a wart. Width of rim 13.5. Ht. to rim *c.* 11, to top of handle 13.5. Very warped and irregular in shape. Grey shading to orange clay with medium-sized grey, red, and white grit; surface black to shades of dark and light brown and reddish; very fine stroke burnish.

1052. (H 26, House IV) Small trough-spouted bowl. Part of rim missing. One wart preserved on carination. Rim class A. Width of rim *c.* 9. Ht. 4.5. Surface light brown to red, burnished but worn. Another similar from III R wall 53, but probably of Period IV, with surface light greyish brown, burnished.

10. *Bowls with short, S-shaped, usually thickened club-like rims* 1053–1062 (FIG. 170)

Bowls with rims of this type were characteristic of Periods VII–VI. A number of such rims were recovered from levels of V and IV. Some of these are almost certainly earlier strays. Others, however, like 1053 do not closely resemble any rims of Periods VII–VI and are more reminiscent of bowl rims of the Tsangli (Dhimini 1) phase of the Thessalian Late Neolithic.

1053. (VI/V H 92) Angle not certain. Hard Silvery Grey Ware; fine burnish.
    Cf. *Arapi* pl. 7: 11, 14, of the Tsangli (Dhimini 1) phase of Thessalian L.N.

1054. (VI/V H 92) Light brown mottling to dusky brown and black; very fine burnish.

1055. (V G/H 85) Light grey; poor burnish.
    Cf. *Poliochni* i pl. iv: e, Black period.

1056. (VII/V X ?130) Angle not certain. Soft fabric; surface light brown, burnished but much worn.

1057. (V/IV X 60/40/25) Grey-brown, burnished.
    Cf. *Poliochni* i pl. vi: r, Black period.

1058. (IV R 35) Light brown shading to red and dusky; fine polish-like burnish.

1059. (IV R 26) Grey-brown; very fine polish-like burnish. Three others similar from levels of V.
    Cf. *Poliochni* i pls. v: q; vi: i, s, t, Black period.

1060. (IV R 26) Light Brown Burnished Ware. Soft fabric; clay grey at core; outside surface grey, inside light brown with abundant straw impressions showing in it, burnished.

1061. (IV R ?39) Soft greyish clay; surface entirely worn away. Clearly an earlier stray.
1062. (IV G 26) Light brown to reddish; fine burnish.

11. *Bowls with inward-curving rims, internally differentiated and usually thickened* 1063–1064 (FIG. 170)

The few rims assignable to this type, which was especially characteristic of Period VII, may all be strays of VII–VI. Most of them came from the lowest levels of V.

1063. (VI/V H 92) Soft fabric; surface red with fine burnish, but worn.
1064. (V R wall 37) Grey-brown with a reddish tinge; high polish-like burnish.

12. *Bowls with straight rims, thickened and usually differentiated on the inside* 1065–1073 (FIGS. 170, 171)

These were at home both in V and in IV. In levels of V rims assignable to this type were if anything more prevalent than rims of the closely related type 13. The elaborate vase 1073 from the Period IV destruction level has a high ring foot, and a projection rising from the rim with a

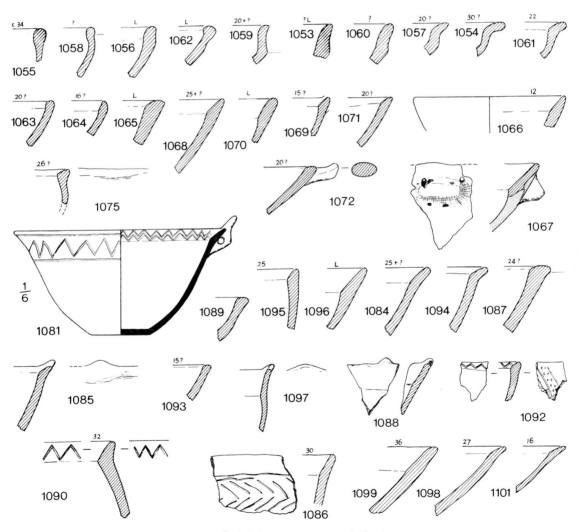

FIG. 170. Periods V–IV. Types 10–13. Scale 1/3.

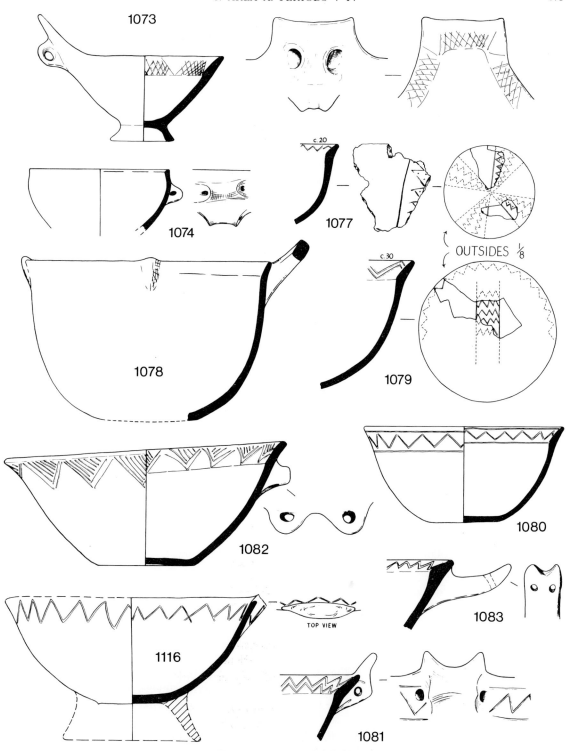

FIG. 171. Periods V–IV. Types 12–14. Scale 1/4.

trumpet lug below it. One or two other type 12 rims had possible indications of similar projections or of handles rising from them; but side handles on the outside of the rim are also attested (e.g. 1072), as are simple vertically perforated lugs (see under 1068).

1065. (V H wall 26) Grey clay; surface light brown to dusky, apparently plain and unburnished.
1066. (V G 54) Soft fabric, with large grit including some white; surface pitted, dark grey-brown, burnished.
1067. (V Q 85) Lug below rim. Irregular; surface light brown, stroke burnished. The lug was evidently planned to have a pair of vertical holes through it, but while the clay was still wet, these were blocked and two holes were cut through the rim above instead, cf. 1311.
1068. (IV G 25) Soft fabric; surface uneven, but well burnished, shades of light and dark brown mottling to red. Three others similar: two (V R 59, VII/V X ?130) with stumps of vertically perforated lugs set well below the rim; one (III H 18, but probably of Period IV) with a red wash, burnished.
1069. (IV G 26/25) Two fragments of rim, apparently from same bowl, one with stump of handle or projection rising from it. Soft fabric; surface black to deep purple-brown with very fine burnish, soapy to feel.
1070. (IV G/H 36) Black, fine burnish.
1071. (IV H 26) Grey-brown; fine burnish. three or four others similar from levels of V.
1072. (IV R 26) (PLATE 58) Stump of side handle. Light brown to red, burnished.
1073. (IV Q 26, House VII) (FIG. 171. PLATE 62) Broken, but complete. Projection from rim with horizontal ribbed trumpet lug below it. High pedestal foot. Width of rim 17. Ht. to rim 9. Dark brown to black; very fine stroke burnish inside and out including underneath base. Outside surface mottled in places to light brown, which may reflect discoloration by fire which destroyed house. Inside of rim with zone of boldly incised cross-hatching filled with white; incisions evidently made after vase burnished, but while clay still soft.
    For similar horned projections above trumpet lugs see *Troy* i fig. 250: 13, late Troy I, and *Thermi* 80 fig. 28: B 9, pl. xxxii: 6, common on bowls of B 9 (cf. Emporio types 4 and 5) in Town III and surviving into Town V. Cf. *Baden Symposium* 387 pl. 6: 14, from the Baden Culture in Moravia, for the same idea. Pairs of projections above horizontal lugs in the Late Chalcolithic of the Konya plain may represent embryonic versions of it (e.g. *AS* xiii (1963) 206 fig. 4: 22).

13. *Bowls with outward-curving rims, internally differentiated and thickened* 1074–1101 (FIGS. 170, 171)

Bowls assignable to this type from levels of V–IV seem to fall into two distinct groups: (1) with rims of variety (a); (2) with rims of varieties (b) and (c) (FIG. 98).

    (1) Bowls with rims of variety (a). The rims are S-shaped in profile, somewhat inward leaning, and with the differentiated part usually short in comparison with that on most rims of the standard varieties (b) and (c). Variety (a) rims are so distinctive that the bowls with them might almost be classified as a separate type. But such rims were rare, and were only represented by a few examples, mostly from levels of V; moreover they appear to merge into rims of the standard varieties (b) and (c) without any sharp line of division. At the same time, rims of variety (a) merge into jar rims of class A III, *d*. Bowls with rims of this kind might have strap handles (1076) or horizontal trumpet lugs on the shoulder (1074).

1074. (V R 59) Section of rim with horizontal trumpet lug on swelling. Grey clay with abundant grit, dominantly white, showing in surface, which pitted, light reddish brown shading to dusky and red; fine stroke burnish.
1075. (V R 59) Very irregular; surface shades of light to dark brown and black, well stroke burnished.
1076. (IV R 35) Rim, apparently of this type, with stump of small vertical strap handle from it to swelling. Soft fabric; surface grey-brown to black, burnished but worn.

    (2) Bowls with rims of varieties (b) and (c). These were not uncommon, and five more or less complete examples were recovered from Period IV destruction levels, with two others from deposits of V. Rims which approximate to those of bowls of type 10 like 1089 and 1093—both much worn—may be earlier strays.
    Some bowls evidently had side handles, as 1078 (see also under 1094); others were provided with lugs of various kinds, including horizontal trumpet lugs (e.g. 1081), a pair of vertically

perforated lugs (1082), and a curious horned lug-handle (1083). Projections rising from the rim appear to have been a characteristic feature of these bowls; that above the trumpet lug on 1081 is large and horned, but small triangular projections, as 1085, 1088, and 1097, are more usual. Warts set on the outside of the rim and slightly projecting above it are found on 1078 of Period V. Bases may be flat or sunk, but the bowls with elaborate incised decoration on the outside like 1077 and 1079 appear to have had rounded bottoms.

All bowls appear to have been burnished, but there was a considerable range in the quality of fabric and finish. A number, especially of the smaller and shallower bowls of classes B and C, had a very fine polish-like burnish, the surface being grey-brown shading to delicate tints of pink and olive green. The bowls with this finish, and others of type 13, often had incised decoration. The relatively common occurrence of incised decoration on bowls of this type and on ones of the allied type 14 is in sharp contrast to its virtual absence on bowls of other types from this horizon.

Incised decoration was normally confined to the rim, where it occurs both inside and outside, or on the inside or outside alone. Bowls with decoration on the outside of the rim alone seem to have been more common in V than in IV. Some bowls of both periods, however, evidently had schemes of incised decoration spreading from beyond the zone of the rim to involve the whole outside surface of the vase (e.g. 1077, 1079).

Large fragments from levels of V
1077. (R 50, H 49) (PLATE 63) Fragments of rim and body with elaborate incised decoration. Fabric as 1079. Clay grey-brown, red-brown at edges in places; surface shades of grey-brown mottling to patches of reddish; fine burnish. Incised decoration in zone round inside of rim and on outside.
1078. (H 49) (PLATE 62) Profile. Stump of side handle set on outside of rim. Diam. *c.* 26. Ht. 16. Soft fabric. Grey-brown clay with grit (some very large) and abundant straw showing in surface, which uneven, with a red wash, stroke burnished.

Complete vases and large fragments from Period IV destruction levels
1079. (G 36, 25, north of wall 50) (PLATE 63) Fragments. Diam. estimated *c.* 30. Grey-brown clay with grit and straw; surface slightly pitted, but with very high polish-like burnish, shades of grey-brown through olive green to purplish red. Bold, deeply incised decoration, made while clay still soft; traces of white fill: double chevrons round inside, single chevron round outside, of rim; a wide band or bands of multiple chevrons running across outside of body.
1080. (G 36, 25, north of wall 50) (PLATE 62) Profile. Only about half vase preserved; some kind of handle or lug probably missing. Flat base. Diam. 22. Ht. 10. Grey-brown surface with high polish-like burnish. Bold incised decoration with traces of white fill: single chevrons between lines round inside and outside of rim.
1081. (Q 26, House VII) (PLATE 64) Broken, but virtually complete. Horned projection from rim with horizontal trumpet lug below it. Flat base. Diam. 36. Ht. 17. Somewhat irregular, and rim uneven, but very good fabric; surface with high burnish, shades of brown tinged with red, discoloured to greyish in parts by fire which destroyed house. Bold incised decoration with white fill unusually well preserved: double chevrons round inside, single chevron between lines round outside of rim, cf. 1079. A similar rim (IV X ?26 south of wall 49) with dark grey brown burnished surface has the same scheme of incised decoration.
For horned projections above trumpet lugs see under 1073.
1082. (Q 26, House VII) (PLATE 64) Broken, but complete. Twin vertically perforated lugs below rim. Sunk base. Diam. 31. Ht. *c.* 12. Somewhat irregular in shape, and rim uneven, but of very fine fabric. Surface with exceptionally high burnish, although marks of burnishing implement everywhere visible; dark brown to black, apart from one area turned light reddish brown by fire which destroyed house. Incised decoration made after vase burnished, and apparently when clay quite hard; abundant remains of white fill: hatched inverted triangles round inside and outside of rim. The hatching on the inside triangles goes in the opposite direction from that on the outside ones, but on one of the inside triangles the direction of the hatching is reversed. Two fragments of a similar rim (V/IV X 60/40/25) with bands of incised lattice inside and out.
1083. (Q 26, House VII) (PLATE 64) Broken, but virtually complete. Horned lug-handle with pair of holes immediately below rim. Flat base. Diam. 33. Ht. 15. Rather irregular in shape and thick-walled; rim uneven.

Clay with grit (some very large) including both red and white. Inside dominantly black, outside shades of brown, well burnished. Bold incised decoration round inside of rim.

Rims from A. Deep and B. Medium bowls

1084. (V R 59) Grey-brown; fine burnish. Five or six rims of this general type from levels of V.

1085. (V R 50) With triangular projection. Soft fabric; grey clay; abundant straw impressions showing in surface, which grey-brown with a deep reddish tinge, worn but with high polish-like burnish. Another similar (V G/Q 85) of harder fabric; sandy grey clay, red-brown at edges; surface purple-brown, burnished.

1086. (V R 50) (PLATE 65) Soft fabric. Grey clay; surface shades of deep red and red-brown, burnished. Band of boldly incised chevrons with white fill round outside. One or two others similar (IV H ?37) with incised decoration on outside.

1087. (V G wall 23) Grey clay with large white and orange grit; burnished surface black inside, light brown round inside of rim and on its top, and apparently outside, which much worn.

1088. (IV H ?37) With triangular projection. Light brown with slight reddish tinge, burnished.

1089. (VI/V G/Q 87) Dark grey clay; surface light brownish grey, much worn.

1090. (V/IV X 60/40/25) Angle not certain. Shades of dark and light brown to red, well burnished. Decorated with single incised chevrons inside and out.
For the rim shape cf. *Poliochni* i 565 pl. xli: c, evolved Blue period.

1091. (V/IV X 60/40/25) (PLATE 65) Light brown shading to darker brown; very fine burnish. Decorated with incised lattice inside and out.

1092. (V/IV X 41/24) Angle not certain. Shades of light and dark brown; fine burnish. Elaborate incised decoration inside and out (cf. FIG. 114 No. 15); traces of white fill.

1093. (V Q 62) Light Brown Burnished Ware; surface with fine burnish, but much worn. Another similar from V H level 49.

1094. (IV G 26) Grey clay with some large grit including red; surface light brown with fine burnish, but much worn. Others similar: one (VI/V G/Q 87) with stump of side handle immediately below rim; another (V X 82/77/60) dark purple-brown with fine burnish.

1095. (IV G 25) Angle not certain. Black; very fine burnish.

1096. (IV G 25) Outside light brown, inside darker brown, burnished.

1097. (IV G 25) With triangular projection. Angle not certain. Sandy grey-brown clay; surface brown shading to red, well burnished outside, less well inside.

Rims from C. Small and shallow bowls

1098. (V R ?73) Cooking pot type ware. Grey-brown clay; surface well burnished but crackled, red to light brown and dusky brown to black. Two others similar (V R wall 37, IV H 37) with burnished surfaces red and light brown to dusky.

1099. (VI/V R ?87) Shades of light and dark brown, burnished.

1100 (IV G 25) As 1534 of Period II. Grey-brown; fine burnish. Four or five similar from levels of IV and V in G and H, with burnished surfaces shades of grey-brown, black, dark red-brown, and light brown.

1101. (IV H 26) Grey-brown, burnished.

14. *Bowls with outward-curving rims, not internally differentiated, but sometimes thickened* 1102–1127
(FIGS. 171, 172)

Bowls of this type were rather more common it seems in the horizon of V–IV than ones of the related type 13 with internally differentiated rims. Diameters ranged from *c.* 30 to less than 10; a good many type 14 bowls were evidently small with diameters under 15, but some of the smaller rims may in fact come from dipper cups of type 16. A number of the larger rims, especially those with handles or lugs, could have belonged to jars: some, notably it would seem those with vertical warts on the outside (e.g. 1125–1127), are clearly from cooking vessels, whether these were jar-like in shape or bowls.

A considerable variety of handles and lugs is attested. There was perhaps in general only one lug or handle to each vase, as in the case of the complete vases of the related type 13 from Period

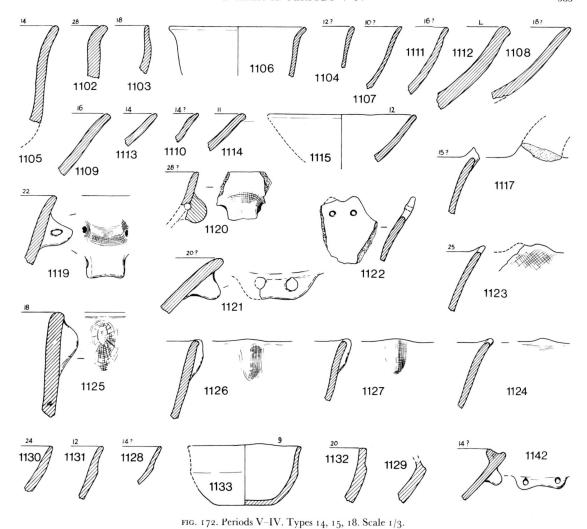

FIG. 172. Periods V–IV. Types 14, 15, 18. Scale 1/3.

IV destruction levels. A wide ring base supported 1116, and also it would seem the little bowl 1107. Incised decoration was evidently not as common as on bowls of type 13, but occurs on 1116.

All type 14 bowls seem to have had burnished surfaces; but there was a considerable range in fabric, from coarse or cooking pot type ware, with irregular shapes, thick walls, uneven surfaces, and poor burnish, to the very finest burnished ware. There also appears to have been a kaleidoscopic variety in surface colour, ranging from black through shades of grey and dark brown and purple-brown, to orange and buff, red and light brown, and even white (e.g. 1104 cf. 1109). The surface on the same vase might display a considerable range in colour.

Rims from A. Deep bowls
1102. (V R 59) Grey clay; surface orange, burnished.
1103. (V R wall 37) Surface grey-brown, pitted, but with fine burnish.

1104. (V H 48) Possibly from a dipper cup of type 16. Grey-brown clay; surface lightish grey-brown with tinge of green mottling to white; high polish-like burnish.

1105. (IV G 25) Fragments including rim. Thick-walled. Coarse fabric; dark grey clay, light brown at edges, with largish grit, dominantly grey; surface uneven but well burnished, light brown to reddish and dark brown. Several other similar rims from levels of V and IV.

1106. (IV H/R 26) Soft fabric; surface grey-brown with very fine burnish.

1107. (IV H 26) Rim, with what may be spring of a pedestal or ring base. Surface rather uneven, grey-brown, with poor burnish.

Rims from B. Medium and C. Shallow bowls

1108. (VI/V H 92) Grey-brown, burnished.

1109. (V R 59) Greyish to orange clay, sandy with fine white grit; surface uneven but well burnished, pale buff to light brown with a slight reddish tinge in places.

1110. (V G wall 51) Dark grey-brown to black with a reddish tinge; high burnish.

1111. (V R ?73) Very rough and uneven; burnished surface irregular and pitted, dull grey-brown outside; light brown to darker around rim inside.

1112. (V G 54/36) Rough and irregular. Grey clay; surface light brown outside, light greyish inside; scored or wiped (but not burnished) inside and out.

1113. (V G/Q 70) Grey-brown to black; fine burnish. Several others similar from levels of V in G and H; shades of grey-brown, light brown, and red, burnished.

1114. (V G/H 85) Grey clay; surface light grey, originally perhaps light brown and burnished, but now very worn.

1115. (IV R 35) Grey-brown with a reddish tinge; fine burnish.

1116. (IV G 25, House VIII) (FIG. 171. PLATE 64) About half of bowl, with some kind of strap handle or lug rising from rim and wide ring base, now missing. Diam. c. 28. Ht. as preserved c. 11. Light brown to reddish; fine burnish. Incised decoration (row of single chevrons) on rim inside and out.

Handles and lugs

1117. (V R ?50) Stump of handle rising, apparently sideways, from top of rim. Grey-brown; fine burnish.

1118. (V R wall 37) (PLATE 58) Projection on rim with vertical strap handle set below it. Grey-brown, stroke burnished.

1119. (V R 59) (PLATE 58) Horizontal, slightly trumpet-shaped lug below rim. Surface minutely pitted, shades of brown, stroke burnished.

1120. (VI/V G/H 88) As 1119. Light greyish brown, burnished.

1121. (V R 50) Double vertically perforated lug below rim. Light brown; fine stroke burnish. Another similar (1121A) from V H level 49 (PLATE 58).

1122. (VI/V H cleaning wall 20) (PLATE 58) Horned projection with two perforations rising from rim. Dark reddish brown mottling to light brown and black, burnished.

    Similar horned lugs with double perforations rising from rims were fairly common on bowls of class A (Towns I–III) at Thermi (*Thermi* 75 fig. 26 class A 6; 77 fig. 27: 6).

1123. (IV H 37) Slight horned projection on rim. Angle not certain. Grey-brown, burnished.

    For a rim of this type with similar projections cf. *Poliochni* i 564 f. pl. xxviii: d, of the evolved Blue period.

1124. (V R 50) Triangular projection on rim. Fabric cf. 1109. Greyish clay; surface pale buff to light brown with a tinge of red, well burnished.

1125. (V/IV X 60/40/25) Large vertical wart below rim. Cooking pot ware; inside surface lightish brown, outside dusky brown, burnished. Probably from a cooking bowl or jar of some kind.

1126. (IV G 25) Large vertical wart on outside of rim. Coarse cooking pot ware; inside surface with faint trace of a red wash, outside dusky brown with hint of burnish. Evidently from a cooking bowl or jar like 1125.

1127. (IV G 25) As 1126. Grey-brown clay; outside surface light brown, well burnished; inside dark brown, much less well burnished. Possibly from a cooking vessel like 1125–6.

15. *Carinated bowls with outward-spreading rims* 1128–1133 (FIG. 172)

A few rims may be grouped here. Most have a hollow above the carination, and seem to come from small bowls; they may have belonged to dipper cups of the following type 16.

1128. (V H 48) Grey clay, red-brown at edges; surface light brown, uneven but with fine burnish although worn.

1129. (V R 50) Carination; rim missing. Dark brown to red; fine burnish.
1130. (V G 54) Shades of dark and light brown to reddish, well burnished.
1131, 1132. (V Q ?70) Grey-brown, burnished.
1133. (IV G 36 north of wall 50) Profile. Grey clay with some large grit (including white) showing in surface, which uneven but with a high stroke burnish, dark brown to light brown and reddish inside, light brown outside.

16. *Dipper cups* 1134–1141 (FIG. 173)

These were in effect small varieties of bowls of several different types (4 or 5, 9, 13, 14, and 15) with large strap handles rising above their rims. A number of the smaller rims (with diameters less than 15) grouped under these types may come from handled dipper cups. In most cases where the classification as a dipper cup was certain, the bowl was like a small hemispherical version of type 5. Some rims with quite small strap handles rising from them (e.g. 1134) can hardly be separated from true dipper cups and are placed here; these all came from levels of V and might reflect a stage in the evolution of dipper cups, but standard dipper cups with large handles were also attested in V.

Handles might be surmounted by warts, which when large approximate to horns (e.g. 1139). Some dipper cup handles were evidently ribbed.

There was a considerable range in fabric and finish among these cups, which tended to be thick-walled, but to have very finely burnished surfaces, sometimes dark brown to black, often light brown to reddish in colour.

1134. (V G/H 85) Rim cf. type 5, with small strap handle. Irregular; surface pitted, lightish brown, burnished. Another similar (V R 59) with surface much pitted, grey-brown, burnished.
1135. (V/IV X 60/40/25) Profile cf. type 14, with rounded base. Most of handle missing. Diam. 11. Ht. to rim *c.* 4. Shades of brown, burnished.

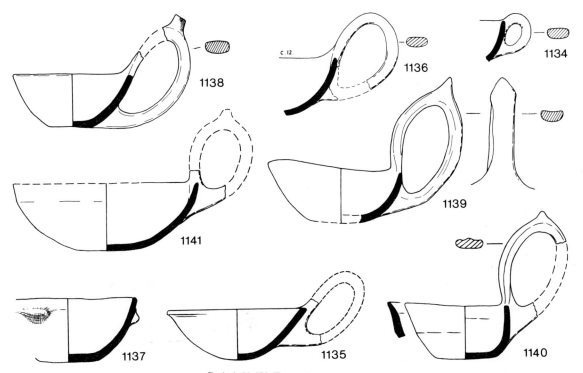

FIG. 173. Periods V–IV. Type 16 (dipper cups). Scale 1/3.

1136. (IV H 26, House IV) Rim cf. type 5, with large strap handle. Grey clay; surface grey-brown, burnished but worn. Others similar from levels of V and IV.

1137. (IV R 26, House V) About half preserved, with three oblong warts on carination and stump of strap handle. Body slightly carinated cf. types 9 and 15. Diam. of rim 11.3. Ht. *c.* 4.7. Unevenly made. Coarse fabric; clay with large grit; surface grey-brown shading to light brown and reddish, burnished.

1138. (IV Q 26, House VII) (PLATE 65) Broken, parts missing. Handle exceptionally large, attached from underneath base to rim, and surmounted by wart. Diam. of rim 10. Ht. to top of rim 9. Clay with grit, dominantly white, but some red; surface light grey with a brownish tinge mottling to black, well burnished.

 Fragments of about twenty other similar cups from the same deposit in House VII; at least four with handles surmounted by warts; mostly rather thick-walled; some with slightly outward curving rims cf. bowls of type 14; all with surfaces grey-brown, often with very fine even burnish.

1139. (III G 19, but presumably of Period IV) (PLATE 65) Broken, parts missing. Horned handle. Diam. of rim 11. Surface with high burnish, shades of dark brown and purplish; traces of what seems to be very thick crimson-red paint applied to surface before burnishing. Fragments of two similar cups (V Q ?70, IV Q 32); surfaces shades of brown to reddish; very fine polish-like burnish.

1140. (III G 19, but presumably of Period IV) (PLATE 65) Broken, but nearly complete. Ribbed handle, surmounted by wart. Diam. of rim 9.5. Dark grey clay with fine white grit; surface dark brown to black, burnished. Fragments of two or three others similar from IV G 26, House VIII, and III G 19.

 Cf. *Thermi* 114 no. 257 pls. viii, xxxvi, Town III. *Poliochni* i 565 pl. xl: b, evolved Blue, is comparable but cruder. One from Troy II f. (*Troy* i 317 fig. 414: 17) seems to have been like this.

1141. (III G 19, but presumably of Period IV) About half preserved; handle missing. Diam. 15. Ht. to top of rim 5.4. Orange clay with prominent white and some grey grit; surface light brown to reddish with dusky patches, burnished. Fragments of several others similar from levels of III and IV in G and H.

18. *Bowls with a ledge below the rim outside* 1142 (FIG. 172)

Only one rim was recognised assignable to this type. This has a double vertically perforated lug set below it. The fabric suggests that it may come from an imported vase.

1142. (V X 61) Black clay with some mica showing in surface, which black, finely burnished. Possibly an import.

(B) JUGS, THERIOMORPHIC VASES, AND TRIPOD COOKING POTS

Jugs 1143–1169 (FIGS. 174–176)

These ranged in height from less than 10 to over 30 to judge from the complete examples recovered from Period IV destruction levels, but a height of *c.* 20 seems to have been average. The necks of some jugs from IV at any rate sloped backwards like those of Early Cycladic jugs (e.g. 1151). Bodies were usually globular; the belly was sometimes carinated (e.g. 1148, 1149, 1164). Spouts were for the most part simple as on the standard type 23A; but some cutaway spouts (as type 24A) occurred in V as well as in IV (e.g. PLATE 66 (*a*) centre, from VI/V H level 92). Cutaway spouts were occasionally it seems elaborate in shape, as seen on 1159 and on PLATE 66 (*b*) (all with black burnished surfaces, from V H levels 48 and 76, and VI/V H level 90). Necks were usually, but not always, more or less sharply differentiated from shoulders.

 In the vast majority of cases handles were set to rims. The handle normally dropped downwards from the rim and did not rise above it, but some jugs evidently had high-swing handles, like 1158 of type 23B. Elbow handles like 1317 may have been of this kind, but did not necessarily come from jugs. Some examples of jug handles set below the rim in the way that became standard in Period II are attested from levels of V as well as IV (e.g. PLATE 66 (*a*) right, from VI/V G/H level 88, and 1156 which is also unusual in having vertical instead of the normal circular warts on the belly). Bases were in general flat, although often not well differentiated (as class 6 C), and might be sunk (class 5).

 Warts were much in evidence on jugs both in V and IV. This is in marked contrast to their

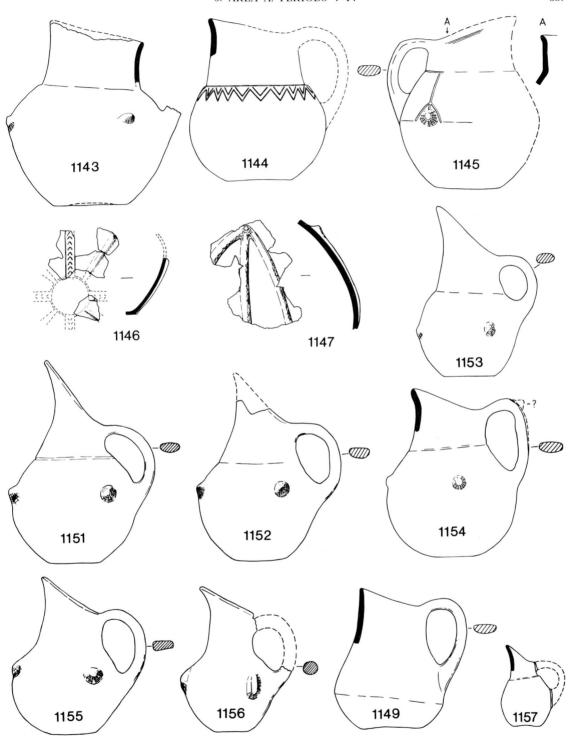

FIG. 174. Periods V–IV. Jugs. Scale 1/4.

comparative rarity on jugs of Periods VII–VI. Not all jugs, however, were adorned with warts, and an absence of warts may have been more frequent in V than in IV, although they are lacking on some of the jugs from the Period IV destruction levels (e.g. 1149, 1157). When warts occur there are normally three of them set on the belly, one opposite the handle, and one in the middle of each side; but 1163 has a vertical row of three warts opposite the handle, making five in all. Warts on jugs are normally circular, but once at least (on 1156) vertical. In one or two instances a large circular wart appears on the side of a jug neck (examples from VI/V Q 88 and V H 24), but this seems to have been unusual.

Decoration. When decoration of any kind (apart from the ubiquitous warts) occurs on jugs from the horizon of V–IV it is normally incised. But a number of fragments, apparently from jugs, recovered from levels of V were decorated with ribs in relief, sometimes combined with incision (e.g. 1146). At least one fragment of a jug with white-painted decoration (1148) from a level of V appears to be of contemporary date and not a stray of VII–VI.

Fabric. The outside surfaces of jugs were invariably it seems burnished like the surfaces of bowls. The colour of the outside surface is in general dark, normally shades of grey-brown or brown. Black, light brown, and red surfaces also occur, but are not so common; light brown and red surfaces are especially characteristic on jugs of comparatively coarse fabric with poor burnish (e.g. PLATE 66 (a) from V H ?86, VI/V H 92 and G/H 88). The insides of jugs often show distinctive marks of wiping, probably with bunches of twigs.

Period V. Fragments of jugs were abundant in levels of V, especially in G and H, but very few shapes could be restored. The rims suggest that most of the jugs were akin to type 23A as in Period IV, but cutaway spouts of various shapes also occurred (FIG. 175). There may have been a tendency for jug mouths to be somewhat wider, more like those of jugs in VII–VI, than was usual

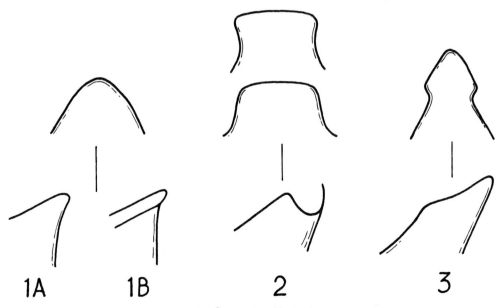

FIG. 175. Jug mouths of Period V.

in IV. Two fragments, apparently from the necks of jugs, from V H levels 76 and 49, had perforations (rivet-holes) bored through them after firing. About twenty five rims, mostly from jugs but including one or two from jars (e.g. 1226), were of Light Brown Burnished Ware like the majority of jugs in VII–VI; but some at any rate of these rims appear to be of contemporary date and not earlier strays.

Period IV. A considerable number of complete jugs came from the destruction levels of this period. These were mostly, where it was possible to judge, of type 23A, but some had cutaway spouts (type 24A). More than a dozen jugs were recovered from House IV, mostly—eleven in all—of type 23A, but including one at least of type 24A, and two which could not be assigned as between types 23A and 24A as their spouts were missing. The deposit in House VII yielded two jugs with cutaway spouts (type 24A), together with the exceptional 1158 of type 23B, and 1168–9 of type 24B. These two jugs (1168–9) with carinated bodies, long elegant necks, and cutaway spouts, have elaborate incised decoration including a pair of stylized eyes. Incised decoration is also found on the large jug 1161 of type 24A and on fragments of jugs of uncertain types from levels of IV. A fragment from IV G level 36, of hard fabric with light brown burnished surface, appeared to come from a ridged throat like those common in Period II.

From levels of Period V (FIG. 174)

1143. (V H 49) Type 23A or 24A. Broken, but virtually complete except for spout and handle. Differentiated neck; three warts on belly; sunk base. Ht. preserved 19.5. Clay with grit, including red; outside surface dark brown to black, occasionally with reddish tinge, burnished.

1144. (V H 49) Type 23A. Large parts including handle and back of neck missing. Ht. 17.5. Grey-brown clay with much straw and some grit; outside surface shades of dark and lightish brown to dusky, well burnished; inside pinkish, wiped (with a bunch of twigs?) except around rim, which is shades of brown, burnished, like the outside. Incised decoration on shoulder: double row of chevrons made while clay still wet.

1145. (V G 85) (PLATE 66) Type 23A or 24A. Profile of back with handle preserved to ht. 16. Rim everted; carinated body; warts on carination. Gritty grey to red-brown clay; outside surface brown to black, burnished; inside wiped (with a bunch of twigs?). Simple incised decoration on shoulder.

1146. (V R 59) (PLATE 66) Fragments of base and body with incised and relief decoration. Gritty grey-brown clay; outside surface dark brown to black with fine burnish; inside wiped (with a bunch of twigs?). Vertical bands of incised chevrons alternating with ribs, apparently four of each. Possible traces of red paint by one of ribs.

1147. (V R wall 37) Shoulder with relief decoration. Outside surface dark purple-brown to black; fine burnish. Three ribs meeting at top in a wart.

1148. (V R 50) (PLATE 66) Fragments from shoulder and carinated belly of large jug with painted decoration in white. Wart preserved on carination. Soft grey-brown clay with some large grit; outside surface brown shading to black with fine burnish; inside rough. Groups of broad vertical stripes in matt white above and below carination.

From Period IV destruction levels

(1) Type 23A. Jugs with sloping mouths and pointed spouts: standard type (FIG. 174)

1149. (H 26, House IV) (PLATE 67) Broken, parts missing. Carinated belly, with no warts; base markedly sunk. Ht. 15. Soft fabric; brownish grey clay; surface grey-brown, burnished but worn. Another (1150) identical from same deposit at north end (R 26) of House IV (PLATE 67).
   For this profile with the exceptionally low swelling cf. *Archaeology* xvii (1964) 247 f., from Müskebi on the coast of Caria.

1151. (R 26, House IV inside pithos) (PLATE 67) Broken, but nearly complete. Ht. 21.5. Outside surface burnished, light brown, but with large areas dusky or black, apparently owing to effects of fire which destroyed house. Another similar from same deposit in House IV.

1152. (R 26, House IV) (PLATE 67) Broken, but nearly complete except for tip of spout. Ht. as preserved 17. Clay with fine grey grit; surface shades of dark to light brown, burnished but much worn.

1153. (R 26, House IV) (PLATE 67) Broken, but virtually complete. Ht. 18.5. Outside shades of light and dark brown with dusky patches, burnished.

1154. (R 26, House IV) (PLATE 67) Broken, but nearly complete. Top of handle worn; originally perhaps surmounted by wart. Ht. 18. Thick-walled. Coarse orange clay with grey, red, and white grit, including large lumps; surface very worn, but with faint traces of original red wash, which no doubt burnished.

1155. (R 26, House IV inside bin) (PLATE 67) Broken, but nearly complete. Ht. 16. Grey clay; surface very much pitted but with fine burnish, warm pale buff to white.

1156. (H 25, west of wall 38 in area of hearth B) (PLATE 67) Broken, but nearly complete except for handle. Three vertical warts on belly. Ht. 15.5. Well made, thin-walled. Orange clay; surface light brown, burnished but rather worn.

1157. (R 26, House IV) (PLATE 67) Miniature. Broken, but complete except for handle. No warts; sunk base. Ht. 8.5. Soft grey clay; surface shades of light and dark brown, burnished.

(2) Type 23B. Jug with sloping mouth and pointed spout: tall, with differentiated neck (FIG. 176)

1158. (Q 26, House VII) (PLATE 67) Broken, but nearly complete. High-swung handle surmounted by large cylindrical wart. Ht. to top of handle 23.2. Thin-walled; very fine fabric. Grey-brown clay; inside surface dark grey, rough; outside black shading to brown with polish-like burnish.

    For the shape, but without warts on handles, cf. *Thermi* 80 fig. 28 class B Jugs 2, pl. viii: 207, 253, Town III. *Poliochni* i 567 f. pl. xlii, evolved Blue period.

(3) Type 24A. Jugs with cutaway spouts: standard type (FIG. 176)

1159. (G 25, north of wall 50) (PLATE 66) Spout, apparently from jug. Grey-brown; fine burnish. Fragment of another larger but similar from IV H level 25, west of wall 38 in area of hearth B.

1160. (R 26, House IV) (PLATE 67) Broken, but complete. Ht. 20. Coarse fabric; rather irregular in shape. Reddish brown clay with very large grit (dominantly red and purplish with some dark grey and white) showing in surface, which is red shading to light brown and blackish, burnished.

1161. (Q 26, House VII) (PLATE 68) Large, with elaborate incised decoration. Lower part missing. Ht. preserved 29. Outside surface dark reddish brown with fine burnish: the strokes of the burnishing implement run vertically on neck and body, which may be intentional for decorative effect. Three warts on belly; bold incised decoration on upper part of body, with rows of stitch-like jabs round base of neck.

1162. (Q 26, House VII) (PLATE 67) Broken, but nearly complete. Ht. 28. Reddish clay, sandy with some grit (including red and white); surface light brown to reddish with fine stroke burnish.

(4) Type 23A or 24A (FIG. 177)

1163. (G 25, north of wall 50) (PLATE 68) Broken, and parts including spout and handle missing. Ht. preserved 26. Single wart on belly each side and vertical row of three warts opposite handle. Dark grey clay; outside surface dark brown to black with very fine polish-like burnish.

1164. (H 26, House IV) (PLATE 67) Broken, but nearly complete except for tip of spout. Carinated belly with three warts on it. Ht. preserved 18.1. Soft brownish grey clay; straw impressions in surface, which dark brown, burnished but much worn.

1165. (Q 26, House VII) (PLATE 68) Rim and spout missing together with handle. Ht. as preserved 18. Outside surface light brown with fine burnish. Incised decoration: double row of dashes on neck; row of diagonal dashes on top of shoulder below join with neck; dot-filled chevrons on body. Stolen from Chios Museum in 1954.

1166. (V/IV X 60/40/25) (PLATE 68) Parts including most of neck and spout missing. Base markedly sunk. Ht. preserved 29. Diam. of body c. 28. Soft grey clay; inside surface dark grey-black, very much pitted; outside worn and pitted but with fine burnish, dark grey-brown to light brown. Three warts on belly; incised decoration on upper part of body: multiple chevrons bisected by a vertical line rising from each wart (FIG. 115 No. 4); bisected chevrons on handle (FIG. 116 No. 11).

(5) Type 24B. Jugs with cutaway spouts: with tall slender necks

Two jugs of this rare type were found together in House VII. These were identical in shape, with

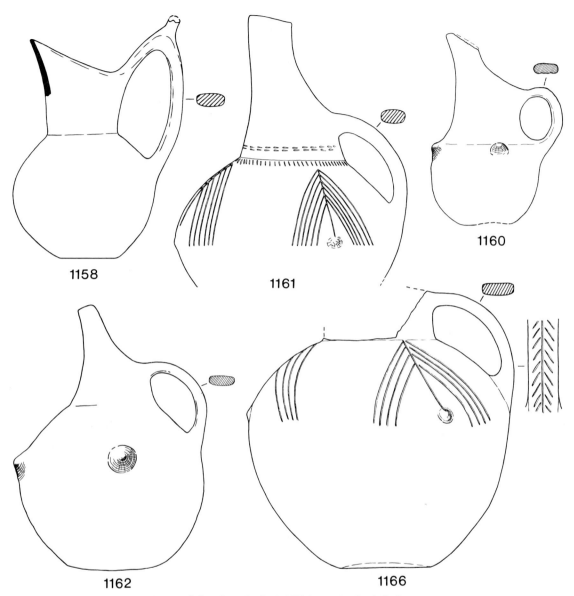

FIG. 176. Jugs from the Period IV destruction level. Scale 1/4.

tall necks, cutaway spouts, and carinated bellies. Three warts adorn the bellies, and the shoulders bear incised decoration, while incised 'eyes' appear on the necks. The long strap handles descending from the rims were 'thrust through' the sides, since the narrow necks made it impossible for the potter to insert a hand once the vase was made.

1168, 1169. (Q 26, House VII) (FIG. 177. PLATE 69) Broken, large parts missing. Ht. 23.5, 24. Grey-brown; fine burnish. Elaborate incised decoration; traces of white fill.

25. *Theriomorphic vases* 1170–1173 (FIG. 177)

Four bird-shaped askoi (type 25A) were recovered from Period IV destruction levels, three

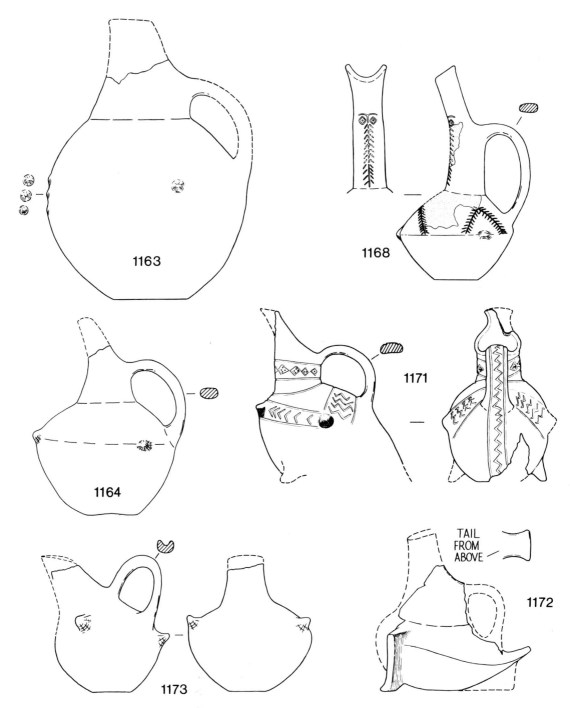

FIG. 177. Jugs and theriomorphic vases from the Period IV destruction level. Scale 1/4.

(1171–3) in the deposit of vases in House VII, the fourth which is by far the smallest (1170) in House IV. The largest (1171) from House VII had elaborate incised decoration. The spouts may all have been of the cutaway type as seen on 1170.

1170. (H/R 26, House IV) (PLATE 68) Large parts including most of rim and handle missing; a non-joining fragment of handle and a wart which may have adorned the tail survive. Cutaway spout. Ht. as preserved *c.* 10. Thin-walled. Grey-brown; fine burnish.

1171. (Q 26, House VII) (PLATE 69) Broken, large parts missing. Spout evidently of cutaway type; strap handle bent over from rim and 'pushed through' body; two short legs, and three warts on belly. Ht. as preserved 18. Grey-brown clay; surface shades of dark brown, well burnished. Bold incised and punctuated decoration, which appears to have been made after vase burnished and when clay already quite hard; abundant traces of white paste in incisions.

1172. (Q 26, House VII) (PLATE 69) Only about half, including one front leg and tail; most of rim missing together with spout, which may have been of cutaway type. L. as preserved 16.5, ht. 14.5. Grey-brown clay with grit, some large (grey, red, and white); inside surface grey, rough; outside silvery grey to light brown, well burnished.

1173. (Q 26, House VII) (PLATE 69) Parts including most of rim missing. Ht. as preserved 14. Finely made; thin-walled; outside surface with high polish-like burnish, apparently light brown, but discoloured by effects of fire which destroyed house.

26. *Cooking jugs* 1174, 1175 (FIG. 178)

Fragments of such jugs would be indistinguishable from those of tripod cooking vases or of jars with rims of class A III; but one complete and another restorable example of this type were recovered from levels of V–IV. Possible fragments of others were recognised from levels of V in G and H.

1174. (V/IV X 60/40/25) (FIG. 178. PLATE 69) Probably of Period IV. Broken, but virtually complete, except for a small section of rim which may have been formed into an open spout opposite the handle. Two low vertical warts on rim, one on each side. Diam. 11.5. Ht. 14. Grey-brown clay with straw impressions and some grit showing in surface, which rather uneven but with good stroke burnish outside and over most of inside, dominantly light reddish brown, mottling to light grey and darker brown and black both inside and out.

1175. (V X 61) (PLATE 70) Part of another similar to 1174, but rather larger. Diam. *c.* 15. Thin-walled. Grey-brown clay with abundant white grit showing in surface, which much pitted but with good stroke burnish, light brown to red.

27. *Tripod cooking pots* 1176–1182 (FIG. 178)

Cooking vessels with three feet for support, already attested in Period VI, came into general use in V. Large fragments of such vessels (1176, 1177) were recovered from levels of V, together with over fifty feet—mostly of crude fabric and roughly oval in section, but five or six square-ended like those of 1176 (PLATE 71 (*f*)). Two feet from V were unusual in having neat triangular sections and curving outwards, like the feet which became standard on cooking pots in Period II (e.g. 1578).

Eight more or less complete or restorable tripod cooking vessels were recovered from deposits of the Period IV destruction. Most of these were crudely made; but 1178 was extremely elegant, with neat triangular-sectioned feet and kidney-sectioned handle. The standard shape to judge from these eight examples was a jug akin to type 26 with legs added to it; wide-mouthed, with S-shaped or short everted rim, and a vertical strap handle. Three vertical warts (one opposite the handle, and one in the middle of each side) were characteristically set on the rim and might project above the line of it; but triangular projections on top of the rim sometimes take the place of warts (e.g. 1181), and sometimes it would seem the wart opposite the handle was replaced by a slight open spout. These tripod cooking pots range from *c.* 17.5–24.5. in height and *c.* 10–15 across the rim.

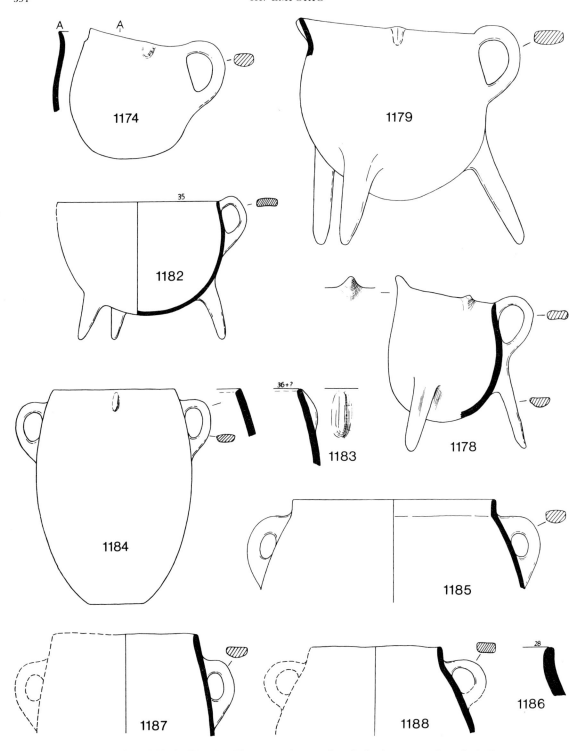

FIG. 178. Periods V–IV. Tripod cooking pots and storage jars. Scale 1/4, except 1182, 1184 (1/8).

Some tripod vessels in use at Emporio at this time were evidently more bowl-like. Thus the receptacle in the case of 1182 is wider than it is high. Similarly the fine burnish on the inside surface of a fragment of a vase to which a large foot from IV R level 39 belonged (PLATE 71 (*f*) left) suggests that it was open and bowl-like. But in general tripod cooking vessels in V–IV appear to have been deep and more like jugs or jars in shape. No evidence was noted for the existence of low-rimmed dish-like tripod bowls.

These vases were made of coarse cooking pot ware. Surfaces normally had a red wash, but often shaded to light brown, and might be discoloured to dusky by the fires in conjunction with which the vessels were evidently used. The vessels were burnished as a rule inside and out, but the burnish was often poor and superficial.

From levels of Period V

1176. (R 59) (PLATE 70) Fragments, including about one-third of rim; two rather elegant square-ended feet apparently belong to the same vase. Diam. of rim *c.* 13. Grey-brown clay; surface with a red wash, varying to light brown and dusky, well smoothed but not truly burnished.
1177. (R ?50) (PLATE 71) Cf. 1178 of Period IV, but cruder. About half body including strap handle preserved; legs missing. Rim slightly everted, with vertical warts rising above it. Diam. of rim 14. Coarse grey clay; surface light brown shading to dusky in places with poor burnish inside and out.

From levels of Period IV

1178. (G 25, north of wall 50) (PLATE 71) Parts including one leg missing. Strap handle of kidney-shaped section; three vertical warts on rim. Max. ht. to rim 17.5. Well made, and light to handle. Clay with fine white, grey, and reddish grit; surface light brown with dusky and reddish patches.
1179. (R 26 and bin in 26, House IV) (PLATE 71) Large parts missing. Strap handle; three vertical warts on rim. Max. ht. to rim 24.5. Grey clay, light brown at edges; surface much pitted, originally light brown to reddish, burnished but worn. Two others similar but smaller from IV G level 26 in House VIII.

   Similar warts rising above the level of the rim are found on tripod cooking pots of the Early and Middle Subperiods of Troy I (*Troy* i 80 figs. 235: 30 (265: 14) (above a handle); 242: 2, 4, 6, 11; 248: 5). They also appear to be a feature of Class A cooking pots at Thermi (*Thermi* 75 fig. 26: Class A Tripod Cooking Cups 2, pl. ix: 210, Town III). Such warts still seem to be in fashion as late as Period II at Emporio (e.g. 1563).

1180. (H 26, House IV) (PLATE 71) Part of rim and handle missing. Three vertical warts on rim. Ht. to rim *c.* 21. Diam. *c.* 15. Grey-brown clay with large grit; surface with a red wash, shading to light brown and dusky; poor burnish.
1181. (H 26, House IV) (PLATE 71) Part of rim and legs missing. Strap handle; three slight triangular projections from rim in place of warts. Diam. *c.* 14. Thick-walled; surface lightish brown to dusky with rough burnish.
1182. (X 41, north of wall 49) (PLATE 71) One leg and most of rim missing. Large. Ht. *c.* 30. Max. diam. *c.* 37. Soft grey-brown clay with large grit (including grey, dusky white, and white); surface with a red to purplish wash inside and out; poor burnish.

(c) JARS

A number of jars of all sizes of which the shapes could be restored came from the Period IV destruction levels. But jars of similar types were already current in V to judge from the fragments of them noted in levels of the period. The great range in the size of these jars no doubt corresponds to the variety of uses which they served.

Large storage jars of types 38–40 had simple rims of classes A I–III. Smaller jars of similar shape, most characteristically with rims of class A I as type 34, were very common; their coarse fabric and poor finish suggest that they were largely used for cooking. Jars with differentiated necks and simple rims of classes B I–II, common and characteristic in earlier periods at Emporio, still occur (types 43–45). Some of these were of very large size, and were evidently used for the storage of food (e.g. types 43, 45); but smaller jars or pyxides of similar shape (type 44) may have held cosmetics. Small pyxis-type jars could also have rims as class B III, and large jars with rims of this class were very much in evidence (types 46, 47). Some of them had fine burnished surfaces and rich incised decoration.

A. *Jars with rims of class A undifferentiated from the rest of the body*

(1) Types 38–40. Large tall storage jars with vertical handles on the shoulder

Restorable examples of such jars were recovered from the Period IV destruction levels, but all three types were evidently in use in Period V as well as in IV. Jars of type 38 with simple rims of class A I appear to have been the most common. These jars might stand *c.* 40 or more high, and normally had a pair of handles set opposite each other, while often at least there were a couple of warts, one on each side of the vase in the spaces between the handles. The warts might be circular or oval, or vertical as on 1183 and 1184.

The fabric is usually coarse, and the vases tend to be irregular in shape (mouths may be oval, as in the case of 1184, although this was evidently not deliberate). Surfaces are shades of grey-brown to dusky, or show traces of a red wash; they are almost invariably burnished, but the rim 1185 is of pithos fabric with an unburnished dark brown wash. The fabric of 1183 from a level of V is akin to Silvery Grey Ware: its rim is cut square and sharp as if in imitation of metalwork.

38. *With simple incurving rims (class A I)* (FIG. 178)

1183. (V R ?73) Fragments, including part of metallic rim with large circular wart. Fabric cf. Silvery Grey Ware; sandy reddish brown to grey clay with grit (dominantly black and red); surface shades of light and dark brown to reddish and dusky, stroke burnished, but with strokes so deep and narrow that burnishing approximates to wiping of surface while clay still soft.

A rim of similar shape and fabric from V H level 78; outside surface dark grey-brown, burnished; inside deep purple-brown, less well burnished.

1184. (IV R 26, House IV inside bin) (PLATE 72) Broken, but nearly complete. Rim somewhat oval (diam. 26–28). Ht. *c.* 48. Soft fabric; clay orange to grey, with grit (including a good deal of large grey and some red and white) showing in surface, which pitted, with a thin red to red-brown wash, appearing in places as streaks; traces of burnish.

39. *With ogival rims (class A II)* (FIG. 178)

1185. (IV H 37, above floor IV. 1 west of wall 38) Large parts, including some of rim with handles preserved. Coarse grey-brown clay with large grit showing in surface, which violently mottled from red to dark brown and dusky black; rough burnish inside and out.

1186. (IV R 35, above floor IV. 1 in House IV) Rim. Pithos fabric; hard sandy red clay, fired an even colour throughout; surface with a thin dark brown wash, unburnished.

1187. (IV G 26, House VIII) Part of rim with one of handles preserved. Shades of dusky brown and red; poor burnish.

1188. (IV G 26, House VIII) Half of rim with one of handles preserved. Shades of brown to reddish with dusky patches; poor burnish.

(2) Type 34. Jars with simple incurving rims (class A I)

Small jars of this type were evidently common and characteristic; but no complete example was recovered from levels of V–IV, although the shapes of several were restorable. The height tended to range from *c.* 10–25 with a concentration around *c.* 15–16. In shape these jars resembled the large storage jars of type 38, and like them might have vertical strap handles set to the rim (e.g. 1190) or just below it (e.g. 1189). Circular, sometimes oblong warts, appear on the shoulders,

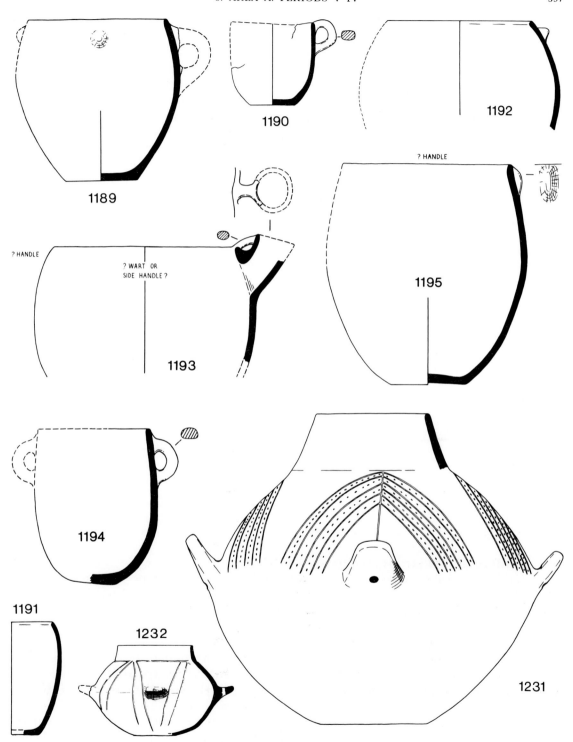

FIG. 179. Periods V–IV. Jars. Scale 1/4.

while vertical warts are commonly found on the rims. Many rims of classes A II–III evidently belonged to jars of related shapes, smaller versions of the storage jars of types 39 and 40; but none could be restored.

Many of these small jars had evidently been used for cooking like similar types in earlier periods. The fabric tends to be hard, the clay coarse, often with abundant grit, shades of grey-brown; the surface grey or dark brown to black, often with a dull purplish tinge, and dusky—no doubt from use of the vessel over a fire. The surface may shade to light brown and reddish, and in some cases at any rate it had clearly been coated with a red wash. Vases were apt to be irregular and uneven, but were almost always burnished inside as well as out, although the burnish might be very poor and superficial. Decoration, apart from warts, does not seem to be attested.

From levels of Period V

1189. (V H 49) Base, and non-joining fragments of rim with stump of one vertical strap handle and wart on shoulder. Diam. *c.* 15. Thick-walled; coarse cooking pot type ware; clay grey-black to brown with grit (including grey and white) some very large, showing in surface, which is shades of dirty brown to dusky (due to use over fire?) with rough stroke burnish outside and round inside of rim.

1190. (V H 76) (PLATE 72) Profile, including part of rim with one vertical strap handle set to it. Ht. to rim 9.5. Rather thin-walled, and irregular in shape. Soft fabric; light sandy greyish brown clay with fine straw impressions showing in surface, which is pale brown shading to dusky and orange in patches, burnished.

1191. (V H 49) Profile, including part of rim. Ht. *c.* 12. Diam. *c.* 10. Unusually good fabric. Sandy grey-brown clay with occasional fine white grit; surface dark grey-brown to black with a purplish tinge cf. Cooking Pot Ware; burnished outside, less well inside.

1192. (V G 85, ?70) (PLATE 70) Fragments of rim. Grey clay; light brown at edges; thin-walled, but with some very large grit (including red and white) showing in surface, which is light reddish brown, rather uneven although stroke burnished outside and less well inside.

1193. (V/IV G 51, 36) (PLATE 72) Fragments of rim, with nozzle spout joined to it at top by small strap handle cf. 1329. Possible indications of side handle or wart. Diam. estimated *c.* 20. Hardish fabric; clay grey, red-brown at edges, with abundant grit (including red and white) some large showing in surface, which is rather pitted, grey-brown to black, stroke burnished inside and out.

From levels of Period IV

1194. (IV X 40/25, House VI) (PLATE 72) Broken, part of rim with one of a presumed pair of handles missing. Rim very uneven, and distinctly oval. Diam. 12–14. Ht. 16.5. Reddish clay with very abundant grit (dominantly grey, but including red and some white); outside surface light brown with patches of black, burnished.

1195. (IV H 25, west of wall 38 in area of hearth B) Base, and part of rim with vertical lug. Grey-brown clay; outside surface lightish brown to dusky, stroke burnished; inside darker, less well burnished.

(3) Undifferentiated jar rims: classes A I–III

Most of the simple rims of class A I appear to come from jars akin to type 34. Some of these are internally thickened and differentiated, perhaps to support lids, as 1199. But internally differentiated rims of this kind are more often of class A II (e.g. 1207–8).

Most of the rims of class A II are of coarse ware with a poor burnish; but one (1206) has a very finely burnished red to light brown surface.

Rims of class A III may be divided into four groups: (a) more or less upright; (b) short, outward curving; (c) long, outward curving; and (d) internally differentiated. The rims 1213–5 of group (a) from mixed levels or early levels of V may be strays of Periods VII–VI. Rims of group (b) merge into ones of variety (a) of type 13 bowls.

Many rims of class A III evidently came from cooking pots of various types like the majority of rims of classes A I–II. A few rims of class A III have vertical warts set on or below them as found on cooking pots of this horizon; sometimes these warts rise above the rim (see under 1228).

Handles are not as much in evidence in conjunction with rims of class A III as they are in the case of ones of classes A I–II.

Rims of class A I

1196. (V R 50) Surface pitted; outside light brown, inside dark brown to black; dull burnish. Many others more or less similar from levels of V.
1197. (V R wall 37) Outside brown to black, inside lighter mushroom-brown, burnished.
1198. (V H 49) Grey clay; surface light brown, burnished.
1199. (V R ?73) Rim with slight internal differentiation and vertical strap handle on outside. Cooking Pot Ware; surface grey-brown, stroke burnished. Others similar from levels of V.
1200. (V R ?73) With handle as 1199. Cooking Pot Ware; very gritty grey clay; surface light brown to reddish, burnished.
1201. (V G ?70) Strap handle below rim. Cooking Pot Ware; surface uneven, dull purple-brown to lighter brown; poor burnish. Several others similar from levels of V.
1202. (VI/V X ?130) Small strap handle on outside. Angle not certain. Coarse fabric; surface grey-brown; poor burnish.
1203. (IV Q 26, House VII) Dark grey-brown clay; surface dusky reddish brown with traces of burnish outside and to lesser extent inside. Others similar from levels of V–IV.

Rims of class A II

1204. (V H 49) Outside purplish brown to black, inside light dusky brown; poor burnish. Many others similar from levels of V.
1205. (V R ?73) Cooking Pot Ware; surface grey-brown, stroke burnished. Several others similar from levels of V.
1206. (IV G 26/25) Red to light brown; very fine burnish.
1207. (V R wall 37) Internally thickened and differentiated. Soft fabric; surface light brown to reddish; fine burnish.
1208. (V H 49) As 1207. Cooking Pot Ware; surface grey-brown, stroke burnished. One or two others similar.
1209. (VI/V R ?87) Vertical strap handle on outside. Surface pitted; outside dark brown to black, inside light brown; dull burnish.
1210. (V H 48) Strap handle. Cooking Pot Ware; surface shades of dark to light brown; dull burnish.
1211. (IV G 25) Strap handle. Grey clay, with fine grit and some large white grit; outside surface buff, inside red due to a wash; rather dull burnish inside and out. Another similar.
1212. (IV R 26) Vertical wart below rim. Cooking pot type ware; clay grey, light brown at edges; surface much pitted, shades of brown, burnished inside and out.

Rims of class A III (FIGS. 180, 181)

Group (a): more or less upright rims
1213. (VI/V G/Q 87) Probably of Period VI. Grey clay; surface light brown with traces of burnish inside and out.
1214. (V R 86) Probably of Period VI. Light Brown Burnished Ware; surface worn.
1215. (VI/V G/Q 87) Probably of Period VI. Irregular and uneven. Surface shades of dark brown to dusky, burnished inside and out.
1216. (IV G 25) Angle very uncertain. Surface uneven, but well burnished; deep purple-brown outside, light brown inside.

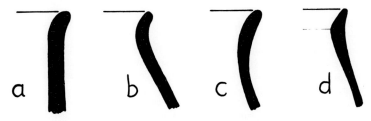

FIG. 180. Periods V–IV. Varieties of jar rims of class A III.

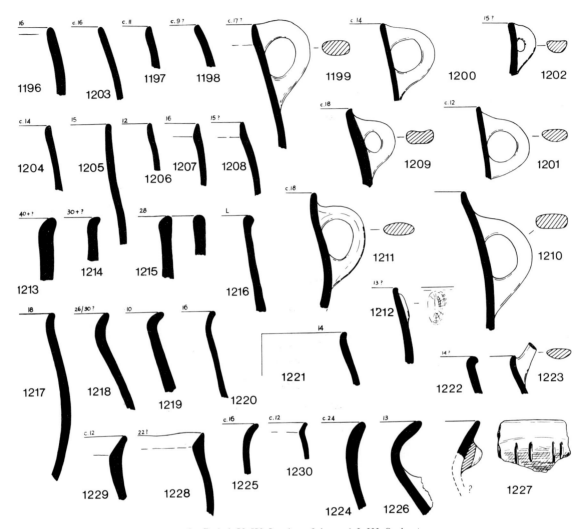

FIG. 181. Periods V–IV. Jar rims of classes A I–III. Scale 1/3.

Group (b): short, outward curving rims

1217. (V X 82/77/60) Outside shades of light brown mottling to red and black with fine burnish; inside light reddish brown, rather less well burnished.

1218. (IV R 39) Hard grey clay; surface much pitted, dusky to light brown, with stroke burnish inside and out.

1219. (VI/V H 92) Angle uncertain. Coarse fabric; abundant straw impressions in surface, which has a pale red wash, unburnished.

1220. (V R ?73) Cooking Pot Ware; clay grey; surface shades of lightish brown, much pitted but well stroke burnished. Several others similar from levels of V.

1221. (IV G 25) Cooking pot type ware; outside surface brown-buff, inside with a reddish tinge, presumably due to a red wash; slight hint of burnish. Two or three others similar from levels of V–IV.

1222. (IV G 25) Sandy orange clay, pitted with tiny holes, but evenly fired throughout; surface with a thick, slightly lustrous, red wash. Possibly an import.

1223. (V R 50) Stump of high-swung vertical strap handle set just below rim. Grey-brown, burnished. Another similar but larger from V Q level 85; surface grey-brown with very fine burnish. Possibly from jugs of some kind cf. 1158 of type 23B.

Group (c): long, outward-curving rims

1224. (V R 50) Cooking Pot Ware; hard grey clay, red-brown at edges; surface dusky to purplish brown, unburnished. Two others similar (V R 50, IV H 37) with burnished red washes.

1225. (IV R 26) Cooking pot type ware; surface shades of dusky, dark and light brown; poor burnish.

1226. (V R 59) Possibly of Period VI. Stump of vertical handle. Light Brown Burnished Ware; outside and inside of rim light brown, burnished; inside below rim with an unburnished red wash.

1227. (IV R 26) (PLATE 75) Large horizontal wart with bold vertical cuts on it. Cooking pot type ware; clay grey, light brown at edges; surface with a red wash.

> Cf. *PMac* 181 fig. 54: c, from Vardaroftsa, E.B.A. *PZ* xlii (1964) 43 fig. 8: 23, from Sitagroi (Fotolivos).

Group (d): internally differentiated rims

For rim profiles like these cf. 1401 and *Poliochni* i pl. lxx: h, i, of the archaic Blue period.

1228. (V R 50) Cooking Pot Ware; clay grey; surface dusky brown to black, well burnished. Several others similar from levels of V in G and H; one (V H 49) with a vertical wart rising above rim level cf. 1178.

1229. (VI/V Q 87) (PLATE 54) Hard gritty grey clay; straw impressions showing in surface, which is reddish brown, well burnished, outside; inside shades of light brown, unburnished except around rim.

1230. (V G 70) Cooking Pot Ware; surface dull brown to black; little or no sign of burnish. Another similar, and perhaps from same vase, but with light brown surface, and vertical wart to rim.

B. *Jars with necks or rims of class B more or less clearly differentiated from the rest of the body*

The unique jar 1231 from the Period IV destruction level in House IV is a late version of the early type 41. The fabric and the style of the incised decoration indicate that it is of more or less contemporary date, not an heirloom from earlier times. One or two rims (e.g. 1244–5) may come from vases of similar shape.

The vase 1231 is also unusual among large jars of V–IV in having lugs instead of handles, resembling in this respect the small jars (pyxides) of the related type 44. These small jars of type 44, usually with surfaces well burnished and often with elaborate incised decoration, were probably for cosmetics. They seem much at home in Periods V–IV, and many of the fragments of small closed vases with incised decoration from this horizon may come from such jars.

Large jars of type 45 with short collar necks were evidently used for storage. They have various arrangements of horizontal and vertical handles and lugs, and may bear incised decoration, as 1233. The jar 1235 assigned to type 46 is in effect a crude variety of the following type 47, which is extremely characteristic of this horizon. It occurs in three main varieties: with vertical strap handles (A) on the shoulder, or (B) on the belly; and (C) with horizontal side handles on the belly. Some jars of this type had very fine burnished surfaces and elaborate incised decoration. Jars with this superior finish tended to have carinated bellies (e.g. 1237, 1239).

(1) Complete or nearly complete jars of types 43–47 from Period IV destruction levels

43. *Large jar with collar neck and four vertically perforated lugs on the belly (rim of class B I)*

1231. (H 26, House IV) (FIG. 179. PLATE 73) Broken, parts missing. Ht. 33. Diam. of rim 12, of belly *c.* 37. Very soft fabric; light grey clay, red-brown at edges, with little or no grit. Abundant pin-holes in the break, and surface much pitted, apparently owing to use of straw temper. Original surface worn away, but probably grey-brown, burnished. Elaborate incised decoration on upper part of body centred upon each of the four lugs.

44. *Small jar (pyxis) with short collar neck and four vertically perforated lugs on belly (rim of class B I)*

1232. (R 26, House IV inside bin) (FIG. 179. PLATE 72) Only about half preserved. Ht. 9.5. Thin-walled. Grey-brown clay with grey, red, and white marble-like grit, some large; surface shades of dark and light brown to red, burnished outside and round inside of rim. Bold incised decoration, made before final firing of vase. The lid 1297 of type 62 evidently belongs with this jar.

This example is not far removed in shape from jars of type 42 which may be ancestral to it. It corresponds to Trojan shape C 27, which occurs throughout the Early Sub-period of Troy I and may possibly be identified in the Late Subperiod (*Troy* i 71).

45. *Large globular jars with short upright collar necks*

1233. (R and R/H 26, House IV) (FIG. 182. PLATE 73) Pair of large side handles on belly, with four smaller ones on shoulder above. Wide low rim cf. class B II. Broken, but complete except for small parts missing including one of the small handles. Ht. *c.* 47. Diam. of rim 24, of belly *c.* 50. Softish fabric; clay black at core, brown at edges, with straw, and grit (some large) dominantly grey, but including marble-like white and red; much grit and straw showing in surface, which is orange-brown except where discoloured black by fire which destroyed house. Outside with faint traces of burnish and possible indications of an original red wash, especially on one of the two large handles. Bold incised decoration: line of chevrons round base of neck, and line running down vertically from it to each of the four small handles, which are hatched. The two large handles on the belly have bold diagonal grooves imitating rope ornament. These rope-ornamented handles suggest that the vase may be an import.

1234. (R 26, House IV) (FIG. 182) Pair of side handles on belly, and pair of vertical strap handles on shoulder between them. Wide low rim cf. class B I. Only about one third preserved, but shape restorable. Ht. *c.* 43–44. Diam. of rim *c.* 22, of belly *c.* 52. Coarse grey-brown clay; surface slightly pitted. Inside dusky, rough and unburnished; outside with a red wash, which in places thick and crackled, elsewhere thin, so that surface shades from red to light brown with dusky patches round base; poor burnish outside and round inside of rim.

A similar rim (diam. 21) from V R level ?73, of very hard fabric; sandy reddish clay fired an even colour throughout, with abundant fine white grit; surface with a red wash and little or no trace of burnish. Possibly from an imported vase.

46. *Jar with tall slightly differentiated neck and outward-curving rim (class B III)*

1235. (R 26, House IV) (FIG. 182. PLATE 73) Two vertical strap handles on shoulder, and two pairs of warts, one on each side in spaces between them. Rim very uneven cf. class B III c–d. Broken, parts including one of two handles missing. Ht. 24. Diam. of rim 20. Roughly made and irregular in shape. Clay with abundant sandy grit (dominantly white, but including grey and red); outside surface dirty shades of light and dark brown mottling to black, with poor burnish.

Type 47. *Globular jars with tall necks and upright or outward-leaning rims*

(A) With vertical strap handles on shoulder

1236. (R 26, House IV) (FIG. 182. PLATE 73) Two vertical strap handles on shoulder, and large circular warts on belly in spaces between them. Rim class B II. Broken, parts missing. Ht. 28. Diam. of rim. 14.5, of belly 25. Orange clay; surface with fine burnish, light brown to red, but much discoloured by fire which destroyed house. The lid 1296 of type 61 appears to belong to this jar.

1237. (G 26, 25, House VIII) (FIG. 182. PLATE 73) Four small strap handles on shoulder, and elaborate incised decoration. Large parts of body preserved; rim, neck, and base missing. Diam. of belly *c.* 28. Hard grey clay, red-brown at edges, with sandy white grit prominent, together with some very large grey lumps. Inside surface purplish, wiped, apparently with bunch of twigs of which marks clearly visible; outside dark brown to black, with very fine burnish. Elaborate incised decoration on shoulder; traces of white fill.

(B) With vertical strap handles on belly

1238. (R 26, House IV) (PLATE 74) Four handles. Lower part missing. Diam. of rim 24, of belly 34. Orange clay; outside surface light brown to red, with fine burnish; inside unburnished, and mostly dusky, apparently owing to effects of fire which destroyed house, as dusky fragments join with others which light brown. Bold incised decoration.

1239. (H 26, House IV) (FIG. 183. PLATE 74) Pair of handles, and wart each side in spaces between them. Rim class B III a 1. Broken, parts missing. Ht. 37. Diam. of rim 21.5, of belly *c.* 36. Well-fired; grey-brown clay with large grit; surface shades of light and dark brown to reddish; very fine burnish. Elaborate incised decoration on upper part of body and handles; traces of original white fill.

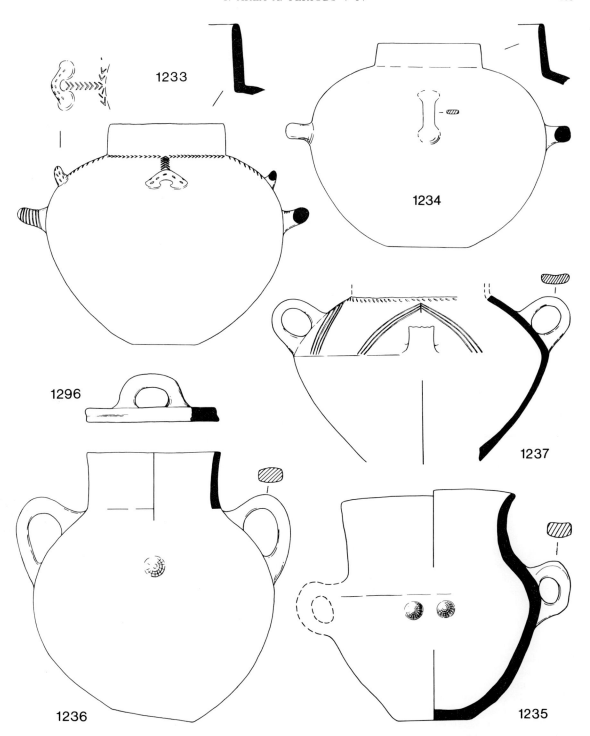

FIG. 182. Jars from the Period IV destruction level. Scale 1/4, except 1233, 1234 (1/8).

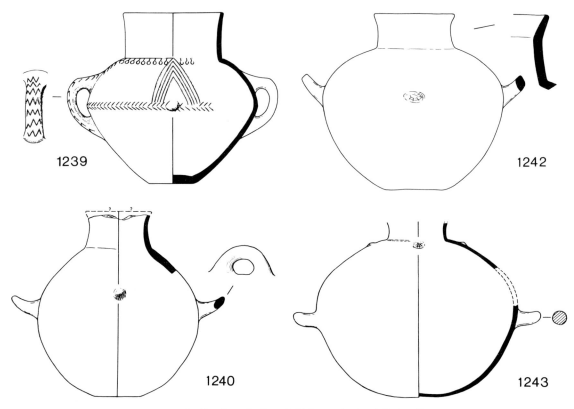

FIG. 183. Jars from the Period IV destruction level. Scale 1/8.

(C) With horizontal side handles on belly

1240. (G 25, House VIII) (FIG. 183. PLATE 73) Pair of handles, and wart on each side in spaces between them. Rim class B III c. Broken, parts including one handle and top of rim missing. Ht. as preserved 38. Diam. of belly 35. Coarse grey clay, brown at edges, with large grit (shades of white, grey, and reddish), often showing in surface, which light brown to red, burnished. Fragments of another similar from IV X level 40/25, House VI.

1241. (R 26, House IV) (PLATE 74) Pair of handles; four warts, one each side in spaces between handles and one above each of them. Rim class III a 3. Broken, but nearly complete. Ht. c. 43.5. Diam. of rim 18.5. Grey clay, light brown at outside edge. Outside with a wash, red to light brown mottling to black, burnished. Fragments of one or two others similar from same deposit in House IV.

1242. (H 26, House IV) (FIG. 183. PLATE 74) Pair of handles, and wart each side, as on 1240. Rim class B III a 1. Broken, but virtually complete. Ht. 38. Diam. of rim 17, of belly 36. Dark grey clay; inside surface grey-black; outside light brown with traces of a red wash, burnished but worn.

   Part of another similar (diam. of rim 16) from same deposit at northern end of House IV. Greyish brown clay with abundant straw and some grit; surface mottling from red to red-brown and light brown with large dusky patches, well burnished inside as well as out. Fragments of two or three others similar from levels of V in G and H.

1243. (V/IV X no level) (FIG. 183) Pair of handles, and apparently four warts high on shoulder. Rim cf. class B III d. Only about one-third preserved; one handle and top of rim missing. Diam. of rim 11, of belly 54. Obsidian Ware; hard sandy grey-brown clay, with some ordinary mica and shiny black particles showing on inside surface. Inside rough with signs of wiping with a bunch of twigs; outside with a red wash, shading to light brown and dusky, well smoothed but not it seems burnished. Probably an import.

(2) **Differentiated jar rims: classes B I–III**

The great majority of these are now of class B III. Rims of class B III from the horizon of V–IV can be divided into six groups (a–f). Most of these B III rims evidently come from jars akin to type 47; but the short everted rims of group f belong to cooking pots, whether round- or flat-bottomed, or with tripod feet. Rims of this group (f) seem to be commoner in the later levels of V than in the earlier ones. Some of the rims assigned to group e of class B III may come from bowls of type 14.

Rims of class V I (FIG. 184)

1244.   (V H 47) Irregular. Grey-black clay; surface brown to black, well stroke burnished inside and out.
1245.   (IV Q 26, House VII) Grey-brown; fine burnish inside and out.
1246.   (V G/H 70) Cooking Pot Ware; surface dusky grey-brown; outside stroke burnished.

Rims of class B I (FIG. 184)

1247.   (IV G 36, north of wall 50) Hard gritty grey clay; outside surface dull lightish brown, stroke burnished; inside reddish with poor burnish.
1248.   (V H 49) Grey-brown clay; surface shades of dark and light brown to reddish; fine burnish.

Rims of class B III a: variety 1 (FIGS. 184, 186)

1249.   (IV G 36, north of wall 50) (FIG. 186) Coarse grey-brown clay; straw impressions abundant in surface, which has a dark purplish wash, unburnished. Another similar from V G level 51; surface orange to red with slight traces of stroke burnish.
1250.   (V H 48) Surface grey-brown with purplish tinge shading to reddish brown around top of rim; fine burnish.
1251.   (V/IV H no level) Surface with a red wash shading to dark and light brown, burnished. An unburnished strip at base of neck may indicate where a string or band of some perishable material was tied round it, cf. 842, 1403, 2086, 2584.
1252.   (IV G 25, House VIII) (FIG. 186) Hard grey-brown clay with abundant grit, including grey, red, and white; surface orange-brown to red; traces of poor burnish.

Rims of class B III a: variety 2 (FIG. 184)

1253.   (V G wall 51) Gritty brown clay; surface light brown with fine burnish. Burnishing on outside careful, with marks running horizontally around rim, vertically on neck, as if for decorative effect.
1254.   (IV G 26, House VIII) Gritty grey clay; surface uneven, with a wash, red to light brown inside, light purplish outside; poor burnish.

Rims of class B III a: variety 3 (FIG. 184)

1255.   (V G 85) Hard grey-brown clay; surface chestnut brown, stroke burnished.
1256.   (V H 48) Cooking Pot Ware; sandy grey-brown clay; surface with purple-brown to red wash, smooth but with only slight trace of burnish.
1257.   (V R wall 37) Diam. *c.* 14. Grey clay; surface light orange-brown, burnished. Another similar from V G wall 23.

Rims of class B III b (FIG. 184)

1258.   (IV G 25) Chocolate brown to dark red, stroke burnished.
        Compare 739 from a level of Period VII. Cf. Eutresis: *Hesperia* xxix (1960) 144 fig. 7: IV. 7, of red-slipped ware assigned to E.H. I. The same type of jar rim is in evidence at Perachora in Phases X and Y which may be E.H. I (*BSA* lxiv (1969) 56 fig. 2: 17, 18; 61 fig. 4: 26–28).
1259.   (V/IV X no level) Four string-holes through top of rim, which evidently from a small jar (pyxis) cf. type 44. Soft fabric; sandy clay, grey at core, red-brown at edges; outside surface black, apparently due to a wash, which does not seem burnished. Irregular line incised round outside.

Rims of class B III c (FIGS. 184, 186)

1260.   (V H 76) Soft fabric; grey-brown clay; surface light brown, presumably once burnished, but worn. Four or five

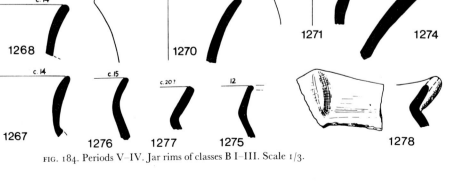

FIG. 184. Periods V–IV. Jar rims of classes B I–III. Scale 1/3.

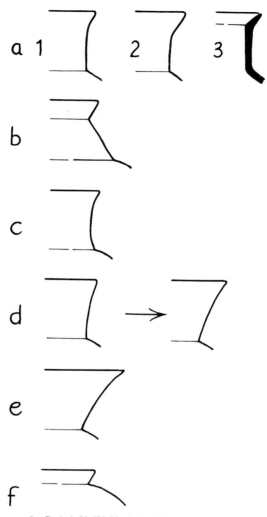

FIG. 185. Periods V–IV. Varieties of jar rims of class B III.

others similar from levels of V; mostly with abundant straw impressions in surfaces, which light brown, burnished, or with unburnished red wash. Possibly all strays of Periods VII–VI.

1261. (V H 49) Grey-brown clay; surface light brown to reddish, smooth and evenly burnished, but worn. Three others similar from levels of V.

1262. (V G/Q 70) Hard grey-brown clay; surface light brown with slight traces of stroke burnish. Two others similar from levels of V.

1263. (IV X ?26, south of wall 49) (FIG. 186) Grey-brown; fine burnish.

1264. (IV H 26, House IV) (FIG. 186) Grey clay, light brown at edges, with grit and straw; surface red to light brown; poor burnish.

1265. (IV Q 26, House VII) Black clay, light brown at edges; surface with a red wash outside and round inside of rim, smoothed or burnished.

Rims of class B III d (FIGS. 184, 186)

1266. (V R ?73) Light brown; fine burnish.

1267. (V R wall 37) Grey-brown clay; surface grey-brown with a purplish tinge shading to reddish brown round top of rim, burnished.

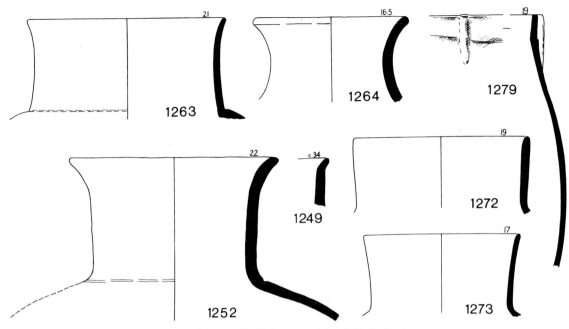

FIG. 186. Periods V–IV. Jar rims of class B III. Scale 1/4.

1268. (V G 70) Grey clay; surface with a red wash, well burnished.
1269. (V G wall 23) Soft grey-brown clay; surface with a thick red wash, burnished.
1270. (V R wall 37) Grey-brown with a reddish tinge, burnished but much worn.
1271. (VI/V G/H 88) Hard grey clay; surface lightish brown shading to dusky; poor burnish.
1272. (IV H 26, 18) (FIG. 186) Soft grey-brown clay; surface with traces of a red wash, burnished but much worn.
1273. (IV H 25, west of wall 38 in area of hearth B) (FIG. 186) Soft grey-brown clay; surface dark brown shading to light brown and reddish; very fine burnish.

Rims of class B III e

1274. (V/IV X 60/40/25) (FIG. 184) Possibly from a bowl of type 14. Shades of light brown to red, burnished but worn.

Rims of class B III f (FIGS. 184, 186)

1275. (V R ?73) Cooking Pot Ware; grey-brown clay with grit and straw; surface dusky reddish with poor burnish.
1276. (V G/Q 85) Gritty grey-brown clay; surface pitted, with grit showing in it; light to darkish brown, burnished on outside.
1277. (IV G 25, north of wall 50) Coarse gritty black clay, red-brown at edges; surface deep purplish red-brown; poor burnish.
1278. (V R 86) (PLATE 75) Rising in triangular projection with bold vertical wart on it. Surface dusky dark brown with a slight reddish tinge; poor burnish.
1279. (V X ?82/77) (FIG. 186) Fragments of large jar; most of rim and all of base missing. Thin-walled. Dark grey clay with large grit; surface with a red wash, dusky in places; slight burnish inside and out.

(D) MISCELLANEOUS

51. *Double vase* 1280

The fragment 1280 was the only evidence noted for the existence of double vases in V–IV. It joined two vases, but there was no channel leading from one to the other.

1280. (V Q ?70) (PLATE 75) Hard fabric; very sandy clay with some mica; surface black, burnished. Incised decoration: horizontal band of chevrons flanked by lines (FIG. 115 No. 13). Possibly an import.

(E) PITHOI 1281–1295 (FIG. 187)

Substantial parts of at least five large storage jars deserving the name of pithoi were recovered from destruction levels of Period IV: 1284 in House VIII, 1292 and 1293 in House IV, 1295 in House V, and the nearly complete 1283 in House VI. Fragments of pithoi from levels of III, but probably of Period IV date, have also been grouped here (e.g. 1290–1).

Several fragments of pithoi recovered from levels of V–IV were over 2 cm thick, and one from V G level 85 measured nearly 4 cm across the break. This suggests that some pithoi by now were very large; the complete example 2332 from the Period IV destruction level in Area D stood 1.40 m high. This, like the other Period IV pithoi of which the outlines could be restored, was bag-shaped, with the swelling low down near the base; the base itself being very narrow, almost pointed, as if made for sinking into the ground. But normally at least it would seem that the bottoms of these pithoi were not sunk very deep below the surface (e.g. PLATE 23 (e)); the spigot holes bored through the sides of several of them just above the bottoms (e.g. 1283, 1287) were presumably above ground level. Some pithoi evidently had rounded bases like 2332 from Area D.

There was a considerable variety in the shapes of pithos rims, but necks were normally it seems differentiated so that rims correspond to jar rims of class B III. Rims akin to class B III a 3 were the most common and characteristic, and one or two fragments of very large rims of this kind were recovered from levels of V–IV. At least one rim (1282) was like class B III b, and another (1293) like class B III d. The simple rim 1281 from an early level of V may be a stray of Periods VII–VI.

Pithoi of V–IV regularly had a pair of vertical strap handles set on the neck or joining neck and shoulder; and, to judge from complete examples like 1283, there was often another pair (or even two pairs, as in the case of 2332 from Area D) of handles set lower on the body below the first one. Handles resembled those of jugs and jars, but were larger in size. Several pithos handles were noted with thin oval, rectangular, and ribbed sections (including examples with single and others with double ribs). Oval and kidney-sectioned pithos handles also occurred.

The clay used for pithoi was coarse with abundant straw or grit, or both combined. Large lumps of grit, and straw impressions, show in the surfaces. White grit is prominent, but grey and red are also noticeable. While the fabric of pithoi shades into that of ordinary coarse ware, the firing tends to be decidedly better than it is in the case of most other vases. This suggests that large storage vessels may have been made by expert craftsmen, perhaps itinerant potters who went from one area to another using the clay of each locality they visited, as makers of pithoi still do today in Crete and some other parts of Greece. The comparatively good firing of pithoi is responsible for the marked reddish or iron-grey colour of the clay in the break; this being in distinct contrast to the shades of brown and black normal in the case of ordinary vases. In many fragments of these pithoi the clay is seen to be fired an even colour throughout, in spite of the great thickness of the walls.

The outside surfaces tended to be red. Normally at least the colour was due to the application of a red wash; but the surface might shade to orange and light brown, dusky and purplish. The outside was often (but not it seems invariably) given a more or less superficial burnish. One fragment from a pithos or large jar (IV H 25, west of wall 38 in the area of hearth B) has what looks like trickle ornament of the type common on Cretan storage vessels from Early Minoan

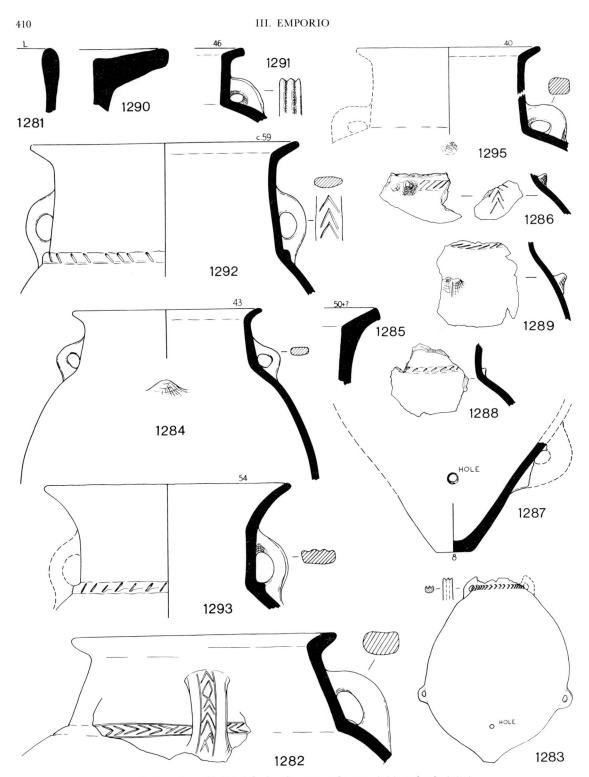

FIG. 187. Periods V–IV. Pithoi. Scale 1/8, except 1281, 1290 (1/4), and 1283 (1/20).

times onwards. The inside surface of this fragment is red to light brown, the outside yellowish, wiped but not burnished. But the streaks of thin darkish paint which appears to have run down the outside may reflect the use of a thin, rather liquid overall wash, rather than an attempt at trickle ornament of the kind found on Cretan vases.

Decoration is restrained. Handles may be adorned with incision, and a strip of incised chevrons is sometimes found at the base of the neck (e.g. 1282); but a rib with diagonal cuts or chevrons on it, imitating the rope used to strengthen such large vessels, is more usual here. Similar rope ornament appears on fragments of a large jar, perhaps akin to type 45, but of coarse fabric like that of pithoi. That more elaborate ornament in relief might be applied to pithoi is suggested by the two fragments of 1294. Warts of various types are found on the shoulders of large jars and pithoi, including at least one example of a hollow-topped wart.

1281. (V G 54) Rim. Hard gritty clay, grey at core; surface dusky orange, with poor burnish.

1282. (V/IV Q 62, 32) Rim, with vertical strap handle (one of a pair?) of kidney-shaped section. Coarse grey to brown clay; abundant straw impressions and grit showing in surface; outside with a red wash, unburnished. Incised decoration: row of chevrons down handle; strip of chevrons at join of neck and shoulder.

1283. (IV X 40/25, House VI) (PLATE 76) Complete, except for rim. Pair of ribbed strap handles joining neck to shoulder; another pair set below them on the swelling. Ht. as preserved c. 85. Diam. of neck c. 30, of belly c. 75, of base 8. Small hole (diam. c. 1.8) in middle of one side just above base, presumably for wooden bung cf. 1287, 2332. Coarse reddish clay with abundant grit showing in surface, which light brown to reddish, apparently with a red wash, unburnished, but much worn. Possible traces of fire lit inside bottom, during firing or perhaps afterwards in cleaning vessel cf. 2332. Rib around base of neck with bold incised chevrons.

1284. (IV G 26, House VIII) (PLATE 76) Upper part of pithos, with pair of vertical strap handles; warts on shoulder between them. Coarse grey clay; abundant straw impressions and grit showing in surface, which is red (apparently due to a wash) shading to light brown and dusky, worn.

1285. (IV G 26, House VIII) Rim, possibly from 1284. Coarse gritty brown to reddish clay; surface with a red wash; little or no trace of burnish.

1286. (IV G 26, House VIII) (PLATE 74) Fragments from shoulder of large jar, apparently cf. type 45. Coarse reddish brown clay; abundant straw impressions showing in surface, which may have had a red wash, but worn. Low rib with diagonal incisions at join of neck and shoulder, interrupted by a prominent wart.

1287. (IV G 26, House VIII) Base, with stump of handle set just above it. Small hole (diam. 2) bored after firing, presumably for wooden bung cf. 1283. Hard fabric; coarse gritty grey clay, shading to reddish at outside edge. Inside surface dusky grey, wiped; outside red (due to a wash?) shading to brown and dusky, roughly smoothed rather than burnished.

1288. (IV G 26, House VIII) (PLATE 74) Join of neck and shoulder of large jar, perhaps as type 45. Coarse gritty reddish clay; inside surface scraped; outside with a red wash, wiped. Rib with diagonal cuts round base of neck.

1289. (IV G 25, House VIII) (PLATE 74) Shoulder of large jar, apparently cf. type 45, with peculiar horned wart. Coarse grey-brown clay with large grit showing in surface, which has a red wash carelessly slapped on outside; splashes of red paint inside. Band of diagonal incisions round base of neck.

1290. (III G 19) Probably of Period IV. Rim. Coarse grey-brown clay, light brown at surface, which is full of straw impressions with traces of a red wash. Another similar from V G/Q level 85 with a red wash.

1291. (III G 19) Probably of Period IV. Rim, with ribbed handle joining neck and shoulder. Coarse brown to red clay; surface with abundant straw impressions; traces of a red wash.

1292. (IV R 26, House IV) (PLATE 76) Neck and rim, with one of a pair of vertical strap handles of thin oval section. Coarse gritty grey-brown clay with grit showing in surface, which has a red wash outside and round inside of neck; outside with poor superficial burnish. Bold incised chevrons on handles; rib with diagonal cuts round base of neck.

1293. (IV R 26, House IV) (PLATE 76) Rim, with vertical strap handle (one of a pair?). Coarse reddish brown clay with grit (some very large) showing in surface, which has a red wash; very poor burnish inside and out. Handle ribbed; rib with diagonal incisions round base of neck.

1294. (IV R 26, House IV) (PLATE 76) Fragments of large pithos with relief decoration. Coarse fabric; outside surface with a red wash.

1295. (IV R 26, House V) About half rim, with one of a pair of vertical strap handles of rectangular section. Hard grey clay, red at surface, which has abundant straw impressions. Parts of outside with very superficial burnish.

Two fragments of shoulder with warts and a large strap handle of rectangular section from the same deposit in House V seem to belong to this vase.

(F) LIDS 1296–1302 (FIG. 188)

Lids were much more in evidence than they had been during previous periods. Several complete or nearly complete ones were recovered from destruction levels of Period IV. These were mostly varieties of type 63, but types 61 and 62 were also represented.

61. *Flat lid with handle*

1296. (IV R 26, House IV) (PLATE 73) This appears to belong to the jar 1236. Complete, except for part of edge missing. Diam. *c.* 14.5. Irregular; soft fabric; orange clay with large white grit; surface light brown to red with dusky patches, well burnished.

62. *Flanged cover*

1297. (IV R 26, House IV) (PLATE 72) Lid of 1232. Pair of string-holes each side. Virtually complete. Ht. 4.2. Diam. 10. Rather coarse gritty grey clay; inside surface black, outside grey-brown shading to light brown and reddish, burnished but much pitted. Bold incised decoration on top surface; no traces of white fill.

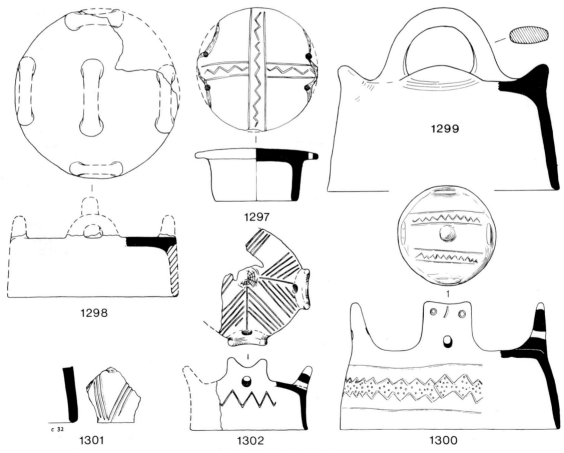

FIG. 188. Periods V–IV. Lids. Scale 1/3.

63. *Covers with handles or lugs on top*

1298. (IV R 26, House IV) Variety B: with central handle and four smaller ones round edge. Only part of top preserved; sides and handles missing. Diam. 13. Orange clay; surface red to light brown, burnished.

1299. (V/IV X 60/40/25) (PLATE 77) Variety C: with central strap handle and four warts round edge. Complete and unbroken. Ht. 14.5. Diam. 19. Outside light brown shading to red, inside dark brown to black, burnished.

1300. (IV G 26, House VIII) (PLATE 77) Variety D: with conical spike-shaped wart in centre of top and four perforated horned lugs round edge. Broken, but virtually complete. Diam. 19. Sandy grey to reddish clay; surface shades of light and dark brown mottling to black and reddish; high burnish inside and out. Elaborate incised and punctuated decoration; white fill very well preserved.

1301. (IV G 25, north of wall 50) (PLATE 75) Fragment of rim from large lid. Surface dark purplish brown; fine burnish on outside. Incised chevrons with white fill.

1302. (IV R 26, House IV) (PLATE 77) Small lid of variety D, with wart in centre of top and four perforated horned lugs round edge. Only half preserved. Ht. 5. Diam. 9.5. Surface grey-brown with a purplish tinge; very fine burnish. Incised zig-zag round side with traces of original white fill.

Cf. *Poliochni* i 576 pls. lxvi: f; lxvii: c, evolved Blue period, for a fragment of a similar lid with a zigzag line incised on the side.

(G) MINIATURE VASES 1303–1305 (FIG. 189)

A few vases from levels of V were of the miniature class which was very well represented at Thermi (*Thermi* pls. xli–xliii). But no examples of miniature vases were recovered from the Period IV destruction levels.

1303. (V H 76) Bowl cf. type 5, with single lug or wart below rim; rounded base. Complete and unbroken. Ht. 3.4. Diam. 4.5. Coarse dark grey clay with large white grit showing in surface, which is light brown to orange, unburnished.

1304. (V R ?73) (PLATE 76) Apparently a jug or jar, with lug or stump of handle 'pushed through' side; flat base. Rim missing. Ht. as preserved 4.1. Diam. 4.5. Dark grey clay; surface light yellowish brown, unburnished.

1305. (VI/V Q wall 22) (PLATE 76) Lid cf. *Thermi* pl. xxxix, type VI *c*; or a bowl with sunk base cf. *Thermi* pl. xli, Nos. 7, 11, 14. Complete and unbroken. Ht. 2.1. Diam. 3. Orange-red clay; surface unburnished.

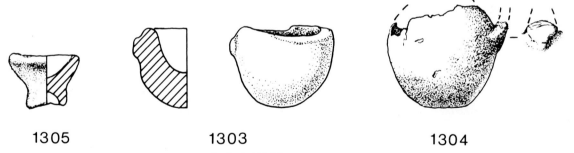

1305 **1303** **1304**

FIG. 189. Period V. Miniature vases. Scale 2/3.

(I) HANDLES AND LUGS

(1) *Bowls* 1306–1315 (FIGS. 106, 190–192)

Handles. In contrast to the situation in Periods VII–VI many bowls now had handles. These were either horizontal, or less commonly vertical.

(a) Vertical. Large vertical handles (FIG. 106: 1) rising from the rim were by definition the hall-mark of dipper cups of type 16, and small bowls of various types were classified as dipper cups because they had such handles. Some of these dipper cup handles were horned or

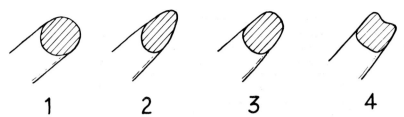

FIG. 190. Periods V–IV. Sections of bowl handles: 1. circular; 2. pointed oval; 3. sub-rectangular; 4. rectangular, hollow.

surmounted by warts. But vertical handles also occurred on several larger bowls, mostly of type 9, either rising from the rim like those of dipper cups, or set below it as FIG. 106: 3.

(b) Horizontal. These were much more common on bowls than vertical handles. They were normally simple and rounded in shape (FIG. 107: 1), but often pointed as FIG. 107: 2 (cf. PLATE 77 (c) 2, from V R level 59); or slightly ogival as FIG. 107: 3, especially it would seem on carinated bowls of the common type 9. Some horizontal bowl handles have a nick (FIG. 107: 4), which if widened gives the handle a pair of horns as FIG. 107: 5 (cf. PLATE 77 (c) 1, from V G level 54). In section these horizontal side handles were normally more or less circular or thick oval (FIG. 190: 1); sometimes pointed oval (2), or rectangular (3); once or twice rectangular with a hollow in the outer face as FIG. 190: 4. Horizontal side handles were usually set on or just below the rim. In a few instances, however, fragments of rim had the stumps of horizontal handles rising from the top of them as commonly in Periods X–VII (FIG. 106: 5) (e.g. 1072 on PLATE 58); but some of these at any rate may be earlier strays. There was only one doubtful example of a horned lug-handle (FIG. 106: 8 b) of the type common in Period II. Two other lug-handles (FIG. 106: 9, 10) were of types more characteristic of Periods X–VIII; one of these (9) is 1308, the other (10) is on 1083 of type 13 from the Period IV destruction level in House VII.

Lugs. Projections rising from the rims of bowls as FIG. 106: 16, 17, and 26, while not common, seem to be characteristic of this horizon. There is a large projection with a vertical strap handle set below it (26) on the fragment 1118 of a bowl of type 14 from V R wall 37. A double projection with a horizontal trumpet lug below it from V H level 49 comes from a bowl of type 5 or 6 with

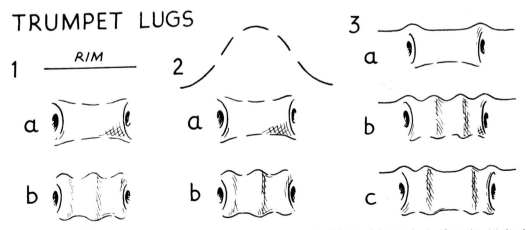

FIG. 191. Periods V–IV. Trumpet lugs on bowls: 1. below rim: (a) simple, (b) ribbed; 2. below projection from rim: (a) simple, (b) ribbed; 3. on rim: (a) simple, (b), (c) ribbed.

grey-brown burnished surface; and large projections with horned (16) or serrated (17) tops and horizontal trumpet lugs below them occur on a few bowls from Period IV destruction levels.

Trumpet lugs, common in Periods VII–VI, were clearly still at home in V–IV. Some twenty were recognized from levels of V, although a number of these may be earlier strays. They are attested, however, on four of the vases from Period IV destruction levels. Most, if not all, trumpet lugs from the horizon of V–IV belonged to bowls, and in every case where it was possible to judge they had been set horizontally; there was no evidence for the existence of vertical trumpet lugs in this horizon. They were placed on the body of the vase below the rim (as FIG. 191: 1), or occasionally below a projection rising from it (2); most of those from levels of V were set on the outside of the rim with the raised ends projecting slightly above the line of it (FIG. 191: 3). But the lugs with the ends rising high above the rim in elegant horns, as found on some vases of Periods VII–VI (FIG. 105: 23), are hardly attested in V–IV. A few trumpet lugs, about half a dozen in all, have one or sometimes two ribs (as FIG. 191: 1 b, 2 b, and 3 b, c). In one case at least a trumpet lug has a wart in the middle.

One or two other lugs with ribs at the sides from levels of V might be considered as varieties of trumpet lugs (e.g. 1310) (FIG. 106: 22). Tubular lugs as FIG. 106: 29 with their tops rising slightly above the level of the rim are attested from levels of V. The tubular lug 913 set below a type 5 bowl rim has finger tip impressions on the outside (FIG. 106: 30). Other horizontally perforated lugs of various kinds seem more characteristic of V than of IV; some may be earlier strays.

1306. (V R 50) Handle, apparently from bowl. Purplish grey-brown, burnished. Decorated with stripes in white paint. Probably a stray of Periods VII–VI.

1307. (V H ?50) (PLATE 78) Fragment, apparently from side handle cf. FIG. 107: 5. Light brown to red; fine burnish. Incised decoration on upper side.

1308. (V/IV G 54/36) Lug handle cf. FIG. 106: 9. Grey-brown, burnished.
     Cf. *Poliochni* i pl. xxxix: f (xl: i), evolved Blue period, but this is horned and has only two perforations.

1309. (V H 84/79/78) Trumpet lug with ribs, from rim of bowl apparently cf. type 6. Fabric akin to Silvery Grey Ware. Grey clay; surface light greyish brown, burnished.

1310. (V H 49) (FIG. 106: 22. PLATE 58) Horizontally perforated lug with vertical ribs, apparently from bowl of type 9. Black clay with white grit; inside surface shades of brown with poor burnish, outside dark brown to black, with high polish-like burnish but much worn.

1311. (V R 50) Horizontally perforated lug, from bowl of types 6–8; apparently begun as a triple vertically perforated lug, but changed to one horizontally perforated while clay still wet (compare 1067). Irregular; surface shades of light and dark brown; fine burnish.

1312. (V R ?73) Horizontally perforated lug as FIG. 106: 28; from bowl of type 9 (?). Grey-brown; fine polish-like burnish.

1313. (IV R 26, House V) Horizontally perforated lug as FIG. 106: 27. Soft fabric; surface much pitted, black, burnished.

1314. (VI/V G/H 88, H 48) (PLATE 65) Double horizontally perforated lug, from bowl of types 13 or 14. Perhaps set below horned projection rising from rim cf. 1081 of type 13. Surface light brown with fine burnish, but worn. Elaborate incised decoration: zigzag flanked by lines on both sides of rim; vertical strip of pointillé-filled diamonds below lug.

1315. (IV H 25, west of wall 38 in area of hearth B) (PLATE 58) Horned lug with double perforations, projecting from rim; apparently from bowl of type 13 or 14. Soft fabric; dark grey clay; surface light brown, burnished but much worn.

(2) *Jugs and jars etc.*

Vertical handles (FIGS. 106, 108, 192). Over 5,600 fragments of vertical handles of the kind found on jugs and jars were recovered from levels of Period V, and several hundred from those of IV. These handles were for the most part more or less oval in section as FIG. 108: 2, sometimes circular (1), semi-circular (6), lunate (7), kidney-shaped (8), or rectangular (10); several were hollow rectangular as FIG. 108: 11. There were also a very few true strap handles, thin and straight as

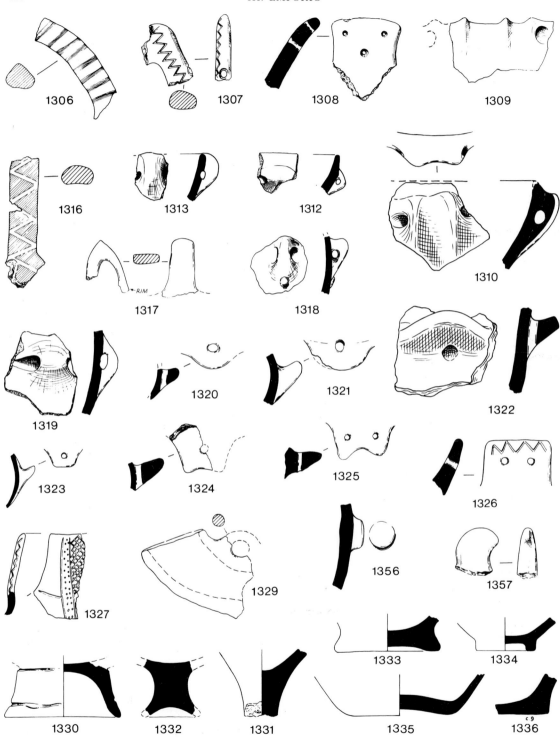

FIG. 192. Periods V–IV. Handles, lugs, spouts and bases. Scale 1/3.

FIG. 108: 4, or hollow (5). One or two handles of rectangular section had a rib (FIG. 108: 12), while four or five others with ribs were oval (13) or ogival (14) in section. One handle of ribbed ogival section from a level of V had a wart on it. A few small lug-handles were noted, mostly from levels of V; some of these at least may have been earlier strays. In several cases the base of a handle was markedly differentiated (e.g. PLATES 79 (a) 1, from IV Q 26, House VII; and 78 (b) 5, from VI/V R ?87); all of these differentiated handles appear to have belonged to jugs.

Although jugs with comparatively narrow necks were now common, very few handles were of the true 'pushed-through' type: only two were noted from levels of V, and four from those of IV, all of them coming from the destruction level (Q 26) in House VII—two being on the unique narrow-necked jugs 1168–9, one on the askos 1171; the fourth (PLATE 79 (a) 3) was evidently from a similar vase.

Some eight horned handles, resembling but not absolutely identical with those characteristic of the lowest levels (Periods X–VIII), were recovered from deposits of V; and similar horned handles occur on one or two of the distinctive dipper cups of type 16 from the Period IV destruction levels (e.g. 1139). Occasionally handles were of the sharp-angled 'elbow' type, which may be a degenerate version of a horned handle (e.g. PLATE 78 (b) 1, from V R ?50).

Warts occurred on some 80 of the 5,627 handle fragments from levels of V— an average of about 1 in 70 (PLATE 78 (a) 2, 3, from V H 78 and IV H 35). Only two of the complete or nearly complete jugs from destruction levels of IV (1154 and 1158) had their handles surmounted by warts, but warts existed on at least four handles of dipper cups (type 16) and on three other fragments of handles from deposits of IV; they were therefore as much in evidence on handles in IV as in V. Two handles from levels of V had a pair of warts in line down the length, while two or three others boasted a pair set across the width. Warts were normally more or less conical, but might be disc-shaped with the top flat or sunk (e.g. PLATE 78 (b) 2, 6, from V G/H 85 and VI/V G/H 88). One handle from V had an oblong wart across the width (PLATE 78 (a) 1, from V H 49). In three or four instances a wart was noted at the base of a handle (PLATES 78 (b) 4, from V G 70; 79 (a) 2, and (b) 2, both from IV G 25: and 1318); but the latter (1318) is a small lug-handle of a type at home in earlier periods, and may be a stray from them.

In six instances, all from levels of V, handles with warts were decorated with incision. Traces of incised decoration were noted on some 75 handles (including the six with warts) from levels of V—an average of about 1 in 75. Decoration in white (e.g. 1316) was very rare, in marked contrast to Periods VII–VI; only four examples of handles with painted decoration in white were recovered from levels of V, and one of these (ribbed, and with wavy lines in white) came from a mixed level (VI/V G 88) and may well be of Period VI date. Three handles from V had traces of holes made before firing like a number of handles from levels of IX–VI (e.g. 347).

Horizontal side handles. These were now common on jars, especially on ones of type 47C. Six slashed handles were recovered from levels of V (e.g. PLATE 78 (a) 4, from V R wall 43); all bore traces of a red wash, except one from a mixed level (VI/V H 92) whose surface was light brown with possible traces of burnish. A pair of slashed handles is also found on the large jar 1233 from the Period IV destruction level in House IV.

Lugs. Perforated lugs were not common in V–IV; they occurred, however, on jars, mostly on small pyxides of type 44, but also in a large form on vases of considerable size like 1231 of type 43 from the Period IV destruction level in House IV; and they were also placed on the lids, large (1300) and small (1302), of type 63D which were designed for such vases. Lugs when they are found on the bodies of jars are regularly upturned, and often square-ended or horned (FIG. 106:

31). The simple perforated lugs as FIG. 106: 32 a, characteristic of earlier periods, are less in evidence, and some, if not all, of the few recovered from the horizon of V–IV may be earlier strays.

String-holes made before firing occurred on lids of type 62 (e.g. 1297), and on a few rims of pyxides of the kind which might have had lids to tie on them (e.g. 1259).

Rivet-holes made after firing, common in the early periods X–VIII and attested in VII–VI, were scarcely noted in V–IV.

1316. (V G/Q 70) Strap handle with painted decoration in white. Roughly made; surface purplish grey-brown, burnished.
    Possibly a stray of Period VI. But a handle and other fragments with white-painted decoration were found in late Troy I contexts (*Troy* i 79 fig. 249: 25).
1317. (VI/V R ?87) (PLATE 78) Elbow handle; from a jug, and probably rising high above rim cf. type 23B. Light brown to reddish, burnished.
    Cf. elbow handles from early but also from late Troy I contexts (*Troy* i 98 figs. 235: 14, 15, Troy, I a; 236: 22, 23, Troy I b. Ibid., 124, 152, 178 fig. 245: 17–20). Cf. *Poliochni* i pl. xlvii: j–l, evolved Blue period, also apparently from jugs. Some handles of the earlier part of the Late Neolithic in Thessaly are not altogether dissimilar (e.g. *Arapi* pl. 8: 22, Tsangli ((Dhimini 1) phase of L.N.). What may be earlier relatives of Trojan elbow handles seem at home in E.B. 1–2 in the Konya plain (*AS* xiii (1963) 217 fig. 9: 34–36, 40, 41).
1318. (V R 59) Small lug-like handle with wart at base. Grey-brown clay; surface uneven, lightish brown, burnished inside and out.
    Possibly a stray of Period VIII, but such handles occur in mature Neolithic and later contexts on the Greek mainland (e.g. *Athenian Agora* xiii 45 pl. 13: 189. *Ayia Sofia Magula* 7 pl. 8: 10, assigned to the Rakhmani period).
1319. (VI/V Q wall 22) Horizontally perforated lug. Hard grey-brown clay; surface shades of dusky and dark to light brown and reddish; traces of burnish. Perhaps an earlier stray.
1320. (VI/V Q wall 22) Vertically perforated lug, upturned; probably from a pyxis cf. type 44. Soft fabric; coarse gritty grey-brown clay; surface purplish brown, unburnished.
1321. (V H 49) Vertically perforated lug, upturned; from large jar or cooking pot. Coarse cooking pot type ware; surface shades of purple-brown and reddish with abundant straw impressions; traces of superficial burnish. Another (V G 85) of similar fabric; outside surface grey-brown, inside reddish with poor burnish.
1322. (IV H 25, west of wall 38 in area of hearth B) Vertically perforated lug, upturned; from large jar. Very coarse dark grey to black clay with grit and abundant straw showing in surface, which has a red wash outside and traces of poor stroke burnish.
1323. (V R 50) Vertically perforated lug, upturned with square end; from body of pyxis cf. type 44. Outside surface black, burnished.
1324. (IV G 26, House VIII) Vertically perforated lug, upturned and horned; apparently from body of pyxis cf. type 44. Inside surface rough, dull black; outside grey with fine burnish. Incised decoration. Two others similar (V Q ?70, IV G 36) from pyxides with incised decoration.
1325. (V/IV X 60/40/25) Double vertically perforated lug, upturned and horned. Irregular. Soft fabric; surface dark brown shading to light brown and red, due to a wash, burnished.
    Similar lugs were common on bowls of class A in Towns I–III at Thermi (*Thermi* 77 fig. 27: 3, 4).
1326. (IV H/R 26, House IV) Double vertically perforated lug with square end. Surface dark to light brown; fine burnish. Incised zigzag on upper side; remains of white fill.

(J) SPOUTS 1327–1329 (FIG. 192)

Jug spouts were of various kinds (FIG. 175). Cutaway spouts like those of jugs of type 24 also occurred on askoi (type 25). Open trough-like spouts akin to them were occasionally found on bowls (e.g. 1051–2 of type 9, and 1327), all apparently of Period IV and not earlier. Some five nozzle spouts, mostly it would seem from jars, were noted from levels of V–IV (e.g. 1328). In two instances (1193 and 1329) these spouts were joined by a small handle on the top to the rim or side of the vase.

1327. (IV X 41) (PLATE 65) Open spout, evidently from bowl. Surface dark shading to light brown, burnished.

Elaborate incised decoration on underneath and sides; traces of white fill. Another similar (IV H 26, House IV) with surface light greyish brown, burnished.

1328. (V R ?73) (PLATE 77) Nozzle spout, from carinated vase. Silvery Grey Ware; surface grey-brown to black, burnished.

1329. (VI/V R ?87) (PLATE 77) Nozzle spout with handle at top: cf. 1193, and one from Stage 3 in area F. Roughly made; surface light greyish brown, burnished.

(K) BASES 1330–1336 (FIGS. 109, 192)

Bases were normally flat or roughly flattened (class 6), often sunk (class 5). The markedly sunk base 1335 may come from a large bowl. Sometimes bases were rounded, especially it would seem in the case of the bowls of type 13 with elaborate incised decoration (e.g. 1077, 1079).

The bowl 859 of type 4 from the Period IV destruction level in House IV has a high pedestal (class 1), and one or two fragments that might come from high pedestals of this class were recovered from levels of V. But pedestal feet of class 2, while not common, appear to be more at home than pedestals of class 1 both in V and IV; most, if not all, of them may come from bowls (e.g. 1050–1 of type 9). A couple of bowls of type 14 (1107 and 1116) appear to have had wide ring bases of some kind.

1330. (V Q 75) Pedestal foot (class 2A); from bowl. Dark grey clay with grit; surface dark brown to black, with fine burnish inside and out. Bold irregular groove round edge of rim, as if cord or twig been tied round it while clay still wet; traces of similar groove at point of junction of foot and bowl.

1331. (V R 59) Solid pedestal foot (class 2B); from bowl (?). Gritty grey-black clay; surface silvery, slightly pitted and stroke burnished inside and out.

1332. (IV R ?39) Solid pedestal foot (class 2B); from bowl (?). Hard fabric; surface grey-brown, burnished. Another similar from VI/V X ?98.

1333. (V H wall 37) High ring foot (class 3A); from bowl. Hard grey-brown clay; inside surface with a red wash, burnished; underneath of foot light brown, burnished.

1334. (V R 59) Low ring foot with straight sides (class 4B); from bowl (?). Surface grey to light brown, stroke burnished inside and out.

1335. (IV R 26) Sunk base (class 5C); from large bowl (?). Coarse grey clay; outside surface light brown and purplish with a tinge of red, inside dusky to reddish; poor burnish.

1336. (V/IV X no level) Flat base (class 6A); from jar (?). Light brownish grey clay; surface light orange-brown with slight stroke burnish. Possibly an earlier stray.

DECORATION 1337–1357

When decoration occurs in V–IV it is normally incised. The incisions often retain traces of a fill of white paste, and this white fill was probably normal; it may have disappeared in many instances where no remains of it are now visible. White-filled incisions would have created much the same effect, but in a more vivid and enduring manner, as the white-painted decoration fashionable during the preceding periods VII–VI. White paint applied to the burnished surfaces of vases must have been very evanescent, and white-filled incisions were no doubt adopted as an improvement. Incisions filled with white paste to form a surface flush with that of the vase as found in Periods V–IV have more in common with the white-painted decoration of Periods VII–VI than with the earlier cycle of incised decoration of Periods X–VIII, which depended for effect on the play of shadows in the hollows of the incisions. In this early phase (X–VIII) at Emporio the use of white paste to fill incisions is only attested in the case of one or two fragments from the top level 139 of VIII in G, and it is excessively rare in VII–VI.

Decoration in relief is common in the horizon of V–IV in the form of warts of various shapes on vases of many different types; but ribs, although somewhat rare, also occur, notably on jugs and pithoi.

Pattern burnish

True pattern burnish of the kind which was common and characteristic in Period VIII appears to have entirely ceased by now. The very few scraps from bowls with pattern burnish—two rims and three or four other fragments—all come from levels of V and appear to be earlier strays. On a few bowl fragments, however, which evidently belong to the horizon of V–IV, the very fine thorough burnishing of the surface has created a rippled effect, and this may, or may not, have been deliberate.

Paint

Decoration in white paint was also rare in V–IV. Some ten fragments with white painted decoration were recovered from levels of V, and three from those of IV. Most of these fragments evidently belonged to jugs of Fine Black Burnished Ware of the kind characteristic of VII–VI; they include the elegant strap handle 1316 of oval section with a zigzag in white down the length of it, and another handle from V with a double chevron on it. Fragments from the bodies of jugs or jars from levels of V are painted with triple chevrons, or in one case (from V H level 59) with a cross-hatched diamond. The large handle 1306 of triangular section evidently comes from a bowl.

While all these fragments might be strays from Periods VII–VI, it is quite possible that the fashion for making vases with white-painted decoration continued into V–IV, if not at Emporio itself, then in some nearby area from which occasional imports reached the site. The jug of which a large fragment (1148) was recovered from V R level 50 certainly seems to be of contemporary date, whether made at Emporio or imported from elsewhere. Similarly at Troy it was suggested that the few pieces with white-painted decoration found in levels of Troy I, roughly corresponding to Emporio V–IV, might have come from imported pots, or reflect the influence of a foreign tradition of vase decoration (*Troy* i 79). There were only 21 of these white-painted fragments in all, but they were recovered from various strata of Troy I ranging from the end of the Early or beginning of the Middle Subperiod to the Late Subperiod (ibid. 52).

Incision

This was by far the commonest type of decoration in both Periods V and IV. Vases with incised decoration, however, were comparatively few in number as compared with those without any form of decoration at all. Incised decoration occurred on jugs and jars of various types, both large and small; but in the case of bowls it was virtually confined to ones of types 13 and 14, and it was especially at home on bowls of type 13 with outward curving rims internally differentiated and thickened. On these bowls the decoration was usually limited to the area of the rim, where zigzags, single (sometimes with flanking lines) as FIG. 114 Nos. 1–3, or double as Nos. 4–6, appear both inside and out, or inside, or outside, alone. A row of chevrons, with or without flanking lines, as FIG. 114 Nos. 8–10, is found on the rims of a few large bowls of types 13–14 from levels of V (e.g. 1086 and PLATE 65 (*a*) 3). Once or twice lattice or cross-hatching occurs, as FIG. 114 No. 11 (e.g. 1073, 1091). In one single instance a bowl of type 9 (1025) had been decorated with rows of zigzags round the outside of the rim and below it (PLATE 65). A solitary bowl rim assigned to type 4 (see under 852) had incised decoration round the inside edge like some rims of bowls of types 13 and 14. On a number of bowls of type 13 vertical strips of incised decoration were carried down the sides (FIG. 114 Nos. 12–19); the strips may have met on the underneath of the bases where these were rounded (e.g. 1077, 1079).

It seems to have been exceptional, however, for the whole outside surface of a vase to be used as a field for decoration in this manner. Some lids (e.g. 1300) and askoi (e.g. 1171), and a number of small jars (pyxides) of type 44, appear indeed to have been covered with incised decoration; while a few jugs had incised and relief decoration running over the whole of the body (e.g. 1146 and 1165). But decoration on jugs and jars when it occurred was normally confined to the shoulder, the lower part of the body being left plain. The whole of the neck and the rim was also usually left plain, but the neck of the large jar 1238 had a band of incised chevrons on it.

As in earlier periods motifs of decoration were almost invariably linear. The one obvious exception is the dot-filled oval (FIG. 115 No. 36) on 1351, which has an exact counterpart from an early level of Troy I, where other similar (although rare) curvilinear designs are also attested (*Troy* i 77 fig. 235: 18). Zigzags, multiple chevrons, and lattice or cross-hatching (FIGS. 114 Nos. 11, 13; 115 No. 25), as found in earlier periods, are well represented in V–IV. Zigzags and rows of chevrons or dashes are often flanked by incised lines (FIGS. 114 Nos. 2, 3, 9, 10; 115 Nos. 9, 12–14, 18–20). Multiple chevrons bisected by a line are not uncommon (FIG. 115 Nos. 4, 5, 16, 17). Wide bands of multiple chevrons of the type noted from levels of the earliest periods (X–VIII) still occur (FIGS. 114 No. 14; 115 No. 26, which is from 1339). Hatched bands and hatched chevrons (FIG. 115 Nos. 27–29) are in evidence, although not common; they were already attested in Period VI (e.g. 803: PLATE 49 (*d*)), but do not seem to occur earlier. Inverted hatched triangles, as FIGS. 114 No. 7 and 115 No. 30, are also found in incision now. A similar hatched triangle, but painted in white, was noted on the inside of a bowl rim (568) from a level of Period VII. Bands or chevrons consisting of a pair of lines with a row of dots or dashes down the centre, as FIG. 115 Nos. 6 and 20, are not uncommon (e.g. 1165); sometimes there are two or more rows of dots (FIGS. 114 No. 15B; 115 No. 32).

Panels or areas of various shapes filled with dots (pointillé), already well attested in Period VI, and occurring it seems as early as VIII, are now common and characteristic. They are normally bounded by incised lines (FIGS. 114 Nos. 16–19; 115 Nos. 33–38). Designs include chevrons (FIGS. 114 No. 17; 115 Nos. 33, 34) and rows of diamonds (FIGS. 114 No. 18; 115 Nos. 35, 38B), which may coalesce to form a continuous serrated band as FIGS. 114 No. 19 and 115 No. 37. Rows or areas of dots also occur without a boundary of incised lines, as on 1340 (FIG. 115 No. 31).

A row of dashes, single or double as FIG. 115 No. 21, is sometimes found on jugs and jars at the top of the shoulder immediately below the join with the neck. Dashes also appear on the necks of some jugs (e.g. 1161, 1165), and on handles of the jar 1233 (cf. FIG. 116 No. 3). Another motif of decoration commonly found at the top of the shoulder where it joins the neck is a row of incisions, either diagonal as on 1354 and the jug 1165, or upright (FIG. 115 No. 22). A row of small chevrons as FIG. 115 No. 10 appears in this position on the large jar 1233; while small circles hanging from stalks (FIG. 115 No. 23) are found here on the finely decorated jar 1239. Small circles like these, made with the end of a reed, were to become a common motif of decoration in Period II; but the only earlier examples of them at Emporio, apart from the fragment 1355 which looks as if it may be a Period II intruder, were on this vase 1239 and on the lid 1300 (where each of the four lugs had a pair of circles on it as FIG. 115 No. 24), both from Period IV destruction levels. Similar reed-made circles, however, occur on vases at Troy from the beginning of Troy I onwards (e.g. *Troy* i fig. 235: 19, from Troy I a).

Pairs of eyes, consisting of a diamond with a dot at the centre, appear on the necks of the two unique jugs 1168–9 of type 24B from the Period IV destruction level in House VII. One other fragment (from V/IV X 60/40/25), apparently a jug mouth, had a similar eye incised on it. Faces with eyes of a comparable sort are found on the rims of bowls similar to our type 12 in Troy I (e.g. *Troy* i figs. 234: 4, 19; 257). The fragment 1353, evidently from the neck of a large jar, has rough pock-marks which seem to have been made on purpose at some point after the vase was fired.

A good many handles from jugs and jars bore incised decoration, usually chevrons (PLATE 79 (*d*), (*e*)). A simple row of chevrons as FIG. 116 No. 8 occurs on about a third of these incised handles, and multiple chevrons (FIG. 116 No. 13) are not uncommon. Motifs like FIG. 116 Nos. 3–6, 14, 15, are rare; while Nos. 16–18 are only represented by a single example each.

1337. (IV/V H 92) (PLATE 79) Fragment of bowl or open jar. Hard fabric; surface light brownish grey, burnished. Two rows of large impressed dots cf. FIG. 115 No. 31.

1338. (VI/V H 92) (PLATE 55) Fragment of small jar, perhaps neck of pyxis cf. type 44. Soft fabric; surface grey-brown, burnished outside, rough inside. Zigzag between lines cf. FIG. 115 No. 9.

1339. (VI/V G 88) (PLATE 49) Fragment from body of large vase. Gritty lightish brown clay; surface pale light brown, with traces of burnish outside. Vertical zone of multiple chevrons cf. FIGS. 114 No. 14; 115 No. 26.

1340. (V G wall 23) (PLATE 80) Fragment of large jar. Surface light brown; rather poor burnish outside. Chevrons made with bold shallow grooves, and group of large dots.

1341. (IV H ?37) (PLATE 80) Fragment of large jar or jug. Surface light greyish; fine burnish. Wide band with five rows of small dots cf. FIG. 115 No. 32.

1342. (V G/Q 70) (PLATE 80) Fragment of jar. Soft fabric; surface light greyish; outside once apparently with burnished red wash, but much worn. Elaborate chevrons with fill of dots cf. FIG. 115 No. 33.

1343. (V R ?50) (PLATE 80) Fragment from neck of jar cf. 1338. Surface grey-brown, very worn. Row of diamonds filled with dots between lines cf. FIG. 115 No. 35.

1344. (V R 50) (PLATE 80) Fragment, perhaps from neck of large jug or jar. Surface dark greyish, very worn. Zigzag running through dot-filled band, above row of diamonds filled with dots as on 1343; incisions with traces of white paste. Cf. FIG. 115 No. 38.

1345. (V H ?50 (PLATE 80) Fragment from body of bowl or jar with rounded carination. Surface light brownish grey; fine burnish inside and out. Row of diagonal cuts on carination like those on FIG. 115 No. 22.

1346. (V G 85) (FIG. 115 No. 25) Fragment, possibly an earlier stray, as surface very worn, light greyish, but perhaps once light brown, burnished.

1347. (V H 48) (FIG. 115 No. 15) Fragment from belly of jug (?). Outside surface dull light brown to greyish, burnished. Wart on swelling flanked by vertical zigzags between lines.

1348. (V R no level) (PLATE 75. FIG. 115 No. 16) Surface black, burnished. Wart on swelling with vertical row of empaled chevrons rising from it.

1349. (V H 49) (PLATE 75, where upside down! FIG. 115 No. 19) Fragment from shoulder of jug (?). Outside surface dark reddish brown with fine burnish. Row of dashes below join with neck; chevron filled with chevrons; white fill.

1350. (V R 50) (PLATE 75) Fragment from shoulder of jug or jar. Surface grey-brown, burnished. Double row of dashes cf. FIG. 115 No. 21 below join with neck.

1351. (V R 50) (PLATE 75) Fragment from neck of jug or jar. Surface grey-brown, burnished but much worn. Oval filled with dots cf. FIG. 115 No. 36.

1352. (V H 78) (PLATE 55. FIG. 115 No. 34) Fragment from shoulder of small jar, perhaps pyxis cf. type 44. Soft fabric; surface black, burnished. Zigzag filled with dots.

1353. (V/IV X 60/40/25) (PLATE 79). Fragment, apparently from neck of large jar. Inside surface red, outside shades of dark and light reddish brown with poor burnish. Roughly pocked designs, evidently deliberate, made after firing.

1354. (V R 50) (PLATE 80) Shoulder of jug or jar. Surface dark brown to reddish, burnished. Row of dashes above row of dots round top of shoulder.

1355. (V H 48) (PLATE 80) Fragment of large jar. Hard fabric; outside surface red-brown, well burnished; inside purple, strongly wiped. Row of reed-stampled circles with lattice above. In fabric and style of decoration cf. Period II from which it may be a stray.

Relief

Warts (FIG. 193) were extremely common, occurring on bowls as well as jars, but especially on jugs which regularly had three warts on the swelling—one opposite the handle, and one in the

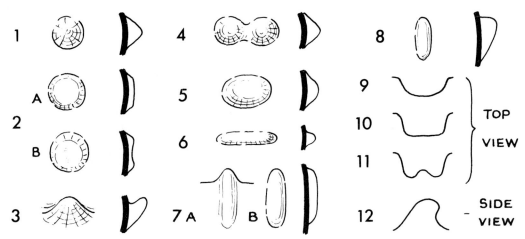

FIG. 193. Periods V–IV. Warts and solid lugs: circular, with pointed (1), flattened (2A), or sunk (2B) top, or upturned (3); double circular (4); oval (5); oblong (6); vertical (7); vertical, akin to animal head (8); semi-circular (9); rectangular (10); horned (11); hooked (12).

centre of each side. Warts were normally circular, either pointed (FIG. 193: 1) or sometimes flat-topped (2A). Hollow-topped circular warts (FIG. 193: 2B) occur on a fragment from IV G level 25 (PLATE 79 (*b*) 1); on the carination of a vase, probably a bowl, with a finely burnished light brown surface from IV R level 35; and on a fragment of pithos from IV: similar hollow-topped warts are attested in Troy I (e.g. *Troy* i figs. 245: 30; 247: 8). Upturned warts as FIG. 193: 3 are often found on bowls, and occasionally on jugs and jars. Pairs of warts, as on 1235, and double warts (FIG. 193: 4), also occur. A row of circular warts appears on a solitary fragment from V R ?50, apparently from the swelling of a large jug, with a finely burnished black surface; while a group of three warts was set vertically on the front of the jug 1163. Oval warts (FIG. 193: 5) commonly occur on bowls, and thinner oblong (6) and vertical (7) warts are attested on vases of all kinds, vertical warts being particularly favoured for the rims of cooking vessels, as 1278 (cf. PLATE 75 (*a*) 1–5). On these they often project above the line of the rim as FIG. 193: 7A; they also sometimes do this when they occur on bowls (e.g. 1050 of type 9).

Vertical warts occasionally have an inverted nose-like profile as FIG. 193: 8. This is seen in its most exaggerated form in an example from a low level of Period V (V G 85). In shape such lugs recall the perforated animal head lugs of Period VIII (365–8) and a comparable one (1723) from a level of II. Solid lugs, of the same shape as the perforated lugs found on small jars of the pyxis type and on lids, also occur (FIG. 193: 9–11); these are usually on bowls. Two carinated bowls of type 9 (1030 and 1045) are provided with horned warts as FIG. 193: 11. The hooked knob 1357 (FIG. 193: 12) is unique, and may have come from the top of a lid.

Ribbed decoration seems to have been virtually confined to jugs and pithoi; but some

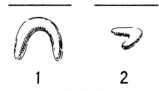

FIG. 194. Periods V–IV. Relief decoration.

fragments of small closed vases with ribbed decoration may have come from jars (pyxides) cf. type 44. About thirty fragments of vases with ribbed decoration (other than pithoi) were recovered from levels of Period V alone. The ribs normally seem to have run vertically down the body of the vase, and might be combined with incision, as on 1146. Examples of more elaborate relief decoration include 1147 where three ribs meet at the top in a wart. Another fragment (IV R 26, House VI) apparently from a jug has a wavy rib in relief like the 'snake' that adorned a pithos (297) of Period X. Some half a dozen fragments of vases (mostly it seems bowls) from levels of V have a horseshoe in relief as found on some bowls of Periods X–VIII (FIG. 194: 1): similar relief decoration appears on Early Bronze Age bowls from Anatolia (e.g. Asarcik Hüyük near Ilica: *Ist. Mitt.* xvi (1966) 61 f. figs. 1: 6, 8; 2: 5, 8, Level V, E.B. 2–3). An arrow-shaped motif (FIG. 194: 2) occurs below a jar rim with a black burnished surface from V R ?73.

1357. (IV R 26, House IV) (PLATE 79 (*b*). FIG. 193: 12) Hooked knob, perhaps from top of lid. Grey-brown to light brown, burnished.

IMPORTS 1358–1366

Some of the slashed jar handles from levels of V–IV may have belonged to imported vases. Possibly the large jar 1233 from the Period IV destruction level with handles of this type was an import, or, if not, a copy of a foreign vase. The double vase 1280, and some of the small jars (pyxides) of type 44 with elaborate incised decoration, of which a number of fragments were recovered from levels of V, may also have been imports, but their fabric was not essentially different from that of local wares. Another possible import already described is the jar rim 1222.

Several fragments of Early Helladic II vases were reported from the Middle and Late Subperiods of Troy I. The Early and Middle Subperiods of Troy I may have more or less overlapped with Emporio V–IV; but only one fragment (1358) from this horizon at Emporio was recognized as likely to be from an Early Helladic II import, although one other might pass for a local imitation of Early Helladic ware (see under 1358).

1358. (V G/Q 70) Fragment of vase. Possibly Early Helladic II imported from Greek mainland. Rather soft fabric; clay grey in break, with abundant grit and straw; many fine straw impressions showing in surface, especially on inside. Outside with dark reddish brown wash with very slight lustre; inside buff, with streaks of same wash, but rather thin and light brown in colour.

   A fragment (VI/V H 92/78) may be a local copy of imported glazed ware. From a jar or jug. Fabric indistinguishable from other local wares. Soft clay, black at core, with abundant straw temper; straw impressions showing in surface, which is pitted. Outside with a dark purplish brown wash, slightly lustrous and not apparently burnished, across which runs a broad stripe (evidently a chance trickle) of the same wash, but lighter orange-brown in colour.

1359. (IV H 26, House IV, or II X 15/14/13/7) (PLATE 90) Fragment of bowl with side handle of thick oval section. Hard orange clay, fired an even colour throughout, but a darker shade of orange-brown at the edges. Abundant white marble-like grit and some grey grit, together with silvery and gold mica, showing in the surface, which has a red wash, mottling to black on the outside, orange to dusky on the inside, well smoothed or burnished.

1360. (VI/V Q 87) (PLATE 80) Large handle of lunate section. Hard sandy grey-brown clay with fine grit and some mica; surface very worn. Possibly from one of the Cycladic islands.

1361. (VI/V Q 88) (PLATE 80) Fragment of large jug or jar. Grey-brown clay; surface reddish, slightly pitted; wiped inside and out; but inside left rough, while outside evidently smoothed or burnished.

1362. (V H 49) (PLATE 80) Four fragments, apparently all from same pithos. Obsidian Ware. Hard sandy clay, shades of light or dark brown in break. Inside surface light or darkish brown, rough, with abundant grit (especially red and white) showing in it together with sharp, angular, shiny black particles; outside with a wash, dark brown to black or red, smoothed but not burnished.

1363. (IV R ?39, House V) Fragment of jug or jar. White Slipped Ware. Orange clay, fired a more or less even colour throughout, with white and large brick-red and some greyish grit. Grit and straw impressions showing in the surface, which has a matt white wash on the outside. Another fragment of similar fabric and appearance from IV Q level 32.

1364. (V R 50) Fragments from neck of jug or jar. Micaceous Ware cf. 1365. Hard fabric; exceptionally sandy grey-brown clay with some mica in it. Inside surface rough; outside with a red wash, smoothed but not burnished.

1365. (V H 48) Fragments of jug with strap handle and wart. Micaceous Ware cf. 1364. Sandy orange clay, dusky at core, with abundant mica. Outside surface with a red mottling to black wash, virtually unburnished.

1366. (V R wall 37) Fragment of vase of uncertain type. Fine Light Grey Burnished Ware. Hard fabric; fine sandy clay, light battleship grey, fired an even colour throughout. Surface of same colour; outside smooth and once it seems burnished, but worn; inside pitted, but with traces of burnishing or careful smoothing. Possibly a stray of Periods VII–VI, but fragments of similar fabric were recovered from levels of II.

PLATE 1. (a) 3. Kalamoti: site to south-west. (b) 6. Piryi: Kastri tou Psellou. (c) View to north-east from 6. (d) Defence wall on west of 6. (e) 9. Olimpoi: Tripanos. (f) 9 and 8. Olimpoi: Tripanos and Petranos.

PLATE 2. (*a*) 14. Langadha: Ayios Isidhoros. (*b*) 15. Nagos: hill to south-east. (*c*) 16. Ayio Gala: church in front of Upper Cave. (*d*) 17. Volissos: Levkathia. (*e*) 18. Volissos: Anemomilos. (*f*) Section on south edge of road through 18.

PLATE 3. Vases and objects from 5. Dotia (4–10), 7. Kato Fana (11, 12), 11. Chios Town (13), and 18. Volissos: Anemomilos (15).

PLATE 4. Ayio Gala: Lower Cave. Scale *c.* 1/2, except 3, 5 (*c.* 1/5).

PLATE 5. Ayio Gala: Lower Cave. Scale *c.* 1/5, except 19, 19A, 21 (*c.* 1/10).

PLATE 6. Ayio Gala: Lower Cave. Scale *c.* 1/2, except bottom right (*c.* 1/4).

PLATE 7. Ayio Gala: Lower Cave.

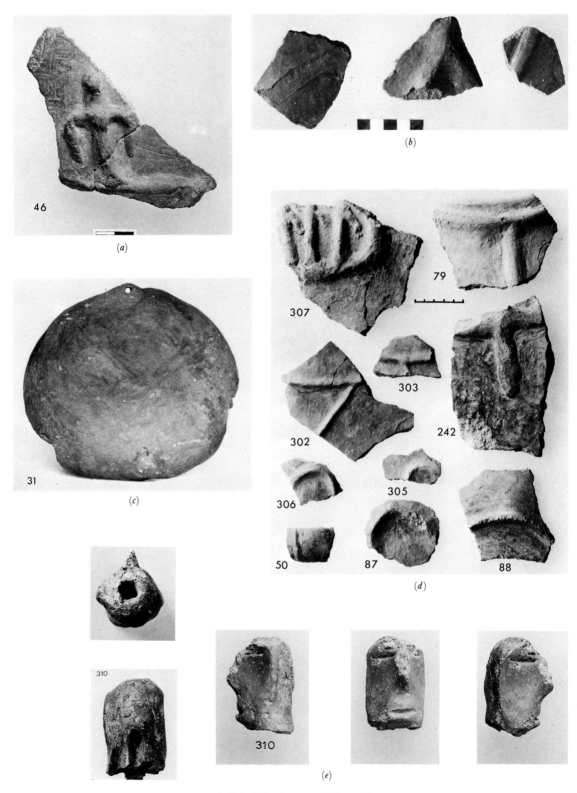

PLATE 8. Ayio Gala: Lower and Upper Caves.

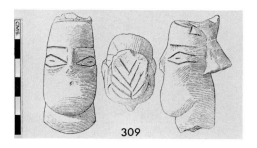

PLATE 9. Ayio Gala: Upper Cave.

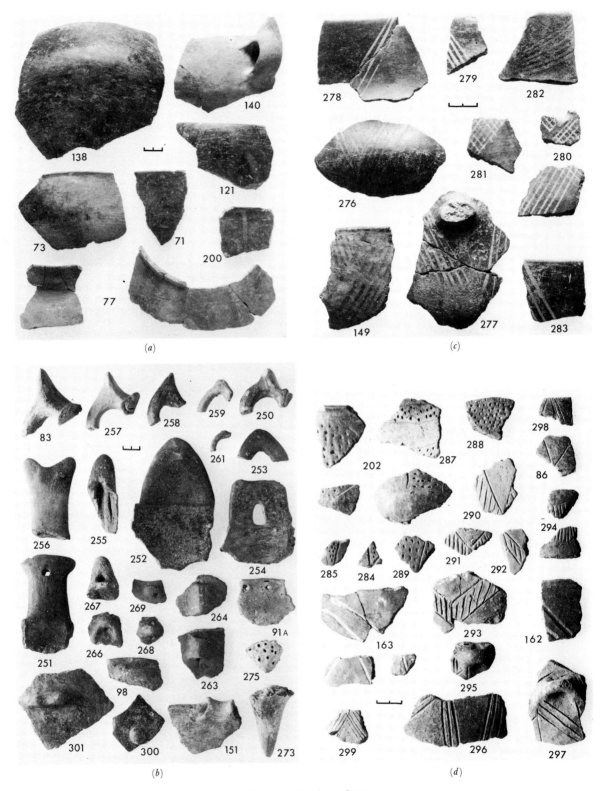

(a)

(c)

(b)

(d)

PLATE 10. Ayio Gala: Upper Cave.

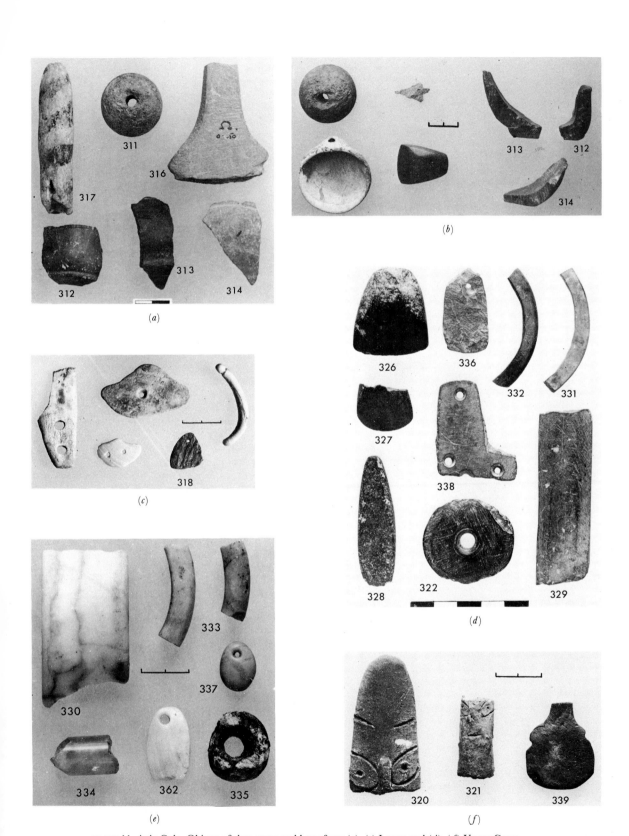

PLATE 11. Ayio Gala. Objects of clay, stone and bone from (a)–(c) Lower and (d)–(f) Upper Caves.

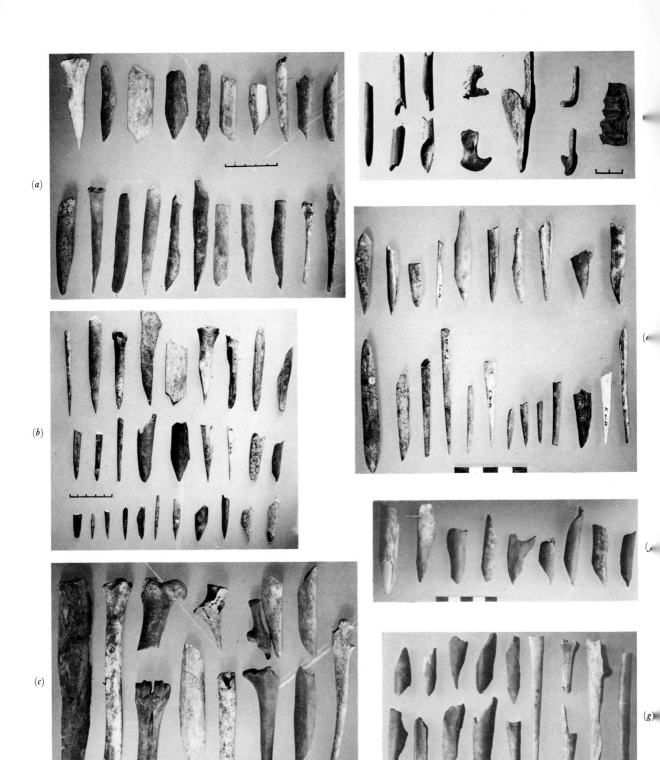

PLATE 12. Ayio Gala: Lower Cave. Bone tools.

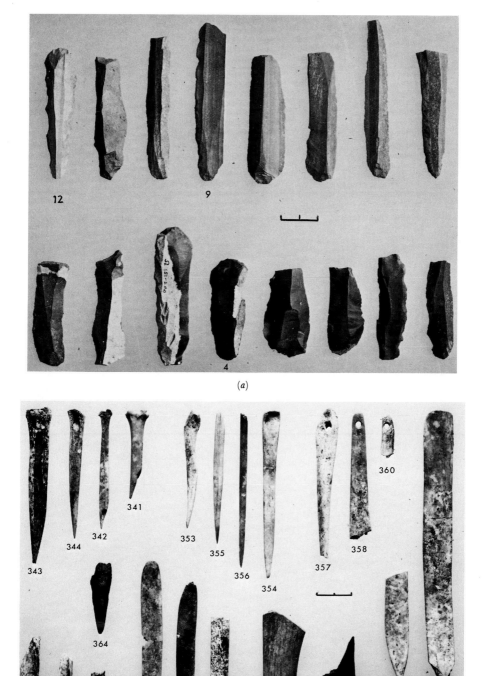

PLATE 13. Ayio Gala. (*a*) Stone implements from Lower Cave. Scale 1/2. (*b*) Bone tools from Upper Cave. Scale *c*. 1/3.

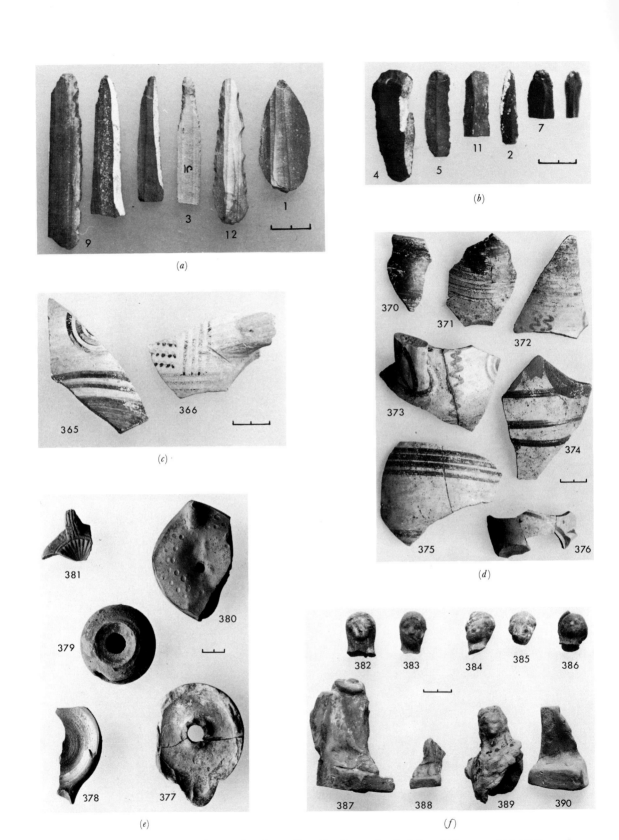

PLATE 14. Ayio Gala. (a), (b) Stone implements from Lower Cave. Post-Bronze Age finds from (c) Lower and (d)-(f) Upper Caves.

(a)

(b)

(c)

PLATE 15. Emporio. (a) Acropolis from north-east. (b) Area A, and (c) Areas B and A, from Acropolis.

PLATE 16. Area A: Periods X–VIII. (a) Trenches Q and G from north-east. (b) Skulls in trench Q and wall 2 behind. (c), (d) Trench G from north and (e) from west, with walls 4, 11, 14.

PLATE 17. Area A: Periods X–VIII. (*a*) Trench G from north-west, with walls 4, 11, 14. (*b*), (*c*) Trench H from north-west, with walls 3, 5, 10, and 20 above. (*d*), (*e*) Quern in D-shaped room of Period VIII in trench G.

PLATE 18. Area A: Period VIII. (*a*) D-shaped room in trench G from north. (*b*) Burial below wall 12 of D-shaped room. (*c*) Door, and (*d*) Stand A, in D-shaped room. (*e*) Vase 156 above D-shaped room.

PLATE 19. Area A: Periods VII–VI. (*a*) Wall 19 from north with wall 15 below on left. (*b*) Well from east. (*c*) Well from south-east with wall 20 behind. (*d*) Wall 20 from south-east. (*e*) Wall 20 above wall 10 from south-east.

PLATE 20. Area A: Periods VI–IV. (*a*) Wall 20 from north-west. (*b*) Walls 20 and 30 from north-east. (*c*) Hearth E in trench Q. (*d*)
House VII with hearth D in trench Q from north. (*e*) Hearth D in trench Q.

PLATE 21. Area A: Periods IV–III. (*a*) House VII and hearth D in trench Q from north-west. (*b*) Vases on floor of House VII. (*c*) Post-hole (C) in wall 47. (*d*) Face 1 of wall 53 from north-east. (*e*), (*f*) Face 1 of wall 53 with face 4 behind, and wall 54 in front, from north-east.

PLATE 22. Area A: Periods IV–III. (*a*) Stone fill of Period III in trench G from east. (*b*) Wall 23 above wall 20 in trench G from south-east. (*c*) Trench G between walls 23 and 50 from south-east. (*d*) Wall 50 (north side). (*e*), (*f*) Pithos fragments and pigs feet found below them in south corner of trench G (House VIII).

PLATE 23. Area A: Periods V–IV. (a), (b) Trench H looking north-west: walls 29, 31, with 26/38 behind. (c) House IV, with vases on floor: wall 38 behind. (d) Bin, and (e), (f) pithos, in House IV.

PLATE 24. Area A: Periods V–IV. (*a*), (*b*) Wall 44 of House V in trench R from north-east. (*c*) East end of trench R. (*d*), (*e*) Post-hole (A) in House IV.

PLATE 25. Area A: Periods V–II. (*a*) Trench X from north-west. (*b*), (*c*) Pithoi in House VI in trench X. (*d*) Vase 1182 by wall 49 in trench X. (*e*) Postern gate of Period II in trench R, with post-hole in wall 53.

PLATE 26. (*a*)–(*c*) Area B: foundations of granary (?) of stage 6. (*d*), (*e*) Area D: trench L: (*d*) from south (Mycenaean stage I); (*e*) wall 5 from north (Mycenaean stage II).

PLATE 27. (*a*) Area D: trench M, with pithoi of Period IV. (*b*)–(*f*) Area F (Acropolis): (*b*), (*c*) door of stage 4 in trench D from north; (*d*) room V in trench F from east; (*e*) vase 2531 below wall 13 in trench B; (*f*) pithos hearth L with jug 2826 in trench B.

PLATE 28. (*a*)–(*d*) Area F (Acropolis): (*a*) Roman levels, looking north; (*b*), (*c*) walls 36, 37, in trench B; (*d*) wall 41. (*e*) Mud with impression of pole or reed from stage 8 in Area B.

PLATE 29. Area E. (*a*)–(*c*) Tomb 1 (Early Bronze Age). (*d*), (*e*) Tomb 3 (Mycenaean).

PLATE 30. Area A: Periods X–VIII.

PLATE 31. Area A: Periods X–VIII.

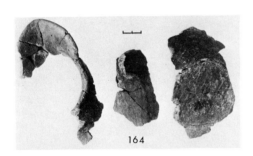

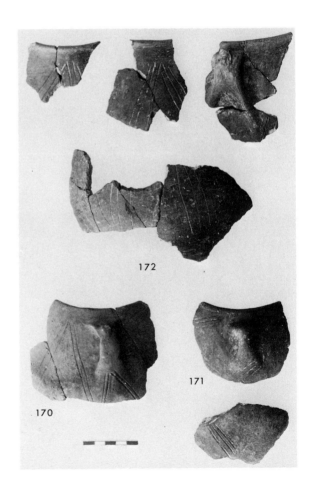

PLATE 32. Area A: Periods X–VIII.

(a)

(b)

(c)

(d)

PLATE 33. Area A: Periods X–VIII.

PLATE 34. Area A: Periods X–VIII.

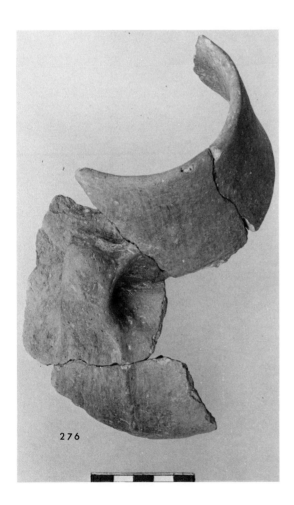

PLATE 35. Area A: Periods X–VIII.

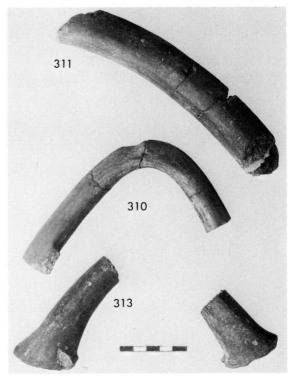

PLATE 36. Area A: Periods X–VIII.

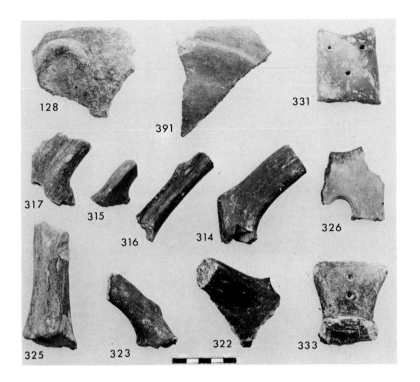

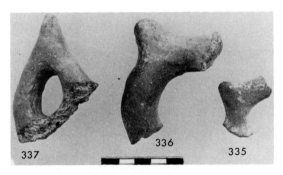

PLATE 37. Area A: Periods X–VIII.

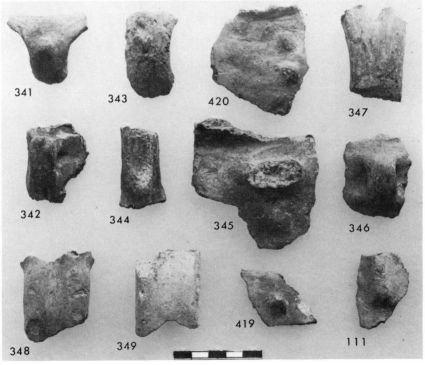

PLATE 38. Area A: Periods X–VIII.

(a)

(b)

PLATE 39. Area A: Periods X–VIII.

(a)

(b)

(c)

(d)

PLATE 40. Area A: Periods X–VIII.

PLATE 41. Area A: Periods X–VIII.

PLATE 42. Area A: Periods X–VIII.

(a)

(b)

PLATE 43. Area A: Periods VII–VI. Light Brown Burnished Ware: (a) Period VII; (b) Period VI.

(a)

(b)   (c)

PLATE 44. Area A: Periods VII–VI. (a) Period VII; (b), (c) Period VI.

(a)

(b)

PLATE 45. Area A: Periods VII–VI. (a) Period VI or later; (b) Period VII.

480

507

570

717

481

658

773

440A

654

655

PLATE 46. Area A: Periods VII–VI.

629

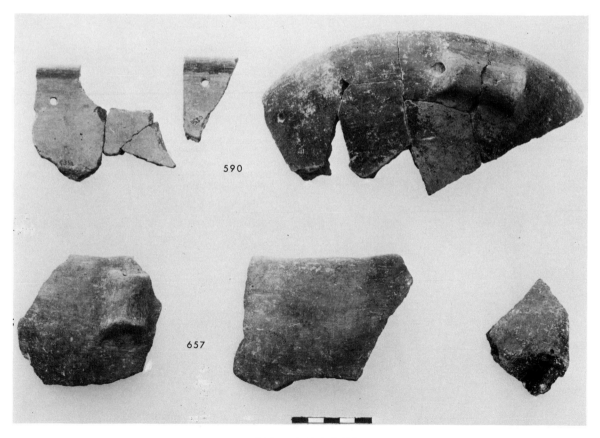

590

657

PLATE 47. Area A: Periods VII–VI.

(a)

(b)

PLATE 48. Area A: Period VII. Jugs of Fine Black Burnished Ware with decoration in white.

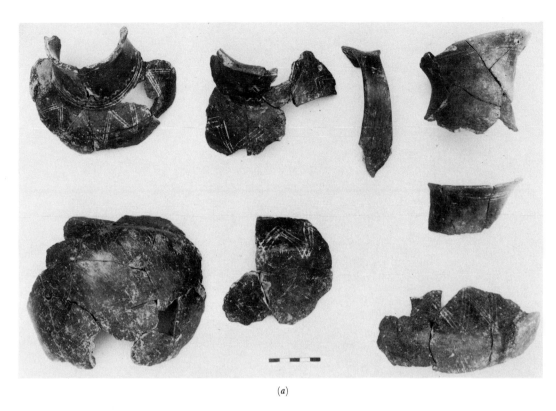

(a)

(b), (c)

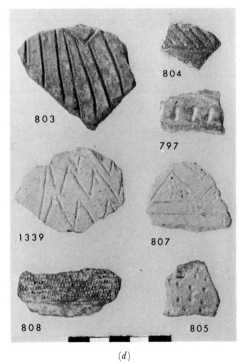

(d)

PLATE 49. Area A: Periods VII–VI. (a)–(c) Jugs of Fine Black Burnished Ware with decoration in white from levels of Period VI. (d) Incised decoration.

(a)

(b)

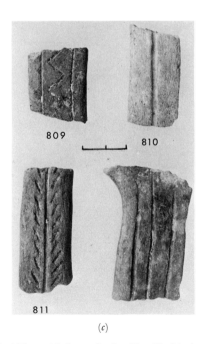

(c)

PLATE 50. Area A: Periods VII–V. Vertical handles (a) from jugs of Fine Black Burnished Ware with decoration in white; (b) ribbed; (c) incised.

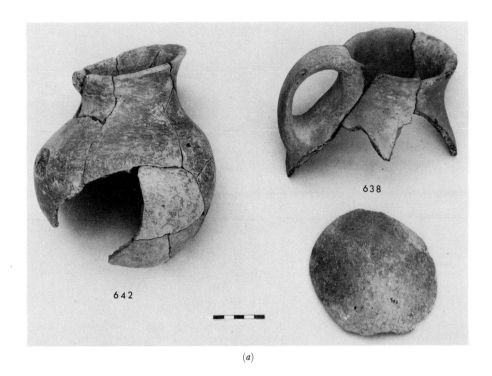

(a)

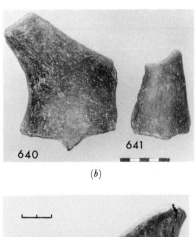

(b)

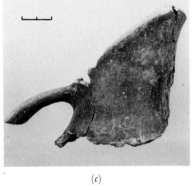

(c)

(d)

PLATE 51. Area A: Periods VII–VI. Jugs.

(a)

(b)

PLATE 52. Area A: Period VII. (a) Unburnished Red Washed Ware. (b) Light Plain Ware.

(a)

753 850 845

435 750

(b)

PLATE 53. Area A: Periods VII–V. (a) Light Plain Ware. (b) Miscellaneous.

701

1229

716

739

486

656

815

PLATE 54. Area A: Periods VII–VI.

PLATE 55. Area A: Periods VII–V. (*a*), (*b*) Incised decoration of Periods VI and V. (*c*) Period VII: Pattern Burnish. (*d*)–(*f*) Period VI.

814

817

728

729

664

748

724

723

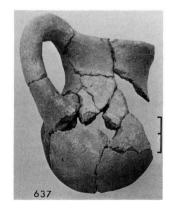

637

PLATE 56. Area A: Periods VII–VI.

859

923

925

924

926A

926

927

PLATE 57. Area A: Period IV.

(a)

(b)

(c)

PLATE 58. Area A: Periods V–IV. (a), (b) Bowls. (c) Silvery Grey Ware.

1026

1028

1030

1029

1032

1033

1034

PLATE 59. Area A: Period IV.

1039   1038

1040   1041

1042

1043

1045

1046

PLATE 60. Area A: Periods V–IV.

1047

1051

1049

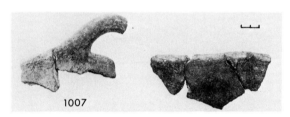

1007

1051

1050

PLATE 61. Area A: Periods V–IV.

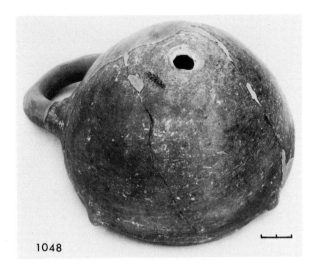

1048

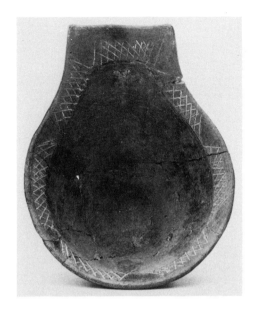

1073

1080

1078

PLATE 62. Area A: Periods V–IV.

961

1079

1077

PLATE 63. Area A: Periods V–IV.

1081

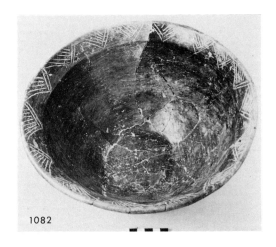

1082

1081

1082

1083

1116

PLATE 64. Area A: Periods V–IV.

(a)

(b)   (c)

(d)

PLATE 65. Area A: Periods V–IV.

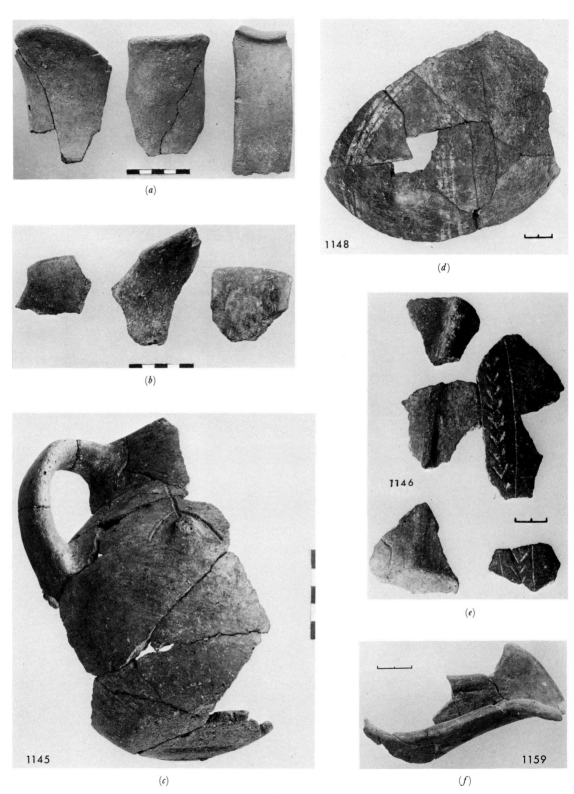

(a)

(b)

1148

(d)

1145

(c)

1146

(e)

1159

(f)

PLATE 66. Area A: Periods V–IV.

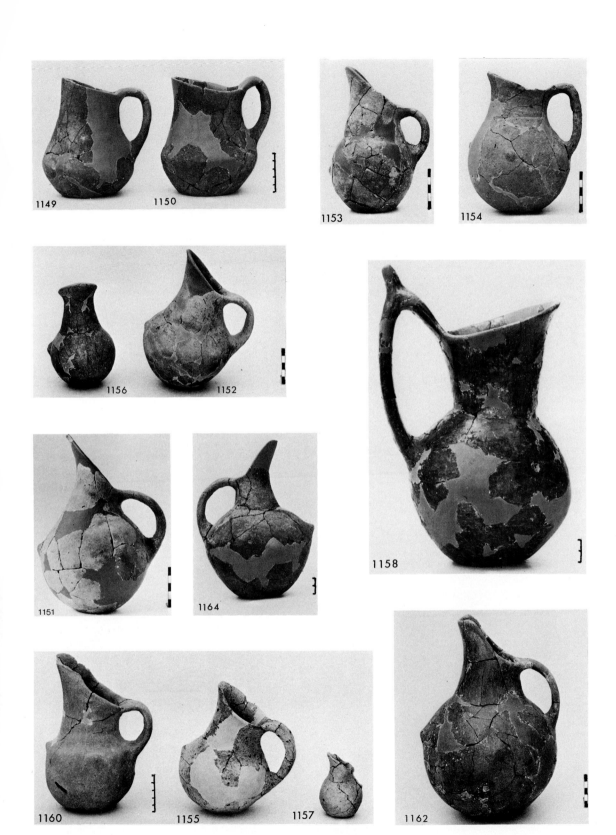

PLATE 67. Area A: Periods V–IV.

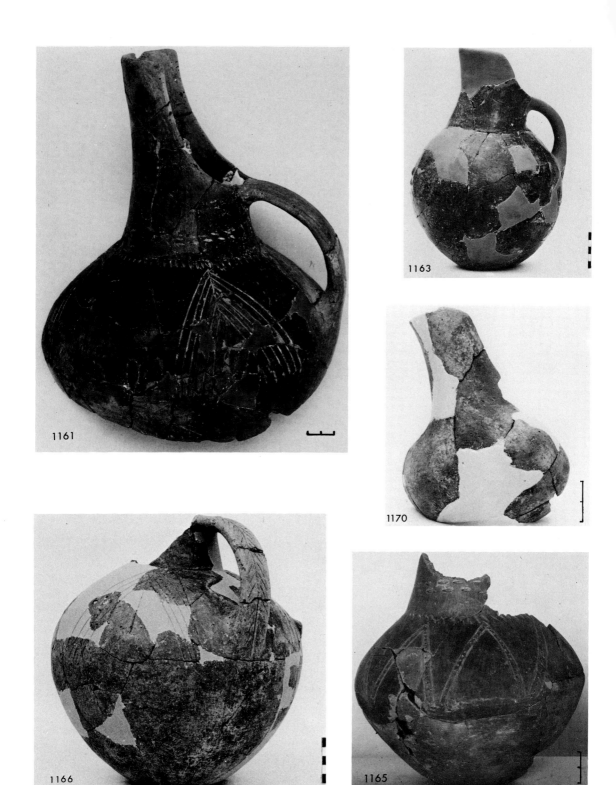

PLATE 68. Area A: Periods V–IV.

PLATE 69. Area A: Periods V–IV.

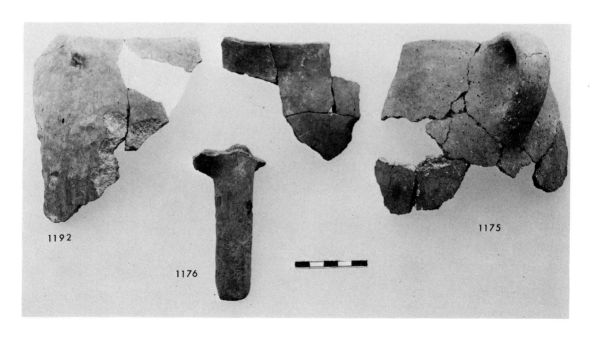

PLATE 70. Area A: Periods V–IV.

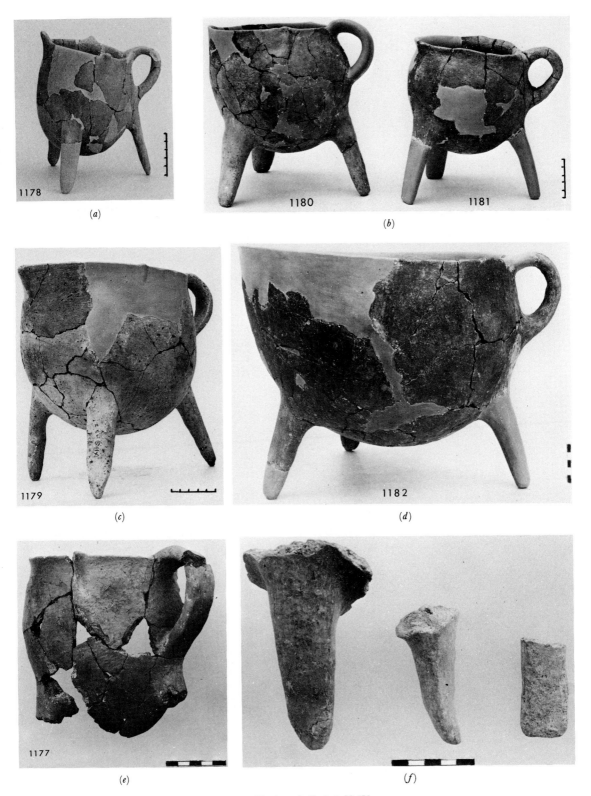

(a)

1178

1180   1181

(b)

1179

(c)

1182

(d)

1177

(e)

(f)

PLATE 71. Area A: Periods V–IV.

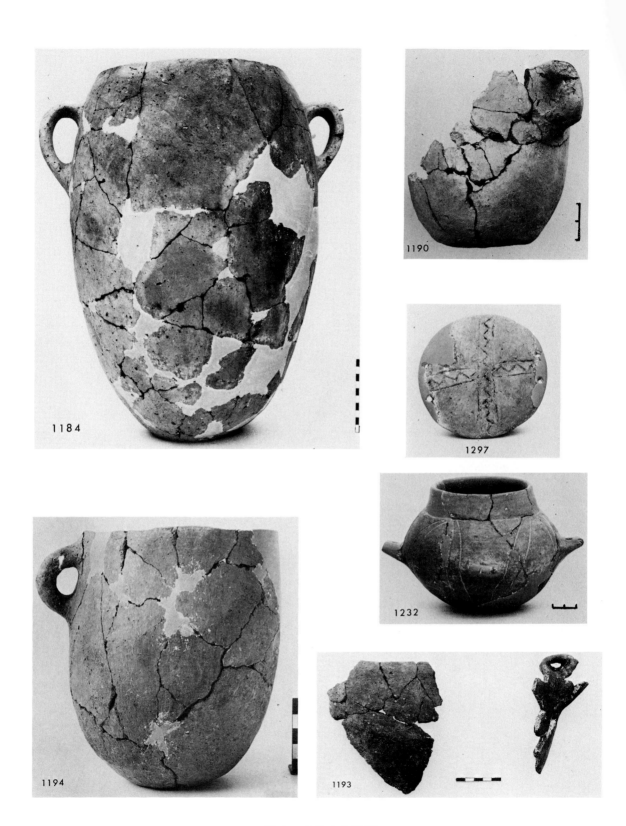

PLATE 72. Area A: Periods V–IV.

1231

1233

1235

1240

1296

1236

1237

PLATE 73. Area A: Periods V–IV.

1239

1241

1238

1242

1289   1286   1288

PLATE 74. Area A: Periods V–IV.

(a)

(b)

PLATE 75. Area A: Periods V–IV.

1283

1292

1284

1304

1305

1293

1294

PLATE 76. Area A: Periods V–IV.

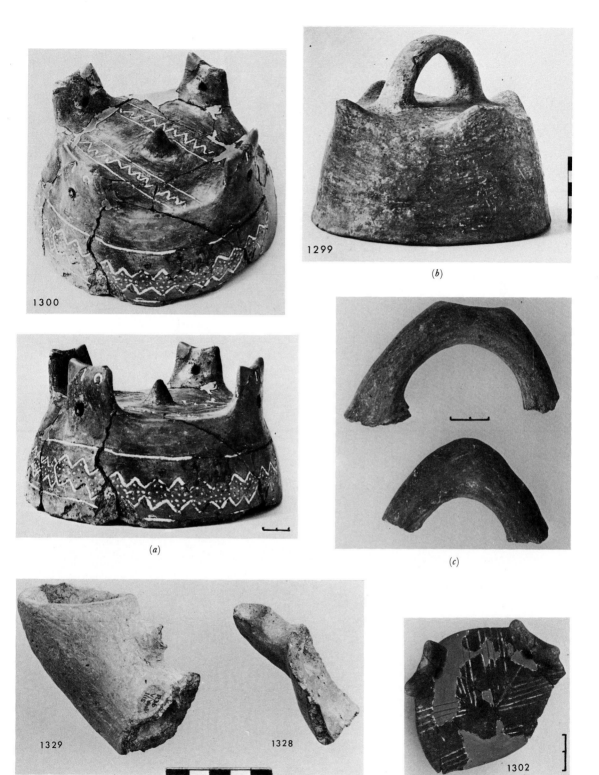

1300

1299

(b)

(a)

(c)

1329   1328

(d)

1302

(e)

PLATE 77. Area A: Periods V–IV.

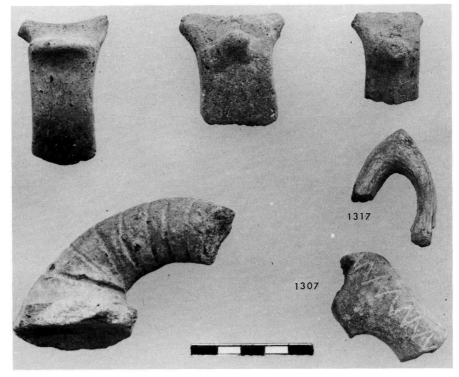

(a)

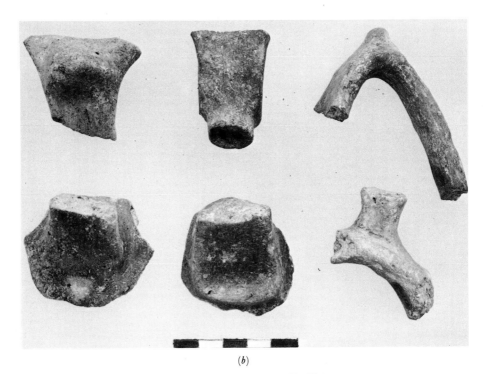

(b)

PLATE 78. Area A: Periods V–IV.

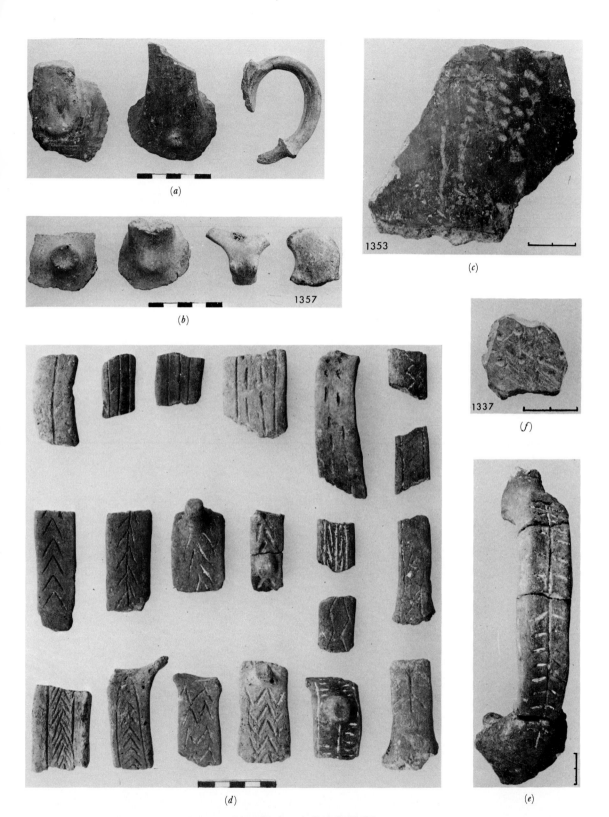

(a)

(b)   1357

(c)   1353

(d)   (e)   (f) 1337

PLATE 79. Area A: Periods V–IV.

PLATE 80. Area A: Periods V–IV.